D0712738

PRINCIPLES OF THE JEWISH FAITH

© Louis Jacobs 1964

Library of Congress Catalog Card Number:
64-23950

Manufactured in Great Britain

PRINCIPLES OF
THE JEWISH FAITH

An Analytical Study

LOUIS JACOBS

Basic Books, Inc., Publishers
New York

Contents

		Page
PREFACE	. . . .	viii
ABBREVIATIONS	. . . . . .	xi
SCHEME OF TRANSLITERATION OF HEBREW	.	xii

Chapter

1. INTRODUCTION 1

2. THE FIRST PRINCIPLE:
   The Existence of God . . 33

3. THE SECOND PRINCIPLE: .
   God's Unity . . . 70

4. THE THIRD PRINCIPLE:
   God's Incorporeality . . . 118

5. THE FOURTH PRINCIPLE:
   God is Eternal . . . 135

6. THE FIFTH PRINCIPLE:
   God Alone is to be Worshipped . 149

7. THE SIXTH PRINCIPLE:
   Prophecy 184

8. THE SEVENTH PRINCIPLE:
   The Superiority of Moses . . 206

Chapter *Page*

9. THE EIGHTH PRINCIPLE:
   The Torah is Divine . . . 216

10. THE NINTH PRINCIPLE:
    The Torah is Unchanging . . 302

11. THE TENTH PRINCIPLE:
    God Knows the Deeds of Men . 320

12. THE ELEVENTH PRINCIPLE:
    Reward and Punishment . . 350

13. THE TWELFTH PRINCIPLE:
    The Coming of the Messiah . 368

14. THE THIRTEENTH PRINCIPLE:
    The Resurrection of the Dead . 398

15. SUMMARY AND CONCLUSIONS . . . 455

INDEX 468

In Memory of
Israel Isaac and Rachel Mintz

ר׳ ישראל יצחק ב״ר אברהם פינחס זעליג ע״ה
מרת רחל בת ר׳ בערל דוב ע״ה

They loved the Torah
And walked in her ways.

PREFACE

THIS book is an attempt to discuss what a modern Jew can believe. By putting the question in this way it is not suggested that the twentieth century Jew is necessarily ill-disposed towards religious faith, still less that Jewish beliefs must be watered down in some way and made 'attractive' in order to win his grudging adherence. One of the most interesting aspects of present-day Jewish life is the search for a deep and abiding faith on the part of intelligent Jews and Jewesses. It is becoming increasingly evident to such people that Judaism is a *religion* and not only what is vaguely referred to as a 'way of life'.

There are, however, obstacles to belief in some of the classic expressions of the Jewish Creed in those areas where the *facts* about the universe, presented by new knowledge, contradict some of the older formulations. In these areas it is futile to invoke the principle of faith or to contrast it with reason. A complete acceptance of ancient formulations where these run contrary to the facts is a *sacrificium intellectus* which the author, and he hopes many of his readers, does not believe Judaism demands.

Nowhere is the conflict between the facts and the older formulation seen more clearly than with regard to Maimonides' eighth principle of faith – that the *Torah* is divine. To give up this principle is to abandon Judaism as a religion. But to accept it in the way it is formulated by the great mediaeval sage of Cordova is to tie Judaism down to fundamentalism and obscurantism. This is not, of course, to denigrate Maimonides by suggesting that he was an obscurantist. On the contrary, the remarkably courageous manner in which he grappled with the intellectual problems of *his* day and his passionate striving for a viable synthesis between what was then the new knowledge and the old, provides sufficient evidence that if Maimonides were alive today and familiar with the range of present-day Bible studies he would face the issues with that same fearlessness.

Much of what is presented here is not particularly original.

viii

After all, distinguished thinkers have faced this kind of problem for a long time now and have had many wise and helpful things to say. But, so far as I am aware, no attempt has hitherto been made to present systematically the thirteen articles of the Jewish faith in reinterpreted form. These articles are here considered in the light of the fresh discoveries in the fields of Bible and Talmudic research and in the history of the Jewish religion. The approach is theological but every effort has been made to be true to history. New philosophical trends, particularly existentialism and linguistic analysis, have been considered and, in part, utilized for the purposes of reinterpretation. The author does not believe that the rabbi has any special competence in these fields. He is convinced that rabbi and 'layman' (the latter term is, after all, unknown in the classic Jewish tradition) must cooperate in discovering the message of Judaism for our day. When William Temple collaborated in a similar volume in the light of his faith, the contributors were criticised for attempting to provide a hypothetical layman, 'Mr. Jones', with a palatable feast. Temple replied: 'It was not my aim to provide Mr. Jones with food. I *am* Mr. Jones asking what there is to eat'.

The first chapter is introductory. In it the history of Creed formulation in Judaism is considered. Each of the following thirteen chapters deals with one of Maimonides' articles and treats it from the point of view of the present state of our knowledge. But the opinions of the great mediaeval thinkers are duly noted and discussed. Needless to say, the scope of the inquiry is so vast that it would be pretentious for an author to imagine that he has given all the answers or even asked correctly all the questions. My ambition has been the far more modest one of trying to formulate my own personal faith and presenting the results to interested readers as a basis for further debate and discussion. The final chapter contains a summary of the tentative conclusions reached. The 'excursi', which are interpolated throughout each chapter, contain biographical material and elaborations of points raised in the text. In them cross-references from chapter to chapter have been almost entirely avoided, so that there is a duplication of the bibliographies: however, this is an advantage for those readers who wish to study in isolation from the rest of the book.

A word perhaps ought to be said regarding theological thinking. One often hears the claim put forward that Judaism has no theology. If this means that, for the reasons stated in this book, there have been very few systematic and highly organised authoritative statements of what Jews must believe, the claim has much truth. But if, as one suspects, it is put forward as an encouragement for Jews to be unconcerned with theological topics the results of heeding such a claim may well prove disastrous. Judaism is not a form of behaviourism. All the practices of traditional Judaism are buttressed by faith. For the precepts to possess religious value they must be carried out as the Word of God.

The religious position I have tried to sketch in this book is that of modernism within traditional Judaism. In its recognition and acceptance of the *Halakhah* this position may be called 'Orthodox' or 'Neo-Orthodox', if the terms are interpreted (as, indeed, they are in some parts of the Jewish world) to cover practice alone. If, on the other hand, the term 'Orthodox' is tied to its etymology and is thereby made to cover complete acceptance of the mediaeval standpoint then I am not 'Orthodox.' But a major theme in this book is that the fundamental principles of the Jewish faith have always received fresh interpretations so that the picture of a completely static system of beliefs handed down from age to age reaching back to Sinai is, in any event, false to the facts of history. Judaism, it has frequently been noted, is, if seen with a historical perspective, a dynamic, not a static, faith. For all that, continuity between past and present must be preserved and the eternal values of the faith expressed. How this is to be done is one of the major theological issues in Jewish religious thought. It is unlikely that all religious Jews will ever agree on the correct solution to the problem. Certainly only a visionary will imagine that something like complete agreement will be forthcoming in our generation. But every addition to the discussion brings the solution a little nearer. If this book serves as some minute contribution to the aim all faithful Jews have at heart – the increasing power of Judaism in bringing men to God – the author will be well satisfied.

ABBREVIATIONS

Biblical books:

Gen.	.. ..	Genesis
Ex.	.. ..	Exodus
Lev.	.. ..	Leviticus
Num.	.. ..	Numbers
Deut.	.. ..	Deuteronomy
Josh.	.. ..	Joshua
Judg.	.. ..	Judges
Sam.	.. ..	Samuel
Is.	.. ..	Isaiah
Jer.	.. ..	Jeremiah
Ezek.	.. ..	Ezekiel
Hos.	.. ..	Hosea
Obad.	.. ..	Obadiah
Jon.	.. ..	Jonah
Mic.	.. ..	Micah
Nah.	.. ..	Nahum
Hab.	.. ..	Habakkuk
Zeph.	.. ..	Zephaniah
Hag.	.. ..	Haggai
Zech.	.. ..	Zechariah
Mal.	.. ..	Malachi
Ps.	.. ..	Psalms
Prov.	.. ..	Proverbs
Cant.	.. ..	Canticles
Lam.	.. ..	Lamentations
Eccl.	.. ..	Ecclesiastes
Esth.	.. ..	Esther
Dan.	.. ..	Daniel
Ez.	.. ..	Ezra
Neh.	.. ..	Nehemiah
Chron.	.. ..	Chronicles

Tractates of the Talmud:

Bek.	.. ..	*Bekhoroth*
Ber.	.. ..	*Berakhoth*
Betz.	.. ..	*Betzah*
Bikk.	.. ..	*Bikkurim*
B.B.	.. ..	*Baba Bathra*
B.Q.	.. ..	*Baba Qama*
B.M.	.. ..	*Baba Metzi'a*

Gitt.	.. ..	*Gittin*
Hor.	.. ..	*Horayoth*
Zeb.	.. ..	*Zebhahim*
Hag.	.. ..	*Hagigah*
Hull.	.. ..	*Hullin*
Toh.	.. ..	*Toharoth*
Yad.	.. ..	*Yadaim*
Jeb.	.. ..	*Jebhamoth*
Yom.	.. ..	*Yoma*
Kil.	.. ..	*Kil'aim*
Ker.	.. ..	*Kerithoth*
Keth.	.. ..	*Kethubboth*
Meg.	.. ..	*Megillah*
Mid.	.. ..	*Middoth*
Makk.	.. ..	*Makkoth*
Mak	.. ..	*Makhshirin*
Men.	.. ..	*Menahoth*
Ma'as.	.. ..	*Ma'asroth*
M.Q.	.. ..	*Mo'ed Qatan*
M. Sh.	.. ..	*Ma'aser Sheni*
Me'il.	.. ..	*Me'ilah*
Miq.	.. ..	*Miqwaoth*
Neg.	.. ..	*Nega'im*
Ned.	.. ..	*Nedarim*
Nidd.	.. ..	*Niddah*
Sanh.	.. ..	*Sanhedrin*
Sukk.	.. ..	*Sukkah*
A.Z.	.. ..	*'Abhodah Zarah*
'Ed.	.. ..	*'Eduyyoth*
'Erub.	.. ..	*'Erubhin*
'Arak.	.. ..	*'Arakhin*
Pes.	.. ..	*Pesahim*
Qidd.	.. ..	*Qiddushin*
R.H.	.. ..	*Rosh Ha-Shanah*
Sheb.	.. ..	*Shebhu'oth*
Sabb.	.. ..	*Shabbath*
Sheq.	.. ..	*Sheqalim*
Ta'an.	.. ..	*Ta'anith*
Tem.	.. ..	*Temurah*
Ter.	.. ..	*Terumoth*

General

ANET	Ancient Near Eastern Texts, ed. J. B. Pritchard
'Arukh, Koh.	*'Arukh*, ed. Kohut
ARN	*'Abhoth* of Rabbi Nathan
A.V.	Authorised Version
b.	born
B.C.E.	before common era
Bell. Jud.	Josephus: 'Bellum Judaicum'
C.C.A.R.	Yearbook of Central Conference of American Rabbis
c.	*circa*, about
C.E.	common era

xi

d.	died
DOTT	Documents from Old Testament Times, ed. D. Winton Thomas
EB	Encyclopedia Britannica
Ecc. R.	*Midrash* Ecclesiastes *Rabbah*
ERE	Hastings' Encyclopedia of Religion and Ethics
ET	*Encyclopedia Talmudith*, ed. S. Sevin
f.	following pages
freq.	frequently
Gen. R.	*Midrash* Genesis *Rabbah*
Ginzberg, Legends	'The Legends of the Jews' by Louis Ginzberg
Hil.	*Hilkhoth*
HTR	Harvard Theological Review
HUCA	Hebrew Union College Annual
ICC	International Critical Commentary
JE	Jewish Encyclopedia
Jer.	Jerusalem
Jer.	Jerusalem Talmud
JJS	Journal of Jewish Studies
JQR	Jewish Quarterly Review
Lam. R.	*Midrash* Lamentations *Rabbah*
Lev. R.	*Midrash* Leviticus *Rabbah*
MGWJ	Monatsschrift für Geschichte und Wissenschaft des Judentums
N.T.	New Testament
N.Y.	New York
O.H.	*Shulhan 'Arukh, 'Orah Hayyim*
op. cit.	work quoted
O.T.	Old Testament
P.B.	Prayer Book
p.	page
pp.	pages
R.V.	Revised Version
S.A.	*Shulhan 'Arukh*
SCM	Student Christian Movement
Teh.	*Tehillim*
Tos.	*Tosephta* or *Tosaphoth*
UJE	Universal Jewish Encyclopedia
Y.D.	*Shulhan 'Arukh, Yoreh De'ah*

SCHEME OF TRANSLITERATION OF HEBREW

'Aleph	=	'	*Teth*	=	*t*	*Pe*	=	*p*
Beth	=	*b*	*Yod*	=	*y* (i)	*Phe*	=	*ph*
Bheth	=	*bh*	*Kaph*	=	*k*	*Tzade*	=	*tz*
Gimel	=	*g*	*Khaph*	=	*kh*	*Qoph*	=	*q*
Daleth	=	*d*	*Lamed*	=	*l*	*Resh*	=	*r*
He	=	*h*	*Mem*	=	*m*	*Sin*	=	*s*
Waw	=	*w* (u)	*Nun*	=	*n*	*Shin*	=	*sh*
Zayin	=	*z*	*Samekh*	=	*s*	*Taw*	=	*t*
Heth	=	*h*	*'Ayin*	=	'	*Thaw*	=	*th*

It has not been possible to maintain complete consistency in transliteration, particularly in cases where a different form of spelling has become popular, e.g. *Akiba*, not *Aqiba*.

[1]

INTRODUCTION

In the year 1889 there appeared, in London, the first issue of the Jewish Quarterly Review, edited by Israel Abrahams and C. G. Montefiore. The editors frankly state that they lay no claims to satisfying an obvious and long-felt need since the Anglo-Jewish community has evinced no desire for a magazine dealing with Jewish history, literature and theology. Nonetheless the editors express the hope that their new venture will provide a medium in which scholars may register the results of their research and theologians the results of their thoughts. Interestingly enough the first issue opens with an essay by the famous Jewish historian, Graetz, entitled: 'The Significance of Judaism for the Present and the Future'. This essay by one of the foremost representatives of the historical school, dealing with the basic ideas of Judaism, may well serve as a starting point for a discussion on the meaning of the Jewish Creed in present-day Judaism.

Graetz points out that Judaism demands severe sacrifices from its followers but readiness to sacrifice for an ideal can only be inspired by the strongest convictions that it is true. The author addresses himself to this question. How can a sceptical and critical generation become possessed of such convictions? To do this a generation must know the essence of Judaism, must be aware of Judaism's characteristic qualities, by which it is distinguished from other forms of religion. In other words, Graetz is here searching for a definition of the basic principles of the Jewish faith.

However, Graetz remarks at the outset that he is not at all happy about the term 'the Jewish faith', though it is not too clear what it is in the term which arouses his ire. Defining 'faith' as the acceptance of an inconceivable miraculous fact, insufficiently established by historical evidence, he proclaims that Judaism has never required such a belief from its adherents.

1

Yet he goes on to speak of Judaism as 'not a *mere* doctrine of faith' (italics mine), thereby implying that some kind of faith is required. The historian's argument becomes somewhat clearer as it develops but it is impossible to deny that his whole presentation suffers from the ambiguity of his definition. This point is worth more than a passing notice. The dangers of ambiguity lurk unpleasantly near in any attempt at interpreting Jewish belief in the light of modern thought and knowledge, which is only another way of saying that the problem of interpreting Judaism in a way in which justice is done to both tradition and progress does not lend itself to an easy solution.

Graetz quotes with approval Renan's aphorism that Judaism is 'a minimum of religion', saying that it hits the mark, 'not only in the sense that Judaism demands few, or no, articles of faith, but also in the sense that its centre of gravity is not to be found in the religious sphere'. By the latter statement Graetz presumably means that the scope of Judaism is far wider than the range covered by ritual. As William Temple said, God is interested in many things apart from religion. His first statement is far more open to question. As we shall see, the question of the dogmas of Judaism cannot be dismissed so lightly. Be that as it may, Graetz quotes, as evidence of Judaism's minimum of religion, such sayings as Micah's: 'Thou askest what the Lord requires of thee? Only to do justly, and to love mercy, and to walk humbly with thy God' (Mic. vi. 8). Another example is Hillel's answer to the heathen who asked him what was the quintessence of Judaism: 'That which is hateful unto thee do not do unto thy neighbour. This is the whole of the Law; all the rest is but commentary on this text' (*Sabb.* 31a). Similarly, in the second century the Council of Lydda ruled that, under certain circumstances, the precepts of the *Torah* may be transgressed in order to save one's life with the exception of three: avoidance of idolatry, avoidance of unchastity, and, finally, avoidance of murder (*Sanh.* 74a). Thus there are two elements in the essence of Judaism, the ethical and the religious, each possessing a positive and a negative side. The ethical includes in its positive side, love of mankind, benevolence, humility, justice, and in its negative aspects, respect for human life, care against unchastity, subdual of selfishness and the beast in man, holiness in deed and thought.

The religious element in its negative aspects includes the prohibition of worshipping a transient being as God and to consider all idolatry as vain and to reject it entirely. The positive side is to regard the highest Being as one and unique, to worship it as the Godhead and the essence of all ethical perfections. The two elements are intimately connected. The divine perfection gives the ideal for the moral life.

Herein lies the unique character of Judaism. It is in the union of the ethical and the religious from its first revelation that Judaism differs from other religions, including Christianity. Can this doctrine, Graetz asks, have lost its influence? He answers with an emphatic negative. The world still desperately needs ethical monotheism, and Judaism alone can provide this in its purest form. Furthermore, absolute monotheism is rationalism. It required a high stage of cultivated intelligence to arrive at the conviction that Baal and Zeus were abominations, as Judaism called them. Idolatry only appears absurd today because Jewish rationalism fought against it. The ruling creed, says Graetz, is likewise anthropolatry with cathedrals, cloisters, and pilgrims' shrines dedicated to it. 'The only defenders of true monotheism, in other words, of rationalism in religion, are still the adherents of Judaism'. In fighting words Graetz continues that Judaism, which is throughout rationalistic, is the sole stronghold of free thought in the religious sphere. While 'millions of men still recognise a representative vicar of God on earth, whose words they credulously accept as an infallible oracle' there are still enough phantoms to be banished from the temples of the nations and the hearts of men.

Finally, in his concluding paragraph, Graetz observes: 'Of course, Judaism contains an elaborate ritual besides these ideal principles, which, unfortunately, owing to the tragic course of history, has developed into a fungoid growth which overlays the ideals. But originally the ritual in its pure form had its justification, and was intended to surround and protect ideals in themselves of an ethereal nature. It must be reserved for a later article to explain the manner in which the ritual was adapted to the ideal'.

Graetz's 'later article' appeared in the second volume of the Jewish Quarterly Review (1890, pp. 257-269). Significantly enough, in the first volume, Solomon Schechter's famous essay on the dogmas of Judaism had also appeared but Graetz refuses to discuss the question of 'what may be considered orthodox or heterodox in Judaism'. His lack of interest in this kind of question (one with which this book is concerned) is evidenced by the rather glib paraphrase of the Rabbinic teachings concerning one who 'denies that the *Torah* is from Heaven' as (Graetz calls this 'in modern phraseology') 'doubt in the supernatural'! According to Graetz, in spite of Schechter, Moses Mendelssohn's dictum that Judaism only judges actions and not religious opinions remains unshaken. All Graetz's nineteenth century rationalism is contained in his remark: 'Whether an intelligent Jew finds more happiness, assurance, and solace from his convinced belief in the ideal principle of Judaism and its ethical consequences than a Russian or Polish Chasid from the mechanical performance of some ritual ceremony, and from a vague messianic hope is purely a matter of sentiment'. (It is automatically and gratuitously assumed that the Chasid's performance will be mechanical and his messianic hope vague). 'Taking as my guides', continues Graetz, 'the Bible, the *Talmud*, and the *intelligent* rabbis, I have endeavoured to prove that this fundamental principle must be sought for in ethical idealism (humanity in the highest sense of the word) and in pure rational monotheism, *adverse to all mysticism and disfigurement*' (italics mine).

The ritual side of Judaism is not, according to Graetz, in the first place an end in itself but a means to an end. For one thing it helps to keep alive the national memory of past glories and thereby provides Jews with a profound sense of their destiny. Only in this way can Israel be constantly reminded of its lofty role in God's scheme. Ideals, even the highest, die away unless they are tied to the concrete. Ethical monotheism is no exception. Furthermore, the ritual has a preservative value. It weaned the Jews away from polytheism and kept them apart as a holy people from pagan contamination. Graetz calls these ceremonies 'prophylactic'. They were intended to keep Jews free from religious and, particularly, ethical contamination. No doubt some of them had base, even pagan, origins but even these were assimilated or metamorphosed by the spiritual energy of Judaism which stamped its mark on all it found.

Therefore, and here comes the most radical part of Graetz's
theory, the ceremonial character was not endemic in the Bible
(with the exception of the book of Leviticus which, for Graetz,
contains a 'foreign' element, unlike the 'beautiful book of
Deuteronomy' which tends to reduce the ceremonial part of
religion). Only in post-exilic days did Judaism receive a
ceremonial character. 'The pure well-spring of Judaism, the
Bible, was so buried under all this accumulation (of ritual
laws) that it almost seemed to have disappeared altogether'.
The conclusion would seem to be that for Graetz the ceremonial
side of Judaism is unimportant. But this is certainly not the
historian's intention. In this very essay he dwells on its value
and he is known to have kept the ceremonial law in his own
private life, to the extent, it is said, of not even carrying a
handkerchief into the street on the Sabbath. His appeal is
rather for the recognition of this side of Judaism as being
subordinate to its essence, pure ethical monotheism.

Since Graetz wrote his essay the world has lived with devastating global wars, concentration camps, gas chambers, the
horrors of genocide and totalitarianism, and all the depravities to
which human beings can sink. An over-optimistic view of human
potentialities is therefore suspect. In the age of Barth and a
fresh interest in Kierkegaard and other existentialist heroes,
rationalism itself is on the defensive. In a generation accustomed
to Otto's 'Numinous' the identification of Judaism with the
'purely rational' can do little service for the ancient faith and is
unlikely to be given a sympathetic hearing. The immense
literature produced on Hasidism in the late nineteenth and
twentieth century reminds us that there is something here of
lasting appeal and renders Graetz's adverse judgement hope-
lessly superficial. The real interest today in mysticism
(a natural consequence, as Dean Inge has said, of the decline
of authoritarian religion) only serves to give prominence to
Graetz's blind spot, evidenced in all his writings, including his
massive History, on this important manifestation of the religious
life. A search for the essence of Judaism conducted in the mid-
twentieth century cannot afford to leave out significant areas of
human experience. For all that, Graetz's attempt is relevant.
His essay is open to criticism on many counts but his recognition
is sound that in the Talmudic statement concerning the three

precepts for which martyrdom is demanded is contained the basic formulation of Judaism's essence. Historically considered this is the formulation of the principles nearest to the realities of Talmudic Judaism. But 'faith', in the sense of 'creed', and 'ritual', in the sense of '*mitzwah*' (divine command), are also basic to what has been called 'traditional Judaism'. The various formulations of a Jewish Creed have undoubtedly been in answer to the contemporary needs of earlier Jewish communities but they, too, have had their effect in moulding the Jewish spirit during the past thousand years. It is for this reason that the more fruitful approach to the question of what a modern Jew can, and should, believe, is to be found in an examination of Maimonides' Creed, with the all-important proviso that Maimonides' formulation requires much re-interpretation and revision in the light of the new knowledge God has given to man since the twelfth century.

Reference has been made to Schechter's essay on the dogmas of Judaism. Graetz, as we have seen, virtually ignores Schechter's hint that the modern Jew desperately needs a *detailed* Creed. Schechter's essay was republished in his 'Studies in Judaism', First Series, Jewish Publication Society of America, Philadelphia, 1905 (reprinted in the Meridian Books edition, New York, 1958, pp' 73–104). In the Introduction to the 'Studies' Schechter develops the idea of a theology for the modern Jew. Prominent in Schechter's presentation is the idea of 'Catholic Israel' – that the 'norm as well as the sanction of Judaism is the practice actually in vogue'. This means that the possibility of reinterpreting Judaism is not to be denied since it is neither Scripture nor early Judasim which is the real guide for Jews but rather Scripture as interpreted by generations of Jews. Schechter admits, however, that in unguarded moments the 'old Adam' still asserts itself in him, causing him to rebel against the new rival of revelation in the shape of history. The theology of the historical school, observes Schechter, may 'do' for his generation but he neither hopes nor believes that it will do for those who come after him. We who have come after him are faced with a mighty dilemma. We can either try to reject totally all the insights of the historical school, without much hope of success, and go back to a dogmatism without roots in Jewish history, or we can try to build a Jewish theology based on firm historical foundations. For a historically minded generation the first alternative is impossible. Having been introduced to the conception of Judaism as a dynamic rather than static faith, with its institutions developing in and through the historical processes of the Jewish people and the nations with whom it came into contact, we are convinced that there are truths here it would be obscurantism to deny. On the other hand, many of us share Schechter's concern for the poverty of historicism. It is Judaism as a living faith, not only as a happy hunting ground for the student of antiquities, that we require. We agree with Schechter that there *are* dogmas in Judaism. But we must try, at least, to take up the matter where Schechter left off and ask ourselves what these dogmas are and if and how they can be re-interpreted for the Jew of today. This book is only an attempt to examine in turn each of the thirteen principles of Maimonides and to try to discover the permanent truth in each, while recognising that in such a re-interpretation questions of *fact* are involved, namely, the facts discovered through the pious labours of thousands of researches into Jewish sources and origins. Before proceeding to the task it is necessary to follow Schechter in sketching briefly the history of dogma in Judaism. To this the remainder of the chapter is devoted.

*   *   *

EXCURSUS

For the literature on the subject of Dogma in Judaism *v.* the sources quoted in Schechter's notes; M. Mendelssohn's 'Jerusalem', Gesammelte Schriften, 1843, Vol. 3, pp. 319 ff.; David Neumark: '*Toledoth Ha-'Iqqarim Be-Yisrael*', Vol. 1, Odessa, 1912, Vol. 2, Odessa, 1919; J. Abelson's trans., with an Introduction and notes, of Maimonides' formulation in JQR (Old Series), Vol. XIX, 1907, pp. 24 ff.; M. Friedländer: 'The Jewish Religion', 2nd. ed., London, 1900, pp. 19–231; Morris Joseph: 'Judaism as Creed and Life', London, 1903, pp. 39–50; Kaufmann Kohler: 'Jewish Theology', Macmillan, New York, 1925, pp. 19–28; J. Holzer: 'Mose Maimuni's Einleitung zu Chelek', Berlin, 1901; Leo Baeck: 'The Essence of Judaism', trans. by V. Grubwieser and L. Paul, London, 1936, pp. 1–76; article 'Articles of Faith' by Emil G. Hirsch and K. Kohler in JE, Vol. II, pp. 148–152; article by Samuel S. Cohon 'Creed' in UJE, Vol. 3, pp. 400–403; Carol Klein: 'The Credo of Maimonides', Philosophical Library, New York, 1958; Hartwig Hirschfeld: 'Creed (Jewish)' in Vol. 4, pp. 244–246; B. Felsenthal:

'Gibt es Dogmen im Judenthum?' in Yearbook C.C.A.R., Vol. 8, 1898, pp. 54–73; Max L. Margolis: 'The Theological Aspect of Reformed Judaism' in Yearbook C.C.A.R., Vol. 13, 1903, pp. 184–308, followed by discussion; Discussion on above in Yearbook C.C.A.R., Vol. 15, 1905, pp. 83 ff; 'Christianity and Judaism Compare Notes' by Harris Franklin Roll and Samuel S. Cohon, Macmillan, New York, 1927, Part II, Chapter III, pp. 43–67. Adolph Harnack's 'History of Dogma,' trans. by Neil Buchanan, Dover Publications, New York, 1961, is, of course, indispensable reading for the Christian approach.

*   *   *

The discussion begins with the statement attributed to Moses Mendelssohn that Judaism has no dogmas. It is not too clear what exactly Mendelssohn intended to convey. He himself suggested that the formal Jewish Creed, containing the thirteen principles of the faith, should be taught to school children, although he was prepared to substitute 'I am convinced' for 'I believe'. One thing is certain. There are far too many Jewish teachings on the value of correct belief and far too many attempts at the classification of articles of faith to allow the superficial 'dogma of dogmalessness' to be accepted. The *Oxford English Dictionary* gives two definitions of 'dogma'. The first is 'an opinion; a belief; a tenet or doctrine'; the second 'the body of opinion formulated and authoritatively stated'. Since there has never been, in Judaism, a central authority moved to formulate a Creed there are no dogmas in the second sense in Judaism. But dogma in the first sense is a very different matter.

The Bible contains no definite command or injunction to 'believe', but beliefs concerning God and His revelation to man are implied throughout the Biblical books. Under the influence of Greek thought Philo (b.c. 20 B.C.E.) was the first Jew, so far as we know, to formulate articles of faith. After describing the teachings of the early chapters of Genesis Philo sums these up as follows: 'By his account of the creation of the world of which we have spoken Moses teaches us among many other things five that are fairest and best of all. Firstly that the Deity is and has been from eternity. This with a view to atheists, some of whom have hesitated and have been of two minds about His eternal existence, while the bolder sort have carried their audacity to the point of declaring that the Deity does not exist at all, but that it is a mere assertion of men obscuring the truth with myth and fiction. Secondly, that God is one. This with a view to the propounders of polytheism, who do not blush to transfer from earth to heaven mob rule, that worst of evil policies. Thirdly, as I have said already, that the world came into being. This because of those who think that it is without beginning and eternal, who thus assign to God no superiority at all. Fourthly, that the world too is one as well as its Maker, who made His work like Himself in its uniqueness, who used up for the creation of the whole all the material that exists; for it would not have been a whole had it not been formed and consisted of parts that were wholes. For there are those who suppose that there are more worlds than one, while some think that they are infinite in number. Such men are themselves in very deed lacking in knowledge of things which it is good to know. Fifthly, that God also exercises fore-thought on the world's behalf. For that the Maker should care for the thing made is required by the laws and ordinances of Nature, and it is in accordance with these that parents take thought beforehand for children. He that has begun by learning these things with his understanding rather than with his hearing, and has stamped on his soul impressions of truth so marvellous and priceless, both that God is and is from eternity, and that He that really IS is One, and that He has made the world and has made it one world, unique as Himself is unique, and that He ever exercises forethought for His creation, will lead a life of bliss and blessedness, because he has a character moulded by the truths that piety and holiness enforce'. (*'De Opificio Mundi'*, trans. F. H. Colson and G. H. Whitaker, Loeb Classical Library, 1949, Chapter LXI, pp. 135-137).

It is worthy of note that Philo's five principles have been formulated in response to views current in his day which he felt to be against the spirit of the Jewish faith. In other words, his statement of what a Jew should believe is conditioned by the special denials of his age, which required to be combated. This was to happen again and again in the history of Jewish Creed formulation. It was never a question of examining the classical sources of Judaism in an objective manner in order to discover the basic principles of Judaism. This would have been an almost impossible task since the Biblical sources are neither speculative nor systematic but organic and dynamic. It was rather a question of emphasising the ideas and beliefs which required to be stressed as principles of faith in a given age because it was in these areas that the challenge to the Jewish spirit was felt to be acute. In reality this is only another way of saying that dogmas in the Catholic sense, for instance, are impossible in Judaism because Judaism has no Church, no central authority with the power to formulate beliefs. (On this *v.* Auguste Sabatier: Outlines of a Philosophy of Religion Based on Psychology and History', Harper Torchbook Edition, New York, 1957, Book III, Chapter 1, pp. 223-237. On Philo's formulation *cf.* H. A. Wolfson: Philo, Harvard University Press, 1948, Vol. I, pp 171 ff., and 312 ff). Philo's idea that there is only one world is based on Plato's argument from an ideal model which Philo has recast in accordance with Jewish monotheistic belief. In this case it is not so much a question of Philo combating a challenge as incorporating into his system an idea, then widely accepted, which had formerly been debated. In any event, our argument is not affected, that Philo's formulation has to be understood not in abstract but against the background of contemporary thinking.

The question of principles of faith in the Rabbinic literature is more complicated. We have noted above Graetz's recognition that in the statement of the three offences for which martyrdom is demanded by the Rabbis we have a formulation of the basic principles of Judaism. Another relevant passage is that dealing with the famous preachment of the third century Palestinian teacher, R. Simlai (*Makk.* 23b-24a). Here we are told that Moses received on Sinai six hundred and thirteen precepts but that David (Ps. xv) reduced them to eleven. (The meaning is undoubtedly that by keeping the eleven principles of David the Jew will, in fact, be led to the keeping of all the other precepts. This applies to all the examples of 'reductions' given in this passage). Isaiah reduced them further to six principles (Is. xxxiii. 15-16), Micah to three (Micah vi. 8), Isaiah again to two (Is. lvi. 1), and Amos (v. 4) to one great principle. Finally, it is said that it was rather Habakkuk who reduced them all to one great principle – 'But the righteous shall live by his faith' (Hab. ii. 4).

Another relevant passage is that concerning the acceptance of proselytes to the Jewish faith (*Yeb.* 47 a-b). Before a prospective proselyte is accepted he is informed that Israel 'at the present time' are afflicted and despised. If he replies: 'I know and yet am unworthy' he is immediately accepted and is given instruction in some of the minor and some of the major commandments. It is noteworthy that in the passage, beyond a homiletical interpretation of Naomi's plea to Ruth in which the former tells her daughter-in-law that Jews are forbidden idolatry, there is no reference to beliefs. Maimonides (*Hil.* '*Issure Bi'ah*', XIV. 2), however, adds that he is to be told the principles of the faith, namely, the unity of God and the prohibition of idolatry. This is Maimonides' own addition, probably based on the actual practice of his day, but the Commentaries remark that this is either an obvious demand or that it is implied in the homily on Ruth (*v. Encyclopedia Talmudith*, Vol. VI, p. 430, note 43).

The *locus classicus*, however, for the question of fundamental beliefs in Judaism, so far as the Rabbinic literature is concerned, is the *Mishnah* in tractate *Sanhedrin* (X. 1): 'All Israelites have a share in the world to come . . . And these are they who have no share in the world to come: he that says there is no resurrection of the dead in the *Torah* (i.e. that the doctrine is without foundation); and he that says that the *Torah* is not from Heaven; and the Epicurean ('*epiqoros*). R. Akiba says: 'Also he that reads the external books (i.e. books not included in the canon of Scripture; the meaning is probably that he reads them in public, thereby suggesting that they enjoy Scriptural authority), or that utters a charm over a wound and says: "I will put none of the diseases upon thee which I have put upon the Egyptians: for I am the Lord that healeth thee" (Ex. xv. 26)' Abba Saul says: 'Also he that pronounces the Name (the Tetragrammaton) with its proper letters'.

*   *   *

EXCURSUS

The term '*epiqoros*, obviously derived from the name of the philosopher Epicurus is, in the Rabbinic literature, applied with no reference to its origin but to one who is licentious and sceptical. *V.* S. J. Rapoport: ' '*Erekh Millin*', Prague, 1852, *s.v.*, p. 181;

Encyclopedia Talmudith, Vol. II, *s.v.* pp. 136–7; Judah Bergmann: *'Shene Shemoth We-Goralam'* in '*Ha-'Am We-Ruho'*, Jer. 1937, pp. 64–69; Ephraim Shmueli: 'Faith and Heresy' (Heb), Tel-Aviv, 1962, pp. 163 ff.; J. Kaempf in MGWJ, Vol. 12, 1863, pp. 143–148; J. Oppenheim in MGWJ, Vol. 13, 1864, pp. 144–149; G. Deutsch in JE, Vol. I, pp. 665–6; J. Bergmann in UJE, Vol. 4, pp. 136–7. Josephus ('Antiquities', Book X, 11. 7, Loeb Classical Library, trans. Ralph Marcus, 1951, pp. 311–313, *cf.* 'Contra Apionem', II 19, Loeb, trans. H. St. J. Thackeray, p. 365) uses the term in the older sense as referring to the followers of the Greek philosopher: 'the Epicureans, who exclude Providence from human life and refuse to believe that God governs its affairs or that the universe is directed by a blessed and immortal Being to the end that the whole of it may endure, but say that the world runs by its own movement without knowing a guide or another's care'. *Cf.* Acts xvii. 18. It is remarkable that the root *paqar* is used in the Rabbinic literature to express 'abandonment' e.g. of property, as in the word *hephqer,* also in the sense of casting off moral and religious restraints. This led Buxtorf and others to suggest that the root is a derivative from '*epiqoros.* Oddly enough Maimonides (*Mishnah* Commentary to *Sanh.* X. 1) suggests that the root is a Semitic one and that the word '*epiqoros* is derived from it. The '*epiqoros* is the person who 'abandons and despises the *Torah* and its students'. Etymologically this can hardly be correct. But the root *paqar* is clearly Semitic, like *baqar, cf.* the term *hebhqer* for *hephqer* in *Pe'ah* VI. 1. The resemblance in sound to '*epiqoros* is purely coincidental but led to a close identification between the two. Although Maimonides connects the word with the root *paqar,* he knows of the existence of Epicurus, whom he quotes in his 'Guide', III. 17, unless it be that Maimonides did not know of the Greek philosopher when he wrote the Commentary to the *Mishnah* in his youth. Rapoport says that the name '*epiqoros* is 'well-known to us as referring to anyone who denies religion or one of its great principles, whether belonging to the written or the oral *Torah'.* The '*Encyclopedia Talmudith*' defines it as 'one who, out of abandon, despises the *Torah* and its students, both in deed and in opinion'. In the Tannaitic period the '*epiqoros* was generally identified with heretical opinions, *v. Mishnah Sanh.* X. 1 and '*Abhoth* II. 14. In the Amoraic period he was identified with one who shows flagrant disrespect to the Rabbis, *v. Sanh.* 99b. In the post-Talmudic period the term was used in various senses until eventually it was used in a very loose fashion to signify one who holds any kind of heretical belief. In the Rabbinic literature the '*epiqoros* is vehemently denounced to the extent that his life is forfeit – 'they may be cast in (into a pit) and need not be brought out', *v.* Maimonides, *Yad, Hil. 'Eduth,* Chapter 11, 10. It is, however, extremely doubtful if this is more than anti-sectarian preachment. There is no record anywhere in the Talmudic literature of a practical application of the law that the heretic's life is forfeit, *v.* the remarks of Louis M. Epstein: 'Marriage Laws in the Bible and Talmud', Harvard University Press, 1942, pp. 214–215. Present-day religious authorities such as the *'Hazon 'Ish'* and Rabbi Kook, embarrassed by these statements, suggest that they do not apply in modern times either because they will have the effect of increasing heresy or because the older type of *'epiqoros* is unknown, *v. Encyclopedia Talmudith, loc. cit.* notes, 30–40.

*   *   *

Schechter is undoubtedly correct in pointing to the semi-Halakhic (legal and obligatory) nature of this passage in the *Mishnah.* It is not to be compared with Aggadic (homiletical) passages in which a person is said to be excluded from the world to come for this or that offence, such as putting a neighbour to shame in public. These are almost certainly hyperbole whereas the statement in the *Mishnah* is recorded as part of this authoritative summary of Judaism. The *Mishnah* here excludes the following offenders from the world to come:

(1) One who denies the resurrection of the dead.

(2) One who denies that the *Torah* is divine.

(3) The *'epiqoros.*

(4) One who reads the external books (R. Akiba).

(5) One who utters a charm over a wound (R. Akiba).

(6) One who pronounces the Name (Abba Saul).

The last three are offenders in deed rather than belief. They throw light on the other three. It seems clear that we do not have in this *Mishnah* an early Rabbinic attempt at formulating a Creed so much as a warning against false opinions and religiously harmful practices current in the time of the *Mishnah.* Here the principle we noted with regard to Philo operates. Dogmatic formulations in Judaism generally appear to have been made in response to a particular situation in which certain ideas, challenged by sectarians, needed to be stressed. Particular stress is then placed on these ideas without necessarily suggesting that other unchallenged beliefs were of lesser significance. As Schechter notes, all the Rabbis looked upon such beliefs as the advent of the Messiah or divine Providence as basic in Judaism. The real impetus to Creed formulation was given in the Middle Ages when Jewish thinkers had to face the challenge presented by Greek philosophic thought, by Christianity and by Islam. It then became essential to define Judaism and to dwell on its unique features. It is somewhat ironic that the earliest formulations of Jewish Creeds in the Middle Ages were by Karaites, themselves sectarians and rebels against Rabbinism. They were the first Jews to come into close contact with non-Jewish systems. Later Rabbinic formulations had the additional motive of combating Karaism.

The most important formulation of articles of faith by a Rabbinate is, of course, that of Moses Maimonides (1135–1204) in his Commentary to the *Mishnah* (actually to the section of the *Mishnah* in tractate *Sanhedrin* we have just considered). Maimonides' Thirteen Articles of the Faith are:

(1) Belief in the existence of God.
(2) Belief in God's unity.
(3) Belief in God's incorporeality.
(4) Belief in God's eternity.
(5) Belief that God alone is to be worshipped.
(6) Belief in prophecy.
(7) Belief in Moses as the greatest of the prophets.
(8) Belief that the *Torah* was given by God to Moses.
(9) Belief that the *Torah* is immutable.
(10) Belief that God knows the thoughts and deeds of men.
(11) Belief that God rewards and punishes.
(12) Belief in the advent of the Messiah.
(13) Belief in the resurrection of the dead.

Maimonides concludes his statement of these principles with this observation: 'When all these principles are in the safe keeping of man, and his conviction of them is well established, he then enters 'into the general body of Israel', and it is incumbent upon us to love him, to care for him, and to do for him all that God commanded us to do for one another in the way of affection and brotherly sympathy. And this, even though he were to be guilty of every transgression possible, by reason of the power of desire or the mastery of the base natural passions. He will receive punishment according to the measure of his perversity, but he will have a portion in the world to come, even though he be of the 'transgressors in Israel'. When, however, a man breaks away from any of these fundamental principles of belief, then of him it is said that 'he has gone out of the general body of Israel', and 'he denies the root truth of Judaism'. And he is then termed 'heretic' (*min*) and 'unbeliever' ('*epiqoros*) and 'hewer of the small plants' (*v. Hag.* 14b), and it is obligatory upon us to hate him and cause him to perish, and it is concerning him that the Scriptural verse says: "Shall I not hate those who hate thee, O Lord?" (Ps. cxxxix. 21)'.

The emphasis of Maimonides is on faith, on correct belief as the supreme value. The believing sinner is included in 'the general body of Israel'. The unbeliever is excluded. It may well be, though this is nowhere stated explicitly by Maimonides, that this thinker's aim in stressing the supreme value of correct beliefs is tied up with his general philosophy, based on Aristotelean modes, of the immortality of the soul. Only that part of man is immortal, on this view, which has engaged in speculative reasoning concerning the metaphysical truths regarding God. It is the intellect acquired by this reasoning process – the 'active intellect' – which alone is immortal. It would seem to follow that only the philosopher can attain to immortality but as a devout Jew Maimonides is unable to accept this proposition. The *Mishnah* to which his comment is attached states clearly that *every* Israelite has a share in the world to come. In order to get round the difficulty Maimonides provides the unreflective Jew with certain basic beliefs of a metaphysical nature. By accepting these the Jew has acquired for himself some measure of divine truth and this suffices to provide him with a degree of the 'active intellect'. This theory has been advanced by Julius Guttmann ('*Ha-Philosophia Shel Ha-Yahaduth*' – Hebrew translation of his earlier German work – Jer. 1953, pp. 165-166) who suggests that Maimonides' aim was to provide a minimum of recognition of truth for the non-philosophic Jew, since in Maimonides' Aristotelean opinion it is only by the intellectual perception of metaphysical truth that the soul of man can acquire immortality. S. Urbach ('The Philosophical Teachings of Crescas' – Hebrew – Jer. 1961, p. 26, note 29) rather cavalierly dismisses this as 'philosophical homiletics' but Guttmann may well be right for all that, particularly since Maimonides deals at length with the Aristotelean view of immortality and its acquisition in this very comment to the *Mishnah* in *Sanhedrin*.

Although the Commentary to the *Mishnah* was written by him in his youth, Maimonides remains consistent in all his subsequent work. In his Code Maimonides elaborates on the heretics who are excluded from the 'general body of Israel' and from the world to come (*Yad, Hil. Teshubhah*, Chapter 3, 6-14): 'The following have no share in the world to come but are cut off and destroyed and punished for ever for their great wickedness and sin: The *Minim*, the *'Epiqorsin*, those who deny the *Torah*, who deny the Resurrection, the coming of the Redeemer, the apostates, those who cause many to sin, those who separate themselves from the ways of the Community, those who sin with a high hand like Jehoakim, the informers, those who terrorise the public for purposes other than the sake of Heaven, those who shed blood, the slanderers, and those who remove the sign of circumcision.'

'Five are called *Minim*: One who says that there is no God; that the world has no Controller; one who agrees that the world has a Controller but believes that there are two or more; one who says that there is one Lord but that He is corporeal and has a likeness; also one who says that He is not the First and the Rock of all, also one who worships a star or planet and so forth as an intercessor between him and the Lord of the Universe. Each one of these is called a *Min* ("sectarian")'. 'Three are called *'Epiqorsin*: One who says that there is no prophecy at all and that there is no knowledge which reaches to the hearts of men from the Creator; one who denies the prophecy of Moses our Teacher; and one who says that the Creator does not know men's deeds. Each one of these three is an *'Epiqoros*. Three are deniers of the *Torah*: One who says that the *Torah* is not from God, even if he refers to no more than one verse or one word, saying that Moses spoke it of his own accord, he is a denier of the *Torah*. The same applies to one who denies its explanation, namely, the Oral *Torah*, or, like Zadok and Boethus, denies its teachers. The same applies to one who says that the Creator changed one precept for another so that even though the *Torah* did once come from God it is no longer valid, like the Christians and the Muslims. Each one of these three is a denier of the *Torah*.'

Maimonides goes on to record the other types of offences he has listed and concludes:

'Each one of the twenty-four persons we have counted, even if he is an Israelite, has no share in the world to come. There are lesser offences than these concerning which the Sages nevertheless said that one who is accustomed to do them has no share in the world to come and it is right to be remote from them and to take care against transgression. They are: Giving one's neighbour an opprobrious nickname; calling him by that nickname; putting him to shame in public; obtaining honour at the expense of a neighbour's shame; despising scholars of the *Torah;* despising one's teachers; despising the festivals; profaning sacred things. The statement that all the above have no share in the world to come applies only if they died without repenting. But if they turned from their wickedness before dying they are repentant sinners and belong to the world to come for nothing can stand in the way of repentance. Even one who had denied the basic principle of Judaism all his days has a share in the world to come if he repented at the end, as it is said: "Peace, peace, to him that is far off and to him that is near, saith the Lord, and I will heal him" (Is. lvii. 19).'

The thirteen principles of Maimonides eventually became authoritative for the majority of Jews, even though various subsequent thinkers challenged Maimonides' formulation. An indication of their significance is that they are found today in most traditional prayer books in two forms. (It goes without saying that their appearance in the prayer book was responsible in large measure for their very wide acceptance). The first of these is the *Yigdal* hymn (The Authorised Daily Prayer Book, ed. S. Singer, p. 2) composed in Italy about the beginning of the fourteenth century, probably by Daniel ben Judah of Rome. The second is in prose form (Singer's P.B. pp. 89–90), almost certainly fashioned on Islamic models, in which the statement of each article begins with the words '*'Ani Ma'amin*' – 'I believe'. This first appeared in 1517 and was incorporated into many liturgies. Its author is unknown. This formulation is less precise, and philosophically far less adequate, than either Maimonides' original version or that of the *Yigdal* hymn. It should be noted that a catechism of the '*'Ani Ma'amin*' type was completely unknown until then in Judaism. The liturgy

certainly contains numerous ideas implying beliefs but this
is the first attempt to introduce into Jewish practice a formal
recital of abstract beliefs and, almost certainly, owes much to
non-Jewish influences (*v.* Neumark, *op. cit.*, Part II, p. 161).

As has been said, various Jewish thinkers took issue with
Maimonides, either because they believed that his reduction of
the principles to thirteen was unjustified, since everything in
the *Torah* is of equal importance, or because they disagreed
with his particular formulation and favoured a different one.
Prominent among the critics was Hasdai Crescas (1340–1410)
in his '*'Or 'Adonai*', 'Light of the Lord' (Vienna, 1859,
Hatza'ah, p. 3b; Book II, Introduction, p. 27b; Book III,
Introduction, p. 61a; Book IV, Introduction, p. 85a. *Cf.* Neumark *op. cit.* Part II, Chapter 9, pp. 163–175; H. A. Wolfson:
'Crescas' Critique of Aristotle', Harvard University Press,
1929, note 1, p. 319; S. B. Urbach: 'The Philosophical Teachings of Crescas' – Hebrew – Jer. 1961, pp. 25 ff.). For Crescas
the basic belief in God – that He exists, is One and is incorporeal – is in a class by itself. In addition to this basic belief
there are three categories of beliefs: (1) *Fundamentals*, without
which the Jewish religion is inconceivable. These are: (*a*)
God's knowledge of His creatures, (*b*) His Providence, (*c*) His
power, (*d*) Prophecy, (*e*) Freewill, (*f*) the *Torah* leads man
to his true hope and final bliss. (2) *True opinions*. These are
divided into beliefs which are independent of any particular
precept and beliefs dependent on a particular precept. To the
first type belong: (*a*) Creation, (*b*) the soul is immortal, (*c*)
Reward and Punishment, (*d*) Resurrection, (*e*) the immutability of the *Torah*, (*f*) Moses, (*g*) that the High Priest had
the oracle of the *Urim We-Thummim* (Ex. xxviii. 30), (*h*) the
Messiah. Of the second type are: (*a*) beliefs implied in Prayer
and the Blessing of the Priests, (*b*) beliefs implied in Repentance, (*c*) beliefs implied in the Day of Atonement and the other
Jewish Festivals. Anyone who denies one of the 'fundamental
beliefs' or one of the 'true opinions' is an unbeliever, the only
difference between the two categories being that the Jewish
faith is inconceivable without the first but not without the
second. (3) *Probabilities*. These are opinions which Crescas
discusses on the basis of Jewish teaching, arriving at certain
conclusions which he is convinced are correct. Nevertheless

since these conclusions are neither obvious nor simple, one
who arrives at different conclusions, though he is mistaken,
is not an unbeliever. These 'probabilities' are thirteen in
number (was Crescas influenced here by Maimonides' number
thirteen?): (*a*) Is the world eternal? (*b*) Are there many
worlds? (*c*) Are the spheres living creatures? (*d*) Have the
stars an influence over human destiny? (*e*) Is there any efficacy
to charms and amulets? (*f*) Do demons exist? (*g*) Is the
doctrine of metempsychosis true? (*h*) Is the soul of an infant
immortal? (*i*) Paradise and Hell, (*j*) Are the Rabbinic 'Works
of Creation' ('*Ma'aseh Bereshith*') and 'Works of the Heavenly
Chariot' ('*Ma'aseh Merkhabhah*') to be identified with 'Physics'
and 'Metaphysics'? (*k*) the nature of comprehension, (*l*) the
First Cause, (*m*) can the true nature of God be comprehended?
All these are discussed in the older sources of Judaism but
Crescas is aware that there are no simple answers to the
problems raised. Consequently, one who does not accept the
right opinion here is not an unbeliever.

Crescas thus differs from Maimonides, not in the very idea
of formulating articles of faith, but in the method of formulation.
Neumark is possibly right in detecting an apologetic, anti-
Christological aim in Crescas' presentation. Crescas may be
saying in so many words that certain institutions known to
Christianity are not unknown to Judaism and that the Jew
has no need to feel his faith inferior in these areas. This would
explain the special emphasis on Repentance, the Day of
Atonement and the Priesthood. The otherwise very odd emphasis
on the *Urim We-Thummim* is also to be explained, probably,
by the apologetic tendency in Crescas' thought (*v.* Neumark
op. cit. pp. 174–175). If this is correct we have a further instance
of the influence of the special requirements of the age in the
formulation of principles of faith.

Another important figure in the history of Creed formulation
in Judaism is Simon ben Zemah Duran (1361-1444). (On
Duran's thought *v.* J. Guttmann: 'Die Stellung des Simon ben
Zemach Duran in der Geschichte der jüdischen Religionsphilo-
sophie' in MGWJ, Vol. 52, 1908, pp. 641–672, Vol. 53, 1909,
pp. 46–79, 199–228). In Duran's view ('*Magen 'Abhoth*',
Leghorn, 1785, p. 2b, end of Introduction) the principles of
the Jewish faith are three in number: (1) The existence of

God, (2) That the *Torah* is divine, (3) Reward and Punishment. Duran sees these three spoken of in the *Mishnah* in *Sanhedrin*. The three persons denied a share in the world to come, it will be recalled, are: the one who denies that the *Torah* is from Heaven, the one who denies the resurrection, and the *'epiqoros*. This latter is taken by Duran to mean one who denies the existence of God, while belief in the resurrection is made to embrace the belief in reward and punishment, hence Duran's formulation in a positive form. But these three are given certain elaborations so as to include other basic beliefs: 'The foundation of faith is to believe in God, blessed be He, that He exists, that He is One, that He is eternal, that He is incorporeal and that it is fitting to worship Him alone. All these are included in the term *'epiqoros*, as we have said. Next, one must believe in the predictions of the prophets and of Moses, in the *Torah* and that it is eternal. These are included in the term "*Torah* from Heaven". Next, one must believe in reward and punishment and their offshoots, which is included in the term "The Resurrection of the dead".' It will be seen that, in fact, Duran manages to include in his three principles the thirteen of Maimonides. He claims that 'earlier teachers' (*'rishonim'*) have invented a mnemonic for these three basic beliefs. This is: *'We –Ha – 'Adamah Lo Thesham'* ('And that the land be not desolate', Gen. xlvii. 19). The word for 'desolate' – *thesham* – is composed of the three letters – *taw, shin* and *mem*. These stand for: *Torah, Sekhar* (='Reward') and *Metzi'uth Ha-Shem* (=the existence of God). Duran gives us no indication of the identity of his predecessors who have invented this mnemonic (*v.* Guttmann, *op. cit.*, Vol. 53, pp. 56-57, note 4).

Joseph Albo (*c.* 1380–*c.* 1445) devotes his book *'Sepher Ha-'Iqqarim'*, 'Book of Principles' (ed. I. Husik, with an English translation and notes, Philadelphia, 1946) to a critique of Maimonides' formulation, differing from the latter in his definition of what is and what is not a 'principle' of Jewish Faith. Albo (Book I, Chapter 2, ed. Husik p. 49 f.) develops an important idea which, in fact, as Husik and Neumark point out, he has taken from Duran without acknowledgment. A person is only called an unbeliever (*kopher*) who knows that the *Torah* lays down a certain principle but wilfully denies its truth. It is the element of rebellion against the clear teaching of the

Torah which constitutes unbelief. 'But a person who upholds
the law of Moses and believes in its principles, but when he
undertakes to investigate these matters with his reason and
scrutinizes the texts, is misled by his speculation and interprets
a given principle otherwise than it is taken to mean at first
sight; or denies the principle because he thinks that it does
not represent a sound theory which the *Torah* obliges us to
believe; or erroneously denies that a given belief is a fundamental principle, which however he believes as he believes
the other dogmas of the *Torah* which are not fundamental
principles; or entertains a certain notion in relation to one of
the miracles of the *Torah* because he thinks that he is not
thereby denying any of the doctrines which it is obligatory upon
us to believe by the authority of the *Torah* – a person of this
sort is not an unbeliever. He is classed with the sages and pious
men of Israel, though he holds erroneous theories. His sin is
due to error and requires atonement'. Albo gives the illustration of one of the sages who appeared to deny *creatio ex nihilo*
but since it was his opinion that this is taught in the *Torah*,
he was not an unbeliever, despite his unconventional views.

Like Duran, Albo considers the principles of the Jewish Faith
to be three in number – belief in God, in Revelation, and in
Reward and Punishment. To each of these a Book of the work
is devoted, Book 2 to the first principle, Book 3 to the second,
and Book 4 to the third. Like Duran again, each of the main
principles is divided into subordinate ones derived from it.
The three benedictions incorporated in the Additional Service
for New Year, going by the name of 'Kingdoms', 'Memorials'
and 'Trumpets' (Singer's P.B. pp. 247–254), represent these
three principles. According to Albo these three blessings were
ordained in order to call our attention to the basic beliefs
of Judaism at the beginning of the year, the traditional period of
divine judgment, 'that by properly believing in these principles
together with the dogmas derived from them we shall win a
favourable verdict in the divine judgment' (Book I, Chapter 4,
Husik, p. 65 f.). Schechter's observation (*op. cit.*, begin. p.
73) that Judaism does not ascribe any saving power to dogmas
requires some modification. It is indubitable that Schechter's
remarks are true of many Jewish thinkers but they are not true
of all of them. We have discussed earlier Guttmann's interpre-

B

tation of the Maimonidean formulation. Here we find Albo
putting forward a doctrine not very far removed from the idea
that true dogmas possess a saving grace in themselves. Of
course, the possibility that Albo is consciously or unconsciously
influenced by contemporary Christian attitudes cannot be ruled
out. The 'Kingdom' benediction, consisting of Scriptural
verses dealing with the theme of God's sovereignty, corresponds to the principle of the existence of God. The 'Memorials'
benediction corresponds to the principle of Reward and Punishment, containing as it does verses dealing with God's 'remembrance' and hence His Providence. The benediction 'Trumpets',
containing verses dealing with the sounding of trumpets,
alludes to the third principle of Revelation, since at the giving
of the *Torah* the loud trumpet was sounded.

Albo concludes (Book I, Chapter 26, Husik p. 202) that the
number of principles, fundamental and derived, i.e. the three
fundamentals and those derived from them, is eleven. These
are: (1) the existence of God, (2) His unity, (3) His incorporeality, (4) His independence of time, (5) His freedom from
defect, (6) prophecy, (7) authenticity of the messenger (the
prophet), (8) revelation, (9) God's knowledge, (10) providence, (11) reward and punishment. Without these the Jewish
religion is inconceivable, hence these are called principles
of the faith. There are, in addition, six dogmas which everyone
professing the law of Moses is obliged to believe (Book I,
Chapter 23, Husik, pp. 181 f.) and one who denies them is a
heretic without a share in the world to come. They are not
called 'principles of the faith', however, since, on Albo's
definition, the only beliefs entitled so to be called are those
without which the Jewish faith is inconceivable. These six are:
(1) *creatio ex nihilo*, (2) the superiority of Moses' prophecy, (3)
the immutability of the *Torah*, (4) that human perfection can
be attained by fulfilling even a single one of the commandments of the *Torah*, (5) the resurrection of the dead, (6) the
coming of the Messiah. Taking issue with Crescas, without
mentioning him by name, Albo refuses to include in either list
beliefs based on specific commandments because no one
commandment should be counted as a dogma rather than
another. Nor does he include beliefs in certain miracles because
these are included in the general belief in miracles which form

part of the belief in the *Torah*. As examples of the former Albo
cites repentance and prayer. As examples of the latter he
cites the fire coming down from heaven upon the altar of the
burnt offering and that the priests received answers from God
through the *Urim We-Thummim!*

The famous preacher Isaac Arama (c. 1420–1494) in his
' '*Aqedath Yitzhaq*' (Gate 55) similarly speaks of *three* fundamental principles. These are: (1) *creatio ex nihilo*, (2) revelation, (3) belief in the world to come. The second of these
is the same as Albo's. For the existence of God Arama substitutes *creatio ex nihilo* which obviously includes it. Similarly, his
third principle includes reward and punishment. Arama
believes that the Sabbath is a cornerstone of Judaism because
in the observance of the day all three principles are given
expression. The Sabbath reminds man of God's creation; He
'rested' on the seventh day after performing the work of creation.
On the Sabbath man has the leisure to engage in *Torah* study
and he is thus reminded of the divine origin of the *Torah*.
Finally, Sabbath bliss is a foretaste of the bliss the righteous
will enjoy in the world to come. Needless to say, historically
speaking, Arama's three principles are selected as arbitrarily as
Albo's.

Isaac Abarbanel's (1437–1508) '*Rosh 'Amanah*', 'Pinnacle of
Faith', is another book devoted to the question of principles
of faith in Judaism. (The work was completed in 1495 and
published in Constantinople in 1505). Twenty-two chapters of
the work are devoted to a defence of Maimonides against his
critics and to a detailed examination of the whole idea of
principles of faith. In chapter twenty-three the author elaborates
his own view that since every part of the *Torah* is of equal
value the very attempt to formulate principles of faith is
misguided. In the last chapter, twenty-four, this view is
defended against its critics. Abarbanel claims (Chapter 23) that
the impetus towards the formulation of articles of faith by
Maimonides and his successors was provided by their study
of the sciences. They concluded from their observation that
each science has its main principles and that certain notions
must form the basis of the science of *Torah*. But, in fact, the
analogy between the *Torah* and other sciences is false. Other
sciences require first principles because they are based solely

on human reasoning which proceeds from axiom to axiom. But it is extremely offensive to suggest that any part of the *Torah* is superior to any other since the *Torah* is not a human work but is divine. 'Therefore I am convinced that it is improper to postulate principles or foundations with regard to God's *Torah*. For we are obliged to believe everything recorded in the *Torah* and we are not permitted to doubt the smallest matter therein that it should be necessary to prove its truth by reference to principles or root ideas. For whoever denies or doubts any matter, small or great, of the beliefs or narratives contained in the *Torah* is a heretic and an unbeliever. Since the *Torah* is true no single belief or narrative in it can be superior to any other'. By speaking of some portions of the *Torah*, suggests Abarbanel, as 'principles' and others as 'derivatives' we tend to imply that the former are in some way more significant than the latter. This contradicts the basic Rabbinic view that there is no distinction between 'severe' and 'light' precepts, both classes being God-given.

David ben Solomon Ibn Abi Zimra (c. 1479–1589) like Abarbanel and the Qabbalists, generally refuses to distinguish between parts of the *Torah* by speaking of some of them as 'principles'. Ibn Abi Zimra was a prolific writer of Responsa, of which he wrote more than three thousand. Responsum No. 344 reads as follows:

'Question:
You ask me, with regard to the matter of principles of faith, whether I accept the formulation of Maimonides or Crescas or Albo.

Answer:
I do not agree that it is right to make any part of the perfect *Torah* into a "principle" since the whole *Torah* is a "principle" from the Mouth of the Almighty. Our Sages say that whoever states that the whole of the *Torah* is from Heaven with the exception of one verse is a heretic. Consequently, each precept is a "principle" and a fundamental idea. Even a light precept has a secret reason which is beyond our understanding. How then dare we suggest that this is inessential and that fundamental? In short, Rabbi Isaac Abarbanel, of blessed memory, wrote correctly in his work *"Rosh 'Amanah"*; consult this

work. There he develops this theme at length, criticising earlier scholars. My opinion is the same as his that every detail and inference of the *Torah* is a "principle", a foundation and a fundamental belief and whoever denies it is an unbeliever and has no share in the world to come. For this reason if heathen force a Jew to transgress any of the precepts of the *Torah*, saying to him that God did not command it or that it was given only for a certain time and no longer has validity, he is obliged to suffer death rather than transgress. This only applies where he is urged to profane the Sabbath in order to transgress against his religion. Rabbi Yom Tobh ben Abraham, of blessed memory, writes accordingly and derives from this that a Jew must suffer death rather than become a Muslim even though Muslims are not idolators. I have written that which seems correct to my puny intellect.'

*   *   *

EXCURSUS

> Here is a suitable place to insert a note on the general question of martyrdom in Judaism, a question of no little importance also in assessing the principles of Judaism as conceived of in Jewish thought and history. Graetz, as we have seen, correctly points to *Sanh.* 74a, in which the ruling is given that the Jew must give his life rather than worship idols, commit murder or offend against the Levitical laws governing sexual relations, as the best indication, from the historical aspect, of the real principles of the Jewish faith. Similarly, Ibn Abi Zimra, above, uses the argument from martyrdom in defence of his view of articles of faith in Judaism. In the book of Maccabees (I Macc. ii. 32–41) we are told that, at first, the Jewish warriors refused to join battle on the Sabbath, allowing themselves to be slaughtered without resistance rather than profane the sacred day but that eventually the ruling was given to permit defence of life even on the Sabbath. (*Cf.* II Macc. xv and Arnold Toynbee's remarks, 'An Historian's Approach to Religion', Oxford University Press, 1956, pp. 100–101, that possibly the first to have laid down their lives for the sake of a god who was not some form of collective human power were the Jewish martyrs who suffered under the Seleucid Monarchy in 167 B.C.). Subsequently, in the Tannaitic period, it became axiomatic that a Jew may transgress the precepts of the *Torah* in order to save his life, Lev. xviii. 5 being quoted in support ('he shall *live* by them', not die by them, *Sanh. ibid.* and freq.). R. Ishmael extends this even to idolatry, permitting the

Jew to worship idols in order to save his life (*Sanh. ibid.*) unless
he was called upon to do it publicly when he is obliged to give his
life in order to avoid a 'profanation of God's Name' (Lev. xxii.
32). R. Eliezer disagrees with R. Ishmael, arguing that Judaism
demands martyrdom rather than idolatry even in private (*Sanh.
ibid.*). Cf. *Mishnah, Ber.* IX. 5. At the Council of Lydda, to which
Graetz refers, the ruling was given that martyrdom must be
chosen, even in private, rather than the transgression of the three
offences mentioned above (*Sanh. ibid.*). All these were Tannaitic
teachers and it seems certain that the issues discussed were practical
ones. In the Amoraic period, R. Johanan, third century, is reported
as expressing one of two opinions. According to the first opinion
attributed to him, the rule that a precept, other than the three,
may be transgressed in order to save life applies only where the
government issued no special decree to this effect. Where there was
a determined effort by the reigning government to uproot Judaism
the Jew was obliged to resist, allowing himself to be martyred even
for a 'light precept'. According to the second opinion, the rule
applies only in private but rather than transgress a precept in
public the Jew must be prepared to suffer martyrdom (*Sanh ibid.*).
Later Amoraim (*Sanh.* 74*b*) give as an example of a 'light precept'
even such a minor Jewish custom of lacing one's shoes in a special
manner. Furthermore, the term 'in public' is defined as where ten
Jews are present. The question is then asked: 'Did not Esther
sin in public?' i.e. since everyone knew that she was with Ahasuerus
(Esther ii. 5–18). To this Abaye replies that she was 'passive' (i.e.
the rule does not apply to the woman victim upon whom sexual
intercourse is forced), while Raba replies that where the heathen
intends it for his own pleasure, not in order to force the Jew to
disobey his religion, the rule does not apply (*Sanh. ibid.*). On
the basis of this passage in *Sanhedrin*, Maimonides (*Yad, Hil.
Yesode Ha-Torah*, Chapter 5, 1–9) rules that a Jew may transgress
the precepts of the *Torah* in order to save his life but that this
does not apply to the three offences nor does it apply in public
if the intention of the heathen is to force the Jew to disobey his
religion. Similarly, where there is a government decree against
Jewish observance the Jew is obliged to suffer martyrdom even
for a 'light precept' in private. Maimonides (*op. cit.* 4) is of the
opinion that where martyrdom is not demanded it is positively
forbidden and that one who allows himself to be killed in such
circumstances is a suicide. Other mediaeval authorities disagree
with Maimonides (*v. Tos.* A.Z. 27b *s.v. yakhol* and *Keseph Mishneh*
to Maimon. *op. cit.* that even Maimonides would agree in the case
of a Jew distinguished for his learning and piety who suffers

martyrdom that others might learn the value of the precepts, *cf.*
Shulhan 'Arukh, Yoreh De'ah, 157. 1). On this whole subject *v.*
the interesting Responsa of Rabbi A. I. Kook, *'Mishpat Kohen',* Jer.,
1937, Nos. 142 and 148, pp. 305 ff. and 354 ff. and the observations
of Rabbi S. Sevin on self-sacrifice in wartime in his *'Le-'Or Ha-
Halakhah',* Jer. 1946, pp. 7–11. Graetz and others (Greenstone
in JE, Vol. VIII, 'Martyrdom, Restriction Of', pp. 353–4, who states
this as 'probably', Lelyveld in UJE, Vol. VI, 'Kiddush Hashem and
Hillul Hashem', pp. 380–381) claim that the famous ruling at
Lydda concerning the three offences took place during the Hadrianic
persecutions. Apart from the fact that this contradicts the later
Halakhah that in times of religious persecution the Jew must give
his life for *any* precept (it might be argued that this is a later
development of the Amoraic *Halakhah*) there is no evidence in
the sources that the meeting at Lydda took place during the persecutions. In fact, there is a Tannaitic source which states that during
the Hadrianic persecutions Jews gave their lives for such precepts as
circumcision, *v. Mekhilta, Yithro,* ed. Friedmann, 68b. On this *v.*
the arguments of C. Z. Reines in *Sinai,* Vol. 16, March-April,
1953, pp. 23–42, *'Mesirath Nephesh Ba-Halakhah'.* The famous
case of the two men travelling through a wilderness with only
one of them having sufficient water to sustain his life (*Siphra,* ed.
Weiss, *Behar,* 109c, *B.M.* 62a) has been widely discussed. Ahad
Ha-Am (*v.* 'Essays, Letters, Memoirs – Ahad Ha-Am', trans. by
Leon Simon, East and West Library, Oxford, 1946, p. 128 f.) draws
the conclusion, completely unwarranted to my mind, from the
case that Jewish teaching would be opposed to 'Greater love hath
no man than this, that a man lay down his life for his friends' (John
xv. 13). In fact, Judaism, too, considers self-sacrifice for another,
where circumstances demand it, to be an act of the greatest piety, *v.*
my book 'Jewish Values', London, 1960, pp. 124 ff. and my debate
with Sir Leon Simon in the correspondence columns of the 'Jewish
Chronicle', Nov. 1961. Cf. *'Sepher Hasidim',* ed. Wistinetzki, 252,
p. 83: 'If a scholar and an unlearned man were sitting together and
heathen wished to kill one of them, it is meritorious (*mitzwah*) for
the unlearned man to say to them: "Kill me and spare my neighbour" ', and C. Z. Reines in the Federbush Jubilee Volume, Jer.
1960, pp. 304–15.

*   *   *

It will be seen from the above that while there are undoubtedly
articles of faith in Judaism there are, nonetheless, fundamental
differences between Judaism and Christianity in the matter of

dogma. The first of these is due to the practical nature of Judaism. Since both Bible and *Talmud*, the classical sources of Judaism, are non-speculative in character, their influence militated against precise formulations of a Creed until comparatively late in the history of Judaism. Even when such formulations were made, they were the work of individual teachers, enjoying only the authority due to them by their learning. There was no Jewish 'Church', no central authority whose opinion in this matter would be binding upon Jews, nothing corresponding to the Athanasian and Nicene Creeds of the Church. To conclude from this that Judaism is unconcerned with belief is erroneous, and much credit is due to Schechter and others who have pointed this out in emphatic terms. In the essay quoted Schechter rightly says: 'We usually urge that in Judaism religion means life; but we forget that a life without guiding principles and thoughts is a life not worth living. At least it was so considered by the greatest Jewish thinkers, and hence their efforts to formulate the creed of Judaism, so that men should not only be able to do the right thing, but also to think the right thing . . . Political economy, hygiene, statistics, are very fine things. But no sane man would for them make those sacrifices which Judaism requires from us. It is only for God's sake, to fulfil His commands and to accomplish His purpose, that religion becomes worth living and dying for. And this can only be possible with a religion which possesses dogmas.'

Schechter's contribution here cannot be sufficiently praised. But it is a pity that he stopped there and made no attempt to describe for the modern Jew the dogmas Judaism requires him to accept. There is not really much point in emphasising both the historical significance of dogmas in Judaism and their importance for Jewish religion in the present unless the dogmas are defined. If it be granted that a religion without beliefs has neither salt nor savour, it is surely essential that we know what these beliefs are. Schechter's admission comes, therefore, as a shock: 'But it was not my purpose to ventilate here the question whether Maimonides' articles are sufficient for us, or whether we ought to add new ones to them. Nor do I attempt to decide what system we ought to prefer for recitation in the Synagogue – that of Maimonides or that of Chasdai, or of any other writer. I do not think that such a recital is of much

use. My object in this sketch has been rather to make the reader
think about Judaism, by proving that it regulates not only our
actions, but also our thoughts'. What Schechter gives with
one hand he takes away with the other. It is well-nigh incredible
that once Schechter's 'old Adam' had asserted itself to point
out that Judaism regulates our thoughts he should be content
to stop short at even attempting to describe the kind of thoughts
it seeks to regulate. The reader convinced by Schechter's
powerful argument that there can be no living Judaism without
articles of faith will be a poor sort of thinker if he is content to
leave it at that. To say that there are dogmas in Judaism but
we neither know or can know what they are is tantamount to
saying that Judaism has no dogmas. The historical school
has always been handicapped by its failure to build theologically
on the very sure foundations its researches have uncovered.
This has only too often meant that our theologians try to
construct systems which have no historical basis while our
historians are uninterested in the theological implications of
their rediscovery of the Jewish past. Theology thus becomes
divorced from historical reality and history of only antiquarian
interest. The theologian takes refuge in his concept of 'eternity'
to ignore the time process. The historian refuses to consider
metaphysics, as beyond his competence. In this 'post-critical'
age an attempt to formulate articles of faith for the modern
Jew is one of the most important tasks facing thinkers who
are not only historians but Jewish believers.

It would be quite wrong, of course, to suggest that nothing
has been done in this field for there are a number of important
studies provided for the Jew interested in theology. But there
is need of a detailed and well-documented examination of the
thirteen principles in the light of modern thought. The following
chapters, then, take up the matter where Schechter left off,
accepting Maimonides' formulation as a basis on which to
build. This seemed to be a far better procedure than to discuss
the possibility of a new formulation of a Jewish Creed since
by now, Maimonides' thirteen principles have more or less
won for themselves a permanent place in Judaism. This does
not mean, of course, that they present no difficulties to moderns
in their present form. In the following chapters these difficulties
will be considered and the possibility of re-interpretation

examined. No claim is made that the result will provide the
thinking Jew with a completely adequate Creed. If it serves to
stimulate thinking on this vital matter the author will feel well
rewarded.

*   *   *

EXCURSUS

Of the older works on this theme are Morris Joseph's 'Judaism
as Creed and Life', London, 1903, recently republished, and M.
Friedländer's 'The Jewish Religion', 2nd. ed., London, 1900. Both
contain material of value but they are both very 'Victorian' in
spirit and much in both of them is dated. Friedländer believes that
Maimonides' thirteen principles must be accepted as they stand
without modification. The book still enjoys a certain popularity but
is very naive. Kaufmann Kohler's 'Jewish Theology', New York,
1925, is much more learned and sophisticated, containing in the
notes a very full survey of the literature on the subject up to his
day, but Kohler is unduly influenced by late nineteenth century
Protestant thought. Leo Baeck's 'The Essence of Judaism',
London, 1936, trans. by Victor Grubwieser and Leonard Paul, is
justly celebrated but the style is rather heavy and the work vague
in parts. Mordecai Kaplan's: 'Judaism as a Civilisation', New York,
1934, 'Judaism in Transition', 1936, and 'The Meaning of God
in Modern Jewish Religion', 1937, have been widely discussed. In
this connection v. Bernard J. Heller: 'The Modernist's Revolt
Against God' in Yearbook of the Central Conference of American
Rabbis, Vol. XL, 1930, p. 323 f. and Max Arzt: 'Dr. Kaplan's
Philosophy of Judaism' in Proceedings of the Rabbinical Assembly
of America, Vol. 5, 1938, pp. 195–219. Ira Eisenstein's
'Judaism Under Freedom', New York, 1956, is a presentation of
Kaplan's philosophy by a prominent disciple. Further material is
to be found in the issues of the magazine 'The Reconstructionist'
devoted to the furtherance of Kaplan's ideas. Maurice H. Far-
bridge's 'Judaism and the Modern Mind', New York, 1927, is a
clearly written, well-balanced investigation of the theme of the
title as is Israel H. Levinthal's 'Judaism: An Analysis and An
Interpretation', New York, 1935. Isidore Epstein's 'The Faith of
Judaism', London, 1954, and his 'Judaism', Pelican Books, 1959,
are well-written and comprehensive, but inadequate in dealing
with all the challenges of modern thought, e.g. in their treatment
of Bible Criticism. The same applies to Samuel Belkin's 'Essays in
Traditional Jewish Thought', New York, 1956 and his 'In His
Image', New York, 1960. It is surprising that so little has been

published on the subject in Hebrew in recent years. A. Barth's
'Dorenu Mul She'eloth Ha-Netzah', 2nd. ed., Jer. 1955, contains a
number of helpful discussions. Jacob B. Agus: 'Guideposts in
Modern Judaism', New York, 1954, is a courageous attempt at
dealing with current trends in Jewish thought. The same author's
'Modern Philosophies of Judaism', New York, 1941, is a profound
interpretation of the philosophies of Hermann Cohen, Franz
Rosenzweig, Martin Buber and Mordecai Kaplan. Existentialism
is represented among Jewish thinkers by Martin Buber, Franz
Rosenzweig and A. J. Heschel, the latter's thought being strongly
influenced by Jewish mysticism. On Buber there is an immense
literature, *v.* his 'I and Thou', trans. by Ronald Gregor Smith,
New York, 1937, his 'Eclipse of God', London, 1935, Maurice
S. Friedman: 'Martin Buber, The Life of Dialogue', London, 1955,
and Malcolm L. Diamond: 'Martin Buber, Jewish Existentialist',
New York, 1960. On Rosenzweig *v.* his 'Der Stern der Erlösung',
Heidelberg, 1954, Nahum H. Glatzer: 'Franz Rosenzweig, His
Life and Thought', New York, 1953, Alexander Altmann: 'Franz
Rosenzweig on History' in 'Between East and West, Essays
Dedicated to the Memory of Bela Horovitz', East and West
Library, London, 1958, pp. 194 ff., Ignaz Maybaum's 'Jewish
Existence', Vallentine, Mitchell, London, 1960. Heschel's well-
known book on the theme of the relevance of the Jewish religion
for modern man is 'God in Search of Man, A Philosophy of Judaism',
London, 1956. Another work of Heschel's is 'Man Is Not Alone',
New York, 1951. Will Herberg's 'Judaism and Modern Man,
An Interpretation of Jewish Religion', New York, 1951, Meridian
Books, 1959, is an existentialist interpretation of Judaism. Milton
Steinberg's 'The Making of the Modern Jew', Routledge, London,
1934, has awakened great interest. *Cf.* Steinberg's collection of
essays, published posthumously, 'Anatomy of Faith', ed. with an
Introduction by Arthur A. Cohen, New York, 1960. 'A Rabbinic
Anthology' by C. G. Montefiore and H. Loewe, Macmillan,
London, 1938, reprinted in Meridian Books, 1960, contains a
fascinating discussion by the two authors, one a Liberal the other an
Orthodox Jew, on Jewish theological topics. Two works by Rabbis
of the old school dealing with a Jewish theology for the present
are Rabbi A. I. Kook's ' *'Oroth Ha-Qodesh'*, 2 Vol., Jer., 1938, and
Rabbi E. Dessler's *'Mikhtabh Me-'Elijahu'*, London, 1955. Refer-
ence should be made to the various volumes of the Yearbook of the
Central Conference of American Rabbis, the Proceedings of the
Rabbinical Assembly of America, and the papers published by the
Chief Rabbi's Standing Conference of Great Britain, which contain
important material. As an example we may quote Max L. Margolis:

'The Theological Aspect of Reformed Judaism', in Year C.C.A.R., Vol. XIII, 1903, pp. 185–308, followed by a discussion. Margolis, after surveying the field of Jewish dogma historically, proceeds to formulate a Creed in the light of 'Reformed Judaism'. The subsequent discussion on his paper only proves how fraught with difficulty is such an enterprise. Particularly objectionable is the suggestion of a Creed for only one part of Jewry, v. The Report of the Committee in Yearbook C.C.A.R., Vol. XV, 1905, pp. 83 ff. 'At the same time your Committee is of the opinion that any attempt at formulating a Creed for one section of Judaism, with the exclusion of the rest, is a dangerous proceeding with should by all means be discouraged, as it tends to create a schism in antagonism to the spirit and tradition of Judaism'. A splendid long article on our theme is that of R. J. Zwi Werblowsky: 'Judaism, or the Religion of Israel' in 'The Concise Encyclopedia of Living Faiths', ed. by R. C. Zaehner, Hutchinson, London, 1959, pp. 23–50. L. Finkelstein's article on 'The Beliefs and Practices of Judaism' in 'The Jews: Their History, Culture and Religion', 2nd. ed., New York, 1950, Vol. 2, pp. 1327–1387, is an important contribution to the subject. Reference might also be made to my 'We Have Reason to Believe', Vallentine, Mitchell, 2nd. ed., London, 1962, and 'Jewish Values', 1960. 'Judaism: a Portrait' by Leon Roth, Faber and Faber, London, 1960, is an interpretation of Judaism which builds on the basis of Maimonides' approach with its strong emphasis on the role of reason in the religious life. Professor Roth has no use for the irrationalism of the *Qabbalah* and has scant respect for present-day admirers of Hasidism. On Maimonides' exclusion of certain classes of unbelievers from Heaven Roth remarks (p. 125): 'For there were (as there are still) many plain people who believe that somewhere "up there" there is a Heaven, and in Heaven there is an "ancient of days" seated on a throne and stretching out a saving hand in order to help a good man out of his difficulties. They might not have thought their position out. They might have had no position to think out. Metaphysically they might be in error. But are they in error *religiously*; and are they, because of a metaphysical error, cut off from eternal bliss? Is the Last Judgment an examination of our knowledge of philosophy or (as the *Talmud* affirmed unequivocally) a weighing of our good and evil deeds?' *Cf.* the chapter on 'Dogmas' in Roth's book, Chapter 8, pp. 117–134.

[2]

THE FIRST PRINCIPLE
The Existence of God

MAIMONIDES (Abelson's translation) thus expresses the first principle: '*The First Principle of Faith.* The existence of the Creator (praised be He!) i.e. that there is an existent Being invested with the highest perfection of existence. He is the cause of all existent things. In Him they exist and from Him emanates their continued existence. If we could suppose the removal of His existence then the existence of all things would entirely cease and there would not be left any independent existence whatsoever. But if on the other hand we could suppose the removal of all existent things but He, His existence (blessed be He!) would not cease to be, neither would it suffer any diminution. For He (exalted be He!) is self-sufficient, and His existence needs the aid of no existence outside His. Whatsoever is outside Him, the intelligences (i.e. the angels) and the bodies of the spheres, and things below these, all of them need Him for their existence. This is the first cardinal doctrine of faith, which is indicated by the commandment: "I am the Lord thy God" (Ex. xx.2, Deut. v. 6)'.

The '*'Ani Ma'amin*' version is: 'I believe with perfect faith that the Creator, blessed be His name, is the Author and Guide of everything that has been created, and that He alone has made, does make, and will make all things'. The *Yigdal* version is: 'Magnified and praised be the living God: He is, and there is no limit in time unto His being'.

Friedländer puts the first principle in these words: 'The first principle: The belief in the existence of the Creator; that is, the belief that there exists a Being who requires no other cause for His existence, but is Himself the cause of all beings'. Werblowsky puts it in this way: 'This article includes the faith in divine Providence and in God's continued sove-

33

reignty over and solicitude for his creation. The term "Creator" must not, therefore, be understood in a deistic sense, although "creation" has usually been held to imply the belief in a divine creative act at a particular date. Traditional Jewish chronology differs slightly from that of Archbishop Usher (A.D. 1959 corresponds to the year of creation 5719 according to the Jewish calender) but the approach is essentially the same. The assumption of geological ages, evolution (in all its forms) and other cosmogonic hypotheses of modern science are still considered heretical by the orthodox. The Kabbalists tended to understand creation as a primeval, non-temporal or supra-temporal act. As such, creation is really eternal and is in no way similar to the construction of a clock or even to keeping it going. Modern theologians, who accept the relevance of the natural sciences in their own sphere, believe that dates are unimportant; they are merely a naive but necessary concrete symbol of the faith in creation and the Creator. Here, one feels, modern Jewish theology is indebted to Kabbalistic concepts'.

In the Middle Ages religious thinkers, Jewish, Christian and Muslim, believed that it was possible to prove the existence of God. The three main types of demonstration used for the purpose, the three traditional proofs for the existence of God, are: the *ontological*, the *cosmological* and the *teleological*. In modern times, particularly since Kant, the traditional proofs have been heavily assailed but they deserve detailed examination if only for the important role they once played in religious thought, quite apart from the fact that some, particularly Catholic, thinkers still believe their validity.

(a) The ontological proof

The ontological proof of God's existence was first posited by St. Anselm of Canterbury (1033-1109). The argument is not found in Jewish sources.

St. Anselm's proof is directed against the 'fool' of the Psalms (xiv. 1) who says in his heart that there is no God. Anselm tries to prove that the existence of God is a conclusion to be reached from the very use of the term 'God' and that the 'fool' in denying God, and thereby using the term, is giving the lie to his own case. This is Anselm's argument. The name 'God' means (and is so understood by all who use it) the Being than which nothing greater can be conceived. From which it must follow that God exists, for if He does not exist it is possible to imagine a greater Being, namely, one who enjoys existence. The use of the term 'God' implies the greatest and most perfect Being *imaginable*. But if God does not exist then it is possible to *imagine* an even greater Being, since a being who exists is obviously greater and more perfect than one who does not.

Among criticisms of the argument is Kant's famous one. The argument assumes that 'existence' is a true predicate, whereas, in fact, if I say that God exists I am not adding anything new that is not already contained in the subject 'God'. I am simply saying: 'God is God'. If, for example, I say: 'The table is square' I am describing the nature of the table by adding a concept not contained in the subject. A table may be round or oblong. By stating that it is square I am calling attention to the special feature of *this* table. But if I say: 'The table exists' I add nothing about the table. I state only that there *is* such a table, that it is a *real* table not an imaginary one, but I do this on grounds other than an examination of the statement 'The table exists'. Consequently, the whole force of the argument falls to the ground since it is not permissible to speak of a Being who enjoys existence as superior to one who does not. The Being who exists is not a more perfect Being than one who does not in the sense that more is attributed to him. The question whether the all-perfect Being does actually exist or is only in the mind is of tremendous importance but this question cannot be decided by recourse to the use of the term 'God'.

In Anselm's own day his argument was criticised by the monk Gaunilo of Marmoutiers, in his 'Apology for the Fool' (*Liber pro Insipiente*), who pointed out that we can quite easily imagine that a marvellously perfect island exists but it would be absurd to conclude from this that there actually is such an island simply because we can imagine it. Centuries later, Kant made the same point when he said that imaginary money will not serve the purpose of real money in the bank. St. Anselm in his reply to Gaunilo tries to show that his argument has only force when applied to the term 'God'. Of course, he says, it is possible to imagine things which do not really exist but it is impossible to account for the idea of God unless He

exists. For all other things do not by definition include the idea of
complete perfection. We can therefore think of them as failing
to enjoy existence. But God is by definition the Being than
whom no greater can be conceived and here the argument
would apply. But the step is still taken from the thought of
God's existence to His actual existence and herein lies the
weakness of the argument. Eric S. Waterhouse ('The Philosophical Approach to Religion', London, 1947) says of the
ontological proof: 'The reason for the failure of Anselm's
argument as a logically necessary demonstration is that it
proceeds from a necessity of thought to a necessity of fact.
To say that if one thinks of God, one must think of an existent
God, is true, but it does not follow that what is necessary
to the consistency of one's thought must be regarded as
existing in any sphere outside thought'.

A determined upholder of the argument will not give up here.
He will claim that the real issue is whether our thought
processes correspond to a reality outside them. As formulated
by Descartes and others the ontological argument puts it
to us that unless an all-perfect Being does actually exist it is
difficult to account for the emergence of the idea of His existence
in the human mind, difficult, indeed, to account for the idea
of God at all. It is quite true that I can think of a dragon, for
instance, even though there is no such creature, but this
fictitious creature is formed of parts taken from the world of
experience. I have seen the bodies of horses, the wings of
birds, the flames of fire, and I can, therefore, imagine a creature
having the body of a horse, the wings of a bird, and a tongue
flashing flames of fire. But how did men come to have the
notion of a Being outside all our experiences and enjoying
every kind of perfection unless such a Being actually exists?
Put in this way the argument is no longer capable of stilling
the doubts of the sceptic but the believer may argue that on
his premises the emergence of the God idea is more reasonable
than any alternative explanation of the rise of the idea.

*   *   *

EXCURSUS

H. A. Wolfson: 'Notes on Proofs of the Existence of God in
Jewish Philosophy' in HUCA, Vol. I, 1924, pp. 575–596, remarks

that two arguments widely resorted to in the Middle Ages were not used by Jewish thinkers, the argument from the innateness of the idea of God and the argument from universal assent, known to Christians and Muslims. The former argument was not used, according to Wolfson, because the Jewish philosophers did not recognise in their theory of knowledge any such thing as an *innate* idea in the sense of an idea which comes from *within* instead of from *without*. As for the argument from universal assent, this was not accepted by the Jewish thinkers because they believed in the *only* God, not in a God above all others, and for this there was no universal assent, quite the contrary. 'It was therefore not to a universal assent that Jewish philosophers appealed but rather to a national assent, or tradition, as they call it, a tradition based upon the evidence of a direct experience shared by the entire race at the foot of Sinai'. On the argument *de consensu gentium*, Jakob J. Petuchowski: 'The Theology of Haham David Nieto', Bloch, New York, 1954, p. 112, says that Nieto (' *'Esh Dath'*, London, 1715, I, 62, p. 9a) is one of the few Jewish thinkers to use this argument under the influence of the Deists, with whom it was popular. In note 17 to Chapter 8 (p. 156) Petuchowski remarks that both Wolfson (*op. cit.*) and Kaufmann Kohler, 'Jewish Theology', p. 69, state that Jewish thinkers did not use this argument at all because the other nations did not worship God but the gods. However, Petuchowski concludes, Samuel S. Cohon has drawn attention to the following passages in which the argument does occur: (1) Malachi i. 11, (2) *Hephetz ben Yatzliah* in B. Halper's 'A Volume of the Book of Precepts by *Hephetz ben Yatzliah'*, Dropsie College, Philadelphia, 1915, pp. 32 and 36, (3) Gabirol's *'Kether Malkhuth'*, Stanza VIII. It is worth noting that Gabirol argues that even idolators are, in reality, desirous of worshipping God but that they are confused. His argument really implies that the urge to worship in the human breast suggests that there is an Object of worship. A very good account of the ontological argument, with full quotations from St. Anselm's *'Proslogion seu Alloquium de Dei existentia'* is given by A. E. Taylor, article 'Theism', in ERE, Vol. 12, pp. 267–269. Kant's critique of the traditional proofs is to be found in his 'Critique of Pure Reason', Book II, Chapter 3, par. 3, 4, 5, 6, quoted in full in 'Selections from the Literature of Theism', Caldecott and Mackintosh, 3rd. ed., Edinburgh, 1931, pp. 179–255. Useful summaries of the arguments are given in a number of books of which the following may be mentioned: W. R. Sorley: 'Moral Values and the Idea of God', Cambridge University Press, 1921, Chapter XII, pp. 299–327; A. C. Ewing: 'The Fundamental Questions of Philosophy', London, 1951; Neal W. Klausner and

Paul G. Kuntz: 'Philosophy: The Study of Alternative Beliefs', New York, 1961, pp. 508–525; Paul Edwards and Arthur Pap: 'A Modern Introduction to Philosophy', The Free Press, London, George Allen and Unwin, 1957, pp. 446 ff, 'Historical Selections in the Philosophy of Religion', N. Smart, SCM Press, London, 1962.

*   *   *

(b) The cosmological proof

The cosmological proof of God's existence, known particularly in the Western world from the treatment it receives in the work of St. Thomas Aquinas, goes back to Aristotle and is found frequently in the mediaeval Jewish philosophers. Philo (*'De Fuga et Inventione'*, Loeb Classical Library, Vol. V, 1949, 2, p. 17) puts it as follows: 'The world has come into being and assuredly it has derived its existence from some cause'. Briefly stated, the argument notes that everything must have a cause. If I observe a table, for instance, and inquire of its cause I am told that it was made by a carpenter. If I go on to ask for the cause of the carpenter one answer would be his parents. But they, too, must have had a cause, in this case their parents, and so on. Thus all existing things are dependent on others. But a dependent thing cannot be a final cause. Therefore, if we are to explain how things came into being we must postulate a final cause that is not itself caused, and this is God.

Two criticisms have been advanced against the cosmological proof. First, the question can be put: 'Who made God?' The conventional reply to this is that God is the Being Who exists without a cause but, on the argument's own premises, this is no answer at all since the argument assumes that there cannot exist anything which has no cause. Defenders of the argument retort that although admittedly we cannot grasp the idea of an uncaused being, the Theistic claim is that, in any event, the nature of God cannot be comprehended. The Theist claims that it is still preferable to assume that God exists and is the causeless Cause rather than accept the only alternative, that we must give up entirely the search for a cause and say that the universe just happened.

The second criticism is that even if the argument is sound it leads only to an Ultimate Cause or Prime Mover. It tells us nothing about the nature of this Cause and in no way leads to the God of conventional Theism. But here the Theist replies that every rational person either accepts the belief in God as the Cause of things or else believes that there is no God (or he may, of course, suspend his judgment on the question). No one seriously accepts the third alternative that there may be a Cause but that this is not God. In other words, if the argument does carry weight and the universe is proved to have a causeless Cause, no one would then doubt that this causeless Cause is the God of Theism. Naturally, once the proof has been subjected to this kind of criticism it no longer possesses the power of demonstrative 'proof', even if the replies demonstrate that it is not without probability.

(c) The teleological argument

The teleological argument, or the argument *from* (or, as some prefer it to avoid question-begging, *to*) design, is probably the best-known of the three traditional proofs for the existence of God, though it is not as popular with the mediaeval Jewish philosophers as the cosmological proof. Kant says of this argument that it always deserves to be mentioned with respect as the oldest, the clearest, and that most in conformity with the common reason of humanity. 'For these reasons', says Kant, 'it would be utterly hopeless to attempt to rob this argument of the authority it has always enjoyed. The mind, unceasingly elevated by these considerations, which, although empirical, are so remarkably powerful and continually adding to their force, will not suffer itself to be depressed by the doubts suggested by subtle speculation; it tears itself out of this state of uncertainty the moment it casts a look upon the wondrous forms of nature and the majesty of the universe, and rises from height to height, from condition to condition, till it has elevated itself to the supreme and unconditioned author of all'. For all that, Kant denies demonstrative certainty to the argument.

Briefly stated, the argument runs as follows. There is evidence of design in nature, that things have been put together by a purposive mind. The human body, for instance, functions in a way which suggests that its various parts are co-ordinated. Food is taken in at the mouth, the teeth chew it to make it digestible, the stomach continues the digestive process, the blood is circulated from the heart, the nervous system is controlled by the brain, all of which suggests that the different organs have been produced by a mind. The same observations are to be made of the animal world and of the universe as a whole. Most convincing of all, there is mind in the universe since man thinks, plans, schemes and hopes, and it is hard to see how mind can have come into existence from matter alone. Consequently, there must be a divine Mind by whose fiat all things were brought into being. Philo uses the teleological argument in two passages. 'Should a man see a house carefully constructed with a gateway, colonnades, men's quarters, women's quarters, and the other buildings, he will get an idea of the artificer, for he will be of the opinion that the house never reached that completeness without the skill of the craftsman; and in like manner in the case of a city and a ship and every smaller or greater construction. Just so anyone entering this world, as it were some vast house or city, and beholding the sky circling round and embracing within it all things, and planets and fixed stars without any variation moving in rhythmical harmony and with advantage to the whole, and earth with the central space assigned to it, water and air flowing in set order as its boundary, and over and above these, living creatures, mortal and immortal beings, plants and fruit in great variety, he will surely argue that these have not been wrought, without consummate art, but that the Maker of this whole universe was and is God. Those, who thus have their reasoning on what is before their eyes, apprehend God by means of a shadow cast, discerning the Artificer by means of His works' (*'Legum Allegoria'*, III, 32, Loeb Classical Library, Vol. I, 1949, pp. 367-369). The passage is important both as the earliest systematic statement of the argument by a Jew and for its beauty. It is interesting, however, to see that some of Philo's sense of order is due to a faulty picture of the nature of the universe, i.e. his conviction that the earth has been 'assigned' to its 'central space'. In another passage (*'De Specialibus Legibus'*, I, 6, Loeb Classical Library, Vol. VII, 1950, p. 119) Philo says: 'Who can look upon statues or paintings without thinking at once of a sculptor or painter? Who can see clothes or ships or houses without getting the idea of a weaver and a shipwright and a housebuilder? And when one enters a well-ordered city in which the arrangements for civil life are very admirably managed, what else will he suppose but that this city is directed by good rulers? So then he who comes to the truly Great City, this world, and beholds hills and plains teeming with animals and plants, the rivers, spring-fed or winter torrents, streaming along, the seas with their expanses, the air with its happily tempered phases, the yearly seasons passing into each other, and then the sun and moon ruling the day and night, and the other heavenly bodies fixed or planetary and the whole firmament revolving in rhythmic order, must he not naturally or rather necessarily gain the conception of the Maker and Father and Ruler also? For none of the works of human art is self-made, and the highest art and knowledge is shown in the universe, so that surely it has been wrought by one of excellent knowledge and absolute perfection. In this way we have the conception of the existence of God'.

While admitting the strong appeal of the teleological argument, modern thinkers like Kant have subjected it to criticism. First, as in the case of the cosmological argument, the proof, even if valid, leads only to a Supreme Architect, not to the God of Theism. But here, too, if we can go so far we will arrive at God. The words of G. H. Joyce ('Principles of Natural Theology', 3rd. ed., Longmans Green, London, 1934, p. 134) are extremely pertinent: 'It is, however, certainly the case that our proof does not directly establish that the Author of our nature is the supreme, self-existent Being. Yet the value of the argument is not really affected. In the first place, no one who grants our conclusion will have any doubt that he has proved the existence of God. He will recognise that He whose wisdom and power fashioned the order of nature, can be no other than the self-existent God. We shall search in vain for a thinker who admits such an ordering Intelligence and yet remains in doubt whether there be a God or not'.

Another more cogent criticism of the argument is that there is evidence of faulty, even of evil, design so that if the argument is accepted it by no means yields the conclusion that there is a benevolent Creator Who is responsible for all that exists. On the other hand, the problem of evil, constituting though it does the severest obstacle to a Theistic faith, is not strictly germane to the teleological proof. Evidence of design in the universe is evidence of a divine Mind. Why that Mind, wholly good according to the Theistic view, should have brought evil as well as good into existence is a terrible question, with which the Theist is obliged to grapple, but it in no way contradicts the evidence for design and purpose in the universe.

A more serious attack on the argument is advanced by the evidence of Natural Selection. The Darwinian theory offers a rival account of how characteristics have been acquired and is sometimes thought to have dealt the death-blow to the whole argument from design. But even on the Darwinian view there is still no accounting for the process as a whole unless a divine Mind is postulated. Even if it is accepted (and the evidence for this is of the strongest) that certain animals are equipped to cope with their surroundings, not because of any special creation for this purpose, but because only those so equipped have been able to survive, it is still necessary to explain why nature is so constituted that the fittest can survive. The survival of the fittest is itself evidence of plan and order and there can be no plan without a mind in which it is conceived. Furthermore, it has been well noted, the fittest must have existed in order to survive; the *'arrival* of the fittest' is evidence of design.

*   *   *

EXCURSUS

For the cosmological proof in the mediaeval Jewish philosophers *v.* *Saadiah*: ' *'Emunoth We-De'oth'*, 'Beliefs and Opinions', Treatise I, Chapter 2, trans. Samuel Rosenblatt, Yale Judaica Series, Vol. I, Yale University Press, New Haven, 1948, p. 46 f.; Maimonides' 'Guide', Part II, Introduction and Chapter 1, trans. M. Friedländer, London, 1904, pp. 145–154; *Bahya Ibn Paqudah: 'Hobhoth Ha-Lebhabhoth'*, 'Duties of the Heart', *Sha'ar Ha-Yihud*, Chapters 4–6; Crescas: ' *'Or 'Adonai'*, 'Light of the Lord', Vienna 1856, Book II, Part 3, Chapter 2, pp. 40b–41a; Joseph Albo's ' *'Iqqarim'*, Book II, Chapters 4 and 5, trans. Isaac Husik, Jewish Publication Society of America, Philadelphia, 1946, pp. 26 ff. As for the argument from design *v.* Wolfson *op. cit.*, p. 573 and 583, who observes that this argument, though not completely overlooked by the mediaeval thinkers, was not used by them as an independent proof of the existence of God but was used either as a reinforcement of the cosmological argument from creation or as evidence of divine goodness, unity, intelligence and the like, after existence had been demonstrated on some other ground. *Bahya*, for instance, uses the argument, *after* he has demonstrated the fact of creation, in reply to the suggestion that the universe may have come into being by chance (*'Hobhoth Ha-Lebhabhoth'*, *Sha'ar Ha-Yihud*, Chapter 6). In no way does he attempt to use it as a proof of God's existence if the world were assumed to be eternal. Judah Ha-Levi in his *'Kuzari'*, III, 11 and V, 20, trans. Hartwig Hirschfeld, London, 1931, pp. 128–9 and pp. 246 f., likewise uses the argument not to demonstrate the existence of God but that since the world has a Creator the evidence of design shows that creation was an act of will and wisdom, not of chance. *Bahya op. cit.* gives the famous illustration of a sheet of paper on which there is writing which makes sense. No reasonable person will accept the view that the writing was caused by ink spilled accidentally on to the paper, forming itself into letters, words and sentences. The conclusion to be drawn from the sheet of paper is that it had an author and this conclusion must be drawn *a fortiori* so far as the universe as a whole is concerned. *Cf.* Gersonides: *'Milhamoth 'Adonai'*, 'The Wars of the Lord', Leipzig, 1866, Book V, Part 3, Chapters 4–6, pp. 247–268. With regard to the teleological argument in Philo *cf. 'De Migratione Abrahami'*, 33–35, Loeb Classical Library, Vol. IV, 1949, pp. 239–249, where Philo argues from the existence of mind in man to the Mind of the universe. *Cf.* in full H. A. Wolfson's 'Philo', Vol. II, Harvard University Press, 1948, Chapter 10, p. 77, note 22, where Philo's illustration of a house is compared with the passage in the *Midrash*, *B.R.* 39.1. Here it is stated that Abraham, who recognised his Creator, was like a man who saw a mansion 'all lighted up' (*'birah doleqeth'*) and said, at first, that there is no owner to the mansion. The owner looked out and said to him: 'I am the owner of this mansion'. In reality, as the commentators to the *Midrash* point out, there are two possible interpretations of the term *'birah doleqeth'*. One is that which Wolfson adopts. But the one to be preferred is that which takes the term to mean that the mansion was 'on fire'. Abraham is compared to the man who saw a mansion on fire, i.e., he could not, at first, help but conclude that God had abandoned His world since there is so much evil in it, just as a burning mansion suggests that the owner has neglected it. This interpretation also gives point to the expression: 'The owner looked out' i.e. after deep reflection Abraham comes to the conclusion that in spite of the evil in the world God is still in control. The *Midrash* is thus a homily on the problem of evil, not on the argument from design. A cogent discussion of the teleological argument is W. R.

Matthews' 'The Purpose of God', Nisbet, London, 1935. At the
end of the book (p. 177) the author observes that the teleological
argument is not necessarily in favour of a design only for man's
benefit, but only for design. 'The universe is, when all is said, full
of darkness and tragedy. It has profound abysses of being which the
plummet of our reason cannot sound. It is not only the "vale of soul
making", it is not only the home of man, it is not even only the
training ground for his home beyond, nor only the sphere where
human values are realised – it is all of these things, but it is much
more. It is the work of a sublime Artist who expresses Himself
in its majesty and in its beauty; and its sublimity is part of its
justification. It is fitting, then, that one who lectures on the purpose
of God should remember at the end the words which came to Job
out of the whirlwind: "Who is this that darkeneth counsel by
words without knowledge? Gird up now thy loins like a man; for I
will demand of thee, and declare thou unto me. Where wast thou
when I laid the foundations of the earth . . . when the morning
stars sang together and all the sons of God shouted for joy?" '
The view that the universe has a purpose apart from man is no
doubt unconventional from the Jewish point of view but it is implied
in the passage from Job and is accepted by no less a thinker than
Maimonides, 'Guide' III, 13, ed. Friedländer, pp. 272–277. Maimonides states, for instance, that the Scriptural passage 'And have
dominion over the fish of the sea' (Gen. i. 28) does not mean that
man was created for this purpose, but only that this was the nature
which God gave man. It is, indeed, hard to believe that the beauty,
variety and abundance of marine life, for example, much of it far
removed from man's habitat and even from his recognition, exists
solely for some human purpose. Various passages in Scripture
suggest an ancient form of the teleological argument, e.g. 'Lift up
your eyes on high, And see: who hath created these? He that
bringeth out their host by number, He calleth them all by name;
By the greatness of His might, and for that He is strong in power,
Not one faileth' (Is. xl. 26). 'The heavens declare the glory of God,
And the firmament showeth His handiwork' (Ps. xix. 2). 'He that
planted the ear, shall He not hear? He that formed the eye, shall
He not see?' (Ps. xciv. 9). Wolfson ('Notes' etc. *op. cit.*, p. 585),
however, understands these as examples of the *cosmological* proof
and gives the Scriptural anticipation as the reason for the popularity
of this proof in mediaeval Jewish philosophy. 'The popularity of
this type of cosmological argument, the readiness with which it was
generally accepted, was due to the fact that it chimed in with the
traditional method of reasoning which had come down from the
Scriptures. To argue from the fact that the world had come into

existence to the existence of the Creator was simply to translate into a syllogistic formula the first verse of the book of Genesis, or to rationalise the emotional appeal of the Prophets to look up into heaven and ask who created it all'. But the verses have generally been understood, surely correctly, as pointing to evidence of design, v. in particular the reference to 'their host by number' and that 'He calleth them by name' and that 'not one faileth', also the comparison in Psalm xix of the 'laws' of nature with the laws of the *Torah*. *Cf.* Is. xl. 12–26 and xlvi. 10.

*   *   *

It is clear that when criticism of the traditional proofs has done its work all demonstrative power has been taken from them. But if they are treated not so much as 'proofs', as definite demonstrations of the truth of God's existence, but as *indications* of its truth, then they do possess power, particularly if taken together, in producing conviction. We are faced with two viewpoints, the Theistic and the atheistic. The three 'proofs' do not demonstrate that the Theistic view is correct but they do show how this view, with all its difficulties, makes greater sense of the universe and human experience in it. Only on the Theistic view have we any indication of how the idea of God came into the human mind (the ontological proof); of how contingent being is possible, because it depends on necessary being (the cosmological proof); and how the evidence of design makes sense (the teleological proof). On the atheistic view all that can be said is that somehow the God idea came into men's minds; that the universe just happened (i.e. there is no explanation of how things came to be); and that the appearance of design is an illusion. We turn now to consider three further 'proofs' which have been advanced by Theists. Like the others, these do not enjoy the force of a demonstration. If they, or the first three, did it would be more than a little odd for defenders of Theism to require so many. If any one 'proof' really *demonstrated* that God exists any further demonstrations would be superfluous. But, though inconclusive in themselves, these further proofs provide additional indications of the truth of the Theistic view. These further three are: (*a*) the argument from the moral sense, (*b*) the argument from religious experience, and (*c*) the argument from tradition.

(a) The moral argument

The argument for God's existence from man's sense of right and wrong has had many advocates, including Kant, who, for all his criticism of the three traditional arguments, attaches great importance to this one. ('Critique of Practical Reason', Book II, Chapter 2, par. 3, 4, 5, 8, Caldecott and Mackintosh, *op. cit.*, pp. 220 f. *Cf.* Sorley, *op. cit.*, particularly Chapter XII, pp. 328-353). We have a feeling that some actions are wrong, others right. The terms right and wrong are not used as synonyms for pleasant and unpleasant. Most of us would say that an act may be unpleasant or hard to carry out and yet be right while another act may be pleasurable and easy and yet wrong. But where does the sense of duty come from unless it were implanted in our nature by God, the ultimate source of the good? Critics of the argument have not been slow in pointing to the very different standards of right and wrong prevailing in different societies. Acts which in our society are considered reprehensible were, and are, looked upon as completely innocent, even praiseworthy, in other civilisations or groups. Conversely, acts considered by us to be quite blameless are viewed in certain societies as deserving the severest condemnation. This is said to prove that all our moral judgments are relative and that there are no absolute standards of right and wrong. If this were correct it would obviously dispose of the moral argument for God's existence. But although it is true that different standards of moral conduct obtain in different societies, all societies have this in common, that they recognise standards to which the terms right and wrong apply. A savage, for instance, may see no harm in killing his enemies but he knows that it is wrong to kill certain other people. He differs from us not in failing to recognise murder as a wrong but on what constitutes murder. Conscience can be all too often misleading but its very existence is a powerful indication that God exists.

A variation of the moral argument is sometimes expressed in these terms. The use of words like 'right' and 'wrong' and the recognition of the 'ought' imply that there are moral standards. Now where are these standards to be found? They cannot inhere in the universe outside of man for the universe is morally neutral; there can be no moral standards in mindless matter. Nor can the standards inhere in individuals, since each

individual recognises standards greater than himself and outside and apart from himself. This is, indeed, what a moral
standard means, that the individual judges his conduct by
norms he has not made himself. To say that the standards
inhere in humanity is similarly absurd, since humanity or
mankind is simply the name we give to a collection of individuals
and if moral standards cannot inhere in any one of them they
cannot do so in the mass, in all individuals collectively. The
conclusion to be drawn is that moral standards must inhere in a
Mind that is not human, and this is God.

It should be noted that, despite frequent misunderstandings
on this score by some supporters of religion, it is no part of
the moral argument to declare that the atheist cannot lead a
moral life or that he has no moral standards. The force of the
argument is to compel the atheist to ask himself what he means by
right and wrong and how these are to be explained without God.

(b) The argument from religious experience

The argument for God's existence from religious experience
is of a two-fold nature. The argument has it that it is possible
for human beings to have a direct experience of God. 'Do you
believe in God?' a Hasidic teacher once asked his astonished
followers. 'I do not', he went on to say, 'any more than I
believe that we are sitting at a table. I *know* that we are sitting
at a table and I *know* that God exists'. (For a good theoretical
discussion of this theme in Hasidic literature *v.* Menahem
Mendel of Lübavitch: '*Derekh Mitzwothekha*', Poltova, 1911,
on the precept of 'Faith in God' in which a distinction is made
between ' *'emunah*', 'faith', and *'da'ath*', 'knowledge'). Persons
who have enjoyed this kind of experience have as little use for
'proofs' of God's existence as a lover for proofs of the existence
of his beloved. But the argument is intended to convince those
with no direct experience of this nature. This it tries to do in
two ways. The first is by pointing to similar experiences which
most of us have from time to time. These are in no way a
direct experience of God but, it is claimed, they only make
sense if God really does exist. There are many descriptions of
such experiences in literature, from Browning's 'Just when we
are safest . . .' to C. S. Lewis's 'Surprised by Joy'. Secondly,
it is claimed that the testimony of the great mystics of diverse

climes and faiths points to a Reality behind the experience
which ought to convince the sceptic. Here we are on rather
shaky ground. For it might be retorted that the experiences
are no doubt authentic but what proof do they really offer
of a Reality apart from themselves? In other words, the
mystics may all suffer from a self-induced delusion, no doubt a
very profound and deeply moving one, but in essence not very
different from the kind of hallucination induced by alcohol and
drugs. The alcoholic, it is argued, drinks and sees pink elephants,
the mystic starves and sees angels. However, many of those
who have claimed to have had these experiences were men and
women of the highest integrity and moral stature and if *their*
experiences were illusory the whole nature of reality is
brought into question. Furthermore, the remarkable resemblance in the testimony of so many mystics of totally different
backgrounds, who can have had no contact with each other,
lends powerful support to the argument that they were in
contact with a Reality not themselves, which they sought to
describe, however inadequately, after having 'been there'. In the
Jewish sources this kind of experience is mentioned frequently,
from the visions of the prophets to the testimonies of the Jewish
mystics, though it should be noted that a marked reticence has
resulted in a huge literature of mystic themes but a remarkable
absence of mystical testimonies among the Jewish mystics.

(c) The argument from tradition

All the arguments hitherto mentioned start, as it were,
from the beginning. They are addressed to the uncommitted
person, trying to make up his mind whether God exists. In
fact, hardly anyone approaches the Theistic question in this
way. People brought up in a Theistic faith and belonging to a
long Theistic tradition either accept it without question or,
in moments of crisis or doubt, then begin to question its
validity. For such persons, and in Western lands at least they
are in the majority, the question whether God exists really
means: 'Can I go on believing in God as my father did before
me?' The argument from tradition is found frequently in the
Jewish sources. In its classic form it runs as follows. Generation
after generation Jews have handed down a tradition that God
revealed Himself to a whole people, the people of Israel, who,

as a result, took upon themselves the 'yoke of His kingdom'. Now tradition can often be a faulty guide. But it is extremely unlikely that if religion were an illusion it would have persisted in the heroic manner in which Judaism has survived among Jews. For here we have a whole people finding its justification as a minority group, sometimes reviled and persecuted for its faith, in its belief that there is a God Who has chosen Israel to help fulfil His purpose. When the Jew of today finds that his belief in God makes sense of his life and enriches it beyond measure he is fortified in his faith to know that what means so much to him has meant the same to the great Jews of the past. Hence the significance in Jewish teaching of the famous verse from the Song of Moses: 'This is my God, and I will glorify Him; My father's God, and I will exalt Him' (Ex. xv. 2).

* * *

EXCURSUS

On the moral argument *cf.* Hastings Rashdall: 'The Theory of Good and Evil', The Clarendon Press, Oxford, 1907; David Elton Trueblood: 'Philosophy of Religion', Rockliff, London, 1957, Part II, Chapter 8, pp. 106 f.; Rudolf Bultmann's essay: 'The Old Testament Heritage' in 'A Modern Introduction to Ethics', ed. Milton K. Munitz, Free Press, George Allen and Unwin, 1958, pp. 226–231. On the argument from religious experience *v.* Edwards and Pap *op. cit.*, pp. 457–463; William James: 'The Varieties of Religious Experience', Longman's, Green, London, 1905; R. C. Zaehner: 'Mysticism Sacred and Profane', The Clarendon Press, Oxford, 1957; Marghanita Laski: 'Ecstasy: A Study of some Secular and Religious Experiences', The Cresset Press, London, 1961; Bertrand Russell: 'Why I Am Not a Christian', George Allen and Unwin, London, 1957; William Temple: 'Religious Experience and Other Essays and Addresses', James Clarke, London, 1958, pp. 57–63; David Elton Trueblood, *op. cit.*, Part II, Chapter 11, pp. 143 f. Browning's famous lines are from his poem 'Bishop Blougram's Apology', Reynard Library ed., Rupert Hart-Davis, London, 1950, p. 300 f.

> *'Just when we are safest, there's a sunset-touch,*
> *A fancy from a flower-bell, some one's death,*
> *A chorus ending from Euripides, —*
> *And that's enough for fifty hopes and fears*
> *As old and new at once as Nature's self,*
> *To rap and knock and enter in our soul . . .'*

C. S. Lewis's 'Surprised by Joy', Geoffrey Bles, London, 1955,
is an account of the author's growing conviction of the truth of
Theism. Bishop Gore: 'Belief in God', Pelican Books, 1939,
Chapter 4, pp. 76 f., argues for the existence of God from the otherwise inexplicable existence of the Hebrew prophets. 'Here, then,
we find a succession of wonderful men, mostly conscious of profound
unpopularity in their contemporary world, who nevertheless, even
in the face of the most determined hostility of courts and people,
delivered a message which we feel to be self-consistent and to
involve the same great principles throughout, about God – His
nature, His will, His purposes – and about human nature, its
dignity, its responsibility, and its sin; a message which they declare,
with the fullest conviction, to be derived not from their own reasoning or speculation, nor from tradition (though they would have
indignantly repudiated the idea that they were its first recipients),
nor from any external source at all, but from God, the God of
Israel, speaking in their own souls, so intensely and clearly that
there could be no mistake about it.' The great representative of
the argument from tradition is, of course, Judah Ha-Levi in his
'*Kuzari*', trans. Hartwig Hirschfeld, Cailingold, London, 1931. *V.*
particularly Part I, 25–117, pp. 41 ff. *Cf.* Rashi's comment to
Ex. xv. 2 and Moses Hayyim Luzzatto's '*Derekh 'Adonai*', 'The
Way of the Lord', *var. ed.*, Book I, Chapter 1, where Luzzatto
states that the existence of God can be proved by references to the
physical sciences but that Israel believes because of tradition. *Bahya*
'*Hobhoth Ha-Lebhabhoth*', *Sha'ar Ha-Yihud*, Chapter 2, holds,
however, that one who believes because of tradition is greatly
inferior to one who arrives at the truth by speculation.

*   *   *

Having examined the question of 'proofs' of God's existence
we turn now to the attacks made on Theism and the Jewish
reply to them. Atheism, the denial of God's existence, was a
rare phenomenon in the ancient world. Significantly enough,
there is no name for it in classical Hebrew. The ancient Greeks
coined the term but they, and the Romans, frequently meant by
it not a denial that the gods existed, but a failure to pay homage
to them in State worship. However, while this is true of the
Greeks before the age of the Sophists, it is not entirely true
after their time (*v.* J. Baillie: 'Our Knowledge of God', Oxford
University Press, 1939, p. 107 f.). Plato ('The Laws', Book X)
is the first in world history to *demonstrate* God's existence and

he is thus generally held to be the founder of 'natural theology' (*v*. A. E. Taylor's trans. in the 'Everyman' edition, and Taylor's account of Plato's views in his 'Introduction', pp. xlix f.). For the Biblical prophets the issue was not between God and no God but between the one God and the many. It is doubtful if we can speak of the ancients *believing* in God. For the ancient polytheists the gods were as real as electricity is to us. For the ancient monotheists the one God was real in the same way. Belief implies some degree of reflection, deliberation and judgment on a matter accepted by some, disputed by others. When a man says: 'I believe in God' he does so because he is aware that his belief is not universally entertained. His protestation of belief has as its aim the negation of God-negation. He is saying in so many words that he has examined the atheistic case and found it wanting, inadequate as a means of making sense of the universe. It is not suggested that every believer has given much time or thought to serious reflection on such matters as the proofs for God's existence or the intellectual refutation of atheism. But, subconsciously at least, the believer's declaration of faith presupposes its denial by others. The ancient Hebrews, however, moved in a world in which no one doubted the existence of supernatural powers or forces. The Hebraic contribution consisted in the conviction that there is only one Power or Force and that He is the God who speaks to man and who reveals Himself in nature and in history. It was only when, as a result of the speculative methods forged by the Greeks, men began to question God's existence, that Theists felt obliged to demonstrate the truth of the proposition that God exists.

It is admittedly difficult for us to understand how the belief in God could have been so obvious to the ancient Hebrews that no one doubted His existence. Surely, it can be argued, human nature cannot have changed to such a degree that a matter upon which there was so much disagreement in mediaeval and modern times should have been so clear to the ancients as to obviate the need for either defence or refutation. The phenomenon is certainly strange but a careful examination of the historical facts reveals its truth. The analogy from electricity, often used by present-day Theists, is not unhelpful. Before electricity was actually used, men might have speculated

as to whether such a force actually existed. Now that it has
been harnessed to man's use such speculation is meaningless.
The nature of the force may be unknown, its workings understood only by the electrical engineer, but since a room can now
be illumined by a flick of the switch the existence of electricity
is never doubted. In some such fashion the question of God
(or, for the polytheist, the gods) must have presented itself
to the ancient mind. Men were convinced beyond the need for
argument or discussion that a supernatural Force or forces
were 'there' in the universe to be used by, or, in higher religion,
to use men and make demands on them in terms of justice
and righteousness. This conviction will be explained by
moderns in terms of their own beliefs. The atheist will explain
it away as an example of mass delusion; the Theist will explain
it as a recognition of or, at least, a groping for a Reality which
enjoys objective existence. What is clear beyond doubt is
that the belief persisted throughout the ancient world.

Thus the doubts expressed in the Biblical book of Ecclesiastes
deal with the injustices evident in the world, which lead men
to question God's concern with human affairs, but not with
God's actual existence. When the ancient Hebrew did have
doubts, his uncertainty was with regard to God's providence,
not His existence:

> 'And thou sayest: What does God know?
> Can He judge through the dark cloud?
> Thick clouds are a covering to Him, that He seeth not;
> And He walketh in the circuit of heaven'
> (Job xxii. 13–14).

Even the verse in Psalm fourteen (1): 'The fool (*nabhal*)
hath said in his heart: There is no God' has to be understood
less as the fool's denial of God's existence than as his affirmation of God's lack of concern with the deeds of man. Consequently, when St. Anselm put his ontological argument for
God's existence in the form of a reply to the fool of the Psalms,
thereby suggesting that the latter was a theoretical atheist,
he was on shaky historical grounds.

What is true of the Bible is true of the Rabbinic literature.
When the Rabbis speak of the man who says 'there is no
judgment and no Judge', and even when they speak of one who

'denies the root principle', they are not thinking primarily of the theoretical atheist but of the person who believes, in Nietzsche's phrase, that 'all is permitted' since God does not care. It was only when Jewish thinkers like Philo came into close contact with Hellenistic philosophy that they felt compelled to argue in favour of God's existence and so refute atheism. In the Middle Ages proofs for the existence of God were advanced by Jewish, Christian and Muslim thinkers precisely because in those ages atheism, while far from being either a widely held or respectable position, was embraced by some whose speculative thought led them to question the hitherto barely questionable. In the mediaeval period the real enemy of the Jewish, Christian and Muslim theologian was no longer the polytheist but the atheist. It is a moot point whether Moses Cordovero (1522–1570) is unusual in treating the atheist as more reprehensible than the idolator, since the latter believes in deity but entertains false notions as to its nature, while the former has no belief at all. (It is possible that Cordovero, as a Qabbalist, feels obliged subconsciously to reply to the charge, frequently made by the oponents of the *Qabbalah*, that the Qabbalistic doctrine of the *Sephiroth*, the 'powers', 'spheres' or 'influences' by means of which the unknown God manifests Himself, borders on polytheism. Cordovero, like all the Qabbalists, naturally repudiates the polytheistic accusation vehemently but he may be suggesting, in so many words, that the Qabbalistic system, for all the dangers to which it exposes its devotees, is still to be preferred to its rival, philosophy, since philosophical speculation can lead to atheism and the atheist is worse than the polytheist).

* * *

EXCURSUS

On the question of atheism in the Bible *v.* Robert Gordis: 'Koheleth – The Man and His World', New York, 1955, p. 112 and p. 377, note 1 and Baillie *op. cit.*, pp. 119–123. Jer. v. 12 has also to be understood in its context. W. O. E. Oesterley in 'The Psalms', London, 1939, pp. 278–281, understands the 'fool' of the Psalms to be a real atheist but, Oesterley himself observes, the Hebrew '*nabhal*' expresses not so much mental as moral stupidity. Maimonides understands the first commandment as an injunction to believe in God. This, too, is historically inaccurate but very interesting

C

in itself, *v.* Schechter's essay on the Dogmas of Judaism *op. cit.* The
two passages in which Maimonides discusses the question should
be quoted in full:
(*a*) 'The first precept is that we have been commanded to believe
in the Deity. This means that we must believe that there is a
Mover and Cause who created all things. This is the meaning of
His saying, may He be exalted: "I am the Lord thy God" '

(*Sepher Ha-Mitzwoth*–I)
(*b*) 'The foundation of foundations and the pillar of wisdom is to
know that there is a prime Being and that it is He who has brought
everything into being and that all creatures in heaven and earth owe
their existence to His true existence'

(*Mishneh Torah, Hil. Yesode Ha-Torah,* I. 1).
The commentaries to the *Sepher Ha-Mitzwoth* point out the logical
absurdity in the idea of a divine command to believe in God. If
one has this belief no command is necessary, if one lacks it there
is no one to issue the command! Some scholars have tried to resolve
the difficulty by suggesting that Maimonides' reference to the
command 'to know' that there is a God is not to a bare assent but to
the demonstrative proof of God's existence. But in the first quotation above Maimonides refers to 'belief' not to 'knowledge'. It is
possible that Maimonides means by his command to believe a
command to *strengthen one's faith.* However, it seems very plausible
to suggest that Maimonides is using the term '*mitzwah*' (lit. 'a
command', 'a precept') in its conventional sense of a 'good deed', a
'meritorious act'. Aware that there can be no command to believe
in God, Maimonides is, in fact, saying that if one does believe in
Him a special *mitzwah* has been fulfilled over and above the *mitzwoth* which will follow from this belief. When man attains to belief
in God he possesses the merit of having attained to it. For the
Rabbinic term 'no judgment and no Judge' *v.* Gen. R. 26. 6. Cf.
George Foot Moore: 'Judaism', Vol. I, Harvard University Press,
1927, pp. 359–360: 'In accordance with the principle of revelation,
the existence of God is not a subject for question or argument;
he has revealed himself in Scripture, and Scripture teaches man to
recognise the manifestations of his power, his wisdom, his goodness, in nature and history and providence. Dogmatic atheism
and theoretical scepticism are the outcome of philosophical thinking,
to which Jews had no inclination. They knew the man who thought
that there was no God and conducted himself accordingly; but what
such men really meant was that no higher power concerned itself
about men's doings – there was no providence and no retribution'.
On the term 'one who denies the root principle', '*kopher ba-'iqqar*',
v. Siphra, Behukkothai, III, end (ed. Weiss, p. 111c); *Tos. Sheb.*

III. 6 (ed. Zuckermandel, p. 449); *Sanh.* 38b. Maimonides (*Yesode Ha-Torah*, I. 6), calls the person who believes in another god 'one who denies the root principles'. For Philo's discussion of atheism *v.* '*De Somnis*', ii. 43, and '*De Opificio Mundi*', 61. For further details of atheism from the Jewish point of view *v.* the article by Emil G. Hirsch in JE, Vol. II, pp. 262–265 and the articles by Max Wiener and Samuel S. Cohon in UJE, Vol. I, pp. 578–579. Cordovero's view is to be found in his ' '*Elimah Rabbathi*', Lemberg, 1881, I. 1, Chapter 1, p. 1: 'His (the atheist's) nature is inferior to that of the idolator who admits that there is a God but is in error as to who is God, making a god for himself according to his belief and opinion. This heretic, on the other hand, does not even worship idols since according to his premise there is no God'. *Cf.* the same author's remarks in I. 1, Chapters 16–17, pp. 12–13: 'We (the Qabbalists) know the truth by tradition (i.e. the mystical lore) unlike the philosophers. Just as they consider it to be meritorious to delve into the proofs for God's existence, so do we, but our data are not those of the physical sciences but of the world of the *Sephiroth*'. On this question *v.* Francis Bacon's 'Essays' (XVII – 'Of Supersition'): 'It were better to have no opinion of God at all than such an opinion as is unworthy of him; for the one is unbelief, the other is contumely: and certainly superstition is the reproach of the Deity' – an exactly opposite view from Cordovero's. Pierre Bayle (1647–1706) has as a main theme of his discourses the idea that idolatry is a greater evil than atheism, *v.* 'Appendix B' ('Bayle on Strabo's "Atheism" ') in Norman Kemp Smith's edition of Hume's 'Dialogues Concerning Natural Religion', The Clarendon Press, Oxford, 1935, pp. 101–109.

*   *   *

In modern times atheism bases itself on the opinion that evidence from nature makes it impossible to believe in God. In great measure this kind of evidence is drawn from the existence of evil in the universe, which appears to conflict with the view that there is an all-wise, benevolent Creator. But while modern atheism bases itself chiefly, in its argument, on the age-old problem of pain (with which Theists have always grappled in the realisation that here lies the strongest challenge to their faith) it advances two further types of argument against the God hypothesis. The first of these is derived from a mechanistic and materialistic picture of the universe which, in turn, is said to emerge from the investigations of modern science. For example, the Darwinian theory of natural selection is said to demonstrate the irrelevance of introducing God into a description of how animals came to acquire the characteristics which enable them to cope with their environment. The second trend in modern atheism seeks to explain why Theism, if it is false, has been capable of winning so many adherents. The Marxist atheist attributes the persistence of Theism to economic forces which make Theism attractive to both the exploiter and his victim by diverting attention from real social evils in this world to an imaginary picture of compensatory bliss in the next. The Freudian atheist explains Theism away as wishful thinking, a yearning for a father figure or substitute, which is projected on to the universe by men insufficiently mature to stand on their own feet.

Ludwig Feuerbach (1804-1874) is generally held to be one of the most influential atheistic thinkers of modern times. Marx, in particular, owes a great debt to Feuerbach. Marx was fond of repeating his pun on Feuerbach's name (*feuer-bach*, 'stream of fire'). Feuerbach's denial of God and his insistence on man's divinity paved the way to the Marxist paradise. (H. de Lubac: 'The Drama of Atheist Humanism', London, Sheed and Ward, 1949, pp. 17 f.). It is easy to be wise after the event but the Theist has no difficulty in showing that an adequate faith in God endows man's life with dignity instead of robbing it of dignity, whereas Marxism ended in a totalitarian denial of the individual. In Feuerbach's view there has been a progressively humanising tendency in modern thought, a determined shift of emphasis from a God-centred to a man-centred universe. Thus, Protestantism dwells on the significance of God for human salvation while Spinoza's pantheism seeks to identity God with nature. Feuerbach claims that he is drawing the necessary conclusions from this trend in urging man now to allow his humanity its full expression free of the fetters of Theism. According to Feuerbach, the worship of God is really the worship of man's unrealised potentialities. Man, when he worshipped God, was really worshipping the essence of the human spirit which he projected on to the universe. Man, argues Feuerbach, must now learn to appreciate this and become his own god. Whereas Hegel, his former master, had said: 'Only the rational is true and actual', Feuerbach says: 'Only the human is true and actual'. Feuerbach denies that he is irreligious or even that he is a true atheist. 'He alone is the true atheist to whom the *predicates* of the Divine Being, for example, love, wisdom and justice are nothing; not he to whom merely the *subject* of these predicates is nothing' ('Essence of Christianity', English Translation, p. 21, quoted in 'Encyclopedia Britannica', Vol. 2, p. 600). Typical is Feuerbach's saying: 'To enrich God, man must become poor; that God may be all, man must be nothing'. For the theist, this antithesis between man's and God's enrichment is false. Numerous believers in God have discovered an enlargement and an enrichment of their own personality, have become God-like in engaging in what Feuerbach calls 'the enrichment of God'. Mention should be made here of Auguste Comte (1798-1857) who similarly developed a religion of humanity, influencing, among others, George Eliot. Feuerbach goes beyond Comte, however, in stating that what men have worshipped in God is really the infinite possibilities of mankind and his thesis is that these can only be realised if they are recognised as the true object of worship.

Another important figure in modern atheistic thought is Friedrich Nietzsche (1844-1900). Nietzsche holds that God is really man's negation of life. Man is a tortured being. There is something in him which desires martyrdom and self-denial and he, consequently, invents God and conscience to inflict punishment on himself. Man's saying 'No' to himself is made into a 'Yes' outside himself. It is certainly true that some religious people have looked upon God as a kind of cosmic policeman but it is against these, rather than against the God concept itself, that Nietzsche's critique has any validity. Furthermore, Nietzsche fails to explain why man should have this need for self-torture. Nietzsche's two best-known and typical aphorisms are: 'God is dead' and 'Body am I entirely, and nothing more; and soul is only the name of something in the body'.

A pioneer of modern atheism was Baron Paul Holbach (1723-1789) who was fond of calling himself 'the personal enemy of God'. His main work on this theme is: 'The System of Nature' (trans. by H. D. Robinson, Matsell, New York, 1835). When David Hume remarked to the Baron that he had never met, and did not believe in, any atheists, Holbach pointed out his eighteen friends at the dinner party to which Hume had been invited, fifteen of whom were atheists, the other three not having made up their minds (Mossner: 'The Life of David Hume', London, 1954, p. 483). W. K. Wright ('A Student's Philosophy of Religion', New York, 1950, p. 367 f.) paraphrases in this way Holbach's 'common sense' argument for atheism. 'If there really were a God, we should have no doubt on the subject at all. Such a Being as God is thought to be, all-wise and powerful, who expects men to believe in Him, would certainly have made Himself known to men in some unmistakable manner, and not merely by the mode of improbable miracles and revelations which are unconvincing to most thoughtful men. If God exists, why has He not declared Himself?' But the Theist has no difficulty in replying that if God were to make Himself known without the possibility of doubt this would have the effect of depriving man of his freedom of choice, for which man could fail to obey if there were no tensions in the life of faith? The *Hasidim* attribute this very question to the *Ba'al Shem Tobh*, the founder of the movement. Why does God allow men to doubt His existence? His reply is reported to have been that if doubt were impossible charity and sympathy would be impossible, for man's faith would be so strong that in every case of need he would be inclined to leave it to God! It is also said by the *Hasidim* that a Hasidic saint, Aaron of Premishlan, once said that it was really wrong for a true servant of God to wish to see Elijah (who appeared to the saints) for this would tend in some measure to interfere with the saint's freedom of choice (*v.* David Ha-Lahmi: '*Hakhme Yisrael*', Tel-Aviv, 1957, p. 160).

*　　　　*　　　　*

EXCURSUS

On the subject of modern atheism *v.* James Collins: 'God in Modern Philosophy', London, 1960, Chapter VIII, 'The Emergence of Atheism', pp. 238–284. There is a good selection from Comte's thoughts on religion, together with useful critical notes, in Caldecott and Mackintosh, *op. cit.*, pp. 316–358. Selections from Feuerbach's thought, together with further references and a short critique, are to be found in 'Philosophers Speak of God' by Charles Hartshorne and William L. Reese, University of Chicago Press, 1953, pp. 448–466. The literature on Marx and Freud is, of course, immense. Of particular interest for the views of Marx and Freud on religion are: 'K. Marx and F. Engels On Religion', Foreign

Languages Publishing House, Moscow, 1957, a selection from the writings of these two men on God and religion; James Collins, *op. cit.*, the bibliography given in notes 10–17, p. 437; David Elton Trueblood, *op. cit.*, Chapter 12, 'The Challenge of Dialectical Materialism', pp. 161–176; Freud's 'Totem and Taboo' (1915), 'The Future of an Illusion' (1928) and 'Moses and Monotheism' (1939); Leslie D. Weatherhead's 'Psychology, Religion and Healing', London, 1952; H. L. Philp: 'Freud and Religious Belief', London, 1956; Victor White: 'God and the Unconscious', London, 1953; Theodor Reik: 'Ritual', London, 1931, and 'Dogma and Compulsion', New York, 1951; Abraham Cronbach: 'Psychoanalytic Study of Judaism' in HUCA, Vol. VIII–IX, 1931–32; Alter Druyanov's Hebrew essays in the periodical '*Reshumoth*', Vol. I, Odessa, 1918, pp. 199–204, Vol. II, Tel-Aviv, pp. 303–357. The editors of the book on Marx and Engels open the selection of writings with these highly revealing words (typical of the 'scientism' on which Marxist critique of religion is based): 'The present collection includes works in which Marx and Engels expressed their views on the essence and origin of religion and its role in class society; these works lay the theoretical foundations of proletarian, Marxist atheism. The world outlook founded by Marx and Engels is based on the objective laws of the development of nature and society. It rests on facts provided by science and is radically opposed to religion'. Marx wrote in 1844: 'Religion is the opium of the people' though some have claimed that Charles Kingsley said this first. Lenin, in a well-known statement, remarked: 'All contemporary religions and churches, all and every kind of religious organisation, Marxism has always viewed as organs of bourgeois reaction, serving as a defence of exploitation and the doping of the working-classes'. 'Modern Atheism' by Etienne Borne, Faith and Fact Books, Burns and Oates, London, 1961, is a Catholic critique of atheism.

*   *   *

Modern atheism thus proceeds to attack Theism on three grounds – that it deprives man of his worth and dignity, that it is irrational, and that it is contrary to the scientific picture of the universe. The Theistic reply to the first charge is, as we have noted, that on any advanced view of Theism its aim is to enrich man's character and personality, not to impoverish it. As for the denial of the use of reason in attaining to truth about God, this is a double-edged weapon. Once argue that men *cannot* arrive at *this* truth by the exercise of their reason, once argue, in fact, that when men imagine that they are reasoning about God they are really indulging in a process of rationalisation, the motives of which are either economic or psychological, and you prohibit *any* type of reasoning. Marxists and Freudians, on their own analysis, may also be governed by emotions affecting their reasoning power. In other words (and this point has often been made without any effective reply from those against whom it is directed), no argument can possibly be valid which questions the power of men to argue, for this places a question mark against the argument itself.

As to the alleged argument from science this is, in reality, in the form of a philosophical position derived, so it is claimed, from science. It is certainly not science itself, which is a *method* not a philosophy. Modern science investigates the facts and draws certain conclusions from them. The argument that the facts are such that only an atheistic interpretation of them is valid is entirely unwarranted, receiving no support from the facts themselves. That there are difficulties in his position no Theist would deny. But Theism offers, at least, an explanation of how the world came into being and what life is about; whereas atheism must be content to say that things just happened, that there is no meaning to life and to the world. But man is so constituted that he is always searching for reasons, for meaning, for purpose. Science itself is based on the view that there is a rationality underlying appearances, that the facts the scientist examines can be given a reasoned explanation. Paul Edwards ('A Modern Introduction to Philosophy', *op. cit.*, p. 447), in a very fair and balanced statement of Theism and opposing theories, observes: 'It should be noted that, in denying the existence of God, an atheist does not necessarily claim to know the answers to such questions as "What is the origin of life?" or "Where does the universe come from?" He merely rules out as false theological answers to these questions. There has been a great deal of confusion on this subject. Clarence Darrow, for example, based his agnosticism partly on the premise that "whether the universe had an origin – and if it had – what the origin was, will never be known by men". An atheist, however, could quite consistently admit that this is an insoluble problem. If somebody asked me "who killed Carlo Tresca?" I could answer "I don't know and it will probably never be discovered" and I could quite consistently add "But I know some people who certainly did not kill him – e.g. Julius Ceasar or General Eisenhower or Bertrand Russell". It seems that the mistake here rests in a confusion between two kinds of insoluble problems. When I say that I know that General Eisenhower did not kill Carlo Tresca but that the identity of the killer will never be known I am not saying that there is no solution to the problem "Who killed Carlo Tresca?", only that no one will ever know the solution. But when the atheist says that he does not know how the universe came about but that he knows it was not brought into being by God he is saying far more than that there is an insoluble problem. For if God is not responsible for the world the only alternative is to say that it just happened or was "there" all the time, i.e. to be content not with a problem to which no one *knows* the solution but a problem to which, in the nature of the case, there can *be* no solution. This would be analogous to saying: "I know that neither Julius Ceasar nor General Eisenhower nor Bertrand Russell *nor anyone else* killed Carlo Tresca but I do not know who killed him". This is, of course, nonsense. If I know that no one killed Carlo Tresca I cannot go on to say that I do not know who killed him and so suggest that he was killed. It is more than a little difficult to see how the impression can be avoided that once one has exhausted the possibilities of attributing the origin of the world to God or accepting that it just happened one has any further possibilities which may be true!'

Modern atheistic theories are not infrequently given the lie by the lives of their own proponents. No one familiar with the biographies of Marx and Freud, for instance, can fail to recognise in the lives of these men a devotion to ideas, in which they believed passionately, which is more than a little difficult to explain on their own premises. For, on the atheistic hypothesis, why should a man be so constituted that he is capable of enduring calumny and hatred in defence of what he holds to be the truth? Why should he deny himself in the pursuit of truth and justice, demonstrating by his endeavours that he believes in values greater than himself? It is impossible to share the opinion of some religionists that the atheist is incapable of leading an ethical life since our experience shows that he can. But why the atheist should demonstrate in his life a self-sacrificing, heroic, at times almost superhuman, devotion to truth and duty – and that he does do this sometimes is also within our experience – is puzzling granted his philosophy since, in his view, there are no absolute standards of value 'out there' in the universe. To reply, as the atheist is bound to do, that man is so constituted as to be obliged to pursue truth, justice and duty, even when the pursuit is painful and against his own interests, is yet further confirmation that the atheistic view really declares that there is no explanation of the universe and of life within it.

This must not be taken to mean that for the Theist values such as truth and justice are not good in themselves but only good because God wills them so. Most modern Theists would say that God, being God, cannot violate His own nature by ordering man to do otherwise than choose the good. But the Theist's case rests on the idea that values such as truth and goodness must be grounded in a Being other than man. The poet declares:

> 'It fortifies my soul to know
> That though I perish truth is so'.

The Theist explains this as due to the grounding of truth and other values in God, so that even if man perishes truth does not perish. The atheist can only say that although this or that individual man perishes truth is so for other men, who will live by the truths discovered by the individual. But other men are also individuals and it is hard to see why one individual should perish in order that other individuals might see the truth.

It is here necessary to consider briefly the philosophy of agnosticism, according to which man is incapable of knowing whether or not there is a God. Everyone knows that the term was coined by T. H. Huxley. Huxley has described amusingly how he came to coin the term for an attitude he had long felt (v. the chapter 'Agnosticism' in Huxley's 'Science and Christian Tradition', New York, 1894, quoted in part in 'Approaches to the Philosophy of Religion' ed. Daniel J. Bronstein and Harold M. Schulweis, Prentice-Hall, New York, 1954, pp. 210-215). He was a member of the Metaphysical Society at which every variety of philosophical and theological opinion was represented. Huxley says that he felt like a fox without a tail. All his colleagues had a label. He was the odd man out.

To remedy this defect and provide himself with a tail like the other foxes Huxley called himself an *agnostic* – one who claimed that the 'gnosis' of the Church, the claim to know so much about things which man cannot, in Huxley's view, know, was mistaken. It is thus unfair to criticise Huxley's agnosticism as a mere evasion. Huxley is not saying that he cannot make up his mind whether or not there is a God but that it is impossible for a man to make up his mind on this question. Both the Theist and the atheist are mistaken. The one affirms that God exists, the other denies that He does. Both are certain that truth can be attained here whereas the true agnostic refuses to admit anything of the kind. All such matters as the existence of God are beyond the scope of human inquiry.

Two fairly obvious criticisms of agnosticism have been made. The first is that a really thoroughgoing agnosticism is inconsistent for if man cannot know anything at all about the God question he cannot know that he cannot know. The second is more serious. If the belief in God were a simple proposition open to denial or affirmation the matter would be different. But it is clear that belief in God demands practical manifestations. The real question is the tenor and quality of a life, not the assent to or dissent from an idea. In the arena of life man has only two possibilities. He can either live in the presence of God or he can deny that God exists. By suspending judgment permanently, as the agnostic is bound to do, he, in fact, comes down on the side of atheism. To refuse to make a decision 'for God' is not to leave the matter in abeyance. It is to decide against God. The existentialists who speak of 'committment' and the 'leap of faith' certainly are justified. Man cannot see life from the outside as a spectator without his missing the whole essence of life's game. It is only man as actor, as participant in life's struggles, who learns the meaning of life.

The illustration has been given of a garden in which flowers are yearly planted. The owner of the garden may deliberate whether to plant the flowers in a particular year or to allow the weeds to grow. For a week or two he may weigh up the pros and cons, balancing the trouble he will be obliged to take if he cultivates the garden against the absence of beauty if he fails to do so. But sooner or later he must decide one way or the other. The one thing he cannot do is to leave the matter in abeyance permanently for by so doing he is, in fact, deciding against the cultivation of flowers in a garden.

It is to the credit of religious existentialism that it has called our attention to the element of decision in the religious life. Religious existentialists have noted that there is all the difference in the world between knowing a 'thing' and knowing a 'person'. A thing can be known through learning in a detached way all there is to know about it. A person can only be known by encounter. The lover 'knows' the object of his affection in an entirely different way from the manner in which a student 'knows' his subject. Love is essentially a meeting of two personalities in which there is a 'life of dialogue'. Religious existentialism claims that God is to be known as a 'person' is known, not as a 'thing' is known. Man does not discover God by arguing about His existence but by staking his life on that existence. The theologian may know a great deal *about* God. It is only the committed who really knows God.

That there is much truth in the existentialist emphasis and much insight it would be futile to deny. We have seen at the beginning of this chapter that in the Hebraic tradition speculation concerning God's existence is a latecomer. The ancient Hebrews 'knew' God through their encounter, and that of their people's history, with Him. But when all has been admitted it is surely going too far to suggest, as some religious existentialists do, that all arguments for the existence of God are utterly futile. Thus Kierkegaard says ('Concluding Unscientific Postscript', Princeton University Press, 1944, p. 485, followed by the Jewish existentialist Will Herberg, 'Judaism and Modern Man', New York, 1951, p. 67, note 6, who says that attempts to 'prove' the existence of God are an impertinence): 'So rather let us mock God out and out; this is always preferable to the disparaging air of importance with which one would prove God's existence. For to prove the existence of one who is present is the most shameless affront, since it is an attempt to make him ridiculous. How could it occur to anybody to prove that he exists unless one had permitted oneself to ignore him and now makes the thing all the worse by proving his existence before his very nose? The existence of a king or his presence is commonly acknowledged by an appropriate expression of subjection and submission; what if, in his presence, one were to prove that he existed? One proves God's existence by worship'. Paul Tillich ('The Religious Situation in Germany Today' *Religion in Life*, Vol. III, No. 2, 1934, p. 167, quoted by Klausner and Kuntz *op. cit*, p. 526) follows the same line of approach: 'God can be proved, or again he can be refuted, by rational methods. But an idea which can be proved by means or arguments that are more or less convincing cannot give me a foundation for my existence in face of eternity. Arguments for the existence of God presuppose the loss of certainty of God. That which I have to prove by argument has no immediate reality for me. Its reality is mediated for me by some other reality about which I cannot be in doubt; so that this other reality is nearer to me than the reality of God'. There appears to be in all this a colossal begging of the question. Of course it is true that once one knows that God exists it is futile and impertinent to 'prove' His existence. Of course it is true that arguments for the existence of God presuppose the loss of certainty of God. But since there are people who deny God's existence and claim that any 'encounter' one has is not real but imaginary it is surely necessary to reason about faith, to consider what cause we have for believing in God's existence. The existentialist is right if all that he is doing is to persuade the believer not to stop at argument but to go on to worship. No true believer requires the admonition. But when the existentialist goes further to suggest that all reasoning about God's existence is an impertinence he is on very uncertain ground. To follow Kierkegaard's illustration of the king, suppose I see the king and desire to give the appropriate tokens of subjection and submission, but I am told by someone present that I am the victim of an hallucination so that the obeisance I intend to make is to a figment of my own imagination. In such circumstances it would be my duty, first, to determine whether there really is a king to whom homage should be paid, to decide by the means given to me whether I am the lunatic or the man who tells me that no king is present. The king, if he knows of my predicament, will not be angry with me for postponing my act of homage for he knows that I am sincerely confused and he will find no pleasure in submission to what might be a mirage so far as I am concerned. He would rather wish that I should attain conviction of his existence first and then my submission to him will be a real submission. If, from time to time, the committed believer still resorts to arguments about God's existence he does so either to help others to attain his conviction or to help himself in the moments when faith falters, for there is an ebb and flow in the life of faith and complete certainty is not given to humans all the time. This latter, I take it, is the meaning of the numerous references in the literature of Jewish piety to *'hizzuq 'emunah'*, 'strengthening of faith'.

Finally, reference must be made to the severe challenge presented to the whole Theistic position by the Logical Positivists. This attack on Theism is not on the grounds of its falsehood but its meaninglessness. By an analysis of the meaning of meaning this school arrives at the conclusion that only those sentences are meaningful which are either analytical or capable of verification. Analytical statements are concerned with the elucidation of the meaning of words and they do not attempt to convey any information about the world. Statements which do attempt to convey information about the world must be capable of empirical verification, so it is claimed, if they are to have meaning. If I say: 'It is going to rain tomorrow' this is a meaningful sentence. I know how to go about verifying it. I wait until tomorrow and if it rains my statement is true, if it does not my statement is false. But a statement which cannot be verified, which cannot be either contradicted or affirmed no matter what test is applied, has no meaning at all. Such a statement is nonsense. If I say: 'There is an invisible blong in this room' someone might deny it. He would challenge me to produce the evidence. I might point to a corner of the room and tell him that the blong is over there. He would then say that he cannot see it and I would reply: 'But of course you can't see it, it is invisible'. By this time we will both probably realise that we are talking nonsense, that it is not really a question of whether an invisible blong is really in the room but that the words 'an invisible blong' are as meaningless as no words at all would be. It is as if I had said: 'There is an . . . in this room'. Now it is claimed that metaphysical statements are incapable of verification and are therefore meaningless. The statement 'God exists' can neither be affirmed nor can it be denied empirically, that is to say, no matter what *facts* are produced the Theist will persist in declaring that there is a God while the atheist will persist in denying that there is a God. But a statement which fits *all* the facts fits *no* facts and is sheer nonsense. Thus we have a much stronger attack on Theism than atheism ever was. The atheist does the Theist the courtesy of agreeing that the Theist is talking sense although he disagrees with him. The Logical Positivist denies that there is anything to discuss in the Theistic statement which, for him, is no statement at all. Indeed, the Logical Positivist would argue that atheism and agnosticism are similarly meaningless. For if the statement 'There is a God' is meaningless so is the statement 'There is no God' and the statement: 'I do not know if there is a God'.

What is the Theistic reply? First, the verification principle has been challenged on the grounds that it contains an inner contradiction. The statement that only a statement capable of verification is a meaningful statement is itself incapable of verification! But leaving such subtleties aside, the Theistic statement can be verified. If the proofs for God's existence are valid then Theism has been verified by these proofs. But, as we have seen, the proofs have been under heavy fire since Kant and few Theists would claim that they amount to empirical verification of the existence of God. In addition there is the question of what we mean by the term 'God'. On the Logical Positivist view no definition capable of verification can be given. However, as someone has rightly said, for the Theist there is a process by means of which the statement 'God exists' can be verified. This process is what we call dying! At death we shall know whether we enter the eternity of God's presence or vanish into nothingness.

The Logical Positivist challenge has served a useful purpose in compelling religious people to be careful in their use of words. For while the Theistic position is not meaningless it is undoubtedly true that many meaningless statements are made in the name of Theism. For instance, one sometimes hears Theists, faced with the problem of pain, arguing that although God is good He is not 'good' in our human sense. This is, indeed, nonsense. For the only meaning we can give to the term 'good' is the human 'sense' of the word. If we say of a being that it is 'good' in a non-human sense and this is totally different from the human we are, in fact, giving no meaning whatever to the word 'good'. On this showing to say 'God is good' is akin to saying 'God is . . .' without completing the sentence. Theists ought to welcome the constant demand, nowadays, for clarity of expression. If the result of the demand is that they must keep silence more often, there is much gain in this, in the worship of the God to whom 'silence is praise'. Moses, said a Hasidic teacher, was 'slow of speech' (Ex. iv. 10) because he knew so much and the more one knows the more one is compelled to be silent.

*   *   *

EXCURSUS

On religious existentialism v. the works of Kierkegaard, particularly: 'Either/Or', trans. by Walter Lowrie, Princeton University Press, 1944; 'Fear and Trembling' and 'The Sickness Unto Death', trans. by Walter Lowrie, Doubleday Anchor Books, New York, 1954; 'The Journals of Soren Kierkegaard: A Selection', ed. and trans. by Alexander Dru, Oxford University Press, 1938; 'A Kierkegaard Anthology', ed. Robert Bretall, Princeton University Press, 1946. Cf. David E. Roberts: 'Existentialism and Religious Belief', Galaxy Books, New York, 1959; John A. Hutchinson: 'Faith, Reason, and Existence', Oxford University Press, New York, 1956; Frederick Copleston, S. J.; 'Contemporary Philosophy, Studies of Logical Positivism and Existentialism', Burns and Oates, London, 1956; Reinhold Niebuhr: 'Leaves From the Notebooks of a Tamed Cynic', Meridian Books, New York, 1957; the works by and on Buber and Rosenzweig cited above; Will Herberg op. cit.; Milton Steinberg's 'Anatomy of Faith' op. cit. Steinberg's essays contain a critique of the 'anti-reason' tendency in modern theological thinking. Steinberg sees in this the inheritance of Christian thought and states that a Jewish thinker should view the whole movement with caution. 'Sanity and spiritual realism – these are special endowments of Judaism from which Christianity, at least traditional Christianity, is by inheritance debarred. In Judaism's case, mystery may attend, but no absurdity mars the simple lines of its essential faith nor the elemental humaneness of its moral aspirations' (p. 212). 'There is, in my view, less necessity for antirationalism in Jewish theology than there is in Christian theology' (p. 230). 'Professing no Gods who are yet men, no vicarious atonement of sins, no trinities that are somehow unities, no justification of one man and damnation of another, though both are equally sinners, professing in sum none of the paradoxes of Christianity, we Jews are subject to little of the motivation which

impels Christians to the glorification of the unintelligible' (p. 168).
The last passage has, with justice from his point of view, been
described by James Parkes ('The Theology of Toleration', Claude
Montefiore Lecture, 1961, Liberal Jewish Synagogue, London,
p. 26) as a 'superb naughtiness about Christianity' from a distinguished Jewish scholar. Parkes turns the tables on Steinberg by
observing: 'How truly delightful as coming from one whose
religion symbolises the entry into a national relationship of unique
responsibility with the Creator of the universe by a primitive
physical mutilation, which indulges in violent religious controversy
over the culinary destination of the pig, which splendidly refuses
to abandon a combination of intense particularity with the most
comprehensive universalism, which combines a history of the
longest and most dreadful persecution with the most illogical
belief in human perfectibility, which, in a word, exhibits in glorious
confusion all the paradox and unintelligibility to outsiders to which
any ancient and living religious tradition is necessarily heir'.
The point is well taken. Steinberg's choice of words is unfortunate.
But, in fairness to Steinberg, the point he is trying to make is
that there is more of the element of 'mystery' about the Godhead in
Christianity than in Judaism, more of the 'paradox' and that,
therefore, an antirational theology will be treated in Christianity
with greater hospitality than in Judaism. Indeed, some Christian
existentialists have referred to Steinberg's examples as evidence of
the correctness of their view. However, it could be argued that this
attitude is not unknown among Jewish thinkers. An extreme
example is that of the Hasidic teacher, Nahman of Bratzlav, who
is similarly fond of the 'paradox' and whose wild piety emphasises
that religion is 'higher than reason'. He was, incidentally, a severe
critic of Maimonides. *Cf.* Joseph Weiss on the 'paradox' in Nahman's thinking in The Schocken Jubilee Volume, Jer. 1952, pp.
245–291. On Logical Positivism *v.* A. J. Ayer: 'Language, Truth
and Logic', 2nd ed., London, 1946; F. Copleston, *op. cit.*, Edwards
and Pap, *op. cit.*, pp. 544 ff.; Trueblood *op. cit.* Part III, Chapter 14
'The Challenge of Logical Positivism', pp. 189 f.; 'Faith and
Logic' ed. Basil Mitchell, George Allen and Unwin, London, 1957;
C. E. M. Joad: 'A Critique of Logical Positivism', University of
Chicago Press, 1950. Frederick Ferré in his 'Language Logic and
God', Eyre and Spottiswoode, London, 1962, brilliantly surveys
the wide field and offers his own justification of the use of Theistic
language. *Cf.* the important symposium, ed. by Sidney Hook,
'Religious Experience and Truth', Oliver and Boyd, Edinburgh,
1962, the papers being those read at the Fourth Annual Meeting of
the New York University Institute of Philosophy.

[3]

THE SECOND PRINCIPLE
God's Unity

M AIMONIDES' (Abelson's translation) statement of the
second principle is: '*The Second Principle of Faith*'.
The Unity of God. This implies that this cause of all is one;
not one of a genus nor of a species, and not as one human
being who is a compound divisible into many unities; not a
unity like the ordinary material body which is one in number but takes on endless divisions and parts. But He, the
exalted one, is a unity in the sense that there is no unity
like His in any way. This is the second cardinal doctrine of
the faith which is indicated by the assertion, "Hear, O Israel,
the Lord our God the Lord is One" (Deut. vi. 4)'.

The '*'Ani Ma'amin*' form is: 'I believe with perfect faith
that the Creator, blessed be His name, is a Unity, and that
there is no unity in any manner like unto His, and that He
alone is our God, who was, is, and will be'. In the *Yigdal*
formula the principle is given as: 'He is One, and there is no
unity like unto His unity; inconceivable is He, and unending is
His unity'.

Friedländer's version is: 'The belief in the Unity of God;
that is, the belief that the Being who is the cause of everything
in existence is One; not like the unity of a group or class,
composed of a certain number of individuals, nor the unity of
one individual consisting of various constituent elements, nor
the unity of one simple thing which is divisible *ad infinitum*,
but as a unity the like of which does not exist'. Werblowsky
puts the second principle as follows: 'The stress on unity has a
theoretical and a practical aspect. Theoretically it excludes
all types of polytheistic, dualistic and trinitarian beliefs and,
according to Maimonides, all positive attributes. God's unity
is an absolutely unique unity. For the Qabbalists the uniqueness
of this unity actually means the mystery of the divine in its

hidden, non-manifest aspect of *En Sof* and in its manifest, dynamic and creative aspect of the *sefiroth*. Divine unity is also usually defined as to exclude all mediators. Nevertheless Qabbalism and folklore are full of angels, demons and spirits which, though never worshipped or adored, are nevertheless addressed and exorcized (by amulets, magic formulae, etc.) respectively'.

The first principle of the Jewish faith, as recorded by Maimonides, is belief in the existence of God. The second principle is belief in God's unity. The two combine to form the doctrine of *monotheism* – the belief in one God. Apart from *atheism* and *agnosticism*, considered in the previous chapter, the rivals to *monotheism* are *deism, pantheism, polytheism, dualism* and *trinitarianism* (trinitarians deny that their belief is non-montheistic but from the Jewish point of view the Christian doctrine offends against the pure monotheistic principle). These we may here consider in turn.

(a) Deism

Traditional Jewish monotheism holds that God is both transcendent and immanent. He is above, beyond and apart from the universe and yet He is also inside the universe, filling it with His spirit. Deism denies the second proposition, pantheism the first. Deism is the belief that God is solely transcendent, that He is outside the universe and can have no concern with those who inhabit the world. In the view of the Deists, God created the world but He does not govern it.

Deism has its antecedents in the ancient world. The Epicureans also taught that the gods were unconcerned with the deeds of man and, as we have seen, the Psalmist's castigation of the *nabhal*, who says in his heart that there is no God, is directed chiefly against one who denies divine Providence. But it was in the eighteenth century that Deism became a popular philosophy. With the rise of modern science and the consequent vividness of a causal explanation of phenomena it seemed plausible to some to draw a distinction between God, the Author and Creator of all which exists, and Nature, which proceeds by its own laws without divine intervention. God, in His relationship to Nature, is thought of as the maker of a machine.

The influence of the maker is limited to the manufacture of the machine, which is then left to work by itself with no more than an occasional check by the maker to see if the machine is functioning properly.

This view is at variance with traditional Jewish Theism, which sees the hand of God constant in all events. God is both transcendent and immanent so that in some sources He is described as the potter who moulds the clay or the jeweller who fashions an intricate piece of jewellery, in other sources as the soul of the universe. He is thought of as being both apart from the universe and yet, at the same time, as being within it. He works on the universe both from without and from within.

Among eighteenth-century Jewish attacks on Deism, one of the most original was that of the Hasidic leader, Schneor Zalman of Liady (1747-1813), whose views we shall shortly note in somewhat greater detail. For our present purpose it is sufficient to quote the passage in his '*Tanya*' (ed. Vilna, 1930, *Sha'ar Ha-Yihud We-Ha-'Emunah*, Chapter 2, pp. 153-154) for its relevance to Jewish anti-Deism. Schneor Zalman does not mention the Deists by name. It is, indeed, extremely unlikely that he had ever heard of them. But Deistic theories were 'in the air' in his day and there can be no doubt that it is these that he is attacking when he writes: 'Here lies the answer to the heretics and here is uncovered the root of their error, in which they deny God's providence over particulars and the miracles and wonders recorded in Scripture. Their false imagination leads them into error, for they compare the work of the Lord, Creator of heaven and earth, to the works of man and his artifices. These stupid persons compare the work of heaven and earth to a vessel which emerges from the hand of the artificer. Once the vessel has been fashioned it no longer requires its maker. Even when the maker has completed his work and goes about his own business the vessel retains the form and appearance it had when it was fashioned. Their eyes are too blind to notice the important distinction between the works of man and his artifices – in which "something" is made from "something", the form alone being changed from a piece of silver into a vessel – and the creation of heaven and earth, which is the creation of "something" out of "nothingness".

This latter is an even greater marvel than the division of the Red Sea, for instance, when the Lord caused a strong east wind to blow all through the night, until the waters were divided to stand as a heap and a wall. If the Lord had stopped the wind for but a moment, the waters, undoubtedly, would have begun to flow again in their normal, natural way and would no longer have stood upright like a wall. Although this nature implanted in the waters is also "something" created out of "nothing", for all that a stone wall does stand upright without the help of the wind, only this is not true of the nature of water. It follows *a fortiori* that with regard to *creatio ex nihilo* – higher than nature and a much greater marvel than the division of the Red Sea – it is certain that the creature would revert to the state of nothingness and negation, God forfend, if the Creator's power were to be removed from it. It is essential, therefore, for the power of the Worker to be in His work constantly if the work is to be kept in existence'. For Schneor Zalman it is impossible to suggest, as the Deists do, that God has created Nature and left it, as it were, to its own devices, since from God's point of view Nature itself is 'unnatural', contrary to the 'nothingness' whence it emerged. As the stone drops to the ground when the restraining hand relinquishes its hold, Nature would 'naturally' revert to nothingness were it not for the hand of God, which keeps Nature permanently suspended over the void. It follows that it is an absurdity to speak of Nature being left to its own devices, for if Nature were 'left alone' by God it would become 'no-Nature', vanishing into the abyss whence it came.

Another eighteenth century Jewish thinker to deal with Deism was Haham David Nieto (1654–1728), who delivered a discourse at the Spanish and Portuguese Synagogue in London in the year 1703, on the theme that was to have far-reaching consequences. A fuller discussion of this famous discourse and the controversy to which it gave rise will be reserved for the following section on Pantheism. Here it suffices to note that the discourse was directed explicitly against the Deists, who regarded Nature as a metaphysical entity apart from God. Nieto observes – and, as we shall see, this caused the charge of Pantheism to be levelled against him – that the word 'Nature' was of fairly recent coinage and is, in reality, only another name for God's providential control over the world He has created.

A well-known anti-Deist comment to the Psalms – I cannot trace the source of this but it is frequently repeated in learned Jewish circles – reads the controversy between Deism and Theism into Psalm cxiii, verses 4 to 6:

> *'The Lord is high above all nations,*
> *His glory is above the heavens.*
> *Who is like unto the Lord our God,*
> *That is enthroned on high,*
> *That looketh down low*
> *Upon heaven and upon earth?'*

The Deist claims that 'God is high', that His glory is above the heavens, and that earth is too lowly for His concern. Israel replies that if it is too low for God to descend upon earth it is as low for Him to descend into heaven, since, so far as God is concerned, the highest heaven is too low. Deism invests the world with a kind of false independence. Traditional Jewish Theism emphasises that the world is dependent upon God.

*   *   *

EXCURSUS

On Deism *v.* George Galloway: 'The Philosophy of Religion', T. & T. Clark, Edinburgh, 1951, pp. 458–460; N. L. Torrey: 'Voltaire and the English Deists', Yale University Press, 1930; J. Orr: 'English Deism: Its Roots and Fruits', Grand Rapids, Michigan, 1934. Carlyle in *'Sartor Resartus'*, Book II, Chapter VII, describes the Deistic God as 'an absentee God, sitting idle, ever since the first Sabbath, at the outside of his universe, and seeing it go'. In the famous *Yom Kippur* hymn by an unknown author God is compared to the potter, the jeweller etc. who work on the material from without, *v.* Festival Prayer Book, ed. Routledge and Kegan Paul, Day of Atonement, Part I, p. 39. But in the *Talmud, Ber.* 10a, in an oft-quoted passage, God's immanence is stressed: 'Just as the Holy One, blessed be He, fills the whole world, so the soul fills the body. Just as the Holy One, blessed be He, sees but is not seen, so the soul sees but is not seen. Just as the Holy One, blessed be He, feeds the whole world, so the soul feeds the whole body. Just as the Holy One, blessed be He, is pure, so the soul is pure. Just as the Holy One, blessed be He, dwells in the innermost recesses, so the soul dwells in the innermost recesses. Let that which has these five qualities come and praise Him who has these five qualities'. On Nieto *v.* Jakob J. Petuchowski: 'The Theology of Haham David Nieto – An Eighteenth Century Defence of the Jewish Tradition', New York, 1954. J. Abelson's 'The Immanence of God in Rabbinical Literature', London, 1912, is a particularly important account of Jewish views on God's immanence.

*   *   *

(b) Pantheism

Deism departs from traditional Theism by its total emphasis on God's transcendence. Pantheism, the doctrine that all is God and God is the all, that God and Nature are the same, departs from the traditional concept in the opposite direction. The Deist believes that God is only 'outside' the universe. The Pantheist believes that He is only 'inside' it, that He is, in fact, to be identified with the universe.

In ancient times Pantheism was found particularly in the Far Eastern religions. Hinduism is the classical example, Pantheism reaching its fullest expression in the Upanishads. Among more recent thinkers the outstanding representative of Pantheism is, of course, Benedict Spinoza (1632–1677). Spinoza's system is among the most difficult to grasp and its detailed study is a task for experts. But it does seem fairly clear that in Spinoza's system God and Nature are treated as different names for the same thing. God is not 'outside' or apart from Nature. He did not *create* Nature but *is* Nature. Neither intellect nor will can be ascribed to God. Indeed, it seems, God, in Spinoza's thought, is the name we give to the totality of things.

It is not surprising that Spinoza has been frequently accused of 'Atheism', an accusation he took pains to deny. In a letter to Jacob Ostens (1625–1678), Lambert Van Velthuysen (1622–1685) of Utrecht, openly states that in his view Spinoza's opinions are nothing more than a disguised form of atheism. 'He (Spinoza) acknowledges God and confesses Him to be the maker and founder of the universe. But he declares that the form, appearance, and order of the world are evidently as necessary as the Nature of God, and the eternal truths, which he holds are established apart from the decision of God. Therefore he also expressly declares that all things come to pass by invincible necessity and inevitable fate . . . He does this in accordance with his principles. For what room can there be for a last judgement? Or what expectation of reward or of punishment, when all things are attributed to fate, and all things are declared to emanate from God with inevitable necessity, or rather, when he declares that this whole universe is God? For I fear that our author is not very far removed from this opinion; at least there is not much difference between declaring that all things emanate necessarily from the nature of God and that the Universe itself is God . . . I think, therefore, that I have not strayed far from the truth, or done any injury to the Author, if I denounce him as teaching pure Atheism with hidden and disguised arguments'.

Ostens sent Spinoza Velthuysen's letter for comment. 'First', replies Spinoza, 'he says *that it concerns him little to know of what nationality I may be or what manner of life I follow.* But if he had known this he would not have persuaded himself so easily that I teach Atheism. For Atheists are wont to desire inordinately honours and riches, which I have always despised, as all those who know me are aware . . .' It appears that in Spinoza's day the atheist was viewed with the strongest reprobation. The charge of practical atheism, with its associations of a loose and morally reprehensible life, Spinoza vehemently denies, and any biography of the Amsterdam thinker will vindicate him here. But on the purely theoretical level it is hard to see how Spinoza's identification of God and the universe can fail to amount to an atheistic philosophy.

We have noted under 'Deism' the fierce controversy which broke out over the anti-Deist sermon preached by Haham David Nieto on Nov. 20th, 1703. Nieto claimed that God and Nature were one and the same. He was really concerned to refute the Deist view that Nature is an intermediary between the world and God. Nieto states that this view is at variance with Judaism and that Nature is a modern term for which the ancient Rabbis used the word 'God'. Opponents of Nieto seized upon this as an acceptance of Spinozism and a query was addressed to Zevi Ashkenazi, the famous Rabbi of Amsterdam, for his opinion. The conclusion arrived at by both Nieto and Zevi Ashkenazi was that the fundamental difference between Spinoza and what Nieto considers to be the Jewish view is that for Spinoza God is the name given to the totality of things, whereas, on the Jewish view, God created Nature and He governs the world. On the Jewish view God is transcendent as well as immanent and particular parts of Nature such as vegetation, clouds and rain are God's creatures, not part of God Himself.

The distinction is important. It will become clearer if a few passages, in Cecil Roth's translation, are given from the letter addressed by Nieto's Wardens to Zevi Ashkenazi and from the latter's reply.

(*1*) *From the letter of the Wardens*

'Rabbi David Nieto, president of the Rabbinical court and guide and teacher of our community, gave a sermon in the synagogue in which he said: "I am reported to have stated in the Rabbinical college that *God and Nature, and Nature and God, are one and the same.* It is true that I have made this statement and I now repeat and confirm it; and I gave as my authority the words of the Psalmist in the 147th Psalm: *He who covereth the heaven with clouds; he who prepareth rain for the earth; he who maketh grass to grow upon the mountains.* You must know, however, as the first principle of our faith, that the word Nature is a modern expression, no more than four or five hundred years old, and is not found in the words of the Talmudical Sages, who said that it is God who *causeth the wind to blow;* and God who *causeth the rain to fall;* and God who *causeth the dew to come forth.* From these passages it is clear that everything attributed by modern thinkers to Nature is due to the action of God; so that in fact there is no such thing as Nature, what they call Nature being nothing other than the providence of God. And so, as I said, God and Nature, and Nature and God, are one and the same". This sermon has given rise to a charge of heterodoxy . . . Such is the case. We ask you to decide with whom is the right'.

(*2*) *From the reply of Zevi Ashkenazi*

'I have listened to the complaints of his (Nieto's) opponents but do not understand them. If they take exception to his statement that apart from God there is no Nature comprehending all existing things, and make this objection on the ground that it is a derogation from the glory of God, the King of Kings, that he should act without intermediary; they must learn that it is those who seek for the mediation of Nature in the general world-order who are likely to fall into perplexity, whereas those who believe in the direct action of God's providence in all things do so securely whithersoever they turn. If, secondly, they think that the words of the sermon referred not to Nature in general but to particular natural things, – the heat of fire, for example, or the wetness of water – and from this understanding force the interpretation that in their natural action fire and water are themselves the Godhead (an opinion which would not be held by the most foolish and brutish of unbelievers, much less by a sage and learned man among the people of God who believe in God and His holy law), – on this count the words of the sermon are perfectly clear, without the need of the defence, seeing that they are centred upon the fundamental principle of the world-order; as he says: *it is God who causeth the winds to blow and bringeth down the rain and dews; from which passages it is clear that everything attributed by modern thinkers to Nature is due to the action of God.* On this point only wilful misconstruction can raise a doubt'.

For Nieto and Zevi Askenazi, then, the basic difference between the Jewish view and that of Spinoza is that for the latter there is really no God, only Nature, and God is only another name for Nature. Whereas in the Jewish view there is, in reality, no such thing as Nature, which is only a modern word for God's providence. This providence, however, is identical with Nature as a whole. But it is heretical to hold the view that particular natural things (the wetness of water etc.) are the Godhead.

Some Jewish thinkers, however, went even beyond this. For them God is actually to be found in the wetness of water and in all particular natural things. In this view, held among others by Schneor Zalman of Liady referred to above, there is no cosmos at all, only God. According to this acosmic view the universe is only appearance, not reality. From our point of view there is, indeed, a universe but from God's point of view, as it were, there is no world at all. 'Know this day, and lay it to thy heart, that the Lord, He is God in heaven above and upon the earth beneath; *there is none else*' (Deut. iv. 39) is interpreted by Schneor Zalman to yield the thought, not that there are no other gods, but that there is, in reality, nothing else but God! Schneor Zalman claims that his view is that of Hasidic thought.

This is one of the grounds on which the opponents of the Hasidic movement declared it to be heretical. Jewishly unconventional it no doubt is, but it differs very profoundly from Spinoza's pantheism. For Schneor Zalman God is *not* the universe, as for Spinoza. On the contrary, from God's point of view there is no universe. A useful term for views like Schneor Zalman's is *panentheism*. Pantheism has it that all is God. Panentheism has it that all is *in* God. The difference is obvious.

*　　　*　　　*

EXCURSUS

The term *panentheism* is used in 'Philosophers Speak of God', by Hartshorne and Reese, University of Chicago Press, 1953, where the idea is discussed with great acumen. The Chapter 'Classical Pantheism' in the same work, pp. 165–210, should be consulted for readings from pantheist thinkers. Older thinkers frequently fail to make a distinction between *pantheism* and *panentheism* and attack the latter under the name of the former, e.g. George Galloway *op. cit.*, pp. 460–466, who writes: 'Those who affirm the self-consciousness of God and of man, and also affirm the inclusion of the latter in the former, are really saddled with a hopeless problem. They have to explain how this limited, imperfect and incomplete experience which I call my own, is really owned by God, and forms part of his perfect and complete experience . . . The crux of the problem is to explain how my specific consciousness at this given moment can, without ceasing to be mine, be also God's consciousness . . . The facts of moral and spiritual experience are really unintelligible on the pantheistic theory that there is only one will in the universe, of which all things, material and human, are the utterance. While religion teaches that true living is conformity to the will of God, it always presupposes in individuals the freedom to obey or fail to obey. Pantheism, on the contrary, if it is consistent, must be fatalistic and can admit neither contingency nor human initiative within the rigid order of the universe'. Schneor Zalman attempts to get round this difficulty by his distinction between the universe from our point of view and the universe from God's point of view. Whether this is really intelligible the reader must judge. For Schneor Zalman's views *v.* his *'Tanya'*, Vilna, 1930, *Sha'ar Ha-Yihud We-Ha-'Emunah*, pp. 152 ff. A good account of this Hasidic thinker and the *Habad* movement in Hasidism which he founded is M. Teitelbaum's *'Ha-Rabh Mi-Ladi'*, Part II, Warsaw, 1913. Teitelbaum, pp. 105 f. points to the following differences between Schneor Zalman and Spinoza:

(1) For Spinoza God and Nature are one and the same but for Schneor Zalman God is transcendent as well as immanent.

(2) For Spinoza there is no creation of the world by God but for Schneor Zalman the Jewish view of *creatio ex nihilo* stands.

(3) For Spinoza the universe is eternal but for Schneor Zalman the world is temporal and God alone is eternal.

(4) For Spinoza it is impossible to attribute will to God but for Schneor Zalman it is God's will which has created the world, i.e. which endows the world with the appearance of reality.

(5) For Spinoza God does not work *through* Nature but *is* Nature; for Schneor Zalman God is revealed *through* Nature.

The best statement of the *Habad* view is to be found in the writings of Menahem Mendel of Lubavitch, Schneor Zalman's grandson, v. his '*Derekh Mitzwothekha*', Poltava, 1911. 'On the Unity of God', pp. 118 ff. Leon Roth uses the term *panentheism* for Spinoza's views in 'The Legacy of Israel', Clarendon Press, Oxford, 1927. p. 455. The term appears to have originated with K. C. F. Krause (1781–1832), v. J. Macquarrie: 'Twentieth Century Religious Thought', SCM Press, 1963, p. 274, note 2.

*　　　*　　　*

(c) Polytheism

Polytheism, the belief in and the worship of many gods, is the enemy of Biblical monotheism. It is against polytheism that all the great prophets of Israel direct their shafts. The older view among Biblical scholars, and still adhered to by some, was that Hebrew monotheism was the result of a long development out of polytheism through the stages of *henotheism* or *monolatry*, the belief in one God but not that He is the only god. There were 'other gods' beside Him who enjoyed an actual existence but who were not to be worshipped by the people of Israel. Only through the efforts of the literary prophets did pure monotheism triumph in Israel. But many scholars today, prominent among whom are Albright and Kaufmann, prefer to think of monotheism as present from the early beginnings of Israel and to think of Moses as a pure monotheist. The problem is of great interest and must be discussed here but it should be said that so far as Jewish theology is concerned the whole question does not matter very much one way or the other. For even if the older view were correct it is undeniable that eventually in Israel it was pure monotheism which was taught and accepted. 'I am the

Lord, and there is none else, Beside Me there is no God; I have girded thee, though thou hast not known Me; That they may know from the rising of the sun, and from the west, That there is none beside Me; I am the Lord, and there is none else' (Is. xlv. 5–6). 'And the Lord shall be King over all the earth; In that day shall the Lord be One, and His name one' (Zech. xiv. 9).

The evolutionary theory holds that the term 'other gods' in the Decalogue means that these have actual existence but that Israel is to worship God alone. It is argued that at first the Israelites were henotheists – people who believed in a special god for each region or nation – or monolatrists – people who worshipped one god among many – and that it was not until the Babylonian exile, after the prophets had purified the early religion, that Israel became purely monotheistic. According to the scholars who reject the evolutionary hypothesis and claim that monotheism erupted in ancient Israel from the very beginning, the term 'other gods' is to be explained only in the sense that the people who believed in them called them 'gods', not that they enjoyed actual existence. Opponents of the evolutionary theory note that it was put forward in the last century by scholars who were unduly influenced by Hegelian categories of thought and that there is no evidence whatsoever that the idea of evolution can be applied to such a world-transforming idea as monotheism. It is certain that in a number of Biblical passages (though questions of dating are obviously important here) the gods the nations worship are referred to as ' 'elilim' meaning literally 'things which are not', 'non-entities', or, as we would say, mere figments of the imagination.

*   *   *

EXCURSUS

The term ' 'elilim' is found in Lev. xxvi. 1; I Chron. xvi. 26; Ps. xcvi. 5; Is. ii. 8; Ezek. xxx. 13; Hab. ii. 18; with the definite article in : Lev. xix 4; Is. xix. 3; Ps. xcvii. 7. Albright's views are to be found in his 'From the Stone Age to Christianity', 2nd. ed., Doubleday Anchor Books, New York, 1957. E. Kaufmann's massive work 'Toledoth Ha-'Emunah Ha-Yisraelith', Tel. Aviv, 1937 and f. has recently been translated into English in an abridged form by Moshe Greenberg: 'The Religion of Israel', University of Chicago Press, 1960. Kaufmann is of the opinion that Israelite monotheism is an original, primary institution which moulded all of Israel's creativity. Israel, in fact, had so firm a conviction of the truth of monotheism that it failed to have any understanding of pagan religion. Pagan mythology, for instance, is conspicuously absent from the pages of the Bible. It is of great interest that there is no word in Biblical Hebrew for 'goddess'. The Biblical passages which appear to restrict God's domain to His land or to the affairs of His people (e.g. Gen. xxxv. 2 ff.; Judg. xi. 24); I Sam. xxvi. 19; II Kings v. 17) on which followers of the evolutionary theory base their case, are explained in quite a different sense by Kaufmann. They do not suggest that God's creation or government is limited to a particular land or people, only that the land and the people are the special *concern* of the God of all the earth (*v.* especially, Greenberg, *op. cit.*, pp. 127 ff.). On this theme *cf.* S. W. Baron: 'A Social and Religious History of the Jews', 2nd. ed., Vol. II, Columbia University Press, New York, 1952, p. 316, note 34; 'Before Philosophy' by Henri Frankfort and others, Pelican Books, 1949, Chapter VIII, pp. 237 f.; J. E. Fison: 'The Faith of the Bible', Pelican Books, 1957, Chapter I, 'The Unity of God', pp. 11 f.; Solomon Goldman: 'The Ten Commandments', ed. by Maurice Samuel, University of Chicago Press, 1956, pp. 133 f.; G. W. Anderson in 'The Old Testament and Modern Study', ed. H. H. Rowley, Clarendon Press, Oxford, 1956, pp. 286 ff.; Edmond Jacob: 'Theology of the Old Testament', trans. by Arthur W. Heathcote and Philip J. Allcock, Hodder and Stoughton, London, 1958, pp. 65–67; 'Moses and Monotheism' in 'From Moses to Qumran', by H. H. Rowley, Lutterworth Press, London, 1963, pp. 35–63.

* * *

(d) Dualism

Dualism is the belief that there are two gods, one of whom was responsible for some part of creation, the other for some other part. Generally, Dualism apportions the good in the universe to the power of good, the evil in the universe to the power of evil. Among the dualistic systems of the ancient world were: Zoroastrianism, with its god of light, Ormuzd, and its god of darkness, Ahriman; Gnosticism, with its supreme God enthroned in unapproachable distance and its Demiurge, who created the world; and Manichaeanism, a composite religion in which Christian (Gnostic) and Zoroastrian elements were combined and whose outstanding feature was a religious dualism. There were Christian Gnostics who taught that the author of the Old Testament was the inferior god of darkness, while the New Testament was the work of the good god of light. It seems almost certain that Deutero-Isaiah's strong affirmation of God's unity is directed against early Persian dualism. 'I form light, and create darkness; I make peace, and create evil; I am the Lord, that doeth all these things' (Is. xlv. 7). This verse was eventually incorporated into the liturgy of the Synagogue (Singer's P.B. p. 37) with the word *'ha-kol'* ('all things') substituted for *'ha-ra''* ('evil'), in order to avoid the direct ascription, in daily prayer, of evil to God. The figure of Satan without doubt came into Judaism under the influence of Dualism but in Judaism Satan is never a rival god, only a servant of God, to Whom he is completely subordinated.

Of all ancient religious philosophies Dualism is nearest to Monotheism, not alone in that it reduces the number of gods to two and no more, but that it encourages men to fight against evil on the side of the good. For all that, Judaism, however it coped with the terrible problem of evil, always refused to accept the doctrine of two powers or gods. There is only one God, Judaism teaches, Who, somehow, created evil as well as good for the fulfilment of His good purposes.

Saadiah Gaon refutes Dualism by a number of arguments which have lost none of their force. First, if the experience of the Dualists leads them to believe that all things can be subsumed under the headings of the useful and the harmful, and they consequently postulate two powers, they could, with the same logic, divide things into further categories, such as the five senses, and arrive at a belief in five or more gods. Furthermore, if there are two gods, neither of which could create without the help of the other, then neither would be a god, since his power would be limited. If, on the other hand, one can act without the other how is it that their desires always coincide and why does it never happen that one wishes to keep a person alive while the other wishes to kill him? Furthermore, if the two powers are connected with one another then they would really be one. If, on the other hand, they are distinct from each other then the separation would have to be produced by a third principle which is neither one nor the other. Saadiah quotes as Scriptural testimony against Dualism, in addition to the verses from Deutero-Isaiah, the verses: 'Unto thee it was shown, that thou mightest know that the Lord, He is God; there is none else beside Him' (Deut. iv. 35). 'Know this day, and lay it to thy heart, that the Lord, He is God in heaven above and upon the earth beneath; there is none else' (Deut. iv. 39). Similarly, Bahya Ibn Paqudah argues that if there are two gods then either each one could create the world without the other's help or he could not do so. If one could have created the world without the other's help then the other is superfluous. If, on the other hand, neither could have created the world without the other's help then each is weak in himself and neither is omnipotent, whereas a god who lacks omnipotence is no god. Furthermore, the profound sense of unity which men have and which they see in the universe would be unintelligible if there were two conflicting powers at work. Actually this kind of argument was expressed in the *Talmud* in its own inimitable way. There we are told that a *Magus*, a Zoroastrian priest, said to Amemar: 'From the middle of thy body upwards thou belongest to Ormuzd; from the middle downwards, to Ahriman.' Amemar replied: 'In that case why does Ahriman permit Ormuzd to send water through his territory?' i.e. how are the digestive and excretory processes possible, how can the human body function as a unity if it belongs to two contending forces?

*   *   *

EXCURSUS

The ruling in the *Mishnah* (*Ber.* V. 3) that if a man said in his prayer 'We give thanks, we give thanks' (i.e. he repeated the words instead of saying them only once) he is to be silenced, is obviously aimed against Dualism, as explained in the Gemara (*Ber.* 33b). *Cf. Ber. ibid.* that the man who says 'May Thy name be mentioned for the good Thou hast wrought' has similarly to be silenced since this implies for the good only and not for the bad, and the statement of R. Zera that the same applies to one who says '*Shema''* twice. The *Gemara* here, and elsewhere, refers to the dualistic heresy as 'two powers' – '*shethe reshuyoth*', *cf. Hag.* 15a. The story of the *Magus* and Amemar is in *Sanh.* 39a. Saadiah's arguments against Dualism are in his ' '*Emunoth We-De'oth*' Treatise II, 2, trans. Samuel Rosenblatt in Yale Judaica Series, Yale University Press, 1955, pp. 96–99, while Bahya's arguments

are in his *'Hobhoth Ha-Lebhabhoth'*, *Sha'ar Ha-Yihud*, Chapter
7. The Qabbalistic doctrine of the *Sephiroth* has frequently been
criticised as Dualism, both because of the conflict between the
Sephiroth of the Right and Left and because of the distinction
between *'En Soph* and the *Sephiroth*, but the Qabbalists are at
pains to stress the essential unity of both the Sephirotic world
in itself and in its connection with *'En Soph*, *v*. e.g. Joseph Gika-
tila's Introduction to his *'Sha'are 'Orah'*, Mantua, 1561, and I.
Tishbi's *'Mishnath Ha-Zohar'*, Jer., 1949. On the influence of
Persian thought on Judaism *v*. S. Bernfeld's *'Da'ath 'Elohim'*,
Warsaw, 1899, Part I, Chapter 4, pp. 71 ff. and the article "Satan"
in JE, Vol. XI, pp. 68–71.

*   *   *

(e) Trinitarianism

While Polytheism has been abandoned, in the Western
world at least, and while Dualism is hardly acceptable as
a religious philosophy anywhere in the world today, *Trinitarianism* is accepted by all Christians. Trinitarianism is the belief
that there are three persons in the Godhead. There have been,
of course, doctrines of a Trinity before Christianity: Brahma,
Siva and Vishnu in Indian religion, Osiris, Isis and Horus in
Egyptian religion. But in Christianity the further doctrine is
accepted that one of the three persons of the Trinity took on
human flesh in Jesus of Nazareth. Christians deny most emphatically, with justice, that theirs is a belief in *Tritheism*, in three
gods. Indeed, such a belief is considered to be grossly heretical
by all Christians. The Christian claim is that the three persons
of the Trinity, though separate, are, for all that, one. But
from the Jewish point of view, the Christian belief is a breach
of pure monotheism and Jewish martyrs have given their lives
rather than embrace the Christian faith. Particular objection
has always been taken, from the Jewish side, to the Christian
doctrine of the Incarnation. In Judaism man can be very near
to God, and God to man, but God and man are still distinct
so that Judaism looks upon it as blasphemy to suggest that at
a certain period in human history the divine became human.
Kaufmann Kohler ('Jewish Theology', p. 87) says in this
connection: 'The medieval Jewish thinkers therefore made
redoubled efforts to express with utmost clearness the doctrine
of God's unity. In this effort they received special encourage-

D

ment from the example of the leaders of Islam, whose victorious march over the globe was a triumph for the one God of Abraham over the triune God of Christianity. A great tide of intellectual progress arose, lending to the faith of the Mohammedans and subsequently also to that of the Jews an impetus which lasted for centuries. The new thought and keen research of that period had a lasting influence upon the whole development of western culture. An alliance was effected between religion and philosophy, particularly by the leading Jewish minds, which proved a liberating and stimulating force in all fields of scientific investigation. Thus the pure idea of monotheism became the basis for modern science and the entire modern world-view'. There is no doubt that Kohler is correct in attributing the emergence of the modern world-view to monotheism. The belief in the basic unity of nature upon which modern science is founded could not have emerged in a polytheistic world. For all that, Kohler's implication that this was almost entirely due to Jewish thinkers and could not have arisen under Christian influence is very one-sided. Christian thinkers have also stressed very effectively the unity of nature based on God's unity. This observation, naturally, does not affect the complete denial of the Christian claim by every Jewish believer. It is quite impossible for a man to be an adherent of Judaism and a Christian at the same time.

As we have seen the Talmudic Rabbis occasionally preached against Dualism. There are few preachments against Trinitarianism, however, probably because the former idea is much earlier and presented a greater challenge to Judaism in Rabbinic times. On the verse: 'I am the first, and I am the last, And beside Me there is no God' (Is. xliv. 6) the Palestinian teacher R. Abahu (d.c. 320) commented, in an obvious anti-Trinitarian and anti-Dualistic polemic, ' "I am the first" for I have no father, "and I am the last" for I have no brother, "And beside Me there is no God" for I have no son' (Ex. R. 29. 5). This is the text as we have it but the more probable reading, confirmed in some editions, is: ' "I am the last" for I have no son, "And beside Me there is no God" for I have no brother', i.e. the first two preachments are against Trinitarianism, the last against Dualism (v. the note of David Luria to Midrash Rabbah ad loc.). The third century teacher R. Simlai similarly taught

that the use of the three names for God ' '*El*', ' '*Elohim*' and the
Tetragrammaton do not, as the Christians of his day claimed,
refer to three persons in the Godhead but they all refer to one
and the same, as one might say 'King, Emperor, Augustus' or
'master, builder and architect' (*Yer. Ber.* ix. 12d and 13a).

During the middle ages the doctrine of the Trinity was often
one of the chief matters of contention in Jewish-Christian
polemics and disputations. In the famous debate, arranged by
King Jayme I of Aragon in 1263, between Pablo Christiani
and Nahmanides, the latter argues against the Trinity. The
King suggests in favour of the doctrine the illustration of wine
which has flavour, colour and bouquet, three things which are
yet one. Nahmanides points out that each of these can be found
without the others and the analogy is therefore misleading.
The three, moreover, are 'accidents' of the wine, which is
separate from them, so that if the analogy were correct it would
lead to a belief in four persons, not three. When Pablo retorts
that the doctrine of the Trinity is so profound that even the
angels cannot comprehend it, Nahmanides replies that no one
can believe that which he cannot comprehend and if Pablo
is right this only means that the angels do not believe in the
Trinity.

Another famous polemic against Christianity is that of
Hasdai Crescas, written originally in Spanish and translated
into Hebrew by Joseph Ibn Shem Tobh with the title: '*Bittul
Iqqere Ha-Notzerim*'. On the question of the Trinity Crescas
writes : 'This principle is opposed to the Jewish religion for God
is One in perfect simplicity and He alone is infinite in power.
He embraces all perfections, to Him alone belong power,
wisdom and will and all other eternal qualities. He has no
partner and is in no way composite. He exists necessarily,
that is to say, He is self-sufficient and owes not His existence
to another. The refutation of the doctrine of the Trinity is as
follows. If, as the Christians say, the Son born of the Father is
like the Father then the Father, too, must have been born of
another. But if so then He is an effect (i.e. not a cause) and has
been created by another and has no necessary existence. The
same applies to the Holy Ghost. If the Holy Ghost emanates
from the Father and the Son and is like them then the Father,
too, must have been emanated and He cannot therefore have

necessary existence. It is also impossible to believe that the
Father has all perfections for if this were so why should it have
been necessary for Him to give birth to the Son who is God
like Him? And why should it have been necessary for Him
to cause the emanation of the Holy Ghost which is also God
like Him? It can be asked further, at which time did the Father
give birth to the Son? If the birth took place within Time it
must follow that the Son did not exist at the beginning of
Time, in which case the Son would not be eternal as the Father
is eternal. If, on the other hand, the birth of the Son took
place at Time's beginning one might just as well say that the
Son gave birth to the Father. Some of them try to explain
the matter by saying that the Father constantly gives birth to the
Son and that the Son is constantly born of the Father. But this
would mean that Time is composed of many times and periods
and it would follow that from time to time the Son loses His
existence and then regains it, so that at one time He is in
existence at another time not. But if this is so then the Son
is not eternal as the Father is eternal. The same kind of contradiction applies to the Holy Ghost, which, they say, emanates
from the Father or from the Father and the Son. We ask them
whether It emanated within Time or at different times. Does it
not follow either way that It is not eternal? A further proof
that the Son is not as perfect as the Father and that the Father
cannot have given all His power to the Son is the following.
The Father had the power of begetting a Son while the Son does
not give birth. If this is because the Son cannot give birth then
He is not perfect. If, on the other hand, it is because He does
not wish to give birth then the power He has is set at naught.
The Holy Ghost, too, is unlike the Father, since the Father
has the power of causing the emanation of the Holy Ghost
while the Holy Ghost either cannot or will not produce such an
emanation. The Christians try to prove the Trinity by the
illustration of a burning coal which has a threefold appearance –
fire, flame and coal. But this is no proof whatsoever. For there
can be a coal without a flame, namely, a dull ember. There can
also be a flame without a coal, the flame in a pan of oil, for
instance. And there can be an ember without either flame or fire'.

The debate between Judaism and Christianity continues.
There are some Jews and Christains who speak of a common

Judeo-Christian tradition, others who claim that for all their points of resemblance and for all the ideas and ideals the two faiths have in common the differences are too great to allow for any such designation. But the doctrinal differences between Judaism and Christianity are quite clear. Thinking Jews and Christians would not wish it to be otherwise, though it goes without saying that believers in both camps can and do find much ground for fruitful endeavour in common.

*   *   *

EXCURSUS

On the subject of the attitude of Judaism towards Trinitarianism *v.* Samuel Krauss in JE, Vol. XIII, pp. 260–261. For the Nahmanides disputation *v.* Morris Goldstein: 'Jesus in the Jewish Tradition', New York, 1950, pp. 202 ff. and the sources given in the notes, and O. S. Rankin: 'Jewish Religious Polemics', Edinburgh University Press, 1956, Chapter IX, pp. 157 f. Crescas's polemic was published by Ephraim Deinard, Kearny, N. J., 1894. Both these works, and others of a similar nature, have been collected in J. D. Eisenstein's *''Otzar Wikuhim'*, New York, 1928, a valuable collection of polemics and disputations. A work recently published is Leon de Modena's (1571–1648) *'Magen Wa–Herebh'*, ed. S. Simonsohn, Jer. 1960, a defence of Jewish monotheism against the Christian doctrine. De Modena suggests that the main Jewish objection to Trinitarianism is to the doctrine of the Incarnation, *v.* Part II, Chapter 4, pp. 25–27, which suggests that there are three *persons* in the Godhead rather than three aspects of God's thought. On the history of the doctrine of the Trinity *v.* W. Fulton's article in ERE, Vol. 12, pp. 458–462. Critics of the *Qabbalah* from the Jewish side have detected a leaning towards a kind of Trinitarianism in the *Qabbalah* though, of course, the Qabbalists deny this most emphatically, *cf.* S. Rubin: 'Heidenthum und Kabbala', Vienna, 1893. Saadiah devotes part of his *''Emunoth We-De'oth'* (Treatise II, Chapters 5–8, Trans. Rosenblatt, *op. cit.*, pp. 103 ff.) to a refutation of the Christian doctrine. Saadiah observes that he presents his refutation only for those Christians whose philosophy is subtle and sophisticated, not for the uneducated who profess a materialistic trinity, actually a belief in Tritheism. J. Katz: 'Exclusiveness and Tolerance, Studies in Jewish-Gentile Relations in Mediaeval and Modern Times', Oxford University Press, 1961, is an important survey.

*   *   *

We have seen that the dualistic philosophy is based chiefly on man's experience of both good and evil. The problem of evil, of why the All-Good should allow evil to exist in His creation, is without doubt the greatest obstacle to Theistic faith. Jewish thinkers have grappled with the problem and have offered partial solutions but they have steadfastly refused to be persuaded to abandon in any way the monotheistic philosophy. Generally speaking the discussions in the Jewish sources are concerned with the more immediate problem of why the righteous suffer, as in the books of Job and Ecclestiastes and in the Rabbinic literature. There is far less discussion on the more ultimate problem of why there should be evil at all in God's creation. This emphasis is no doubt due to the 'organic' nature of Biblical and Rabbinic thinking. Abstract and systematic thinking was introduced into the mainstream of Jewish thought at a much later period. Deutero-Isaiah is the exception as we have noted above.

The real problem has been formulated in many ways. There are three propositions, all of which cannot be true. God is omnipotent. God is wholly good. Evil exists. An adequate solution to the problem of evil must reject, or at least qualify, one of these three propositions. For if God is wholly good how can He be responsible for evil, unless He lacks the power to remove it? Or if God is omnipotent and can therefore remove evil it can only be because He does not choose to remove it, in which case how can He be wholly good? Or if God is both omnipotent and wholly good, if, in other words, He chooses to have no evil in His creation and has the power to remove it, why is there any evil, unless it is an illusion?

From time to time the attempt has been made by religious thinkers to deny the third proposition. Evil, it is claimed, does not really exist, it only appears to do so. A good and all-powerful Being cannot tolerate evil in His creation and, indeed, does not do so. That which men call evil is not real, it is an illusion. But the delusion that evil exists is real at all events and this is in itself an evil. As J. M. E. McTaggart put it: 'Supposing that it could be proved that all we think evil was in reality good, the fact would still remain that we think it evil. This may be called a delusion or a mistake. But a delusion or mistake is as *real* as anything else. A savage's erroneous belief that the earth is stationary is just as real a fact as an astronomer's correct belief that it moves. The delusion that evil exists, then, is real. But then, to me at least it seems certain that a delusion or an error which hid from us the goodness of the universe would itself be evil. And so there would be evil after all. If, again, the existence of the delusion is pronounced to be a delusion, then this second delusion, which would be admitted to be real, must be pronounced evil, since it is now this delusion which deceives us about the true nature of reality, and hides its goodness from us. And so on indefinitely. However many times we pronounce evil unreal, we always leave a reality behind, which in its turn is to be pronounced evil'.

Nor would any representative Jewish Theist deny the second proposition, that God is wholly good. It is possible to think of God as a sublime Artist concerned only with the design and harmony of the universe and indifferent to its moral aspects but this is not as Judaism conceives of God. To say this does not necessarily imply, however, that the universe exists only for man and that good and evil are to be judged solely from the human standpoint. Many, probably the majority, of Jewish thinkers do not hesitate to describe man as the purpose of creation. But no less a thinker than Maimonides, as we have noted above, denies that man is the purpose of creation. According to this thinker all one can say in reply to the question: 'What is the purpose of creation?' is that the universe came into being at God's will. Thus, for Maimonides, it is possible that there are evils which can serve no possible purpose so far as man is concerned but which have their place in a universe which does not exist solely for man. But this in no way solves the problem of evil. For it might be asked why it is God's will that for the fulfilment of His purpose some of His creatures should suffer. Maimonides would not reply that God is neutral so far as good and evil is concerned nor would he attempt to deny that God is wholly good. Thus no Jewish believer can find his way out of the dilemma by denying God's goodness. All this is apart from the difficulty of whether one can worship a Being who is, in some measure, at least, indifferent to evil, and the difficulty of believing in a Being who is so intelligent as to have created all things and who yet is indifferent to evil.

Consequently, hardly any Theists have tried to solve the problem in this way.

Any adequate solution, from the Jewish point of view, must, then, if not deny at least qualify the first proposition – that God is omnipotent. Accordingly, when a solution suggests that evil is necessary for some good purpose it will not do to ask why an omnipotent God cannot achieve the purpose without the evil, for if the solution is really sound this would involve a contradiction. We cannot live in a world in which certain goods, unrealisable without evil, can come into being, unless there is evil in that world. Even God cannot let us have our cake and eat it, because this is an absurdity. God can do that which is impossible to us. He cannot do that which is impossible to Him, not because there are any limitations to His power but because the absolutely impossible, the impossible to Him, is meaningless. There cannot be any such thing. To expect God to do the impossible to Him because He is omnipotent is like expecting God to will Himself out of existence because He is omnipotent.

The most convincing attempt at a solution to the problem of evil, long popular with Theists, particularly since the Middle Ages, is that which suggests that for man to have freedom of choice there must be evil in the universe he inhabits. God wishes to be worshipped by creatures with some measure of independence, not by machines or automata. Such creatures must be the authors of their own good, that is to say, they must have made it their own by choosing it freely even though they could have chosen evil. Only a creature whose goodness is self-acquired in this way is worthy of enjoying God's goodness for ever, for only the self-acquired type of goodness can in any way resemble God's self-authenticating goodness. Now if there is to be a choice between good and evil the universe must contain evil as well as good. As we have seen, it is impossible even for God to give His creatures the power to choose between good and evil if there is no evil to be rejected. This is not because of any limitations of God's power but simply because the very idea of choosing between good and evil is meaningless if there is no evil to choose. Nor is it possible for man to make the good his own in fighting evil unless he inhabits a world in which there is evil to be fought.

It has been argued, granted that *some* evil is necessary for free choice of the good, was it really necessary for the all-good God to have created so much of it? To this the only reply is that God alone knows the amount of evil necessary in the universe to make it a testing ground for man's struggle for the good. This is presumably what Leibnitz meant when he said that this was the best of all possible worlds. The operative word here is *possible*. If the claim is made that this is the best world *imaginable* it is easy to show, as Voltaire did in 'Candide', that the claim is ridiculous. But the real question to be considered is whether the necessary conditions for freedom of choice for all men could be fulfilled in a world other than this. The Theistic view holds that God in His wisdom can alone know the amount of evil required if freedom of choice is to be possible. It is in this sense that it is claimed that this is the best possible of worlds.

No truly religious person dares to approach this terrible problem of suffering without a profound awareness of human limitations. From the earliest times, believers in God have held on to their faith in His goodness even though the way was dark. It is all too easy when discussing this problem academically to forget that one is dealing with human torment and tragedy. Someone once said that he would make it compulsory for every theologian to visit a large hospital and witness children in agony before writing on the subject and teaching the answers. In a very real sense the religious mind must be content to express total inability to comprehend, and to follow the Scriptural example of Aaron who, when his sons died, was silent (Lev. x. 3). 'If I knew Him I would be Him' as the old Jewish saying has it. This is where faith comes in. Faith in God means that in spite of the evidence to the contrary the believer does not lose his conviction that God is good and that He is on the side of the good who fight against evil and that in doing so they are doing His will. As an attitude to life, it is this the devout Jew means when he affirms daily the unity of God.

*   *   *

EXCURSUS

The classical Talmudic passage on why the righteous suffer is *Ber.* 7a, *cf.* '*Abhoth*, IV. 19. A survey of Jewish teachings on the problem of evil is contained in Hillel Zeitlin's profound essay:

'*Ha-Tobh We-Ha-Ra'* ', 'Good and Evil', Warsaw, 1911. On the 'organic' nature of Rabbinic thinking the best work is Max Kadushin's justly famed: 'Organic Thinking', New York, 1938. *Cf.* the same author's 'The Rabbinic Mind', New York, 1952. A good modern statement of the age-old problem of pain is that of J. L. Mackie: 'Evil and Omnipotence' in '*Mind*', Vol. LXIV, No. 254, April, 1955, p. 200 f. *Cf.* the replies in subsequent issues of the magazine. McTaggart's observation is in his 'Some Dogmas of Religion', 1930, section 171, pp. 209–210. Maimonides' views are to be found in his 'Guide', III. 13–14, *cf.* III. 15. A clear, if somewhat mechanical statement of the argument for freedom of choice is that of M. H. Luzzatto in his '*Derekh 'Adonai*', *Mosad Ha-Rav Kook*, Jer., 1949, Part I, Chapters 2–3, pp. 15 f. The problem of evil occupies a prominent place in Qabbalistic thought. The Lurianic doctrine of God's withdrawal into Himself to make room for the world – *Tzimtzum* – seeks to explain the origin of evil as the result of the necessary withdrawal of the divine light, necessary because without such withdrawal there could be no finite world. On this *v*. G. Scholem: 'Major Trends in Jewish Mysticism', Thames and Hudson, London, 3rd. ed., 1955, pp. 244 f. Scholem (p. 237) thus explains the Zoharic teaching on the fundamental causes of evil: 'The totality of divine potencies forms a harmonious whole, and as long as each stays in relation to all others, it is sacred and good. This is true also of the quality of strict justice, rigor and judgment in and by God, which is the fundamental cause of evil. The wrath of God is symbolized by His left hand, while the quality of mercy and love, with which it is intimately bound up, is called His right hand. The one cannot manifest itself without involving the other. Thus the quality of stern judgment represents the great fire of wrath which burns in God but is always tempered by His mercy. When it ceases to be tempered, when in its measureless hypertrophical outbreak it tears itself loose from the quality of mercy, then it breaks away from God altogether and is transformed into the radically evil, into Gehenna and the dark world of Satan'. This 'tempering' of the divine judgment is caused by the deeds of man which have a cosmic effect according to the *Qabbalah. Cf.* I. Tishbi's '*Mishnath Ha-Zohar*', Vol. I, Jer. 1949, Part II, pp. 285 ff. and the same author's '*Torah Ha-Ra' We-Ha-Qeliphah Be-Qabbalath Ha-'Ari*', Tel-Aviv, 1952. The idea that God has a purpose apart from man alone makes explicable in some measure the very difficult problem of animal suffering – 'nature red in tooth and claw'. Indeed, it is difficult to see the need for the teeming millions in the animal Kingdom if man is made the sole measure of all things. Judah Ha-Levi, *Kuzari*, III. 11, dealing with animals preying on each other, observes that while reason compels us to see the wisdom of the Creator in the very means by which the strong animals are able to devour the weak, the apparent injustice remains unexplained. But reason assures us that if there is evidence of divine wisdom in the means used by the lion to capture and kill its victims these acts must also have their place in God's scheme though their purpose is unknown to us. *Cf.* the remarks of W. R. Matthews in the note on the teleological argument above. Otto's observations ('The Idea of the Holy', London, 1957, pp. 78–80) are also relevant. Otto notes that in God's reply to Job the glorious illustrations from the animal kingdom in Job afford little help if we are seeking *purpose* in nature, but they rely on the sheer absolute wondrousness that transcends thought, on the *mysterium*, presented in its pure, non-rational form. The mediaeval thinkers, e.g. Bahya, *Sha'ar Ha-Behinah'*, Chapter 4, quote this passage as evidence of teleology but Otto's fresh insight is extremely valuable. The mediaeval thinkers discussed the question of the 'impossible' for God, *v.* Saadiah: *'Emunah We-De'oth*, II. 13, ed. Rosenblatt, Yale. University Press, 1948, p. 134; Maimonides 'Guide' III. 15; Crescas *'Or 'Adonai V*, 2. 3.

*　　*　　*

Since the affirmation of the unity of God is given in the *Shema'*, there can be no better way to an understanding of what unity has meant to the Jew than by noting the comments of the great Jewish teachers on the *Shema'*. The following is a fairly comprehensive survey of comments on the *Shema'* throughout the ages.

' *Hear, O Israel: The Lord our God is one Lord'* (A.V.).
' *Hear, O Israel: The Lord our God, the Lord is one'*. (Jewish Pub. Soc. Vers.)
'*Listen, Israel: the Eternal, the Eternal alone, is our God'* (Moffatt).
'*Hear, O Israel! The LORD is our God, the LORD alone'*. (New Jewish trans.)

The verse which became known, after its opening word, as the *Shema'* (the term is also used frequently for the subsequent verses and two other paragraphs, Deut. xi. 13–21, Num. xv. 37–41, recited daily by the devout Jew in the morning and at night) occurs in the book of Deuteronomy, chapter six, verse four. It can be seen from the translations quoted above that the verse is capable of bearing several meanings. The verse contains the name whose pronunciation is unknown, YHWH, and the Hebrew, in transliteration, is: '*Shema' Yisrael YHWH 'elohenu YHWH 'ehad'*. S.R. Driver ('Deuteronomy' in the I.C.C. Series, 3rd. ed., T. and T. Clark, Edinburgh, 1902, pp. 89–91) quotes four possible meanings:

(1) 'The Lord our God (even) the Lord, is one' (R.V. 1st margin, Ewald)

(2) 'The Lord is our God, the Lord is one' (R.V. 2nd m.)

(3) 'The Lord is our God, the Lord alone' (Ibn Ezra, R.V. 3rd m.)

(4) 'The Lord our God is one Lord' (Schultz, Keil, Baudissin, A.V.)

If (3) were correct the word we would have expected is: *lebhado*, 'alone', rather than *'ehad*, 'one'. Driver concludes that, in his opinion, (4) is the most probable meaning. The term 'one' may only express the *unity* of God (Ewald, Schultz) or it may refer also to the *uniqueness* of God (Keil, Oehler, Baudissin, König). Driver favours the second explanation which includes the first. 'The verse is thus a great declaration of Monotheism (in the sense both that there is only one God, and that the God who exists is truly one)'.

Naturally such an important text has received many interpretations, some of them close to the plain meaning of the text, others of a more homiletical, even far-fetched, character. We shall here examine the more important of these from the days of the Rabbis down to more recent exponents of the Jewish faith. The value of such an investigation lies not alone, or primarily, in the light the comments throw on the text, but in the information it conveys of how representative Jewish teachers faced challenges to Jewish monotheism and of how they dwelt lovingly on a popular text, reading out of it guidance for their religious life and into it ideas of their own.

(1) *Siphre, Wa-'Ethhanan,* vi. 4.

The problem discussed in this early *Midrash* is the apparent contradiction between the concept '*our* God' and that of 'the Lord is one', a difficulty not of Biblical exegesis alone but one which must have presented itself with particular force to Jewish religious leaders in the Roman world – the issue of particularism versus universalism in Judaism. 'Our God' denotes the God of Israel, the God recognised by the Jewish people and unrecognised by the majority of mankind at the time. 'The Lord is one' denotes that God is the Father of all men. The tensions between particularism and universalism were not unknown, of course, to the Biblical writers. But the Rabbis, in fairly close contact with Roman manners and society, must have found the question of the most immediate concern for them and their followers. The *Siphre* endeavours to solve the contradiction in two ways. First, it is suggested, although God is the Lord of the whole universe, His 'name rests upon Israel in particular'. This probably signifies that it is Israel which keeps the God idea alive. Israel is especially devoted to the one God (a truism in the time of the *Siphre* in contrast with contemporary paganism and polytheism), His name 'rests upon them'. Secondly, although in this world God is acknowledged by Israel alone, in the Messianic age all mankind will worship Him. Then God will be truly 'one'. ' "The Lord is our God" – in this world. "The Lord is one" – in the world to come. And so it is said: "In that day shall the Lord be One and His name One" (Zech. xiv. 9)'.

(2) *Midrash Rabbah, Wa–'Ethhanan*, II, 31–35.

This is a *Midrash* of much later date than the *Siphre*, though the exact period of its compilation is still uncertain. The passage here referred to consists of a number of homilies on the *Shema'*. First it is suggested that the *Shema'* was originally said by Israel at the foot of Sinai when God declared to His people: 'I am the Lord thy God' (Deut. v. 6). God said to them: 'Hear this, O Israel' and they replied: 'The Lord our God, the Lord is one'. The *Shema'* is here thought of as a dialogue, God supplying the first part, Israel the second. Another explanation is then given to the effect that the *Shema'* stresses the uniqueness of God. 'God said to Israel: "My sons, I have created all things in pairs. Heaven and earth; sun and moon; Adam and Eve; this world and the next; but My glory is one and unique" (*'ehad u-meyuhad*). This we read in the *Shema'*". Another explanation follows. God, at Sinai, opened up the seven heavens to show Israel that there is no other god. Israel replied that just as there is no other god in Heaven they will testify, by reciting the *Shema'*, that there is no other god upon earth. Still another explanation, plainly both anti-dualistic and anti-Christological, is directed against the rival philosophies to the faith of the compilers. The verse is quoted: 'There is one that is alone, and he hath not a second; yea, he hath neither son nor brother' (Eccl. iv. 8). 'God has neither son nor brother but: "Hear, O Israel . . ." ' Finally, it is suggested that the words: 'Hear, O Israel' are addressed to the Patriarch Jacob, called 'Israel'. When reciting the *Shema'*, his descendants declare to their progenitor, Jacob, that they remain true to his faith in God.

(*3*) *Yalqut Shimeoni*, sec. 834–835

This is a collection of early and later *Midrashim* compiled by Simeon Kara of Frankfort in the 13th century. Both comments have for their theme the reciprocal love of God and Israel and Israel's constant loyalty to God.

(*a*) A good man married to a good woman praises his wife by saying: 'There is no woman as good as my wife', while she, in her turn, declares that there is no man as good as hers. Similarly, God says that there is no people like Israel and Israel recites the *Shema'* in praise of God.

(*b*) The legions of a human king only go out to battle on his behalf if he provides them with their rations but Israel fights the Lord's battles even if He allows them to go hungry. It is to convey this thought that the *Shema'* uses two divine names – the Tetragrammaton and *'elohim*, 'God'. Generally in the Rabbinic literature the former is said to refer to God's mercy, the latter to His judgment. Hence the meaning of the *Shema'* is: 'The Lord' (=the quality of mercy) and 'our God' (=the quality of judgment) are one, i.e. it is all one to Israel whether God is merciful to them or sits in stern judgment on them. Whatever their fate they remain loyal to His trust.

(*4*) *Saadiah Gaon* (b. Dilaz, Upper Egypt, 882; d. 942), ' '*Emunoth We-De'oth*', Treatise II, Chapter 1, beg. (trans. Samuel Rosenblatt, Yale Judaica Series, Yale University Press, New Haven, p. 94).

Saadiah in his classic defence of Judaism against Christianity
and Islam works out a theological system in the light of the
Arabic philosophy of his day. His statement, in this passage, of
the essential beliefs about God runs as follows: 'We have been
told by our Lord, magnified and exalted be He, through the
pronouncements of his prophets that He is one, living, omnipotent and omniscient, that there is nothing that resembles
Him, and that He does not resemble any of His works'. Saadiah,
fond of Scriptural proof-texts, proceeds to quote Biblical
verses in support of each of these ideas. In support of the first –
that God is one – he quotes the *Shema'*. Thus, for Saadiah, the
Shema' is essentially a declaration of monotheism, in the sense
that there are no other gods.

(*5*) *Bahya Ibn Paqudah* (prob. end of eleventh century),
'Duties of the Heart', Gate I (devoted to the theme of God's
unity).

The first 'Gate' of Bahya's work is a philosophical exposition,
displaying considerable originality and real profundity, of
the true meaning of God's unity. His account of the *Shema'*
is found in the Introduction to this 'Gate'. Bahya first observes
that the injunction to 'hear' refers to the echo of faith in the
heart rather than to physical audition. It means 'to believe in
this and accept it'. Implied in monotheism are three great
ideas: (1) That God exists, (2) That He is our God, (3) That
He is one. All three ideas are contained in the *Shema'*. Furthermore, included in the last is the belief that God is unique,
unlike any of His creatures ('Gate' I, Chapters 9 and 10).
For Bahya the *Shema'* gives expression to the basic beliefs
Judaism holds of God. God exists. He brought the world into
being and is concerned with it. There is only one God and He
is a unique Being, totally different from His creatures.

(*6*) *Rashi* (b. Troyes, France, 1040; d. Troyes, 1105).

Rabbi Solomon Yitzhaqi (called *Rashi* after the initial letters
of his name) is the best-known and most popular of the Jewish
mediaeval commentators to the Bible. In his commentary to
the *Shema'* (Deut. *ad loc.*) he leans (as in other passages in
his commentary to Deuteronomy) on the *Siphre*. *Rashi's*
comment reads: 'The Lord who is now *our* God and not the

God of the peoples will be the only God in the future (i.e. in the Messianic age). As it is said: "For then I will turn to the peoples a pure language that they may all call upon the name of the Lord" (Zeph. iii. 9). And it is said further: "In that day shall the Lord be One and His name One" ' (Zech. xiv. 9). *Rashi* thus paraphrases the *Siphre* but adds the proof-text from Zechariah.

(7) *Abraham Ibn Ezra* (b. Toledo, Spain, 1092; d. 1167).

This commentator is unusually cryptic. With some difficulty the following meaning can be extracted from his brief note to the *Shema'*. The verse means that the Lord *alone* is God, i.e., there are no other gods. Ibn Ezra is aware, of course, of the verse in Zechariah (xiv. 9) quoted by *Rashi* above. When the verse states that the Lord will be one in *that* day it does not mean to suggest that He is not one here and now but that in the present many peoples do not acknowledge Him as God, whereas in the Messianic age His sovereignty will be recognised by the whole of mankind. Furthermore, the verse in Zephaniah (iii. 9), quoted above, suggests that in that age all peoples will have the same language and then God's name will be one (the same) for all of them.

(8) *Samuel ben Meir* (b. Rameru, France, c. 1080; d. after 1158).

Samuel ben Meir (*Rashbam*), *Rashi*'s grandson, wrote a commentary to the Pentateuch distinguished for its adherence to the plain meaning of the text. In the section to the *Shema'*, *Rashbam* explains the verse in this fashion. 'The *Lord* is our God' means that we have only one God. Ibn Ezra, quoted above, derives this thought from the words 'the Lord is one', which he understands as 'the Lord *alone*'. But *Rashbam* is of the opinion that, by emphasis on the word 'Lord', the idea that there is only one God can be derived from the first part of the verse. As for the second part of the verse: 'the Lord is one', *Rashbam* appears to take it in the sense of 'alone' but not to yield the thought that only God exists (for this has been derived adequately from the first part of the verse) but that only God is to be *worshipped*. *Rashbam* adds an interesting point. Man may believe in God and yet use other gods for magical purposes,

believing in their talismanic properties. It is against this that
the second part of the *Shema'* inveighs. Similarly, *Rashbam*
explains the second commandment to mean that the fashioning
of idols for magical purposes is forbidden even if it accompanies
belief in God (*v.* his comment to Deut. v. 7).

(9) '*Da'ath Zeqenim Mi-Ba'ale Ha-Tosaphoth*' (in Pentateuch,
ed. David Balaban, Lemberg, 1902).

These glosses belong to the French school of Talmudists
which flourished from the 12th century onwards. We know
from various sources that Christian writers in the middle ages
sought to demonstrate that the doctrine of the Trinity was
hinted at in the *Shema'*, which contains three divine names
where one would have sufficed (*v.* 'Jewish Encyclopedia',
Vol. XII, p. 261 and Jacob Katz: Exclusiveness and Tolerance',
Oxford University Press, 1961, p. 19). In a Christian environment it was natural for the Tosaphists to be concerned with
the alleged hint. In their comment to the verse they raise
the difficulty of the three divine names and reply that all three
are required if the verse is to yield its full meaning. If the
verse had simply said; 'Hear, O Israel, the Lord is one', each
of the nations would have claimed that the term 'the Lord'
refers to their god. Hence the verse must state: 'Hear, O
Israel: the Lord *our* God' i.e. the God of Israel. Nor could
Scripture have been content with: 'Hear, O Israel: the Lord
our God is one' for this may have been taken to mean that He
is one among many. Now that the verse contains all three
divine names the meaning is beyond ambiguity: 'Hear, O Israel:
the Lord who is our God is the only Lord and there is no other'.

(10) *Maimonides* (1135-1204), '*Sepher Ha-Mitzwoth*', II.

In Maimonides' great classification of the precepts of the
Torah he records the following under the heading of the second
positive command: 'The second precept is the command to
believe in the Unity. This means that we must believe that He
who brought all things into being and who is their First Cause
is one. This precept is contained in His saying, may He be
exalted: "Hear, O Israel: the Lord our God, the Lord is one".
You will find that in numerous *Midrashim* the Rabbis use expressions such as: "In order to unify My name" or "In order to

testify to My unity" and many similar. They intend to convey the thought that God verily did bring us out of bondage and performed goodness and mercy on our behalf in order that we might believe in His unity, for this is our obligation. There are, consequently, numerous references to the "precept of unity". The Rabbis call this precept, too, "the acknowledgment of God's sovereignty", hence they say: "In order to accept the sovereignty of Heaven", namely, acknowledgment of His unity and belief in it.' Thus, according to Maimonides, the *Shema'* is in the nature of a command. It is a religious obligation to believe in God's unity and this is successfully fulfilled whenever the Jew recites the *Shema'*.

(11) *Bahya Ibn Asher* (b.c. 1260; d. Saragossa, 1340)

Bahya's commentary to the Pentateuch was written in 1261 and has been printed in a number of editions. This author, too, deals with the difficulty of the three-fold repetition of the divine name. All are necessary, he remarks, for if the verse had said: 'Hear, O Israel: the Lord is one' it would have provided an opportunity for the nations to claim that the reference was to their god, called by them 'the Lord'. Consequently, the verse must add 'our God' to denote the God of Israel. Nor would it have sufficed to have said: 'Hear, O Israel: the Lord our God is one' for that might have been taken to mean that both the God of Israel and the god of the nations are one. Now that there are three divine names in the verse the meaning is beyond doubt. The God of Israel alone is the Lord who is one 'and there is none else, blessed be He, for His unity is perfect in every respect, without any compositeness, and none among the higher or lower beings are like unto Him'. The anti-Christological *motif* is here, once again, clearly seen. *Bahya* then quotes an interpretation of the three divine names in the name of R. Eleazar of Worms (1160–1238). According to this the meaning of the verse is: 'Hear, O Israel: the Lord (who existed before the world came into being), our God (in the world), the Lord (after the world has come to an end) is one (in all worlds)'. Finally, *Bahya* explains the term 'Israel', like others before him, as referring to the Patriarch Jacob. 'Hear, O Israel in the Cave of Machpelah, the Lord our God, the Lord is one'.

(12) *Zohar*, III, 263 a-b.

Here is a good place to record the teachings of the *Zohar* on the *Shema'*. This work, the 'Bible of the Jewish mystics', as it has been called, first saw the light through the efforts of Moses de Leon (b. 1250; d. Arevalo, Spain, 1305), considered by G. Scholem, the world-famous authority on the subject, to be the true author of the book. It is impossible to understand Zoharic ideas without some reference to the doctrine of the *Ten Sephiroth* upon which the whole thought of the work rests. Here it is impossible to give anything like an adequate survey of the doctrine. (By far the best account in English is to be found in Scholem's 'Major Trends in Jewish Mysticism' 3rd ed., Thames and Hudson, London, 1955, Chapter 6, pp. 205–243). But for the purpose of grasping the Zoharic comment to the *Shema'* the following very brief account may suffice.

God as He is in Himself is unknown to man. He is the 'Limit-less', *'En Soph*, of which nothing can be postulated. But *'En Soph* becomes revealed by means of 'attributes' or 'qualities', known as *'Sephiroth'*, 'numbers'. The relationship between these aspects of the Deity are worked out in great detail and the Scriptural references to God by different divine names are, in fact, according to the Zohar, references to the different *'Sephiroth'*.

Of the *Ten Sephiroth* the *Zohar* sees four hinted at in the *Shema'*. 'Israel' is said to be the Patriarch Jacob but the mystical meaning here, as elsewhere in the *Zohar*, is almost certainly that this is the name for the *Sephirah, Tiphereth*, 'Beauty', symbolised by the name 'Jacob'. This *Sephirah* is, at it were, at the centre of the divine activity in self-revelation. Hence it is called 'the body of the Tree' and is hinted at again in the second 'the Lord' in the *Shema'*. The first 'the Lord' is the *Sephirah, Hokhmah*, 'Wisdom', the divine wisdom as it thinks of creation. The term 'our God' refers to the *Sephirah, Binah*, 'Under-standing', the actualisation in divine thought of the potential divine wisdom. Finally, the term 'one' refers to the 'Community of Israel', the *Sephirah, Malkhuth*, 'Sovereignty', the archetype of the community of Israel down below. It is basic to the Zoharic idea that the 'impulse from below brings about the impulse from above', i.e. man's deeds have a cosmic effect.

By living the good life he has an influence on the 'upper world' of the *Sephiroth* and brings down the divine grace. Since the *Shema'* contains the names of the *Sephiroth* which become united in God's Sovereignty, when man recites the *Shema'* he helps, as it were, to create harmony not alone here on earth but also in the divine realm.

The dangers of this kind of teaching to Jewish monotheism are evident. On not infrequent occasions, as we have seen above, the Qabbalists feel bound to refute the accusation levelled against them of worshipping a plurality of gods. Their apology always takes the form of a strict emphasis on the basic unity of *'En Soph* and the *Sephiroth*. Among illustrations given to express this unity are those of the water poured into coloured bottles or the multi-coloured flames in one glowing coal.

(13) *Hezekiah ben Manoah—'Hazzequni'* (Commentary to the Pentateuch, written c. 1240, various ed.).

This famous French commentator observes, in his comment on the *Shema'*, that the word 'Hear' means 'Reflect'. He follows the interpretation that the three divine names refer to God in the past, present and future. God alone is Infinite so that the verse means that God alone exists in past, present and future, He alone is Infinite. Another explanation of the three divine names resembles those quoted previously (this appears to have been the current reply to the Christian polemicists who endeavoured to read the Trinity into the *Shema'*). If Scripture had said: 'Hear, O Israel: the Lord is one' the nations might have argued that the reference is to their god. To have said: 'The Lord our God is one' or simply 'Our God is one' might have been taken to mean that He is one among many. To avoid ambiguity all three divine names are recorded, yielding the thought: 'Hear, O Israel: the Lord who is our God (the God of Israel) is the only Lord'.

(14) *Aaron Ha-Levi of Barcelona* (d. c. 1300).

Aaron Ha-Levi of Barcelona is the author of a work on the precepts of the *Torah* ('*Sepher Ha-Hinnukh*', first ed. Venice, 1523, and various ed.) in which the laws of each precept are briefly described together with the ethical and religious ideas they exist to promote. These latter are called by Aaron

the 'root' of the precept. The purpose of the *Shema‛* is thus
described in Section 420: 'The root idea behind this precept
is that God desired to allow His people to acquire merit by
accepting upon themselves the yoke of His sovereignty and
unity, each day and night for all their days. For since man's
nature is material he is tempted by worldy vanities and attracted
by his lusts. He needs, at least, some permanent reminder of the
sovereignty of Heaven to keep him from sin. Consequently,
God in His mercy allowed us to possess this merit by commanding us to remember Him at these times in a constant
manner and with true inwardness. The first of these times is
by day, that all our actions during the day might benefit.
For if man remembers God's unity and sovereignty, in the
morning, and that God's power and providence are over all,
and if he considers, in the morning, that God's eyes are open
upon all his ways and that God counts every step that man
takes, nothing being hidden from Him and no thought concealed, then this idea and the verbal assent he gives to it will
become as a charge to him for the whole day. Similarly, man's
assent to the idea at night will be as a charge to him for the
whole of the night'.

Thus far Aaron Ha-Levi discusses the precept of reciting
the *Shema‛* and its purpose. The *Shema‛* itself he understands,
following Maimonides, as a command to believe in God's
unity. In Section 417 Aaron writes: 'This is a command to
believe that God, blessed be He, the author of creation, the
Lord of all, is one without any partner. As it is said: "The Lord
our God, the Lord is one". This is a positive precept, not a
mere homiletical embellishment of the verse. The meaning of
the verse is: "Hear", that is, "Accept this idea and believe in
it" – "the Lord who is God is one". As proof that this is a
positive precept we may quote the frequent saying of the
Rabbis in the *Midrash:* "In order to express the unity of My
name" or "In order to accept upon himself the Sovereignty
of Heaven", that is, acknowledgment of God's unity and faith
in it. The root of the precept is obvious for this is the main
object of the faith of mankind. This is the strong pillar upon
which the heart of every intelligent person replies. Included in
the laws appertaining to this precept is the rule laid down by the
Rabbis, of blessed memory, that every Jew is obliged to suffer

martyrdom if need be for the sake of God's unity. For whoever fails to acknowledge God's unity, blessed be He, it is as if he denies the fundamental principle of faith, for without complete unity there can be no perfect sovereignty or glory. This will be admitted by all the wise-hearted. Consequently, this precept embraces the prohibition of idolatry. We are obliged at any time or place to give our lives rather than offend against the prohibition. Further details are scattered in the *Midrash* and *Talmud*. In those sources many stories are to be found concerning persons, great and small, who allowed themselves to be slaughtered for the sake of God's holy unity, blessed be He. May the memory of them all be for a blessing. This precept applies at all times and places and to both males and females. Whoever transgresses this precept by failing to believe in God's unity, blessed be He, has annulled this positive precept and, together with it, all the other precepts of the *Torah*, for they all depend on belief in God and His unity, blessed be He. Such a person is called a denier of the fundamental principle. He is not to be included among the children of Israel but belongs to the heretics and God will set him apart for evil. But whoever believes in God and trusts in Him will be exalted. This is one of those precepts, to which we have called attention at the beginning of this work, which man is obliged to observe constantly, that is to say, their obligation never ceases for one moment'.

(15) *Joseph Caspi* (b. France, 1297–d. 1340).

Caspi in his Commentary to the Pentateuch (ed. Isaac Last, Cracow, 1905, '*Mishneh Keseph*', p. 280) remarks: ' "Hear, O Israel; the Lord our God, the Lord is one". It would be quite impossible to find a more perfect form of expression to convey the idea of God's existence and His unity'.

(16) *David ben Joseph Abudraham* (middle of 14th century, Seville, Spain).

David Abudraham's popular commentary to the Synagogue liturgy (written 1340, first ed. Lisbon, 1489, Jer. 1959) contains the following note to the *Shema'* (Jer. ed. p. 80):

'It is customary to recite the *Shema'* aloud in order to awaken concentration during the recitation of the first verse when it is especially required. It is also necessary to raise the voice because the *Shema'* is in the nature of testimony. It is as if each man says to his neighbour: 'Hear that I believe that the Lord our God is one in His world'.

(17) *Joseph Albo* (b.c. 1380; d.c. 1444) in *'Sepher Ha-'Iqqarim'*, ed. I. Husik, Jewish Publication Society of America, Philadelphia, 1946, Vol. I, Chapter 14, pp. 127–8.

Albo observes that belief in God's unity involves two ideas: (1) That there is only one God and there is no other equal or similar to Him. (2) That though God is one without any plurality or compositeness whatsoever, He is, nonetheless, *our* God, i.e. He is the cause of the plurality of all existing things. The verse of the *Shema'* refers to the second idea, the meaning being: 'The Lord is our God (He brought the universe into being and is thus the cause of its plurality and compositeness) and yet the Lord is one'. (*Cf.* Vol. II, Chapter 10, p. 58 and Chapter 13, pp. 80–81). This interpretation is obviously at variance with the plain meaning of the text but is one with appeal to a philosophic mind in the fourteenth century concerned with evidence of dualism and compositeness in a universe which stems from the One.

(18) *Isaac Arama* (b. Northern Spain, c. 1420; d. Naples, 1494) in his '*'Aqedath Yitzhaq'*, Pressburg, 1849, Vol. V, Deuteronomy, Gate 90, p. 21f.)

On page 24b Arama notes that the *Shema'* occurs in the book of Deuteronomy soon after the Ten Commandments and its purpose is to emphasise the first two – that God is unique and that there are no other gods. The meaning of the verse is: 'Hear, (=reflect, consider, understand thoroughly) O Israel; the Lord is *our* God (He controls the world by His will, He is God) *and* He is the one Lord' (i.e. unlike any creature, without any compositeness in His nature). A second meaning is then given according to which the term 'one' is synonymous with 'perfection' ('one' = 'complete', 'whole', 'perfect'). God is the only Being who can be called 'one' in the sense of utter perfection. Apart from Him there is no true perfection. The first meaning, says Arama, that God is unique and that there are no other gods, is the popular one and it must suffice for the majority since the 'masses' (*ha-hamon*) are incapable of grasping the abstract idea of complete perfection and lack of any compositeness in God. The second meaning implies that in spite of the evidence of both diversity and imperfection in the universe God is both without any diversity and is wholly perfect. How this is possible has puzzled the finest minds. It is, as Arama remarks, the central problem of the *Qabbalah* which speaks of the *Sephiroth* as ten in number and yet united in their Source. Such a difficult idea can hardly be present in the mind of the ordinary Jew when he recites the *Shema'* and he must perforce have recourse to the simpler meaning of the text. The more advanced meaning is reserved for the thinking Jew whose mind quests for unity in the midst of diversity.

(19) *Obadiah ben Jacob Sforno* (b. Cesena, Italy, c. 1475; d. Bologna, Italy, c. 1550), Commentary to Pentateuch, various ed.

Sforno remarks, like others before him, that 'hear' means much more than mere physical audition. It means rather to reflect, to consider, to ponder deeply. The meaning of the *Shema'*, according to this author, is two-fold – that God alone is to be worshipped ('our God') and that He is unique, totally distinct from His creatures, 'wholly other' ('the Lord is one' = unique, *'ehad*). In Sforno's own words: '*Hear, O Israel* – Reflect on this and understand it. *The Lord* who created all things and brought them into being is *our God*. He is supreme and from Him alone can we hope for our desires to be fulfilled without any intermediary. Since He is supreme in His creative power, to Him alone it is right to bow, and since our hope is in Him, without any intermediary, it is proper for our prayer to be directed to Him alone and that only He should be worshipped. *The Lord is one*. Since He brought everything into being from complete nothingness it follows that there is no other being like unto Him and that He is different in kind from the world of transient being, from the world of the spheres, and from the angelic world, existing alone in the fourth world of His own'. Once again we have a philosophical interpretation, far removed from the simplicity of the original, but satisfying to the mind nurtured on mediaeval thinking about God's nature.

(20) *Moses Alshech* (Safed, Palestine, 2nd half of the sixteenth century) in his Commentary to the Pentateuch, entitled '*Torath Mosheh*', various ed.

This famous preacher first notes that the *Shema'* is in the singular, addressed to *one* person. This is to denote that in God all hearts are united since He is both 'our God' (= the quality of judgment) and 'the Lord' (= the quality of mercy). Just as these two qualities are united in Him so should we transcend our divergent viewpoints and individual egos in the imitation of God. Furthermore, although God is the Creator of all, He is, for all that, 'our God', the God of Israel. Developing the idea of God's unity in His judgment and mercy, Alshech remarks that from God's point of view His stern judgment is also compassion, it is for man's ultimate benefit and in no way vindictive. Another point made by our author is that the word 'Hear' and the word for 'And thou shalt love' in the next verse are in the second person whereas the term 'the Lord *our* God' is in the first person. This is to convey the thought that although there are many incapable of rising to the heights of either reflecting deeply on God's unity or really loving Him, for all that, He is still their God since they acknowledge Him as such. Finally, two mystical thoughts are read into the *Shema'*. The first of these, to which we have previously referred, is that man's deeds on earth have an influence on the 'upper worlds'. When man obeys God's will he causes an increase in the flow of divine grace and he thereby converts, as it were, God's judgment into His mercy. The verse means then: 'Hear, O Israel (= obey) and by so doing the Lord (= the quality of mercy) and our God (= the quality of judgment) will become one Lord'! Furthermore, although God is the God of Israel as a whole yet He loves each individual: 'Hear, O Israel (= the individual Jew) although the Lord is our God (and loves all Israel) yet the Lord is one' (He is thy God alone). For divine love is unlike human love. It is not weakened by an increase in its objects and extends to the many with the same abundance as to the few.

(21) *Shabbethai Horowitz* (c. 1565–1619) in his '*Nishmath Shabbethai Ha-Levi*', Prague, 1616, Jer. 1850 (?), Chapter 7.

In this intriguing little book Shabbethai Horowitz defends

his radical opinion, stated in an earlier work, that there is a 'spark of the divine' in every Jewish soul. In Chapter 7 he claims, with great boldness, that Moses himself was the first to refer to this doctrine in the *Shema'*. The author appears to interpret the verse: 'Hear! Israel and the Lord our God are one' i.e. completely united since the spark of the Jewish soul is itself divine!

(22) *Leon de Modena* (1571–1648) in his *'Magen Wa-Herebh'*, ed. S. Simonsohn, Jer. 1960, Part II, Chapter 7, pp. 31–32.

We have seen that Christian writers in the middle ages were fond of quoting the *Shema'* in proof of the Trinity and that, as a result, Jewish scholars were at pains to defend the use of the three divine names in the text. Nowhere, to my knowledge, is this theme treated more comprehensively than in the anti-Christian polemic of the Renaissance scholar, Leon de Modena, entitled *'Magen Wa-Herebh'* ('Shield and Sword'), mentioned above, recently published from manuscripts by S. Simonsohn. De Modena begins by quoting those Christian writers who see in the three divine names in the *Shema'* a reference to the Father, Son and Holy Ghost who though three are 'one'. The term *'our* God' in this Christian interpretation refers to the Son who was clothed in flesh and was 'with us'. De Modena expresses his astonishment that a verse so obviously intended to convey the pure monotheistic view against contemporary polytheism and dualism should be interpreted in this fashion, implying a weakening of monotheism in the very verse in which it receives its fullest formulation. The true meaning of the verse, declares the author, is: 'Hear, O Israel: (i.e. understand this well and consider that here is stated the great principle of faith, therefore, be not led astray like other nations); the Lord, both in His role as our God (who loves us and extends His providence to us) and the Lord (as He is in Himself) is one from every aspect'. In fact, de Modena goes on to say, the verse has the very opposite intention from that read into it by the polemicists in that its purpose is expressly to forbid any suggestion of plurality in God. Furthermore, such an important idea, if it were true and if men could only be saved by belief in it, would hardly have been conveyed by Moses in such ambiguous fashion but would have received the detailed treatment the Law of

Moses gives even to the simple precepts and regulations required for man's happiness. The attempt has been made, he observes, to reply to this that Israel, at that time, were unready to receive the full truth which might have led them, in their primitive state, to a belief in three gods. But this is surely untenable since the people of Israel at the time of Moses had a far more advanced faith than the pagan peoples in the days of the Apostles and if the latter could have been trusted with the secret why not the former?

(23) *Hayyim ben Moses Ibn Attar* (b. Morocco, 1696; d. Jerusalem, 1743) in his Commentary to the Pentateuch, entitled *"Or Ha-Hayyim'*, var. ed. e.g. Lemberg, published David Balaban, 1909).

Ibn Attar states that there are two reasons for accepting the Lord as our God. (1) He is '*our* God' i.e. He is good to us, so that even if there were other gods we should still worship Him. (2) He is the *only* God, so that even if He did not do good to us we would worship Him since there is no other object of worship. How much more so must we worship Him now that He is both 'our God' and the only God, the Being who alone is deserving of our worship and who alone is good to us. The *Shema'* means: 'The Lord is both our God (who loves us) and the Lord alone (the only God) and He alone is, therefore, to be worshipped.'

(24) *Moses Hayyim Luzzatto* (b. Padua, 1707; d. Acco, Palestine, 1746) in his '*Derekh 'Adonai*', 'The Way of the Lord', var. ed., Jer. Tel-Aviv, 1949, Part IV, Chapter 4, pp. 151–161.

Luzzatto, mystic, poet and theologian, compiled his '*Derekh 'Adonai*', referred to above, as a summary of Jewish theology, particularly in the light of the *Qabbalah*, (though the Qabbalistic references are always veiled). This is Luzzatto's scheme as it touches on the duty of reciting the *Shema'*. (There is not much original thought here except in the systematic and lucid presentation. Luzzatto draws very heavily in his theology on earlier Jewish teachers but as a summary his work is unrivalled). The existence of evil in God's creation appears to be in conflict with God's purpose, which must be good for God is all-good. But evil is necessary for it is only by conquering

it that freely-choosing human beings can acquire the good by
their own efforts. There must be a *striving* after the good and
free rejection of evil. Both of these would be impossible were
there no evil. Only goodness acquired by man through his own
efforts is true goodness, resembling, in faint measure, the
goodness of God himself which is self-validating and unbestowed
by another. Evil, essential though it is, is only the result of the
concealment of God's unity. In the true light of this unity there
is only good. At the end of days the full process of the conquest
of evil by the good through man's efforts will be complete.
At that time all will see evil for what it is in reality, the hand-
maiden of the good. This truth, that the good God is truly one,
is concealed from the majority of men at the present, but Israel
knows the truth here and now. Therefore, Israel is bound to
testify to the truth. By virtue of this testimony, in the *Shema'*,
Israel draws down from above divine grace and thereby they
not only testify in theory to God's unity but actually help
the cosmic process in which, under God, evil is vanished and the
good emerges victorious. By declaring that God is one, in
spite of the appearance of evil, Israel assists God, as it were, to
make His unity truly perceived by all mankind. Seen in this
light every recitation of the *Shema'* brings the Messiah a step
nearer.

Furthermore, if the Jew, while reciting the *Shema'*, is ready
in thought to offer himself as a martyr, if need be, in defence
of God's unity, this brings about such a mighty flow of grace
that the cosmic drama is hastened towards its culmination.
In Luzzatto's own words: 'It follows that the general idea
contained in the first verse of the *Shema'* is testimony to, and
acknowledgment of, God's blessed unity in all its aspects.
That is to say, man accepts upon himself the yoke of the
Kingdom, which means that he acknowledges God as Sovereign of all and firmly resolves to sacrifice his very life, if need
be, for the sanctification of God's name. The result of all this
is that the Lord, blessed be He, strengthens the domination
of His unity over all creation so that forces of evil are humbled
and subdued and good grows stronger and prevails. God
thereby comes nearer to His creation that it might be dependent
on Him to become perfected by Him in His perfection. Then
there is drawn down from on high the flow which elevates

creatures to the degree required of them, giving them purity and holiness to the degree that is needed'. The Qabbalistic idea, noted earlier, of the cosmic significance of the precepts is here clearly stated. By reciting the *Shema*', which testifies to God's dominion over all, man helps God, as it were, to fulfil His purpose of bestowing true goodness on His creatures.

(25) *Alexander Süsskind ben Moses* of Grodno (d. Grodno, Lithuania, 1794) in his '*Yesod We-Shoresh Ha-'Abhodah*' ('The Foundation and Root of Divine Worship'), Novydvor, 1782, Warsaw, 1870, Gate IV, Chapter 4, Warsaw ed., pp. 28–29.

Alexander Süsskind's work is a devotional treatise of great popularity. (On this '*Hasid* before Hasidism' *v*. Joseph Klausner in '*Sepher 'Asaph*', Jer. 1953, pp. 427–432). The author, in the section on the *Shema*', quotes his predecessors on the three possible meanings of the word 'Israel' in the verse. (1) The Jew addresses his fellow – 'Israel' referring to the reciter's neighbour. (2) The reciter addresses the Patriarch Jacob (as above, *cf*. Maimonides, *Yad, Hil. Qeriath Shema*', I. 4). (3) God is called 'Israel' (*cf*. the Zoharic passage quoted above, III, 263a) so that the meaning is: 'Hear, O God: I testify to Thee that Thou art one'. The author, having quoted the three possible meanings, leaves it to the reader to choose the one he prefers 'provided that he recites the *Shema*' with true inwardness'.

The author continues: 'The root principle of unification involves two matters; the first, belief, the second, acknowledgment. Faith implies that when man recites the words "the Lord our God, the Lord is one" he should convince himself that this is really true, that the Lord is truly one, alone, and unique. Acknowledgment implies that he should accept upon himself the yoke of the Kingdom of Heaven in completeness, that is to say, the acceptance of the yoke of God's sovereignty, divinity and lordship, blessed and exalted be He, upon himself and upon his children after him. As soon as he finishes reciting the word "one" he should concentrate on the following with all his mind's power and with great joy: "I believe with perfect faith, pure and true, that Thou art one and unique and that Thou hast created all worlds, upper and lower, without end, and thou art in past, present and future. I make Thee my King over each

of my limbs that it might keep and perform the precepts of
Thy holy *Torah* and I make Thee King over my children and
children's children to the end of time. I will, therefore, command
my children and grandchildren to accept upon themselves the
yoke of Thy kingdom, divinity and lordship and I will command them to command, in turn, their children up to the last
generation to accept, all of them, the yoke of thy kingdom,
divinity and lordship" '.

Alexander continues that a man should be ready to offer
up his life for God, if need be, and he should have this readiness in mind after he has finished reciting the first verse of the
Shema'. In extremely realistic fashion he gives the following
illustration of the kind of thought that should be in the mind
at this point: 'He should depict to himself that he is standing
at the top of a very high tower and opposite him there stand
idolators with idols in their hands. These order him to bow
to the idols or else be cast off the tower to the ground. He
replies: "I refuse to bow to an image made by man, for our
God is called the God of all the earth, the God of Israel, He is
God in the heavens above and the earth beneath and there is
none else. To Him will I bow and bend the knee". He should
then imagine immediately that they push him off the tower so
that he hurtles to the ground and he should also have in mind
the horrible sufferings he will endure as a result of this unnatural death' (end of first 'Gate'). Similar pictures should be
in the mind to bring home the other three forms of capital
punishment recorded in the *Talmud*. 'Burning' should be
depicted as the pouring of molten lead down the throat and
being cast into a fiery furnace. 'The sword' should be depicted
as decapitation, 'strangulation' by hanging or by drowning.
The author concludes that all this should be with perfect
sincerity otherwise it is valueless.

(26) *Moses Mendelssohn* (b. Dessau, Germany, 1729; d. Berlin,
1786) in his Commentary to the Bible, '*Bi'ur*', Prague, 1862.

Mendelssohn's Commentary was the first in the modern
period to attempt an exposition of the plain text of the Bible.
The following is his interpretation of the first verse of the
Shema': 'The Lord our God, to whom we hope for all goodness
and all that we desire, is the only Lord, and no other god may

be associated with Him, for He is of one and unique Essence, the Source of all goodness without any intermediary or partner whatever'.

(27) '*Sepher Ba'al Shem Tobh*', Lodz, 1938, p. 175.

The Hasidic movement, rising to prominence during the eighteenth century and eventually capturing millions of adherents among Eastern European Jewries, was a pietistic, mystical movement with a strong emphasis on the all-pervading nature of the Deity. The following two quotations from an anthology of Hasidic teachings (the first in the name of the early Hasidic saint, Phinehas of Koretz, the second from Solomon Zalman of Kaputs' '*Magen Abhoth*', Berditchev, 1902) convey the panentheistic tendencies in Hasidic thought.

(*a*) 'The following should be in man's thought when he recites the word "One" in the *Shema'*. He should contemplate that there is nothing else in the whole world but the Holy One, blessed be He, whose glory fills the whole earth. Man's chief intention should be that he looks upon himself as nothingness and utter negation, only his soul, the portion of God from above, his main being, from which it follows that there is nothing else in the whole world but the Holy One, blessed be He. His main intention when he recites the word "one" should be that the whole earth is full of God's glory and that there is nothing from which God is absent'.

(*b*) Solomon Zalman, in the name of the 'disciples of the *Ba'al Shem Tobh*', the founder of Hasidism, states that the meaning of the word 'one' in the *Shema'*, according to Hasidic thought, differs from that of conventional Theism. In the latter 'the Lord is one' means that there is only one God but in Hasidic thought the meaning is rather that there is only one – God, i.e. only God alone enjoys true existence and His creatures only appear to exist because of the screening of the divine light which embraces them all ('as the rays of the sun have no independent existence in the sun itself').

This idea of Hasidism, as we have noted earlier, was dubbed heretical by the opponents of the movement who believed it to be a radical departure from traditional Theism. To suggest that God is in all things or that all things are in God is to blur the distinction between God and His creation and between

good and evil. That God's glory fills the earth was taken
to mean, by the opponents of Hasidism, that His providence is
over all, not that He is found, as it were, in material things.
But the Hasidic teachers did not hesitate to teach that from
the point of view of God, as it were, there is no world and
that the purpose of man's worship is to pierce the veils of
illusion until he sees only the divine in all things. We have
noted in earlier quotations that the *Shema'* can be taken to
mean either that God is one or that God is unique. The Hasidic
teachers go further to teach that God is all, 'one' being used
in the sense that in ultimate reality God is all that there is.
He alone is true Being.

(28) *Elimelech of Lizianka* (b. 1717; d. Lizianka, Galicia, 1787)
in his '*Tzetil Qatan*' ('Small Note'), printed at end of his
'*No'am 'Elimelekh*', Jer. 1865.

This note on the *Shema'* is part of a regimen of spiritual
discipline drawn up by this famous Hasidic saint for his own
spiritual advancement. 'Whenever a man is not engaged in
studying the *Torah*, and particularly when he sits alone in his
room or when he lies on his bed without sleep coming to him
he should contemplate on the precept of sanctifying God's
name. He should imagine that a great and terrible fire, its
flames reaching to the heavens, burns in front of him and that
he breaks his nature, for the sake of God's holy name, to throw
himself as a martyr into the flames. When he recites the first
verse of the *Shema'* he should have the same idea in mind. He
should have the further intention that if the nations of the world
were to torture him with every kind of severe torture and if
they were to flay him alive unless he denied, God forfend,
the unity of God, he would be ready to suffer all their tortures
rather than admit that they are right, God forfend. He should
imagine them actually doing this to him and he will in this way
fulfil properly the duty of reciting the *Shema''*.

(29) *M. L. Malbim* (b. Russia, 1809; d. Kiev, Russia, 1879) in
his Commentary to the Pentateuch, Warsaw, 1880.

Malbim is of the opinion that the *Shema'* was aimed originally
against dualism. In his own words: ' "The Lord our God, the
Lord is one", – the Tetragrammaton refers to the quality of

mercy, responsible for the good, and "God" refers to the quality of judgment, responsible for judgment and punishment. They are "one", the God who is only good and doeth only goodness and mercy, hence the Tetragrammaton is repeated. Since all is united in perfect unity, the second verse goes on to say: "And thou shalt love the *Lord* thy *God*" '

(30) '*Siddur 'Otzar Ha-Tephilloth*' (Vilna, 1914), Prayer Book with Commentaries by Hanoch Zundel ben Joseph – (*a*) and (*b*) – ' '*Etz Yoseph*' and '*Anaph Yoseph*' – and Aryeh Laib ben Solomon Gordon – (*c*) – ' '*Iyyon Tephillah*'.

(*a*) The Hebrew letters of the word for 'one' – '*ehad* – have the numerical value of 1–8–4. When reciting the first verse of the *Shema'* man should have the following intention: 'The Lord who is our God is one, unique in all seven heavens, in the earth and its four corners (1 = God, 8 = seven heavens and earth, 4 = four corners of the earth) and this I believe with perfect faith'.

(*b*) 'When one says "the Lord our God" he should have in mind that he accepts the commandment "I am the Lord thy God" (Ex. xx. 2), and when one says "the Lord is one" he should have in mind that he accepts the command "Thou shalt have no other gods" (Ex. xx. 3). And he should have as his trust neither angel nor planet and should rely on no other to help him, only God alone, who is one and to whom there is no second'.

(*c*) The word 'Hear' means to 'understand'. The subject of the verse is 'the Lord', its predicates are: 'our God' and the second 'the Lord'. Hence the verse states: (1) The Lord is our God. (2) The Lord is one. The verse refutes both the idea of a plurality of gods and the idea that God is unconcerned with the universe He set into motion. He is both one and *our* God.

E

[4]

THE THIRD PRINCIPLE
God's Incorporeality

MAIMONIDES' statement of the third principle (Abelsons' translation) is: '*The Third Principle of Faith. The removal of materiality from God.* This signifies that this unity is not a body nor the power of a body, nor can the accidents of bodies overtake Him, as, e.g., motion and rest, whether in the essential or accidental sense. It was for this reason that the Sages (peace to them!) denied to Him both cohesion and separation of parts, when they remarked (*Hag.* 15a) that above there is no sitting and no standing, no division and no cohesion (*v.* Abelson *loc. cit.*). The prophet again said, "And unto whom will ye liken God" (Is. xl. 18) etc., "and unto whom will ye liken Me that I may be like, saith the Holy One" (Is. xl. 25). If God were a body He would be like a body. Wherever in the Scriptures God is spoken of with the attributes of material bodies, like motion, standing, sitting, speaking, and such like, all these are figures of speech, as the Sages (*Ber.* 31b) said: "The *Torah* speaks in the language of men". People have said a great deal on this point. This third fundamental article of faith is indicated by the Scriptural expression (Deut. iv. 15), "for ye have seen no likeness", i.e. you have not comprehended Him as one who possesses a likeness, for, as we have remarked, He is not a body nor a bodily power'.

The '*Ani Ma'amin*' formula is: 'I believe with perfect faith that the Creator, blessed be His name, is not a body, and that He is free from all the accidents of matter, and that He has not any form whatsoever'. The *Yigdal* form is: 'He hath neither bodily form nor substance: we can compare nought unto Him in His holiness'. Friedländer says: 'The strict Unity of God, in the sense explained above, implies His Incorporeality, which forms the subject of the third article. Corporeality implies substance and form, a dualism which must be rigidly excluded from God. It would not have been necessary to formulate a special article for the exclusion of corporeality from the idea of God but for the fact that many erroneous notions have been entertained on the subject. Besides the fact that the corporeality of God was assumed by certain religious sects, there have been scholars among the Jews who defended the literal sense of anthropomorphic phrases in the Scriptures'. Werblowsky describes articles three and four together: 'These two articles express, among other things, the severely non-mythological character of God in Judaism. God has no form, no family, no history. In a way the two articles are corollaries of art. 2. The divine is beyond time (i.e. generation and corruption) and space (i.e. composite matter). As our language is derived from the world of our experience, it can never describe nor adequately express the divine. Maimonides would probably have denied the possibility of a theology of analogy. Other thinkers did not go so far. The Qabbalists, whose thinking bears an unmistakably Platonic mark, would say that anthropomorphisms are legitimate because language as such (i.e. the Holy Tongue, Hebrew) is essentially a system of mystic symbols of the divine reality. It is only by derivation and by analogy that language is also applied to human conditions; essentially and ultimately it is "theomorphic". In modern philosophical and theological writing, the idea of God is treated either in orthodox, mediaeval-Aristotelian fashion, or else in accordance with the philosophical background (Kantian, Hegelian, existentialist or dialectical) of the various authors'.

A number of Theists have been prepared, rightly, it seems to me, to recognise the value of atheistic attacks of various kinds on their own faith. It may be a remarkably bold view to hold that if there were no atheism it would be necessary to invent it for the sake of Theism, but this is, nonetheless, a view which commends itself to some serious Theistic thinkers. For people who call themselves atheists are frequently in revolt against an inferior concept of God to which they have been introduced, and this kind of rebellion causes the Theist to examine more carefully his concept of God in favour of a more refined view. It must be obvious, for instance, that any denial of God as a colossal old man in the sky, wearing a crown and a long white beard, seated upon a throne surrounded by winged creatures who praise Him all day long, is a denial which sophisticated Theists would themselves accept. We think in pictures and cannot avoid such mental images as that of the old man in the sky in one form or another. But, according to any refined Theistic view, it is essential that we recognise the image for what it is, a symbol of the Deity, not an actual representation. There is an analogy from algebra. In an algebraic formula the letters x, y and z may represent, let us say, quantities of wall-paper to be used in papering a room. In the process of working out the sum the letters are manipulated as if they had an identity of their own and the quantities of paper they represent is forgotten. $3x$ is considered as if the letter x were being multiplied and this is inevitable if the extremely cumbersome method of multiplying the actual quantities of paper is to be avoided. But the mathematician must eventually relate his symbols to the actual wall-paper, or, at least, someone must do this, unless the whole exercise is to remain purely academic. Language about God can only be a kind of algebraic symbol. Even the most sophisticated Theist is bound to have in his mind, whenever he uses the word 'God', an image not very different from that of the old man in the sky, since this is the way the human mind functions. Provided the symbol is recognised for what it is no harm is done and the positive good results that God is spoken of, so that the reality of God is kept before the mind. But the symbol must be related constantly to the Reality it is intended to represent, and here the atheistic attack is of value to Theism for it compels the Theist so to refine his conception of that Reality as to leave no room for a challenge to vulgar or unworthy notions. I take it that Tillich ('Theology of Culture', p. 131) had something like this in mind when he said that without an element of 'atheism' no 'Theism' can be maintained. It might, indeed, be said with justice that a critical Theism, which seeks to remove misconceptions about the Deity, frequently proceeds on lines not too dissimilar from atheistic attacks on crude notions and no ist infrequently dubbed atheistic by a more popular and credulous Theism, exactly as the Jews were called atheists by certain Romans who were unable to see how one can worship an invisible God.

Maimonides is so insistent on the rejection of God's corporeality that, in his great Code, he rules (*Yad, Hil. Teshubhah*, III. 7) that one who believes in God's corporeality is a heretic and has no share in the world to come. His famous critic, Abraham Ibn David (*ad. loc.*) observes: 'Why does he call such a person a "heretic"? Men greater and better than he have adopted this view because they have seen God so described in Scripture and even more so in legendary works which confuse the mind'. Clearly, Abraham Ibn David does not himself believe in God's corporeality but he feels that a more charitable attitude than Maimonides' should be cultivated since the 'plain meaning' of both Scripture and Rabbinic legend can easily persuade the unphilosophic student that the notion of corporeality is taught in the great classical sources of Judaism. In fact, the Talmudist Moses Taku, Maimonides' contemporary, takes strong issue both with Maimonides and with Saadiah for daring to defy this 'plain meaning'. This writer upheld the legitimacy of anthropomorphic expressions used of the Deity, claiming for them far more than symbolic value, e.g. he appears to suggest that God, somehow, actually does dwell, or at any rate, makes Himself dwell occasionally, on a great Throne in Heaven. (Moses Taku's '*Kethabh Tamim*', in which these views are adumbrated, has been published from the manuscript with an Introduction and notes by R. Kirchheim in ' '*Otzar Nehmad*', Vol. III, Vienna, 1860, pp. 54–99).

Taku (p. 59 f.) states that man was created in 'God's image after His likeness' (Gen. i. 26) and that this is testified to in both Scripture and the Rabbinic literature. The book of Genesis leaves us in no doubt on this score: 'And God created man in His own image, in the image of God created He him' (Gen. i. 27). Similarly the precepts of the *Torah* were given 'from the *mouth* of the Holy One' – 'like a father who issues commands to his son'. Verses such as 'And behold, the Lord stood beside him' (Gen. xxviii. 13) and 'with him do I speak mouth to mouth' (Num. xii. 8) provide further support that God has an image and form. Isaiah saw the Lord 'sitting upon a throne' (Is. vi. 1). Another verse says: 'I saw the Lord sitting on His throne, and all the host of Heaven standing by Him on His right hand and on His left' (I Kings xxii. 19). So, too, in the book of Daniel we read: 'I beheld, till thrones were placed,

and one that was ancient of days did sit, His raiment was as
white snow, and the hair of His head like pure wool' (Dan. vii.
9). In the Rabbinic literature we find further support, particularly in Rabbi Meir's famous illustration on the verse in
Deuteronomy xxi. 22–23. Twin brothers closely resembled
each other; one became king, the other was arrested for robbery
and was hanged. Whoever saw the thief on the gallows thought
that the king was hanged (*Sanh.* 46b). The Talmudic explanation of the prohibition against drawing a portrait of the full
human face (*R.H.* 24b) is based on the verse: 'Ye shall not make
with Me' (Ex. xx. 20), which is said to imply: 'Ye shall not
make Me' i.e. the human face is a copy of the divine. Further
passages are quoted which, if taken literally, and Moses of
Taku does so take them, all suggest that in some sense, at
least, it can be said that God is corporeal. The author goes on
to ask (p. 61), if God fills Heaven and earth how can He
assume or appear in the form of a man? To this the reply is
given, again supported by passages from the Rabbinic literature taken quite literally, that just as the sun, one of God's
servants, can appear in many places at once, so can the Creator
appear in many forms. Angels, too, and even demons, observes
the author, have this power of assuming different guises and
human magicians can turn themselves into animals! It is more
than a little difficult to know exactly what Moses of Taku
means when he insists on God's corporeality. In more than
one passage in his book he is at pains to point out that God's
greatness is far above all human conception. Indeed, he takes
issue with Maimonides and Saadiah on precisely this point,
arguing that they are all too ready to tell us that God cannot
be perceived by man's senses and thereby they, paradoxically,
place arbitrary limits to His power. Moses seems to be saying
that God is great – even infinitely great – but in a corporeal
sense. Thus he gives the illustration (p. 62) of the flame of a
wick in comparison to a great bonfire. The nature of the fire
is the same in both instances even though one is so much more
powerful than the other. Similarly, the divine fire sometimes
appears, as the Rabbis say, in the form of a lion on the altar
but it constantly eludes any attempt at comprehension so that
even the angels cannot grasp it and it is too high even for
beings higher than the angels. In other words, Moses of Taku

was a non-philosophical Talmudist who believed very strongly that all the words of Scripture regarding the nature of God, as well as the passages on the same theme in the Rabbinic literature, are to be taken literally. For philosophic minds like Saadiah and Maimonides this was quite impossible. It was the view of the philosophers which finally won out so that the Jew of today finds Moses Taku's protest very strange reading.

We have seen that Maimonides quotes the Rabbinic '*the Torah speaks in the language of men*' in explanation of Biblical anthropomorphisms. In this he follows distinguished predecessors. But in his 'Guide for the Perplexed' Maimonides is, apparently, dissatisfied with this general solution to the problem but devotes a large portion of the work to an explanation of the detailed anthropomorphic terms used of the Deity, interpreting these in a transcendental and metaphorical sense (*v.* 'Guide', I, Introduction and Chapter I f.). Furthermore, Maimonides is of the opinion that whatever attributes we use of God are to be understood in a negative sense. They do not tell us what God is but what He is not. Thus when we say that God is one we do not really mean to imply that we know anything about God's true nature but we merely affirm that He is not a plurality of beings. Or when we say that God is compassionate we refer to His acts, which if done by humans would be due to compassion, and that He is not cruel. Even when we say that God exists we mean that He is not non-existent ('Guide', I, Chapters LI–LX). Maimonides' attitude is not, of course, an agnostic one. At the most it can be termed religious agnosticism. We do know that there is a God but we cannot say anything about His essence. What we can do is to reject all inadequate conceptions of Him and this we do by stating, albeit in positive form, what He is not. Thus when the Jew says: 'The Lord is one' he is really saying, according to Maimonides, 'I do not know anything about God's true nature but this I do know: that any attempt to explain that nature in a plural sense is false'. Critics of the doctrine of negative attributes have argued that if we cannot say anything positive about God how can we even negate anything from His nature since negation, too, is a positive affirmation about His nature? Can we really negate anything from that of which we have no knowledge at all? This objection is far from cogent. Maimonides himself supplies us with a helpful illustration. If I am told that there is a being in a house and I am then told that whatever else it is it is not a plant or a mineral I am a little nearer to understanding its true nature even though I have no knowledge of what that nature may be. Maimonides believes that man can have an increasing knowledge of God but such increase must always be obtained through negations. 'The following question might perhaps be asked. Since there is no possibility of obtaining a knowledge of the true essence of God, and since it has also been proved that the only thing that man can apprehend of Him is the fact that He exists, and that all positive attributes are inadmissible, as has been shown; what is the difference among those who have obtained a knowledge of God? Must not the knowledge obtained by our teacher Moses, and by Solomon, be the same as that obtained by the lowest class of philosophers, since there can be no addition to this knowledge? But, on the other hand, it is generally accepted among theologians and also among philosophers, that there can be a great difference between the knowledge of God obtained by two different men. Know that this is really the case, that those who have obtained a knowledge of God differ greatly from each other; for in the same way as by each individual attribute an object is more specified, and is brought nearer to the true apprehension of the observer, so by each additional negative attribute you advance toward the knowledge of God, and you are nearer to it than he who does not negative, in reference to God, those qualities which you are convinced by proof must be negatived' (Friedländer's trans.).

It is in the *Qabbalah* that the *via negativa* receives its most radical expression. The *Qabbalah* distinguishes, as we have seen earlier, between God as He is in Himself and God as He manifests Himself through the *Sephiroth*. When referring to the Sephirotic realm man can, and should, use positive attributes. God in His manifestation is, for example, compassionate in a positive sense. But *'En Soph*, the Limitless, God as He is in Himself, is completely unknown. He is not even spoken of in the Bible, He is utterly beyond all human comprehension (on this theme *v.* particularly I. Tishbi: '*Mishnath Ha-Zohar*', Vol. I, Jer. 1949, pp. 75 ff.). True to this teaching,

the *Zohar*, while it has much to say on the *Sephiroth*, is almost
completely silent on the subject of *'En Soph*, anticipating
Wittgenstein's famous aphorism: 'Whereof one cannot speak
thereof one must be silent'! There are, however, one or two
passages in the *Zohar* which hint at *'En Soph* and that He cannot
be known. Thus in one passage a distinction is drawn between
'The Causes of causes', the name given to the highest of the
Sephiroth, and 'The Cause above all causes', which is *'En Soph*.
Similarly, of *'En Soph* it is said that He 'fills all worlds' and
yet 'surrounds all worlds' (these two passages, quoted and
explained in detail by Tishbi, *op. cit.* are: *Zohar* I, 22b and
Zohar III, 225a). Following in the same tradition the famous
Qabbalist, Moses Cordovero (' *'Elimah Rabbathi'*, I. 10, p. 4b),
remarks: 'When your intellect conceives of God do not permit
yourself to imagine that there is a God as depicted by you. For
if you do this you will have a finite and corporeal conception,
God forfend. Instead your mind must dwell only on the affirmation of God's existence and then recoil. To do more than this
is to allow the imagination to reflect on God as He is in Himself and such reflection is bound to result in imaginative limita-
tion and corporeality. Put reins, therefore, on your intellect
and do not allow it too great a freedom, but assert God's
existence and deny your intellect the possibility of comprehending Him. The mind should run to and fro – running to affirm
God's existence and recoiling from any limitations produced
by the imagination, since man's imagination pursues his
intellect'.

*   *   *

EXCURSUS

On the whole subject the splendid article by Louis Ginzberg:
'Anthropomorphism and Anthropopathism' in JE, Vol. I, pp.
621–625, should be consulted. When the early Rabbis wished to say
something particularly bold about God they qualified whatever they
said by the term *kebheyakhol* ('as though it were possible') as if to
say, this must not be taken literally but is a poetic way of giving
expression to the idea, *cf.* e.g. *Mekh. Yithro, 4, Mishnah, Sanh. VI.
5*, but this latter source is based on a very doubtful reading, *v.*
'Arukh, Kohut, *s.v. yakhol* and the further sources quoted there.
Kohut rightly compares the expression with the German *wenn
man so sagen kann*. In the well-known 'Speech of Elijah', *Tiqqune*

Zohar, second Introduction, 12b, the utter incomprehensibility of *'En Soph* is expressed as follows: 'Elijah began his discourse saying: Master of the Worlds! Thou art one but not by enumeration! Thou art He who is exalted above all exalted ones, mysterious above all mysteries. Thought cannot grasp Thee at all!'. For a vivid latter-day mystic's approach to the *via negativa v.* the long quotation from the writings of Rabbi Kook in *'Peraqim Be-Mahashebheth Yisrael'*, ed. S. Israeli, Israel, 1952, pp. 77–78: 'Faith chiefly involves the conception of God's greatness so that whatever the heart conceives is as nought compared with that which it is fitting to conceive, and this, in turn, is as nought compared to the Reality. All the divine names, whether in Hebrew or in other languages, convey no more than a faint spark of the hidden light for which the soul longs and which it gives the name "God". Every definition of the divine leads to denial and all attempts at defining the divine are spiritual idolatry. Even the definition of divine intellect and will and even the divine itself and even the name "God" are definitions and lead to denial unless they are qualified by the higher knowledge that these are but the light of sparks flashing from that which is above definition . . . It is a natural thing for all creatures to be submissive to the divine, for all particular being to be as nought before Being in general, how much more before the Source of all general being? In this there is nothing of pain or repression but only delight and strength, majesty and inner power . . . When the central point of the recognition of the divine is weak the divine Existence is thought of as no more than a tyrannical force from which there is no escape and before which one must be humbled. One who approaches the service of God in this empty situation, when the lower fear of God is torn from its source in the higher fear through the dark conception of the divine, arrived at as a result of lack of intelligence and of *Torah*, gradually loses the illumination of his world. The majesty of God cannot then be revealed in the soul, only the degraded conceptions of an unbridled imagination, which portrays an obscure and false image calculated to confuse whoever believes in it, to crush his spirit and remove all the divine splendour from his soul. Even if such a person proclaims the whole day long that this is belief in the one God this is no more than an empty phrase of which the soul knows nothing'. On Moses of Taku *v.* S. Bernfeld: *'Da'ath 'Elohim'*, Warsaw, 1898, pp. 343–346 and A. Marcus: *'Ha-Hasiduh'* (Heb-trans.), Tel-Aviv, 1954, Chapter 25, pp. 335–338.

*   *   *

However, Theism must always be on guard against a
negation of the God idea in the name of sophistication. It
must not capitulate to atheism by refining the God concept
out of existence. Various attempts have been made in modern
times at retaining the term 'God' but using it in what is said
to be a non-supernatural sense, i.e. as describing the total
of those forces in the universe which make for righteousness,
human growth and happiness, or as the process by means of
which these are achieved. Conventional Theists have rightly
pointed out the semantic confusion to which this kind of thinking
leads and have not hesitated to call the affirmation of a non-
supernatural God atheism, even though the advocates of such a
position angrily deny the charge. In a world dominated by
science and technology it is natural to imagine that terms such
as 'Power' or 'Energy' or 'Force' are better suited to describe
the Reality we call God than highly charged emotional terms
such as 'Father'. Furthermore, the term 'Father', or any
personal term, suggests a grossly anthropomorphic conception
of the Deity, a conception the best Jewish thinkers have ruled
out of court, as we have seen. A *person* is easily moved to change.
He feels strongly, is frequently irrational, loses his temper,
becomes childish, is capricious and arbitrary in his likes and
dislikes. Is it not better, it is argued, to substitute impersonal
for personal terms in speaking of the Changeless Being who is,
in Pascal's words, the 'God of the geometers'?

Now from the standpoint of traditional Theism it is true
that God can only be described on His own terms and, since
these are known only to God, He cannot really be described
at all in human language, a totally inadequate instrument for
speaking of God. Inadequate though it is, however, we have
no other instrument. It might be objected that, in the event, we
should never speak of God. But the Theist cannot afford to
dispense with prayer, worship and the study of his religion,
all of which would be impossible if he were forbidden to speak
of God. The Theist's only resort is to use human language
while being aware always of its inadequacy. He is obliged,
therefore, to use the symbols expressing the highest he knows
when he speaks of God, thereby suggesting that although God's
nature cannot be known by man He is at least as elevated as
the highest possible symbol suggests.

It is here that the supernaturalist parts company with the
naturalist conception. For whether we use the terms 'Father'
or 'Force' we are thinking in picture language and it is hard
to see why the non-human symbol should be preferred to the
human. Human personality is the highest thing we know in
the universe. To speak of God as 'It', instead of 'He', is,
in a sense, perfectly legitimate since any term we use is adequate and since a too literal interpretation of 'He' as applied
to God suggests the ascription of sex to Him, a conclusion
that is certainly at variance with traditional Theism. But when
'It' is used of God there is a failure to convey the idea that
He is *more* than personality, not *less*, as an 'it' is less. For in our
use of language an 'it' is an inanimate thing to which a person
is superior. It is precisely here that the naturalist interpretation fails. Naturalists repeatedly speak and write as if the life
forces were themselves 'God' and this not only commits the
absurdity of personalising natural forces – which may be
excused as poetic licence – but fails to satisfy the religious
mind, which can find anchorage only in the supernatural. 'The
Lord is my shepherd' has been used as a hymn of praise and
adoration by millions of devout souls, endowing them with
faith's courage to cope with life's uncertainties. 'Force is my
shepherd' offends against the most elementary canons of both
taste and religious sensibility.

In world literature there are three well-known attacks on
the idea of a personal God, all aimed at demonstrating its
alleged absurdity by appealing to the animal world:

'The Aethiopians say that their Gods are snub-nosed and black-
skinned, and the Thracians that theirs are blue-eyed and red-
haired. If only oxen and horses had hands and wanted to draw
with their hands or to make the works of art that men make, then
horses would draw the figures of their Gods like horses, and
oxen like oxen, and would make their bodies on the model of
their own'.   (*Xenophanes*).

'The BRAHMINS assert, that the world arose from an infinite
spider, who spun this whole complicated mass from his bowels,
and annihilates afterwards the whole or any part of it, by
absorbing it again, and resolving it into his own essence.
Here is a species of cosmogony, which appears to us ridiculous;

because a spider is a little contemptible animal, whose opera-
tions we are never likely to take for a model of the whole
universe. But still here is a new species of analogy, even in
our globe. And were there a planet wholly inhabitated by
spiders (which is very possible), this inference would there
appear as natural and irrefragable as that which in our planet
ascribes the origin of all things to design and intelligence, as
explained by Cleanthes. Why an orderly system may not be
spun from the belly as well as from the brain, it will be
difficult for him to give a satisfactory reason'.

(*David Hume*: 'Dialogues Concerning Natural Religion', ed.
Norman Kemp Smith, Oxford, Clarendon Press, 1935, p. 223).

'HEAVEN'

'Fish (fly-replete, in depth of June,
Dawdling away their wat'ry noon)
Ponder deep wisdom, dark or clear,
Each secret fishy hope or fear.
Fish say, they have their Stream and Pond;
But is there anything Beyond?
This life cannot be All, they swear,
For how unpleasant, if it were!
One may not doubt that, somehow, Good
Shall come of Water and of Mud;
And, sure, the reverent eye must see
A Purpose in Liquidity.
We darkly know, by Faith we cry,
The future is not Wholly Dry.
Mud unto Mud! – Death eddies near –
Not here the appointed End, not here! –
But somewhere, beyond Space and Time,
In wetter water, slimier slime!
And there (they trust) there swimmeth One
Who swam ere rivers were begun,
Immense, of fishy form and mind,
Squamous, omnipotent and kind;
And under that Almighty Fin,
The littlest fish may enter in.
Oh! never fly conceals a hook,
Fish say, in the Eternal Brook,

But more than mundane weeds are there,
And mud, celestially fair;
Fat caterpillars drift around,
And Paradisal grubs are found;
Unfading moths, immortal flies,
And the worm that never dies.
And in that Heaven of all their wish,
There shall be no more land, say fish'.

                                        (Rupert Brooke)

Now all three passages are surely correct in implying that *if* horses, oxen, spiders and fish could think as humans do they would describe God in terms resembling a horse, an ox, a spider or a fish. If there could be such a creature as a thinking fish he might well be superior both rationally and morally to human beings and then, indeed, he would be obliged to think of God as a fish since this would be to think of God in the highest terms he knew. But he would also be obliged to add to his mental picture that God is *more* than fish just as the human must to his conception that God is *more* than a *He*. In all three passages there is clever legerdemain. First, horses, oxen, spiders and fish are endowed with intelligence and made to think like humans and then humans are invited to say: 'Poor horses, oxen, spiders and fish! They imagine themselves to be the apex of creation and fashion God in their own image. How little do they know of higher forms of life!' All this is put forward that humans might draw their own conclusions that all thoughts of God are due to colossal human arrogance. But, so far as we know, human beings are the highest forms of life in the universe while horses, oxen and the rest cannot think and behave as humans do. If it be granted that there exist in the universe beings superior to man, angels, for instance, or the inhabitants of other planets, then, indeed, these would be compelled to conceive of God on their own terms, and for them the human image would be as inadequate as the fish image is for humans. It is not the anthropomorphic image that the Theist wishes to preserve but the implication it suggests of intelligence and moral nature, of a Being deserving our worship. Discussing the failure of the ancient Greeks to build up an all-comprehensive philosophical explanation of the world without at the same time losing their religion, Etienne Gilson points out that this was due to their description of all phenomena as 'things' and 'things' cannot be worshipped:'In the light of what precedes, the reason for their failure is at hand. A Greek philosophical interpretation of the world is an explanation of what natures are, by what a certain nature is; in other words, the Greeks have consistently tried to explain all things by means of one or several principles themselves considered as things. Now, men can be preached into worshipping any living being, from a wholly imaginary one like Zeus to a wholly ridiculous one like the Golden Calf. Provided only it be somebody or something which they can mistake for some-body, they may eventually worship it. What men cannot possibly bring themselves to do is to worship a thing' ('God and Philosophy', Yale University Press, New Haven, 1941, p. 37). This is the great contribution of the Hebrews. They always thought of God as a Person, that is as a Being who can be worshipped.

E. S. Brightman ('A Philosophy of Religion', Skeffington, London, 1947, Chapter 7, 'The problem of Belief in God', *par.* II: 'Is God a Person?', pp. 129–135) has some very helpful things to say on the idea of a personal God. He defines this concept as meaning that 'the unbegun and unending energy of the universe is conscious rational will' and goes on to say: 'The concept of a personal God is said to be *an expression of man's arrogance.* Why should the God of all resemble man in any way? If this argument be valid, it stands in curious contradiction with the empirical fact that in general religious persons have regarded all expressions of arrogance as irreligious. Believers in God have practised and taught humility and meekness. It is true that churches have often been arrogant and have allied themselves with arrogant secularism and wealth. But in so doing they were contradicting rather than expressing the implications of their belief in God. It is difficult to see why religious thinking is more arrogant than any thinking by scientists and philosophers, which lays claim to objectivity and reasonings that go on in the minds of puny creatures such as we. What is sauce for the goose is sauce for the gander'. It is hardly necessary to refer in this connection to such verses in Scripture as: 'Behold now, I have taken upon me to speak unto the Lord, who am but dust and ashes' (Gen. xviii. 27).

It should be noted that there is no term in classical Hebrew for 'person' and that the term 'personal God' had its origin in the Christian description of the Trinity. It would be, of course, a gross error to conclude from this that the God of Judaism is not personal. Clement C. J. Webb ('God and Personality', George Allen and Unwin, London, 1918, pp. 85–86) is certainly right in saying in his Gifford Lectures: 'Though Jewish theology has never, I believe, made use in describing God of any word exactly corresponding to Personality and has ever offered a resolute opposition to the Christian doctrine with which the term as employed in theology was first associated, of a plurality of Persons in God, few would hesitate to describe Judaism as a religion with a personal God. Long before the rise of Christianity the prophets of Israel had succeeded in a task which the Greek philosophers failed to accomplish, or indeed had scarcely attempted . . . The fear of "making God too much a man", a fear stimulated by aversion to the Christian doctrine of Incarnation, combined with the influence of Aristotle on the thought of mediaeval Jewish thinkers, such as Maimonides, in emphasising the distance between God and man, may have imposed a greater restraint upon developments of personal religion, which in Christianity were at once encouraged and directed by the ascription of Godhead to its historical Founder. But it would be absurd to deny that a religion has a personal God which has ever taken as its ideal the great Lawgiver to whom his God "spoke face to face as a man speaketh unto his friend" '. This is truly well said except that Judaism, of course, considers the Christian doctrine no advance but quite the opposite. In fact it is highly probable to suggest that Maimonides intended his third principle concerning God's incorporeality to refute the doctrine of the Incarnation. Judaism strikes the mean between the doctrine that God is an impersonal force or power and the doctrine which thinks of Him as so like a man that He is capable of assuming human flesh. Classical Judaism looks upon the first doctrine as atheistic and upon the second as blasphemous. This is why Maimonides, like the great Jews who preceded and followed him, refers to God as a *He* while insisting on His incorporeality.

*   *   *

On the 'non-Personal' interpretation of the God idea *v*. James Collins, *op. cit.*, Chapter VIII. 4, 'American Naturalism as a Methodological Atheism', pp. 268–284 and the bibliography given in the notes on p. 441, to which should be added Julian Huxley's 'Religion Without Revelation', London, 1957. The best-known Jewish exponent of a non-supernaturalist Theism is Mordecai M. Kaplan (b. 1882), particularly in his 'The Meaning of God in Modern Jewish Religion', Jewish Reconstructionist Foundation, New York, 2nd. printing, 1947. *V*. my critique of the 'Reconstructionist' viewpoint in 'We Have Reason to Believe', Vallentine, Mitchell, London, 1957, pp. 18 f. An early Jewish statement of the psychological advantages of the use of anthropomorphisms is that of *Bahya Ibn Paqudah*, 'Duties of the Heart', *Sha'ar Ha-Yihud*, Chapter 10, Warsaw ed., 1875, p. 80. 'Necessity compels us to describe the Creator in corporeal terms', says Bahya, 'and to speak of Him as possessing creaturely attributes in order that we might conceive in our souls the idea that the blessed Creator exists. Therefore the prophetic books express His nature in words drawn from the physical world which are near to man's intellect and his power of understanding. Were they to describe God in a manner suitable for Him, namely, by using spiritual words and ideas, no one would understand either the words or the ideas. It would not be possible to worship the unknown for how can one serve that which is uncomprehended? Consequently, it was necessary for the words and ideas used to be in accordance with their hearer's intellectual capacity so that, at first, the idea is comprehended in a corporeal sense through the use of words drawn from the physical universe. Afterwards, we can increase his wisdom by encouraging him to grasp that all this is purely figurative and symbolic and that the true idea is far more refined, advanced, elevated and remote than one can possibly understand by virtue of its extremely subtle nature'. C. D. Broad ('Religion, Philosophy and Psychical Research', Routledge and Kegan Paul, London, 1953, pp. 159–174) has an acute analysis of the term 'person' as applied to God. Broad observes that we use the term of a substance if it fulfils the following conditions: (1) It must think, feel, will etc. (2) Its various contemporary states must have that peculiar kind of unity which we express by saying that they 'together make up a single total of mind'. (3) Its successive total states must have that peculiar kind of unity with each other which we express by saying that they are 'so many different stages in the history of a single mind'. (4) These two kinds of unity must be recognised by itself, and not only by some external observer, i.e. it must also know that it is a mind

Thus we call a sane grown man a 'person' but we refuse to call any inanimate object, such as a chair, a 'person' and we also refuse to call a cat, a dog or a horse a 'person'. When Theists speak of God as a 'Person' then they mean that He is *not less* a Being than one in whom these conditions are fulfilled. But they go on to say that He is *more* than a person. A good statement of the Theistic position in this matter is that of Hastings Rashdall ('Philosophy and Religion', London, 1914, p. 56) : 'If we are justified in thinking of God after the analogy of the highest existence within our knowledge, we had better call Him a Person. The word is no doubt inadequate to the reality, as is all the language we can employ about God; but it is at least more adequate than the terms employed by those who scruple to speak of God as a Person. It is at least more adequate and more intelligent than to speak of Him as a force, a substance, a "something not ourselves which makes for righteousness'. *Things* do not "make for righteousness"; and in using the term Person we shall at least make it clear that we do not think of Him as a "thing", or a collection of things, or a vague substratum of things, or even a mere totality of minds like our own'.

[5]

THE FOURTH PRINCIPLE

God is Eternal

$\mathbf{M}$AIMONIDES' fourth principle (Abelson's translation) is: 'The Fourth Principle of Faith. The priority of God. This means that the unity whom we have described is first in the absolute sense. No existent thing outside Him is primary in relation to Him. The proofs of this in the Scriptures are numerous. This fourth principle is indicated by the phrase: "The eternal God is a refuge" (Deut. xxxiii. 27)'.

In the ' 'Ani Ma'amin' formulation the fourth principle is: 'I believe with perfect faith that the Creator, blessed be His name, is the first and the last'. The Yigdal formula is: 'He was before anything that hath been created – even the first: but His existence had no beginning'.

Friedländer thus states the fourth principle: 'The next property we declare of God in the Creed is the eternity of God. As He is the cause of everything in existence, and requires no cause for His existence, and as it is impossible to separate the idea of existence from the idea of God, it follows that God is always in existence, and that neither beginning nor end can be fixed to His existence'.

In the ancient world Plato and Aristotle held differing views on the creation of the world. Plato was of the opinion that the world was created by God but that creation out of nothing – creatio ex nihilo – is impossible even for God and he, therefore, postulates that God created the world out of a hylic substance. In this view the world had a beginning in time and time itself is a creation of God but the world will have no end. Aristotle, on the other hand, rejects the whole notion of creation. For Aristotle the world is eternal and co-existent with God but is dependent on God who is its Final Cause. This whole question was a fundamental one in mediaeval Jewish philosophy. The traditional Jewish view as recorded in the Bible and the Rabbinic literature appears to be at variance with both Plato and Aristotle. In the Jewish sources God alone is eternal and the world is His creation. Maimonides devotes a considerable section of his 'Guide' to the elucidation of this problem. Briefly stated, Maimonides' view is that of Plato with one very important qualification. For Maimonides there was no hylic substance out of which God created the world. *Creatio ex nihilo* has to be accepted literally. The world and time are both creations out of nothing by God. But Maimonides agrees with Plato that once time has been created the world will endure endlessly in time. The world had a beginning but it will have no end.

Maimonides writes ('Guide', Friedlander's trans. II, 13, pp. 171–172): 'In the beginning God alone existed and nothing else; neither angels nor spheres, nor the things that are contained within the spheres existed. He then produced from nothing all existing things such as they are, by His will and desire. Even time itself is among the things created; for time depends on motion, i.e. on an accident in things which move, and the things upon whose motion time depends are themselves created beings, which have passed from non-existence into existence. We say that God *existed* before the creation of the Universe, although the verb *existed* appears to imply the notion of time; we also believe that He existed an infinite space of time before the Universe was created; but in these cases we do not mean time in its true sense. We only use the term to signify something analogous or similar to time . . . We consider time a thing created; it comes into existence in the same manner as other accidents, and the substances which form the substratum for the accidents. For this reason, viz., because time belongs to the things created, it cannot be said that God produced the Universe *in the beginning*'.

In the same portion of his great work Maimonides argues that the theory of a future destruction of the Universe is not part of the religious belief taught in the Bible. On the contrary, Scripture teaching is in favour of the indestructibility of the Universe and those passages in the Bible which appear to suggest the opposite view have to be interpreted to accord with the correct belief that the Universe is indestructible. (*V.* 'Guide' II, 27–29, pp. 201–212). Since the world owes its existence to the will of God, argues Maimonides, there is no reason to suppose that God wills to destroy the Universe in the future, any more than He wills to destroy individual souls. The belief in the indestructibility of the Universe is not, of course, an article of faith. Anyone who believes that God will one day destroy His Universe is at liberty to do so since various Scriptural passages, at a superficial reading, appear to lend support to this thesis, but Maimonides is himself convinced that the Bible really teaches the indestructibility of the Universe. Maimonides goes on to quote verses such as: 'He laid the foundations of the earth, that it should not be moved for ever' (Ps. civ. 5) in support of his theory. Similarly, in the book of Ecclesiastes we read: 'Whatsoever God doeth it shall be for ever; nothing can be put to it, nor anything taken away from it' (Eccl. iii. 14). Since the world is God's creation out of nothing and time, too, is His creation, the opening verse of Genesis must not be taken to mean 'In the beginning'. The true explanation of the verse, according to Maimonides, is: 'In creating a principle (*be-reshith*) God created the beings above and the things below'. The term '*bara*' is used of the creation of the heavens and the earth because this term implies '*creatio ex nihilo*' ('Guide', II, 30 end, Friedländer, p. 218).

Eternity in philosophical thought has been given two distinct meanings. The first is that of endless duration in time. If this is what is meant by God's eternity, the meaning is that He existed always and will always exist. Maimonides, as we have seen, does not quite see it in this way. He speaks of time itself as a creation. But, on the other hand, he thinks of the Universe lasting for ever *in time*, the idea being, evidently, that once time has been created it endures for ever. This gives rise to various philosophical difficulties not least of which is to reconcile the notion of a 'time' before time was created with that of endless duration in time. In other words the idea developed by many thinkers, the mystics in particular, that God is outside the time process altogether, is touched upon by Maimonides but is not developed fully by him.

The classical Jewish expression of God as the eternal in time is found in the popular Synagogal hymn '*Adon 'Olam*:

> *'He is Lord of the universe, who reigned ere any*
> *creature yet was formed:*
> *At the time when all things were made by His desire,*
> *then was His name proclaimed King.*
> *And after all things shall have had an end,*
> *He alone, the dreaded one, shall reign;*
> *Who was, who is, and who will be in glory'.*

The mind reels at the thought of time without end. We all allow our minds to dwell occasionally on this thought only to recoil with a kind of horror – on and on and on and yet still no end! I once heard a *Maggid* preaching on this view of eternity. He gave the illustration of a huge mountain formed entirely of mustardseeds. Imagine now, he said, a bird coming once every million years and taking one grain of mustardseed and think how long it would take before the whole mountain had been removed, and this would still not be eternity. Imagine further, he said, that the whole vastness of time represented by the mountain were itself as a 'mustardseed' in an immensely bigger mountain and think of the enormous distance of time this would represent, and you would be as far from eternity as ever. Go on in this way *ad infinitum* and eternity would still not have been reached.

The other view of eternity sees it as outside the time process altogether. In this view God's eternity does not mean only that He lives for ever, in the sense of enduring through endless time, but that He is outside time, that time itself, as Maimonides says, is God's creation. God, in this view, surveys the whole of time as but a 'moment'. He inhabits, as it were, what the mystics are fond of calling 'the Eternal Now'. It is true that we find this concept impossible to grasp but the idea of endless temporal duration is similarly beyond all our comprehension. Some thinkers have tried to convey the idea by asking us to imagine two-dimensional beings, inhabiting a world in which there is only length and breadth but no height. The philosophers among such beings might appreciate that there might well be a three-dimensional world but having no conception of height they would be obliged to speak of that world, if they spoke of it at all, in terms of either length or breadth. They would refer gropingly to a different kind of 'length' or 'breadth' just as

Maimonides speaks of a different kind of 'time' before time
was created. Similarly, it is argued, our three-dimensional
world may be only a very small part of a world of more dimensions and so far as God is concerned the whole of our time is
seen at once.

> 'I saw Eternity the other night,
> Like a great ring of pure and endless light,
>   All calm, as it was bright;
> And round beneath it, Time in hours, days, years,
>   Driv'n by the spheres
> Like a vast shadow mov'd; in which the world
>   And all her train were hurl'd'.

(Vaughan)

A remarkable attempt at describing God's eternity on these
lines was made by the Hasidic teacher Nahman of Bratzlav
(1772–1811). Nahman ('Liqqute Moharan', Ostrog, 1821,
Part II, 61) says: 'God is higher than time, as is known.
This matter is truly marvellous and utterly incomprehensible.
It is impossible for the human intellect to grasp such an idea.
Know, however, that time is, in the main, the product of
ignorance, that is to say, time appears to us as real because our
intellect is so small. The greater the intellect the smaller and
more insignificant time becomes. Take, for instance, a dream.
Here the intellect is dormant and the imaginative faculty
alone functions. In the dream it is possible for seventy years to
pass by in a quarter of an hour. In the dream it seems as if a
great space of time has elapsed but in reality only a very short
time has passed. On awakening after a dream one sees that
the whole seventy year period of the dream occupied in reality
but a minute fraction of time. This is because man's intellect has
been restored to him in his waking life and, so far as his intellect
is concerned, the whole seventy year period of the dream is
no more than a quarter of an hour . . . There is a Mind so
elevated that the whole of time is counted as nought, for that
Mind is so great that for it the whole of time is as nothing
whatsoever. Just as the seventy years which pass in the dream
are, so far as we are concerned, no more than a quarter of an
hour in reality, as we have seen, so it is with regard to that
Mind, which is so far above mind that time has no existence

for it whatsoever'. Schneor Zalman of Liady similarly states
(*Tanya'*, Vilna, 1930, *'Sha'ar Ha-Yihud We-Ha-'Emunah'*,
Chapter VII, pp. 162 f.) that God is 'higher' than Space and
Time although He is found in Space and Time. The Tetragrammaton, writes this author, which comes from a root meaning 'to be', refers to this aspect of the Deity – 'He was, is, and
will be, all at once' – the term used is 'in one *rega'*', 'one
moment', reminding us of the 'Eternal Now'. Of course these
ideas are ancient. They occupy an important place, particularly,
in Neo-Platonic philosophy. We find Boethius, for instance,
saying: 'Since God hath always an eternal and present state,
His knowledge, surpassing time's notions, remaineth in the
simplicity of His presence and, comprehending the infinite of
what is past and to come, considereth all things as though they
were in the act of being accomplished'.

*   *   *

EXCURSUS

The mediaeval Jewish Bible commentators discuss the meaning
of the Hebrew *'bara'*, 'created' in Gen. i. 1. Does it suggest *creatio
ex nihilo? V.* the important article by Emil G. Hirsch in JE, Vol. IV,
pp. 336–9. Nahmanides in his first comment to Gen. i. 1 states that
one who does not believe in *creatio ex nihilo* is a heretic, one who
denies the *Torah.* The very early Synagogal hymn – *'Barukh She-
'Amar'* – begins: 'Blessed be He who spake, and the world existed:
blessed be He: blessed be He who was the Maker of the world
in the beginning' (Singer's Prayer Book, p. 16). The term *'bara'*
certainly is used only for 'the production of something fundamentally
new, by the exercise of a sovereign originative power, altogether
transcending that possessed by man' (Driver: 'The Book of
Genesis', Westminster Commentaries, 1954, p. 3). *Cf.* T. H.
Robinson's acute observation in 'The Old Testament and Modern
Study', ed. H. H. Rowley, Oxford, Clarendon Press, p. 351: 'On
the one hand we have a dignified, philosophical, scientific, almost
evolutionary statement, in which the divine act of "creation", i.e.
the introduction of a totally new factor which cannot be explained by
anything earlier, occurs only at three crucial points, the provision of
sheer matter, the introduction of animal life, and the formation
of that personality which man shares only with God Himself.
What follows is a simple story in which God models the objects of
creation as a potter fashions his vessels of clay. Many people, it is
true, succeed in harmonizing the two, but to others the only valid

explanation of the facts seems to be that the one is addressed to a highly "sophisticated" audience, while the other is intended for hearers who are still in the intellectual nursery. But (and this is what matters) both insist that the physical universe and man himself are directly and expressly made by God; He is the author of all being other than His own, and He is eternal and self-existent. That truth is as valid today as it was when the Genesis stories were first told, though for its own sake the modern mind might need to have it expressed in terms which did not correspond to those either of Gen. i or Gen. ii.' On current scientific theories and their relation to philosophical thinking about creation *v.* Milton K. Munitz: 'Space, Time and Creation', The Free Press, Glencoe, Illinois, 1957. The idea of cycles of time, i.e. that the world passes through a cycle again and again is known, of course, in Qabbalistic thought though, on the whole, this is very unconventional from the standpoint of 'normative' Judaism, *v.* especially the essays in 'Man and Time – Papers From the Eranos Yearbooks', Routledge & Kegan Paul, London, 1958, and the treatment of this theme with quotations from Qabbalistic sources in Israel Lipshütz's '*Tiphereth Yisrael*', the famous Commentary to the *Mishnah*, '*Derush 'Or Ha-Hayyim*', printed at the end of the Order *Neziqin*, p. 281. A good though rather unhistorical account of Rabbinic views on Time & Eternity is 'The Concept of Time in Rabbinic Literature' (Heb.) by M. M. Kasher in '*Talpioth*', Vol. V, 1952, pp. 799–827.

*   *   *

Implied in the fourth article of faith is the belief that God is infinite. Various philosophies of God as a finite being have been put forward throughout the ages but they do not accord with the traditional Theist view of Judaism. However, it is necessary to discuss these theories as well as the doctrine of an emergent Deity.

Samuel Alexander ('Space, Time and Deity', Macmillan, London, 1920, Vol. I and II) is the great representative of the view that God is always in the process of evolving. Alexander's views are very difficult and they are shared by very few thinkers today but an examination of them is very worthwhile since it helps to throw light on important questions connected with the basic idea of the fourth article of faith – that the God of Judaism is an eternal and self-existent Being who is the Maker of the universe and, in the words of Scripture, the Possessor of heaven and earth.

According to Alexander, an empirical approach to the meaning of Deity demands first that we recognise a quality, which he calls that of deity (with a small 'd'). This quality is present in man's experience of the universe. The highest quality so far produced in Time is mind or consciousness. But in Space-Time there is a *nisus*, a striving, which has borne its creatures forward through matter and life to mind and, since Time is infinite, will not stop there. There is always a next higher empirical quality to the highest we know and this is the quality of deity. When this will have been attained there will be a next higher quality to that, which in turn will be deity. Deity as a quality is thus constantly emerging. Alexander claims that something of this kind is behind the belief in angels, i.e. beings higher than mind who can contemplate mind in the same way as mind contemplates life and lower levels of existence. In Alexander's own words: 'Deity is thus the next higher empirical quality to mind, which the universe is engaged in bringing to birth. That the universe is pregnant with such a quality we are speculatively assured. What that quality is we cannot know; for we can neither enjoy nor still less contemplate it. Our human altars are still raised to the unknown God. If we could know what deity is, how it feels to be divine, we should first have to become as gods. What we know of it is but its relation to the other empirical qualities which precede it in time. Its nature we cannot penetrate'. Religious emotion, which undeniably exists and which must have a real object just as hunger has food as its object, is, on this view, our going out or striving towards something higher than ourselves, namely towards the quality of deity. God is, then, in Alexander's definition, 'the infinite world with its *nisus* towards deity, or, to adapt a phrase of Leibnitz, as big as, or in travail with deity'.

Alexander recognises that his God is not the God of traditional Theism. Traditional Theism, he says, makes appeal to the personal or egotistic side of the religious consciousness, the feeling that in surrender the worshipper still retains his individuality. This is the strength of Theism. Its weakness, on the other hand, according to Alexander, is that if God's acts are those of His creatures how can He also lead a separate existence from them? But to this difficulty Theism replies by reminding us that man cannot know the nature of God. The real objection to Alexander's emergent Deity is the objection noted earlier, in our discussion of the third principle, to the non-personal or naturalistic interpretation of God. God as a 'person' can be worshipped. It is difficult to see how the emergent Deity of Alexander really satisfies that very religious emotion on which his argument is based.

Alexander claims, further, that on his view alone the problem of pain is rendered intelligible. On the traditional Theistic view, in which God precedes the world and all things are determined by His will, why should a benevolent being not take a course which spares His creatures pain, why did He not plan it differently from the beginning? But, says Alexander, if God is the outcome of human striving, as in his system, then both the striving and the suffering acquire meaning. 'It is not God then who allows the struggle, but the struggle which is to determine, it may not be at once but in the end, what deity is to be'. The problem of pain is, indeed, a torment for the traditional Theist but here again the traditional replies, some of which have been stated earlier, are not to be brushed aside. It is worth noting that in Jewish teaching there is a sense in which it can be said that man by his deeds makes God real, but this has to be understood as making Him real *for men*, not actually *making Him*, as in Alexander's system. God, in Jewish teaching, exists, of course, independently of man (*v.* the discussion on this theme in my book 'Jewish Values', Vallentine, Mitchell, London, 1960, Chapter V: 'The Sanctification of the Name', pp. 74–85).

The real issue here, on the empirical level, is whether Alexander's conception really does justice to the religious emotion by which he himself arrives at his conception. Does his conception justify prayer, for instance? Alexander claims that it does: 'Nor is it otherwise than natural that men so engaged should send up their prayers to a God whom they suppose to be already in being and to favour their particular ideals. They embody the forecast of what they hope in a present form. The God they pray to is the God to whose nature they contribute, but the call of their ideal is the call of the universe as a whole as it appears to them'. This is precisely the question. Can one really pray to a God to whose nature one contributes or respond, *in prayer*, to the call of the universe as a whole?

Alexander finally offers a 'brief index' to his great book. The sentences on his conception of Deity read: 'In the hierarchy of qualities the next higher quality to the highest attained is deity. God is the whole universe engaged in process towards the emergence of this new quality, and religion is the sentiment in us that we are drawn towards him, and caught in the movement of the world to a higher level of existence'. Profound though this idea is it is emphatically not the view of Judaism and its rejection is implied in the fourth article of the faith we are here considering.

Alexander's view is that of emergent Deity. Another thinker of note in modern times whose ideas are germinal, even though unacceptable so far as traditional Jewish Theism is concerned, is Edgar Sheffield Brightman. Brightman believes in a personal God and in this he belongs in the complete line of traditional Theism. He differs from the latter in following Plato and similar thinkers who conceive of God as finite rather than infinite, of Him as possessing great but not unlimited power.

For Brightman the problem of evil prevents us from accepting the notion of God as omnipotent. It is not so much the question of why the righteous suffer which bothers him, for here traditional Theism has put forward more or less convincing explanations. But there is an element of irrationality about evil, the meaningless phenomenon of a mongoloid child, for instance. Brightman has coined an expression to describe such meaningless suffering. This is the term 'dysteleological surd'. A surd in mathematics is an irrational number, a number which neither makes sense within itself nor makes sense in terms of other numbers. In God's creation, too, according to Brightman, there are features incapable of being explained rationally. Although there is evidence of design in the universe, evidence of teleology, there are factors which do not yield to any kind of teleological explanation. These are 'dysteleological surds'. Their existence can only be explained, according to Brightman, if we think of God as an immensely good and powerful Being who is not responsible for *everything* in the universe but has to cope with either the limitations of His own being or the limitations of the material with which He works. These limitations Brightman calls *The Given*. *The Given* is 'there', yielding to no

rational explanation. On this view God Himself is at constant
war with evil which is not of His making and man 'helps' God in
the struggle for the good. We saw that in Alexander's opinion
the practices of religion such as prayer are difficult to defend.
Not so in Brightman's view. On the contrary, the whole
human struggle, with its hopes, fears and prayers, assumes
tremendous dramatic significance because man is truly a 'co-
worker' with God and man truly helps God to achieve His
purpose. The sense of the dramatic is heightened, in Brightman's view, because, unlike in conventional Theism, the outcome of the struggle is undetermined beforehand. God cannot
guarantee that He will 'win out' in the struggle against evil
but He has created man to help Him 'win out'.

Brightman thinks that unless we modify in some measure
the idea of God's complete unity and inner bliss we must
limit God's relations with the actual world, since it is clear
that in the world of experience there is disunity, evil, and human
struggle against evil. He claims that the superficial and more
blindly optimistic of religious thinkers have never been able
to tolerate the thought of any compromise of the absolute
unity of the divine nature and yet there have been profound
minds which, though making the unity of God their central
belief, have conceived of that unity in such a way as to provide
for contrasts within the life of God. The older Theistic reply
to the problem of evil, that evil comes either from man's
freedom of choice or is a disguised good, strikes Brightman
as superficial, although he says that the fact of evil being due,
in some measure, to man's freedom is confirmed in experience.
The benevolence of God is derived from experience whereas
the idea of His omnipotence is derived from abstract thought.
Why not, therefore, reject this idea in favour of one which
tallies with experience to a far greater degree? Because of
these and similar objections to the traditional Theistic view
Brightman expresses his own theory as follows: 'God is a
conscious Person of perfect good will. He is the source of all
value and so is worthy of worship and devotion. He is the
creator of all other persons and gives them the power of free
choice. Therefore his purpose controls the outcome of the
universe. His purpose and his nature must be inferred from
the way in which experience reveals them, namely, as being

gradually attained through effort, difficulty and suffering.
Hence there is in God's very nature something which makes
the effort and pain of life necessary. There is within him, in
addition to his reason and his active creative will, a passive
element which enters into every one of his conscious states,
as sensation, instinct, and impulse enter into ours, and constitutes a problem for him. This element we call *The Given*.
The evils of life and the delays in the attainment of value,
insofar as they come from God and not from human freedom,
are thus due to his nature, yet not wholly to his deliberate
choice. His will and reason acting on *The Given* produce
the world and achieve value in it'.

The difficulty of Brightman's view lies in the concept of
The Given. If God is to give meaning to existence it is hard
to see how the postulate of an irrational factor either in God or
apart from Him, which frustrates His will and which He is
powerless to hinder, can do anything but obscure life's meaning-
fulness. In reality the idea of *The Given* is the old Dualism,
against which Judaism set its face, in a modern guise. We have
noted earlier, in our discussion of the problem of evil, that
certain qualifications in the term 'omnipotence', as applied
to God, are required. But Brightman goes a good deal further
in treating God as finite and although ideas not too far removed
from the conception are found here and there in Jewish thought
it remains true that the doctrine of traditional Jewish Theism
is utterly opposed to the notion of a finite God.

*   *   *

EXCURSUS

On the literary level the great exponent of an 'emergent' doctrine
of Deity is, of course, George Bernard Shaw, particularly in 'Back
to Methuselah'. *Cf.* William K. Wright: 'A Student's Philosophy
of Religion', rev. ed., Macmillan, New York, 1950, pp. 362 f. W. R.
Matthews: 'The Purpose of God', Nisbet, London, 1935, p. 37,
rightly says that Professor Alexander's system leaves fundamental
problems unsolved and questions unanswered, for instance, why
the marvellous potentialities of which Alexander speaks should
reside in the simplest 'stuff'. 'We are given description but not
explanation'. The same author writes (p. 89): 'The newer conceptions of evolution which have transcended the merely mechanical
point of view have been fertile in speculative philosophies of nature

which recognise a certain teleological character in the universe but refuse to attribute that character to Creative Mind. In many forms this thought is presented to us: that a "direction in evolution" may be the product of the process itself; or that it may be the working of a Life Force which seeks an aim which it does not know'. *Cf.* the whole critique, pp. 89–96, and Lillith's famous speech at the end of 'Back to Methuselah' in which she says: 'Sufficient that there is a Beyond'. How can a blind force work for a 'beyond'? Brightman's views are to be found in his 'The Problem of God', Abingdon Press, New York, 1930, and 'A Philosophy of Religion', Skeffington, London, 1940, Chapter X, 'Is God Finite?', pp. 170–180. A short summary with extracts and a critique is found in Charles Hartshorne and William L. Reese: 'Philosophers Speak of God', University of Chicago Press, 1953, pp. 358–364. *Cf.* Wright's account of Brightman's views, *op. cit.*, pp. 394–401, and the account of Brightman's and other theories of a 'finite' God, particularly that of Whitehead, in James Collins: 'God in Modern Philosophy', Routledge and Kegan Paul, London, 1960, pp. 315–324. One of the earliest modern thinkers to put forward the theory of a 'finite' God was John Stuart Mill in 'Three Essays on Religion', Longmans, Green, London, 1874. Mill holds that the very argument from design supports this conclusion since an omnipotent Creator would not require to overcome difficulties but would create without them. The very notion of a plan or purpose, according to Mill, suggests that God has to 'devise' ways and means of accomplishing His purpose and He cannot therefore be omnipotent. From the traditional Theistic position it can be argued that God 'designs' the universe so that His creatures might see the evidence of His wisdom and that such design is for their benefit and not because of His needs or limitations. *Cf.* an early Rabbinic statement of a similar point of view in *'Abhoth*, V. 1: 'With ten Sayings the world was created. What does this teach us? Could it not have been created with one Saying? It is to make known the punishment that will befall the wicked who destroy the world that was created with ten Sayings, as well as the goodly reward that will be bestowed upon the righteous who preserve the world that was created with ten Sayings'. A useful summary of the whole argument for and against the idea of a 'finite' God is David Elton Trueblood's in his 'Philosophy of Religion', Rokcliff, London, 1957, pp. 240–243. Trueblood effectively summarises five specific religious values which finitism safeguards:

(*a*) There is greater assurance of divine sympathy and love.
(*b*) There is something awe-inspiring about the magnificent cosmic struggle.

(c) Finitism furnishes incentives to co-operative endeavour.

(d) Belief in a finite God affords grounds for belief in cosmic advance.

(e) It is more natural to pray to a finite God who may be moved by our infirmities.

However, Trueblood observes that, for all this, the weight of opinion in philosophical theology is critical of the doctrine of divine finitude. The doctrine is opposed by all Roman Catholic thinkers, all the leaders of Islam, and many influential Protestant and Jewish thinkers. The basic objection to the idea is that a finite God would not be God at all, just as a slightly flat circle would not be a circle at all. Milton Steinberg: 'Anatomy of Faith', ed. with an Introduction by Arthur A. Cohen, Harcourt, Brace, New York, 1960, pp. 267 f. takes issue with most theories of a non-absolute God but inclines towards the acceptance of Brightman's principle of the surd. Steinberg says: 'Having come to religion from philosophy, I now feel, if it does not sound unduly arrogant, that I have religiously outgrown philosophy. The kind of God with which one ends in Spinoza, Hegel, or even Whitehead may be suggestive and illuminating for the religious man, but in itself is of no particular religious use'. Naturally if one believed in a primordial 'stuff' out of which God created the world this would contain something of Brightman's *The Given*, but practically all the great mediaeval Jewish thinkers believe in *creatio ex nihilo*. The exception is Levi ben Gershon (Gersonides) in his *'Milhamoth 'Adonai'*, who believes that there existed from eternity inert undetermined matter, devoid of form and attribute, upon which God, at a given moment, bestowed essence, form, motion and life. He endeavours to show that his theory agrees with the account in Genesis. For this and similar unconventional theories Gersonides' work was frequently said to be heretical, *v.* JE, Vol. VIII, p. 31 f., Isaac Husik: 'A History of Mediaeval Jewish Philosophy', Jewish Publication Society and Meridian Books, New York, 1958, p. 352 f. and S. Bernfeld: *'Da'ath 'Elohim'*, Warsaw, 1899, Book III, Chapter 5, pp. 417–442.

[6]

THE FIFTH PRINCIPLE
God Alone is to be Worshipped

MAIMONIDES' (Abelson's trans.) states the fifth principle as follows: '*The Fifth Principle of Faith.* That it is He (be He exalted!) who must be worshipped, aggrandized, and made known by His greatness and the obedience shown to Him. This must not be done to any existing beings lower than He – not to the angels nor the spheres nor the elements, nor the things which are compounded from them. For these are all fashioned in accordance with the works they are intended to perform. They have no judgment or free-will, but only a love for Him (be He exalted!). Let us adopt no mediators to enable ourselves to draw near unto God, but let the thoughts be directed to Him, and turned away from whatsoever is below Him. The fifth principle is a prohibition of idolatry. The greater part of the *Torah* is taken up with the prohibition of idol-worship'.

The fifth principle in the ' *'Ani Ma'amin'* formulation reads: 'I believe with perfect faith that to the Creator, blessed be His name, and to Him alone it is right to pray, and that it is not right to pray to any being besides Him'. The *Yigdal* formulation has it: 'Behold He is the Lord of the universe: to every creature He teacheth His greatness and His sovereignty'.

Friedländer expresses the fifth principle in this way. 'After having declared our faith in God as the sole Ruler of the universe, who is One, incorporeal and eternal, we proclaim Him as our Supreme Master, who alone is capable of granting our petitions. All existing things are under His control; all forces in nature only work at His will and by His command. No other being possesses the power and independence to fulfil our wishes of its own accord, if it were approached by us with our prayers. It is, therefore, to Him alone that we can reasonably address our petitions, and in doing so we have confidence

F   149

in the efficacy of our prayers, for "the Lord is nigh to all those who call upon Him, to all who call upon Him in truth" (Ps. cxlv. 18)'.

Werblowsky's lengthy summary of the fifth principle reads: '*The Obligation to worship God alone.* This article actually embodies the practical corollary of monotheism – the duty to serve God and God alone. It not only excludes other divinities (already ruled out by the denial of their existence in art. 2) but forbids the worship of or even appeal to other powers, forces and intermediaries. The few instances in the liturgy in which angels are addressed and requested to bring our prayers before the throne of the Almighty have given rise to controversy. Thinkers like *Bahya* even denied the existence of intermediaries or "secondary causes" '.

'In its simple and popular formulation the article merely states that God is the only object of prayer. It does not say anything about the nature, meaning, value or efficiency of prayer. Here again all sorts of views have been held, varying with the philosophical outlook and religious temperament of the authors concerned. The efficacy of petitionary prayer is usually taken for granted, in spite of the serious theological problems which it raises. Rabbinic tradition sees in prayer a divine *Mitzwah* or commandment: God desires man to express his love of him, dependence on him and wish to commune with him in this form. In every prayer, then, there is the purest and most concentrated expression of what life as a whole, understood as the service of God, should signify. The Rabbis deduced the duty of daily prayer from the more generalized Biblical injunction "to serve him with all thine heart". "Which is the service of the heart?" they ask, and reply: "This is prayer". The order and character of prayer was regulated by the Rabbis so as to include praise, thanksgiving and petition. Both the proportion of these elements and their detailed contents varied, with the individual worshipper, though for public worship a unified fixed liturgy developed. Jewish tradition insists on the value of public worship and, in fact, full liturgical proceedings are only possible in the presence of the "Congregation of Israel" which must be represented by a quorum of at least ten adult males. The Qabbalists consider prayer as the occasion of the most intense mystical meditation;

in their inner life, "serving god" signified the mystical intention which turned every prayer or religious performance into a redemptive act. Later, modernist writers occasionally explained the meaning of prayer as "self-examination" and the like; in the place of the dialogue with God they put an edifying monologue'.

The fifth article of faith actually contains three ideas: (1) That God is to be worshipped. (2) That God is not to be worshipped through an intermediary. (3) That no other being, apart from God, is to be worshipped. A discussion of the fifth article ought to consider each of these propositions.

(1) *God is to be worshipped.*

Issac Bashevis Singer tells of a Hasidic Jew he knew in his youth who was wont to say: 'It is good to be a Jew. What greater pleasure can there be than being a Jew? I'll give up all theatres, all riches, all delicacies for one *Mincha* prayer, for one chapter of Psalms, one *Asher Yatzar*! If a person were to offer me all the gold in the world, all the palaces and forttresses and soldiers and Cossacks, on condition that I skip one blessing, I would laugh in his face. These are vanity, trifles, not worth an empty egg-shell. But when I recite the blessing: "By whose word all things exist", I feel renewed strength in my very bones. Just think of it: "Blessed art Thou, O Lord our God, King of the Universe, by Whose word all things exist". All things, all! The heavens, the earth, I, you, even – forgive the comparison – the dog in the street. All were created by Him, the Creator, and to us He gave the power to praise Him. Is not this sufficient earthly pleasure?' ('Commentary', April, 1962, p. 302). Singer pokes gentle fun at his elderly hero but anyone acquainted with Eastern European Jews of the old school, whether *Hasidim* or their opponents, knows that for very many of them the worship of God through the performance of His commandments was, in truth, the greatest joy of their lives. Another anecdote with the same theme tells of an elderly Jewish woman who complained to Rabbi Hertzog, the late Chief Rabbi of Israel, that her sons were not observant Jews, they did not keep the *mitzwoth*. The Rabbi, wishing to console the poor woman, told her that her sons had behaved with such bravery in the War of Liberation that, he assured her, they would have a share in the Life to Come. 'Rabbi', the old lady replied, 'it is not their Life to Come I am concerned about. It is this life I want them to enjoy, and how can life be enjoyed without the *mitzwoth*?'

These observations are not irrelevant to the theme of worship. The person who approaches the matter from the outside finds the whole conception of worship strange, even ludicrous. Is worship for God's benefit or for man's? To reply that it is for man's benefit and to attempt an evaluation of ritual in this light, inevitably results in absurdity. Great names in the past have lent the power of their authority to an interpretation of the dietary laws, for example, as an aid to good health, but if the matter is left at that the inadequacy of the explanation becomes apparent. For the very concept of worship suggests man's *service* of the Creator, man's giving of himself for the sake of Heaven. If all the details of divine worship are so interpreted that they are seen to have as their sole purpose the enrichment of human life then the man who carries them out is a self-worshipper, or, at best, a worshipper of human society, rather than a worshipper of God. If, on the other hand, worship is for God's sake the obvious theological difficulty arises, how can God be said to need man's worship? The dilemma is insoluble for one who sees it from the outside. But for the Jews, like those we have mentioned, who see it all from within, who *live* by the *Torah* and in the performance of the *mitzwoth*, the difficulty is unreal. For them there is no doubt that worship is for God's sake in the sense that it is a giving of the self to the Creator. Much of it is, indeed, 'useless' so far as man is concerned. Even where worship does have the effect of enriching man's life, either materially or mentally, such enrichment is a by-product, not an aim. But the giving of the self in worship of the Highest is in itself the greatest enrichment of the human personality there is. God wants us to worship Him because man can have no higher privilege than the opportunity to reach out towards the Infinite. As Evelyn Underhill ('Worship', Nisbet, London, 1958, p. 5) finely puts it: 'It is true that from first to last self-regarding elements are mixed with human worship; but these are no real part of it. Not man's needs and wishes, but

God's presence and incitement, first invoke it. As it rises towards purity and leaves egotistic piety behind, He becomes more and more the only Fact of existence, the one Reality; and the very meaning of Creation is seen to be an act of worship, a devoted proclamation of the splendour, the wonder, and the beauty of God. In this great *Sanctus*, all things justify their being and have their place. God alone matters, God alone Is – creation only matters because of Him'.

The question we are considering, whether worship is for God's sake or for man's, was answered by the Qabbalists according to their frequently occurring distinction between God as He is in Himself – *'En Soph* – and God in His manifestations, in His *Sephiroth*, the means by which He reveals Himself to others. We have touched on this Qabbalistic doctrine earlier. So far as our present theme is concerned, the Qabbalistic teaching is that while *'En Soph* cannot be said to *need* human worship, the harmony of the Sephirotic world depends, in some measure at least, on the deeds of men. If man leads a virtuous life he draws down the divine influence from above, producing harmony and balance in the whole of God's creation. The *Shekhinah*, the Divine Presence of God, exiled from her source, is restored to her rightful place and peace reigns in all worlds. If man leads a vicious life his evil deeds help to promote an imbalance in the Sephirotic world. The *Shekhinah* remains in exile and the divine grace cannot flow. The whole of God's creation suffers as a result and the divine purpose is frustrated. Thus man is placed at the centre of the cosmic drama. Every evil deed on earth is a hindrance to redemption. Every good deed paves the way for the coming of the Messiah. When the work of reclaiming the 'divine sparks', which fell into all things at the beginning of creation, is completed, redemption will come and the exile of the *Shekhinah* will be ended. All this has been dubbed 'magical' by critics of the *Qabbalah* and there is much substance in the critique. For all that there is grandeur in the idea that somehow man's deeds really 'help' God and that worship is truly for God's sake, that He might fulfil His purpose.

The above ideas are put forward in all the great classical Qabbalistic works and are usefully summarised in Isaiah Horowitz's (c. 1555–1628) *'Shene Luhoth Ha-Berith'*, called after its initial letters, *Shelah* or 'The Holy *Shelah*', a gigantic compendium of Rabbinic and Qabbalistic teachings. The *Shelah* deals with our theme in the section of the work near the beginning known as the 'Ten Words' – ' '*Asarah Ma'-amaroth*'. These are principles of divine worship of which the fourth is entitled 'Worship for the needs of the Most High, for the sake of God'. Horowitz begins by describing the purpose of man's creation. This was that man might serve God. When Adam and his descendants sinned God chose the Patriarchs and sent their offspring into Egypt, the house of bondage, that they might there learn the bitter lesson of human bondage and thereby become equipped to serve God. Horowitz defines his conception of 'worship for the needs of the Most High' to mean that it is not enough for man to carry out God's precepts with joy and delight. In addition, he must intend to bring about the harmony in the upper worlds which his deeds can help to promote, for this is the tremendous power given to man. When harmony prevails in the upper worlds God's name is perfected and as a result all worlds become perfected and enjoy peace and blessing. God then rejoices in His creation and His purpose is fulfilled since He created all things for His glory and brought into being creatures capable of recognising His majesty. Then the greatest blessing will be theirs for such is the will of the Source of all goodness. The sinner, on the other hand, brings about a 'flaw' – *pegam* – in the upper worlds through each sin he commits with the result that God's name is imperfect, His blessing withheld and His purpose frustrated. 'The true worshipper does not serve God for his own sake but because God needs his worship for the perfection of His name. Such a worshipper never departs from God's service, day and night; he neither slumbers nor sleeps. He never ceases from observing the severe precepts and the light, the Biblical and the Rabbinic, as well as later enactments of the Sages and the "fences" around the Law, and he takes care against sinning even unwittingly since atonement is required even for an unwitting sin'. The followers of the *Qabbalah*, particularly the *Hasidim*, still stress ideas of this kind, offering their prayers and performing the precepts of the *Torah* in firm belief that these acts of man have cosmic significance and satisfy, as it were, the need of God to be loved and worshipped by man so that His goodness and grace might flow through all the worlds. But such views, though popular in Qabbalistic circles, are certainly unconventional. Usually Judaism prefers to speak of man's need to worship rather than God's need of man's worship. But, as we have noted, the problem is really far too complicated to permit of a simple division into man's needs and the 'needs' of God. God wants man to worship Him because only in this way can man reach out to the divine, be aware of God's presence and His majesty, and become God-like.

Worship, in Judaism, is expressed in three ways: in prayer, in the study of the *Torah*, and in the performance of the precepts of the *Torah*. To consider how each of these operates in Jewish life is beyond the scope of this work. An investigation into all the phases of Jewish worship would involve a number of lengthy treatises, would, in reality, involve the fullest examination of the whole range of Judaism. A more satisfactory approach for our purpose is to study in some detail the meaning of worship as interpreted in one of the finest summaries in Jewish devotional literature – Alexander Süsskind of Grodno's *'Yesod We-Shoresh Ha-'Abhodah'*, the work referred to in our discussion of the second article of faith.

Alexander Süsskind's work is divided into a number of 'Gates', most of which are in the form of devotional commentaries to the Jewish liturgy. The first of these, called 'The Great Gate', he describes as: 'A great introduction which has as its aim the inflammation of men's hearts for divine worship in love and fear, including divine worship in heart and mind' (The edition used is that of Warsaw, 1870).

The author begins (p. 3b) by stating that God's purpose in creating the world was for man to serve God so that God might derive satisfaction – *nahath ruah* – from man's worship. The author supports this thesis by quotations from Bible, *Talmud* and the mediaeval thinkers. In particular the author relies on a passage in the *Zohar* (III, 111b) in which it is said that Israel is called both 'son' and 'servant' of the Most High; 'son' because men can know the supernal mysteries, and 'servant' because it is man's duty to worship God, in Temple times with sacrifices and at other times with prayer and the perform-ance of the precepts. Although he is no philosopher, Alexander

Süsskind is not unaware of the theological difficulties inherent in the idea that God 'needs' man's worship. His attempted solution is that God does not actually need man's deeds but that He is 'pleased' when man affords Him the satisfaction of doing His will. In this connection the author quotes the Rabbinic saying that the term 'a pleasing odour unto the Lord' (Lev. i. 9) is used of animal sacrifices to signify 'satisfaction (*nahath ruah*) to Me by the knowledge that I gave the command and My will was executed' (*Siphra ad loc., Zeb.* 46b). No attempt is made to analyse the concept still further, to ask, for example, why God should be thought to 'derive satisfaction' from man's deeds or how God can be said to 'derive satisfaction' at all? The language of simple piety is content with the idea that man in his worship of God provides God, as it were, with *nahath ruah*, the satisfaction of knowing that His will has been done.

Alexander Süsskind continues (4a) that the nature of the 'satisfaction' man affords God consists in man's love and fear of Him. Fearing God means the avoidance of sin, i.e. the observance of the negative precepts of the *Torah*, while love means keeping the positive precepts. God derives special pleasure from man's study of the *Torah* and from man's praise of Him. Although God has created the angelic hosts and worlds without number, all of which join in praise of Him, He derives greater satisfaction from the praises of puny man, occupying a physical body in the material world, than from all of these. Indeed, the very harmony of the upper worlds depends on man's worship. Alexander Süsskind sums it up as follows: 'The main intention of the Creator, blessed be He, and His main purpose in creation, is for the sake of man, that he might by his worship give satisfaction to God, blessed be His name. Happy is the man who fears the Lord and delights exceedingly in His commandments, who is mighty upon earth to perfect the upper worlds by his thought and utterance all the days of his life in this world. This note is sufficient for the intelligent'.

In the second chapter of this 'Gate' (4a) the author notices that there are degrees in men's worship, not all men being equal in the stages they can attain. The greater man's recognition of God's glory and majesty the greater his delight in the privilege that has been granted to him of worshipping God.

The man of deep religious feeling is nowadays able to contemplate on the vastnesses of space revealed by modern astronomy to evoke his sense of wonder at God's majesty. He is able to reflect on such facts as the tremendous distances covered by the light of the stars before it reaches our planet and the enormous size of the heavenly bodies beside which our tiny world pales into insignificance. Alexander Süsskind, not having these means at his disposal, seeks to recall his readers to a profound sense of their creatureliness and God's awful majesty by describing the numerous worlds which the *Zohar* states as existing. Thus it is said in the portion of the *Zohar* known as the 'Great Assembly', ' '*Idra Rabba*' (III, 128b), that there is a certain most elevated and fearful world from which proceeds a million times seventeen thousand five hundred brilliant and pure lights, each of which is, in turn, divided into four hundred and ten parts (the numerical value of the Hebrew term '*qadosh*', 'holy') and each of these particles of light powerfully illumines four hundred and ten worlds. Each of these worlds is hidden, only the highest world from which the lights proceed knowing their secret. The author concludes (5a): 'It is fitting that every Jew, a member of the holy people, should give thanks with all his might to the blessed Creator for choosing him and giving him the portion of worshipping God by means of the performance of His precepts and the study of His holy *Torah*, thus endowing him with the capacity to apprehend some small portion of the greatness of the Creator, blessed be He. For this was the blessed Creator's intention in creating man in this world to recognise God's greatness and His majesty'.

A further means by which man can recognise God's glory (5b) and avoid having a God who is 'too small' is the contemplation of the wonders of God as revealed in the marvels of nature, the miracle of the human mind, for instance. Here the author follows Bahya Ibn Paqudah who devotes a section of his 'Duties of the Heart' ('Gate II, *Sha'ar Ha-Behinah*') to the duty of 'examination', i.e. of discerning the wisdom of the Creator in His creation.

Chapter three (5b) deals with the idea of the 'higher fear' of God, '*yirath ha-romamuth*', which appears to correspond with Otto's idea of the 'numinous'. Alexander Süsskind gives this illustration. Imagine a man renowned for his saintliness, holiness and great wisdom so that others stand in awe of him and fear to approach him. Such fear is not of what the holy man may do, for a sage of his calibre will certainly avoid doing anything harmful. It is simply the awareness of one's own insignificance in the presence of such greatness which acts an an inhibiting factor. And yet, for all that, the holy man exercises a powerful fascination over others who, embarrassed though they are by their own unworthiness in his presence, wish to be near to him. At the slightest token of encouragement they will overcome their natural apprehensions and seek to approach him and enjoy the privilege of serving him. The same two elements of recoil and fascination are present in man's 'higher fear' of God. This is not fear of what God may do but a deep feeling of sheer creatureliness and unworthiness coupled with a tremendous longing to be near to Him. In Scripture God has given man the token of encouragement for which he yearns if he is to draw near to offer his supplications before God's throne, since in many Scriptural verses it is implied that God is nigh to those who call on Him in truth.

Chapter four (6a) offers counsel to the man desirous of making the 'higher fear' of God his own. First, he should contemplate on God's power, glory and majesty, as stated above. Secondly, he should reflect that God knows all the deeds and thoughts of men, penetrating even to the most secret recesses of the heart. Even the Gentiles admit that God knows all man's thoughts, just as the watchmaker is certainly familiar with all the complicated workings of the time-pieces he fashions. Whenever man is tempted to do a forbidden thing or to have an unworthy thought he should reflect that God knows of this, that his offence takes place in God's very presence and banishes the *Shekhinah*.

Chapter five (6b) offers counsel on how man can find many opportunities for God's worship. The author gives a number of illustrations and hopes that his readers will discover for themselves similar means of affording God the 'satisfaction' of which he has spoken. For instance, whenever a man notices that a regular worshipper in his Synagogue is absent through sickness or some other mishap he should feel aggrieved that some of the praise due to God is lacking. Particularly, if the absent one is a scholar he should be grieved at all the *Torah* which cannot now be studied and all the deep praises of the Creator which cannot now be offered. Conversely, his heart should overflow with joy whenever he notices that a fellow-congregant is offering his prayers with profound concentration and thereby giving great delight to his Father in Heaven. It is said of a certain saint that he would rejoice whenever he heard that a male child had been born in a Jewish home for a new recruit had been added to the hosts of the Lord. Rather ungallantly the author observes that the same saint would rejoice 'even' if a girl had been born for women, too, are capable of offering their share of God's praises and thus add to God's delight that His will has been done. It goes without saying the child's father should rejoice that he has brought another of God's servants into the world. The father's heart should similarly be full to overflowing whenever his child reaches some stage in the spiritual life of a Jew, when, for instance, he begins to pray or to study the *Torah*. Conversely a man should grieve whenever he hears of a death, particularly the death of a scholar, for all God's glory which now goes unrecognised and unsung. Similarly, if man hears that someone has had good fortune in his business he should rejoice at the increase in God's glory, for the fortunate one will surely give thanks to God for His goodness and will use part of his fortune in good deeds and charity. Conversely, when he hears that someone has suffered financial loss he should grieve at the loss of opportunity of acknowledging God's goodness. Whenever he notices someone in pain he should grieve both because a human being suffers and because God, being with him in his pain, suffers too. This affords God great '*nahath ruah*', that man suffers with Him. Before the advent of a festival man should delight at the opportunity that is about to be given him of carrying out God's will in the performance of the special precepts of the festival, the eating of unleavened bread on Passover for example.

Chapter six (7b) gives further illustrations of the '*nahath ruah*' idea. Whenever a man comes upon a difficult passage in a holy book and, after concentrated effort, is able to grasp the meaning, he should say: 'Sovereign of all worlds, I give thanks and praise to Thy great name for having given me the power

of understanding Thy holy and perfect *Torah*'. Similarly, whenever he reads a marvellously profound interpretation of the
Torah in a holy book he should give thanks to God for having
endowed the author of the book with the intelligence required
to reveal the wonders of God's *Torah* and he should reflect
in astonishment, if such is the achievement of mortal wisdom,
how great is the divine wisdom! At all times man should
accustom himself to say: 'I believe with perfect faith that
Thou art One and Unique' and in this way he will serve God
all the time. At every step man takes he should open his eyes
to gaze on the wondrous wisdom of the Creator, in the grass
which grows, in the food he eats, even in the stone, which is
but the lowest form in the physical world of some divine aspect
of God's creation in the supernal realms, and he should proclaim constantly: 'The mighty deeds of God, the mighty deeds
of God!'

So far Alexander Süsskind might be accused of neglecting
his fellow-men for God. In fact, in his view, the whole idea
of giving God '*nahath ruah*' is impossible unless human relationships are themselves seen as opportunities for worship. Alexander Süsskind is a great believer in (as Walt Whitman was
later to put it) seeing God in the faces of men and women.
In Chapter seven (8a) he develops this theme at length. Man
must accustom himself to carry out constantly two positive
precepts of the *Torah* – 'Thou shalt love thy neighbour as
thyself' (Lev. xix. 18) and 'In righteousness shalt thou judge
thy neighbour' (Lev. xix. 15). Both these precepts are to be
found in the Holiness Code in Leviticus, for if man accustoms
himself to fulfil them he will certainly attain the highest stage
of all, becoming a holy man. He should love his neighbour
as himself, that is to say, he should be as delighted with his
neighbour's good fortune as he is with his own and should
grieve at his neighbour's bad fortune as if the mishap had
befallen him. Just as he dislikes the thwarting of his own
desires he should never do anything to his neighbour which
does not meet with the latter's approval. If he observes his
neighbour doing wrong and there appear to be no mitigating
circumstances he should, nonetheless, find any excuses he can
rather than judge his neighbour guilty of wrong-doing.
Whenever man rejoices at his neighbour's good fortune

and grieves at his loss he fulfils the precept of loving his neighbour as himself. Unlike other precepts of the *Torah* this one can be fulfilled at all times, even when he is in an unclean place in which it is forbidden to have in mind sacred things. These two precepts are among the most difficult to carry out since men are by nature envious of one another. How great, then, is the reward of the man capable of self-mastery in his desire to obey his Creator!

In Chapter eight (8b) the theme is developed further. It is obvious that when others share the grief of one in sorrow his load is lessened whereas lack of concern for his misery on the part of others only serves to increase his trouble. It is sound Rabbinic teaching that God is pained at human sorrow. Consequently, by participating in his neighbour's woes man shares the grief of the *Shekhinah* and he lessens thereby, as it were, God's sorrows. Similarly, by rejoicing in his neighbour's joys he increases God's joy since God rejoices in human happiness. The author claims that if man will only fulfil these two precepts as they should be carried out his prayers will be pure and free from all extraneous and disturbing thoughts.

Chapter nine (9a) describes a further means of worshipping God at all times and in every act. *Bahya Ibn Paqudah* ('Gate of Divine Worship', Chapter 4) makes the point that although from the legal aspect of Judaism all acts are divided into the licit, the illicit and the obligatory, from the moral point of view there is no such thing as the licit, in the sense of a *neutral* act which is neither good nor bad. For the devout Jew every one of his deeds is either essential, in which case it is obligatory, or inessential, in which case it is illicit. For the true worshipper of God there can be no area in which man is left to himself with God excluded, no opportunity for men to have a holiday from moral decision, no possibility of self-indulgence with the claim that the deed he performs is not in itself contrary to Jewish law. Alexander Süsskind gives a number of examples, for instance the act of eating. If man eats in order to gain strength for God's service, eating no forbidden food and enjoying only sufficient for his physical needs, and if, in addition, he conducts himself properly at his table, then in the very act of eating he carries out divine worship. Where one of these conditions remains unfulfilled the act of eating becomes sinful.

Gluttony, for instance, even if it involves permitted food, is a sin because it is both harmful to health and because it encourages man in his slothful and gross habits and thereby hinders him from serving God. In similar fashion all five senses have their illicit and obligatory aspects. Whenever man engages his senses in due proportion and with proper intention he carries out a religious duty, he performs an act of divine worship. If the senses are indulged in illicit or uncontrolled fashion they are the causes of sin.

In Chapter ten (9b) the author observes that it is impossible to be a true worshipper of God unless one has acquired the quality of equanimity in the sense of complete imperviousness to human praise or blame. It should be the same to the true worshipper of God whether people praise or blame him. He should neither attach any value to human praise nor fear human censure, otherwise his pure intention in carrying out good deeds will be sullied since part of his mind will be engaged in considering whether the deeds he does will bring him fame or condemnation. The antidote has been given, states the author, by *Bahya Ibn Paqudah* ('Gate on Unification of Action', Chapter 5). This consists of a constant reminder of the illusory nature of human fame. How can human beings be of any real help to others? Even if a man wins world-wide renown his deeds are still as grass and he will soon be forgotten. If a man succeeds in praying with great devotion in the Synagogue he should never be tempted to enjoy the admiration of his fellow-congregants but should imagine that he is offering his prayers in a forest among trees where it would be absurd to feel pride at the admiration of the trees. However, man should never cut short his good deed out of fear that people might look upon him as a saint for this is a pretext of the evil inclination.

Chapter eleven (10a) deals with man's intention of sacrificing himself in theory. We have noted earlier, in the section dealing with the second principle of faith, Alexander Süsskind's views on this matter. His views on worship in this section of his work have been quoted here in full because they are a more or less typical example of Jewish piety at its best in the pre-Emancipation era. Worship according to our author consists, then, in giving God the satisfaction of doing His will. This

aim is achieved in various ways – through contemplation on
God's greatness and His providence; through recognising and
acknowledging His goodness at all times; through loving one's
neighbour as oneself; through sanctifying the licit; through
being impervious to human praise and blame; and through
firm resolve to be prepared to suffer martyrdom, if need be,
for God's sake. This type of piety is not to everyone's taste.
There are sufficient theological objections, for instance, to
the whole idea of God desiring '*nahath ruah*'. It is also questionable whether it is psychologically possible for man to rejoice
and be grieved at events in his neighbour's life as if these
had happened to him. Since there are 'neighbours' without
number one who tried to live by the saint's counsel would
always be in a state of both intense joy and profound sorrow.
Furthermore, to urge men to cultivate indifference to praise
or blame is to deprive life of one of its great incentives and is
certainly a hindrance to the kind of life in society that Judaism,
in its normative form, seeks to inculcate. This is part of the
spiritual problem of the modern Jew. He wishes to lead a
normal life and to participate in the world's work. And yet,
unless he is completely lacking in spiritual sensitivity, he
cannot help seeing the grandeur and spiritual beauty in an
approach such as that of Alexander Süsskind. He will try to
work out his own solution to the problem of devoutness but
works such as this will help serve as a powerful reminder of the
role which worship should occupy in Jewish life and that
religion is more than good conduct and ethical behaviour.

William James's discussion of the value of saintliness ('The
Varieties of Religious Experience', Longmans, Green, London,
1905, Lectures XIV and XV, pp. 326 ff.) is germane here.
James refers to the impression of extravagance produced by
the kind of pietistic literature we have been considering. Is it
necessary to be quite so fantastically good as that? We are
glad that saints existed to show us the way but they did so
at the cost of a one-sidedness for which others must make
amends. Devoutness, for example, may lead to fanaticism,
purity to a neglect of family and social relationships, tenderness
and charity to indulgence of evil in society, and asceticism
to a morbid violation of human nature. So far as this world
is concerned, says James, any one who makes an out-and-out

saint of himself does so at his peril. For all that, life's saints
and spiritual heroes bring an irridation into the world, a
profounder sense of mystery, wonder and goodness without
which we would all be the poorer. Not all Jews can be expected
to live as Alexander Süsskind would have them do, nor is it
desirable that they should do so. But a Judaism without such
men and the ideal of worship they represent would be a poor
faith incapable of providing its adherents with that satisfaction
of man's yearning for the Infinite on which all true religion
is based.

Mention must here be made of Maimonides' famous chapter
on 'How God is worshipped by a Perfect Man' ('Guide', III,
51, ed. Friedländer, pp. 384–391). Maimonides begins with a
parable. A king is enthroned in his palace. Some of his subjects
are abroad and some have their backs to the palace and are
bent on travelling away from it. Others desire to enter the
palace to minister to the king but have not even seen the face
of the wall which surrounds it. Others go around the palace
wall without discovering the entrance. Others again have
proceeded farther into the ante-rooms of the palace while still
others have succeeded in entering into the monarch's presence.
But even the latter cannot converse with the king until they
have made the effort required of those to whom the privilege of
conversation with the king is granted. The parable is applied
to the religious life of mankind. The subjects of the King of
kings who are 'abroad' are those with no religion at all. Worse
than these are those who hold false doctrines in religion. They
have their 'backs to the palace'. A son of his age, Maimonides
remarks that under certain circumstances it may become
necessary to slay them, and to extirpate their doctrines, in order
to prevent them misleading others. Those who desire to
enter the palace but have not seen it are the mass of religious
people, who observe the divine commandments but are ignorant.
Those who go around the palace are the traditionalists who
observe all the practical demands of the *Torah* and study it
thoroughly but who are unversed in philosophy. Others again
have used their reasoning powers to prove the truths of religion
and have thus entered the ante-chamber of the palace. But
those who have proved as much of religion as is humanly
possible, who have attained in this way a true knowledge of

God, have reached the goal and are in the palace in which
lives the king. Thus, for Maimonides, true worship is for the
intellectual aristocrat, the metaphysician whose thoughts are
centred on God, who understands the proofs for God's existence
and how God controls the world. The more such a man reflects
on God and the more he thinks on Him the more is he engaged
in worship. True worship of God is only possible when correct
notions of Him have previously been conceived. In other words,
only the philosopher can truly worship God, both because the
worship of the unphilosophical mind is not really directed
towards God but towards a figment of the human imagination,
and because the essence of worship is intellectual perception
of the truths about God. Since it is the intellect which is the
link that joins man to God, the true worshipper will spend as
much time as he possibly can in meditation upon God's name.
'We must bear in mind,' says Maimonides in an oft-quoted
passage, 'that all such religious acts as reading the Law,
praying, and the performance of other precepts, serve exclusively
as the means of causing us to occupy and fill our mind with
the precepts of God, and free it from worldly business; for
we are then, as it were, in communication with God, and
undisturbed by any other thing. If we, however, pray with
the motion of our lips, and our face toward the wall, but at
the same time think of our business; if we read the Law with
our tongue, whilst our heart is occupied with the building of
our house, and we do not think of what we are reading; if
we perform the commandments only with our limbs, we are
like those who are engaged in digging the ground, or hewing
wood in the forest, without reflecting on the nature of those
acts, or by whom they were commanded, or what is their
object'. Man should train himself gradually, continues Maimonides, to recite some of his prayers with proper inwardness.
Once he has mastered this art he should go on to include
other prayers and the benedictions until all acts of divine
worship are performed with the mind entirely abstracted
from worldly affairs. 'When you are alone by yourself, when
you are awake on your couch, be careful to meditate in such
precious moments on nothing but the intellectual worship of
God, viz., to approach Him and to minister before Him in
the true manner which I have described to you – not in hollow

emotions. This I consider as the highest perfection wise men can attain by the above training'. Maimonides goes on to claim that one who has really reached the elevated stage of constantly being with God in his thoughts has attained the spiritual degree of a prophet and nothing in the world can harm him. He is, indeed, immune from mental and physical mishap and cannot be touched by evil.

If the objections to the views on worship of Alexander Süsskind are that they are too naive the opposite objection can be levelled against Maimonides' ideas on the same subject. On his view, true worship is impossible to all but a few rare souls equipped with the spiritual resources and intellectual gifts to engage in prolonged meditation and rigorous metaphysical studies. The true worshipper is a kind of Yogi. But traditional Judaism is a religion for 'all the community of Israel' and is, indeed, so described by Maimonides himself in his great Code of Law. It would be superficial and altogether too facile an approach to consider whether it is Alexander Süsskind or Maimonides who is best suited to be the spiritual mentor of the modern Jew in this matter of worship. Judaism is far too complex to permit of a simple either/or in this field. The truth of the matter is rather that in the teachings of these two men, and of many other masters of the devout life, there is rich nourishment for hungry souls. But, like physical nourishment, it must be taken in proper measure. A man's spiritual diet must be balanced, to suit his temperament; it must be rich in spiritual vitamins but not over-rich. Here, as in matters of physical diet, one man's meat is another's poison. The great idea which emerges from these and from all similar descriptions of Jewish worship is that it must be God-orientated to deserve the name.

*   *   *

EXCURSUS

The Chapter on 'Jewish Worship' in Evelyn Underhill's book, *op. cit.*, pp. 193 f., is stimulating but is written from the Christian standpoint, besides needing supplementation and correction in several details. The author remarks that the Jewish soul, as disclosed to us in its records, was from the beginning peculiarly sensitive towards God. She notes that the connection of Fire with

Divine Presence runs right through the Hebrew Bible: e.g. the Burning Bush, the Pillar of Fire, the flame and smoke of Sinai, on which God descended in His glory 'like devouring fire' (Ex. 17; *cf.* Ex. xix. 18, Deut. ix. 15 and xviii. 16), the sacrifices of Elijah on Mount Carmel, the visions of Ezekiel and Daniel. For Semitic thought, she says, fire and light were essential attributes of the divine self-disclosure: and this conception has had a marked influence on Jewish ritual worship. No examples are given by the author but one might refer to the Sabbath and Festival lights, the blessing over fire at the conclusion of the Sabbath (Singer's P.B. p. 108 and 216), the light kindled in a house of mourning and on the anniversary of a death, the candles before the ark in the Synagogue, the 'Perpetual Lamp' in the Synagogue, the prohibition of the use of fire on the Sabbath (Ex. xxxv. 3), the kindling of the *Hanukkah* lights, the rejoicing in Temple times on the feast of Tabernacles (*v. Mishnah, Sukk.* V. 2–4), and the burning of leaven on the eve of Passover. The favourite symbol of which the Qabbalists represent the Sephirotic world is 'light'. *Cf.* the *Habhdalah* prayer recited at the conclusion of the Sabbath (Singer's P.B. p. 216): 'Blessed art Thou, O Lord our God, King of the universe, who makest a distinction between holy and profane, between light and darkness, between Israel and other nations, between the seventh day and the six working days'. Evelyn Underhill further remarks that the strange history of Israel is of a people dominated by that thirst for God, that certitude of God and that sense of obligation to God, which form the raw material of all worship. Among all the religions of antiquity Israel's alone is based upon that confident dependence on the Unseen which is the essence of the theocentric life. In a remarkable passage the author describes the famous vision of Isaiah (Is. vi. 1–8): 'Here God is revealed to His prophet as the Wholly Other, the Object of man's awestruck adoration, and also as the Wholly Good, setting a standard of holiness and convicting man of sin: and a step forward is taken in that total sanctification and redemption of experience, which is the manward aim of worship. Before Him the seraphim veil their faces; yet He asks for the willing and open-eyed co-operation of imperfect men. His nature is indeed disclosed in those theophanies which show something of His ineffable glory, glints of a world of living splendour beyond the conception of man: but also, in the demand for purity, mercy, truth, and devotedness which He makes upon His human creatures. In both, in different ways, He requires their unlimited self-offering: an inward dedication of personality expressed by outward signs. Therefore, the *Torah*, the Law, is itself a disclosure of the supernatural, God's will for men. It is not a creature in the ordinary sense, but a revelation of the Eternal, a reflection of the Divine Mind, final and immutable: and the rigid obedience it demands and secures – whether in the sphere of ritual or of morals – is not mere submission to a code, but an act of adoration'. (*Cf.* on this theme C. S. Lewis's popular 'Reflections on the Psalms', G. Bles, London, 1958, particularly Chapter VI: 'Sweeter than Honey', pp. 54 f). It is doubtful, however, to say the least, whether the author is justified in seeing the names of the twelve tribes on the shoulder-straps of the High Priest as a 'first hint of the ministry of mediation'. What is the author's source for the statement (p. 201, note 2) that blue 'was and is for Jewish thought the colour of the *Shekhinah*'? A further important point made by the author is that it is a mark of Israel's spiritual genius that from the first the Jew placed reality within mystery and had an intense aversion to all images of the Divine. There follows a vivid description of Synagogal worship centering around the reading of the *Torah*. The author is not, of course, entirely correct when she observes that the 'non-sacerdotal' character of Synagogal worship is such that 'the priest as such has no prerogative and that any member may be called to the reading or exposition of the Law' (p. 209, note 1). The first '*aliyah* is always given to the *kohen*, the descendant of the priests, and the second to a Levite. The priestly blessing is still performed by the *kohanim*. Evelyn Underhill concludes that if worship is to be true to the Jewish conception it will not be all bright and clear, thin in colour, humanistic and this-world in feeling. It will retain the ancient sense of cloud and darkness, other-worldly fire and light, which still lives in the Psalter; the awe before a sacred mystery which is with us yet never of us, the deep sense of imperfection, and above all the unconquerable trust and the adoring love for a God who has set His glory above the heavens and yet is mindful of the children of men'. It is, indeed, a pity that so few Synagogue buildings have been successful in capturing the mood of which Evelyn Underhill speaks. Ideally a Synagogue ought not to give those who worship within its walls merely a sense of comfort and ease. There ought to be something of the 'numinous' about the edifice, leading them to exclaim: 'How full of awe is this place! this is none other than the house of God, and this is the gate of heaven' (Gen. xxviii. 17). In this connection, too, perhaps the modern Synagogue has, in its attempt at the 'modernisation' or 'Westernisation' of the services, gone too far in virtually abolishing all sense of the mysterious. The older type of chant, the prayer shawl worn over the head, even the swaying of the body, frowned upon by certain mediaeval scholars, did produce an atmosphere of 'other-worldliness' painfully absent from today's Synagogues in which all such practices are declared 'out-landish'. There is no easy solution to this problem. Few would suggest a return to the old pattern but many Jews sensitive to the prayerful mood feel that something ought to be done to recapture it for the modern Synagogue. On swaying in prayer *v.* the article by J. D. Eisenstein in JE, Vol. XI, p. 607. Eisenstein's quotation, with approval from Simon Brainin, who suggests that the purpose of swaying in prayer was to afford exercise during study and prayer, is incredibly banal. Bodily movements in prayer are, of course, found very frequently in the East, the 'dancing dervishes' being only the best-known example. The main Jewish sources for the custom are: *Zohar* III, 118b–119a; Judah Ha-Levi's *'Kuzari'*, II, 80; Jacob ben Asher's Commentary (*'Ba'al Ha-Turim'*) to Ex. xx. 18; note of Moses Isserles to *'Orah Hayyim* 46, 1 and *Magen 'Abhraham ad loc.; Mishnah Berurah ad loc. Cf.* the interesting but rather tendentious work of S. Piker: *'Tephillah Ba-'Aretz'*, Jer. 1962, pp. 232–244. It is well-known that the Hasidic movement which arose in the latter half of the eighteenth century attached the greatest significance to prayer. A very comprehensive anthology of the more important early Hasidic teachings on prayer is contained in *'Sepher Ba'al Shem Tobh'*, Sotmar, 1943, in the section to *Noah*, pp. 118 ff., from which the following is taken. The worshipper should give all his strength to the words he utters in prayer, proceeding from letter to letter until he forgets his bodily sensations. The *Ba'al Shem* attained to his knowledge of the higher worlds not because of his learning but because he prayed at all times with the profoundest inwardness and concentration. Even when man prays with great love and fear he should be humble at the same time. Man should remember God in all that he does. Even when he is about to enter the privy he should think to himself that he is about to separate the evil from the good so as to serve God with the good which remains after the evil has been removed. It once happened that the prosecutor presented his case before the heavenly court, claiming that Jews were prepared to be distracted by petty business matters even on their way to pray in the Synagogue. The defence had no reply until the *Ba'al Shem* acknowledged the justice of the prosecutor's plea but added that it was also true that once a Jew has carried out a *mitzwah*, a divine precept, he would not sell it for all the money in the world. A little *Torah* study before prayer helps to prepare the mind for its devotions but too much study can be detrimental to prayer if it has the effect of exhausting the mind. The worshipper should learn to assess for himself the delicate balance in this matter. The true worshipper should be ready to put so much of himself into his prayers that it should only be by a

miracle that he can recite them without expiring on the spot. When
a man has reached but a humble stage on the ladder of prayer he
should recite his prayers from the prayer book which will assist
him in his devotions. But once he has reached the stage of attachment to the upper world he should recite his prayers with closed
eyes that he be not distracted even by the prayer book. Sometimes a
man finds that he cannot pray with deep contemplation. He should
then content himself with the thought that God's glory fills all
worlds and that God is near to him. When man begins to pray it
should be with the fear of God in his heart for this is the gateway to
God's presence. He should say to himself: 'To whom do I wish
to cleave? It is to the Creator by whose word all things were made,
who brought all things into being and who sustains them all'.
He should concentrate on God's greatness and majesty and he will
then be equipped to enter the higher worlds. The person afflicted
with a melancholy disposition imagines that he prays with the fear
of God. Similarly, a sanguine man imagines that he has attained
to the love of God. But both these are spurious states. The fear
of God descends upon man without any effort on man's part. As a
result of such dread he no longer is aware of himself and his tears
flow of their own accord. Only that love of God which stems from
this kind of fear is true love of God. The man who says that he will
pray with devotion and inwardness only on the Sabbath is like
the king's servant who is only prepared to serve his master in his
presence. A man should get into the habit of 'shouting to God
in silence' i.e. he should put all his strength into profound concentration without necessarily giving his cry any external expression.
Whenever 'strange thoughts' (i.e. extraneous thoughts) enter
man's mind during prayer he should experience a sense of great
shame for he has been expelled from the royal palace. With great
embarrassment he should seek to return to the palace with an
overwhelming sense of his unworthiness. On the other hand, he
should not allow himself to become unduly disturbed by the 'strange
thought' but should shatter it and cleave to God. By so doing he
redeems the 'holy spark' present in every 'strange thought'. When
man suffers, the *Shekhinah* suffers with him. Consequently, one's
prayers on behalf of a neighbour in trouble should be intended for
the *Shekhinah* who grieves with the neighbour. 'He will fulfil the
desire of them that fear Him; He will also hear their cry, and will
save them' (Ps. cxlv. 19). The *Ba'al Shem* interpreted this verse
as follows. A man may pray for something he believes is good for
him but may find it harmful when the request has been granted.
He should not then be ashamed to entreat God to help him, even
though the harm is, as it were, of his own making, since God 'hears

their cry and saves them'. When man has prayed in fear of God the fear that is awakened can lead to anger. Similarly, when he has prayed in love of God the love that is awakened can lead him to illicit loves. The antidote is for man to engage in work or study as soon as possible after his prayers. If man feels joyful after his prayers he should know that his prayers have been answered.

These and other elevated thoughts in the *Ba'al Shem* and his followers' system must not be allowed to blind us to the fact that the whole system is based on the Qabbalistic belief in the thaumar-turgic power of the words of prayer. Written in the sacred tongue by divinely inspired authors, the very letters of the prayer book, it was held, contained far more than their plain meaning as symbols representing human needs and human ideas. The letters were, in fact, combinations of divine names and their utterance had the power of bringing down the flow of divine grace from above. For this purpose profound inwardness and concentration were required. To utter the words of prayer without concentration, said the *Ba'al Shem* (*op. cit.* pp. 128–9), was spiritual masturbation. The divine seed was thereby prevented from producing fruit. It is impossible to understand early Hasidic thought without a realisation of its occult and semi-magical nature. It is not difficult to produce an anthology of beautiful Hasidic tales and maxims on the subject of prayer, but to do this without reference to the system as a whole is to present a half-truth. To say this is not, of course, to deny that the modern Jew can find spiritual help in Hasidic devotional doctrine even if he cannot accept some of the basic ideas of the move-ment. Most of the material we have quoted, for example, is capable of being applied in his prayer life by the devout modern since the early Hasidic masters were true adepts in prayer. On the meaning of worship for the Jew of today *v.* Chapter 34: 'The Meaning of Observance' in Abraham J. Heschel's 'God in Search of Man', John Calder, London, 1956, p. 348 f. Heschel defines a *mitzwah* as a 'sacred deed where earth and heaven meet'. It is 'a deed in the form of a prayer'. 'Jewish observance is a liturgy of deeds'. 'All *Mitzwoth* are means of evoking in us the awareness of living in the neighbour-hood of God, of living in the holy dimension. They call to mind the inconspicuous mystery of things and acts, and are reminders of our being the stewards, rather than the landlords of the universe; reminders of the fact that man does not live in a spiritual wilderness, that *every act* of man is an encounter of the human and the holy'. On the question discussed in the text of God's *need* of human worship *cf.* Maimonides' 'Guide', III. 13. *Cf.* Heschel's recent book: *Torah Min Ha-Shamayim*, Vol. I, Soncino Press, London, 1962, pp. 76 f.

* * *

(2) *God is not to be worshipped through an intermediary.*

This principle does not necessarily state that there are no intermediaries, only that these are not to be worshipped. It is clear, for instance, that throughout the Biblical and Rabbinic periods the majority of the people, including their spiritual leaders, believed in the existence of angels through whom God, as it were, carries out His work. Philo, it is well-known, believed in the divine word, the *Logos,* through which God creates and controls the world. It is, however, of much interest that in the whole of the *Mishnah,* the great compendium of Jewish teaching compiled by Rabbi Judah the Prince at the end of the second century, there is no reference to angels. The argument from silence is always a precarious one. It is not certain that scholars like David Neumark who see this as a conscious protest against a belief in angels are correct. But there is unanimity in the sources that the angels and other intermediaries, even if they do exist, are not to be worshipped. There can be little doubt that Maimonides' insistence on this principle is in conscious reaction to the Christian doctrine of the Incarnation and prayers to and through Jesus. Maimonides is emphatic that prayers are not to be offered to angels but departures from this are not unknown in Jewish practice when, albeit on rare occasions, angels are entreated to offer prayer to God on man's behalf. Part of the objection to the Hasidic movement by its opponents was to the doctrine of the *Tzaddiq,* the Hasidic saint and leader, to whom his followers' petitions were addressed in the first instance in the belief that the holy man's prayers would be more acceptable to God. The opponents of the movement saw in this a breach in the idea that God is to be approached directly and that He is near to all who call upon Him in truth.

It is generally held that the Palestinian teachers in Talmudic times had, on the whole, a more refined faith than their Babylonian colleagues. There is far less emphasis, for instance, on a belief in demons in the Palestinian than in the Babylonian *Talmud.* With regard to the use of angels as intermediaries, scholars like Louis Ginzberg see a fundamental difference in approach between the two centres of Jewish life. Thus we read in the Palestinian *Talmud:* 'R. Judah said: "A man in trouble who has a great man for a patron stands at the door awaiting the answer the servants will bring, whether or not he will be permitted to approach him for aid. But he who needs God's help ought not to ask the assistance of either Michael or Gabriel or any other angel, but should turn immediately to God: for whosoever shall call on the name of God will be delivered" '. (*Jer. Ber.* ix, 13a). In the Babylonian *Talmud*, on the other hand, we read: 'He who prays in the Aramaic language will not be helped by the ministering angels, for the ministering angels do not know Aramaic' (*Sabb.* 12b). However, it is more than a little difficult to accept this as different attitudes on the part of the Palestinian and Babylonian authorities since the Babylonian *Talmud* quotes the saying in the name of the famous Palestinian teacher, R. Johanan. It is by no means far-fetched to understand the passage in the Babylonian *Talmud* as referring to the angels *carrying* the prayers to God, not as prayer *directed* to angels. Be that as it may, here and there in the Jewish liturgy one does find prayers to angels and, although these scandalised Rabbinic authorities, protests against them appear to have been of no avail.

It would be erroneous to conclude, therefore, that Jewish life knows nothing of intercessors. Even a kind of saint cult is not unknown, the ceremonies at the grave of Rabbi Simeon ben Yohai at Meron in Israel on *Lag Ba-'Omer*, for instance. In other parts of the Jewish world, too, it is not unknown for candles to be burned at the tombs of holy men and for petitions to be thrown into the tomb through a special aperture for the purpose. Two things, however, can safely be said. The first is that all these activities would without doubt have been considered extremely offensive by a teacher like Maimonides and would have been construed by him as a breach of his fifth article of faith. The second is that even in its crudest and most superstitious phases the cult of the dead saint is never allowed to degenerate into worship of him.

*   *   *

EXCURSUS

On the idea of an intermediary in Judaism *v.* Kaufmann Kohler's article 'Mediator' in JE, Vol. VIII, pp. 406–409. On the role of angels *v.* JE, Vol. I, pp. 583–597 and UJE, Vol. I, pp. 304–314; Israel Abraham's note in his 'Companion to the Authorised Daily

Prayer Book', rev. ed., Eyre and Spottiswoode, London, 1922, pp. xliv–xlvii; and A. Cohen's 'Everyman's Talmud', Dent, London, 1949, pp. 47–58. In the latter work there is an anthology of Rabbinic ideas on angels. The only place in the prayer book in which angels are designated by name is the night prayer, which reads: 'In the name of the Lord, the God of Israel, may Michael be at my right hand, Gabriel at my left, before me Uriel, behind me Raphael, and above my head the divine presence of God' (Singer's P.B. p. 297). Zunz-Albeck: *'Ha-Derashoth Be-Yisrael'*, Jer. 1947, p. 546, note 100, gives some of the sources on the Rabbinic opposition to the invocation of angels. The thirteenth century Jacob Anatoli in his *'Malmed Ha-Talmidim'*, Lyck, 1866, p. 68a, in his commentary to the second commandment, observes that this implies a prohibition against the invocation of angels. He attacks the custom obtaining in 'some places' of reciting the prayer calling upon the angels to bring the prayers of Israel to God – *makhnise rahamim*. Anatoli says that in the prayers of Moses and the other prophets and in the statutory Synagogal prayers there is not the slightest trace of prayers to angels. The difficulty of Jacob's prayer (Gen. xlviii. 16) is answered in two ways: (1) The meaning of the verse is: 'God who sent His angel to redeem me' or (2) The term 'angel' here refers to the 'will of God'. *Cf.* R. Isaac ben Shesheth (*Ribash*) (1326–1408), No. 157 (given wrongly in JE as 159). The Responsum deals with the question of the propriety of the Qabbalistic doctrine of the *Sephiroth* and whether it is right to pray to them. *Ribash* quotes his teacher, R. Peretz Ha-Kohen, who never spoke of the *Sephiroth* and never thought of them. R. Peretz further told of R. Samson of Chinon, 'the greatest of his generation', who used to say that he prayed 'like a child', namely, not as the Qabbalists with their complicated prayers, now to one *Sephirah*, now to another. The Qabbalists interpret the Rabbinic saying: 'He who desires wisdom should face south when praying and he who desires wealth should face north' as referring to the requisite *Sephiroth*. All this, observes *Ribash*, is very strange to the non-Qabbalist, who suspects a dualism here. He once heard, he says, someone influenced by philosophy (*'ehad min ha-mithpalsephim*) attack the Qabbalists on the grounds that while the Christians believe in 'three' the Qabbalists deviate still further to believe in 'ten'. *Ribash* describes a meeting he had with the elderly sage, Don Joseph Ibn Shoshan, who is described as a Talmudic sage, familiar with philosophy, and a great Qabbalist and saint. *Ribash* put to him the question: how can the Qabbalists have one *Sephirah* in mind when reciting one benediction and a different *Sephirah* in mind when reciting another benediction? Is it not

forbidden for a Jew to pray to the *Sephiroth*, thereby suggesting that
they are deities? Don Joseph replied that, of course, the prayer
of the Qabbalist is directed to the Cause of causes but concentration
on the different *Sephiroth* can be compared to a petition presented to
a king in which the monarch is requested to command that the
suppliant's wish be carried out through the lord appointed for that
purpose. Thus when the Qabbalist thinks of the *Sephirah* of 'Lovingkindness', when praying for the righteous, and the *Sephirah* of
'Power' when praying for the downfall of the wicked, his intention
is to pray to God to draw down His influence into the requisite
Sephirah. *Ribash* praises the ingenuity of the reply but expresses
his dissatisfaction with it. Surely, he argues, it is far better to pray
to God with simple intention without appearing to advise Him
how to grant the bequest! *Ribash* concludes that he personally
favours simple, unsophisticated concentration in prayer. This does
not mean that *Ribash* rejects the Qabbalistic system but, as he
remarks in this Responsum, since he has not had the advantage
of learning the system at the feet of a master he prefers to avoid
the subject. On the prayers of the Qabbalists with their concentration on the *Sephiroth v.* the comprehensive essay of J. G. Weiss in
Journal of Jewish Studies, Vol. IX, 1958, 'The Kavvanoth of
Prayer in Early Hasidism', pp. 163–192. *Cf.* a discussion of this
topic from the standpoint of orthodox Qabbalism in Menahem
Mendel of Lübavitch's '*Derekh Mitzwothekha*', Poltava, 1911, pp.
234 ff. It is a very widespread custom among Jews to visit the
graves of parents and relatives, particularly during the penitential
season. This raises the question of praying through an intermediary
as well as appearing to offend against the prohibition of necro-
mancy (*v.* Deut. xviii. 11). Despite opposition, however, the
custom persisted (*v. Hokhmath 'Adam*, 89. 7, *Zohar* III, 71b, *Sot.*
34b and the other sources quoted in *ET*, Vol. VII, p. 247). There
was a good deal of Rabbinic opposition in the last century to the
custom in Palestine of visiting the grave of R. Simeon b. Yohai
on the thirty-third day of the '*Omer*, the traditional anniversary of
his death (as mentioned above), to offer prayers and to burn
valuable garments! *V.* the survey of the literature on the subject in
S. Sevin's '*Ha-Mo'adim Ba-Halakhah*', 2nd. ed., Tel-Aviv, 1949,
pp. 300–304.

*   *   *

(3) *No other being, apart from God, is to be worshipped.*

From the days of the great Hebrew prophets who fought
against idolatry there has been determined opposition in

Judaism to any image of God or any kind of plastic representation of the divine. Idolatry in Hebrew is *'abhodah zarah*, literally, 'strange worship'. It embraces both the worship of heathen deities and the worship of an idol as God or as the image of God. On the whole, hardly any attempt is made, in the classical Jewish sources, to distinguish between different kinds of pagan or primitive worship such as animism, fetishism and polytheism. All forms of worship that are not purely monotheistic as well as any type of representation of the divine are treated together as idolatry and severely condemned.

Maimonides devotes a whole section of his great Code to the prohibition of idolatry. His remarks in the first chapter of this section (*Hil. 'Abhodah Zarah*, Chapter I) are worth quoting for the light they shed on Jewish thinking on idolatry in the Middle Ages. It hardly needs stating that Maimonides was working with the facts as known to him. He cannot be expected to have known modern anthropological studies or to have anticipated the findings of comparative religion, so that some of his conclusions on the rise of polytheism or idolatry cannot now be accepted. (It might be noted, however, that Maimonides in his 'Guide for the Perplexed' was the first scholar to attempt a systematic presentation of Biblical prohibitions in the light of contemporary idolatrous practices. With sure instinct, Maimonides was the first to see fully that many of the Biblical regulations can only be understood against their background. In this he influenced John Spencer who acknowledges, indeed, his debt to the great mediaeval thinker. Spencer, in turn, influenced both Robertson Smith and James Fraser, so that Maimonides, as we have noted later, has been heralded, with some justice, as the real founder of comparative religion). 'In the days of Enosh' (*v.* Gen. iv. 26), writes Maimonides, 'men fell into great error and the counsel of the sages of that generation was exceedingly foolish, Enosh himself belonging to those who went astray. The following was the nature of their error. They argued thus: Since God created the spheres and stars to control therewith the world, placing them on high and allotting glory to them, and since they are servants who minister in God's presence, it is only right to praise them and glorify them and accord them honour. It must be the will of God, those people argued, that men should aggrandize and pay homage to those He has honoured, just as a king desires homage to be paid to his ministers so that to carry out this wish is to honour the king himself. No sooner had they reasoned in this way than they began to erect temples to the stars and to offer sacrifices to them, and they began to sing praises and hymns to them and bow down to them, in order to fulfil, according to their base reasoning, the will of the Creator. This was the chief idea behind idolatry and this is how the idolators who knew this idea argued. They did not argue that apart from this star there is no God. Hence Jeremiah says: "Who would not fear Thee, O King of the nations? For it befitteth Thee; Forasmuch as among all the wise men of the nations, and in all their royalty, There is none like unto Thee. But they are altogether brutish and foolish: The vanities by which they are instructed are but a stock" (Jer. x. 7–8). The prophet means to imply: All know that Thou art alone but their error and folly consists in imagining that this vanity is Thy will'.

Maimonides continues: 'After some time had elapsed false prophets arose among the children of men who claimed that God had spoken to them commanding that a certain star, or all stars, should be worshipped and that libations and sacrifices be offered to the star which is worshipped and that a temple be erected to it with representations of its form, in order that all the people might bow down before it – the women and children and all other ignorant people. The false prophet would furthermore impart to them an image of the star he had himself invented, saying to them: This is the image of such-and-such a star which has been made known to me. Thus they began to make images in temples and under trees, at the tops of mountains and upon the hills. There they would gather to bow down to the images and they would proclaim to all the people that this image has the power of doing good and evil and it is therefore right to worship and fear it. Their priests would inform them that as a result of their worship they would increase and prosper and they would order the people to worship in this manner and not in that. Other liars arose who claimed that the star, sphere, or angel itself, ordered them to worship it in such-and-such a manner. And the false prophet would thus instruct the people to worship in this manner and not in that. Eventually, this idea spread to the whole world, that images should be worshipped in diverse ways and that men ought to offer sacrifices to them and bow down before them. In the course of time the glorious and fearful Name was forgotten from mouth and mind of all creatures so that none recognised it. The result was that all the people and their women and children knew only of the image of wood and stone and the temple of stone in which they had been trained from infancy to bow down to the image, to worship it and to swear in its name. As for the sages among them, the priests for example, they imagined that there was no other god than the stars and spheres in whose honour the images had been fashioned. But the Rock of Ages remained unknown and un-recognised except to a few individuals such as Enoch and Methuselah, Noah, Shem and Eber. This is how human history developed until the birth of Abraham our father, the pillar of the world'.

'No sooner was this mighty man weaned than, child though he was, his mind began to probe. Day and night he engaged in reflection, expressing his astonishment that the sphere should move without cause or controller since it could not have caused itself. Submerged as he was among the foolish idolators of Ur of the Chaldees, he had neither teacher nor mentor. Both his father and his mother as well as the rest of the people worshipped idols and he followed them. But all the time his mind was probing and deepening in understanding until he attained to the proper way and grasped the truth by his own correct discernment. He then realised that there is only one God who controls the sphere. He created the world and there is no other god in all creation. Abraham then realised that all the world was in error, an error brought about by star and image worship until the truth had been lost. Abraham was forty years of age when he recognised his Creator. At once he began to refute the theories of the Chaldeans and to argue with them that their way was untrue. Breaking the images, he began to make it known that God alone is to be worshipped and that only to Him is it right to bow down, to sacrifice and to offer libations that all creatures of the future might know Him, breaking all the images to pieces that people might not be led astray by them into believing that beside

them there is no God. When Abraham's proofs began to convince others the king sought to murder him, but a miracle
happened and he escaped to Haran. Here he began to proclaim
to the whole world that there is only one God for all mankind
and that He is to be worshipped. Thus would he wander from
town to town and from kingdom to kingdom, gathering the
people together and proclaiming the truth to them, until he
reached the land of Canaan, as it is said: "And called there on
the name of the Lord, the everlasting God" (Gen. xxi. 33)'.
Maimonides concludes this chapter with an account of how
Abraham handed down these truths to Isaac and Jacob and how
the people of Israel came into being, to whom Moses disclosed
the true way in which God is to be worshipped and idolatry
rejected.

Maimonides is, of course, recording here the traditional
Jewish view, based chiefly on Rabbinic legend, that Abraham
was the first great iconoclast with his descendants continuing
the fight against idolatry in all its forms. In Biblical times the
fight was directed against the pagan deities of Egypt, Canaan,
Babylonia and Assyria. In later, Rabbinic, times the protest
was against the worship of the Greek and Roman pantheon, a
whole tractate of the *Mishnah* and *Gemara*, tractate '*Abhodah
Zarah*, being devoted to this theme. Maimonides' definition
of idolatry (*Hil. A.Z.* II. 1) reads: 'The chief command with
regard to idolatry is that one should not worship any creature,
neither angel nor sphere nor star, neither one of the four elements
nor anything formed from them. Even if the worshipper knows
that the Lord is God and he only worships this creature in the
manner in which Enosh and his contemporaries worshipped
at first, he is still an idolator. The *Torah* warns us against this
when it says: "And lest thou lift up thine eyes unto heaven,
and when thou seest the sun and the moon and the stars . . .
which the Lord thy God hath allotted unto all the peoples"
(Deut. iv. 19). This means: You might observe that these
control the world and that the Lord has allotted them to all
mankind that men might live and that they suffer no decomposi-
tion, and you might conclude from this that it is right and proper
to bow down to them and to worship them. It is in connection
with this matter that the *Torah* enjoins: "Take heed to yourselves, lest your heart be deceived" (Deut. xi. 16), that is to

say, you should not be led astray through the reflections of your heart to worship these to serve as intermediaries between you and your Creator'.

Opposition to anything which savoured of idolatry was very fierce during the period of the second Temple. Josephus (*Ant.* xviii. 3. 1) tells us that when Hadrian introduced the Roman ensigns into Jerusalem the protest was such that he was compelled to withdraw them. Some idea of the way in which the Talmudic sages viewed idolatry is to be gleaned from the *Mishnah* of which, as we have seen, a whole tractate is devoted to this theme. For three days before Gentile festivals it was forbidden to have business dealings with them (*A.Z.*I.1).
It was forbidden to sell articles to Gentiles before their festivals which they might use in idolatrous worship, e.g. fir-cones, white figs, frankincense or a white cock (*A.Z.* I. 5). Wine of Gentiles and certain of their foods were forbidden (*A.Z.* II and V). However, we are told that Rabban Gamaliel in Acre bathed in the Bath of Aphrodite because the Gentiles do not say: 'Let us make a bath for Aphrodite' but 'Let us make an Aphrodite as an adornment for the bath' (*A.Z.* III. 4). There are many references in the Talmudic literature to the prohibition of casting a stone at a *Merqolis* (e.g. *Sanh.* VIII. 7, *A.Z.* IV. I) which appears to have been a pillar to Mercury, the Greek Hermes, who was the patron deity of travellers at whose shrine the grateful passers-by cast a stone. It is said that the Jewish elders were asked in Rome why God does not destroy idols if He hates them so. To this they replied that men worship the sun, moon and stars and God refuses to destroy the world He has created 'because of fools'. If, on the other hand, He were to destroy only those idols of which the world has no use this would only confirm the worshippers of those which were not destroyed that these alone have power (*A.Z.* IV. 7).

Among further details, numerous in the extreme, of Rabbinic abhorrence of idolatry, the following might be mentioned. R. Menahem b. R. Simai was given the appellation 'the son of the holy' because he refused to gaze even upon the image on a coin (*A.Z.* 50a). Not alone was idolatry itself treated with the greatest severity by the Rabbis but anything appertaining to it was strictly prohibited ('*abizraihu*). Thus it was forbidden to use the leaves of an idolatrous grove ('*asherah*) even if the leaves were used for their medicinal properties, so that any other leaves could have served the same purpose (*Pes.* 25a, *Jer. A.Z.* 2.5). The high priest in Temple times did not wear the garments of gold when he entered the holy of holies (*v.* Ex. xxviii. 6 f. and Lev. xvi. 4) because these might serve as a reminder of the golden calf and 'a prosecutor cannot act as a defender' (*R.H.* 26a). Some later authorities infer from this that it is forbidden to write prayers on paper used previously for idolatrous books even if the original writing has been erased (*Yoreh De'ah*, 139. 14). If an idol has been desecrated (i.e. by defacing it) by its worshipper it is permitted to have use of it (*Tos. A.Z.* VI, *A.Z.* 52a) but this only applies to an idol belonging to a Gentile. The idol of a Jew is permanently forbidden even after its defacement by the owner (*ibid.*). R. Nahman said that although obscene scoffing is generally forbidden it is permitted when directed against idolatry (*Meg.* 25b). If a person sees a place in Palestine from which idolatry has been uprooted he should say: 'Blessed be He who uprooted idolatry from our land; and as it has been uprooted from this place, so might it be uprooted from all places belonging to Israel; and do Thou turn the heart of those that serve them to serve Thee' (*Ber.* 57b). Although the intention of committing a sin is not counted a sin this does not apply to idolatry where even the mere thought of worshipping idols is accounted sin (*Qidd.* 40a, *Ber.* 12b). The Rabbis were not unaware that the older pagan cults had lost much of their force, hence the saying of R. Johanan that Gentiles outside Palestine are not true idolators but simply continue in the customs of their ancestors (*Hull* 13b).

*   *   *

EXCURSUS

On idolatry in the Biblical period *v.* Ludwig Blau's article in JE, Vol. XII, pp. 568–9 and Yehezkel Kaufmann's massive '*Toledoth Ha-'Emunah Ha-Yisraelith*', Tel-Aviv, 1937 f., now translated into English in an abridged form by Moshe Greenberg, University of Chicago Press, 1960. According to Kaufmann the faith of Israel was monotheistic from the beginning, i.e. from the time of Moses, but on the Biblical view the universalistic God could only be worshipped properly in the holy land. Furthermore, it is only Israel He wishes to reject idolatry. The 'other nations' are permitted

G

by Him to worship idols. Kaufmann's views are stimulating but it is doubtful whether he has proved his case. *Cf.* Edmond Jacob: 'Theology of the Old Testament', Hodder and Stoughton, London, 1958: 'The invective of the prophets against the gods of the nations are not motivated by hate or arrogance, but by the convictions that these gods are powerless to grant to the nations the place to which they have a right in the order of creation; with still more reason these gods could not be of any help to members of the people of Israel who committed the folly of forsaking *Yahweh* to put themselves under their protection' (p. 67). Rabbinic teachings on the severity of idolatry are legion, among them that whoever acknowledges idolatry denies the whole *Torah* (*Ned.* 25a, *cf. Hor.* 8a). Such a person is treated as a *mumar* (apostate) to the whole *Torah* so that any act of ritual slaughter he carries out is invalid (*Hull.* 5a). The prohibition of idolatry is one of the 'seven precepts of the sons of Noah' i.e. and is, therefore, binding upon Gentiles as well as Jews. The *Shulhan 'Arukh, Yoreh De'ah*, 179, records the prohibitions associated with idolatry and idolatrous practices. Following earlier Rabbinic teachings, it rules that there is a prohibition against consulting astrologers. Under certain circumstances, however, it is permitted to utter incantations, not because these are really efficacious but because of their psychological value to one who believes in them. Here the *Shulhan 'Arukh* follows Maimonides, *v.* his Commentary to the *Mishnah A.Z.* IV. *Cf.* the well-known and very interesting stricture of Maimonides contained in the note of the Vilna Gaon (*S.A. ad loc., Biur Ha-Gra*, note 13) who points to the numerous incantations found in the Babylonian *Talmud* and claims that Maimonides was misled by 'philosophy' to interpret these in an over-rational spirit. The whole subject is a very complicated one. Despite determined efforts on the part of Rabbinic authorities to root out superstitious practices some of these gained a foothold in Jewish life, *v.* Joshua Trachtenberg's 'Jewish Magic and Superstition', New York, 1939 and H. J. Zimmels: 'Magicians, Theologians and Doctors', Goldston, London, 1952; S. Rubin: 'Geschichte der Aberglauber', Vienna, 1887. Reference should here be made to the bold interpretation of the Kotzker Rabbi to Deut. iv. 23: 'Take heed unto yourselves, lest ye forget the covenant of the Lord your God, which He made with you, and make you a graven image, *even the likeness of any thing which the Lord thy God hath commanded thee*'. The Kotzker interprets this to mean that man should not make an idol of a command of God! *V.* M. Buber: 'Tales of the Hasidim', Vol. II, Schocken Books, New York, 1948, p. 279. Rabbi A. I. Kook, the late Chief Rabbi of Palestine, has an interesting observation on the impulse to man's self-worship which leads him to a denial of God. According to Kook ('*Oroth Ha-Qodesh*', 2 Vol., ed. D. Cohen, Jer. 1938, Vol. 2, pp. 411–412) there is sometimes to be found deep in the heart of man a bizarre form of envy – envy of God. Man in the wretchedness of his finite situation and human plight envies God His infinite nature and bliss. This leads, among other things, to a denial of God and a deification of man. There are two antidotes, remarks Kook, to this poison, the first intellectual, the second moral. The intellectual antidote consists in the recognition that the difference between God and the world depends on degrees of comprehension. The greater man's comprehension of truth the fuller will be his comprehension that God is in all, that the happiness and well-being of each individual belongs to the happiness which pervades all things, since all have their source in God. The moral antidote is to be found by the man who *freely* develops his own nature so that of his own accord he longs for the triumph of justice and righteousness in the world. Man's free longing is then in accord with the true nature of reality and there is no longer any reason for envy of the divine. According to Rabbi Schneor Zalman of Liady idolatry is not a denial of God but an attempt at insubordination. Man desires to have a little corner of life apart from God's all-embracing power and the idols he sets up are his means of effecting the separation he desires between God and that part of life man wishes to call completely his own. For its worshippers the idol becomes an ultimate instead of the true ultimate, God. Hence, for the Rabbis, pride is equal to idolatry because both commit the same offence of insubordination. 'Pride is equal to idolatry in very truth. For the main root principle of idolatry consists in man's acknowledgment of something as existing in its own right apart and separate from God's holiness, and is not complete denial of God' ('*Tanya*', ed. Vilna, 1930, Chapter 22, p. 55, *v*. J. B. Agus in '*Sepher Ha-Shanah*', Vol. VIII–IX, New York, 1946, p. 273).

[7]

THE SIXTH PRINCIPLE
Prophecy

M AIMONIDES (Abelson's translation) thus expresses the sixth principle of the faith: '*The sixth principle of Faith*. Prophecy. This implies that it should be known that among this human species there exist persons of very intellectual natures and possessing much perfection. Their souls are predisposed for receiving the form of the intellect. Then this human intellect joins itself with the active intellect, and an exalted emanation is shed upon them. These are the prophets. This is prophecy, and this is its meaning. The complete elucidation of this principle of faith would be very long, and it is not our purpose to bring proofs for every principle or to elucidate the means of comprehending them, for this affair includes the totality of the sciences. We shall give them a passing mention only. The verses of the *Torah* which testify concerning the prophecy of prophets are many'.

The '*Yigdal*' formulation reads: 'The rich gift (*shephaʻ*) of his prophecy He gave to the men of His choice, in whom He gloried'. The ' *'Ani Ma'amin'* formulation is: 'I believe with perfect faith that all the words of the prophets are true'.

Friedländer says: 'In the sixth principle we declare our belief in the fact that the Almighty has communicated His Will to human beings, although we are incapable of forming a clear and definite idea of the manner in which such communication took place. The selection of the individual for the office of a prophet, as well as of the time, the place, and the object of the Divine communication, is dependent solely on the Will of God, whose Wisdom and Plan no mortals are able to fathom. We know only that Malachi closed the series of Prophets, but are ignorant of the reason why since Malachi no human being has "found a vision from the Lord". Mankind is, however, not altogether deprived of the benefit of prophecy; the holy

184

book need only be opened, and the message of the prophets
is heard once more'.

Werblowsky has this to say: 'This article is plainly meant
as the methodological premise of the validity of the actual,
concrete Jewish religion. God communicates with man.
Maimonides would even hold that prophecy is not a free
divine *charisma* but is merely the technical term for the highest
level of communion with God arrived at through the intellectual
love of God. Other thinkers would distinguish between communion with God, various types of illumination and the very
specific *charisma* of prophecy. According to Yehudah Halevi
the capacity for prophecy is an innate hereditary characteristic
of the Jewish people; his conception is almost biological, and
involves the notion of a spiritual super-race. Modern liberal
theologians tend to dilute the conception of prophecy to the
rather vague idea of inspiration or "progressive revelation"
or "worship of the divine in the hearts of men". These concepts, however, belong to the history of modern liberal religion
and to none of the great religions in their historic forms. As
the article stands it does not specify the nature and function
of prophecy. It merely asserts that the words of the prophets
as handed down to us, are true. It does not even raise the question by what criteria true prophecy can be distinguished from
false. This problem is treated in the Bible as well as in Talmudic and later literature'.

It should first of all be noted that in Maimonides' formulation
the emphasis is on the possibility of that form of communication
between God and man known as prophecy. Naturally Maimonides would wish to call attention to the classical prophets and
the truth of their message. In this he is at one with the author
of the ' *'Ani Ma'amin'* formulation. But it seems clear from
Maimonides' discussion of prophecy in his other works that
prophecy is possible even after the close of the Canon and that
even in his own day a man could become a prophet. It is true
that the traditional Jewish teaching, as Friedländer observes,
has it that prophecy came to an end in Israel after the Biblical
prophets but there was an equally widely held view that it would
be restored, to usher in the Messianic age, during the thirteenth
century, i.e. possibly during Maimonides' own lifetime.

It should be noted further, as Werblowsky states, that for
Maimonides no special divine gift is involved in prophecy.
Any human being who makes the necessary efforts and who is
endowed with the requisite moral, intellectual and physical
qualities can become a prophet. To the scandal of many subsequent teachers Maimonides goes so far as to write that, far
from prophecy being in any way miraculous, the miracle is
that, on occasion, one who has attained the stage of prophecy
may be prevented by God from becoming a prophet. Here
Maimonides is at complete variance with Yehudah Ha-Levi
who considers prophecy to be an innate faculty of the Jewish
soul. Only a Jew can become a prophet because, through his
ancestry, he possesses the special prophetic talent which
requires to be roused, after due preparation, by God's grace.

Maimonides was fascinated by the problem of prophecy
all his life. Already in his youth he had promised to write a
work on the subject which he actually began but did not finish.
Many of his views on prophecy are, however, to be found in the
work of his old age, his 'Guide for the Perplexed'. A. J.
Heschel may well be right in claiming that Maimonides'
interest in the subject was more than academic and that he
came to believe not only that the prophetic vision would be
restored in his day but that he personally had attained to it,
in its lower stages, on rare occasions in his life.

A section of the 'Guide' (II. 32–48) is devoted to the theme
of prophecy. Maimonides quotes here three opinions about
prophecy among believers in God. Non-believers, who reject
the belief in God, will naturally reject the existence of the
prophetic faculty. The ignorant, says Maimonides, imagine
that God simply selects a person and inspires him to be a
prophet. No qualifications are necessary, other than those of
moral goodness, since no one maintains that a wicked person
can be a prophet. The philosophers (i.e. the Arabic Aristotelians), on the other hand, hold that anyone who attains
intellectual and moral perfection *must* become a prophet. It is
not at all a question of divine grace but of human capacity and
attainment. It is as impossible that a man who is capable of
prophecy not to attain it as it is for a healthy person to be fed
well without assimilating his food. Maimonides accepts the view
of the philosophers with but one qualification. His reading of

Scripture convinces him that only certain persons are chosen
to be prophets. This he explains, as stated, by suggesting that
God may withold prophecy from one suited to attain it by means
of a miracle.

An interesting feature of the Maimonidean view of prophecy
is the role played by the imagination. The prophetic vision
comes through the intellect but strong imaginative powers
are required before it can be realised. 'Prophecy is, in truth and
reality, an emanation sent forth by the Divine Being through
the medium of the active intellect, in the first instance to man's
rational faculty, and then to his imaginative faculty; it is the
highest degree and greatest perfection man can attain; it
consists in the most perfect development of the imaginative
faculty' (II. 36). When the vision comes to the prophet he
trembles greatly and his senses cease to act (II. 41). The
descriptions in the Bible of the prophets performing bizarre
acts are to be understood as part of their vision. They saw, in a
vision, that they performed those acts. Isaiah did not really
go about naked (Is. xx. 3), Jeremiah did not really hide his
girdle (Jer. xiii. 4–7) in the Euphrates, nor did Ezekiel carry
out any of the acts he is said to have performed, except in a vision.
'God forbid to assume that God would make his prophets
appear as objects of ridicule and sport in the eyes of the ignorant,
and order them to perform foolish acts' (II. 46).

The reference to the 'active intellect' has to be understood
as follows. In the view of the Arabic Aristotelians, whose
views here Maimonides relies on, there are ten Intelligences,
that is to say, ten immaterial beings through which God
exercises His control of the universe. Each of these has a
sphere allotted to it. The lowest of these is known as the 'active
intellect' (sekhel ha-po'el). Its sphere is the material world and
the human soul is derived from it. At first, however, in man,
his soul depends on his body. His rational faculties require to
be developed. As they develop by means of intellectual perception the potential soul becomes actual. It is possible for a
man so to develop his soul that it gradually frees itself of the
body to become reunited with the 'active intellect' whence it
originated. When this takes place man has attained to the
degree of prophecy. Thus, anyone who makes the effort
and has the necessary moral perfection and physical and imagina-

188 PRINCIPLES OF THE JEWISH FAITH

tive endowments must prophesy since the 'active intellect' is bound to do its work, unless, as Maimonides stipulates, God prevents this by a miracle.

Far different is the view of Yehudah Ha-Levi. Ha-Levi denies that prophecy is a natural process but looks upon it as a gift from God. Nor is intellectual perfection essential to the attainment of the prophetic vision. Furthermore, prophecy is confined to the Jewish race so that even a convert to Judaism cannot be a prophet. H. A. Wolfson has pointed out that this 'nationalistic' view is not found at all clearly in the Rabbinic sources (in fact, there are in those sources references to prophets of the nations) but is found, oddly enough, at first in Christian sources. The Church Fathers do speak occasionally of prophecy as confined to the Jewish people, probably to enable them to transfer it, after the rejection of Jesus by the Jews, exclusively to Christians. Secondly, in Ha-Levi's view geographical as well as biological considerations are involved. The prophet must belong to the line of prophets, reaching from Adam through Seth, Enosh, Noah, Shem, Abraham, Isaac and Jacob down to the members of the Jewish race, and he must reside in the holy land. (Ha-Levi's references to prophecy are scattered throughout his *'Kuzari'* but *v.* especially: I. 47, 95, 115; II. 14, 49; III. 1, 5, 11, 23; V. 21).

Hasdai Crescas occupies a midway position between Maimonides and Ha-Levi. Disagreeing with Maimonides' view that prophecy is 'natural' and a matter of human training in the main, Crescas agrees with Ha-Levi that only Jews can become prophets. But it is not due to a special mystic, almost biological, faculty that prophecy is limited to Jews but because the type of moral training required can only be provided by the *Torah*, the possession of the Jewish people. (*'Or 'Adonai'*, Part II, Chapter 4, ed. Vienna, 1859, p. 46a). Other Jewish thinkers take issue with Maimonides. Nahmanides (Commentary to Gen. xviii. 1) objects to his statement that the events recorded of the prophets did not really take place but were part of the prophetic vision. Gersonides (*'Milhamoth'*, II. 6) and Albo (*'Iqqarim'*, III. 8) are critical of the role allotted by Maimonides to the imaginative faculty in prophecy.

Moses Hayyim Luzzatto in his *'Derekh 'Adonai'* leans heavily on his predecessors, particularly on Maimonides and the

Qabbalah, in his description of the prophetic faculty. Luzzatto
(III. 3. par. 4) defines the prophetic experience as a 'cleaving
to God'. As a result of this attachment the prophet acquires a
superhuman insight. The prophetic experience is thus described
(III. 3. par. 6): 'When God reveals Himself to the prophet
and pours out on him His influence the prophet is seized by a
tremendous power; his material form and bodily organs
tremble and feel as if they are about to be overcome. For it
belongs to the nature of matter that it cannot endure the revelation of anything spiritual, still less the revelation of God's
glory. The prophet's senses become numb and even his psychic
faculties no longer operate automatically but become dependent
on God and on His influence which pours down on to him'.
Luzzatto goes on to say that the prophet acquires superhuman
knowledge as a result of his experience and this remains with
him even after his return to normality. It is not necessary,
says Luzzatto (III. 4. par. 6) for a prophet to be sent with a
message from God to His people. The essence of prophecy
is attachment to God but it is sometimes incidental to the prophetic experience that God delivers to the prophet a message to
others which he is then obliged to carry to them. On the literary
side of the prophecy, Luzzatto (III. 4. par. 8) remarks that a
prophet may attain to superhuman knowledge of some matter
which he then puts into words of his own choosing. But the
great literary prophets, whose prophecy concerns future
generations, were the recipients of a 'verbal inspiration', the
very words belonging to the content of their message, even
though these are mediated through the personality of the
prophet.

The discussions among the classical Jewish writers on the
nature of prophecy are of interest but the results of modern
investigations are at least as important and probably more
rewarding. Nor are any particular views of the nature of the
prophetic experience relevant to the theological question of
what is involved in the acceptance of the sixth principle of
faith. Many Jews today would be prepared to argue, with
plausibility, that not being prophets ourselves we cannot hope
to comprehend the exact nature of the prophetic experience.
But for all that, we acknowledge the sacredness of Scripture
with its record of revelation *to* and *through* the prophets and we

see that however these men received their revelation, their
message concerning the God who demands holiness, justice and
mercy in human affairs contains the highest demands made upon
man. Consequently, we accept the sixth principle of faith as a
principle of revelation. This is far different from the opinion
of 'liberal' theology (of which Werblowsky speaks) that
Isaiah was inspired as Shakespeare was inspired. The tendency
in a good deal of present-day theological thinking attempts
to do justice to the unique character of Scripture as the 'word
of God' without failing to recognise the human element in
revelation. In fact, thousands of devoted modern scholars have
shed new light on the Biblical record and the idea of prophecy
and their findings are indispensable for a proper appraisal
of what the Bible actually says concerning the prophetic
experience. Some of these views we must now examine but
although this kind of investigation is important, and must
be pursued as rigorously and as objectively as possible, we
can approach it as religious Jews with a completely free
attitude of mind. For, after all has been said, there remains
an element of mystery about the prophetic experience and the
words of the prophets still speak, as do no other, to the human
situation.

*   *   *

EXCURSUS

It should be noted in any discussion of the role of the prophets from
the Jewish point of view that in the Rabbinic tradition the *Torah*
contains the complete revelation so that the Rabbis could say that
if Israel had not sinned no further revelation through prophets and
kethubhim would have been required (*Ned.* 22b). No prophet was
able to make any innovations, since the revelation to Moses was
complete (*Sabb.* 104a, *Meg.* 2b). *Cf.* on this theme G. F. Moore,
'Judaism', Harvard University Press, 1958, Vol. I, pp. 239 f. An
excellent survey of Rabbinic and mediaeval views on prophecy is
that of Emil G. Hirsch in JE, Vol. X, pp. 215–219. *Cf.* the index
under 'Prophecy' in I. Husik's 'A History of Mediaeval Jewish
Philosophy', Philadelphia, 1940. For Maimonides' views on
prophecy the best works are: Z. Diesendruck: 'Maimonides Lehre
von der Prophetie' in 'Jewish Studies in Memory of Israel Abrahams', New York, 1927, pp. 74–148; H. A. Wolfson: 'Hallevi
and Maimonides on Prophecy' in JQR, New Series, Vol. 32, pp.
345–370 and Vol. 33, pp. 49–82; A. J. Heschel: '*Ha-He' emin Ha-*

Rambam She-Zakhah Li-Nebhu'ah' in the Louis Ginzberg Jubilee
Volume, Heb. sec., New York, 1946, pp. 159–188. Abraham
Abulafia (b. 1240) was greatly influenced by Maimonides and
became the author of prophetical writings through which he made
many enemies, *v.* G. Scholem: 'Major Trends in Jewish Mysticism',
London, Thames and Hudson, London, 1955, pp. 126–155. On
Crescas *v.* S. B. Urbach: 'The Philosophic Teachings of Rabbi
Hasdai Crescas' (Hebrew)' Jer. 1961, Chapter 8, pp. 249–272.
Albo's views on prophecy are to be found in his '*Iqqarim*', Book III,
Chapters 8–12, ed. I Husik, Philadelphia, 1946, Vol. III, pp. 64 f.
Albo (III.9) deals with the question of how God reveals Himself
to different prophets in different ways. Quoting *Ber. R.* 4 Albo says
that just as a man's form is seen differently in mirrors of different
shapes and sizes so does God appear to the prophets under many
and various forms according to the brightness and purity of the
media, though God Himself does not multiply or change. Hence
the Rabbis say: 'Many prophets have one idea, though no two
prophets use the same expression' (*Sanh.* 89a). Albo (III. 11)
agrees that prophecy is only possible in the holy land and among
the Jewish people but his reason for this opinion is novel. The
illumination which comes to the prophet derives from the *Shekhinah*
which rested upon the ark and the tablets of stone, like a spark of
sunlight reflected in a mirror. The prophet who had in him a
certain preparation analogous to the contents of the ark, namely,
who had really made the *Torah* ideas his own, was able to receive
this reflected glory. It follows that prophecy could only be found
among Israel in the holy land since the two conditions of the ark
and the *Torah* personality were required.

*   *   *

The term *nabhi* occurs as a noun with the meaning of a
prophet over four hundred times in the Hebrew Bible as well
as more than one hundred and ten times in verbal form. It is
used of Abraham (Gen. xx. 7), Aaron (Ex. vii. 1), Moses,
Miriam (Ex. xv. 20), of Elijah and Elisha and the great
literary prophets. What is the history of the term? Part of the
difficulty in attempting to answer this question belongs to the
problem of dating the various Biblical books. For instance, the
well-known text we shall now consider from the book of
Samuel would be more helpful to the investigation if we could
determine the exact date when it was recorded and this we
cannot do. In the first book of Samuel it is told how Saul,

searching for the lost asses of his father, decided to ask Samuel where they were to be found. It appears from the narrative that one of the functions of the prophet, here called a *ro'eh* ('seer'), was to assist people by means of his clairvoyant powers. As a gloss to the story the verse (I Sam. ix. 9) states: 'Beforetime in Israel, when a man went to inquire of God, thus he said: "Come and let us go to the seer (*ro'eh*)"; for he that is now called a prophet (*nabhi*) was beforetime called a seer (*ro'eh*)'. It would seem from this that a development took place in the role and functions of the prophet, that in earlier times he was called a *ro'eh*, with the emphasis on his clairvoyant powers, and later he assumed the role of *nabhi*. But, apart from the problem of chronology to which we have referred, it appears from the use of the term *ro'eh* of later prophets that it is precarious to infer any hard and fast or clear-cut distinction between the two types of prophet. Be that as it may, it is important to consider the function of the *nabhi* on the basis of the evidence presented by the Bible itself and the study of this evidence against the general background of ancient Near Eastern cultural and religious patterns.

Elijah, one of the earliest *nebhi'im*, is distinguished by his strangeness and the unusual nature of his dress. He is said to have worn 'a girdle of leather about his loins' (I Kings i. 8). This strangeness of the *nabhi*, setting him apart from his fellows as a man infused with God's spirit (*ruah*) is repeatedly implied in many Scriptural passages. Of great significance are the references to the 'sons of the prophets' (*bene ha-nebhi'im*) i.e. the aspirants for the role of *nabhi* who would gather round a *nabhi* to learn his methods (v. II Kings ii. 3, iv. 1). The prophets resorted to music (II Kings iii. 15) and dancing (I Kings xviii. 26) in order to awaken the spirit. Although this last verse refers to the 'false prophets' it is significant that the term *nabhi* is used in Scripture of both the prophets of God and the prophets of Baal. This only confirms what we know from the picture of Near Eastern religion in ancient times as revealed by the many archaeological discoveries, that the phenomenon of "*nebhi'ism*" was not confined to Israel and that in Israel itself there were sufficient common characteristics between true and false prophets to justify the use of the same term for both.

This leads to the question of whether it is legitimate to

speak of the prophets as 'ecstatics', on which there has been so much discussion in recent years. The older view was that the very word *nabhi* came from a root meaning 'to bubble forth' and was held as referring to the pouring forth of words in a frenzy of ecstasy or even to foaming at the mouth in a kind of fit. This view has now been generally abandoned. Many moderns prefer, following in this some of the mediaeval Jewish commentators, to understand the root meaning of *nabhi* as signifying 'to call'. There is, in fact, an Akkadian root *nabu* meaning 'to call'. The meaning of the term *nabhi* according to this would be 'one who calls', 'one who has a message to deliver'. Albright, on the basis of the same Akkadian root, understands the term to mean 'one who has received "a call" '. (H. Wheeler Robinson: 'Inspiration and Revelation in the Old Testament', Clarendon Press, 1946, page 173, note 1, with justice, however, says that this seems to import too much 'theology' into what must have been a primitive term).

Much depends on what is meant by 'ecstatic' in this connection. If by 'ecstatic' is meant 'abnormal' behaviour it is difficult to see how it can be ignored that the *nebhi'im* did engage in such behaviour. But if by 'ecstatic' is meant the kind of phenomena associated with the mystics we are on more shaky ground. J. Muilenburg ('Peake's Commentary on the Bible', ed. Matthew Black and H. H. Rowley, Thomas Nelson and Sons, London, 1962, pp. 475–483) rightly says that there is no clear instance anywhere in the whole of the prophetic literature of the personality of the prophet being effaced. Consequently, he argues that a term like 'ecstasy' should be used with caution of the prophets although it perhaps best describes the type of phenomenon we have been considering. In recent years, too, there has been a great deal of discussion on the role of the 'cultic prophets'. Abandoning the older view of a severe conflict between prophet and priest, modern scholars, on the analogy of Near Eastern patterns as revealed in cultic texts and on the many hints in the Bible itself (e.g. I Kings i. 34, Nathan the prophet and Zadok the priest; II Kings xxiii. 2; Is. xxviii. 7; Lam. ii. 20; Jer. xxiii), have argued with considerable conviction for the existence of cultic prophets in ancient Israel.

A further question to be considered before examining the role of the great 'classical prophets' or 'literary prophets' is the nature of the 'false prophets'. How did these differ from the true prophets? The difference between the two on the Biblical evidence appears to be that the false prophets (who may have been cultic prophets) told the people only that which they wanted to hear instead of speaking to their conscience as did the true prophets. The false prophets 'speak of peace where there is no peace' (Jer. vi. 14, Ez. xiii. 10 and 16). In Buber's words, the true prophets were 'Realpolitiker', the false prophets 'Illusion-politiker'. The whole of the thirteenth chapter of Ezekiel is important in this connection. Here it is stated that the false prophets say 'the Lord saith' whereas He had not, in fact, sent them (Ezek. xiii. 6). They engaged not in the Lord's battle and failed to repair the hedges (Ezek. xiii. 5).

The picture we have in the Bible of conditions before the rise of the literary prophets is that of bands of *nebhi'im*, probably grouped in some way around the shrines, who were the spokes-men of God. Some of these were 'true' prophets, serving as the conscience of the nation, others were 'false' prophets, failing to remind the people of God's demand on them. All of them appear to have cultivated something resembling the ecstatic state.

The important question now to be considered is the precise relationship between the older groups of *nebhi'im* and the great 'classical' prophets. The classical prophets may also have been ecstatics, though this element is definitely played down in the Scriptural descriptions of their character and work. Were the great classical prophets, Amos, Hosea, Isaiah, Jeremiah and Ezekiel, members of a prophetic guild, distinguished from other *nebhi'im* only by the special quality of their message, or did they belong to an entirely different type of prophet? In the light of the evidence it is by no means easy to answer this question. A good deal turns on the precise meaning of Amos vii. 14–15, the famous declaration of the first of the literary prophets: 'Then answered Amos, and said to Amaziah: "I was no *nabhi*, neither was I a *ben nabhi* ('*son of a nabhi*', i.e. disciple of a *nabhi*); but I was a herdman, and a dresser of sycamore-trees; and the Lord took me from following the flock, and the Lord said unto me: Go, prophesy unto My people Israel" '. Does Amos mean that he *was* not a *nabhi* until God called him (i.e. as he had no prophetic ambitions he had not joined a prophetic

guild) but *now* that he has been called he *is* a *nabhi*? Or does
he mean that he *is* no *nabhi* but someone whom God has called
for a special purpose (the Hebrew bears both meanings)? If
the second interpretation is correct it may well be that in the
great classical prophets we have a completely new type of
messenger from God to the people, called *nebhi'im* only by
analogy with the members of the prophetic guild. However, it
will not do to overstress the differences in character between the
earlier *nebhi'im* and the later 'classical' prophets. The latter
grew out of the former and it is not at all surprising to find many
features common to both.

Perhaps the most remarkable thing to be observed of the
classical prophets is the assurance with which they speak of their
message as coming directly from God. 'The lion hath roared',
says Amos, 'who will not fear? The Lord God hath spoken,
who can but prophesy?' (Amos iii. 8). Isaiah tells of the Lord
speaking to him 'with a strong hand' (Is. viii. 11). Jeremiah
tells how the Lord put His words into his mouth (Jer. i. 9) and
how God imparted to him words of fire (Jer. xxiii. 29). The
book of Ezekiel contains a vivid description of how God's
message comes to the prophet so that he is compelled to speak
(Ezek. iii). The message which comes to the prophet is, in
the first instance, to his contemporaries and it frequently has
to do with future events. It is consequently too superficial to
draw the common distinction between 'forthtellers' and 'fore-
tellers' and to claim that the classical prophets belonged only
to the former group. There is an element of prediction in the
work of the classical prophets, too, though, as Professor
Rowley says, the predictions are of a future arising out of the
present rather than a distant, unrelated future. The 'foretelling'
aspect, so common in Near Eastern prophecy and in Greek, is
by no means absent from Israelite prophecy. However, detailed
prognostication of events hidden in the future is alien to the
Hebrew prophets (the second part of Isaiah is, on these grounds
and others, generally considered by scholars to belong to
another prophet, the 'prophet of exile'). But, seeing as they
did the hand of God in human history, the prophets described
for their people their insight into the way in which human history
unfolds itself pregnant with God's purpose. Very few will
consult the prophets today in order to read modern political

events out of the ancient pages. The significance of the prophets lies in the unique way in which they teach that God is the Lord of history. Professor Muilenburg (*op. cit.*) has put this most effectively: 'The Hebrew prophets tower head and shoulders over their contemporaries both in ancient Israel and in the ancient Near East. Kings, priests, sages and psalmists have their distinctive place in the life and religion of Israel, but none rise to the stature of the prophets or continue to exercise so major an influence on subsequent history. Whether we view them in the light of the phenomenology of religion or in the context of human culture or in the frame of the history of literature, they occupy a position in the thought and faith of mankind unmatched by any other single group. They belong to their own times, but are not confined by them; they are in many way typical members of their race, yet they often transcend the characteristic features of their Semitic cultural heritage and environment. They address themselves to the needs and crises of the ancient world of men in which they lived, but their words continue to stir the conscience of men, to call them to responsibility, to assert the claims of the divine imperative'.

*   *   *

EXCURSUS

The best survey of modern literature on the ecstatic nature of Hebrew prophecy is that of H. H. Rowley: 'The Nature of Prophecy in the Light of Recent Study' in the Harvard Theological Review, Vol. XXXVIII, 1945, pp. 1–38. Rowley quotes Wheeler Robinson who prefers to speak of 'abnormal experience' since the term 'ecstasy' rightly belongs to Greek psychology with its sharper distinction than the Hebrew between soul and body. Rowley (p. 6) rightly observes that even if the term *nabhi* does have an etymology which suggests the idea of ecstasy, words have a history as well as a derivation, and the question is not what the word originally meant but what it came to represent. On the other hand there are undoubtedly abnormal behaviour patterns to be observed even among the great literary prophets, e.g. Isaiah walking naked in the streets, Jeremiah hiding his girdle, Ezekiel eating dung, the symbolic names given to Isaiah's and Hosea's children, which, as Rowley says, 'would seem a little hard on the children'. We have seen that it was considerations of this sort that led Maimonides to deny that these events actually happened except in a vision. J. Lindblom: 'Grundfragen der Altestestamentlichen Wissenschaft' in

Festschrift Alfred Bertholet, Tubingen, 1950, p. 327, makes a
famous distinction between two kinds of ecstasy. 'Absorption
ecstasy' belongs to the *unio mystica* but is not that of the prophet,
whereas 'concentration ecstasy' is that of the prophet. In 'concentration ecstasy' there is an absolute concentration on an idea or
group of ideas during which normal consciousness ceases to operate.
Cf. 'The Prophets of Israel' by Curt Kuhl, trans. by Rudolf J.
Ehrlich and J. P. Smith, Oliver and Boyd, Edinburgh and London,
1960, p. 20. H. Wheeler Robinson: 'Inspiration and Revelation in
the Old Testament', Oxford, Clarendon Press, 1946, pp. 187–198:
The Theological Validity of Prophecy', Chapter XIV, is helpful.
Wheeler Robinson does well to remind us that: 'We may be so
occupied with the psychological process that we forget the most
important of all, that God in His own way, whatever that was, has
brought to birth by human travail a truth which man needed to
know' (p. 192). Aage Bentzen ('Introduction to the Old Testament',
2nd. ed., Copenhagen, 1952, Vol. I, pp. 191–202, similarly argues
that it is only a deficiency in modern man's religious experience
which brings him to label the prophetic experience as 'abnormal';
this is only another way of saying, as we have done, that one must
be a prophet in order to understand fully the prophetic experience.
'It is certainly necessary', observes Bentzen (p. 192), 'to make it
plain that the psychological condition of the prophets is not so
'abnormal' as generally supposed. That word can only be used of
the very exaggerated cases of ecstasy, which are, however, seldom'.
Bentzen (p. 195) also makes the important point, for which he
acknowledges his indebtedness to earlier scholars, particularly
Lindblom, that the ecstatic style of the prophetic oracle demands
frequently a rough language with the pictures chasing one another
and resulting in grammatical incongruities. Thus it is a mistake for
the scholar to be tempted on to 'the slippery road of textual
emendations'. It should be noted that the ancient view did not see
the prophets as abnormal. We have already noted Maimonides'
views in this connection. St. Jerome (Introduction to Prophecy of
Nahum, quoted by R. A. Knox: 'Enthusiasm', Oxford, Clarendon
Press, 1957, p. 35) states that the Old Testament prophets had all
their wits about them. Yehezkel Kaufmann: 'The Religion of
Israel', translated and abridged by Moshe Greenberg, University
of Chicago Press, 1960, is original on his ideas of Hebrew prophecy.
Kaufmann points out (p. 94) that in ancient Israel there was no
science of oneirocriticism – dream interpretation. The only two
oneirocritics among the Biblical heroes are Joseph and Daniel
and they both belong to the court of heathen kings. Even here the
Bible assimilates the oneirocriticism to the word of God, it is God

who inspires them to interpret the dream. Kaufmann notes (pp. 92–101) that all forms of Israelite prophecy contain mantic features, yet there is, for all that, an essential difference between the Israelite and pagan conceptions of prophecy. In pagan religion prophecy is regarded as deriving from a special mantic source of power. The prophet has the gift provided by this power either from birth or by acquisition. But in Israel the prophetic spirit 'comes upon' the prophet and is in no way a native talent. The prophetic ideal of the Bible is Moses (Deut. xxxiv. 10) and yet of him no ecstatic phenomena are related (Kaufmann, pp. 98–9). A very important survey of the whole subject is that of O. Eissfeldt in 'The Old Testament and Modern Study', ed. by H. H. Rowley, Oxford, Clarendon Press, 1956, pp. 115–161. *V.* the discussion on pp. 136–145 on the religious evaluation of the prophetic message and particularly the quotation from Mowinckel on p. 141: 'I am no longer primarily interested in unravelling the processes of the prophet's psychological experiences, in discussing how far the factors hold good in general, that caused the particular experience to take on an ecstatic character and to assume the form of visions, auditions, etc., etc., etc. That is a task for the psychologist, and it is not the duty of a theologian to become a professional psychologist'. A. J. Heschel's work on the prophets, 'Die Prophetie', Krakow, 1936, has attracted a good deal of attention. Heschel looks upon the prophet not as an ecstatic at all but as a special type of man sharing the divine *pathos*. In the sympathy they feel with this the prophets enter into the very experience of God Himself. In fact, according to Heschel, the *sympatheticos* is the exact opposite of the ecstatic. The prophetic state, as Heschel sees it, is a constant one, totally different from the tumultuous state of ecstasy which is for the moment. *V.* now Heschel's book 'The Prophets', Jew. Pub. Soc., Philadelphia, 1962.

*   *   *

Mowinckel (The Old Testament as Word of God', trans. by Reidar B. Bjornard, Blackwell, Oxford, 1960) has recently elaborated on the important theme of the 'word' (*dabhar*) of the Lord which 'comes' to the prophet. The Hebrew word *dabhar* means both 'word' and 'thing'. The more general sense in which *dabhar* is used of prophetic experience calls attention not so much to the 'word' as to the 'thing', the prophetic *dabhar*, the prophetic 'thing', being a situation in which the prophet encounters God. As a result of this experience it becomes clear to him what it is that God would have him do and the nature of the message God would have him bring to his people. The confrontation with God is the 'thing of the Lord', the encounter with the divine, which imparts to the prophet super-human powers of insight and perception so that he now observes the situation in which his people finds itself with a clarity quite beyond the normal human understanding. It is not so much that actual *words* are imparted to him as that he himself finds the suitable words to express his experience and the message it implies. However, it is the content of the experience, the nature of the message which results from it, which gives the experience its validation as a message from God. As Mowinckel (quoted by Rowley, HTR, *op. cit.*, p. 36, note 149) puts it: 'The content is the deciding factor, which makes the prophet's experience an experience of God. The experience of an empty and more or less unutterable *mysterium tremendum et fascinosum* would not make the prophets essentially different from the common *nabhi*; the ecstatic *nebhi'im* had purely "numinous" experiences, but these were of no value as revela-tions. What is merely "numinous" may just as well be "Ba'al" as Yahweh; it may just as well be a "lying spirit" as the spirit of Yahweh, and of this the great prophets are fully aware. The content of an experience makes it an experience of Yahweh, or rather, proves that it is one. In other words, *the certitude of the experience depends upon whether it has a definite content, capable of being apprehended by the mind and tested by religious and moral standards'*.

This point of view, and it has much to commend it as true to the account given of prophecy in the Biblical record, lies midway between the interpretation of prophecy as a simple experience of the numinous and that of verbal inspiration. It is the *content* of the experience, not the experience itself, which gives it its validation as coming from God, but it is not a case of divine dictation of the actual words in which the message is later conveyed. There is no question of verbal dictation to the prophet. The prophetic experience is not, to use Coleridge's phrase, supernatural ventriloquism. If it were, it is difficult to see why each prophet expresses the vision he has seen in terms of his own cultural background, Amos as a herdman, Isaiah as a nobleman, and so forth. The prophet retains his individuality. Although the basic experience is more or less the same for all the prophets, the content is different, and its formulation differs according to the prophet's personality and the particular application of his message. We have seen that Albo develops the illustration of a figure seen in different mirrors. Rowley (*op. cit.* p. 30) uses the illustration of light passing through a piece of coloured glass where the light is from without yet coloured by the glass.

Another problem of importance in connection with prophecy is that of the relationship between the prophetic experience and message and the actual record of it we now have in the prophetic books. Did the prophets themselves write the books which now appear under their name in the Bible? Already in the famous *Baraitha* quoted in the Babylonian *Talmud* (*B.B.* 14b–15a) it is suggested that some of the prophetic books, at least, were edited by later teachers rather than written down by the prophets whose names they bear. Thus Hezekiah and his colleagues are said to have written the book of Isaiah and the Men of the Great Assembly the book of Ezekiel. Eissfeldt (*op. cit.* p. 117), in a survey of the whole question in the light of recent researches, observes that no countenance is now given to the theory that the prophets themselves put down in writing their individual oracles or collections of them. The stress is now on oral traditions, i.e., the words of the master were treasured in the memories of his disciples and transmitted to later times by word of mouth. These sayings were enlarged and expanded from time to time. Only after the books had attained their final form in the oral tradition did writing take place so that the books named after the earlier prophets were not put down in writing until post-exilic times (*cf.* Eissfeldt, *op. cit*, pp. 126–134). A rather less extreme view is taken by Curt Kuhl (*op. cit.*, pp. 36–40). Kuhl discusses the question, what is the relationship between the *ipsissima verba* of the prophets and the literary work in the Bible under their name? He states that there are two opinions among modern scholars. (1) No literature was produced by the prophets themselves. The words of the prophets were handed down in the form of oral traditions and were only written down in post-exilic times. In the course of transmission the material underwent certain modifications and addition, e.g. eschatological material was added. But the difficulty of this view is to account for the personal elements such as the autobiographical material. Why should this kind of material have been preserved as part of the oral tradition since the personal life of the prophet cannot have had much relevance to the situation of posterity? Furthermore the stress among certain modern scholars on oral traditions is based in part on the erroneous assumption that writing was virtually unknown in ancient Israel. (2) The prophet's words were recorded in writing by his disciples. But various oracles were incorporated from other sources and adaptations were later made for the relevance to the contemporary situation in later times. If we keep in mind, concludes Kuhl, the glosses, the additions, the adaptations to the contemporary situation, as well as such things as textual corruptions, the discovery of the *ipsissima verba* of the prophets is very difficult. But Kuhl calls special attention to the great reliability of the autobiographical sections of the prophetic books. These were probably written by the prophet himself or by his disciples.

For further understanding of this important question the following considerations should be noted. Autobiographical material is found in Isaiah vi. and viii; Jeremiah i, ii and xxxvi; Hosea i. 2–9 and iii; and Amos vii. The book of Ezekiel is entirely autobiographical. Isaiah (xxx. 8) is told to write his message on a tablet and inscribe it in a book that it might endure. The same prophet is told to 'bind the testimony, seal the instruction among My disciples' (Is. viii. 16). This may well suggest that at first the prophet's words were recorded, either by himself or by his disciples, and that at some later date the various messages, given at different times, were gathered together. In the collected sayings of the prophet the editors may have incorporated pieces from other sources. This is the most probable explanation of passages duplicated in the books of two prophets. Thus, the famous passage containing the prophetic vision of war being banished from earth is found in almost identical words in the book of Micah (iv. 1 f.) and Isaiah (ii. 2 f.). It is also possible, however, that one prophet is quoting from the other, or they may both be quoting from another source. It is interesting to note that we find in two prophetic books virtually identical messages but directed in each case against a different nation. A good example of this is the comparison of Isaiah against Egypt (xxxi. 3) with

Ezekiel against Tyre (xxviii. 2), where both prophets scorn-
fully declare that the nations to which their prophecies are
directed are 'men and not God'. Further remarkable duplica-
tions in the work of two prophets are: Obadiah's prediction of
Edom's downfall couched in the identical words of Jeremiah's
prediction of the same event (Jer. xlix. 7 f.) and Isaiah's
'burden of Moab' (Is. xv) compared with that of Jeremiah
(Jer. xlviii). All this indicates how complicated the whole
question of discovering the *ipsissima verba* of the prophets is
and how difficult it is to answer with any degree of certainty
the question of how the books as we know them came to assume
their present form.

In a generation greatly interested in psychology it is but
natural to endeavour to investigate the psychological processes
of the great classical prophets. We have touched upon this
question earlier in our discussion. Attempts at psychoanalysing
the prophets have been made and it can hardly be denied that a
study of the autobiographical material in the prophetic books
occasionally yields the picture of psychic abnormality. (*Cf.*
Rowley HTR, *op. cit.* pp. 24 f. and notes and pp. 27 f. and notes).
Superficial investigators have sometimes permitted themselves
to question the value of work produced by men whose psychological makeup was so different from our own. But, as William
James observed long ago, the value of the pearl is not affected
by the clinical description of a pearl as a disease in the oyster.
The prophets are recognised as inspired men because of the
timelessness of their message and its permanent validity.
Professor Broad has even argued that for a man to have windows
to heaven he must be a little 'cracked' in the head! Which is
only another way of saying that the prophets were 'abnormal'
because the average man is no prophet. No perceptive student of
prophecy in Israel will compare the prophetic message with
the rantings of a psychopath, if only because the resultant
message of the prophets contains the ripest wisdom, the richest
insight, and so deep an understanding of the human situation
that generations of men have found it to be the word of God.

To sum up, no violence whatsoever is done to our reason
when we accept Maimonides' sixth principle of the faith.
However we understand, or fail to understand, the exact
nature of the prophetic experience, however much we become

aware of the human element in the experience itself and its
transmission to us, however conscious we are of the great
difficulty of knowing the *ipsissima verba* of the prophets, however strong our recognition that Hebrew prophecy has its
roots in a common Near Eastern pattern, the fact remains
that the succession of strange figures which emerged in
ancient Israel, whom we call the prophets, brought a message,
expressed now in deathless language, of God's love for mankind and His demands of them of holiness, justice and mercy. As
we have noted, Bishop Gore says in his profound book 'Belief
in God' ('Pelican Books', 1939, pp. 79–80): 'Here, then, we
find a succession of wonderful men, mostly conscious of profound unpopularity in their contemporary world, who nevertheless, even in the face of the most determined hostility of
courts and people, delivered a message which we feel to be
self-consistent and to involve the same great principles throughout, about God – His nature, His will, His purposes – and
about human nature – its dignity, its responsiblity, and its sin;
a message which they declare, with the fullest conviction, to be
derived not from their own reasoning or speculation, nor from
tradition (though they would have indignantly repudiated
the idea that they were its first recipients), nor from any
external source at all, but from God, the God of Israel, speaking
in their own souls, so intensely and clearly that there could
be no mistake about it'. Of all the thirteen principles, this is
probably the one which presents no difficulties whatsoever.
For the words of the prophets are there for us and our descendants to read, and sensitive readers throughout the ages have
accepted that these words are true because they have found the
response to them in their own hearts and have recognised in
them a challenge calling forth the highest of which they are
capable.

*   *   *

EXCURSUS

Good bibliographies of modern works on the prophets are to be
found in Eissfeldt, *op. cit.*, Rowley, *HTR*, *op. cit.*, and compiled by
N. W. Porteous, in Kuhl, *op. cit.*, pp. 192–196. Martin Buber: 'The
Prophetic Faith', translated from the Hebrew by Carlyle Witton-
Davies, Macmillan, New York, 1949, is a penetrating interpretation
of Hebrew prophecy. *Cf.* 'Studies in Old Testament Prophecy' –

presented to Professor T. H. Robinson, ed. H. H. Rowley and T.
Clark, Edinburgh, 1950; 'Israel's Prophetic Heritage' – Essays in
honor of James Muilenberg, ed. Bernard W. Anderson and
Walter Harrelson, Harper, New York, 1962; 'Introduction to the
Old Testament' by Artur Weiser, translated by Dorothea M.
Barton, Darton, Longman and Todd, London, 1961, section on:
'The Prophetic Saying', pp. 44–50. Of older works, two of the most
important are 'The Prophets of Israel' by W. Robinson Smith,
2nd. ed., Adam and Charles Black, London, 1895, and 'Prophecy
and Religion' by James Skinner, Cambridge University Press, 1930.
On the relationship between the earlier *nebhi'im* and the classical
prophets Skinner's words (p. 4 note 1) are still relevant: 'The real
point at issue, however, is whether a great and even sudden
advance in religious enlightenment involves an absolute breach of
continuity with the kind of experience which was admittedly
characteristic of the earlier "*nabhi'ism*". The case is closely analogous to the development of self-conscious reason in man from the
rudimentary intelligence of the lower animals. The two are
separated by an immeasurable chasm, so that the higher can never
be *explained* in terms of the lower; and yet the persistence of
animal appetites and instincts in the mental life of man proves
conclusively that somehow it has sprung from that of the animals.
Similarly in the spiritual prophecy of the Old Testament we find
traces of ecstasy, visions and auditions, which are obviously
survivals of states of consciousness belonging to prophecy of a
lower grade. And the fact that the great prophets far surpassed
their predecessors in their apprehension of religious truth is no
reason for denying the reality of the ecstatic element in their experience, or for explaining it away as a mere rhetorical accom-
modation to traditional modes of expression'. A profound study of
the prophetic experience is that of Adolphe Lods: 'The Prophets
and the Rise of Judaism', translated by S. H. Hooke, Kegan Paul,
London, 1937. On the question of the 'sanity of the prophets'
Lods writes (p. 57): 'It would be necessary to disregard the
evidence of history, and to forget the instances of Paul, Mahommed,
Luther, Pascal, in order to maintain that a tendency to ecstasy is
incompatible with a sane and vigorous mind. According to modern
psychology, hallucination is nothing but the awakening of a *memory*
with particular intensity: what the ecstatic sees and hears in trance
is the expression of his personality: it is the fruit, perhaps ripened
in unconsciousness, of his reflections, of his previous religious
experiences, of the deep tendencies of his whole being, rising to the
threshold of consciousness like something which appears to him to
come from outside himself'. Lods notes that both Hosea and

Jeremiah were called 'madmen' by their contemporaries (Hos. ix. 7; Jer. xxix. 26) as had been the 'sons of the prophets' in the time of Elisha (II Kings ix. 11). The characteristic mark of the great prophets is their conviction that they are interpreters and instruments of the righteous God who reveals Himself to them. On the question of the characteristics of the great prophets *v*. H. Wheeler Robinson: 'Inspiration and Revelation in the Old Testament', Clarendon Press, Oxford, 1946, pp. 164–172. Here three important implications of the prophet's call are noted: (a) *God takes the initiative*. The prophet feels himself compelled to undertake his task against his will. The very opposite of magic is here seen since magic is the human attempt to coerce the divine. (b) *There is an intimate association of the prophet with God*. Thus, in the prophetic books the 'I' of the prophet is frequently interchangeable with the 'I' of God. (c) *The word of God becomes as it were 'depersonalised' with an objective power of its own*. The prophet is quite unlike an author interested in questions of 'copyright' and acquiring 'immortality' through his work.

[8]

THE SEVENTH PRINCIPLE
The Superiority of Moses

MAIMONIDES devotes a great deal of space to the formulation of this principle. Here it is in Abelson's translation:

'*The seventh Principle of Faith*. The Prophecy of Moses our Teacher. This implies that we must believe that he was the father of all the prophets before him and that those who came after him were all beneath him in rank. He (Moses) was chosen by God from the whole human kind. He comprehended more of God than any man in the past or future ever comprehended or will comprehend. And we must believe that he reached a state of exaltedness beyond the sphere of humanity, so that he attained to the angelic rank and became included in the order of the angels. There was no veil which he did not pierce. No material hindrance stood in his way, and no defect whether small or great mingled itself with him. The imaginative and sensual powers of his perceptive faculty were stripped from him. His desiderative power was still and he remained pure intellect only. It is in this significance that it is remarked of him that he discoursed with God without any angelic intermediary.'

'We had it in our mind to explain this strange subject here and to unlock the secrets firmly enclosed in Scriptural verses; to expound the meaning of "mouth to mouth"; and the whole of this verse and other things belonging to the same theme. But I see that this theme is very subtle; it would need abundant development and introductions and illustrations. The existence of angels would first have to be made clear and the distinction between their ranks and that of the Creator. The soul would have to be explained and all its powers. The circle would then grow wider until we should have to say a word about the forms which the prophets attribute to the Creator and the angels. The *Shi'ur Qomah* ("divine measurements") and its meaning would have to enter into our survey. And even if this one subject were shortened into the narrowest compass it could not receive sufficient justice, even in a hundred pages. For this reason I shall leave it to its place, either in the book of the interpretation of the "discourses", which I have promised, or in the book on prophecy which I have begun, or in the book which I shall compose for explaining these fundamental articles of faith'.

'I shall now come back to the purpose of this seventh principle and say that the prophecy of Moses differs from that of all other prophets in four respects:

(1) Whosoever the prophet, God spake not with him but by an intermediary. But Moses had no intermediary, as it is said (Num. xii. 8): "mouth to mouth did I speak with him".

(2) Every other prophet received his inspiration only when in a state of sleep, as it is asserted in various parts of Scripture, "in a dream of the night" (Gen. xx. 3), "in a dream of a vision of a night" (Job xxxiii. 15), and many other phrases with similar significance; or in the day when deep sleep has fallen upon the prophet and his condition is that in which there is a removal of his sense-perceptions, and his mind is a blank like a sleep. This state is styled *mahazeh* and *mar'eh*, and is alluded to in the expressions "in visions of God". But to Moses the word came in the day-time when "he was standing between the two cherubim", as God had promised him in the words (Ex. xxv. 22): "And there I will meet with thee and I will commune with thee". And God further said (Num. xii. 6–8): "If there be a prophet among you, I the Lord will make myself known unto him in a vision and will speak unto him in a dream. My servant Moses is not so, who is faithful in all mine house. With him I will speak mouth to mouth . . ."

(3) When the inspiration comes to the prophet, although it is in a vision and by means of an angel, his strength becomes enfeebled, his physique becomes deranged. And very great terror falls upon him so that he is almost broken through it, as is illustrated in the case of Daniel. When Gabriel speaks to him in a vision, Daniel says (Dan. x. 8): "And there remained no strength in me; for my comeliness was turned in me into corruption and I retained no strength". And he further says (Dan. x. 9): "Then was I in a deep sleep on my face, and my

face towards the ground". And further (Dan. x. 16): "By the vision my sorrows are turned upon me". But not so with Moses. The word came unto him and no confusion in any way overtook him, as we are told in the verse (Ex. xxxiii. 11): "And the Lord spoke unto Moses face unto face as a man speaketh unto his neighbour". This means that just as no man feels disquieted when his neighbour talks with him, so he (peace to him!) had no fright at the discourse of God, although it was face to face; this being the case by reason of the strong bond uniting him with the intellect, as we have described.

(4) To all the prophets the inspiration came not at their own choice but by the will of God. The prophet at times waits a number of years without an inspiration reaching him. And it is sometimes asked of the prophet that he should communicate a message (he has received), but the prophet waits some days or months before doing so or does not make it known at all. We have seen cases where the prophet prepares himself by enlivening his soul and purifying his spirit, as did Elisha in the incident when he declared (II Kings iii. 15): "But now bring me a minstrel!" and then the inspiration came to him. He does not necessarily receive the inspiration at the time that he is ready for it. But Moses our teacher was able to say at whatsoever time he wished, "Stand, and I shall hear what God shall command concerning you" (Num. ix. 8). It is again said (Lev. xvi. 2): "Speak unto Aaron thy brother that he come not at all times into the sanctuary"; with reference to which verse the *Talmud* remarks that the prohibition ("That he come not at all times") applies only to Aaron. But Moses may enter the sanctuary at all times'.

In the *Yigdal* formulation the seventh principle reads: 'There hath never yet arisen in Israel a prophet like unto Moses, one who hath beheld His similitude'.

In the *'Ani Ma'amin* the form of the seventh principle is: 'I believe with perfect faith that the prophecy of Moses our teacher, peace be unto him, was true, and that he was chief of the prophets, both of those that preceded and of those that followed him'.

Friedländer puts the principles as follows: 'All that has been said with regard to the sixth article applies to the prophecy of Moses. There is, however, this distinction between the words of

Moses and the words of other prophets: Whilst other prophets chiefly addressed their own generation, blaming their brethren for disobedience to the Divine Law, threatening with punishments and comforting with blessings of which experience was to be made in the remote future, Moses addresses all times and generations, communicating to them laws "for all generations", "everlasting statutes", "the things which have been revealed for us and our children for ever". He is therefore proclaimed by the Almighty as the greatest prophet'.

Werblowsky observes: 'The Superiority of the Prophecy of Moses. This is an intensification of the preceding article. It flows naturally from the position which the Pentateuch (the "Law") occupied in Judaism in relation to the other books of the Bible. Whereas the prophetic books are "inspired", the Pentateuch is God's very Word, literally spoken or dictated to "my servant Moses" to whom God did not speak, as to all prophets, "in a vision or a dream" but "mouth to mouth, even apparently and not in dark speeches" (Num. xii. 6–8). For "the Lord spoke unto Moses face to face, as a man speaketh to his friend" (Ex. xxxiii. 11). On the revelation to Moses is based the authoritative and binding character of the Law. His superiority as a prophet safeguards the Law from the possibility of abrogation by claimants to greater authority'.

The seventh article of faith is bound up with the question of the Mosaic authorship of the Pentateuch and the historical accuracy of the latter. These questions we shall be obliged to consider in the next chapter. Here we shall only touch on the problem insofar as it concerns the question of the historical Moses.

Obviously the seventh article of the faith can have no meaning to those who believe that there was no such person as Moses. In the last century there were a number of scholars who questioned whether Moses ever existed, since our sole source of information about him is the Bible record and subsequent elaborations on it and these, at the very least, contain some legendary material. In a famous essay Ahad Ha-Am observed that he was unmoved by such speculations. Whether or not there was an historical figure called Moses was, in this author's view, irrelevant. The Moses who mattered, the Moses who was

a potent force in the moulding of the Jewish character, was
the ideal figure around which the legends had gathered. In
present-day Biblical scholarship there has been a decided shift
of opinion towards conservatism in this matter. Very few
scholars are now prepared to deny either the historicity of
Moses or his role as the true founder of Israel's religion.
For all the legendary accretions the details are far too circumstantial to admit of any explanation other than that there
actually lived a great leader called Moses who imparted laws
to his people, who led them out of bondage, and to whom later
generations looked back as the founder figure in their history
as a nation. There is nothing whatever in the historical facts
to contradict such conclusions. There is, indeed, everything
to support them. The modern believer will not fail to recognise
that the records we have are less sober history than *Heilsgeschichte*, the sacred saga in which the historical events are
retold. But he will also recognise a hard core of historical
truth in the great Pentateuchal themes of the Exodus and the
Revelation at Sinai. Furthermore, he will see in the sacred
saga itself a continuation of the original events through which
Israel encountered God, the way in which Israel read its own
history and saw in it the finger of the Almighty. The modern
believer will thus adopt a position midway between the complete acceptance of the Pentateuchal record as factual history
and the view of thinkers like Ahad Ha-Am that it is all legendary
material, or that it may be such, albeit of the greatest significance
through its influence on Jewish life and thought. The difficulties
in accepting the Pentateuch at face value will be dealt with in
the next chapter. The difficulties of the Ahad Ha-Am position
are no less severe for the believer than for the historian.
Judaism is an historical faith and as such it must be grounded
at least in events which actually transpired. A good deal of the
very influence of which Ahad Ha-Am speaks is vitiated if the
record is treated in terms of *as if – as if* Moses had lived, *as if*
the Exodus had happened, *as if* the Decalogue was revealed to
Moses. Our position is that the main events actually did happen
(though it is frequently difficult to disentangle the historical
facts from the later elaborations), that God really did reveal
Himself to His servant Moses, but that the record as we have it
is not a contemporaneous account of those events but a saga

in which they are retold, composed by pious Israelites, at different times in their history, as they reflected on the way in which God delivered His people and gave them His Law. If we suppose, for instance, that a group of devout believers wished to retell the story of Dunkirk in terms of God's miraculous acts through which He saved mankind from the horrors of Hitlerism, naturally they would not treat the events as would the factual historian. They would highlight certain events, they might sing special hymns of praise to the heroic little boats which snatched the soldiers out of the jaws of death and captivity. They might perhaps exaggerate the numbers of these or, conversely, they might describe the might of the foe in terms unwarranted by the evidence. If we then imagine that the resulting saga was added to from time to time and that later events in which the devout saw God's hand were somehow fitted into the picture, we have some idea of how a record can be at one and the same time grounded in actual events and yet partake of the nature of a fictitious narrative.

The biographical details in the Rabbinic *Midrash*, for instance, concerning Moses are generally recognised to be no factual records of real events in Moses' life (though, of course, they may contain much ancient material, some of it even going back to the days of Moses) but the use of the ancient hero and his life as pegs on which to hang ideas and principles which the Rabbis felt to be relevant and valuable for their own day and a natural consequence of Moses' teaching for their day. Thus if the Rabbis in the *Midrash* describe anachronistically the complaints of Korah against Moses in terms which could have had no meaning in the wilderness (the story of the widow who was deprived of her *tithes* by Moses and Aaron), they must have been aware that these were not actually put forward by the ancient rebel to the ancient lawgiver but were examples of rebels against religious authority in their own day. We do not go to the Rabbinic *Midrash* so much for information about Moses as for information about how the character of Moses made its impression on the Midrashic interpreters themselves. It is certainly unconventional to suggest that this kind of 'Midrashic' material is found in the Pentateuchal record itself but this is the only point of view which does justice both to the facts of history and the demands of religious belief and conviction.

A further aspect of the question must also be noted. David Neumark (*'Toledoth Ha-'Iqqarim Be-Yisrael'*, Vol. I, Odessa, 1912, Vol. II, Odessa, 1919, particularly, Vol. II, Chapter 8, pp. 82 ff.) has pointed out that the attitude of Jewish teachers towards the personality of Moses varied and that it was influenced by the attitudes of Christianity and Islam towards their Founders. Thus, according to Neumark, the term *'Mosheh Rabenu'* ('Moses our teacher' or 'Moses our master'), found so frequently in the Rabbinic literature, came into use as a conscious reaction against the term 'Master' as applied to Jesus (*v.* Acts ii. 36). On the other hand, Neumark claims, the *Mishnah* 'plays down', in some measure, the significance of Moses in order to avoid the impression that any human being occupies the central role in God's revelation to man. As examples Neumark quotes the Mishnaic denial that the hands of Moses had anything to do with Israel's victory (*R.H.* III. 8) and the Mishnaic claim (*Qidd.* IV. 14) that, long before Moses, Abraham kept the whole *Torah*. Furthermore, the term *Mosheh Rabenu*, so frequent in other Tannaitic sources (e.g. *Siphre*, Num. 157, Deut. 11, 12, 25, 29, *Tos. A.Z.* 3 (4): 19) is never found in the *Mishnah*. This is more than an argument from silence since the *Mishnah* on one occasion uses the otherwise unknown term *'Mosheh Ha-Tzaddiq'* ('Moses the Just') as a substitute for the term *'Mosheh Rabenu'* found in a parallel Tannaitic source (*v. Mishnah Ned.* III and *Gem.* 31b). In Maimonides' day, however, it was necessary to elevate the personality of Moses. The danger of attaching any kind of divinity to the great leader had passed. On the contrary, the challenge now to be faced was that of an implicit denigration of his role in comparison with those of Jesus and Mohammed. It appears that Maimonides was especially influenced by the role Mohammed occupies in Islam. It was essential, Maimonides appears to argue, for Moses to be put forward as the greatest of the prophets. It is not surprising if in his zeal for the honour of the *Torah* Maimonides goes occasionally beyond his sources. Thus, for Maimonides, as in the formulation of the seventh principle, Moses becomes an angelic being. Whether Neumark is right in every detail is irrelevant. In the nature of the case there can be no direct evidence of the kind of influence Neumark attempts to see. It is clear, nonetheless, that in the seventh principle we do not have so much a definite theological formulation as a challenge to contemporary viewpoints of danger to Judaism.

If we attempt to summarise the implications of the seventh principle in the light of Jewish history something of the following emerges. Moses is an historical figure. He was chosen by God to reveal His will to His people. Moses led God's people out of bondage. But Moses was a human being with no divine claims whatsoever. Furthermore, the status of Moses as God's messenger remains unaffected by the rise of Christianity and Islam. None of these propositions run counter to the facts. On the contrary, they afford the best explanation of the facts as we know them. There is no reason, therefore, for a rejection by the modern Jew of this principle of faith. The modern Jew will differ profoundly, of course, from the mediaeval Jew on the *extent* of Moses' role, particularly on the contents of God's revelation to Moses, but this has to do with the eighth principle concerning the *Torah* (to be considered in the next chapter) rather than the seventh.

*   *   *

EXCURSUS

George A. Barton in JE, Vol. IX, p. 56, gives an impressive list of modern scholars who hold not only to the reality of Moses as an historical figure but to the reality of his work, though, of course, they differ in matters of detail. They include Wellhausen, W. R. Smith, Kittel, Cornill and Budde. For the verdict of more recent scholarship *v.* the 1959 ed. of the EB, Vol. 15, pp. 838–9 (article by S. A. Cook and T. H. Robinson): 'Yet, with all this doubt, the fact remains that Moses stands out as one of the greatest figures in history'. It is generally recognised by Biblical scholars that Freud's interpretation in 'Moses and Monotheism', London, 1939, is based on groundless hypotheses. The best treatment of the whole subject from the modern point of view is Martin Buber's 'Moses', East and West Library, Oxford, 1947. *V.* Buber's fine description (p. 8) of the qualities and activities peculiar to the God of Moses: 'He is the One who brings His own out, He is their leader and advance guard; prince of the people, legislator and the sender of a great message. He acts on the level of history on the peoples and between the peoples. What He aims at and cares for is a people. He makes His demand that the people shall be entirely "His" people, a "holy" people; that means, a people whose entire life is hallowed by

H

justice and loyalty, a people for God and for the world. And He is
and does all this as a manifesting, addressing and revealing God.
He is invisible and "lets Himself be seen", whatever may be the
natural phenomena or historical process in which He may desire to
let Himself be seen on any given occasion. He makes His word
known to the men He summons, in such a fashion that it bursts
forth in them and they become His "mouth". He lets His spirit
possess the one whom He has chosen, and in this and through this
lets him make the work divine. That Moses experiences Him in
this fashion and serves Him accordingly is what has set that man
apart as a living and effective force at all times; and that is what
places him thus apart in our own day, which possibly requires him
more than any earlier day has ever done'. Especially important is
Buber's distinction (pp. 13–19) between the 'saga' and 'history'.
The 'saga' is not history but it is not fiction either. It follows in the
footsteps of the historical events and describes the impact they had.
Creative memory is at work in the saga. But the saga is not
simply a matter of group psychology. We can get behind it to the
actual historical events which made such an impact on the people
that they could only explain these events as of divine power at work
in them. It is not a case of 'historization of myth' as of 'mythization
of history'. At the same time, in the Moses saga, the 'mythical'
element is not a myth of the gods. The human figure is not trans-
figured, so that the element of sober historical recording is still
present. But it should also be noted that the saga is itself of historical
value since this was how the original events made their impact.
In other words, Ahad Ha-Am's position is far too extreme. There
was an historical Moses but the later legends told of him also
belong to creative historical appreciation. As Buber puts it: 'The
Moses who had his being long ago is properly expanded by the one
who has come into being in the course of long ages'. Among the
cogent arguments which have been advanced for the basic historicity
of the Exodus is that no people would invent so ignominious a
chapter of its own history. *Cf.* Gerhard Von Rad: 'Old Testament
Theology', Vol. I, translated by D. M. G. Stalker, Oliver and Boyd,
Edinburgh and London, 1962, pp. 289 ff. Ahad Ha-Am's essay
was first printed in *Ha-Shiloah*, Vol. 13, and reprinted in his collected
essays, Vol. III, Berlin, 1921, pp. 210–221. Among the legendary
material in the Moses saga is the story of the finding of Moses with
its remarkable parallel to the story of Sargon, *v.* JE, *loc. cit.*, and
Pritchard *ANET*, p. 119. Another interpretation of the role of
Moses is the 'existential' one of André Neher in the 'Men of
Wisdom' Series, translated by Irene Marinoff, Longmans, Green,
London, 1959. Maimonides' views on the superiority of Moses

are to be found, in addition to his Commentary to the *Mishnah* we
have noted, in *Yad, Madda'*, I. vii. 6 and in his 'Guide' II. 35. *Cf.*
his interpretation of Moses' death by a divine kiss in 'Guide' III.
51. *Cf.* Albo ' '*Iqqarim'*, III. 17, on the distinction between Moses
and the other prophets. Israel Lipschütz, in his Commentary to the
Mishnah, Tiphereth Yisrael, end of *Qidd.*, note 77, tells the following
legend of Moses without stating his source. A certain king, hearing
of Moses' fame, sent a renowned painter to portray Moses'
features. On the painter's return with the portrait the king showed
it to his sages, who unanimously proclaimed that the features
portrayed were those of a degenerate. The astonished king
journeyed to the camp of Moses and observed for himself that the
portrait did not lie. Moses admitted that the sages were right and
that he had been given from birth many evil traits of character but
that he had held them under control and succeeded in conquering
them. This, the narrative concludes, was Moses' greatness, that in
spite of his tremendous handicaps he managed to become the man of
God. It is well-known that during the last century a number of
Russian and Polish Rabbis wished to issue a ban on the further
publication of this legend as a denigration of Moses' character.
Cf. Ginzberg 'Legends', Vol. V, p. 403, note 68, for further
references to the legend and for parallels. *V. Siphre* to Deut. xxxiv. 10
where it is stated that no prophet arose in *Israel* like Moses but
among the nations of the world there did arise one like Moses. In
fact, the *Siphre* suggests that in the matter of the knowledge of God
Balaam was superior to Moses. This statement of the *Siphre*, so
embarrassing to later Jewish teachers, is, in fact, qualified by the
Siphre itself, wherein it is said that Balaam is to be compared to the
king's butcher who is more conversant with the king's expense
account for food than the king's minister. Baruch Epstein in his
'*Torah Temimah*' to Deut. *ad loc.* states that during his student days
in the great *Yeshiba* of Volhozhyn he heard the following interpretation of the *Siphre* in the name of Hayyim of Volhozhyn. Both the bat
and the eagle await the dawn, the one to rise and fly, the other to
hide from the light. Similarly, they both await the dusk, the eagle to
hide, the bat to fly. Both Moses and Balaam were conversant with
the times of God's grace and anger but they used their knowledge
for different purposes, Moses to bless Israel, Balaam to curse them.

[9]

THE EIGHTH PRINCIPLE
The Torah is Divine

Maimonides' statement of the eighth principle of the faith
is as follows (in Abelson's translation with the exception
of the word *mehoqeq* which Abelson gives as 'lawgiver' but
which, it is clear, Maimonides is using in the sense of
'copyist'): '*The eighth principle of faith*. That the *Torah* has
been revealed from heaven. This implies our belief that the
whole of this *Torah* found in our hands this day is the *Torah*
that was handed down by Moses and that it is all of divine
origin. By this I mean that the whole of the *Torah* came unto
him from before God in a manner which is metaphorically
called "speaking"; but the real nature of that communication is
unknown to everybody except to Moses (peace to him!) to
whom it came. In handing down the *Torah*, Moses was like a
scribe writing from dictation the whole of it, its chronicles, its
narratives and its precepts. It is in this sense that he is termed
mehoqeq (= "copyist"). And there is no difference between
verses like "And the sons of Ham were Cush and Mizraim,
Phut and Canaan" (Gen. x. 6.), or "And his wife's name was
Mehetabel, daughter of Matred" (Gen. xxxvi. 39), or "And
Timna was concubine" (Gen. xxvi. 12), and verses like "I am
the Lord thy God" (Ex. xx. 2), and "Hear, O Israel" (Deut.
vi. 4). They are all equally of divine origin and all belong to "The
Law of God which is perfect, pure, holy, and true". In the opinion
of the Rabbis, Manasseh was the most renegade and the greatest
of all infidels because he thought that in the *Torah* there were a
kernel and a husk, and that these histories and anecdotes have
no value and emanate from Moses. This is the significance of
the expression "The *Torah* does not come from heaven", which,
say the Rabbis (*Sanh.* 99a), is the remark of one who believes
that all the *Torah* is of divine origin save a certain verse which
(says he) was not spoken by God but by Moses himself. And

of such a one the verse says "For he hath despised the word of
the Lord" (Num. xv. 31). May God be exalted far above and
beyond the speech of the infidels! For truly in every letter of the
Torah there reside wise maxims and admirable truths for him
to whom God has given understanding. You cannot grasp
the uttermost bounds of its wisdom. "It is larger in measure
than the earth, and wider than the sea" (Job xi. 9). Man has
but to follow in the footsteps of the anointed one of the God
of Jacob, who prayed "Open my eyes and I shall behold wonderful things from thy Law" (Ps. cxix. 18). The interpretation of
traditional law is in like manner of divine origin. And that
which we know today of the nature of Sukkah, Lulab, Shophar,
Fringes, and Phylacteries is essentially the same as that which
God commanded Moses, and which the latter told us. In the
success of his mission Moses realised the mission of a *ne'eman*
(a faithful servant of God) (Num. xii. 7). The text in which
the eighth principle of faith is indicated is: "Hereby ye shall
know that the Lord hath sent me to do all these works; for I
have not done them of mine own mind" (Num. xvi. 28).'

In the *Yigdal* formulation the eighth principle reads: 'The
Law of truth God gave unto His people by the hand of his
prophet who was faithful in his house '.

The *'Ani Ma'amin* formulation reads: 'I believe with perfect
faith that the whole Law now in our possession, is the same that
was given to Moses our teacher, peace be unto him'.

Friedländer states the eighth principle in these words: 'The
whole *Torah*, including both history and precepts, is of Divine
origin; nothing is contained in the *Torah* that was not revealed
to Moses by the Almighty, although we do not know in what
manner Moses received the information. The history of preceding generations was probably handed down to his time by
tradition: in fact it may have been contained in documents
then extant, as is likely to have been the case with the various
genealogies mentioned in the Pentateuch. But it was by Divine
inspiration that Moses knew to distinguish between truth and
error, between fiction and reality. The events recorded in the
Pentateuch are to demonstrate and to keep constantly before
our eyes the fact that there is a higher Power that ordains
the fate of men and nations according to their deeds. Everything
is described in a simple and objective manner. Although the

whole *Torah* is the work of Moses, the great prophet speaks of himself everywhere in the third person, except in the Book of Deuteronomy, in which he records his addresses to the people in the last year of his life.

The last few verses, which describe the death of Moses, the mourning of the Israelites for the death of their teacher, and his exaltation above all other prophets, have been added to the *Torah* by Joshua the son of Nun, the leader of the Israelites after the death of Moses. Thus, from that day until the present the *Torah*, in its integrity, has been in the hands of the children of Israel. It was guarded as the most valuable national treasure, and although there have been not a few generations which were corrupt and idolatrous, Israel has never been entirely bereaved of pious and faithful worshippers of the true God; and when in one generation or period the study and practice of the *Torah* were neglected, they were resumed with greater vigour and zeal in the next.'

Werblowsky states the principle as follows: '8. *The Torah is God's Revelation to Moses.* This article guarantees the validity of the Law as actually known and practised at present. Jewish orthodoxy has therefore always staunchly upheld the theory of verbal inspiration in its extremist form – at least so far as the Pentateuch is concerned. "Higher Criticism" of the Pentateuch is flatly rejected and is considered a major heresy. The underlying assumption is that the whole fabric of traditional Judaism would crumble if its foundation, the notion of divine legislation to Moses, were to be exchanged for modernist ideas about historical growth and the composite nature of sacred texts. As a matter of fact Liberal and Reform Judaism once welcomed Biblical criticism for precisely that reason. They found in criticism a welcome ally in their struggle to get rid of the Law and to substitute for it a purely ethical (and so-called "prophetic") Judaism. Conservative Judaism, as distinct from Orthodoxy and Liberalism, is concerned at present with adapting itself to the climate of Biblical Scholarship and with re-defining the meaning of the terms Law, Revelation, Mosaic teaching etc., in a way that would conserve their significance and validity.'

Of all the principles of faith none presents so many difficulties to the modern Jew as the eighth. Fundamentalism and the doctrine of verbal inspiration have been very widely discredited. It is impossible for most Jews properly acquainted with the facts to accept Maimonides' eighth principle in the form given to it by the great mediaeval thinker. At the same time, Judaism as a religion surely does depend on belief in '*Torah Min Ha-Shamayim*', 'the *Torah* is from Heaven', which is only another way of saying that in Judaism, at least, there can be no religion without revelation. There is, of course, no *a priori* reason why God could not have revealed Himself to man and the modern believer will refuse to challenge the belief that He did so. The problem becomes acute only when the question of the *content* of revelation is considered. As we shall see, Maimonides is true to his Rabbinic sources in stating his eighth principle. From early Rabbinic times down to the modern period, it was held that the whole of the Pentateuch was dictated word by word and letter by letter by God to Moses. Moreover it was believed that the statements contained in the Pentateuch, being the word of God, were infallible. It is hardly necessary to point out that the challenges to the doctrine of Pentateuchal infallibility are now numerous. The question of the new account of the age of the earth which does not tally with Genesis; the ancient civilisations which reach back far beyond the six thousand years of human history as recorded in the Pentateuch; the fossil remains and the evidence for the existence of prehistoric man; the archaeological evidence which has produced incontrovertible proof that both Pentateuchal narrative and law have to be understood against their oriental background; the history of textual and higher criticism; all of these unite to produce a convincing picture of the Pentateuch as a work with a human history and coloured by human ideas, including human errors. For all that, the Pentateuch is a unique record of man's encounter with God and God's revelation to man. It is widely recognised today that there is a divine as well as a human element in the Pentateuch. To understand the problem and the way to its solution it is necessary to study the history of Pentateuchal interpretation. This is the task upon which we now embark.

In tractate *Baba Bathra* (14b), the *Talmud* quotes a *Baraitha*, dated not later than the end of the second century C.E., in which it is said that 'Moses wrote his book, and the portion of Balaam,

and Job; Joshua wrote his book and the last eight verses of the
Torah' (i.e. the final Pentateuchal verses dealing with the death
of Moses). The rather strange reference to the portion of
Balaam has long puzzled the commentators. The probable
meaning is that since Balaam was a prophet it might have been
held that the whole portion of the book of Numbers in which his
prophecies are found, was written by him. Hence the *Baraitha*
states that Moses himself wrote this portion together with the
rest of the Pentateuch. However, in the parallel passage in the
Jerusalem *Talmud* (*Sot.* V. 6) it is said that 'Moses wrote the
five books of the *Torah* and *then* he wrote the portion of Balak
and Balaam and he wrote the book of Job'! In the comment of
the *Gemara* (*B.B.* 15a, the passage can only be dated approxi-
mately but it is certainly not earlier than the beginning of the
third century and not later than the end of the fifth) it is stated
that the *Baraitha* follows the Tannaitic opinion which holds that
Moses did not write the account of his own death. But another
Baraitha is quoted in which this matter is disputed. The second
Baraitha reads: ' *"So Moses the servant of the Lord died there"*
(Deut. xxxiv. 5.). Is it possible that Moses, being dead,
could have written *"Moses died there"?* But up to this point
Moses wrote, from this point Joshua wrote. This is the view
of R. Judah, or, according to others, of R. Nehemiah (both
second century C.E.) R. Simeon said to him: Can a Scroll of the
Torah be valid if even one letter is missing and yet it is written:
"Take this book of the *Torah*" (Deut. xxxi. 26)? We must
rather say that up to this point the Holy One, blessed be He,
dictated and Moses wrote it down, and from this point the
Holy One, blessed be He, dictated and Moses wrote it down
with tears in his eyes, as it is said elsewhere: *"Then Baruch
answered them, He pronounced all these words to me with his
mouth, and I wrote them with ink in the book"* (Jer. xxxvi. 18)'.
The quotation from Jeremiah is evidently intended to convey
the thought that just as Baruch served as Jeremiah's amanuensis
Moses acted in the same fashion at God's dictation. In the
parallel passage in tractate *Menahoth* (30a) R. Simeon's remarks
are more clearly stated: 'Up to this point the Holy One, blessed
be He, dictated and Moses repeated it and then wrote it down;
from this point the Holy One, blessed be He, dictated it and
Moses wrote it down (i.e. Moses repeated verbally all the

rest of the *Torah* but he did not do so with regard to the account of his death but simply wrote it down without repeating it).

Another *Baraitha*, quoted in tractate *Sanhedrin* (99a) is even more emphatic that the belief in '*Torah from Heaven*' means that the whole Pentateuch was dictated by God to Moses: '*Because he hath despised the word of the Lord*' (Num. xv. 31). This verse refers to one who maintains that the *Torah* is not from heaven. And even if he maintains that the whole *Torah* is from heaven but that a certain verse was not dictated by the Holy One, blessed be He, but is from Moses himself, he is included under '*Because he hath despised the word of the Lord*'. And even if he admits that the whole *Torah* is from heaven with the exception of a single point, a particular argument from minor to major (*qal wa-homer*), or a certain analogy (*gezerah shawah*), he is still included in '*Because he hath despised the word of the Lord*'. It should also be noted that in numerous passages in the *Talmud* a Pentateuchal verse is introduced with the formula 'The Compassionate says' (*rahamana 'amar*), implying that the words are God's and not Moses' own. It cannot be too strongly stressed that in Rabbinic times, with the exception of the problem of the last eight verses, the question of the Mosaic authorship of the Pentateuch was not raised by anyone. Even the heretic, against whom the above passage is directed, did not think of denying that Moses wrote the Pentateuch. It would be false to the historical facts, therefore, to maintain that the Rabbis were concerned with establishing the Mosaic authorship of the Pentateuch. Rather they were concerned to emphasize that Moses wrote the Pentateuch at divine dictation, that he did not invent it himself.

Two early third century Palestinian teachers debate whether the whole *Torah* was given at once or whether it was composed at different times during the Israelites' stay in the wilderness (*Gitt.* 60a). 'R. Johanan said in the name of R. Bara'ah: the *Torah* was transmitted in separate scrolls (i.e. each portion was dictated to Moses at the time of the events it records), as it says: "Then said I, Lo I am come, in the roll of the book it is written of me" (Ps. xl. 8); i.e. the *Torah* is composed of different rolls, of various documents written at diverse times. R. Simeon b. Laqish said: The *Torah* was transmitted entire (*hathumah* = "sealed") as it says: "*Take this book of the law*"

(Deut. xxxi. 26) i.e. the whole *Torah* was transmitted as one book'.

Another *Baraitha* of relevance to the Rabbinic attitude is the following (*Makk* 11a): ' *"And Joshua wrote these words in the book of the Law of God"* (Josh. xxiv. 26). R. Judah and R. Nehemiah are divided on the interpretation thereof, one taking them as referring to the final eight verses of the Pentateuch, while the other takes them to be the section on the cities of refuge (Josh. xx. 1–9)'. Although the *Gemara* (*ibid.* 11a) takes this latter idea to mean that Joshua wrote *in his own book* the words which are already found in the book of the Law of God (= the Pentateuch) it is fairly obvious that this is not the plain meaning of the *Baraitha* but an Amoraic interpretation dating from a period when it had become axiomatic that no Jewish teacher could hold that any part of the Pentateuch (with the possible exception of the last eight verses) was written by anyone but Moses. The plain meaning is, however, that according to either R. Judah or R. Nehemiah the whole section dealing with the laws of the refuge cities in the Pentateuch (Num. xxxv. 9–43, Deut. xix. 1–13) is a later addition made by Joshua. This explains the reference in the earlier *Baraitha* to either R. Judah or R. Nehemiah holding that the last eight verses were added by Joshua, i.e. since one of them holds that the addition by Joshua was that of the portion dealing with the cities of refuge! We thus have three second century opinions, if we take the two *Baraithoth* together. (1) R. Simeon: The whole Pentateuch was written by Moses. (2) R. Judah or R. Nehemiah: The exception is the last portion dealing with Moses' death. (3) R. Judah or R. Nehemiah: The exception is the portion dealing with the refuge cities.

The view that Moses wrote the whole of the Pentateuch at divine dictation was the view of both Judaism and Christianity for a very long time, with hardly a dissenting voice. The references to 'the Law of Moses' in the late book of Chronicles (II Chron. xxiii. 18; II Chron. xxx. 16; *cf.* II Chron. xxxiii. 8) are almost certainly to the whole of the Pentateuch, as are the references in the book of Daniel (ix. 11 and 13). The same applies to the reference in Ecclesiasticus to the 'Law which Moses commanded for an heritage unto the congregations of Jacob' (Ecclesiasticus xxiv. 23). Philo generally speaks less of divine dictation than of Moses' utterances but it is clear that both Philo and Josephus share the universally held view of their day that the whole of the Pentateuch is of Mosaic authorship under divine inspiration (v. Philo: 'Life of Moses' II. 51, Loeb Classical Series p. 595; Josephus: *'Antiquities'* IV 48, Loeb Classical Series, p. 633). In the gospels the same view is accepted (*v.* Matt. xix. 8; Mark xii. 26; Luke xxiv. 27 and 44; *cf.* Acts xiii. 39; xv. 5; xxviii. 23). It is no part of this work to consider in detail the views of Christian thinkers on the problem we are discussing, but it might be mentioned in passing that, in some respects, the readjustment required in a critical appraisal of the Pentateuch is more severe for Christians than for Jews, since Jesus is described as believing in the Mosaic authorship of the Pentateuch. On the whole modernists in the Church either adopt the position that it was no part of Jesus' message to teach criticism to the Jews or they maintain that Jesus was liable to error so far as his human nature was concerned. If devout Christians are prepared to undertake such radical re-interpretations of their traditional faith for the sake of intellectual integrity devout Jews should not remain religious ostriches.

In the Middle Ages, the Mosaic authorship of the Pentateuch was continually upheld; the few dissidents we shall presently consider. We have already seen how emphatic Maimonides is on this question. Nahmanides in the Introduction to his renowned Commentary to the Pentateuch is similarly uncompromising. There (*v.* ed. C. B. Chavel, Vol. I, 'Genesis, Exodus,' Mosad Ha-Rav Kook, Jerusalem, 1959, 1–7). Nahmanides observes that Moses wrote this book (i.e. Genesis) together with the rest of the Pentateuch at God's dictation. It is probable, remarks Nahmanides, that Moses wrote the book of Genesis and part of Exodus on his descent from Mount Sinai. The rest of the Pentateuch Moses completed at the end of the forty years in the wilderness. This opinion, observes Nahmanides, follows the Rabbinic view (mentioned above) that the *Torah* was given scroll by scroll. In the other view that the *Torah* was given in its entirety, Moses wrote down the whole of the Pentateuch at the end of the forty years' stay in the wilderness. We might have expected the Pentateuch to have begun, says Nahmanides, with some such introductory passage as: 'And God spoke unto

Moses all these words saying'. But Moses wrote the Pentateuch, including the narrative portions dealing with his own life, in the third person, unlike the prophets who use the first person and who consequently preface their remarks with an introductory phrase stating that the word of the Lord had come to them. Thus Moses does not write 'And the word of the Lord came to me' but 'And the Lord spoke unto Moses'. For the same reason there is no reference to Moses in the Pentateuch until the narration of his birth in the book of Exodus. Even the book of Deuteronomy is no exception, for although here Moses uses the first person, in fact the book begins in the third person and uses the first person passages in the form of reported speech. If it be asked why Moses should have written the Pentateuch in the third person, Nahmanides (relying on Talmudic and Midrashic passages which owe much to the Philonic idea of the *Logos*) replies that the *Torah* preceded the creation of the world, to say nothing of the birth of Moses (v. *Zeb.* 116a, *Hag.* 13b. Gen. R. 8. 2).

Hence Moses is to be compared to a scribe who simply copies an older work. Here we have the mystical view of the *Torah*, widely held in the Middle Ages, that over and above the historical events narrated in the Pentateuch there is the primordial *Torah* which contained the words describing these events long before they happened. The whole record was 'there' in heaven, so to speak, and there it would naturally be recorded in the third person since before the creation of the world Moses and the other heroes of the Pentateuch were yet unborn. Moses did no more than copy down the words of the primordial *Torah*. It is true, beyond doubt, concludes Nahmanides, that the whole of the Pentateuch, from the beginning of Genesis to the final words of Deuteronomy, 'reached the ear of Moses from the mouth of the Holy One, blessed be He'. (This appears to mean that although the primordial *Torah* was in existence Moses could not read it and hence God's dictation to him was necessary). The secrets of the *Torah*, says Nahmanides, were revealed to Moses who either recorded them in the *Torah* explicitly or hinted at them in the *Torah*. The nature of the hints by means of which these profound mysteries are referred to in the *Torah* consists of such things as the use of special letters, larger or smaller than others, in the numerical value

of words and letters by a kind of divine code, and in the adorn-
ments of the Hebrew characters. Furthermore, we have a true
tradition that, in reality, the whole of the *Torah* is composed of
letters which combine to form various divine names. It is for
this reason that every single letter of the *Torah* has its own
significance and a Scroll of the *Torah* is invalid if even one letter
is missing. Even though the plain meaning may be unaffected
the requisite number of letters is required to make up the total
of the divine names.

There can be little doubt that this mystical view of the *Torah*,
which goes far beyond Maimonides' formulation of the eighth
principle, had much influence in maintaining the traditional
conception. It effectively prevented any attempt to regard the
Pentateuch like any other book, at least on its human side.
For how can one compare the divine names of God to a work
of human composition? To this day there are to be found devout
Jews who remain unmoved by such matters as contradictions
both in the different parts of the Pentateuch and by the
findings of modern science in their belief that the *Torah* is no
factual account of ancient events alone (though, of course, these
events will not be denied) but a divine text of the profoundest
meaning, containing sublime mysteries beyond all human ken.
In a well-known passage in the *Zohar* (III. 152a) this view is
put forward in these words: 'Said R. Simeon: "Alas for the
man who regards the *Torah* as a book of mere tales and everyday matters! If that were so, we, even we could compose a
torah dealing with everyday affairs, and of even greater
excellence. Nay, even the princes of the world possess books of
greater worth which we could use as a model for composing
some such *torah*. The *Torah*, however, contains in all its words
supernal truths and sublime mysteries . . . Thus had the *Torah*
not clothed herself in garments of this world the world could not
endure it. The stories of the *Torah* are thus only her outer garments, and whoever looks upon that garment as being the *Torah*
itself, woe to that man – such a one will have no portion in
the next world". David thus said: "Open thou mine eyes, that
I may behold wondrous things out of thy Law" (Ps. cxix. 18),
to wit, the things that are beneath the garment. Observe this.
The garments worn by a man are the most visible part of him,
and senseless people looking at the man do not seem to see

more in him than the garments. But in truth the pride of the garments is the body of the man, and the pride of the body is the soul. Similarly, the *Torah* has a body made up of the precepts of the *Torah*, called *guphe Torah* (bodies, main principles of the *Torah*), and that body is enveloped in garments made up of worldly narrations. The senseless people see only the garment, the mere narrations; those who are somewhat wiser penetrate as far as the body. But the really wise, the servants of the most high King, those who stood on Mount Sinai, penetrate right through to the soul, the root principle of all, namely, to the real *Torah*" '.

*   *   *

EXCURSUS

On the *Torah* as a collection of divine names *v. Zohar* II. 87a. Of relevance to Rabbinic views on the Pentateuchal revelation is the dispute between R. Akiba and R. Ishmael: whether only the general principles of the laws were given on Sinai, with the details given later in the Tent of Meeting, or whether the details, too, were given at Sinai (*Hag.* 6a). On the whole subject *v.* Chapter II in George Foot Moore's 'Judaism', Vol. I, Harvard University Press, 1958, pp. 235 ff. Moore rightly says that it was an uncontested axiom with the Rabbinical schools that every syllable of Scripture has the verity and authenticity of the word of God. The contents of the sacred books were held to be throughout consentaneous and homogeneous. There were no contradictions in them and no real differences. The revelation to Moses was thought of as complete and final and the notion of progressive revelation was impossible. No prophet could make any innovation in the law, *Sabb.* 104a, *Meg.* 2b. Moore concludes (p. 25): 'In fact the application of modern historical and critical methods to the Scriptures, and above all the introduction of the idea of development, involves, consciously or unconsciously, a complete change in the idea of revelation, a change which Orthodoxy, whether Jewish or Christian, has resisted with the instinct of self-preservation'. The statement in *Meg.* 31b that Moses uttered the curses in Deuteronomy himself (unlike those in Leviticus which were from 'the mouth of the Almighty') is, of course, no contradiction to the general Rabbinic view, for the meaning is that Moses uttered them himself after having been told them by God, *v.* note of Jacob Emden in the Vilna ed. of *Sanh.* 99a, who remarks that 'the *Shekhinah* spoke out of the throat of Moses'. In fact Emden has been anticipated by the *Tos.* to *Meg.* 31b, *s.v.*

Mosh me' atzmo. The *Tos.* observe that Moses said them by the aid of the 'Holy Spirit'. The expression used by Emden is not found in the Rabbinic sources but is frequently used by later Jewish, as well as Muslim, authorities, *v.* Ginzberg's 'Legends', Vol. VI, p. 36 note 201. A good example of how the mediaeval mystical view of the *Torah* persists even in non-mystical circles is the statement of the highly revered *Haphetz Hayyim* (d. 1933) that the *Torah* is to be compared to the architect's plans ('God looked into the *Torah* and created the world'). Hence, a Scroll of the *Torah* from which even one letter is missing is invalid since a single letter represents a portion of the universe, much as a stroke or line in the architect's plans represents a whole wall in the completed building, *v.* '*Sepher Haphetz Hayyim* '*Al Ha-Torah*', ed. S. Greiniman, 2nd. ed., Bene Berak, 1954, pp. 25–26, *cf.* p. 24. A formidable 'either/or' on the question of the Mosaic authorship and divine character of the whole of the Pentateuch was launched by the great German leader, Samson Raphael Hirsch, in the last century (*v.* 'Judaism Eternal, Selected Essays from the Writings of Rabbi Samson Raphael Hirsch', trans. by Dayan Dr. I. Grunfeld, Vol. II, Soncino Press, London, 1956, pp. 213 ff). 'Let us not deceive ourselves. The whole question is simply this. Is the statement "And God spoke to Moses saying", with which all the laws of the Jewish Bible commence, true or not true? Do we really and truly believe that God, the Omnipotent and Holy, spoke thus to Moses? Do we speak the truth when in front of our brethren we lay our hand on the scroll containing these words and say that God has given us this *Torah*, that His *Torah*, the *Torah* of truth and with it of eternal life, is planted in our midst? If this is to be no mere lip-service, no mere rhetorical flourish, then we must keep and carry out this *Torah* without omission and without carping, in all circumstances and at all times. This word of God must be our eternal rule superior to all human judgment, the rule to which all our actions must at all times conform; and instead of complaining that it is no longer suitable to the times, our only complaint must be that the times are no longer suitable to it'. In England, the late Chief Rabbi Dr. Hertz was a doughty upholder of the Mosaic authorship of the Pentateuch. *V.* in particular his frequent observations in his Commentary to the Pentateuch, Soncino Press, London, 1937 and subsequently, and his sermon preached on May 22nd, 1926, at the Dalston Synagogue, London (printed in Hertz's 'Affirmations of Judaism', Oxford University Press, London, 1927, pp. 39–54). Among Hertz's remarks in this sermon are the following: 'Wellhausen and his followers thus tear the *Torah* to tatters and reduce its contents to legend and fiction'. 'Every attack on the *Torah* is at the same time an assault against Israel, as well as

a revolt against the Spiritual and the Divine in history and human
life. It is as if the pagan forces of our age had assembled together,
and in their heathen rage resolved to break the bonds of the
Hebrew heritage to humanity, and cast away the moral restraints
which Israel first taught mankind'. Hertz concludes: 'And we, the
descendants of those who stood at the foot of Sinai, will continue
to bless Him who is the God of truth, whose Law is a Law of truth,
whose prophets are prophets of truth, and who aboundeth in deeds
of goodness and truth. We will continue to lift the *Sepher Torah* on
high and exclaim: "This is the Law which Moses set before the
children of Israel at the command of the Lord". We will continue to
sing – and teach our children to sing –

"A true *Torah* God gave unto His people,
By the hand of Moses, his faithful prophet" '.

One can compare this with Dean Burgon's sermon preached in
Oxford in 1861: 'The Bible is none other than the voice of Him
that sitteth upon the throne. Every book of it, every chapter of it,
every verse of it, every syllable of it (where are we to stop?), every
letter of it, is the direct utterance of the Most High. The Bible is
none other than the Word of God, – not some part of it more, some
part of it less, but all alike the utterance of Him who sitteth upon
the throne, faultless, unerring, supreme'. In the last century many
Christians recognised the strength of the critical position and were
prepared to accept it but were held back owing to their belief that
it challenged the authority of Jesus. He had referred to Moses, to
David and to Daniel (Mark xiii. 14) and therefore considered these
to be the authors of the Pentateuch, the Psalms and the book of
Daniel respectively, *v.* L. E. Elliot-Binns: 'English Thought 1860–
1900: 'The Theological Aspect', Longmans, Green, London, 1956,
p. 146. It is one of the oddities of Jewish apologetics that an ultra-
conservative like M. Friedlander in his 'Jewish Religion', 2nd. ed.,
Vallentine, London, pp. 205 ff. feels compelled to defend specifically
the traditional authorship of the book of Daniel, which indeed
presents a problem for Christians, for the reason stated, but which
presents hardly any problem at all to Jews. W. Robertson Smith
(1846–94) was charged with heresy because of his article 'Bible'
in the Encyclopedia Britannica (1875) in which he accepted the
Higher Criticism. He was finally removed from his professorial chair,
in the free Church College at Aberdeen. For the whole fascinating
story *v.* 'The Life of William Robertson Smith', by J. S. Black and
G. Chrystal, Adam and Charles Black, London, 1912, and 'Lectures
and Essays of William Robertson Smith', same authors and pub-

lishers, 1912. It should finally be noted that Muslim theologians, in the Middle Ages, were wont to claim that the Rabbis had falsified the *Torah*. It is almost certain that Maimonides' emphasis in the eighth article on the complete perfectibility of the *Torah* is aimed, in part at least, against this view, *v.* H. Hirschfeld: 'Mohammedan Criticism of the Bible' in JQR (Old Series), Vol. XIII, 1901, pp. 222–240. *Cf.* M. Soloweitchick and Z. Rubashov: *Toledoth Biggoreth Ha-Migra*, Berlin, 1928. On Rabbinic views Abraham J. Heschel: '*Torah Min Ha-Shamayim*', Soncino Press, London, 1962, should be consulted.

*   *   *

It is obvious that the main challenge to the traditional view of the Pentateuch as an infallible book dictated by God to Moses has only come to the fore in modern times. The sciences of geology, zoology and biology, the new astronomy, the profounder sense of history, the anthropological and archaeological evidence, the emergence of Biblical criticism, all of which demand a revision of the traditional picture, are all comparatively recent developments. It is more than a little naive to ask why God did not choose to reveal this knowledge to earlier generations. If the question is put the only possible answer is that He did not choose to do so. In actuality the demand for God to have revealed all truth about all things at once is a demand for the total abolition of human history. Consequently, we can hardly expect the ancients to have had the reasons we have for re-examining and re-interpreting the doctrine of '*Torah from Heaven*'. It is the recognition of this which renders so fatuous the retort to the modernist sometimes advanced by the traditionalist: 'Are you better than Maimonides?' or 'Are you better informed about the nature of the *Torah* than the Rabbis?' For it is not at all a question of what Maimonides or the Rabbis *said* but of what they would have said were they alive today. It should further be noted that the aim of a true Biblical criticism is not to sit in judgment on the Bible (as the rather unfortunate term 'Higher Criticism' might imply and as some of its practitioners might at times have believed) but to discover what the Bible, including the Pentateuch, has to tell us about its own composition. Bible criticism seeks the answer to the question: When were these books written? To whom were they addressed in the first instance? What was their original meaning? It is in the light of these observations that we proceed to examine the history of the challenge to the traditional view as recorded in Maimonides' eighth article of the faith.

It must first be noted that, with the exception of the very late books of Chronicles and Daniel mentioned earlier, there is no claim anywhere in the Hebrew Bible that Moses wrote the whole of the Pentateuch. From this point of view modern criticism, while untraditional so far as the teaching of the past two thousand years is concerned, is really an attempt to rediscover the original Biblical tradition. (It hardly needs to be said that the recognition of this truth has no relevance to the question we shall be discussing later of the significance of Jewish observance as practised during the past two thousand years. This has acquired a validity of its own). Furthermore, although, as we have seen, the virtually unanimous opinion in Rabbinic times and in the Middle Ages was as stated by Maimonides we do hear faint echoes of other views, and even, on occasion, a challenge to the traditional view, even in the Middle Ages.

In the Apocryphal second book of Esdras a strange story is told of how Ezra was ordered by God to rewrite the Law of God which had been burned (v. II Esdras, xiv). In the Rabbinical literature, too, there is a reference to the *Torah* being forgotten and then restored by Ezra (*Sukk.* 20a) and there is a saying to the effect that if the *Torah* had not been given through Moses it would have been given through Ezra (*Sanh.* 21b). It would be going far beyond the evidence to suggest that in these passages we have anything like an anticipation of modern critical views which see the hand of Ezra and his associates in the Pentateuch as we have it, but it is interesting to note that in early times there was a widespread recognition of the importance of Ezra and his time in the history of Judaism and that Ezra's work was compared to that of Moses.

As far as we know the first Jew to challenge the traditional view openly was *Hiwi Al-Balkhi*, who was born in Balkh in Persia in the ninth century. Hiwi offered two hundred objections to the doctrine of the divine origin of the Bible. This work has been lost but is known to us from quotations from it and refutations of its arguments in the works of mediaeval authors. The great Saadiah Gaon composed a special work in refutation of *Hiwi*'s views. The objections of *Hiwi* known to us are of an extremely rationalistic character, such as his explanation of the parting of the Red Sea as due to the ebb and flood tide and the shine on Moses's face as due to the dryness of his skin through prolonged fasting. *Hiwi* also noted contradictions between different parts of Scripture. It is very probable that *Hiwi* was influenced by rationalistic anti-Jewish literature popular in his day. In Jewish circles *Hiwi* was regarded as a heretic and was often referred to, by a pun on his name, as 'the dog', *Al-Kalbi* for *Al-Balkhi*. (On Hiwi *v.* JE, Vol. VI, pp. 429–430 and the literature cited there). In the Cairo Geniza there was found a collection of Bible difficulties by an ancient critic of a similar frame of mind to that of *Hiwi*. Solomon Schechter published this material under the title: 'Geniza Specimens – The Oldest Collection of Bible Difficulties, by a Jew' (J. Q. R., Old Series, Vol. XIII, 1901, pp. 345–374). The document presents a puzzle as to its author. Schechter does not accept a Karaite authorship since it is not the Rabbinical tradition which is attacked but the Scriptures themselves. The tone of the polemic is very sceptical and aggressive with a marked anti-Scriptural bias. Among the difficulties recorded by this unknown author (whom Schechter suggests belongs to the school of *Hiwi Al-Balkhi*) are the following:

(1) The arrangement of the forbidden marriages is different in Lev. xx and Lev. xviii, while in Deut. xxvii only four of the forbidden degrees are mentioned.

(2) The Pentateuch forbids meat which is torn or which is not slaughtered in the proper manner and yet the ravens fed Elijah with meat (I Kings xvii. 6, *cf. Hull.* 5a).

(3) The Day of Atonement and the Day of Sounding the Horn, though mentioned in the list of festivals in Leviticus and Numbers (Lev. xxiii. 23–32; Num. xxix. 1–11), are not mentioned in the list of festivals in Deuteronomy (Deut. xvi).

(4) There are moral difficulties in Scripture such as the pestilence which resulted from David numbering the people (II Sam. xxiv. 1, 13 and 14).

For all his criticism, the author does not appear to reject Scripture entirely. Schechter ironically remarks that the author's position vis-à-vis the Bible 'would resemble very much the one held in modern times by many a Broad Churchman who has long ago accepted Wellhausen and Stade as the infallible authorities on the interpretation of the History of Israel, but would continue out of mere force of habit, or out of regard for his fellow citizens, to speak of the "Word of God", the "Holy Writ", the "Divine Revelation of the Bible" '. (It need hardly be said that Schechter's interpretation of their position would have been repudiated by many a Broad Churchman of his day. And this is of more than passing interest since our problem, as theirs, is to safeguard the idea of the Bible as the 'Word of God' – '*Torah Min Ha-Shamayim*' – without surrendering to fundamentalism. Schechter had many helpful things to say but he was not always at his best when riding his hobby horse of the 'Higher Anti-Semitism', as he dubbed the 'Higher Criticism').

Hiwi Al-Balkhi and Schechter's unknown author had little influence in the traditional Jewish camp. In any event the tone they adopted was anti-Scriptural. Far otherwise is it with regard to one of the greatest Jews of the Middle Ages, Abraham Ibn Ezra (1088–1167), justly hailed by many as the real father of Bible Criticism. Although there were not lacking Jewish teachers who viewed Ibn Ezra with suspicion, the facts are that his famous Commentary is printed in the better editions of the Hebrew Bible and he is accepted today as a foremost 'orthodox' exponent of Judaism. Ibn Ezra's comments are cryptic in the extreme and his more orthodox commentators have sought to explain his views in more conservative fashion, but there can be little doubt that beneath all his veiled language, Ibn Ezra gives expression to the idea, remarkably bold for its day, that there are post-Mosaic additions in the Pentateuch. It is true that in his Commentary to Gen. xxxvi. 31 Ibn Ezra attacks a certain Isaac (of Toledo? 982–1057) for suggesting that the whole passage concerning the kings of Edom dates from the reign of Jehoshaphat; yet, for all that, Ibn Ezra himself does accept a later date than the time of Moses for some passages in the Pentateuch. We shall see presently the attempt of Joseph Bonfils to solve the contradiction between Ibn Ezra's own opinions and his fierce attack on Isaac.

In his Commentary to Deut. i. 2 Ibn Ezra is puzzled by the words of Deut. i. 1: 'These are the words which Moses spoke

unto all Israel *beyond the Jordan*'. In Moses' day the Israelites
had not yet entered the Promised Land and the term 'beyond the
Jordan' would not have been used for the side of the Jordan
on which they were encamped. In an admittedly cryptic and
difficult passage, Ibn Ezra remarks: 'If you know the secret
of the twelve, and of "And Moses wrote", and of "And the
Canaanite was then in the land", and of "In the mount where
the Lord is seen", and of "Behold his bedstead was a bedstead
of iron", you will discover the truth'. Spinoza, who, as we shall
see, was anticipated by the fourteenth century scholar, Joseph
Bonfils, gives this, surely correct, explanation of Ibn Ezra's
riddle. 'The secret of the twelve' refers to the last twelve verses
of the Pentateuch which deal with the death of Moses and which
could not have been written by Moses himself. Similarly, the
words 'And Moses wrote' (Ex. xxiv. 4; Num. xxxiii. 2; Deut.
xxxi. 9) presuppose another author. 'And the Canaanite was
then in the land' (Gen. xii. 6) is hard to explain if this verse
were written by Moses because in his day the Canaanites
were still in the land. 'In the mount where the Lord is seen'
(Gen. xxii. 14) is understood as referring to the Temple
which, of course, did not exist in Moses' day. 'Behold his bedstead was a bedstead of iron' (Deut. iii. 11) speaks of the bedstead of Og, king of Bashan, who was slain by Moses towards
the end of the latter's life, while the words seem to imply that
the bedstead was pointed out as a landmark, or as an exhibit
in the equivalent of the local museum, many years after Og
had been slain. In his comment to Gen. xii. 6 'And the Canaanite was *then* in the land', Ibn Ezra first says that it is possible
that the meaning is that Canaan had just seized the land from
another (i.e. and the meaning is, therefore, 'And the Canaanite
was *just then* in the land'). If this is not satisfying, he goes on
to say, there is a secret here and the wise will be silent! But
apart from these passages, Ibn Ezra to Num. xxi. 1 ('And the
Canaanite, the king of Arad, who dwelt in the South, heard that
Israel came by way of Atharim.') remarks that 'many say this
portion was written by Joshua and their proof is 'the king of
Arad, one' (Josh. xii. 14), i.e. it is stated in the book of Joshua
that it was Joshua, not Moses, who killed the king of Arad.
Going beyond the above-mentioned Tannaitic view that only
the last eight verses of the Pentateuch were written by Joshua,

Ibn Ezra in his comments to Deut. xxxiv. 1 argues that Joshua
wrote the whole of the last chapter of the Pentateuch, since
the first verse of this last chapter speaks of Moses' ascent
to the mount on which he was to die and once he had ascended
the mount he could not have written anything for posterity.
(Since there are twelve verses in the last chapter there can
hardly be any doubt that this is the 'secret of the twelve').
Joshua, continues Ibn Ezra, wrote this portion 'after the manner
of a prophet' i.e. Joshua wrote as a prophet under divine
inspiration. Finally, there is Ibn Ezra's comment to Deut.
xxxiv. 6: 'And he was buried in the valley in the land of Moab
over against Bethpeor; and no man knoweth of his sepulchre
unto this day'. This, says Ibn Ezra, must have been written
by Joshua, probably towards the end of his life, so that sufficient
time would have elapsed since the death of Moses to refer to it,
as is implied by the use of 'unto this day', as an event in the
distant past.

In spite of attempts by Dr. Friedländer and others to explain
these passages differently the unprejudiced reader will see that
Ibn Ezra's intention is as we have explained it. It is certainly
significant that the fourteenth century teacher, Joseph Bonfils,
to whom we have referred, interprets Ibn Ezra in this way.
Joseph Bonfils, otherwise known as Joseph ben Eliezer Ha-
Sephardi, wrote his Commentary to Ibn Ezra, entitled '*Tzoph-
nath Paneah*', at the request of David ben Joshua, Rabbi of
Damascus, who was, incidentally, a great-grandson of Maimon-
ides (The '*Tzophnath Paneah*' was edited by D. Herzog and
published in Heidelberg, 1911, Vol. I; Vol. II in Berlin, 1930.
V. M. Z. Segal's review in *Qiryath Sepher*, Vol. 9, pp. 302–4.
For the work of Bonfils *v*. Herzog's German Introduction to
Vol. II and M. Friedländer: 'Essays on the Writings of Ibn
Ezra', Vol. IV, Trübner, London, 1877, pp. 219–220). Ibn
Ezra's comment on 'And the Canaanite was then in the land' is
taken by Bonfils (Vol. I, pp. 92–93) to mean that this was
written by a prophet who lived after Moses. 'Since we are
obliged to believe in the words of tradition and in the words of
prophecy', elaborates Bonfils, 'what difference can there be if
Moses wrote it or another prophet, since the words of every
prophet are true and divinely inspired?' But Bonfils goes on to
ask, what of the prohibition of adding to the *Torah* (Deut.

xiii. 1)? His reply is that the prohibition refers only to an addition of new *precepts*, not found in the *Torah*, not to an expansion of the narrative portions. Similarly, the *Baraitha* in tractate *Sanhedrin*, which treats the person who denies the Mosaic authorship of even one letter of the Pentateuch as a heretic, refers only to the words and letters of the *precepts*, not of the narrative portions of the Pentateuch. In support of this novel view, Bonfils quotes the *Baraitha* in *Makk.* 11a, in which Tannaitic teachers do not hesitate to ascribe either the last eight verses of the Pentateuch or the portion dealing with the refuge cities to Joshua. As for Ibn Ezra's dark reference to a 'secret' and the need for the 'wise' to be 'silent', Bonfils comments: 'This secret should not be made known to ordinary people in order that they be not led to treat the *Torah* offhandedly, since one who is not wise cannot distinguish between verses containing precepts and those of a purely narrative character. Furthermore, secrecy is necessary because if the nations get to hear of it they will taunt us that our *Torah* was once true but we have changed it. (We have seen that Muslim theologians frequently levelled the charge against the Jews that they had falsified the *Torah*). Consequently, Ibn Ezra says "And the wise will be silent" for the sage understands how harmless all this really is and it is only the fools who make it a matter of guilt'. Ibn Ezra's comment on Gen. xxii. 14, the reference to the mount of the Lord, is simply to refer the reader to his comment to the beginning of Deuteronomy, i.e. Ibn Ezra's aforementioned lengthy comment on the whole question. Bonfils (Vol. I, p. 112) states: 'According to this, the verse was not written by Moses but the later prophets wrote it'. By the later prophets are meant prophets other than Joshua who lived at a time when the Temple stood.

Elaborating on Ibn Ezra's comments to the beginning of Deuteronomy, Bonfils (Vol. II, pp. 65–66) explains: 'The author's meaning is that if you understand the secret of these verses to be that they were not written by Moses you will understand that the five verses from the beginning of Deuteronomy to "The Lord our God spoke unto us" were not written by Moses but by one of the later prophets. The verse "The Lord our God", with which the subject matter really begins, follows on the verse "These are the commandments and the ordinances"

(Num. xxxvi. 13), the end of the book of "And the Lord
spoke" (= Numbers). Whoever investigates carefully the
subject matter of these verses will grasp the truth. As evidence
of this it can be seen that all these five verses use the third
person as if someone else is describing what happened. If you
object that all the rest of the *Torah* is in the third person, you
must surely see the difference. For here indications are given
to identify the places in which these precepts were uttered,
the indications being: "in the wilderness, in the Arabah" etc.
and if Moses had written this no indications would have been
necessary since all Israel were there and they knew the places.
What reason can Moses have had, therefore, for giving them
means of identifying places where they themselves had been and
of which they knew? It was this consideration which forced Ibn
Ezra to explain the verses as he did'. It is really beside the
point whether Ibn Ezra really did have all this in mind. The
important fact to recognise is that a Jewish teacher, as early
as the fourteenth century, saw no objections to 'dissecting'
the Pentateuch with critical acumen and coming to the conclusion, on the internal evidence, that the first five verses of
Deuteronomy were a later interpolation!

If this is so, observes Bonfils (Vol. I, p. 149), why does Ibn
Ezra vent his spleen, in his Commentary to Gen. xxxvi, on
Isaac, who suggests that the portion was written in the days
of Jehoshaphat? Why does Ibn Ezra in his wrath declare that
Isaac's book deserves to be burnt? Bonfils claims that Ibn Ezra
makes a distinction between the addition of explanatory
glosses to Moses's original words and the addition of a whole
portion by later prophets. The latter would offend against the
prohibition of adding to the *Torah*. While Bonfils is probably
correct in attributing this distinction to Ibn Ezra, he himself
is somewhat confused. As we have noted earlier, he quotes in
support of his and Ibn Ezra's views the *Baraitha* in *Makkoth*
concerning the refuge cities. Here there is an addition of a
whole portion, an addition which is moreover inconsistent
with Bonfils' further distinction between the precepts of the
Pentateuch and its narrative portions. Unless we are to say
Bonfils did not follow his ideas to their logical conclusion, we
must suppose that Bonfils distinguishes between a completely
new portion added to the *Torah*, or a completely new precept,

and the portion dealing with the refuge cities which is simply a record of the *Mosaic* law, written down in Joshua's day but given by God to Moses.

Before we take leave of Ibn Ezra it might be noticed in passing that this great exegete was gifted with critical powers far in excess of his non-critical age. Among other matters, he anticipated, in his Commentary to Isaiah, the opinion of modern scholars, who generally acknowledge their debt to him, that the second part of the book of Isaiah (from Chapter xl) was not written by the prophet Isaiah. Ibn Ezra's comment in his Introduction to the book of Psalms (*v.* Friedländer, *op. cit.*, p. 60 f.) is also of interest. There he notes that he fails to see why the Commentators should be surprised at the absence of a superscription to the book of Psalms stating that they were written by David. There is no doubt among Jews that Moses wrote the book of Genesis, as our forefathers were taught by tradition, and yet it does not begin 'And the Lord spake unto Moses'.

Long before, then, the rise of modern Biblical criticism here were two Jewish Bible scholars, Ibn Ezra and Bonfils, who applied critical methods to questions of Biblical authorship. Modern criticism goes a good deal further than either of these two pioneers could have gone in their day. As it is they were in advance of their age by centuries. But basically the methods are the same. When the question of authorship is considered it is the task of the student to examine the available evidence and form his conclusions from it. It is facts such as these which make so hollow the battle-cry of Jewish fundamentalism that modern critics are governed by anti-Semitic considerations and by the need for demonstrating the superiority of the New Testament over the Old. One would be naive in the extreme not to recognise that both these motives are sometimes at work in the writings of non-Jewish Bible scholars. But this demands caution and discernment on the part of the Jewish scholar, not an outright rejection of the whole critical position or an attempt to prejudge the issue in the name of faith. It should be seen that many modern Bible scholars approached their task with a wholly admirable blending of objectivity and reverence for the Bible and that the pioneering work was done by Jewish scholars in the Middle Ages. It would be too much to claim Ibn Ezra and Bonfils for the ranks of objective scholarship. This was completely unknown in both Jewish and Christian circles until modern times. For all their independence and self-reliance, both Ibn Ezra and Bonfils are careful not to offend against tradition and they claim, indeed, that their views are supported by tradition. For all that, it is a source of pride for critically-minded Jews that two Jewish scholars entertained, for their day, highly unconventional views in obedience to the truth as they saw it.

Serious Pentateuchal criticism really began in the time of the Reformation. A number of scholars began to see that the problem was far too complicated to admit of the simple solution that certain anachronisms are to be explained as later glosses to Moses' original work. In 1520 A. B. Carlstadt pointed out that both the *style* and the *diction* were the same in the Pentateuchal passage dealing with Moses' death and in the preceding passages. The Catholic A. Masius in his Commentary to Joshua (1574) conjectured that the Pentateuch was compiled by Ezra from ancient documents. Among the anachronisms noted by Masius were the references to the city of Dan in Gen. xiv. 14 and Deut. xxxiv. 1. But according to the book of Joshua (xix. 47) the name of the city was Leshem until the children of Dan conquered it after Moses' death. Thomas Hobbes in his 'Leviathan', published in 1651, Chapter 32, accepts the Mosaic authorship of the Pentateuch but not of the anachronisms, of which he lists Gen. xii. 6 ('And the Canaanite was *then* in the land') and Deut. xxxiv. 6, which states that no man knows of Moses' sepulchre unto this day. Hobbes also pointed to Num. xxi. 14, in which a song is quoted by the author illustrating events which took place towards the end of Moses' life. This does not make sense if Moses was the author of the passage in which the song is quoted. Baruch Spinoza in his 'Tractatus Theologico-politicus' (Hamburg, 1670) quotes Ibn Ezra's brief comments in Chapter 8 and holds that Pentateuch is a composite work compiled in the days of Ezra. Spinoza noted that some of the Pentateuchal stories are repeated more than once with differences in the accounts. Richard Simon, a Catholic priest, published a work in 1678 in which he put forward the view that the Pentateuch was a compilation of a great number of documents of different dates. In Simon's

opinion the commandments of the Pentateuch were inspired
by God but the narratives are purely human.

Thus so far two ideas had been advanced, both contradicting
the traditional view. The first of these consisted of a serious
questioning of the ascription of the whole of the Pentateuch
to Moses, the second, a growing recognition that the Pentateuch was not a homogeneous but a composite work. It cannot
be too strongly stressed that the later Documentary Hypothesis was advanced as a *solution* to questions which had been
raised long before the nineteenth century. Modifications of
Wellhausen, and they are many, or even his complete over-
throw, do not affect the existence of the problem, which is,
if Moses did not write the Pentateuch and it is a composite
work, who did write it and how were its parts put together?

A further matter of importance must be mentioned. Part of the
aim of modern Bible scholarship is to see the Bible against
its Oriental background. A pioneer in this field was John
Spencer of Ely and Cambridge (1630–1695) whose work
'The Laws of the Hebrews' laid the foundations of Comparative
Religion. In the Prolegomena to the work Spencer states his
aim: 'To show that the laws and rites of the Jews were not
instituted of God without *reasonable* ends'. Many of these
reasonable ends were in the nature of a determined opposition
to idolatrous practices which it was the aim of Pentateuchal
legislation to eradicate in the interests of a pure faith. Now
John Spencer acknowledges his indebtedness to Maimonides, a
major portion of whose 'Guide' is devoted to this very theme.
Spencer influenced in turn both W. Robertson Smith and James
Frazer. It is thus no exaggeration to hail Maimonides as the
pioneer in the field of Comparative Religion, as Ibn Ezra was
the pioneer in the field of Biblical criticism. So much for the
parrot-cry that present-day Jewish Bible critics are merely
aping Christian scholars of dubious motives. In any event,
the issue is one of truth and integrity. If the notion 'accept the
truth from whichever source it comes' is acceptable to Jews, and
the saying is itself of Jewish origin and has often been held up
as an ideal by Jewish teachers, then, painful though it may be to
have to make the necessary adjustments, Jews concerned with
the truth must be prepared to make them. Needless to say, all
this has little to do with the question of loyalty to one's faith

or with the question of whether reason should reign supreme in matters of faith. The question of dating the Pentateuch and understanding how it came to be is a matter of fact, not of faith. That God is good, for example, is an affirmation of faith and the true believer will hold fast in this faith even in the face of suffering and evil. That God revealed Himself in the *Torah* is similarly a matter of faith and there can be no Judaism without revelation. But that God dictated the whole of the Pentateuch to Moses is a belief which has become increasingly difficult to maintain because it appears to be in flat contradiction to the facts, these facts consisting of a considerable body of internal evidence as well as the mass of external evidence provided by the physical sciences, by comparative religion, by historical studies and archaeology. To persist in the traditional belief in the teeth of this kind of evidence is just as much an abuse of faith as it would be to continue to hold that the earth is flat or no more than about six thousand years old because it says so in the Bible. When all is said and done the factual evidence is so convincing that it can be claimed that every serious scholar accepts it, that hardly any Jewish Bible scholar of note today entertains for one moment the fundamentalist position. Whether or not Jewish scholars are followers of Wellhausen is beside the point. Whatever the theory of the scholar concerning the composition of the Pentateuch, he has arrived at it by scientific, not dogmatic, grounds. The only alternative to a scientific approach in these matters (which after all, only means an unprejudiced and unbiased examination of the facts, allowing these to speak for themselves) is to believe that God dictated the Pentateuch to Moses in such a manner as to allow it to give the *impression* of being a post-Mosaic and composite work. It is true that on any conception of God His ways are mysterious and unfathomable but it is neither a general religious nor a Jewish view that He wilfully misleads His creatures.

*　　　　　*　　　　　*

EXCURSUS

　　Louis Ginzberg 'Legends', Vol. VI, p. 48 has called attention to an unknown mediaeval chronicler who held that Moses used written and oral sources for the compilation of the history prior to his time, Neubauer: 'Medieval Jewish Chronicles', I. 163. It should be noted

that the fact that the Commentary of Ibn Ezra was printed together
with those of Rashi, Nahmanides etc. caused it to enjoy equal
authority with them in spite of its unconventional views, *v.* Naphtali
Ben-Menham's list of Hasidic Rabbis who spoke of Ibn Ezra with
great respect in '*Sepher Ha-Ba'al Shem Tobh*', ed. J. L. Maimon, Jer.
1960, pp. 107–111. In addition to the anachronisms noted by Ibn
Ezra and Bonfils the following have been noted by a succession of
scholars. The mention of camels in the Patriarchal narratives is
anachronistic since camels were not domesticated until much later.
But Cyrus H. Gordon: 'Hebrew Origins in Biblical and Other
Studies', ed. A. Altmann, Harvard Univ. Press, 1963, p. 10, proves
from contemporary sources that this is no anachronism. The
centralisation of worship as taught in Deuteronomy is unknown
in prophetic times e.g. Elijah at Carmel, Amos does not protest
against the very existence of Beth-El. The Day of Atonement
appears to be unknown during the whole of the Monarchical period.
Deut. ii. 12 is anachronistic for Moses' day as is Deut. xxiii. 5 and
the references to 'unto this day' in Deut. iii. 9–11, 14. Similarly, the
reference to 'the days of old' in Deut. xxxii. 7 and the reference to
folly done in *Israel* in Gen. xxxiv. 7. Further examples are: Gen.
xxviii. 14 and elsewhere (geographical terms which really mean
'seaward' and 'towards the *Negebh*' and are Palestinian terms); Gen.
xl. 15 ('the land of the*Hebrews*'); Num. xxi. 27 f; the references to
the Philistines, Gen. xxi. 34; xxvi. 14, 15, 18; Ex. xiii. 17, who did
not inhabit the lands until later; the references to Amalek in Gen.
xiv. 7 since Amalek was Esau's grandson; the use of the Persian
word *dath* in Deut. xxxiii. 2 (unless the text is at fault); the terms
in which Moses is spoken of in Ex. xi. 3 and Num. xii. 3. The
duplicates in the Pentateuch are very hard to account for on the view
that it is homogeneous and the discrepancies are even more
puzzling. Of duplicates the following have been noted: the two
creation accounts in Gen. i. 1–ii. 4 with Gen. ii. 5–25; Gen. xii.
10–20 with Gen. x, Abraham and Sarah as his sister, *cf.* Gen. xxvi.
6–14; the two Hagar Stories, Gen. xvi. 4–14 with Gen. xxi. 8–21;
Beersheba and Bethel in Gen. xxi. 22–34; xxvi. 26–34; xxviii. 19;
xxxv. 14 f; the Joseph narrative; the accounts of 'laughter' in Gen.
xvii. 17; xviii. 12; xxi. 6–7; the call of Moses, Ex. iii with Ex. vi.
Of discrepancies the following have been noted: Aaron's death in
Num. xxxiii. 31–39 with Deut. x. 6; the appointment of a king
sanctioned in Deut. xvii. 16–20 but opposed in I Sam. viii. 47; the
sending of the spies in Num. xiii. 1–3 at the command of God but not
in Deut. i. 22–23; Isaac must have spent eighty years on his death
bed, *v.* Gen. xxv. 26; xxvi. 34; xxxv. 28; on sacrifices Deut. xii.
13 f; contradicts Ex. xx. 24; Tabernacles is for 7 days in Deut. xvi.

15 but for 8 days in Lev. xxiii. 36; on the Levites *v.* Deut. xviii. 6–8; Ex. xxviii. 1 f; Num. iii. 5–10; the divine name unknown before Moses. Ex. vi. 2 f but *v.* Gen. iv. 1 and 26 and Gen. xv. 7; the 'pillar' forbidden in Ex. xxiii. 24; Ex. xxxiv. 13 and Deut. vii 5 but erected in Gen. xxxi. 45, 51; Gen. xxxv. 20; Ex. xxiv. 4; Josh. xxiv. 25–27; I Sam. vii. 12; II Sam. xviii. 18; Hos. iii. 4; Sarah young in Gen. xii. 10–20 and xx. 1–8 but very old in Gen. xvii. 7; the two accounts of the Decalogue, Ex. xx. 1–14 and Deut. *v.* 6–18. It is, of course, possible to account for each of these difficulties separately and fundamentalists generally try to do so but it runs counter to all scientific method to explain each detail in separate fashion and to ignore a solution which makes sense of them all by means of one idea. Such a solution is that the Pentateuch is a composite work of post-Mosaic date. The Pentateuch itself, it must be reiterated, makes no other claim. It has often been objected that there is no evidence elsewhere in ancient times of the existence of this kind of composite work. This objection cannot be taken seriously. One need only examine the books of Kings and Chronicles, for example, to see that the 'Chronicler' used 'sources' for his own purposes. Further illustrations are the book of Isaiah, the Psalms, Homer, the Gospels, and (this has been insufficiently noted) the *Mishnah* and the *Talmud.* The difficulties of the unhistorical nature of some of the Pentateuchal material, hard, indeed, to reconcile with the doctrine of divine dictation, have often been noted and were, in part, the cause of the Religion versus Science controversy in Victorian times, e.g. on the cosmogony of Genesis *v.* S. R. Driver: 'The Book of Genesis', in the Westminster Commentaries, Methuen, London, 1954, pp. 19 f. and on the antiquity of man *v.* Driver, *op. cit.,* pp. xxxi f.

*   *   *

We turn now to the solution of these difficulties advanced by modern scholars. It should be noted that two factors had their influence in determining the course of modern Biblical criticism. The first of these was the progress made in Homeric studies where critical methods were applied with success. The second was the growing recognition that the Bible was a collection of 'Oriental' books, i.e. that it was futile to attempt to understand the question of how the Bible was composed without trying to see it against its Oriental background. In other words, the question is not how *we* would have written the Biblical books but how they were, in fact, compiled by their ancient authors. It has well been said by Ernest Trattner that in earlier times people saw the Bible from 'outside' while the Bible scholarship of the past two hundred years is a tremendous attempt to see it from 'inside' i.e. as the Bible describes itself.

Although he is not entirely original, Jean Astruc is generally held to be the founder of modern Bible criticism. Astruc, a Catholic physician, probably of Jewish stock, anxious to defend the Mosaic authorship of the Pentateuch but bothered by the evidence of its composite nature, particularly in the book of Genesis, put forward the theory that Moses used ancient documents as the sources for his work. This theory was advocated by Astruc in his 'Conjectures sur les memoires originaux dont il paroit que Moyse se servit pour composer le livre de la Genèse', published in 1753. Astruc noticed that whole portions of Genesis use the divine name *'Elohim* (translated in English as 'God') while in other portions the Tetragrammaton (translated in English as 'the Lord') is used. This led Astruc to suggest that one of the documents used by Moses was the *'Elohist'* i.e. the document describing the origins of the world in which God is referred to as *' 'Elohim'*. Although this document is now part of the Pentateuch it can be detected apart from the other component parts of the Pentateuch. Astruc, indeed, believed that he could detect thirteen different documents from which Moses drew his material. Astruc's theory is referred to in the history of criticism as 'The First Documentary Hypothesis'. Eichorn added his contribution to the theory by detecting other criteria besides the divine names. Astruc's Elohist document comprised the following chapters of Genesis: i. 1 – ii. 3; v. 1–end; vi. 9–22; vii. 6–10; 19; 22; 24; viii. 1–19; ix. 1–10; 12; 16 f.; 28 f.; xi. 10–26; xvii. 3–27. Other theories, building on the findings of Astruc and Eichorn, suggested that various fragments of documents were to be detected in the Pentateuch (the 'Fragment Theory') or that an original work of Moses had been *enlarged* at different times. But eventually two main documents were detected, the one using the divine name *' 'Elohim'*, hence called *'E'*, the other using the Tetragrammaton, spelled in German JHWH, hence called *'J'*. Now it had long been recognised that the book of Deuteronomy differed in style and language from the other books of the Pentateuch. Furthermore, various ancient authors had held that the book found in the Temple in the days of Josiah (621 B.C.E.) which caused the king to introduce his reformation (*v*. II Kings, Chapters xxii and xxiii) was the book of Deuteronomy. In the year 1805 De Wette published his graduation dissertation at Jena University, entitled 'Discourse on Deuteronomy', in which he claimed that Deuteronomy was a work compiled shortly before its finding in the days of Josiah. Thus, three documents were now recognised in the Pentateuch and were given the symbols '*E*', '*J*' and '*D*'. '*E*' was looked upon as the main document (the 'Foundation Document') with '*J*' and '*D*' as additions. Each of the three documents was held to have been compiled at a different time. At first it seemed as if '*E*' comprised all the legal material in the books of Exodus, Leviticus and Numbers. '*J*' was held to be a later supplement and '*D*' a still later one. But Hupfeld ('Quellen der Genesis', Berlin, 1853) pointed out that '*E*' itself contains duplicates and discrepancies (e.g. the name Beth-El is explained differently in the two '*E*' sources of Gen. xxviii and Gen. xxxv, also the name Israel in the two '*E*' sources of Gen. xxxii. 24–29 and Gen. xxxv. 9–11), hence he postulated the existence of two '*E*' documents. The second of these was called '*P*' (= 'Priestly document' because of the priestly nature of its content) and Graf argued that '*P*' was both the framework of the rest of the Pentateuch and its latest document. Wellhausen described the dating and history of the four documents with great erudition, so that the 'Second Documentary Hypothesis' is known as the 'Graf-Wellhausen Hypothesis'. On this view the four documents, which once existed separately, were combined by a series of 'Redactors' or editors, to whom the symbol '*R*' was given. First there was a prophetic Redactor who combined *J* and *E* so skilfully that it is sometimes difficult to detect the two apart. Subsequent Redactors edited the other documents which were eventually welded into our present Pentateuch.

The question of dating the four documents is very complicated. Briefly, the followers of the Documentary Hypothesis point to the following facts in attempting to ascertain the dates. (a) The prophets refer to the narratives of the Pentateuch (= *J E*) but never, before Jeremiah, to the laws of the main part. (b) Jere-

miah does refer to the laws but always to those in Deuteronomy.
(c) Jeremiah and Deuteronomy know of no distinction between
priests and Levites but Ezekiel knows of the distinction.
Leviticus (= P) knows also of a 'High Priest'. Hence the
chronological order of the documents is held to be: (1) JE,
(2) D, (before Jeremiah), (3) P, (after Ezekiel). On De
Wette's contention we know the approximate date of Deuteronomy. We are able, therefore, to construct the following
chronological scheme:

(1) J (c. 850 B.C.E.)
(2) E (c. 750)
    Combined JE (c. 650)
(3) D (c. 621)
    added by RD (c. 550)
(4) P (c. 500–450)
    RP (c. 400)

The book of Joshua was held to show signs of the same scheme,
hence the term Hexateuch, used by critics, referring to the five
books of the Pentateuch and the book of Joshua. It will be seen
at once that this hypothesis suggests a complete reversal of
the traditional view; the Pentateuch, as we have it, being a
later work than the prophets and influenced by their teaching.

Stated baldly in this fashion the Wellhausen hypothesis
seems altogether too artificial, even preposterous. But attention
to the following details reveals that the theory is endowed with
a high degree of plausibility, although, as we shall see, many
more recent scholars have abandoned it, in part, at least.

If we set side by side the two accounts of the sending away
of Hagar it will be seen that apart from the different divine
names used there are stylistic and theological differences
between the two accounts. In 'J' (Gen. xvi. 4–14) the divine
name used is the Tetragrammaton, the Hebrew word used for
'maidservant' is *shiphhah* and God is depicted as being very
near. In 'E' (Gen. xxi. 8–21), on the other hand, the divine
name used is ' '*Elohim*', the Hebrew word for 'maidservant'
is '*amah*, and God is depicted as more distant. Followers of the
Documentary Hypothesis point out that there are characteristics such as these in the documents *appearing together* with a
great degree of consistency. On the view that the Pentateuch

I

is non-composite in character it is necessary to say not only
that events such as the sending away of Hagar happened twice
but that each 'sending away' is described, for no apparent
reason, in different styles. When these differences in style are
noted in other duplicates, too, the only possible conclusion,
even if it is not precisely Wellhausen's, is that we do not have
one account of two events but two accounts of one.

The following characteristics have been detected in *J*, *E*, *D*,
and *P*:

(1) *J*

Anthropomorphisms.

A simple style.

The divine name used (before Moses) is '*J*'.

There is an occasional mention of angels but this is
infrequent.

There is an interest in the South of Palestine e.g. Abraham
in Hebron, the spies go to Hebron, Judah takes the lead
in the Joseph story. (Hence it is claimed that '*J*' originated
in the South and the symbol '*J*' is made to serve as representing, too, the tribe of *J*udah).

(2) *E*

Less anthropomorphic.

Special interest in angels and dreams.

Fond of scenes of blessings.

The divine name used (before Moses) is '*E*'.

There is a special interest in the North of Palestine, e.g
Reuben takes the lead in the Joseph story, Joshua figures
prominently, Beth-El and Shechem figure in the Jacob
Story. (Hence it is claimed that '*E*' originated in the North
and the symbol '*E*' is applied also to represent the tribe of
'*E*phraim').

(3) *D*

Interest in purity of religion.

One sanctuary.

Levites serve as priests.

Humanitarian.

Levite always counted among the 'needy' together with
the 'stranger' because no special provision made for him
(as in '*P*').

(4) *P*

Interest in sacrificial system and priesthood.

Fond of genealogies.

Transcendent view of God.

Formal style.

No sacrifices offered before Moses and Aaron.

Only *Kohanim* ('priests'), not Levites, offer sacrifices in the Temple.

Tithes given to both priests and Levites, hence no reference to 'Levite' together with 'stranger' (as in '*D*') because provision made through tithes.

Knows of 'High Priest'.

If we proceed to examine the first chapter of Genesis ('*P*') we notice some of these characteristics. The divine name used is *'Elohim*. The style is of a majestic formalism. The view of God is transcendent. The whole is a sublime description of God as Creator and appears to suggest a liturgical composition (which it may well have been) for recitation by the priests in the Temple. In chapter five of Genesis, to give one further example, we find the same formalistic style, the same use of the divine name, and the same setting out of the material in carefully measured periods. If we turn to the second account of creation in Genesis ii–iii the style is totally different. God is here very near to man. The view of God is anthropomorphic. (This is not to say that '*J*' takes the descriptions of God 'walking in the garden' or 'breathing' literally, only that '*J*' is concerned with describing the Deity in the most vivid terms). The style is 'impressionistic' rather than formal. There is a great interest in human psychology.

Another example may be given to illustrate '*D*' and '*P*'. There are two passages in the Pentateuch containing the detailed laws governing manslaughter, one in Numbers (chapter xxxv), the other in Deuteronomy (chapter xix. 1–13). The two most striking differences between the passages are the provision in Numbers for the cities of the Levites to act as refuge cities and the law there concerning the death of the High Priest. Now on the Documentary Hypothesis the differences are explicable for '*D*' does not know of a 'High Priest' and the Levites offer sacrifices whereas in '*P*' (to which this part of Numbers belongs) there is a 'High Priest' and the Levites do not offer sacrifices.

It is impossible, even absurd, to try, as some scholars once did, to apply these criteria to every verse in the Pentateuch, but the claim of the Documentary Hypothesis is that if they can be *recognised* even now so clearly this shows that they *once existed*, i.e. that the Pentateuch is a composite, not a homogeneous, work, although it has been fashioned into a unity by the work of the Redactors. The whole position has here found some severe criticism. Does it not make of the Redactor an imbecile? Did he not see that he was combining different accounts with discrepancies and contradictions? This is to fail to see that Oriental compilers did just that and we must not judge their methods by ours. A modern historian also uses sources but he recasts them entirely in a style and language of his own. Ancient writers frequently preferred to dovetail the sources into each other, sometimes placing two sources side by side or, even when combining them, leaving the 'joints' showing. We have noted earlier the example of the book of Chronicles and that of the *Mishnah*. All in all, there can be no denying that the Documentary Hypothesis, as described in minute detail by Wellhausen and his followers, is a work of extraordinary genius. That in the view of many more recent scholars it has had its day is only to be expected. The essence of a scientific approach to historical problems is that progress is constantly being made as a result of further investigation. The Documentary Hypothesis was put forward as a *hypothesis* to be tested. In the view of many scholars even today it is still the best way of accounting for the facts and will not be overthrown until a better way of accounting for them is found. In the view of others better ways have been found. But the new theories, too, take note of the facts in a way in which fundamentalism does not and they are as 'untraditional' as the old. It is completely mistaken to imagine that because the Documentary Hypothesis is modified or even abandoned by modern scholars they now proceed as if nothing had happened since the Middle Ages, as mistaken as it would be to suggest that because of Einstein's critique of Newtonian physics we are back in the days of the alchemists. Before we go on to examine the new theories which have been advanced it is necessary for something to be said about the question of textual criticism.

Textual criticism of the Bible is known as the 'Lower Criticism' to distinguish it from the 'Higher Criticism', the name given to the analysis of the composition and dating of the Biblical books. Up to now we have been considering the 'Higher Criticism'. The terms, taken from Classical Studies, are perhaps unfortunate, implying, as they might seem to do, that scholars sit in judgment on the Bible and find it wanting. Actually, the proper aim of Higher Criticism is, as we have seen, to determine by whom the Biblical books were written and at which date. Far from sitting in judgment on the Bible, critics endeavour to let the Bible speak for itself. (We might here repeat what has been said earlier that this does not mean that all modern scholars have been completely loyal to the ideal – a difficult one to follow – of pure, objective scholarship. Bias is particularly strong in Bible studies for the very reason that the Bible is tied up with man's religious outlook). Textual or Lower Criticism seeks to establish the original text of the Biblical books.

The implication of the *'Ani Ma'amin* formulation of the eighth article of faith is that the *present* text found in the Scrolls of the Law in the Synagogue today is the identical text delivered to Moses. 'I believe with perfect faith that the whole *Torah*, now in our possession, is the same that was given to Moses our teacher, peace be unto him'. Seen in this light (Maimonides' original formula is quite different) the eighth article implies a belief in a completely infallible book protected from error not alone with regard to its contents but also with regard to its text. Such a view can only be maintained today by those totally unacquainted with the history of the Biblical text.

The present Scrolls in the Synagogue are written in the square script known as *ketabh 'ashuri*, a term explained, as we shall see, in the Rabbinic literature. Another name for this script is, in fact, the 'square script' – *ketabh meruba'*. The early Hebrew script was, however, different in form. This more ancient script is known in the Rabbinic literature as *ketabh 'ibhri*, 'Hebrew script', or *ro'etz*, a difficult term meaning possibly 'broken script' after the manner in which its letters are formed. Tables showing the differences between the two scripts are to be found at the beginning of Gesenius' Hebrew Grammar. The

following ancient writings are in the Hebrew script; the Gezer
calendar (*c.* 950 B.C.E.), the Moabite Stone (c. 840 B.C.E.),
the Siloam inscription (c. 700 B.C.E.) and the Lachish Letters
(c. 588 B.C.E.). The Nash Papyrus, containing the *Shema'* and
the Ten Commandments (c. second century B.C.E. but, according to Albright, much earlier) is written in square script. Thus
the evidence provided by archaeology suggests that the Hebrew
script is earlier than the square script. There are, however,
examples of both scripts being in use at the same time, on Bar
Kochba coins (132–135 C.E.) for instance. From Matthew v. 18
we learn that the square script (which alone uses the *tittle*)
was then in use. It is interesting that in the Habakkuk Commentary and the *Hodayoth* ('Songs of Praise') found at Qumran
(the 'Dead Sea Scrolls') the square script is used but the divine
name is in the old Hebrew letters (a usage referred to in the
Church Fathers). The *Mishnah* (*Yad.* IV. 5), on the other hand,
states that a Scroll written in the old Hebrew script is invalid,
which shows that the Rabbi required the use of the square
script, and this is the practice of the Synagogue.

From the above it follows that the older script of the Pentateuch was in the old Hebrew characters. The square script
was not adopted until much later, probably under Aramaic
influence, the Aramaic form of the square script, in use everywhere in the Near East, being gradually adopted. There are
traces of all this in the Rabbinic literature. In a passage in
tractate *Sanhedrin* of the Babylonian Talmud (21b) it is said
that the *Torah* was given to Israel originally in Hebrew and in
the Hebrew script but that it was given once again in the days
of Ezra in Aramaic and in the square script. Israel eventually
chose for itself, the passage continues, the Hebrew language
and the square script. In another passage (*Zeb.* 62a) it is said
that a prophet who came up out of exile testified that the square
script should be used for the *Torah*. In still another source
(*Tos. Sanh.* IV. 7) it is said that the square script is called
ketabh 'ashuri because it came from Assyria. The opinion of
Rabbi Judah the Prince is also quoted. This teacher holds that
originally the *Torah* was given in the square script but when
Israel sinned this was exchanged for the 'broken' script and the
original script was restored in the days of Ezra (*cf. Jer. Meg.*
1. 9, 71b). Thus it can be seen that even according to many

of the Rabbis there is no question of the *script* of the present-day Scrolls being the original script and all the evidence we have bears out the correctness of this opinion.

The text of the Hebrew Bible now in use is known as the Masoretic text, from the root 'masar' meaning 'to deliver', 'to hand down'. The Masoretes were the Jewish scholars who, in the first thousand years of the present era, preserved carefully the established text. The result of their labours, as well as the very stringent rules governing the scrupulous copying of Scrolls of the *Torah*, has been an astonishing uniformity in Jewish Scrolls wherever they are found. The Masoretic text (abbreviated MT) is consequently treated with the greatest respect by all serious Biblical scholars. That it possesses the highest degree of reliability no scholar would deny. But to conclude from this that the Masoretic text is entirely free from error in all its parts is to ignore both the evidence of the ancient versions, which frequently give readings different from those of MT, and the possibility that errors may have crept in *before* the Masoretes had succeeded in their tremendous efforts at establishing a correct text.

The Biblical text edited by Jacob b. Hayyim, printed by Daniel Bomberg in Venice 1524/5, depended on late mediaeval manuscripts. Kittel's 'Biblia Hebraica', from the 3rd edition onwards, uses the text of the Leningrad manuscript written in 1008 C.E. There is no manuscript of the *complete* Hebrew Bible earlier than this, though fragments of an earlier date were found in the Cairo Geniza. At the Dead Sea there were found very early manuscripts of the whole book of Isaiah, the first two chapters of Habakkuk, and various smaller fragments. Although all these exhibit a truly remarkable affinity with MT, increasing our respect for its reliability, there are, nonetheless, some variants. The Masoretic text goes back to the efforts of Rabbi Akiba in the second century C.E. From the ancient versions and the Dead Sea Isaiah we know that the text must have passed through editorial revision because there are readings in these, as we have said, different from those of MT. It is very probable that there once circulated 'popular', but incorrect, versions of the text and the Masoretic text appears to rely on older, more correct versions. Certainly an early version is no guarantee of authenticity. Among further evidence of textual uncertainty in the Bible, are the textual doublets, where the same passage is repeated in two pieces in the Bible in slightly different words (e.g. II Sam. xxii and Ps. xviii; Is. ii. 2–4 and Mic. iv. 1–4; *'Ishbosheth* in II Sam. ii. 8 and *'Eshba'al* in I Chron. viii. 33). (On the whole subject *v.* S. R. Driver: 'Notes on the Hebrew Text of the Book of Samuel', Clarendon Press, Oxford, 1890, Introduction, and Ernst Würthwein: 'The Text of the Old Testament', trans. by Peter R. Ackroyd, Basil Blackwell, Oxford, 1957).

Of particular interest and importance are the special punctuation marks found in the early Scrolls and still preserved in the Scrolls of today. Certain words or letters, for instance, have dots over them. In a remarkable Rabbinic passage (*ARN* I. 34) it is suggested that these were added by Ezra *because the reading was doubtful:* 'Thus said Ezra: "If Elijah will come and say to me: Why did you write this? I shall say to him: I have placed dots over the letters (i.e. I, too, was in doubt as to the correct reading). But if he will say to me: You have written well, I shall simply erase the dots" '! The *nun inversum* added to the text (Num. x. 35 f., Ps. cvii. 23–28, 39) is said (*Siphre* I. 84, *cf. Sabb.* 115b) to indicate either that the passage has been misplaced or that it is really a separate work. Saul Lieberman has pointed to Greek parallels here, the Greeks treating the text of Homer in more or less the same way. That editorial work on the text was undertaken even in Temple times is seen from the reference (*Jer. Ta'an.* 4. 2) to the three Scrolls of the *Torah*, with variant readings, in the courtyard of the Temple. The remarkable uniformity in manuscripts of the Middle Ages led Paul Legarde (1863) to postulate the existence of a *Musterkodex*, namely, that all these manuscripts go back to a single copy, the archetype produced at the beginning of the second century C.E. in the time of Akiba. But, against this, we know from the Cairo Geniza and from the *Talmud* that there were variant readings in manuscripts of a later date. (In a gloss to *Sabb.* 55b, R. Akiba Eger, Vilna ed., gives a list of Talmudic variant readings, i.e. where the *Talmud* has a reading slightly different from our present text). This makes it highly probable that the consonantal text established in Akiba's day did not immediately supersede all others but only won final acceptance because of the work of the Masoretes.

The vowel points, now found in printed texts but not in the Synagogue Scrolls, are post-Talmudic. The pointing and accents as we have them today were only achieved in the 9th and 10th centuries. The words of the text were not divided originally but ran together. The division into verses was, however, known in Talmudic times. Chapter divisions are of Christian origin. They are found in the Vulgate but are not found in Hebrew manuscripts until the 14th century, while the numbering of verses dates from the 16th century. In fact, Jews only adopted the use of chapter divisions for the purpose of disputations with Christians, the use of the Christian division into chapters facilitating the references for the purpose of the disputation. Not only this, but the divisions into chapters were, at times, made originally with Christian doctrine in mind. Thus the first verses of Genesis, Chapter ii, dealing with the Sabbath, really belong to the first chapter and are clearly in the form of its conclusion. There is little need to point to the Christian motive in severing the passage concerning the Sabbath from the rest of the Creation story. Similarly, Genesis Chapter iii begins with the words: 'Now the serpent', because of the significance of this passage to the Christian doctrine of the 'Fall of Man'! And yet some Jewish ultra-conservatives in the last century sought to defend the very chapter divisions on the grounds that these were 'a law given to Moses on Sinai'. (On this question *v.* the illuminating article by S. Weingarten in *'Sinai'*, Vol. XXI, Feb. 1958, p. 281 f.).

All the ancient versions have many readings different from the Masoretic text. The Samaritan Pentateuch is the 'Bible' of the Samaritans, who broke with the Jewish community, probably in the fourth century B.C.E., adopting only the Pentateuch as their Scripture, not the rest of the Bible. The Samaritan Pentateuch was written in the old Hebrew script in a modified form. It is obvious that many of the variant readings in the Samaritan Pentateuch are not true variants but are due to a reworking of the original text in the name of Samaritan doctrine. Thus, after Exodus xx. 17 the Samaritan Pentateuch contains a commandment to build a Sanctuary on Mount Gerizim (where the Samaritan Sanctuary was actually situated). On the other hand, nearly two thousand examples of variants have been counted in which the Samaritan Pentateuch agrees

with the Greek translation, the Septuagint. Two examples
may be given. In Gen. iv. 8 we read: 'And Cain spoke unto
Abel his brother. And it came to pass, when they were in the
field, that Cain rose up against Abel his brother, and slew
him'. The question which strikes every reader is, what did
Cain say to Abel? The statement is omitted from MT. But in
the Samaritan Pentateuch the words: 'Let us go into the field'
are added after 'Abel his brother'. This reading is found, too,
in the Septuagint, the Vulgate and in Targum Jonathan. It
might still be argued that MT is correct and that the versions
do not contain an authentic reading but an attempt to supply an
apparent deficiency in the text. Yet there are so many of these
variants in the ancient versions that it is extremely unlikely,
to say the least, that the versions are always wrong and MT
always right. Another example is Gen. xxi. 13: 'And also
the son of the bondwoman I will make a nation'. Here the
Samaritan Pentateuch, the Septuagint, the Vulgate and the
Syriac version all read: 'I will make a *great* nation' (*cf.* verse
18).

The Greek version of the Bible known as the Septuagint (the
symbol used for this is LXX) is so called because of the legend
that it was composed by seventy elders. In the 'Letter of
Aristeas' it is related that Demetrius reported to King Ptolemy
II (285–247 B.C.E.) that the Jewish Law was worthy of a
place in the royal library. Envoys, among whom were the
author of the letter, were sent to the High Priest Eliazar in
Jerusalem. As a result, seventy-two elders, six from each of the
twelve tribes, were sent to Alexandria and they, after a royal
welcome, translated the Law in seventy-two days. The translation produced was shown to the Jewish Community of
Alexandria by whom it was approved. The legend is known by
both Josephus and Philo, the latter adding that the elders
worked independently but, by a miracle, produced an identical
translation. The *Talmud* (*Meg.* 9b) also refers to the identical
changes introduced by the elders in passages which, if taken
as they stood, might lead to misunderstanding. There has been
a good deal of discussion among scholars regarding the 'Letter of
Aristeas' but the consensus of opinion now is that its legendary
nature can clearly be seen. The author of the letter was probably
a Jew who lived more than a century after Ptolemy. This date

is arrived at by a consideration of the style and language used
in the letter. The Septuagint was almost certainly produced
by Alexandrian Jews whose everyday language was Greek. But
the date of the translation given in the letter may well be correct,
as well as the suggestion that the Septuagint was produced in
Alexandria.

The matter is, however, further complicated. There are
traces of different hands at work in the LXX, to the extent
that it is better described as a *'collection* of translations'. Early
in its history the Church used the LXX and this fact helps to
explain the later Jewish attitude of hostility towards it. The
Talmud (*Meg.* 9b), for instance, remarks that when the translation was made the world became dark. There is also some
evidence that the LXX has been 'doctored' by Christian writers;
a famous example is the LXX translation of 'virgin' in Isaiah
vii. 14 instead of 'young woman' as in the Hebrew original.
It would not be incorrect to speak of the LXX as a Christian
text to which the name Septuagint has been given. There is the
further complication which results from the attempt to discover
the 'Proto-Septuagint' i.e. the original text made in Alexandria.
The quotations in ancient authors from the LXX (in Josephus
and Philo, for instance) do not tally with the text of the LXX
we now have. It should also be realised that we have different
versions of the LXX.

In addition to the LXX there are other Greek versions of
the Hebrew Scriptures, such as those of Aquila, a pupil of
Akiba, known to us from quotations in the *Midrash* and the
Church Fathers; of Theodotion, a revision of the LXX, compiled at the end of the second century and mentioned in the Church
Fathers; and of Symmachus (c. 170 C.E.) which is preserved
only in a few fragments. The Alexandrian theologian, Origen
(b.c. 185, d. 254) compiled his *Hexapla* between the years
230 and 240 C.E. In this work there were six columns containing
the following: (1) The Hebrew text (in one or two words to a
line), (2) The transliteration of the Hebrew text in Greek
letters, (3) Aquila, the nearest Greek translation to the Hebrew,
(4) Symmachus, (5) The LXX, (6) Theodotion. The *Hexapla*
has only survived in fragments.

It would be tempting to conclude that the LXX, being
earlier than MT (which, as we have seen, goes back to the

editorial work done at the beginning of the second century
C.E.), is superior to the MT and that where the LXX reading
contradicts a reading in the MT the former should be preferred.
Many nineteenth century scholars took, in fact, this view but it is
untenable on a number of grounds. First, the manuscripts of
MT are all uniform whereas the manuscripts of LXX differ
among themselves. Even if the LXX is an earlier text there is
no guarantee, as we have noticed above, that an early text
is necessarily a correct one. The aim of the Masoretes was,
in fact, in part at least, to eliminate the 'popular' but incorrect
versions which were current at the time. Then, as we have
noted, the LXX as we now have it is a Christian text, sometimes
altered with set purpose from the original. Finally, the apparent
variant in LXX may not be a true variant but a mistaken
translation of the original Hebrew by translators who were not
over-familiar with the Hebrew language. For all these reasons
modern scholars today employ the LXX with a great deal of
caution and generally prefer the far more reliable MT. But
it is more than difficult to believe that in the many thousands of
variants between LXX and MT the former is always wrong, the
latter always right. Thus, in Gen. ii. 2, MT has: 'And on
the *seventh* day God finished His work'. This was the reading
in Rabbinic times and it led the Rabbis to put forward the
beautiful interpretation that rest is itself a creation and God
thus finished His work in the very act of resting from it. But
it is highly significant that LXX reads: 'And on the *sixth*
day God finished His work', a reading found also in Philo and
in the Samaritan Pentateuch. It is still possible to maintain
that for all this the versions are mistaken (and that a 'difficult'
but profound text has been altered and made artificially simple
by insensitive translators, and there may be some truth in this)
but to adopt this kind of attitude to every variant in the LXX
and the other versions is to be thoroughly unscientific in up-
holding the dogma of the infallibility of the Masoretic text.

The other ancient versions are the Targumim, the Peshitta
and the Vulgate. The Targumim are the Aramaic paraphrases
of the Hebrew Bible, produced in order to help people with
scanty knowledge of Hebrew. In the ancient Synagogue the
Hebrew was translated into Aramaic by a special functionary
but, at first, there was no standard form or edition, each

individual preparing his own Targum. (*V. Mishnah, Meg.* IV. 4; *Jer. Meg.* IV. 1; *Yad.* IV. 5; *Qidd.* 49a; *Ber.* 8b; *Sabb.* 115a). Eventually, standard editions began to appear. Of these we still have the Targumim of Onkelos (ed. in Babylon not earlier than the third century C.E.); Jonathan (or 'Pseudo-Jonathan', finally redacted in the Islamic period, *v.* Pseudo-Jonathan to Gen. xxi. 21, where there is a reference to Mohammed's wife and daughter); *Yerushalmi* (a Palestinian product with a Babylonian element). The Peshitta ('plain' or 'simple' translation) is the translation in Syriac used by Syrian Christians. The LXX had a great influence on the Peshitta, hence when these two versions agree there is no evidence of a separate version. The Peshitta may well have copied the LXX reading and it would be fallacious to adduce the two as a majority reading against that of MT. Finally, there is the Latin translation, the Vulgate, of Jerome (b. between 330–340 C.E.). Jerome was commissioned to prepare his translation, for the purpose of theological disputations and liturgical use, by Pope Damasus I (366–384). He began the work in Rome in 382 and completed it when he was head of a monastery in Bethlehem. Jerome had a good knowledge of Hebrew but there are still some lapses due to a misunderstanding of the original.

Würthwein (*op. cit.*) to whose splendid presentation I am indebted in the above, explains very clearly how it came about that errors crept into the text and he suggests rules (naturally of a tentative nature) for textual criticism. Some textual errors are due to the copyist mistaking one letter for another which it resembles. Sometimes the error is caused by the copyist inverting the letters of a word. A good example of this is to be found in Isaiah xxxii. 19. MT reads: 'And it shall hail, in the downfall of the forest; But the city shall descend into the valley'. The reference to the 'forest' is obscure. If, however, the Hebrew word *ha-ya'ar* is changed, by a simple transposition of its letters, to read *ha-'ir* ('the city'), the very same word which occurs in the second part of the verse, the improved reading is: 'And it shall hail, in the downfall of the *city*; But (or 'And') the city shall descend into the valley'. It is fascinating to find this reading corroborated in the Dead Sea Isaiah. Other causes of error are: dittography (the accidental repetition of a word or letter), marginal notes accidentally incorporated into the text, homoeo-

teleuton (where the eye of the copyist strays through similar
endings in two different verses, *homoetel* = 'similar ending'),
vowel letters mistaken for consonants, and the wrong joining of
words. An oft-quoted and impressive illustration of this last
type of textual error is the verse in Amos vi. 12: 'Do horses
run upon the rock? Doth one plough with oxen?' The difficulty
in the second part of the verse is obvious. The English versions
add the word 'there', not in the Hebrew text, and read: 'Doth
one plough *there* with oxen?' But the Hebrew word for 'oxen',
babeqarim, can be divided into two separate words (as we have
seen, word divisions were unknown in ancient times and the
words ran together) to read '*babaqar yam*' ('with an ox the sea')
and the verse now makes excellent sense: 'Do horses run upon
the rock? Doth one plough the sea with an ox?'

No serious scholar today will indulge in textual emendation
without sound reasons for so doing. There is no doubt whatsoever that MT is the best witness to the original text. However,
since the vowel signs are much later than the consonants it is
much less precarious to emend the vowels of the text. Where
MT and all the ancient versions agree in offering the same,
unobjectionable text no one would find reason for suggesting
an emendation. To do so would be to follow the man who
produced an 'enlarged and improved' edition of Shakespeare.
Where the other versions differ from MT but it can be seen
that the differences are due to an error in the understanding
of the text MT should be preferred. Where MT is incomprehensible and the other versions make sense they should be
preferred, particularly if it can be shown how the error in MT
crept in. But this will not apply where it can be shown that the
translator was faced with the same difficulty we have and simply
altered the text because he could not grasp its meaning. Where
MT and all the versions agree in preserving an incomprehensible text it may be amended by conjecture; but here the
greatest caution is necessary since the agreement of all the
versions show that the 'difficult' text is very early. Further
points not to be lost sight of are the following: The versions,
too, like MT itself, may also suffer from dittography and the
like. There are early and late recensions of the versions. Versions
such as LXX may go back to a *different* Hebrew text from MT
but not necessarily to the *original* text.

It is by rules such as these that scholars proceed nowadays. To give many examples would be beyond the scope of this work but one very interesting further example may be quoted. In Deut. xxxi. i we read: 'And Moses went and spoke these words unto all Israel'. The words occur after Moses' farewell speech to his people before his death. The difficulty is, where did he go? The LXX reads, however, 'And Moses finished speaking these words unto all Israel'. The LXX version makes far better sense than that of MT. But our willingness to prefer the LXX is increased when we consider how the error in MT may have arisen. The Hebrew for 'And he went' is *wa-yelekh*, the Hebrew for 'And he finished' is *wa-yekhal*. The Hebrew letters are the same in both words and we see how a copyist may have transposed the letters inadvertently. When we find that a fragment discovered at the Dead Sea corroborates the LXX reading the evidence of its correctness becomes overwhelming. That the very great degree of caution in emendation advised by Würthwein and many other scholars is necessary few would deny. Nor would anyone wish to deny the basic reliability of MT for the reasons we have discussed. But it is quite impossible to dismiss every emendation of MT contained in Kittel's 'Biblia Hebraica', based on the ancient versions, and there is no serious Bible scholar in the world who would consider such an outright dismissal as anything but a complete betrayal of the scholarly ideal. That MT is always correct and that all ancient variants are due to error is a belief so preposterous that it would hardly have been necessary to refute it were it not for the fact that it is implied in the standard formulation of the eighth article of the faith.

To revert now to the question of the Higher Criticism of the Pentateuch, it is necessary to consider the state of present-day Pentateuchal criticism. One sometimes hears the view expressed that the Documentary Hypothesis has been ruled completely out of court and that it is held nowadays only by a few diehards. How much truth is there in this? More to the point, is it at all correct to say that the present position in Biblical scholarship has made the Maimonidean view regarding the authorship of the Pentateuch tenable once again?

It is important to distinguish between two theories which in Wellhausen are united but which do not necessarily hang together. The first of these is the analysis of the Pentateuch into its component parts, i.e. into '*JE*', '*D*' and '*P*'. The second theory is an attempt at dating the parts which depends on an evolutionary view of Israelite religion through animism, henotheism into ethical monotheism through the work of the prophets. According to this second theory the more complex and highly developed ideas are always the result of development and evolution from the simple, so that progress from the primitive is always in a straight line. '*P*', with its complex ritual and developed monotheism is thus seen as later than '*D*' and both '*D*' and '*P*' later than '*JE*'. Each document, moreover, reflects conditions in the age in which it was composed, not those of the earlier period or periods it purports to describe. The influence of Hegel and his school in this latter theory is all too evident. This has much more to do with a particular philosophical outlook than with objective historical investigation. It would be correct to say that the majority of thinkers today see little truth in the all too simple evolutionary theory of religious development. Our experiences during this century have shattered forever the opinion that a later age is necessarily ethically and morally superior to an earlier one. Thus the philosophical basis of Wellhausen's method of dating the documents is now seriously questioned. With regard to the first theory, too, there has been a marked reaction against the ridiculous extremes to which analysis has been carried. Attempts at allotting every single verse in the Pentateuch to one of the four documents are generally seen to be futile. Even if separate documents once existed they have been so skilfully woven together that it is now impossible to disentangle them completely. This applies especially to '*J*' and '*E*'. Many scholars, indeed, prefer not to speak of *documents* at all but of circles of tradition. On this view, it is very doubtful if there were ever in existence the actual documents of '*JE*', '*D*' and '*P*'. These represent rather oral traditions compiled at different times and in different circles. Furthermore, the older view that the documents tell us very little about the events they purport to describe, and reflect almost entirely the conditions which obtained when they were written, has now been gradually abandoned. Archaeological discoveries show conclusively that whatever the date and historical value of the documents, they certainly contain much early material (and this includes the '*P*' document) reflecting conditions which obtained in the *second millennium* B.C.E. It follows that to date the documents as Wellhausen did is not to date the material they contain. It is now seen that each of the documents contains much early material, so that it is no longer possible to detect in them a Wellhausenian neat sequence for everything. The result of all this has been a very severe challenge both to the evolutionary approach and to the relative dating of the documents. But the facts we have noted above regarding the *differences* in style, language and ideas, between the parts of the Pentateuch are not denied by any of the challengers. The truth is that very few scholars indeed fail to recognise the existence of either *documents*, or *traditions*, emanating from different circles, and even those who do find it impossible, for the adequate reasons given above, to accept either the Mosaic authorship of the whole of the Pentateuch or the theory that it is a completely homogeneous work.

Among developments in the ranks of those scholars who still accept the Documentary Hypothesis are that '*D*' is sometimes dated later than the seventh century (e.g. by Hölscher), sometimes as early as Samuel (Robertson). '*P*' is still given a late (= post-exilic) date but, as has been said, it is generally recognised that much of the material it contains is centuries older than the date of composition. (A good illustration in this connection is that of the book of Psalms. Nineteenth century scholarship tended to conclude from the late date of the *compilation* of the Psalms into the book as we now have it that the individual Psalms were all very late. Twentieth century scholarship sees that this does not follow by any means). Kaufmann, indeed, while accepting the Documentary Hypothesis, prefers to date '*P*' earlier than '*D*' and to argue that '*D*' presupposes '*P*'.

The Uppsala School rejects the Documentary Hypothesis entirely. The Scandinavian scholars belonging to this school prefer to speak of oral traditions, not of documents. These circulated in ancient Palestine and received elaborations and additions as time went on. The material was not cast into written form until post-exilic times. The Uppsala School has been very critical of what it calls the 'writing-desk logic' of the followers of Wellhausen. It does not follow at all that the ancient Hebrews compiled their literature in the manner in which we compose ours. Repetitions, for instance, may not be due to different documents but to the method of oral reiteration so essential in verbal narration. Some members of this school, instead of speaking of '*J*' '*E*', '*D*' and '*P*', and of a *Hexateuch*, prefer to speak of a '*P-work*', comprising a '*Tetrateuch*' of the books of Genesis to Numbers, and a '*D-work*', comprising the books from Deuteronomy to Kings. '*D*' and '*P*' here do not stand for documents but as symbols of circles of tradition. It is not denied that here and there in the '*P-work*' materials of '*J*' and '*E*' may be detected, but it is now quite impossible to isolate these since they have been fused at the stage of oral transmission. Two prominent Jewish scholars, B. Jacob and U. Cassuto, have been very critical of the Documentary Hypothesis. But a careful study of their own opinions reveal that they, too, see the Pentateuch as composite in some measure, differing from the older theory only on the question of how the Pentateuch came to be compiled. Cassuto, for instance, believes the Pentateuch to have been written by an unknown genius in the days of David, who welded the material containing the different traditions of his people, much as Dante (the revealing illustration is Cassuto's) utilized various sources to construct a fresh and original work of genius. Thus Cassuto accounts for the differences in style, language and interest in the two creation accounts (Gen. i-ii. 4; Gen. ii. 4 f.) on the grounds that the inspired author built on the 'philosophical' tradition in his first account and on the 'poetic' tradition in his second. This is not very different from the idea of a *Redactor* in the earlier theory. The difference is only in this, that whereas in the older theory someone welded separate documents into a unity, in this theory someone imposed a single viewpoint on various types of sources.

*   *   *

EXCURSUS

For an appraisal of modern Bible Criticism the standard 'Introductions' are important. The following works are particularly helpful to an understanding of the problem. G. W. Anderson: 'A Critical Introduction to the Old Testament' Duckworth, London, 1959; J. W. Colenso: 'The Pentateuch and the Book of Joshua Critically

Examined', London, 1862–79; S. R. Driver: 'Introduction to the Old Testament', 1891; F. H. Woods: 'Hexateuch' in Hastings Dic. Bible, Vol. II, pp. 363–376; Joseph Jacobs: 'Pentateuch' in JE, Vol. IX, pp. 589–592; W. Robertson Smith: 'The Old Testament in the Jewish Church', Block, Edinburgh, 1881; A. Bentzen: 'Introduction to the Old Testament', Eng. ed., Copenhagen, 2nd. ed., 1952; Oesterley, W. O. E. and Robinson, T. H.: 'An Introduction to the Books of the Old Testament', London, 1946; H. H. Rowley: 'The Growth of the Old Testament', Hutchinson, London, 1950; Carpenter, J. E. and Harford, G.: 'The Composition of the Hexateuch', Longmans, Green, London, 1902 (here, p. 26 f., the very interesting illustration is given of a cathedral which exhibits the different styles of different periods to the trained eye although the building is now a unity); A. S. Peake ed.: 'The People and The Book', Clarendon Press, Oxford, 1925; H. Wheeler Robinson ed.: 'Record and Revelation', Clarendon Press, Oxford, 1938; H. H. Rowley ed.: 'The Old Testament and Modern Study', Clarendon Press, Oxford, 1958; R. H. Pfeiffer: 'Introduction to the Old Testament', rev. ed., London, 1948; A Weiser: 'Introduction to the Old Testament,' Darton, Longman and Todd, London, 1961. A more 'Jewish' illustration than that of the cathedral is that of the Jewish Prayer Book. Through the work and activities of editors and publishers it is now a unity, but scholars have no difficulty in uncovering the different layers it contains and allotting different dates to the hymns and prayers it contains. Thus the *Shema'* was already old two thousand years ago, while the *Lekho Dodi* hymn dates from sixteenth century Safed. An excellent popular account of the Documentary Hypothesis is Ernest R. Trattner's 'Unravelling the Book of Books', Scribners, New York, 1929. Another is Archibald Duff's 'History of Old Testament Criticism', Watts, London, 1910. Both of these are, however, now very 'dated' and for more information about modern tendencies in Biblical scholarship the reader must have recourse to more recent introductions. Three very useful surveys of the present state of Pentateuchal criticism are: C. R. North: 'Pentateuchal Criticism' in 'The Old Testament and Modern Study', *op. cit.*, pp. 48–83; John Bright: 'Modern Study of Old Testament Literature' in 'The Bible and the Ancient Near East – Essays in Honour of William Foxwell Albright', ed. G. Ernest Wright, Routledge and Kegan Paul, London, 1961, pp. 13–31; of A. Bentzen, *op. cit.*, Vol. II, pp. 18 ff. Bright observes: 'One should begin by warning the reader that is is impossible to make general statements regarding any phase of Biblical criticism today without running the risk of oversimplification. The whole field is in a state of flux. It is moving, certainly, but it is not always easy to say in what direction. Sometimes it gives the impression that it is moving in several mutually cancelling directions at once. Even upon major problems there is often very little unanimity to be observed. As a result, scarcely a single statement can be made about the state of the field that would not be subject to qualification. Indeed, perhaps the only safe generalisation possible is that the critical orthodoxy of a generation ago, with its apparent certainties and assured results, has gone, but that no new consensus has taken its place. Nevertheless, in spite of confusion and disagreement, certain significant trends can perhaps be charted'. A cautious statement such as this on the part of a modern critic has sometimes been heralded by fundamentalists as evidence that the whole of modern criticism is a colossal error and that we can now safely go back to the 'traditional' view but, as we have seen, there is not the slightest warrant for thus putting the clock back. Among the 'assured results' of modern criticism (in the sense that no Bible scholar of note denies any of them) are: that Moses did not write the whole of the Pentateuch, that it is a composite not a homogeneous work, that some of the material contained in it is unhistorical. Bentzen (*op. cit.*, pp. 23–4) says: 'The present situation concerning the Pentateuch – according to the short review now given – is rather in suspense. Especially among scholars of the younger generation there exists a definite scepticism towards the Documentary Hypothesis. But another thing must also be noticed: There often seems to be no real understanding of the problems that led to the hypothesis. And on the other hand, very often the solutions offered are very sketchy. Too often we get postulates and not arguments, often accompanied by rather unpleasant, scornful words against the maintainers of other views'. There are clearly certain phenomena, says Bentzen, of different kinds occurring again and again and grouping themselves in such a manner as to combine into collections (be they 'documents' or 'oral traditions' or 'sources'). Following Humbert, Bentzen calls these 'constants' (e.g. the different divine names, linguistic criteria, ideas and theological concepts). On p. 31 Bentzen says: '*I think we must stop speaking of "documents"*. I am deliberately more inclined to say "strata", indicating that I am a little more optimistic concerning the task of getting behind the "last tradents", back to the story-tellers whose traditions they have taken up in their collections'. For B. Jacob's views, his massive work on Genesis in German should be read, but a summary of his ideas is to be obtained from his articles in JE on the individual Pentateuchal books, Genesis, Exodus etc. Cassuto's views may be studied in his Hebrew works (now partly translated into English by I. Abrahams): 'The Documentary Hypothesis', 3rd ed., Jer.

1959, 'From Adam to Noah', 1959, 'From Noah to Abraham', 1959, and 'The Book of Exodus', 1959, all Hebrew University Press. Y. Kaufmann's *'Toledoth Ha-'Emunah Ha-Yisraelith'*, Tel-Aviv, 1937 ff. has now been abridged and translated into English by Moshe Greenberg: 'The Religion of Israel', University of Chicago Press, 1960. H. F. Hahn's 'The Old Testament in Modern Research', S.C.M. Press, London, 1956, is an illuminating survey of the different approaches to the O. T. Hahn distinguishes between the following types of approach (which demonstrate incidentally that there has been a decided shift in modern Biblical scholarship away from the whole question of literary analysis into other areas): (1) The Critical, (2) The Anthropological, (3) The Religio-Historical, (4) Form Criticism, (5) The Sociological, (6) The Theological. An important idea, stressed particularly by the Uppsala School, is that of *Heilsgeschichte*, i.e. that the Pentateuch is not history in the 'pragmatic' sense but a 'cultic glorification' of God's deliverance of His people. Since the core of the '*P-work*', the members of the Uppsala School have argued, is the cultic glorification of Exodus 1-xv, produced by the priestly circles, to cut this up as in the Documentary Hypothesis is to destroy the cultic unity. The '*P*' and '*D*' circles worked rather side by side, each imposing its special viewpoint on the traditional material. *Cf.* 'The Ten Commandments', by Solomon Goldman, ed. with an introduction by Maurice Samuel, University of Chicago Press, 1956, and 'Moses and the Original Torah' by Abba Hillel Silver, Macmillan, New York, 1961. Silver's book is a not very convincing attempt at reconstructing the original *Torah* of Moses from the Pentateuch and the references to his *Torah* in the prophets. *Cf.* 'Contemporary Trends in Jewish Bible Study', by Felix A. Levy in 'The Study of the Bible Today and Tomorrow', ed. by Harold R. Willoughby, University of Chicago Press, 1947, Chapter 5, pp. 98–115. Levy remarks that since Bible Criticism had become a branch of Protestant dogmatics and the Christian student was anxious to prove the superiority of Christianity to Judaism, the first reaction of Jewish scholars to Biblical Criticism was natural resentment.

*   *   *

An important aspect of modern Bible scholarship is the attempt to detect the influence of ancient Near Eastern cultural patterns on the Biblical record. In view of the archaeological evidence there can be no doubt that the Bible was not produced in a vacuum, as it were. The striking parallels in the Biblical record to laws, stories, poems and myths, found in Babylon,

Canaan, Egypt and elsewhere in the Near East are far too many and the similarities far too close for them to be dismissed as coincidental. But the truly remarkable thing about the Biblical record is not that it uses this Near Eastern material but that it transforms it utterly, using it as a vehicle to convey the specific insights the Biblical authors had regarding the One God and His relationship to men. The following examples will serve to illustrate both the influence of the Near Eastern background on the Bible and the transformation it undergoes. ('Ancient Near Eastern Texts Relating to the Old Testament' – abbreviated *ANET* – ed. by James Pritchard, 2nd. ed., Princeton University Press, 1955, is the best collection of the material in adequate English translation. James Pritchard's 'Archaeology and the Old Testament' – abbreviated 'Pritchard, Archaeology' – Princeton University Press, 1958, is an excellent summary of the striking parallels based on the earlier work. W. F. Albright's 'The Archaeology of Palestine',Pelican Books, 1949, is a classic in the field. 'Documents from Old Testament Times' – abbreviated *DOTT* – ed. D. Winton Thomas, Nelson, London, 1958, is similarly very helpful on this subject).

(1) *The Babylonian Story of the Flood*

The 'Epic of Gilgamesh', containing the Babylonian Story of the Flood (on the eleventh of the twelve tablets which make up the 'Epic'), was discovered by G. Smith in 1872, among the ruins of Ashurbanipal's library. Ashurbanipal reigned at Nineveh towards the end of the seventh century B.C.E. (*V*. J. Skinner: 'Genesis' in the ICC Series, pp. 174 ff.; S. R. Driver: 'Genesis' in the Westminster Series, Methuen, 1954, pp. 99–103; *ANET*, pp. 72–99, 104–106; Pritchard: 'Archaeology', pp. 165–170; *DOTT*, pp. 17–26; A. Parrot: 'The Flood and Noah's Ark', S.C.M. Press, London, 1955). Here the story is told of how the gods resolve to destroy mankind by a flood. The god Ea advises Utnapishtim (the Babylonian Noah) to build a ship. This vessel was made of timber and strengthened against the water with pitch. Utnapishtim took aboard his ship of the species of all living creatures he had and he entered the vessel and closed down the doorway. The deluge came and even the gods were afeared. They 'took to flight and went up to the heaven of Anu, cowered they like dogs and crouched down at the outer

defences'. The storm raged for six days until the whole of
mankind had returned unto clay. When the flood had abated the
ship became grounded on Mount Nisir. Utnapishtim then
released a dove but the dove found no resting-place and it
returned to the ship. A swallow was then released with the
same result. Finally a raven was released and the raven did
not return because the flood had completely abated. Utnapishtim poured a libation and scattered a food-offering on the height
of the mountain. 'Seven and seven did I lay the vessels, heaped
into their incense-basins, sweet-cane, cedarwood and myrtle.
And the gods smelled the savour, the gods gathered like flies
about the priest of the offering'. The god Enlil then arrived
and was furious to discover that Utnapishtim and his family
had survived the deluge. Ea explains that it was through his
design that Utnapishtim was saved. Whereupon Enlil went up
into the vessel and blessed Utnapishtim and his wife, saying:
'Hitherto Utnapishtim has been but a man; but now Utnapishtim and his wife shall be as gods like ourselves'.

One has only to read the Biblical story of the flood in Gen.
vi. 5–ix. 17 to notice the strong similarity between the two
accounts even with regard to the details. But the religious
concepts behind the Hebrew account are totally different from
the Babylonian. Noah is not saved, like Utnapishtim, through
favouritism but because he is the only righteous man in an age
when the earth is filled with violence. There is nothing of such
gruesome mythological ideas as of the gods 'gathering like
flies'. Instead of a multiplicity of gods bent on destroying all
men, whether innocent or guilty, there is One God of justice
and righteousness who wishes to keep these ideals alive. That
the Biblical account is a version of a popular Near Eastern
tale of the Flood can no longer be doubted, but its religious
values shine forth to even greater effect through the transformation it has undergone. It is, of course, an open question
how exactly the Biblical narrative ties up with the Babylonian.
It can either be maintained that the latter travelled westwards
or that both accounts are based on one common earlier version.

(2) Seething a kid in its mother's milk.

'*Thou shalt not seethe a kid in its mother's milk*' (Ex. xxiii. 19;
Ex. xxxiv. 26; Deut. xiv. 21). This Pentateuchal injunction

was explained long ago by Maimonides ('Guide', III. 48, ed. Friedländer p. 371) in an inspired guess as a protest against idolatrous practices. The Rabbis interpret the relevant verses so as to prohibit all meat cooked in milk. Maimonides thus explains the prohibition: 'Meat boiled in milk is indubitably gross food, and makes overfull; but I think that most probably it is also prohibited because it is somehow connected with idolatry, forming perhaps part of the service, or being used on some festival of the heathen. I find a support for this view in the circumstances that the Law mentions the prohibition twice after the commandment given concerning the festivals: "Three times in the year all thy males shall appear before the Lord God" (Ex. xxiii. 17 and Ex. xxxiv. 23), as if to say, "When you come before me on your festivals do not seethe your food in the manner as the heathen used to do". This I consider as the best reason for the prohibition; but as far as I have seen the books on Sabean rites, nothing is mentioned of this custom'. In the years between 1929 and 1939 there was discovered at Ras Shamra in Syria an astonishing collection of clay tablets belonging to a Canaanite temple in ancient Ugarit, dating from the second half of the second millennium B.C.E. (*V. DOTT*, pp. 118–133; *ANET*, pp. 129–155). R. Dussaud in 'Révue d'histoire des religions', Vol. 108, p. 7 f., was the first to notice that from the Ras Shamra text 'Birth of the Gods' i. 14, it appears that a kid was cooked by the Canaanite priests in its mother's milk to procure the fertility of the fields, which were sprinkled with the substance which resulted. (*Cf.* S. W. Baron: 'A Social and Religious History of the Jews', Columbia University Press, 2nd. ed., Vol. I, 1952, p. 328, note 22 and Cassuto in '*Encyclopedia Miqra'ith*', *Vol. I, par.* 1950, p. 89). It should however, be noted that the reading in the Ras Shamra text is rather uncertain, so that it would be going too far to say that the text definitely states this.

(3) *The goring ox.*

Among the ancient Near Eastern texts there are codes of law dealing, among many other matters, with the goring ox. This is how the law is recorded in two of these texts (Pritchard, 'Archaeology', pp. 225–6; *ANET*, p. 163, par. 54 and p. 176 par. 251; *DOTT*, p. 35, par. 250–251).

(*a*) *Law of Eshnunna.*

'If an ox is known to gore habitually and the authorities
have brought the fact to the knowledge of its owner, but he
does not have his ox dehorned, and it gores a man and causes his
death, then the owner of the ox shall pay ⅔ of a mina of silver'.

(*b*) *Code of Hammurabi.*

'If a seignior's ox was a gorer and his city council made it
known to him that it was a gorer, but he did not pad its horns
or tie up his ox, and that ox gored to death a member of the
aristocracy, he shall give ½ mina of silver'.

(*c*) In Ex. xxi. 29–30 we read: 'But if the ox was wont to gore
in time past, and warning hath been given to its owner, and
he hath not kept it in, but it hath killed a man or a woman;
the ox shall be stoned, and its owner also shall be put to death.
If there be laid on him a ransom, then he shall give for the
redemption of his life whatsoever is laid upon him'.

The law of Exodus is thus seen not in isolation but against
its background. The famous stele of Hammurabi (c. 1792–1750
B.C.E.), on which his law code was inscribed, was discovered
in 1901–2 by V. Scheil at Susa. The Eshnunna code is about a
century earlier. Of particular interest is the comparison between
par. 282 of the code of Hammurabi (*DOTT*, p. 35) and the law
of Ex. xxi. 5–6. In the Hammurabi code we read: 'If a serf
has declared to his master – "Thou art not my master", his
master shall confirm him (to be) his serf and shall cut off his
ear'. In Exodus, on the other hand, we read: 'But if the servant
shall plainly say: I love my master, my wife, and my children; I
will not go out free; then his master shall bring him unto God
(i.e. to the judges), and shall bring him to the door, or unto
the door-post; and his master shall bore his ear through with
an awl; and he shall serve him for ever'. Particularly to be
noticed is that in Exodus the ear is bored, not cut off, and the
penalty is not for the slave wishing to be free but for his desire
to remain a slave (*cf*. Deut. xv. 12 f.).

(4) *The Hittite Code.*

In the Hittite Code from the fourteenth century B.C.E. (*ANET*,
p. 196, par. 197; Pritchard, 'Archaeology', p. 224) we read: 'If
a man seizes a woman in the mountains, it is the man's crime
and he will be killed. But if he seizes her in her house, it is the

woman's crime and the woman shall be killed'. The parallel
to this is found in Deut. xxii. 23–27: 'If there be a damsel
that is a virgin betrothed unto a man, and a man find her in the
city and lie with her; then ye shall bring them both out unto
the gate of that city, and ye shall stone them with stones
that they die: the damsel, because she cried not, being in the
city; and the man, because he hath humbled his neighbour's
wife; so thou shalt put away the evil from the midst of thee. But
if the man find the damsel that is bethrothed in the field, and
the man take hold of her and lie with her; then the man only
that lay with her shall die. But unto the damsel thou shalt
do nothing; there is in the damsel no sin worthy of death;
for as when a man riseth against his neighbour and slayeth
him, even so is this matter. For he found her in the field; the
betrothed damsel cried, and there was none to save her'.

What are we to make of this material, of which the above
are but a few examples, easily multiplied? While it must be
recognised that even the most striking parallels between the
Pentateuchal records and the Near Eastern Texts provide no
evidence of direct borrowing, they do compel us to see that
the Pentateuch was produced in a particular *milieu* and that
the language, style and ideas used are those of that *milieu*
albeit transformed, as we have seen, in the light of the monotheistic ideal. Apart from the reasons mentioned earlier, this
is yet another reason for rejecting the doctrine of verbal
inspiration. It is obvious that there is a human, as well as a
divine, element in the Bible. This idea has sometimes been
put nowadays in the following way. The Bible is 'Eternity
expressing itself in Time'. That is to say, the encounter
between God and man which produced, over a long period,
the Hebrew Bible, gave rise to eternal truths by which man
should live. These are contained, however, in the framework
of a particular period in human history, the ideas and language
of which naturally colour the account which has come down to
us. Revelation, on this view, is not the communication of
words to man, not a kind of divine dictation to a passive human
recipient, but a meeting of God and man in history, a meeting
producing results of eternal significance. It is undeniable that,
as we have seen, the older Jewish view (not, however, the view
of Scripture itself), recorded by Maimonides, was that of

verbal dictation or communication. To this it was possible to hold on only for as long as the facts afforded it no contradiction. Nowadays, the facts we know do contradict the doctrine of verbal inspiration and, painful though the process is, the modern Jewish believer is obliged to reinterpret the whole idea of revelation. But to reinterpret does not mean to abandon. It was always recognised by those who thought at all deeply on the subject that the tremendous fact of God's revelation to man was so profound that no single mind, no single generation could hope to grasp the whole truth. It is the severe error of the fundamentalist that he presents us with an either/or, that he accuses those of us who have been compelled to give up the notion of verbal inspiration with giving up our belief in revelation. But the Hebrew Bible is unique for us as well as for him. If man believes in God he cannot help but see that it is in *this* book or, better, collection of books, that He has revealed Himself to man. It is this book, or collection of books, He has chosen as His vehicle. That the record is humanly mediated, that it is coloured by its human background and the minds of its human authors, that it contains error as well as truth, does not affect its claim, or the claim made for it in Jewish tradition, to contain the word of God. We must stress the word 'contain' for the new view of revelation – of '*Torah from Heaven*' – is that this is *contained* in the Bible, not that the Bible itself is revelation. The words are human, they have a history, there are contradictions and discrepancies in them, the view they present of ancient times is frequently limited by the degree of knowledge their authors possessed, but, for all that, in this collection of books, as in no other, the account is there for all to read how man found God and how God helped man to find Him.

The eternal truths first firmly enunciated in the Bible are that: God is One; there are no other gods; God is a Being who is holy and just and who demands these qualities of man; the people of Israel have a significant role to play in the fulfilment of God's purpose; the Sabbath is His witness, testifying to His creative power; the strong and the fortunately placed must help the weak and the unfortunate; God cannot bear the sight of evil and wishes those who serve Him to combat evil; God is constantly at work in human history of which He is Lord; those who trust

in Him shall be blessed. It is these which make us see that the
Bible is unique. If we have been obliged to give up that other
picture of a magic book, perfect in all its details, its very letters
in existence before the creation of the world, containing all
truth and infallible in all its statements, there is gain to religion
as well as loss in the readjustment required. No longer need the
believer torture himself in attempting the reconciliation of the
sublime creation account in Genesis with the findings of modern
science; no longer need he be puzzled by divine commands
to exterminate little children; no longer need he push away
from the centre of his mind the evidence provided by history,
geology, archaeology and the other disciplines which challenge
the factual accuracy of Scripture. The picture which has now
emerged, after a hundred years and more of devoted scholarship,
is of divine truth enunciated in Scripture through weak human
minds and penned by weak human hands. The older view was of
the Bible as a precious jewel beyond all price. The new view
is that it is rather to be compared to a precious jewel in a
setting. If we now have less of the jewel we need no longer be
confused through identification of the jewel with its setting
and the true jewel can now be seen to shine in all its splendour.

When the facts mitigating against the belief in verbal
inspiration and direct divine dictation first became widely
recognised, liberal theologians accepted them and, as a result,
felt that the only way in which they could understand the Bible
to be inspired was the way in which all great literary works
can be said to be inspired, no more and no less. The Bible is
true in the sense in which Shakespeare and Dante are true. But
this way of looking at the Bible has been widely rejected, and
rightly so, by many recent religious thinkers on the grounds
that it fails utterly to do justice to the unique character both
of the Biblical teachings themselves and the way in which
they come to us pregnant with the imperatives of the divine.
There is the further fact that the Bible has meant far more both
in human life in general and in Jewish life in particular than
any other work of literary art. It was not for its aesthetic
value that the Jews honoured the Scroll of the *Torah* but
because through the pages of this book God had spoken to
their ancestors and to them.

Now much of what has been said here is commonplace

among theologians, but it hardly needs saying that the believing Jew will reject that further 'refinement', which, from the Jewish point of view, is no 'refinement' at all, in which the 'Old Testament' is seen as a dim anticipation of the 'New Testament'. Christian thinkers are perfectly justified in the name of the faith which is theirs, to see the 'Old Testament' view of God as inadequate. But by the same token the Jew is entitled to see a 'decline' in the 'New Testament' of the loftier concept of God found in the 'Old'. There God is depicted as the Lord of Hosts and it would have been considered by the 'Old Testament' authors blasphemous in the extreme to suggest that God can ever become man. It must be admitted that practically all the work done today in the field of 'Old Testament' theology is being done by Christians, many of them Bible scholars of renown. All the more urgent and necessary it is, therefore, for the religious Jew to engage in this work from the standpoint of his own faith. As a believer who accepts the findings of objective scholarship, he will refuse to confuse the dogmatic theological interpretations of the Hebrew Bible with the facts as established by scholarship. The facts are sacred. Even where they conflict with sacred traditions they must be upheld by both Jewish and Christian interpreters anxious to retain their intellectual integrity. But naturally the Jew will reject the Christian interpretation of the facts and will interpret these in the light of his own faith. That this needs to be said at all is due to the very strong Christian colouring of so much 'Old Testament' scholarship and the unfortunate neglect of Biblical studies by Jews in modern times.

As an illustration of the point we are trying to make the following quotation from Sigmund Mowinckel's profound, popular account of the issues raised by modern scholarship ('The Old Testament as Word of God', translated by Reidar B. Bjornard, Oxford, Blackwell, 1960) is pertinent. On pages 70–71 Mowinckel writes: 'When we look at the Old Testament as a whole from the standpoint of the history of revelation, it does not matter, for instance, what a tradition concerning a historical incident intended to say as *historical tradition*; but what does matter is why it is *given to us* as a part of the word of God by virtue of a divinely directed history. For example, the original narrators of the story of the sons of God and the daughters of men (Gen. 6: 1–4) or of the Tower of Babel (Gen. 11) perhaps wanted primarily only to tell their listeners something that to them was interesting and belonged to history, about the giants of ancient days, about the reason for the many languages in the world, or the reason for the ruined tower over in Babylonia. But in addition to this certainly the compilers of the source material – the Yahwist and the Elohist and perhaps already the ancient saga tellers – wanted to give examples of the human urge to transgress the limits set by God and to testify to the perversity of the human heart (Gen. 8. 21). For those who wrote down the sagas this was doubtless the main point. But even if they should not have seen this as the main task, it is still *this* meaning that the stories as a whole convey as parts of the totality of Holy Writ and that draws for us the line of revelation from the ancient days through Christ to the consummation, from Genesis through the Gospels to the Revelation of John. In the purpose that *God* had for the Bible to accomplish, *this* is what the stories are meant to tell us'. Now Mowinckel is writing as a Christian for Christians and he is justified in interpreting the record in accordance with his own faith. But this has nothing whatsoever to do with objective scholarship bent on determining the facts. Mowinckel, the objective Bible scholar, has arrived at a knowledge of the facts which he thus uses, perfectly justifiably, for his interpretation as a devout Christian. The Jewish scholar will be faced with the same data as Mowinckel but he, too, will be justified in interpreting them in the light of *his* faith. He may well agree with all that Mowinckel says up to the words 'Holy Writ' but this will mean for him the 'Old Testament' since he acknowledges no 'New Testament'. For him the 'line of revelation' will be drawn from the ancient days to the great Rabbinic period, the 'Oral Law' playing for him the role the 'New Testament' plays for the Christian.

Mowinckel's distinction between the intention of the original narrators and the intention of the compilers who, under God's guidance, made use of it, is perfectly valid and extremely helpful. It was no doubt something of the kind that Franz Rosenzweig meant when he said that the story of Balaam's ass is a fairy-tale for him during the rest of the year but it is the word of God speaking to him when it is read, as part of the Synagogue service, from the Scroll of the *Torah*. It was Rosenzweig, too, who said that for him the symbol '*R*' does not stand for '*Redactor*' but for '*Rabenu*' (= 'our teacher'), for the compilers of the ancient material were doing God's work in utilising the old records to express the great, eternal truths upon which Judaism stands. Similarly, in a letter to Jacob Rosenheim, the Agudath Yisrael leader, dated April 21st, 1927, Rosenzweig wrote: 'Where we differ from orthodoxy is our reluctance to draw from our belief in the holiness or uniqueness of the *Torah*, and in its character of revelation, any conclusions as to its literary genesis and the philological value of the text as it has come down to us. If all of Wellhausen's theories were correct and the Samaritans really had the better text, our faith would not be shaken in the least' ('Franz Rosenzweig: His Life and Thought', presented by Nahum N. Glatzer, Shocken, New York, 1953, p. 158. *V*. p. 246 for the remark about Balaam's ass. Rosenzweig's remark about *Redactor-Rabenu* has often been quoted).

*   *   *

EXCURSUS

Frequent attention has been drawn in recent years to the whole question of 'myth' in the Bible. There was, in ancient times, on the Babylonian New Year festival a great ritual to mark the turning point of the agricultural year. The ritual was performed with the intention of controlling nature and the king took part in certain ritual acts, e.g., those representing the original victory of the god over chaos and the chaos dragon, Tiamat. By repeating the myth it was believed that the situation of the god's victory over chaos was maintained. *V. ANET*, pp. 60–72; *DOTT*, pp. 3–16; Henri Frankfort and others: 'Before Philosophy', Pelican Books, 1949. Whether there are traces of all this in the Bible is still debated. The following passages have been noted in particular: Zech. xiv. 16 f.; Is. li. 9–10; Ps. xciii. 3–4; Ps. lxxv: 12–17; Ps. lxxxix: 10–15; Ps. civ. It seems extremely probable that, at least, the Biblical authors made use of the Babylonian myths but transformed them, as above. *Cf.* 'Myth and Ritual', ed. S. H. Hooke, Clarendon Press, Oxford, 1933; 'Myth, Ritual and Kingship', ed. S. H. Hooke, Clarendon Press, Oxford, 1958. In the latter volume Hooke (pp. 1 f.) gives a survey of the whole 'Myth and Ritual' controversy. *Cf.* the essay by S. G. F. Brandon in the same volume: 'The Myth and Ritual Position Critically Examined', pp. 261 f. In any event the term 'myth' is frequently used nowadays of stories in the Bible such as that of Adam and Eve in the garden. Some thinkers prefer to use the less ambiguous term 'parable' but *v.* the wise observation of S. H. Hooke in his Commentary to Genesis in 'Peake's Commentary to the Bible', revised ed., ed. Matthew Black and H. H. Rowley, Thomas Nelson and Son, London, 1962, pp. 177 f. 'In common usage to say that something is a myth, or mythical, implies that it is not true, and hence many thoughtful people feel that to say the Bible contains myths is the same as saying the Bible contains what is not true. But such an attitude is based on a mistaken idea of the true nature of myth, and also on a mistaken idea of what the Hebrew writer had in mind when he made use of myths, not only in the first eleven chapters of Genesis, but elsewhere in the Bible'. Hooke continues: 'But historical truth, important though it is, is not the only kind of truth, and a myth can, and often does, represent a kind of truth which cannot be expressed in historical categories'. *Cf.* B. S. Childs: 'Myths and Reality in the O.T.', S.C.M. Press, London, 1960 and S. H. Hooke: 'Middle Eastern Mythology', Penguin Books, 1963, particularly Chapter 5, 'Hebrew Mythology', pp. 103–160. Jewish thinkers in modern times have had various attitudes to the problem of the Bible, particularly the Pentateuch. Not all conservative thinkers, for instance, were opposed either to the evolutionary idea or that of man's simian ancestry. Rabbi A. I. Kook appears to accept the doctrine of evolution as completely compatible with the Qabbalistic doctrines in which he believed, *v.* his observations in ' '*Oroth Ha-Qodesh*', Vol. II, Jer. 1938, pp. 555 f. Similarly, Dr. J. H. Hertz: 'The Pentateuch and Haftorahs', Soncino Press, London, 1958, pp. 194–5, adopts a positive attitude to evolution, as does Dr. I. Epstein: 'The Faith of Judaism', Soncino Press, London, 1954, pp. 194–208. But all these writers reject Bible Criticism out of hand as sheer heresy. Among conservative Jewish thinkers who accept modern Bible scholarship but recognise the Bible as the 'Word of God' are the following: H. Loewe: 'A Rabbinic Anthology' ed. together with C. G. Montefiore, Cambridge University Press, 1938, pp. lvi f.; Will Herberg: 'Judaism and Modern Man', Meridian Books, New York, 1959, pp. 243 f.; Ernst Simon: '*Torath Hayyim*, Some Thoughts on the Teaching of the Bible', in 'Conservative Judaism', Vol. XII, Spring, 1958, pp. 1–19; Jakob J. Petuchowsky: 'Ever Since Sinai', Scribe Publications, N.Y., 1961. *V.* in particular Simon's statement on page 4: 'If the Bible is a human translation of God's word, then its proper teaching must fulfil a double task. On the one hand it has to continue the business of translating and keeping the Bible understandable to the various "tongues of human beings", i.e. to the "seventy languages" of cultural environments, intellectual levels, and age groups, by adapting it and interpreting it to them. But, on the other hand – and this second task is in our time much less heeded than the first one, even though it is clearly preconditional to it – proper teaching of the Bible should always try to penetrate as deeply as possible into the underlying meaning of the Divine original which is present but hidden under the layers of human translations, interpretations and adaptations. I believe that this is a conservative approach to the problem of Revelation, as differentiated from the Orthodox viewpoint which identifies the actual text of the Hebrew Bible with the Divine original as well as from the radically humanistic – including the Reconstructionist and Reform theories – which seem to strip the Bible altogether of its Divine character. We claim neither that the Divine original is in our hand nor do we admit that there is no such original. We read and teach the Bible as a palimpsest, discovering in it again and again traces of the original word of God. The text we possess reveals this hidden, authentic writ as well as conceals it.' Despite Solomon Schechter's fierce opposition to 'Higher Anti-Semitism', his attitude to Bible Criticism was not at all negative. In the introduction to his 'Studies in Judaism', First Series, Jewish Publication Society of America and Meridian Books, 1958, Schechter deals with the problem. 'Some years ago when the waves of the Higher Criticism of the Old Testament reached the shores of this country, and such questions as the heterogeneous composition of the Pentateuch, the comparative late date of the Levitical Legislation, and the post-exilic origin of certain Prophecies as well as of the Psalms began to be freely discussed by the press and even in the pulpit, the invidious remark was often made: What will now become of Judaism when its last stronghold, the Law, is being shaken to its very foundations?' Schechter notes that such a remark shows a very superficial acquaintance with the nature of an old historical religion like Judaism, and the richness of the resources it has to fall back upon in cases of emergency. Schechter finds these resources in what he calls the 'Secondary Meaning' of Scripture, i.e. Scripture as interpreted in the Synagogue. In Judaism, according to Schechter, it is not the original or plain meaning of Scripture which is really the authority but the interpretation of Scripture in Jewish history. Women are not put to death for witchcraft, for example, in spite of the injunction in Scripture, because Jewish practice, the practice of 'Catholic Israel', does not interpret the Biblical verse to be applied permanently. Jews do not keep the Sabbath so much because it is in the Bible but because of the emphasis the Biblical iujunctions concerning the Sabbath receive in the history of Jewish life, thought and experience. We have noted above the inadequacy

K

of Schechter's view if left without elaboration but the point he makes is weighty. It is not a mere coincidence, says Schechter, that the first representatives of the historical school were also the first Jewish scholars, who proved themselves ready to join the modern school of Bible Criticism and even to contribute their share to it (i.e. because of their conviction that *origins* did not really matter but that the true centre of authority lies in Jewish historical experience). One of the great founders of *Judische Wissenschaft* is quoted in support of this. Zunz (*'Gesammelte Schriften'*, i, pp. 217–29) expressed the view 'that the Book of Leviticus dates from a later period than the Book of Deuteronomy, later even than Ezekiel, having been composed during the age of the Second Temple, when there already existed a well-established priesthood which superintended the sacrificial worship'. It is painful to have to disagree with the deservedly popular writings of Dr. J. H. Hertz but it is necessary, nonetheless, in the interests of sound scholarship and scholarly integrity, to point out that his total rejection of all Pentateuchal Criticism is biased out of all proportion. This is especially serious since the Hertz Commentary is used in English-speaking communities all over the world. Already in his Preface to the Commentary, *op. cit.*, Hertz states that he is prepared to 'accept the truth from whatever source it come', even from the pages of a devout Christian expositor or an iconoclastic Bible scholar, but his conviction is unshaken that 'the criticism of the Pentateuch associated with the name of Wellhausen is a perversion of history and a desecration of religion.' On page 196 Dr. Hertz accepts the story of the Deluge as historical fact, overlooking entirely the overwhelming objections to this, *v.* S. R. Driver 'Genesis', *op. cit.*, pp. 99–108. On page 198 we are told by Hertz that the followers of Higher Criticism maintain, in the face of all archaeological evidence to the contrary, that the art of writing was not known in Israel before the days of David. Actually, only a very few of the more extreme critics have maintained this and it is no part of the critical position. Hertz's polemic on p. 199 overlooks entirely the question of the other characteristics beside the divine names occurring together which, as we have noted above, makes the critical position so plausible; nor is it correct to say that the differences in the divine names is one of the two main reasons for distinguishing diverse sources in the Pentateuch, for if this were so there would be no means of distinguishing between '*E*' and '*P*'. On page 200 Hertz quotes with approval John Skinner's view that the patriarchal period has been so illuminated by recent discoveries that it is no longer possible to doubt its substantial historicity. But on the traditional view, which Dr. Hertz so doughtily defends, it is as heretical to speak of the Patriarchal narratives being *substantially* correct as it is to deny their historicity completely. If Moses wrote the Pentateuch at divine dictation the stories are not *substantially* correct but unerring records of factual events in all their details. On page 554 Dr. Hertz writes: 'The whole Critical theory is today being questioned on fundamental issues'. We have noticed above the nature of this questioning. It has to do chiefly with the over-neat division into documents typical of the older views. It is in no sense at all a return to the traditional view. Because of his rejection of all critical theories, Hertz is obliged to indulge in a naive and ex-ceedingly weak defence of Bible 'difficulties'. The account of the war with Midian, Num. xxxi, is recognised as unhistorical by practically all critics. Twelve thousand warriors, a thousand from each tribe, go to battle against the whole people of Midian, slaying every male and suffering no loss themselves. And yet we meet with the Midianites subsequently in Israelite history (*Cf.* Judges vi–viii; I Kings xi. 18; Is. lx. 6). Moses is angry with the soldiers for sparing the females. He orders them to kill forthwith every male child and all the women who have known a man, sparing only the little girls. The moral difficulty is obvious. But according to most critical views this whole passage is not a factual account dictated by God but a much later narrative which may or may not be based on an actual event in the past. Thus according to the Documentary Hypothesis this section belongs to ' *P* ', according to the Uppsala school it is part of the ' *P-work* '. In any event, it is a fiction, composed perhaps with a view to bringing home to the later Israelites the truth that God hates immorality. Its purpose is to serve as a warning to *them* not to fall short of the standards deman-ded by the God of holiness. It is *Midrash* that we have here not sober history. There is nothing surprising about this, nothing offensive, once we have noticed the character of the narrative. But Hertz is prevented from seeing this obvious solution to the diffi-culty by his conception of the Pentateuch as a book dictated by God. Hence we find him saying (p. 704) : 'The war against the Midianites presents peculiar difficulties. We are no longer acquainted with the circumstances that justified the ruthlessness with which it was waged, and therefore we cannot satisfactorily meet the various objections that have been raised in that connection. "Perhaps the recollection of what took place after the Indian Mutiny, when Great Britain was in the same temper, may throw light on this question. The soldiers then, bent on punishing the cruelty and lust of the rebels, partly in patriotism, partly in revenge, set mercy altogether aside" (Expositor's Bible). The Midianites affected were only the clans that lived in the neigbourhood of Moab. This accounts for the persistence of Midianites in later periods of Israelite history'. This will satisfy only the over-credulous. There is not the slightest suggestion in the narrative that the war was only waged against certain clans. The whole tenor of the story points to the opposite (*v.* verse 10). As for the 'apology' quoted from the Expositor's Bible it baffles belief that this could have been thought satisfactory. A questionable attempt to find some justification for the ruthlessness of British soldiers during the Indian Mutiny can hardly throw light on deeds which, if the account is taken as history, were done at the direct command of God. It is not at all a question of men doing things 'partly in patriotism, partly in revenge' but of God commanding them to do so and of His servant urging them at His command to complete the slaughter. What possible comfort the fundamentalist Jew can derive from all this it is very hard to see. If this is the best that fundamentalism can do surely the far more reasonable approach is to accept the readjustment required by modern criticism of whatever school; for, in the new picture of Scripture that is then revealed there is great gain as well as loss. Not least of the gains is that it frees the modernist believer from the harrowing difficulties raised by Hertz and the tortured attempts at finding extenuation in ways which convince no one. Particularly confusing is Hertz's habit of quoting authorities of note who reject the critical view, without stating that these authorities are, in many cases, themselves critics who, while rejecting the Documentary Hypothesis, reject, just as much as Wellhausen, the traditional view as well, offering in its stead a new *critical* theory. Thus, Weiner, whom Hertz quotes with approval (p. 554, 558 and elsewhere) criticizes Wellhausen by a ruthless and unscholarly emendation of the traditional text. Similarly B. Jacob, whom Hertz quotes with approval on p. 398 and elsewhere, is hardly a defender of the traditional view of the Pentateuch, as any reader of his articles on the separate five books (Genesis etc.) in JE can ascertain. As for Naville, whom Hertz quotes with approval on p. 399 and elsewhere, it is difficult to see what comfort the traditionalist can obtain from Naville's curious view that part of Genesis consisted originally of separate cuneiform tablets until Ezra translated the Pentateuch from the cuneiform. The same kind of disingenuous apologetic is to be found in I. Epstein's 'The Faith of Judaism', The Soncino Press, London, 1954, pp. 112–3. Epstein quotes in his support Engnell of Uppsala, B. Jacob and Cassuto and then goes on to say that there is 'nothing in its (i.e. the Higher Critical view) still so-called "assured results" to upset the traditional acceptance of the unity and Mosaic authorship of the Pentateuch'. No one would guess from reading this note of Epstein that neither Engnell, Jacob nor Cassuto accept the traditional view. The method of Hertz and Epstein is simple. You show that various scholars have challenged the Documentary Hypothesis and suggest that because this is so we can all go safely back to the traditional view without giving your readers the slightest indication that your very heroes have untraditional views of their own. It should be noted that there is evidence enough that the ancient Rabbis were not unaware of the idea that there is a human element in the Bible though, of course, this for them was strictly limited. Apart from the material I have quoted in this connection in my book 'We Have Reason to Believe', Vallentine, Mitchell, London, 1957, pp. 78–81, reference should be made to the numerous passages in which words ascribed by Scripture to the Biblical heroes are criticised, e.g. in *Pes.* 66b, with regard to Deborah and Moses, *Gen. R.* 44.4. and 44.18 with regard to Abraham, *Gen. R.* 71.7, with regard to Jacob, also *Gen. R.* 80.4, *Gen. R.* 100.3, with regard to Joseph, *Sot.* 35a with regard to David. *Cf.* A. J. Heschel: 'God in Search of Man', John Calder, London, 1956, p. 268 and the sources quoted in note 27, p. 278. *Cf.* The phenomenon of parallelism in Hebrew poetry which was noted by the mediaeval commentators as 'the same matter is repeated in different words', e.g. *Kimbi* to Is. *v.* 9., *v.* I. Heinemann '*Darkhe Ha-' Aggadah*,' 2nd ed., Jan. 1954, pp. 96–97.

* * *

So far we have dealt with the problems raised by modern Biblical scholarship and modern science for the traditional view of how the Pentateuch and the rest of Scripture came into being. But it is clear both from Maimonides' formulation of the eighth principle and from the general Rabbinic view that the belief in '*Torah from Heaven*', in the sense of direct communication in detail to Moses, embraced not alone the Pentateuch but its traditional explanation. This latter the Rabbis call the 'Oral Law', '*Torah She-Be-'Al Peh*', in contradistinction to the 'Written Law', '*Torah She-Bi-Kethabh*'. On the traditional view God gave to Moses the laws contained in the Pentateuch together with their explanations. Thus Moses was told on Sinai not only the general law concerning Sabbath observance but all the details concerning the thirty-nine different categories of work forbidden on the Sabbath as well as the offshoots to be derived from them. This belief is assumed everywhere in the Rabbinic literature. In tractate *Berakhoth* (5a) we read that R. Levi b. Hama said in the name of R. Simeon b. Laqish: 'The verse: "And I will give thee the tables of stone, and the law and the commandment, which I have written that thou mayest teach them" (Ex. xxiv. 12) means as follows: "The tables of stone" are the ten commandments, "the law" is the Pentateuch, "the commandment" is the *Mishnah*, "which I have written" are the Prophets and the Hagiographa, "that thou mayest teach them" is the *Gemara* (i.e. the *Talmud*). This teaches us that all these things were given on Sinai'. Allowing for the element of hyperbole and anachronism of a more or less conscious nature in a passage such as this, it remains true that in the whole of the Rabbinic literature the view is unchallenged that the laws recorded in that literature were given to Moses and enjoy the same divine authority as the laws in the Pentateuch itself. Indeed it would be more correct to say that it is not at all the bare Pentateuchal laws which enjoy authority for the Rabbis but the Pentateuchal law as interpreted by the Jewish teachers. Naturally such a belief did not preclude the possibility of Rabbinic interpretation and elaboration of the laws, nor did it prevent the Rabbis from introducing new laws of their own, but the belief was held by all the Rabbis that the core of the 'Oral Law' was dictated by God to Moses in exactly the same manner as the 'Written Law', the only difference between them being that the one set of laws was written down by Moses, the others, too numerous to be written down, were taught by him to the people. The famous statement in the *Mishnah* (*'Abhoth*. I. 1) that Moses received the *Torah* on Sinai and delivered it to Joshua who, in turn, delivered it to the Elders, the Elders to the Prophets, and the Prophets to the Men of the Great Synagogue, was always understood as referring to the 'Oral Law' as well as to the 'Written Law' and was evidently so intended from the beginning.

Whether there existed an 'Oral Law' was, in fact, one of the major differences between the Pharisees and Sadducees, attested to many times in the Rabbinic literature. Josephus (*Antiq.* XIII. 10. 6) similarly records: 'The Pharisees have delivered to the people by tradition from their fathers a great many observances which are not written in the law of Moses; and for that reason the Sadducean group reject them, saying that only those observances are obligatory which are in the written word, but that those derived from the tradition of the forefathers need not be kept'. Among the many Rabbinic passages, an oft-quoted and very typical one is the story (*Sabb.* 31a) of the heathen who wanted to become a convert to Judaism but wished to accept the 'Written Law' alone. On the first day Hillel taught him the letters of the Hebrew alphabet but on the second day he reversed them. When the pupil objected Hillel replied: 'You see that you have to rely on me, too, with respect to the Oral Law'.

Now there can be no doubt that there actually existed an 'Oral Law' and that this whole concept is not, as some scholars suggested in the last century, an invention of the Pharisees. Many of the Pentateuchal laws are incomplete without supplementary details which must have been known from the earliest times. There are Pentateuchal laws, for instance, dealing with the buying and selling of fields, chattels and slaves, with no indication of how the legal transfer was to be effected. There are references to marriage without any indication of how a legal marriage was to be instituted. There are laws concerning sacrifices which require a detailed tradition kept by the priests. The festivals are recorded but the details of the calendar are left to tradition. In fact, on the hypothesis of the Uppsala School of modern criticism, the 'Oral Law' preceded the 'Written Law', the latter being written down only in post-exilic times. But to note these facts is not to obscure the Rabbinic belief that the 'Oral Law' was given to Moses on Sinai. If the modern Jew finds the eighth principle of the faith impossible of acceptance in Maimonides' formulation with regard to the 'Written Law', he finds it no less a surrender of his reason to accept it with regard to the 'Oral Law'. For modern scholarship is unanimous in seeing the 'Oral Law' as a developing tradition, with a definite history, not something given once and for all.

However, the picture of a static transmission of laws and practices from generation to generation reaching back to Moses in every detail is, in any event, challenged here and there in the Rabbinic sources themselves and modern scholarship in this matter builds, in fact, on *their* earlier foundations. It has long been noted that on occasion, at least, the Rabbis speak of 'a law given to Moses on Sinai' (*halakhah le-moshe mi-sinai*) without taking this literally but simply as pointing to the great antiquity of the law. The famous mediaeval codifier, Asher ben Yehiel (d. 1327), for instance, has this to say on the ruling of the *Mishnah* (*Yad.* IV. 3), that it is a 'law given to Moses on Sinai' that Poorman's tithe must be given in Ammon and Moab, although the law is much later than Moses. Asher b. Yehiel (*Hil. Mikwaoth*, 1) remarks that the meaning is simply that the law is so clear and obvious that it is *as if* it had been given to Moses on Sinai. Modern scholars like Nahman Krochmal, Zechariah Frankel, Isaac Hirsch Weiss, Hayyim Tzernowitz, Louis Ginzberg and Saul Lieberman have proved conclusively that the *Halakhah*, the legal side of Judaism, was not transmitted intact in an unbroken chain of tradition but that its institutions were influenced by the social, political, economic and religious conditions obtaining in different ages.

To make all this clearer it is necessary to give one or two illustrations.

(1) The famous Babylonian teacher, Samuel (third century C.E.) promulgated a rule which was to have the most important consequences for Jewish survival. This was the maxim that 'the law of the kingdom is law' i.e. that the civil laws of the countries in which Jews reside have the full force of Jewish law and have to be obeyed by Jews (*B.B.* 54a, 55a, *B.Q.* 113a and freq.). The *Talmud* everywhere appears to assume that this law existed from the earliest times and that Samuel's task was simply to record it, not to introduce it. Thus, it is assumed that the law was in practice in Palestine under Roman rule and that it was upheld by the Tannaim. But it is typical of the approach favoured by the 'Jüdische Wissenschaft' School that it seeks to get behind the apparent homogeneity of the Talmudic records to unravel the very complex forces which were at work in the development of the *Halakhah*. Once the matter is studied in the light of historical research it is seen that the Palestinian teachers never acquiesced in the conquest of Palestine by the Romans to the extent of recognising the validity of the Roman imposition of laws on the Jews. Perforce Jews had to accept Roman rule but their teachers resolutely refused to give rules imposed by their conquerers the sanction of Jewish law. It was only in Babylon that Samuel taught that the law of the kingdom is law.

(2) The *Talmud* (*Sabb.* 21b) gives the well-known reason for the observance of *Hanukkah* that the 'Greeks' defiled all the oils when they entered the Temple and when the Hasmoneans defeated them they found one cruse of pure oil which, by a miracle, burned for eight days. The whole of the subsequent *Halakhah* regarding *Hanukkah* is based on this reason. But from the historical point of view the real reason for the institution of eight days of *Hanukkah* was on the analogy of the eight days of Tabernacles, as is clearly stated in the Book of Maccabees (*v.* II Macc. i. 9, and JE, Vol. VI, pp. 223 f.), the legend of the oil being a later interpretation of an old custom. It is to be noted that such an approach is not necessarily based on an arbitrary denial that a miracle could have happened. With God all things are possible. It is rather a realisation that the most plausible explanation of the eight days of *Hanukkah*, given in a much earlier source than the Talmudic passage, is the correct one and that there is nothing strange or surprising in the ascription of ancient events of great significance to a miracle. This is an excellent illustration of how the historian learns to view his sources with a sense of history. It is his business to discover what actually happened. He is concerned, and as an historian he must be so concerned, with *origins*. But this does not prevent the theologian, while recognising the 'origin' of *Hanukkah*, from seeing, at the same time, that the legend of the miracle of the oil, with its implications of the enduring effects of the spirit, has become the keynote of *Hanukkah*.

(3) Of much greater significance than the previous two illustrations is one drawn from the Sabbath laws. For the Rabbis the *locus classicus* for determining the term 'work', used in Scripture with regard to the Sabbath, was Chapter 35 of the book of Exodus in which the command to observe the Sabbath is placed in juxtaposition with the instructions concerning the building of the Sanctuary. By the exegetical principle known as '*heqesh*' ('comparison') the Rabbis derive that all the types of labour required for the building of the Sanctuary are forbidden

on the Sabbath, hence Scripture places these two together to
suggest that all work on the Sanctuary must cease on the Sabbath.
This produces a list of thirty-nine main categories of work
(' *'abhoth'*, *'fathers'*) and from these many further types are
derived by analogy. These are called 'offspring' (*'toledoth'*).
All these types of work are, according to the Rabbis, forbidden
by Biblical law. They are Scriptural (*de-'oraitha*) as opposed
to Rabbinic enactments, such as handling money on the Sabbath,
which enjoy only the status of Rabbinic law – *de-rabbanan*.The
thirty-nine main classes of work are stated thus in the *Mishnah*
(*Sabb.* VII. 2): 'Sowing, ploughing, reaping, binding sheaves,
threshing, winnowing, cleansing crops, grinding, sifting,
kneading, baking, shearing wool, washing or beating or dyeing
it, spinning, weaving, making two loops, weaving two threads,
separating two threads, tying a knot, loosening a knot, sewing
two stitches, tearing in order to sew two stitches, hunting a
gazelle, slaughtering or flaying or salting it and curing its
skin, scraping it and cutting it up, writing two letters, erasing in
order to write two letters, building, pulling down, putting out
a fire, lighting a fire, striking with a hammer and taking ought
from one domain into another'.

Now the *Halakhah* generally assumes that all this really
goes back to the law given to Moses on Sinai. The actual
prohibition of work was recorded by Moses in the Pentateuch
as part of the 'Written Law', whereas the details were told
to him as part of the 'Oral Law'. Consequently, all these prohibitions are Biblical – *de-'oraitha* – and in subsequent ages
various teachers added further prohibitions which are Rabbinic –
de-rabbanan. But anyone with the slightest historical sense will
see that the thirty-nine classes of work recorded in the *Mishnah*
all belong to the types of activity common to agricultural
communities in *Rabbinic* times. This does not mean that the
Rabbis were consciously attempting to further their own ideas
under the cloak of Scripture. It means rather that since, in
Rabbinic times, these were the main types of work it was
assumed that their prohibition reached back to Scripture
itself. And, indeed, it goes without saying that many of these
types must have been included in the Scriptural definition of
work. It remains true nonetheless that the classification reflects
conditions in Rabbinic rather than in Biblical times. The Rabbis,

in recording the types of work which must have been forbidden at a time anterior to their own day, if they thought about this matter at all, would have argued that conditions in their day could not have been so very different from those in Moses' day. But to the historian all this is clearly a *reading* by the Rabbis of the ancient Scriptural text, not an actual tradition handed down from generation to generation reaching back to Moses. From the point of view of the historian, in other words, the distinction between *de'oraitha* and *de-rabbanan* is a legal, not an historical, distinction.

(4) Another illustration of far-reaching consequence may here be mentioned. The *Halakhah* generally assumes that six hundred and thirteen precepts (*taryag mitzwoth*) were given to Moses on Sinai. The *locus classicus* for this is the saying of the third century Palestinian teacher, R. Simlai, that six hundred and thirteen *mitzwoth* were 'said' to Moses, three hundred and sixty-five negative precepts, corresponding to the days of the solar year, and two hundred and forty-eight positive precepts, corresponding to the members of a man's body (*Makk.* 23b). R. Simlai's statement is clearly homiletical. His intention is almost certainly to convey the idea that the *mitzwoth* embrace the whole of man's life and his being (the days of his year and the limbs of his body). Although the number six hundred and thirteen was known before R. Simlai (*v.* JE, Vol. IV, p. 181 and S. W. Baron's 'A Social and Religious History of the Jews', Vol. VI, Columbia University Press, 1958, p. 371, note 103) there is no suggestion anywhere that this is anything but a homiletical device and it is significant in this connection that it appears in a Midrashic-Aggadic context. But the great Codifiers of the Middle Ages took it literally so that we find them engaging in prolonged and detailed discussions as to which *mitzwoth* are to be included in the six hundred and thirteen and which excluded. Here, once again, we have a term which belongs to Jewish *law* rather than Jewish *history*. From the historical point of view it is futile to discuss which of the many precepts classified later as *mitzwoth* were given to Moses. In Moses' day the whole concept of '*taryag mitzwoth*' was unknown. It is disconcerting, therefore, to find Dr Hertz ('Commentary', *op. cit.*, p. 862) observing on the command to write

the words of the law on the great stones (Deut. xxvii. 3):
'Some commentators have held that only a brief summary
of the Law could have been inscribed on the stones. However,
since the discovery of the Hammurabi Code, consisting of 232
paragraphs, with a lengthy introduction and conclusion, in all
about 8,000 words, engraved on one block of diorite, it is
seen that the laws of Deuteronomy, or even the whole *Torah*,
could have been written on twelve stones . . . There is, therefore,
no reasonable doubt that, as Saadyah and Ibn Ezra hold, the
613 Precepts of the Torah were inscribed on those great stones'.
In view of what we have said the last sentence contains an
incredible anachronism.

(5) One final illustration may be given. The *Mishnah* (*Sanh.*
III. 3) rules that the following are ineligible to be witnesses or
judges: A gambler with dice, a usurer, a pigeon-trainer, and
traders in the produce of the Sabbatical year. All these, it
should be noted, are people who commit wrong for monetary
gain and they are consequently held suspect. In the later
Amoraic period (*v.* Gem. *ad. loc.* and freq.) people guilty of
purely religious offences, the consumption of forbidden food
for example, were included in the list of invalid witnesses.
The verse said to include these was Ex. xxiii. 1 which excluded
the *rasha'*, the wicked. The subsequent *Halakhah* accepts this
and it is generally assumed that the later Amoraim were
recording a genuine tradition, reaching back to Moses, that,
in other words, the verse in Exodus really was intended to
include religious offenders among those disqualified to serve
as witnesses. But the historian sees in the disqualification of
these a *development* in the law. From the historical point of
view the whole idea of disqualifying those guilty of religious
offences was unknown in the earlier Tannaitic period. It is,
indeed, highly plausible that the Amoraim who did introduce
it were concerned with strengthening the religious life of
their own day. Be that as it may, there is clearly a development
in the law and this notion of development can be discerned with
equal or greater clarity in many others so that the new picture
of the 'Oral Law' which emerges from the researches of modern
scholars is not of static transmission but of dynamic evolution.

*   *   *

The literature on the subject of the 'Oral Law' is immense. A pioneering work is that of I. H. Weiss: *'Dor Dor We-Doreshaw'*, New York–Berlin, 1924, 5 volumes. Further important works are cited in the bibliography at the end of J. Z. Lauterbach's article in JE, Vol. IX, pp. 423–426. *Cf.* the same author's article 'Sinaitic Commandments' in JE, Vol. XI, p. 383; Louis Finkelstein: 'The Pharisees', Jewish Publication Society, Philadelphia, 1940, Chapter XIII, pp. 261–280; George Foot Moore: 'Judaism', Harvard University Press, 1958, Part I, Chapter III, pp. 251–262; Louis Ginzberg's essays on Zechariah Frankel and I. H. Weiss in 'Students, Scholars and Saints', Jewish Publication Society, Philadelphia, 1928, pp. 195–240; Solomon Schechter's review of I. H. Weiss's book in 'Studies in Judaism', Meridian Books, New York, 1958, pp. 25–52; Chaim Tchernowitz: *'Toledoth Ha-Halakhah'*, Vol. I, New York, 1934, pp. 1–136. For the views of earlier writers, in addition to Asher b. Yehiel quoted above, *v.* Maimonides, Introduction to *Mishnah* Commentary, *Rashi, Gitt.* 14a; *Hull.* 12b; *B.Q.* 3b. Of particular interest are the remarks of Yom Tobh Lippmann Heller (Introduction to his famous Commentary to the *Mishnah, Tos. Yom Tobh*, ed. Warsaw, 1881, beg.). This author comments on the saying of R. Hiyya b. Abba in the name of R. Johanan that the Holy One, blessed be He, showed Moses the minutiae of the *Torah*, and the minutiae of the Scribes, and the innovations which would be introduced by the Scribes; and what are these? The reading of the *Megillah* (*Meg.* 19b). After observing that in spite of the complete nature of the exposition of the *Torah* given to Moses there are innovations and new laws in each generation, Heller continues: 'And do not refute me from the saying of the Rabbis in the second Chapter of *Megillah* that the Holy One, blessed be He, showed Moses the minutiae of the *Torah*, and the minutiae of the Scribes etc. For in my opinion Moses did not hand these over to others at all. A careful examination of the Rabbis' words demonstrates that this is so, for they say that God *showed* Moses, not *delivered* to Moses, or *taught* to Moses, but *showed* to him. This means that God only showed these matters to Moses but did not deliver them to him. It can be compared to a man who lets his neighbour see something, allowing him only to gaze at it without actually giving it to him'! *V.* Tchernowitz, *op. cit.*, pp. 30 f.

*   *   *

From what has been said up till now it will be obvious that the eighth principle of Maimonides cannot be accepted as it stands by the Jew with even a rudimentary sense of history. To say this is no reflection on Maimonides any more than it is a reflection on him to point out that he was unable to use electricity, fly in an aeroplane or watch television. Nor have we any grounds for self-congratulation, still less for feeling superior to Maimonides, in that we can do all these things and we do have a sense of historical development. God in His wisdom evidently does not choose to reveal all the truth about all matters at once. But, for all that, Judaism does stand or fall on the belief in Revelation and Maimonides is certainly right in declaring the doctrine of '*Torah* from Heaven' to be a basic article of the Jewish faith. What is required is a re-interpretation of the doctrine in the light of the new knowledge. We have touched upon this very difficult problem more than once in this survey. Here we are obliged to consider the fresh interpretation required in greater detail with particular reference to Jewish practice.

In brief, the problem we have to consider is how the distinction between the older and the new view of revelation affects Jewish observance. Despite the qualifications we have noted, the older view is, on the whole, that of a more or less static body of laws, embracing the whole of life and every aspect of human conduct, dictated by God to Moses on Sinai and handed down from generation to generation. These laws are recorded in the Pentateuch, the 'Written Law', and have their elaboration in the 'Oral Law', the latter being recorded in the Talmudic literature. New enactments and fresh interpretations were, to be sure, introduced by the great Rabbinic teachers in each generation, but the core of the teaching found in the later codes of Jewish law, such as the *Shulhan 'Arukh*, reaches back to a direct communication by God to Moses at a given date in human history. The new knowledge affords us a very different picture of how Jewish observances came into being. The Pentateuch is seen to be a post-Mosaic and composite work, divine, it is true, in its unique character of God- Israel encounter, but with a strong human element. The laws, customs and observances are seen to be the product of historical circumstances. The influence of other civilisations on the Hebraic cannot be overlooked. Moreover, it can be seen that some of the laws had lowly or primitive origins, though they were developed by subsequent teachers as vehicles for the transmission of sublime truths. On the older view the problem of Jewish observance was only difficult from the practical point of view. The discipline demanded by correct Sabbath observance was, no doubt, hard but there was no uncertainty about the divine nature of each of its laws, and this served as a powerful stimulus to strict observance. On the newer view, a major part of the problem of Jewish observance is to see how these laws, so obviously conditioned in and by time, can serve as divine commands possessing eternal validity. In other words, for the modern Jew there is a problem of *Halakhah* over and above the practical difficulties of implementing the *Halakhah*. The Jew who is convinced that the *Halakhah* is the direct will of God will still find it difficult to obey the *Halakhah* in all circumstances, but he will do his utmost to find a way to strict observance because of his conviction that it is God's will that he should do so. Far more complicated is the situation in which that Jew finds himself who feels compelled to consider whether, and in what way, the *Halakhah* is the will of God.

With varying degrees of emphasis, the attitude of Reform and Liberal Judaism is, on the whole, one of rejection of the Halakhic element in Judaism. Arguing that Jewish observances grow in a purely natural way, Reform teachers prefer to think of Judaism as a *prophetic* religion, with all the emphasis on moral conduct and the demands of justice and righteousness together, of course, with prayer and worship. This is not to say that every branch of Reform Judaism today rejects all *Halakhah*. There have been a number of interesting developments in the Reform camp in recent years in which a far greater appreciation than hitherto of the value of Jewish observances and traditional practices is evident. There have even been volumes of Reform Responsa. It remains true, nonetheless, that the *Halakhah* is not considered as binding upon Jews in any authoritative sense according to the Reform interpretation of Judaism.

Jewish Orthodoxy, on the other hand, refuses to accept anything of modern criticism and stands firmly committed to the older view. All the *mitzwoth* are God-given in the sense that they were dictated by God. There is undoubtedly much grandeur in the Orthodox position and a refreshing absence of sentimentality. The *mitzwoth* are not, for the Orthodox Jew,

beautiful ceremonies but divine commands. By carrying them
out he is brought near to God. He is a servant of the Most
High whose commands he obeys unquestioningly. But the
price Orthodoxy has to pay is, from the standpoint of modern
knowledge and modern thought, a definite sacrifice of intellect-
tual integrity. It is no doubt powerful and majestic to believe
in a direct communication of all the six hundred and thirteen
mitzwoth on Sinai but, if human reasoning is to be trusted at
all, such a belief is contrary to the facts.

There are to be found many Jews today who are convinced
that a third way is possible, that one can be perfectly free to
investigate the *origins* of Jewish observances and come to
conclusions concerning these which are at variance with tradition, without giving up the concept of the *mitzwoth* as divine
commands. This middle way, which the present author accepts,
is adopted in one form or another by the vast majority of
serious scholars who keep the *mitzwoth*. In the United States
of America it is represented chiefly by the Conservative Movement. Elsewhere, particularly in Germany, it has been known as
'Historic Judaism', represented among others by the 'Breslau
School'. It is sometimes called 'Orthopraxy' as opposed to
'Orthodoxy', but the term is rather unfortunate in its implication
that theory is unimportant. There cannot be much point in
keeping the *mitzwoth* without a sound philosophy of Jewish
observance. Followers of the 'middle way' will emphatically
deny that they have no theory. They claim that they have a
theory different from that of 'Orthodoxy' but perfectly valid
from the standpoint of traditional Judaism. They would go
further and claim that their dynamic concept of the growth of
the *mitzwoth* is the more authentic and the more in accord with
the facts and the only approach which does justice to both the
claims of the intellect and those of the *Halakhah* as binding upon
Jews. Sometimes, particularly in Great Britain and in certain
circles in Israel, the followers of the middle way speak of themselves as Orthodox Jews, since the term 'Orthodoxy' nowadays
is used, imprecisely it is true, as synonymous with 'observant'.
We have noted earlier some of the famous names associated
with the 'Middle Way' approach.

Probably the best way to delineate the differences between
the three schools is to give the example, already mentioned,

of the Sabbath laws. A simple 'harmless' act like smoking a cigarette would not be considered to be a breach of the Sabbath by anyone approaching the matter from outside the Halakhic framework. Within the *Halakhah* such an act is a severe desecration of the Sabbath and an offence against the verse in Exodus xxxv. 2, carrying with it, according to some Talmudic authorities, the death penalty in the days of the *Sanhedrin* (*v. Sabb.* 70a). Orthodoxy takes all this quite literally. God commanded Moses that kindling a fire on the Sabbath is strictly forbidden and although there were no cigarettes in the days of Moses the principle behind the prohibition is the same today as in ancient times – man is using his creative powers to produce fire and on the Sabbath this is precisely what the Jew must refrain from doing since it is the purpose of the Sabbath to acknowledge God as Creator. If it be asked why the good God would wish one of His creatures to be stoned to death for such an offence, the Orthodox Jew would probably reply that it is not for us to fathom the will of God. But he would probably go on to say that in any event there is no *Sanhedrin* nowadays and that even in the days of the *Sanhedrin* the death penalty for such offences was never carried out in practice (*v. Tos. Makk.*, 7a, *s.v. kemikhahol*). All this is perfectly logical once the basic premises have been accepted. The Reform Jew, on the other hand, will point to the late date of the verse in Exodus. This, according to him, is not so much a command of God as a human law which was seen as the command of God. The Prophetic protest against the 'ritual' carries with it the implication of a rejection of that excessive scrupulousness which would forbid such a harmless act. Furthermore, he would argue, to suggest that even in theory the act carries with it the death penalty is to have both an inferior concept of the Deity (can one believe, he would ask, in a God who condemns a cigarette smoker to death?) and a false scale of values. There is no death penalty, even in theory, for one who gravely wrongs his fellow. The Reform Jew will, of course, see the tremendous value of the Sabbath and he will keep the Sabbath according to his own lights, but he will refuse to accept the Sabbath *Halakhah* which so sternly prohibits quite innocent pursuits. The followers of the 'Middle Way' will accept the late date of the original prohibition, or rather they will prefer to leave this to the Bible scholars and historians as a question which, in itself, cannot be decided by faith but by investigation. They will also point out that there is a human element in Scripture and will agree with the Reform Jew that it is not God who has decreed the death penalty for the offence but human beings who wished to call attention to the seriousness of the offence. But they will differ from the Reform Jew in seeing great value in the continued prohibition. This is how Jews keep the Sabbath. There is something sublime in Jews refraining from creative activity on the Sabbath. From the earliest times the making of fire was typical of man's creative use of nature's resources. Judaism is the religion of the Jewish people and, whatever its origin, the Jewish people have turned this act into a profound expression of recognition of God's power as Creator. For this reason the Jew who follows the 'Middle Way' will refrain from smoking on the Sabbath just as strongly as his Orthodox neighbour and he, too, will see in the prohibition the command of God. He, too, accepts the positive and the negative commandments but he knows that these did not simply drop down from heaven but had a history.

Both Reform and Orthodoxy commit what is known as the 'genetic fallacy'. This is to judge an idea or an institution by its origin. Medicine, for instance, had its origin in the practices of the primitive witchdoctor, but no one in his right senses would use this as a reason for refusing when sick to consult a physician. Reform points to the lowly origin of certain Jewish practices and draws the conclusion that these are now outdated. Orthodoxy accepts the logic of the conclusion and feels obliged to reject the premises on which it is based. The 'Middle Way' position cannot in all honesty deny the premises but it sees the conclusion as fallacious. Supposing it is true, as the majority of modern scholars think, that *Yom Kippur* as the highly developed spiritual institution we know today is very late and certainly post-Mosaic and that even in the Pentateuchal account there are traces of primitive elements? But do the prayers of Israel over centuries count for nothing? Is there a soul so insensitive to the spiritual power of the day as to reject its great spiritual beauty, its message of God's nearness, its lesson that man needs pardon and God in His mercy is ready to grant it? It is not at all a question of what the day *was* in the beginning but of what it has become. The same applies to circumcision. Whatever its origin it has become for Jews, as Z. Frankel once said, a *sacrament*. It is the visible sign in the flesh of God's covenant with Israel. Direct dictation at a given time in history or not, this rite is God's will for Israel. The Jew who believes in God and in the role Israel is to play in helping the fulfilment of His purpose, and without these two beliefs Judaism as a religion can have little meaning, cannot help seeing the hand of God in the evolution of Jewish observance.

There is the further point to be considered that, in rudimentary form at least, the rite, even in its primitive origin, contained the germs of the later development. G. F. Moore ('Judaism', *op. cit.*, Vol. II, pp. 21–22) has well said with regard to the question of the origin of the Sabbath: 'Here, as in the case of circumcision and for the same reason, an exploration of the antecedents of the Jewish Sabbath and of analogous customs or institutions among other races is irrelevant. Days or seasons in which ordinary licit acts and enterprises, or all ordinary occupations, are interdicted are common upon all planes of culture and acquire a fixed place in the calendar of many peoples. The origin and motives of such interdictions are obviously diverse. To huddle them all together under the title ancient "taboo-days" is to deceive one's self with the imagination that where one has put a label – preferably a jargon label – on a phenomenon he has explained it, or dispensed himself from the necessity of understanding it. The jargon of anthropologists (and anthropological theologians) is getting to be as portentous as that of the mediaeval alchemists, with this difference, that the alchemists' jargon was for the mystification of outsiders, while the anthropologists mystify not only the unlearned but themselves unawares with their Totem, Mana, Taboo, and the rest. The sabbath as a "taboo-day" means nothing but that it was a day on which certain doings were interdicted under a supernatural sanction, which is the very definition of the sabbath, as everybody knew before'. Even if it is true that the Israelites borrowed the idea of a day of cessation from work in obedience to higher powers from their Babylonian neighbours, the facts are that over a long period the institution was so infused with the spirit of ethical monotheism that it became something quite different from anything that Babylon ever had, a day of 'delight in the Lord', a day in which God is acknowledged as Creator, a day providing, as the Rabbis phrased it, a foretaste of spiritual bliss in Paradise.

There are, naturally enough, a variety of emphases within the 'Middle Way' position. The standpoint of the present writer is that of Zechariah Frankel, the great pioneer of the 'historical school', but with a stronger theological emphasis. On this view the *mitzwoth* are divine commands for me both because they have come to be such through the long history of my people and because they speak to my own situation as a human being in need of God. I keep the Sabbath, irrespective of its origins, because it is the fundamental religious institution of my people, as a people dedicated to God's service, because of the wealth of meaning the prophets and poets, the saints and sages of Israel, have read into it, and because my personal religious life is enriched immeasurably by the weekly reminder that God is my Maker and Creator of all there is. Although Frankel lived and worked in the last century and was not un-influenced by Protestant religious tendencies in nineteenth-century Germany, much of what he taught is still of the utmost relevance to the twentieth century Jew. One of the best accounts of Frankel's position in this matter is that of Isaac Heinemann in his '*Ta'ame Ha-Mitzwoth*', Vol. II, Jer. 1956, Chapter V, pp. 161–181. Heinemann is followed, on the whole, in this exposition of Frankel's views.

There are, according to Frankel, two kinds of Revelation. The first is the direct Revelation found in Scripture, the second an indirect form through the acceptance of certain observances by the whole Community of Israel. Since it is God who is at work in human history and since He has revealed Himself in a special way in the history of Israel then the forms of religious expression which Israel came gradually to adopt are themselves the will of God. A later disciple of Frankel, Solomon Schechter, was to develop the idea of 'Catholic Israel'. Whether or not Schechter quite meant this, it is true that in Roman Catholicism, for example, the real seat of authority is to be found in the Church rather than the Bible. The Bible itself is interpreted by the Church and it is believed that the latter enjoys divine guidance. In somewhat similar fashion in Judaism it is in the Synagogue that authority resides, that is to say, in the consensus of opinion among the faithful of Israel. Thus, for Frankel, there is, in fact, little difference between Biblical laws – *de-'oraitha* – and Rabbinic laws – *de-rabbanan* (to use the terms found in the Rabbinic literature) since, in the final analysis, both owe their authority to their acceptance by the Jewish people. It should be said that there are faint anticipations of this attitude in the Rabbinic literature. We find the Rabbis, for instance, attaching greater significance to a prohibition which has been universally accepted among Jews (*A.Z.* 36a); we find them occasionally relying on the practice of the people where the law is in doubt (*Ber.* 45a and *par.*); and we find them referring to the people of Israel in their observances to 'the sons of the prophets' (*Pes.* 10a). Frankel's critics were not slow to note the ambiguities in his position. If, one of these critics argued, authority rests with the people then it should follow that where the Jewish people were faithless this very faithlessness would be the will of God. In Ahab's day it should have been right to have worshipped Baal. This is to misunderstand Frankel entirely. In a very real sense Frankel did believe in *vox populi vox Dei* but he was careful to point out that by 'the people' he meant the faithful in Israel, those who wished to preserve Judaism, those who lived by it and who were prepared to die for it. In Ahab's day the 'people' were not represented by the faithless Baal-worshippers but by Elijah and the handful of true prophets of the Lord.

It is interesting to observe the difference in attitude towards folk-customs between Frankel and his famous 'Orthodox' opponent, Samson Raphael Hirsch. Hirsch (*v.* Heinemann, *op. cit.,* p. 168) had a rather lukewarm attitude towards Jewish customs, as opposed to Jewish laws, whereas Frankel always spoke highly of the value of Jewish folk-customs. This is a necessary conclusion from the different approaches of the two men. Hirsch's theology places all the stress on the direct communication of the divine will. The role of the people is purely passive. They are merely the recipients of the divine commands. In Frankel's theology the people have a far more active role. They have their part to play in the creative process by which the laws become binding as the word of God. (This does not mean that there are no differences, for Frankel, between laws and customs. The very fact that the people of

Israel made a strong and clear distinction between the two
means in itself that the laws possess a higher degree of sanctity
and authority – a more powerful indication of the divine will –
than the customs). Although Frankel himself does not seem
to have been bothered by the problems raised by Biblical
Criticism, which in his day was in a rather elementary stage,
it follows that he would not have been unduly concerned by any
results which an impartial investigation of the Bible happened
to yield. Even if the result of such investigation were to demonstrate beyond reasonable doubt that some Jewish observances
are later in date than the Rabbis thought they were, there is
nothing alarming for faith, on Frankel's premises, since the
Shekhinah is at work, as it were, in the very development of the
law. On the centenary of Frankel's birth (he was born in the
year 1801) Louis Ginzberg delivered an important address
on Frankel's thought (published in Ginzberg's 'Students,
Scholars and Saints', *op. cit.*, pp. 195–216). Ginzberg states
that Frankel himself gave the best definition of his 'positive-
historic' school of Judaism when he defined Judaism as 'the
religion of the Jews'. The Law became, in the course of Jewish
history, the specific Jewish expression of religiousness. As
Ginzberg says, developing Frankel's thought: 'The dietary
laws are not incumbent upon us because they conduce to modera-
tion, nor the family laws because they further chastity and
purity of morals. The law as a whole is not the means to an
end, but an end in itself; the Law is active religiousness, and
in active religion must lie what is specifically Jewish'. Ginzberg
continues: 'One may, for instance, conceive of the origin and
idea of Sabbath rest as the professor of Protestant theology
at a German university would conceive it, and yet minutely
observe the smallest detail of the Sabbath observances known
to strict Orthodoxy. For an adherent of this school the sanctity
of the Sabbath reposes not upon the fact that it was proclaimed
on Sinai, but on the fact that the Jewish Sabbath idea found for
thousands of years its expression in Jewish souls. It is the task
of the historian to examine into the beginnings and developments of the numerous customs and observances of the Jews;
practical Judaism on the other hand is not concerned with origins,
but regards the institutions as they have come to be. If we are
convinced that Judaism is a religion of deed, expressing itself

in observances which are designed to achieve the moral elevation of man and give reality to his religious spirit, we have a principle in obedience to which reforms in Judaism are possible. From this point of view the evaluation of a law is independent of its origin, and thus the demarcation between biblical and rabbinical law almost disappears'.

In fact, Jews have, with the exception of groups like the Karaites, accepted Rabbinic law as binding even though this was clearly not dictated to Moses on Sinai. Consciously or otherwise Jews seem to have suggested that since the Rabbinic enactments further the cause of Judaism they belong to God's will, even though we can trace their emergence and see their human development. On the 'Middle Way' point of view what is required is an extension of this principle so as to include Biblical law.

It is by no means suggested that the 'middle way' approach is without its difficulties. Psychologically, for example, it is undeniable that a clear recognition of the human element involved in the development of Jewish practice and observance is bound to produce a somewhat weaker sense of the importance of the minutiae of Jewish law. For the Orthodox Jew, every single detail is a direct expression of the divine will. He will go to the utmost limits to keep every detail of the dietary laws, for instance, since they are part of the divine will. But for the Jew who sees the dietary laws as having *evolved*, although he, too, will recognise them as divine, it will be difficult to be so scrupulous. To take a simple example. Both the Orthodox and the 'Middle-Way' Jew will refrain from eating meat and milk together, but for the former the law is an expression of unfathomable divine mysteries, while for the latter the practice of separation has developed from the original prohibition against seething a kid in its mother's milk. The practical outcome may well be that the one will wait the full six hours after a meat meal before partaking of dairy food, while the other may be inclined to be satisfied with the more lenient view which bids him wait only three or less hours. It might be argued that to give up excessive scrupulousness in these matters is no real loss but then what becomes of the grand old idea of the 'fear of Heaven' expressing itself in great concern and scrupulous regard for every detail of God's law? Furthermore, if developments once took place in Jewish law why should there be no development in Jewish law today? Part of the answer to this second question is that if all Jews shared the 'middle way' philosophy there would indeed be development in Jewish law. But the importance of the Community of Israel stressed by the followers of the 'middle way' demands the recognition that there are *Orthodox* Jews who reject the idea of development and whose views as part of 'Catholic Israel' have to be taken into account, particularly since it is these Jews who are the staunchest upholders of Jewish law in their lives. But for all the difficulties, the 'middle way' approach is the only one possible for the Jew who refuses to fetter the spirit of free, unbiased inquiry into origins but who, at the same time, loves Jewish observance and recognises its tremendous spiritual power.

The *Midrash* records a discussion on the verse in Psalms: 'The *Torah* of the Lord is perfect, restoring the soul' (Ps. xix. 8). One Rabbi says the meaning is that because the *Torah* of the Lord is perfect, *therefore* it restores the soul. The other Rabbi interprets the verse to mean, *because* it restores the soul, therefore it is perfect (*Yalqut, Teh.*, 674). It is not suggested that the Rabbis of the *Midrash* could have anticipated our problem but here in a nutshell you have the difference between the mediaeval and the modern approach to Jewish observance. Maimonides and mediaeval Jews generally, and most of those who follow the 'Orthodox' position today, have as their basis the conception of a perfect, infallible *Torah* dictated by God to Moses on Sinai. All questions of *why* one should keep the *Torah* were really irrelevant. God has given Israel a perfect *Torah* and that was the end of the matter. You might increase your understanding of the *Torah*, you might begin dimly to grasp some of its inner meaning, you might discover or invent satisfying 'reasons' for the *mitzwoth*, but your real reason for keeping them was because God has said so in the *Torah*. Because the *Torah* is perfect it restores the soul; the subtle alchemy by means of which this is achieved is known only to God who gave the *Torah*. For the modern Jew the perfection which inheres in the *Torah* cannot be separated from the *effect* the *Torah* has had on Jewish life and Jewish history. Its perfection lies in its soul-restoring power. On the deeper level the question of whether the *Torah* is God's gift to Israel or Israel's gift to God is seen to be irrelevant, for on a profounder view of what is involved in Revelation the two are seen to be the same many-splendoured thing.

*   *   *

EXCURSUS

Among modern proponents of the 'Middle Way' are: Will Herberg: 'Judaism and Modern Man', Meridian Books, New York, 1959; Boaz Cohen: 'Law and Tradition in Judaism', Jewish Theological Seminary of America, New York, 1959; Jakob J. Petuchowsky: 'Ever Since Sinai', Scribe Publications, New York, 1961; 'God in Search of Man', John Calder, London, 1956; Jacob J. Agus: 'Guideposts in Modern Judaism', Bloch, New York, 1954; Milton Steinberg: 'The Making of the Modern Jew', Routledge, London, 1934; Franz Rosenzweig: 'Frank Rosenzweig: His Life and Thought', presented by Nahum N. Glatzer, Schocken Books, New York, 1953; Herbert Loewe: 'A Rabbinic Anthology', ed. C. G. Montefiore and H. Loewe, Cambridge University Press, 1938. Needless to say these writers differ from each other in matters of emphasis but they all affirm two things, the right of free inquiry into the classical Jewish sources and the acceptance of the *Halakhah*. The papers and essays in the 'Proceedings of the Rabbinical Assembly of America', and 'Conservative Judaism' contain many stimulating discussions on the 'Middle Way' position. In addition to Solomon Schechter's 'Studies in Judaism', to which reference has been made, his 'Seminary Addresses and Other Papers', with an Introduction by Louis Finkelstein, The Burning Bush Press, New York, 1959, should be consulted. *Cf.* the address by Louis Finkelstein: 'Tradition in the Making' in 'The Jewish Theological Seminary of America. Semi-Centennial Volume', ed. Cyrus Adler, Jewish Theological Seminary of America, New York, 1939, pp. 22–34. Israel H. Levinthal's 'Judaism: An Analysis and Interpretation', Funk and Wagnalls, New York, 1935, contains a good popular account of this point of view.

[10]

THE NINTH PRINCIPLE
The Torah is Unchanging

MAIMONIDES' formulation of the ninth principle of the faith is as follows: '*The ninth Principle of Faith.* The abrogation of the *Torah*. This implies that this Law of Moses will not be abrogated and that no other law will come from before God. Nothing is to be added to it nor taken away from it, neither in the written nor oral law, as it is said: "Thou shalt not add to it nor diminish from it" (Deut. xiii. 1). In the beginning of this treatise we have already explained that which requires explanation in this principle of faith'.

The *Yigdal* formulation is: 'This law God will not alter, will not change for any other through time's utmost range'.

The *'Ani Ma'amin* formulation is: 'I believe with perfect faith that this *Torah* will not be changed, and that there will never be any other law from the Creator, blessed be His name'.

Friedländer observes: 'In this article we prounounce our belief in the immutability of the Law. Over and over again the phrase "an everlasting statute" occurs in the Pentateuch. It is true that the Hebrew term " *'olam*" is used in the Bible in the sense of "a very long time", but in the phrase *huqath 'olam* the word cannot have that meaning. Some indication would have been necessary to inform the people when the laws would cease to be in force. On the contrary, the test of a prophet addressing his brethren in the name of God, as a Divine messenger, consists in the harmony of his words with the precepts of the Pentateuch. A prophet who, speaking in the name of God, abrogates any of the laws of the Pentateuch is a false prophet . . . It is useless to investigate whether it would be in harmony with the immutability of the Divine Being to change the laws or any of them, or to grant a new revelation. Certainly the words "I, the Lord, have not changed" (Mal. iii. 6) have great weight; so also, "For God is not a son of man

that he should change his mind" (Num. xxiii. 19). But the
fact that the laws were given by God as "an everlasting
statute for all generations" makes all philosophical speculation
on that point superfluous. Persons who address us in the name
of God as His messengers, and bid us turn away from any of
the laws commanded in the Pentateuch, are in our eyes impostors,
who, knowingly or unknowingly, give forth their own opinions
as Divine inspirations'.

Werblowsky states: '9. *The Torah is immutable.* The implications of this article are many and significant. On the surface
it merely asserts the continued validity of Judaism against
the claims of other religions, Christianity in particular, to have
brought final and fuller revelations superseding or "fulfilling"
the Jewish religion. On a deeper level the article depends on
certain conceptions concerning the *Torah* as the divine *logos*.
As the expression of God's eternal wisdom, *Torah* thus shares
the immutability of God. A theology less indebted to a Greek
evaluation of *ratio* and immutability may more easily admit
the possibility of changes in the divine will and dispensation.
Some mystical and Kabbalistic systems, bearing a certain
resemblance to the ideas of Joachim of Fiore, allowed different
manifestations of the same divine *Torah* in different world-
cycles. But the "different" age *par excellence* is the Messianic
aeon following upon the present era; consequently, the problem
of the "new law" and the abrogation of the old became acute
when Messianic movements claimed to have fulfilled the times.
Towards the end of the Middle Age Messianic movements
were distrusted because they harboured the danger of
antinomianism.'

It is clear that the primary aim of the ninth principle is to
affirm that Judaism is an eternal faith in the sense that it has not
been, and never will be, superseded. It implies a particular
rejection of the claims of both Christianity and Islam. These
'daughter religions' of Judaism did not deny that God had once
revealed Himself to Israel, but in their separate ways they
claimed that a new revelation had taken place which now was
to take over from the old. This Judaism denies. The terms
yahaliph and *yamir*, used for 'alter' and 'change' in the *Yigdal*
hymn, really mean 'to *ex*change'. The words are found, for

instance, in the book of Leviticus: 'He shall not alter it, nor change it, a good for a bad, or a bad for a good; and if he shall at all change beast for beast, then both it and that for which it is changed shall be holy' (Lev. xxvii. 10). Here the meaning is that if a beast had been set aside as a sacrifice it was not to be *exchanged* for another. Similarly, in the ninth principle, the basic idea is that Judaism is an evergreen faith and not one which was merely to herald any other.

It is equally clear, however, that in Maimonides' formulation another idea is contained, that the *Torah* is immutable, that its precepts are binding upon Jews for all time. These two ideas do not necessarily follow one from the other. It does not follow that because no other faith can ever take the place of Judaism there can be no changes within Judaism itself. But Maimonides clearly does think of these two ideas as complementary. Since God does not change He does not allow a law He has once revealed to be superseded and by the same token that law must itself be immutable. This second idea presents certain difficulties, not unrecognised by Maimonides. A good deal depends on what kind of change is meant. In view of the numerous Rabbinic enactments to meet new conditions, for example, it is quite impossible to maintain that there have never been any changes in Judaism. Modern scholarship in particular, as we have noted in the previous chapter, reveals a picture of Judaism as a dynamic rather than a static faith. And yet there must be a profound sense of continuity between the Judaism of one age and that of another, otherwise the two would not be the same, unchanging faith. Thus the whole question of change and development in Judaism is involved in this principle and it is worth while devoting some of our discussion to this intricate question.

The whole question of the immutability of the *Torah* is discussed at length, with particular reference to Maimonides' formulation, by Joseph Albo in his '*Sepher Ha-'Iqqarim*', Vol. III, Chapter 13–23, ed. I. Husik, Jewish Publication Society, Philadelphia, 1946, pp. 112 ff. Albo begins by giving three reasons why it seems to many that there can be no change in the *Torah*. The first is that God who gave the *Torah* does not change and it should follow that the *Torah* which comes from Him does not change. Secondly, the *Torah* was given to the *people* of Israel and, unlike an individual, a people does not change. Thirdly, since the *Torah* is truth it cannot suffer change, for truth is eternal. If it is true, for instance, that there is only one God it is inconceivable that there should come a time when this will no longer be true and there will be many gods. For all that, Albo believes that there is no *a priori* reason why a divine law should not change since it is directed to recipients whose conditions in life are not always the same and who require, therefore, different rules of conduct in their different situations. He gives the telling illustration of a physician who may prescribe a certain regimen for one period and a different one at a later stage of his patient's cure. It is not that the physician has changed his mind but that there are stages in the patient's restoration to health. Similarly, as Maimonides ('Guide', III. 32) says, a sound pedagogue will suit his teaching to the growing capacities of his charges and God adopts the same procedure in His dealings with men. Albo gives examples of even a divine law suffering change. Thus while Adam was only permitted vegetable food (Gen. i. 29), Noah was permitted animal food (Gen. ix. 3). Abraham was given the additional precept of circumcision and to Moses many new precepts were revealed. But from Moses to the present there have been no changes in the divine law. According to Maimonides the *Torah* of Moses will never change and since, as we have seen, a divine law can change this must mean that the *Torah* of Moses is the sole exception to this rule.

Maimonides' source for his teaching, as he himself states, is the verse in Deut. xiii. 1, forbidding any additions or subtractions. This is implied, according to Maimonides (*cf.* 'Guide', III. 34) in the conception of a perfect *Torah*, for that which is perfect cannot suffer change. The famous eighteenth-century preacher, the Dubner Maggid, gave a well-known, rather naive but very typical, parable to illustrate this point. A man asked his friend to lend him a spoon. After a day or two he returned two spoons, remarking that the first had given birth to the second. The astonished lender was prepared to accept the borrower's folly as of benefit to himself and he took both spoons. At a subsequent date the request was made for the loan of a valuable vase. Thinking that there would be a repetition of the earlier event the lender allowed the borrower to have

the vase. To the lender's surprise he was told after a time that the
borrower was very sorry but the vase had died. 'But how can a
vase die?' 'How can a spoon give birth to a spoon?' If you can
believe, concluded Dubner Maggid, that you can add to the
Torah you must think of the *Torah* as imperfect. And if you
think of the *Torah* as imperfect then you will eventually sub-
tract from it.

Albo observes that if Maimonides has this conception of the
immutability of the *Torah* as a traditional interpretation of
the verse in Deuteronomy then we must accept it. But if he
has arrived at his interpretation by his own ratiocination then
we can beg to differ. The verse, in fact, should not be taken to
mean that no new precepts can be added to the *Torah* or that
no precepts can ever be taken away from it. The verse does not
speak of this at all but of adding to or subtracting from the
precepts themselves, e.g. having *Tephillin* with either five or
three paragraphs instead of the statutory four. It is clear that
this is how the Rabbis understood the verse since they say
(*Yeb.* 90a-b) that where there is a strong need a certain precept
may be set aside as the occasion demands. 'In short, I do not
see any evidence in the passages cited by Maimonides that
immutability is a dogma of the Mosaic law at all, as Maimonides
thinks' (Albo p. 126). Moreover even if it be granted that *we*
cannot change the law there is no reason why God should not
change it. As for expressions like 'an everlasting statute' and
so forth (e.g. in Lev. xxiii. 14 and 31, Ex. xxxi. 17, Ex. xii.
24), even if the term ' *'olam'* means 'for ever', which is very
far from certain, it might be argued that the other precepts,
apart from those to which the term is applied, may be abolished
one day. The Rabbis in one place (*Yalqut* on Prov. 9, *par*. 944)
say that all the festivals will be abolished in the Messianic
age except *Yom Kippur* and *Purim*. Moreover, in Ezra's day
two very far-reaching changes were introduced in memory
of the new deliverance. The 'square script' was used for
the Scrolls of the *Torah* instead of the ancient Hebrew
script and the Babylonian months were substituted for the
Hebrew.

Although so far Albo disagrees with Maimonides in fact,
he goes on to say that his own view is that of his master
Crescas (*'Or 'Adonai*, III. 5). Crescas differs from Maimonides

in refusing to count the immutability of the *Torah* as an article
of faith, since on Crescas' definition such an article means one
without which Judaism would be inconceivable. It can hardly
be maintained that Judaism would be inconceivable unless
this dogma were accepted. But Crescas, followed by Albo,
agrees that the belief in the immutability of the *Torah* must be
accepted by the believing Jew. In fact, the difference is only
one of classification. After further discussion of individual
points (in which there is some ambiguity) Albo (Chapter 19)
comes to the conclusion that the first two commandments of the
Decalogue cannot be changed even temporarily. The other
eight can only be changed by a prophet speaking in the name of
God and that only temporarily. As for the other precepts of the
Torah, they can be changed even permanently, as Ezra changed
the script of the *Torah* and the names of the months, but this
can only be done by a prophet.

It will be seen from the above sketch of Albo's views and of
his critique of Maimonides that the whole mediaeval discussion,
as evidenced by Albo, on the immutability of the *Torah*, has
to do with the question of whether a law promulgated by
God will ever be repeated and the response to the challenge
of Christianity is stated explicitly. The later chapters of Albo's
work in this connection are, in fact, devoted to a consideration
of the meaning of the ninth principle as aimed against the
Christian claims. The modern view, we have considered in
the previous chapter, of *development* of the *mitzwoth* is entirely
different both from the view that God *can* or *will* change a
law He has given and the view that He *cannot* or *will not* do so.
It is anachronistic, therefore, to quote the ninth principle as an
argument against change in Judaism itself. The problem for
Jews today is not whether a prophet will one day come from
God to abrogate certain *mitzwoth* or to add new *mitzwoth* but
to see whether the *Halakhah* is capable of being interpreted
in as flexible a manner in the present as it was in the past.
Quite apart from the researches of the historical school, it is
axiomatic to every student of the *Halakhah* that this has never
been a static thing and that it has taken into account new
conditions and new situations.

One of the most interesting tendencies in modern Jewish
theological thinking is the increasing awareness of the role

of law in Judaism. Writing in 1934, Mordecai Kaplan voiced this critique of Reform Judaism: "Although Reformism departs radically from the traditional conceptions of God and Israel, it considers these conceptions in their modernised form, and all that they imply in terms of belief and practice, as constituting the very substance of Judaism. But with regard to the concept 'Torah' and to all that it implies concerning the form and authority of Judaism's social and cultural institutions, traditional Judaism and Reformism seem to have nothing in common. Reformism practically dispenses with the concept of 'Torah'. In the platform of the Pittsburgh Conference the very mention of Torah is omitted, and all that is remembered of the part it played in Judaism is referred to by the colourless term 'Mosaic Legislation'." ('Judaism as a Civilisation,' New York, 1934, pp. 103–4).

Since then, however, there has been religious re-thinking and Reform Judaism has acquired a new respect for Halakhah. On the other hand Orthodoxy and Conservatism are searching for a more flexible interpretation of the Din and one need not be a prophet or the son of a prophet to see the Judaism of the future, of whatever shade of opinion, as a 'religion of law', but law interpreted in a more or less broad humanitarian spirit.

In view of this new interest in law an investigation of the flexibility of the traditional Din and its humanity does not come amiss. There are, of course, many problems to be solved. At the moment little use is made of historical researches into the origins and development of the Halakhah as a basis for the practical Din and this will continue until the historical school and the older Halakhists come into a closer relationship with each other, until we produce more scholars who are lomedim and more lomedim who are scholars. In Israel, for example, progressive religious circles constantly discuss a new working out of Halakhah, which will take into account the changed conditions arising out of the emergence of the State, and more and more thinking people are looking for a solution in terms of a natural extension of the old system, in accordance with its own principles of growth, rather than in the forced, artificial panacea of a *'Sanhedrin'*. It can be shown that, in fact, the traditional *Halakhah*, at least as interpreted by those of its distinguished authorities who were alert to the need for change and adaptation, is flexible rather than rigid.

Every student of the *Halakhah* knows that the maxim that a *Beth Din* cannot annul the decisions of another *Beth Din* unless its members are of greater number and wisdom has been a powerful and unfortunate force for rigidity in *Halakhah*. It has been plausibly suggested by I. H. Weiss (*Dor.* Vol. II, pp. 61 f. *Cf.* H. Tchernowitz: *Toledoth Ha-Halachah*, N.Y., 1934, p. 194 f.) that the original saying was applied to two contemporary Courts only, but be that as it may, in the course of time it came to mean that no *Beth Din* has the power to set aside the rulings of an earlier *Beth Din*. The whole position was further complicated by the notion of the degeneration of the ages, elevated almost to a dogma, so that no later *Beth Din* would acknowledge itself the equal, still less the superior, of a former *Beth Din*. This meant that a law once established could never be set aside, even if the conditions which caused its introduction no longer obtained. A good example of this is the *Din* concerning milk bought from a non-Jew. This milk was originally prohibited out of the fear that the Gentile may mix with it milk obtained from an unclean animal (*A.Z.* II. 6). And yet in spite of a recognition by our modern authorities that nowadays there is little danger of this, the majority of them persist in forbidding it on the grounds that later Rabbis have no powers to change a law instituted by earlier Rabbis. (*Yoreh De'ah*, 15. 1. However, some authorities permit it. *Pithhe Teshubhah*, 115. 3).

This would seem to mean that there is no possibility of any change whatsoever within the traditional framework of the *Halakhah*. Yet, fortunately, there is little consistency in this matter and we have numerous examples of laws being set aside in the past by the most representative authorities where the conditions which compelled their original formulation no longer obtain. The first modern scholar to make a detailed investigation into these laws was Eliezer Zweifel (1815–1888) in his work *Sanegor*, published in Warsaw in 1885, which deserves to be far better known than it is. The following are examples, some of which are taken from Zweifel, of how the *Din* retains its flexibility:

L

The laws of evidence in respect to a husband lost at sea are very strictly applied in the *Talmud*. Yet such a determined opponent of Reform as Rabbi Moses Sofer, ('anything new is forbidden by the *Torah'*), suggests that in these days of improved communications it is not necessary to be so strict, for were the husband alive he would inform his wife. (*Hatam Sofer, E. Ha-' Ezer* 58, *cf.* 'Printing in the *Halakhah'* [Hebrew] in *Sinai*, Shevat-Adar, 570 f, p. 156).

The *Mishnah* prohibits dancing on a festival. (*Betz. v.* 2). The reason given in the *Talmud* is that one of the participants may fashion a musical instrument out of a tree branch. Later authorities were inclined to set this rule aside on the grounds that few people today are skilled at this kind of improvisation. (*Tos. Betz.* 30a. s.v. '*en*).

Despite Talmudic prohibition of child marriages (*Qidd.* 41a) the mediaeval authorities sanctioned the practise of Jewish fathers who married off their daughters while they were still minors on the grounds that the unfortunate situation of the Jewish community made such marriages imperative. (*Tos. ad loc. s.v. 'asur*).

The detailed Talmudical regulations concerning reclining on the Seder Eve were ignored by a distinguished mediaeval authority who argued that in western lands, where it was not the custom to recline at meals, such leaning would be no expression of 'freedom'. (*Shulhan 'Arukh. O.H.* 472. 4.).

No less an authority than Rabbi Joseph Karo, (1488–1575), the celebrated author of the *Shulhan 'Arukh*, suggests that although the *Talmud* always describes the *Bimah* in the Synagogue as belonging in the centre this was due to the size of the Synagogues in those days, the places of worship being so vast that the reading of the law had to take place on a central platform. In the days of smaller Synagogues, he argues, it is preferable on aesthetic grounds to have the Bimah at the end of the building. (*Keseph Mish. to Hil. Teph.* 11. 3.).

In Talmudic law the deaf-mute is treated as an imbecile. When the son of Rabbi Moses Sofer, the author of *Kethash Sopher*, (1815–1871) visited an institution for the deaf in Vienna, he was so impressed by their response to treatment that he seriously questioned if the older law should still obtain today when such people can acquire a good education (*Shebthe*

Sepher, II. 21. *V*. H. J. Zimmels: 'Magicians, Theologians and Doctors', London, 1952, pp. 21–22).

The *Talmud*, on the basis of Deut. xxii. 5, prohibits the use of a mirror by a man. Yet the view is recorded in the *Shulhan 'Arukh* that in later times when men as well as women use mirrors there can be no objection to its use by a man. (*Y. De'ah*, 156. 2).

In Germany, in the last century, the problem of the Sabbath-breaker was an acute one. In Talmudic law, as interpreted by the earlier authorities, he was to be treated as a non-Jew which, of course, made social intercourse with him a most delicate affair. Jacob Ettlinger (1798–1871), who is said to have been the first Orthodox Rabbi to obtain a University Degree, expressed the view that nowadays when, unfortunately, many Jews profaned the Sabbath its profanation, though much to be deplored, could hardly be treated as an act of open defiance of the Jewish Community and the Jewish faith. (*Binyan Zion* [New Series] *c.f. Kitzur S.A.* ed. D. Feldman, Leipzig, 1933, p. 80 note).

The late Rabbi Karelitz, author of the *Hazon 'Ish*, who was the recognised leader of right-wing Orthodoxy in Israel and outside it, opted, as we have noticed earlier, for a more humane attitude to the *'epiqoros* than was adopted in the past for, he said, the unbeliever can only be attracted to Judaism in these days by a calm, tolerant approach (*Encyclopedia Talmudith*, Vol. II, p. 137, note 39).

In Talmudic times it was the rule that not only meals be partaken of in the *Sukkah* on the festival of Tabernacles, but that it was necessary to sleep in the *Sukkah*. In Western lands this rule was set aside (*Kitzur S. A.* 135. 8). Similarly in colder climates the *Din* permits a fire to be lit by a Gentile in the Jewish home on the Sabbath for, it was argued, if a Gentile may do forbidden work on behalf of a sick Jew he should certainly be allowed to do such work in order to prevent sickness. (*S. Arukh, O. H.* 276. 5).

Where Jews who lived among non-Jews would have been ridiculed for their bizarre customs, it was not considered necessary for a Jew to go to the Synagogue wearing *Tallith* and *Tephillin*. For the same reason it was permitted to don shoes for street wear on *Yom Kippur* and the Fast of Ab. (*Mish. Ber.* 25. 8. *Hayye 'Adam, Hil. Tishe Be-'abh*).

It is well-known that in Talmudic times the Rabbis discouraged social intercourse with the heathen. It was forbidden for the Jew to have business dealings with them three days before their festivals, to enter into partnership with them or to use for any purpose whatsoever the wine they had handled. When Jews no longer resided among heathens but among Christians or Muslims, there was a relaxation of these severities on the grounds that the adherents of these two faiths were not idolators. In this connection it is instructive to note how sociological conditions determined the *Halakhah*. In France, where Jews engaged extensively in the cultivation of the vine, and were obliged to rely on Gentile labour, the authorities were in favour of a liberal interpretation of the *Din* so as to permit non-Jewish workers to help them in the production of the wine. The Spanish authorities, on the other hand, who had no social or economic pressure to compel them, upheld the application of the older law in all its severity (*see* S. Zeitlin in JQR, 1952, Vol. XLII, p. 361).

The *Talmud* can always provide ammunition for the enemies of the Jew. It is undoubtedly true that it contains many derogatory sayings about the Gentiles and this aversion found its expression in many laws. But successive generations of scholars took pains to point out that these applied to the heathens only, not to 'the nations among whom we reside'. Though some of these apologies may have been written with one eye on the censor, they are so numerous and have been expressed by so many different authorities that it is certain that they mirror an authentic change of attitude to the non-Jew, which rendered much of the older *Halakhah* in these matters obsolete. (See 'Israel and the Nations' by J. Bloch, Berlin, 1927, Chap. IV. pp. 42 f.) and F. Katz: 'Exclusiveness and Tolerance', Clarendon Press, Oxford, 1961).

Talmudic law is very strict on the prohibition of liquid that has been left uncovered on the grounds that a poisonous snake may have projected its venom into it. Nowadays, in Western lands, where this possibility is extremely remote, the prohibition no longer has force (*Y.D.* 116. 1).

The law of the *Mishnah* (*Ta'an.* III. 4) that in times of an epidemic public fasts should be held is set aside by Abraham Gombiner of Kalisch, seventeenth century, the famous author of the glosses to the *Shulhan' Arukh*, on the grounds that nowadays the loss of strength would be dangerous. (*O.H. 576.2*). This is an interesting point. Precisely because it was believed that the ancients were almost super-men, not alone intellectually superior to us but possessing greater physical powers, what was good law for them is not good law for us. The view of Gombiner is upheld by Hayyim Joseph David Azulai (1723–1806) (*Birke Joseph 576. 4*, quoted by G. Deutsch in C.C.A.R. Vol. XXIX, 1919, p. 92).

Soon after the invention of printing, the question was raised whether it could be used for those purposes where Jewish law demands that a thing be 'written' e.g. a *Sepher Torah*, a *Mezuzah*, *Tefillin*. Among others who deal with this question, Ezekiel Katzenellenbogen (1670–1749) argues that printing is not valid for the above purpose for if it were why was it not invented by Moses, than whom there was no greater in prophecy, or by King Solomon, the wisest of men. It follows, this Rabbi argues, that in Moses' day when, according to the *Talmud*, there was a ban on the writing of the Oral *Torah*, there was no need for this invention for the written *Torah* had to be copied by hand. Only after the removal of the ban on the writing of the Oral *Torah* did God reveal printing to makind. (*Keneseth Yehezqel 37*). Rabbi Zewi Hirsch Chajes (1805–1855), one of the pioneers of Jüdische Wissenschaft, refused to accept this anachronistic viewpoint. 'This is not the way', writes Chajes. 'True that Moses had no equal in prophecy and Solomon had no equal in wisdom but the Almighty foresaw everything at the beginning of Creation and set aside periods for the perfection of all the sciences. Not all periods are alike in this matter. There are silent ages when the vision of wisdom is not widespread and ages expressive in understanding when many sages are abroad. There is nothing which has not its proper time and place according to the will of God who summoned the generations from the beginning'. (Responsa, II, quoted by Kahana, '*Printing in the Halakhah*' loc. cit.).

Yom Tob Lippmann Heller (1579–1654), the author of one of the best commentaries to the *Mishnah*, gives, as we have noted above, in his introduction an original and profound turn to the ancient Rabbinic saying that God showed to Moses the interpretations of later generations of scholars. This does not mean, says Heller, that the rabbis believed that the *Halakhah* was rigid and that each generation received a complete Halakhic tradition from its predecessors. 'Although there existed a complete interpretation of the *Torah* and its commands there is no generation in which something new is not added and which is without its own legal problems. Do not contradict me by pointing to the Rabbinic saying that God showed Moses the minutiae of the *Torah* and the minutiae of the Scribes and the innovations which would be introduced by the Scribes, for I say that this was not handed down by Moses to anyone else. A careful examination of the Rabbinic saying shows that they spoke of God "showing" Moses, not "teaching" or "handing down" . . . by using the word "showing" they meant that these teachings were revealed to Moses but not 'given' to him, like a man who "shows" his friend an object but does not give it to him.'

Enough has been said, it is hoped, to demonstrate that the *Din*, even as traditionally applied, is flexible, in the hands of its liberal interpreters. Moreover the examples quoted are all from post-Talmudic works. It is not very helpful to note examples of flexibility in Talmudic times alone (and there are many) for a great part of the problem today consists in the fact that since the 'close' of the *Talmud* that work has been the final court of appeal in *Halakhah*. If, nonetheless, we see Rabbinic leaders deviating from the Talmudic rules, as above, this gives us good reason to hope that with an extension of this method of liberal interpretation, coupled with the application of modern historical investigations into *Halakhah* origins, our problem of adjustment will be nearer to solution.

The important thing is to have a sufficient number of scholars who are qualified to 'revise' the *Halakhah* because of their knowledge of the times in which we live and their allegiance to *Halakhah*. The latter qualifications must be insisted on. If you accept the law you can interpret it in a liberal fashion but there is no sort of liberality in the complete disregard of the Halakhic side of Judaism. And this has been the trouble up till now. On the one hand the less liberal school of Halakhic interpretation had gained strength while on the other hand a Judaism was preached which had no use for *Halakhah*. One of the most unfortunate by-products of this state of affairs is

that if you speak today of a liberal interpretation of *Halakhah*
you are almost automatically understood as referring to a
religion of expediency which seeks to make things smooth
and easy for its adherents. Whereas, in fact, the application
of *Halakhah* to the life of our times, though it will undoubtedly
remove some unnecessary restrictions, will also, if it is true to
its own development, introduce some new *humroth*, which our
spiritual mood requires. As Dr Robert Gordis remarked some
years ago, the feverish activity which is life in modern large
cities demands, in many ways, a stricter interpretation of the
Sabbath laws if Jews in those cities are to derive full benefit
from the Sabbath rest. Or to take another example, if *Halakhah*
today recognises, as it should, Israel Independence Day as
a religious festival, this will surely involve the '*humroth*' of
reciting special prayers and attending the Synagogue on that
day.

There are, of course, difficulties both in giving proper
direction to change and obtaining something like a consensus
of opinion on the changes to be made. The present situation
in Jewish life is hardly conducive to anything like a solution
to these problems. Perhaps for this generation of Jews the most
that can be achieved is the cultivation of a climate of opinion
in which loyalty to the eternal in Judaism does not prevent a
frank acknowledgment of the ephemeral. The prayer of the
English Admiral should be the prayer of every Jew concerned
with the revitalisation of his faith: 'O God! Give us the courage
to change those things which can and should be changed.
Give us the serenity of mind to accept those things which cannot
be changed. And give us the wisdom to distinguish one from
the other'.

*   *   *

EXCURSUS

On the whole subject of change in Jewish law *v.* especially Boaz
Cohen: 'Law and Tradition in Judaism', Jewish Theological
Seminary of America, New York, 1959. Among the many changes
in the law owing to new circumstances which are listed in the
Talmudic literature, the following may be quoted as examples:
Yad, Iv. 4; *Yeb.* 86b; *Sot.* IX. 9; *Ber.* IX. 5; *Tem.* 14b and *Gitt.*
60a. *Nidd.* 61b regarding the abrogation of the *mitzwoth* in 'the
future' is not really relevant to our problem, dealing as it does with

the Messianic age. Apart from the mediaeval authors mentioned above on the question of *Torah* immutability, reference should be made to the following: Maimonides, *Yad, Hil. Yesode Ha-Torah*, IX. 1; Saadiah, *'Emunoth We-De'oth*, III, 7–9; Ha-Levi: *Kuzari*, III. 39–74; Nahmanides, Commentary to Deut. iv. 2. Ibn Ezra, Commentary to Ex. xii. 1. Cf. *Encyclopedia Talmudith*, s.v. *bal tosiph*, Vol. III, pp. 326–330. On the discussions surrounding this article of faith in the early days of the Reform movement *v.* the two articles on 'Reform Judaism' in JE, Vol. X, pp. 347–359 and the literature cited there and the articles on Orthodox, Reform and Conservative Judaism in UJE, Vol, VI, pp. 238–245. Chapter IV, 'The Perpetuity of the Law', in G. F. Moore's 'Judaism', Harvard University Press, 1958, Vol. I, pp. 263–280, contains much important material on the Rabbinic view.

* * *

To say, as the ninth principle does, that Judaism is an eternal faith which will never be superseded is not to imply that all other religious faiths have no value. The narrower opinion that all faiths apart from Judaism contain no truth whatsoever may have been held by some Jews at different periods of Jewish history but it is certainly no part of Jewish belief. The famous debate between R. Eliezar and R. Joshua on whether the 'righteous of the nations' have a share in the life to come is relevant here. Against R. Eliezer's exclusiveness R. Joshua argued, and this, on the whole, became the official view of Judaism, that the righteous of all nations have a share in Paradise (*Tos. Sanh.* xiii. 2). It is true that Maimonides (*Yad, Hil. Melakhim*, VIII. 11) rules that this only applies if there is a recognition on the part of the non-Jew that the precepts he keeps (the 'seven precepts of the sons of Noah') were given by God to Moses but that if he keeps them because he has arrived at their truth through his own ratiocination, he is not a 'saint of the nations of the world'. If this were to be accepted it would certainly exclude many good men of other faiths. But, as the commentators point out, Maimonides expresses here his own opinion and has no authority in the sources. (It should be noted that the frequently quoted term *'haside 'ummoth ha-'olam'* – 'the *saints* among the nations of the world' – is erroneous. In the *Tos. loc. cit.* the reading is *'tzaddiqe 'ummoth*

ha-ʿolam' – 'the *righteous* of the nations of the world'. *V.* ed.
Zuckermandel, Pasewalk, 1881. The current term is found
only in late sources, e.g. Jellinek's *'Beth Ha-Midrash'*, *Seder
Gan 'Eden*, Maimonides, *op. cit.*, Bertinoro to *Sanh.* X. 2.
It is extremely doubtful whether any of the Rabbis would have
referred to a Gentile as a *'hasid'*. *Cf.* my article 'The Concept of
Hasid in the Biblical and Rabbinic Literatures' in J.J.S., Vol.
VIII, 3 and 4, 1957, p. 154, note 60.)

The claim of Judaism, as implied in the ninth principle, is
not, then, that there is no truth in any other religion but that
the *fullest* revelation of God is contained in the *Torah*. Every
student of Judaism knows that the great Jewish thinkers were
not averse to quoting religious ideas from adherents of other
faiths. Bahya Ibn Paqudah's 'Duties of the Heart', for instance,
is strongly based on Sufi teachings and Sufi sayings are quoted
in the work. But to say this does not mean that Judaism sees
the other faiths as free from error. The Jewish religious outlook
is certainly not one of relativism, in which each religion is
true for its own adherents. From the point of view of Judaism
the Far Eastern religions – Confucianism, Shintoism, Taoism,
Hinduism and Buddhism – are either atheistic, in their more
subtle forms, or polytheistic and idolatrous in their lower forms.
Islam, for all its similarities with Jewish monotheism, is both
too fatalistic and in error so far as the claims of Mohammed
are concerned. Christianity is held to be in error both in its
doctrine of the Trinity and the Incarnation and in its scheme
of salvation. It hardly needs saying that all this has nothing to
do with the question of co-operation among the different
religious faiths of mankind. There are many areas of human
endeavour – the abolition of war is the most cogent example –
where all religious men, indeed, all decent human beings
religious or not, will wish to co-operate. In these areas all
the higher religions can work fruitfully together.

*   *   *

EXCURSUS

In Christian-Jewish polemics in the Middle Ages Jer. xxxi. 30–31
was often quoted. The standard Jewish answer was that the verses
did not refer to the Christian New Testament but to a renewal of
the old *Torah*, *v. Kimhi ad loc.* The mystics sometimes refer to the

spiritual form of the *Torah* which is the same *Torah* but realised in a more spiritual fashion in a world of greater spirituality. For this theme *v.* e.g. *Siddur 'Sha'ar Ha-Shamayyim'* by Isaiah Horowitz (c. 1555–1628), the author of *'Shelah'*, New York, 1952, p. 62. Here Horowitz gives a mystical commentary to the thirteen principles of the faith. On the ninth principle he quotes Cordovero to the effect that when Adam sinned the *Torah* became coarser and of a more material nature. If Adam had not sinned the *Torah* would have been interpreted by him in a far more spiritual form suitable to his lofty spiritual nature. Laws such as the prohibition of ploughing with an ox and ass linked together would have been meaningless for Adam with his 'garments of light' in the Garden of Eden. In this spiritual state there are no oxen and asses and no ploughing. But the reference would have been to the spiritual entities known as 'ox' and 'ass' i.e. the realities in the spiritual world of which oxen and asses in our world are but the lowest physical manifestation. In the Hereafter the new *Torah* will consist of this spiritual meaning suitable for man's Paradise regained. Much has, of course, been written on Jewish-Christian relations during the Middle Ages and the earlier and later periods. *V.* James Parkes: 'The Foundations of Judaism and Christianity', Vallentine, Mitchell, London, 1960; article 'Better Understanding' by Everett R. Clinchy in UJE, Vol. 2, pp. 257–270; the bibliography appended to the above; J. Katz: 'Exclusiveness and Tolerance', Clarendon Press, Oxford, 1961. Katz (Chapters III–IV, pp. 24–47) shows that most Jewish teachers in the Middle Ages considered Christianity to be idolatry, although for certain practical purposes (e.g. the Talmudic laws governing business dealings with idolators before their festivals) it was not regarded as such. But in later centuries there was a new evaluation of Christianity so that later teachers declare that it is not idolatrous, *v.* Katz, pp. 162 f. For instance, there is a ruling of the Tosaphists (*Sanh.* s.v. *'asur*) that Gentiles are not forbidden to associate another name with that of God. The term used is *shittuph*, and this originally meant simple association in an oath of the name of God with any other in one sentence. But in mediaeval philosophical literature (unknown to the Tosaphists) the term *shittuph* was used in a broader sense to mean a duality of the Godhead. Seventeenth and eighteenth century scholars, familiar with this latter sense, read the meaning into the Tosaphists with the result that they understood the Tosaphists to be saying that Christianity was not idolatry so far as Gentiles were concerned. Gentiles are not forbidden *shittuph*, i.e. it is not idolatry for Gentiles to believe in the Incarnation. *V.* the sources in Katz, p. 163, n. 2 and p. 164, n. 1. Katz thus explains the emergence of what he calls 'a convenient theory' – 'permitting Jewish tolerance of Christianity as the faith of others, but retaining absolute monotheism as obligatory upon the Jew.' Katz also shows that the true pioneer in the recognition of Christianity as a non-idolatrous faith was Menahem ben Solomon Me'iri (1249–1306). *V*. Katz, Chapter X, pp. 114–128.

[11]

THE TENTH PRINCIPLE
God Knows the Deeds of Men

MAIMONIDES' formulation of the tenth principle is as follows: '*The tenth Principle of Faith.* That He, the exalted one, knows the works of men and is not unmindful of them. Not as they thought who said: "The Lord hath forsaken the earth" (Ezek. viii. 12; ix. 9), but as he declared who exclaimed: "Great in counsel, and mighty in work; for thine eyes are upon all the ways of the sons of men" (Jer. xxxii. 19). It is further said: "And the Lord saw that the wickedness of man was great in the earth" (Gen. vi. 5). And again: "The cry of Sodom and Gomorrah is great" (Gen. xviii. 20). This indicates our tenth principle of faith.'

The *Yigdal* formulation is: 'He watcheth and knoweth our secret thoughts: He beholdeth the end of a thing before it existeth'. The *'Ani Ma'amin* formulation reads: 'I believe with perfect faith that the Creator, blessed be His name, knows every deed of the children of men, and all their thoughts, as it is said, It is He that fashioneth the hearts of them all, that giveth heed to all their deeds (Ps. xxxiii. 15)'.

Friedländer, after quoting the *Yigdal* version, remarks: 'Here the author proclaims not only the Omniscience of God, but also His foresight; His knowledge is not limited, like the knowledge of mortal beings, by space and time. The entire past and future lies unrolled before His eyes, and nothing is hidden from Him. Although we may form a faint idea of the knowledge of God by considering that faculty of man that enables him, within a limited space of time, to look backward and forward, and to unroll before him the past and the future, as if the events that have happened and those that will come to pass were going on in the present moment, yet the true nature of God's knowledge no man can conceive. "God considereth all the deeds of man", without depriving him of his free-will;

he may in this respect be compared to a person who observes and notices the actions and the conduct of his fellow-men, without interfering with them. It is the Will of God that man should have free-will and should be responsible for his actions; and His foresight does not necessarily include predetermination. In some cases the fate of nations or of individual men is predetermined; we may even say that the ultimate fate or development of mankind is part of the design of the Creation. But as the actual design in the Creation is concealed from man's searching eye, so is also the extent of the predetermination a mystery to him. To solve this problem is beyond the intellectual powers of short-sighted mortals; it is one of "the hidden things that belong to the Lord our God" '.

Werblowsky thus states the tenth principle: '10. *God's Omniscience.* Divine omniscience is part of the complex of ideas that includes omnipotence and omnipresence; on the other hand it is a condition of the belief in a special providence and in individual reward and punishment (art. 11). Since God knows the heart and the innermost thoughts, purity of heart and holiness of thoughts are as significant as physical acts of omission or commission. On a more religious or mystical level the stress is less on God's knowledge of each individual than on the concomitant solicitude and readiness for personal communion. Thus the love of God, fear of God and practice of the presence of God become personal relationships instead of reactions to certain "attributes" '.

Maimonides devotes a chapter of his 'Guide' (III. 20, Friedländer, pp. 292–295) to his conception of God's knowledge. On Maimonides' theory of divine omniscience God, being perfect, cannot acquire new knowledge He did not previously possess. He must therefore know all things before they take place, otherwise His knowledge would change as things come into existence. But philosophers, says Maimonides, have found various difficulties in ascribing the knowledge of particular things to God. Some have argued that God can only know that which is constant and unchangeable. He cannot know any transient thing for if He did it would mean that His knowledge suffers change. Others have taken a more extreme view and have argued that God cannot even know things

which remain constant for since these are many God's knowledge of them would involve a plurality of ideas incompatible
with the oneness of God. According to these thinkers God only
knows His own essence. It is obvious that religion teaches that
God does know all individual things. In Maimonides' opinion
the mistake the philosophers make is to compare divine knowledge with human. But God does not know things as humans
do. When a human being knows something he himself and the
object of his knowledge are two separate things. But God's
knowledge and his essence are one and the same. It follows
that just as it is impossible for man to grasp God's essence
it is impossible for him to grasp God's knowledge. It is impossible for us to see how God who is unchanging can know
transient things, how His oneness can encompass a plurality
of things, but this is to be expected since man cannot know the
true essence of God. In fact, according to Maimonides, the
term 'knowledge' used of God and man is a homonym; the
words are the same but are used to represent two quite different
things. Here modern verification-analytical theories might
well object that you cannot use the same term of two different
things without talking nonsense. If, when we say that God
'knows', we mean that He 'knows' in a sense other than human,
we are not giving expression to a significant statement. For
if human language is being used, and this is the only language
we have, the term 'know' has a precise meaning and is applied
to human perception. If God's knowledge is so different from
the human surely it must not be called 'knowledge'? But a
careful reading of Maimonides, particularly his well-known
remarks on the doctrine of negative attributes to which reference has already been made, shows that our author is not
suggesting that there is no point of contact at all between
divine and human knowledge. The two do mean the same thing
in their negative aspects, i.e. the term knowledge when used
of God and man implies the negation of ignorance. In this
negative sense there is no homonymity. It is only when we
try to describe God's knowledge in a positive sense that we
fall into difficulties by using ideas taken from human experience
which cannot be applied to God. Thus when Maimonides
says that God knows all the deeds of men this has to be taken
to mean that He is not ignorant of all men's deeds but it is not

meant to suggest that we can understand fully how God's knowledge can embrace all men. To do this latter we would have to know God's essence and this is impossible for man.

Maimonides goes on to say that since God's knowledge cannot be comprehended by man the difficulty of accounting for human free-will is considerably lessened. If only we could really know what God's knowledge means we would see how His foreknowledge is not incompatible with human freedom. 'In short, as we cannot accurately comprehend His essence, and yet we know that His existence is most perfect, free from all admixture of deficiency, change, or passiveness, so we have no correct notion of His knowledge, because it is nothing but His essence, and yet we are convinced that He does not at one time obtain knowledge which He had not before; i.e., He obtains no new knowledge, He does not increase it, and it is not finite; nothing of all existing things escapes His knowledge, but their nature is not changed thereby; that which is possible remains possible'.

Maimonides is consistent through all his writings on both divine omniscience and the freedom of the human will. The doctrine of divine omniscience is stated in the tenth principle. The doctrine of free-will is implied in the eleventh principle. Reward and punishment would be impossible unless the human will is free. Of course, the problem of reconciling divine foreknowledge with human freedom was a central problem in mediaeval religious thought, Christian and Muslim as well as Jewish. Islamic fatalists were prepared to deny human freedom. In Christian thought the extreme position is taken in Calvinism. The Calvinist insists on God's omnipotence and omniscience to the extent of holding that God elected certain people to be 'saved', through no merit on their part, and the rest of mankind to be doomed. Some Calvinists – the *supralapsarians* – held that God decreed the sin and fall of man as a means to the salvation of the elect. Others – the *infralapsarians* – held that God merely permitted the fall of man. With very few exceptions Jewish teachers have insisted on man's freedom, some of them even compromising, as a result, God's complete omniscience. But Maimonides accepts both parts of the dilemma. Man is free *and* God has foreknowledge. This seems impossible to us but it is not impossible to God whose knowledge is not our knowledge.

In addition to his statement in the 'Guide' Maimonides has discussed this question in his 'Code' (*Hil. Teshubhah*, Chapter V. 5) but before examining his very important statement here it will be useful to examine his general statement concerning human freedom in the earlier part of this chapter (1–4).

Maimonides begins by stating that every man can choose for himself whether to be good or evil. Following the *Targum* of Onqelos, Maimonides gives a novel turn to the verse in Gen. iii. 22, which is made to read: 'Behold man is unique in that he knoweth good and evil of his own accord' (*'mimmennu'*). Do not accept for one moment, he goes on to say, the opinion of "the fools of the nations of the world (i.e. the fatalists) and the majority of the unsophisticated among the Jews" that it is decreed at man's creation whether he is to be good or evil. This is not so but each human being can become as righteous as Moses or as wicked as Jeroboam. He can, by his own efforts, be wise or foolish, kind or cruel, miserly or generous. As the commentators rightly point out, Maimonides does not necessarily mean here that it depends entirely upon man whether or not he is to become a sage. Obviously some are endowed with greater gifts of intellect than others. The meaning is rather that man by his own free choice can develop the intellectual capacity he has or allow it to become atrophied. This is said to be the meaning of the verse: 'Out of the mouth of the Most High proceedeth not evil and good' (Lam. iii. 38) i.e. it is not by God's decree but through the exercise of his own free-will that man becomes good or evil. This doctrine is a great principle of the faith and the foundation of the *Torah* and the *mitzwoth*. It is interesting to find Maimonides referring to the doctrine of free-will as a 'principle of the faith' (' *'iqqar'*) even though it is not enumerated among his thirteen principles. It is, in fact, implied in the tenth and eleventh principles. As Maimonides himself states, the doctrine that God knows all men's deeds suggests that He is concerned with what men do and the doctrine of reward and punishment suggests that they are responsible for what they do. This does not mean, Maimonides goes on to say, that there is an area – that in which free-will operates – which is not covered by the divine will but that it is by the divine will that man has freedom of choice. The very freedom of man is part of God's purpose in exactly the same way that it is His purpose that fire should ascend, for instance. The paradox here is that man's freedom from God's control in the management of his moral life is itself part of God's control, part of the divine ordering of the universe.

There then occurs Maimonides' famous statement of the divine foreknowledge and human free-will dilemma, which must here be quoted in full: 'You may ask: God knows all that will happen. Before someone becomes a good or a bad man God either knows that this will happen or He does not know it. If He knows that the person will be good is it impossible for that person to be bad? If you reply that while God knows that he will be good it is still possible for him to be bad, then God has no clear foreknowledge. You must know that the solution to this problem is larger than the earth and wider than the sea, many main principles of faith and lofty mountains of thought depend upon it. But it is essential for you to grasp thoroughly that which I am about to say. We have already explained in the second chapter of "*Hilkhoth Yesode Ha-Torah*" that God does not "know" with a knowledge that is apart from Him, like human beings whose self and knowledge are distinct one from the other. God's knowledge and His Self are one and the same though no human being is capable of clearly comprehending this matter. Just as it is beyond the human capacity to comprehend or discover God's true nature, as it said: "For man shall not see Me and live" (Ex. xxxiii. 20), so is it beyond human capacity to comprehend or discover the Creator's knowledge. It is to this that the prophet refers when he says: "For My thoughts are not your thoughts, Neither are your ways My ways" (Is. lv. 8). It follows that we are incapable of comprehending how God knows all creatures and all deeds. But this we do know beyond any doubt, that man's deeds are in his own hands, God neither compelling him nor determining that he should behave in a certain way. It is not alone through religious tradition that we know this to be so but by means of clear philosophical truths. Because of this, prophecy teaches that man is judged on his deeds according to those deeds, whether good or evil. All the words of prophecy depend on this principle'.

The dilemma of which Maimonides speaks may be put in this way. Long before Hitler was born, God must have known what he would become. It cannot be said that God only knew that Hitler *might* turn out to be a monster of iniquity for this would imply that God did not really *know* and it belongs to the doctrine of divine omniscience that God knows all things and is not in any way uncertain about any of them. How can this *certain* knowledge by God of what Hitler was to become be reconciled with Hitler's freedom of choice? If we know that someone will behave in a certain way – if we really know it – that person cannot be free to behave in any other way. Maimonides' solution is that we must not compare God's knowledge to ours. We can only know that someone will behave in a certain way in the future if he is bound to behave in that way but God can know this without depriving him of his freedom of choice.

Abraham Ibn David, Maimonides' great critic, immediately objects: 'This author did not conduct himself in the manner of a sage, according to which no one should embark on a discussion of a problem unless he is capable of seeing it through to the end. He began by setting problems but ended by leaving the problems unsolved and relying on faith. It would have been better for him to have left the unsophisticated in their simple faith, without awakening their curiosity and leaving them with uncertainty, so that for a time doubt may enter their minds. Now although there is no convincing answer to this question it may be worthwhile attempting some slight solution as follows. If man's goodness or badness depended on God's decree we would be obliged to say that for God to know it is to decree it and then the problem would indeed present the greatest difficulty. Since, however, God relinquishes His sovereignty in this matter and has given it into the hands of man, His knowledge is not in the nature of a compelling decree but can be compared to the knowledge of the astrologers who know, by virtue of some other power, how a certain person will behave. It is well-known that God has given the stars power over everything, small or great, which befalls man. But He also gives man intelligence and this provides him with the power of emerging from the control of the stars. This is power given to man through which he can be good or evil. God knows the force of the star and its moments and He knows whether or not man's intelligence is strong enough to break free from the star's control. This kind of knowledge is not in the nature of a decree. But all this is not really worth much'.

Abraham Ibn David's solution, by which he himself sets no great store, is, in fact, the standard answer given by the Mutakallims, the Islamic theologians, and accepted by Saadiah Gaon among others. God's knowledge is not determinative or causative. This is no doubt true but it does not really solve anything as, Abraham Ibn David sees. It is all very well to say that God's knowledge is not determinative but this is the very problem, for how can sure knowledge of an event long before it occurs fail to be determinative? Abraham Ibn David reads Maimonides' statement to mean that there is a difficulty but Maimonides does not know the answer. Various later thinkers have rightly noted that Maimonides is surely saying something more than this.

There is much in the idea which has been advanced periodically that Maimonides is really bent on noting that it is not *impossible* for God to have foreknowledge and man to have free-will. If God's knowledge were the same as human knowledge it would indeed be impossible for man to have free-will. God can do that which is impossible for us. He cannot do that which is impossible to Him since there cannot be any such thing. According to this Maimonides' intention is to point out that there is no impossibility involved here in any absolute sense since God's knowledge – of which we know nothing – is compatible with human free-will, even though we cannot comprehend this compatibility.

Some of the commentators go further and endeavour to show how even we can have a faint glimmer of understanding of why the two are not incompatible. It should first be noted that so far as we know the first Jewish teacher to seize unambiguously both horns of the dilemma was Rabbi Akiba. His saying is given in the *Mishnah* (*'Abhoth* III. 19): 'Everything is foreseen, yet freedom of choice is given'. Maimonides in his Commentary to this *Mishnah* remarks: '*Everything is foreseen.* All the deeds of men, both those of the past and those of the future, are all revealed to Him. But you should not say: Since God knows what man will do he is compelled to be good or bad for *freedom of choice is given* into man's hands to do good or evil without any compulsion whatsoever'. Yom Tobh

Lippmann Heller, in his commentary, *Tos. Yom Tobh*, remarks that this *Mishnah* anticipates Maimonides in raising the problem and in suggesting, as Maimonides does, that *both* divine foreknowledge and free-will are true even though we cannot see how they can both be true. The '*Midrash Shemuel*' of Samuel b. Isaac of Uceda is quoted. Here the idea is put forward that God is outside time and therefore sees all events in the eternal 'Now'. 'When a man sees someone else doing something the fact that he sees it exercises no compulsion on the thing that is done. In exactly the same way the fact that God sees man doing the act exercises no compulsion over him to do it. For before God there is no early and late since He is not governed by time'. This idea is found in connection with this very problem in the writings of Thomas Aquinas who gives the well-known illustration of men passing one in front of the other along a deep gorge. Someone at the top overlooking the gorge sees them all at once even though they pass through the gorge in single file. Finally, the opinion of Moses Almosnino (1510–1580) is quoted. This author believes that a similar idea was in the mind of Maimonides, and he may well be right. 'This is the meaning of Maimonides' distinction between God's knowledge and ours which is on this very point that as God's knowledge is always in the present and before Him there is no future but always the present. Just as relative to us, our knowledge of the present is not determinative so God's knowledge, which is always in the present, is not determinative. Difficulties are only caused for humans by the fact that we are incapable of imagining how God's knowledge can always be in the present even of that which for us is in the future. Consequently, Maimonides reminds us that God's knowledge is unlike our knowledge so that we should not be led astray in this matter. For the same reason the *Mishnah* says: "Everything *has been* foreseen" in the past tense. For it is not a question of God gazing into the future but of seeing everything at once'. It is relevant to quote in this connection the early prayer of *Zikhronoth*, recited on the New Year festival. In this prayer the whole idea of God's omniscience is thus described: 'Thou rememberest what was wrought from eternity and art mindful of all that hath been formed of old: before thee all secrets are revealed, and the multitude of hidden things since the creation;

for there is no forgetfulness before the throne of thy glory, nor is there ought hidden from thine eyes. Thou rememberest every deed that hath been done: not a creature is concealed from thee: all things are manifest and known unto thee, O Lord our God, *who lookest and seest to the end of all the ages'*.

The classical formulation of man's capacity to choose between good and evil is, of course, Deut. xi. 26–28: 'Behold, I set before you this day a blessing and a curse: the blessing, if ye shall hearken unto the commandments of the Lord your God, which I command you this day; and the curse, if ye shall not hearken unto the commandments of the Lord your God, but turn aside out of the way which I command you this day, to go after other gods, which ye have not known'. The idea of a choice is similarly stated in Deut. xxx. 15–20: 'See, I have set before thee this day life and good, and death and evil, in that I command thee this day to love the Lord thy God, to walk in His ways, and to keep His commandments and His statutes and His ordinances; then thou shalt live and multiply, and the Lord thy God shall bless thee in the land whither thou goest in to possess it. But if thy heart turn away, and thou wilst not hear, but shalt be drawn away, and worship other gods, and serve them; I declare unto you this day, that ye shall surely perish; ye shall not prolong your days upon the land, whither thou passest over the Jordan to go in to possess it. I call heaven and earth to witness against you this day, that I have set before thee life and death, the blessing and the curse; therefore choose life, that thou mayest live, thou and thy seed; to love the Lord thy God, to hearken to His voice, and to cleave unto Him; for that is thy life, and the length of thy days; that thou mayest dwell in the land which the Lord swore unto thy fathers, to Abraham, to Isaac, and to Jacob, to give them'. It hardly needs saying that the Biblical writers were not concerned with the philosophical problem of reconciling human free-will with God's omniscience, any more than they were concerned to demonstrate by means of 'proofs' the existence of God or to discuss philosophically the nature of God. It was only when Jews came into contact with the upholders of philosophical systems that attempts at any of these were considered necessary. The Rabbis naturally continued in the Biblical tradition, emphasising, like Akiba, that God knows all but never faltering in their belief that man is free. A typical saying is that of the third century teacher R. Hanina: 'Everything is in the power of Heaven except the fear of Heaven' (*Ber.* 33b; *Meg.* 25a; *Nidd.* 16b). The proof-text quoted is: 'Now, O Israel, what doth the Lord thy God require of thee but to fear the Lord thy God . . .' (Deut. x. 12). R. Simeon b. Laqish quotes Prov. iii. 34 to yield the thought that if man wishes to defile himself God gives him the opportunity of doing so but if he wishes to purify himself God helps him to do so (*Sabb.* 104a). The idea behind the saying appears to be that although man's choice is entirely free he will be positively assisted by God if he chooses the good life whereas God will merely permit him to do so, without aiding him in any way, if he chooses to lead an evil life.

Josephus records that the three major sects, the Essenes, Pharisees and Sadducees, were divided on the question of determination or destiny in human affairs (*Ant.* xiii. 5, 9; xviii. 1, 3, *Bell. Jud.* 8, 14). It would appear from Josephus that the Sadducees held that man is entirely free, that the Essenes were complete determinists, while the Pharisees held that some of men's actions were determined by fate, others by his own free choice, or, according to a different account by the same author, man has freedom of choice but destiny or fate enters somehow into every choice. Since Josephus is not clear as to the precise differences between the sects on this matter and appears indeed to contradict himself we can only conclude that this perennial problem exercised men's minds two thousand years ago as it still does today and that various attempts were made to deal with the problem. For all that, while there are a number of later Rabbinic teachings which seem to accept a form of fatalism in some areas of human life it would be very difficult to find anywhere in the later Rabbinic literature a denial that the human will is free.

Although the mediaeval thinkers discuss the problem of free-will in connection with divine foreknowledge there is another aspect of the problem on which modern thinkers have dwelt in particular. Indeterminists like William James appeal to our experience in which we assume both psychological and moral freedom. We blame ourselves and others for wrongdoing and we offer praise for right-doing, thereby implying that man can freely choose the course he adopts and the acts he performs. As Chesterton once said, we demonstrate that we are indeterminists whenever we say: 'Pass the mustard'. Determinists, on the other hand, have argued that all this is an illusion. We only imagine that we are free to choose. For, the determinists argue, it is impermissible to speak of a choice without cause. We must not think of a man faced with two courses of action deciding upon one of them *without any cause*. His very choice is determined by his character, by what he is, and if all the factors of environment and heredity and so forth which have had their effect on him could be known it would be possible to predict accurately *beforehand* the choice he will make. Many determinists have been at pains to point out that theirs is not an attitude of fatalism. When they speak of determinism they mean *self-determinism* not a *mechanical* determinism. If, for instance, I am tempted to steal a large sum of money but choose not to do so the indeterminist would say that the two possibilities of stealing or refraining from doing so were both open to me and my decision not to steal is the result of my own free choice, operating, as it were, in a vacuum. The fatalist would say that my choice has nothing to do with it. Everything has been determined from the beginning. If it had been destined for me to steal the money I would have stolen it. I refrained from doing so because this had been destined. The determinist argues that it is true I had no option but to *choose* to refrain from stealing but the choice is a real one for all that. But the difficulty of the determinist view is that if we go back far enough a determinist philosophy would seem to make nonsense of man's freedom of choice. If it is true that I make the choice because of my character and this in turn has been determined by other factors, the character of my parents and the nature of my environment, for example, it is hard to see how this really differs from fatalism at least so far as my freedom of choice is concerned.

Now this is a very involved question and it is more than a little difficult to speak of the Jewish view. But the following consideration may be found helpful. On the one hand it is undeniable that the nature of a man's character has a good deal to do with his freedom of choice. It is known from experience that if a man engages habitually in certain acts they no longer seem wrong to him even if at one time he was worried by

conscience whenever he carried out these acts. There is the
famous Rabbinic saying that if a man commits a sin more than
twice it seems to him as if it has been permitted (*Yom.* 86b).
The Rabbis know, too, and speak frequently of, the child
who was 'captured in infancy by heathen' and cannot be blamed
for many of the offences he commits (*Sabb.* 68a). The facts
of experience and the teachings of Judaism appear to be at one,
therefore, in pointing to freedom of choice in certain areas
and lack of freedom in others. From the theological point of
view this means that each person has his own area of choice.
It may well be that the child reared by thieves is compelled
to steal by his upbringing and training. He will not see stealing
as wrong and for him free-will does not operate in this area.
But he, too, will come to see, for instance, that it is wrong to do
violence while stealing and his area of choice may be confined to
whether or no he will do violence. Similarly, a man who has
spent all his life in strict Jewish observance may find after a
time that there is no real choice in his observance of the Sabbath.
It should be mentioned that the *Halakhah* seems to recognise
that on frequent occasions there is no freedom of choice, as can
be seen from the numerous detailed Halakhic discussions concerning what constitutes 'free-will' in law and when a person is
exempt from the demands of the law because he could not help
himself (*'ones*).

*   *   *

EXCURSUS

   The statement in the *Mishnah, R.H.* I. 2 and the discussion on this in
the *Gemara R. H.* 18a are relevant to the tenth principle.The
Mishnah states that at the New Year all mankind pass before God
'*like children of Maron*', the meaning being that they are investigated
and judged one by one. The *Gemara* gives a number of explanations
of this term, thus, 'like a flock of sheep', 'as in the ascent of Beth
Maron' (where travellers have to pass in single file) 'like troops
of soldiers'. In the same passage in the *Gemara* it is said that 'they
are all seen with a single glance'. The proof-text for this is quoted:
'He that fashioneth the hearts of them all, that considereth all
their doings' (Ps. xxxiii. 15). For the question of free-will in the
Apocrypha *v.* Ecclus. xv. 11–17; Psalms of Solomon ix. 4; IV
Esdras viii. 55 f. For the whole question in post-Biblical literature
v. G. F. Moore 'Judaism', Vol I, p. 453 f.; Louis Finkelstein: 'The

Pharisees', Vol. I, Philadelphia, 1940, Chapter XI, pp. 195–260;
A. Cohen: 'Everyman's Talmud', Dent, London, 1949, pp. 93–95.
Cf. I. Broyde in JE, Vol. V, pp. 505–506; Samuel J. B. Wolk in
UJE, Vol. IV, pp. 428–431 and the literature cited in these two
articles. Saadiah's discussion of divine foreknowledge and human
free-will is to be found in his *Emunoth We-De'oth*, IV, Chapter 4,
trans. Samuel Rosenblatt, Yale University Press, 1948, pp. 188–191.
Saadiah, as stated above, gives the familiar answer that God's
knowledge is not determinative. 'What God foreknows is the final
denouement of man's activity as it turns out after all his
planning, anticipations, and delays'. Saadiah evidently means by
this that it is not of the particular act in itself which man does
that God has foreknowledge but of the act *as chosen by man*. E.g. if
God knows before a man will speak that he will speak then that man
cannot help but speak. What God knows is rather that man will
speak after he has himself chosen to do so. Very few later thinkers
were as confident as Saadiah in believing that this disposes of the
problem. *Cf.* Henry Malter: 'Saadia Gaon, His Life and Works',
Jewish Publication Society, Philadelphia, 1942, pp. 215–6. Bahya
Ibn Paqudah deals with the problem in his 'Duties of the Heart',
III, Chapter 8. Bahya's statement of the problem is not with
reference to God's omniscience but to His omnipotence. If everything which happens is ordained by God how can man be free?
(*Cf.* Austin Farrer's statement of the problem in 'The Freedom of
the Will', The Gifford Lectures, Adam and Charles Black, London,
1958, p. 310: 'God (it is the theist's belief) is making our neighbour. And yet our neighbour is, in some measure at least, making
himself. The same thing is true, we suppose, of ourselves; a
providence shapes us, and it is this very work of God upon us
which commands our obedience in the ordering of our lives. But
how, in the creating of a single life, can we accommodate two wills,
one all-knowing and divine, the other fallible and human? Not,
perhaps we should say, two wills side by side, for that would be a
blasphemous equalisation; but rather, as it were, ranged in depth,
the one behind the other, the one acting through and in the other').
Bahya can only reply that this is beyond man's capacity and that he
must rely on faith that somehow the two can be reconciled. If God
knew that our knowledge of the solution to the problem were
necessary and of advantage to us He would have revealed it to us.
Since He did not do so it can have no relevance to the practical life
of religion. We should conduct ourselves in the belief that we are
free to do good or evil and at the same time, so far as the question
of trusting in God is concerned, we should have complete trust in
Him in all that we do. Yeudah Ha-Levi discusses the question in his

'*Kuzari*', Part V, 19–20. The Khazar King asks the Rabbi to discuss questions of faith and he says that it will not be possible to omit the question of predestination and free-will. He quotes the opinions of the Mutakallims who considered this matter in detail. The knowledge of events to come is no more a cause of those events than the knowledge of events which have taken place is a cause of those events. God does know the future but His knowledge is not causative. These thinkers, together with Maimonides, grapple with the dilemma of God being omniscient and omnipotent *and* that the human will is free. But some mediaeval Jewish thinkers appear to have held that the only solution was to compromise in some measure one of the two propositions. For them either God is not completely omniscient or man is not entirely free. Thus Abraham Ibn David's '*'Emunah Ramah*', with German trans. by S. Weil, Frankfurt, 1852, as he states in the introduction, was written at the request of a friend who was bothered by the dilemma. After a lengthy philosophical introduction Ibn David deals with the problem (p. 93 f., *cf.* I. Husik: 'A History of Mediaeval Jewish Philosophy', Jewish Publication Society, Philadelphia, 1940, pp. 228 f.). According to this author man is free. He says that all the ancient sages of our nation were in favour of freedom. But since man is free to choose this means, according to Ibn David, that those events which are the result of man's freedom of choice are not, in fact, known beforehand to God. In other words Ibn David sacrifices the doctrine of God's foreknowledge in favour of that of human free-will. Does this not mean that there is imperfection in God? Ibn David replies that God cannot be ignorant in the sense of inability to know that which can be known. But if there is to be a category of the contingent at all, and without this man can have no freedom of choice, by definition this means that there are things which even God cannot know beforehand. God knows all that can be known. He does not know that which by definition cannot be known. This is a startling doctrine for a Jewish thinker to uphold. What Abraham Ibn David appears to be saying is that in order to make man's free choice possible God voluntarily left certain actions undecided in His own mind. The difficulties inherent in the idea of a God whose mind is undecided are too obvious to need stating and it is not surprising that this solution was held to be unacceptable by the other thinkers. Levi ben Gerson (Gersonides) in his '*Milhamoth 'Adonai*', Leipzig, 1866, III, Chapters 1–6, pp. 120–150, similarly argues that God does not know the contingent. God knows all things as they are and since the very idea of the possible means that it cannot be known beforehand with certainty it is no defect in God to say that He only knows the possible as possible, i.e. this, too, He

knows as it is. God knows the coming of events as they are determined apart from man's freedom of choice. But man's freedom may
succeed in counteracting this order of nature. *Cf.* I. Husik, *op. cit.*,
pp. 343 f. Hasdai Crescas, in his ' *'Or 'Adonai*', Book II, 4 f. (*v.*
Husik, *op. cit*, p. 395 f.) is the only Jewish thinker of note who is
prepared to sacrifice, or at least to limit, human free-will in defer-
ence to the doctrine of God's omniscience. But how then can God's
justice be vindicated? How can He reward and punish man unless
man is responsible for what he does? Crescas's answer appears to
be very similar to the theories of later determinists like Spinoza
(who, incidentally, was influenced by Crescas). As we have seen,
determinism is not fatalism and Crescas thinks that a deterministic
philosophy is not incompatible with Judaism. On a fatalistic theory
both effort and reward and punishment would be impossible. But
on a deterministic theory both effort and reward and punishment
are *causes*, man acts differently because of them, and they therefore
have their place in God's scheme. In a surprising analogy Crescas
says that it is no more unjust for man to receive reward and
punishment, even though his actions are determined by antecedent
causes, than it is for him to be burnt when he comes near to fire by
accident! Crescas is not unaware of the difficulty. Even though, he
says, every act is determined the compulsion towards the act is not
an external one. The act is the person's own and he is identified
with it in a way that he cannot be with regard to the act he is
compelled to do from without. The analogy with the burning fire
must not be pressed too far. Joseph Albo, ''*Iqqarim*', Book IV,
Chapter 3, ed. I. Husik, Jewish Publication Society, Philadelphia,
1946, pp. 12–24, follows Maimonides in his treatment of the
problem. 'But if you ask, how is it possible to maintain both of these
opinions, viz. to maintain the reality of the contingent and at the
same time to hold that God's knowledge embraces it? Our answer
is the same as that of Maimonides, who says that since God's
knowledge is essential in Him and not something added to His
essence, the investigation of the character of His knowledge is
tantamount to an investigation of His essence. But His essence is
absolutely unknown, hence the character of His knowledge is also
absolutely unknown. As there is no comparison or similarity between
His existence and the existence of other things, so there is no
comparison between His knowledge and the knowledge of others.
Hence though if we picture His knowledge on the analogy of our
own, a great many objections follow, such as that we must either
deny the reality of the contingent or assume that His knowledge
embraces that which we cannot conceive as knowable, for He would
have to know the infinite, or His knowledge would change with the

change of the objects, and other difficulties of this sort – this would
follow only if we conceive of His knowledge on the analogy of our
own, but since His knowledge is not of the same kind as ours, these
difficulties do not follow. God's knowledge is infinite, and infinite
knowledge is not liable to these difficulties'. Albo in the same chapter
(p. 22) deals with the question we have raised above that if God's
knowledge is so utterly different from human knowledge what is
the point of calling it 'knowledge'? Albo gives the solution we have
quoted above that divine and human knowledge are alike in their
negative aspects – they both imply the negation of ignorance – but
not in their positive aspects. An acute discussion of the whole
question of human freedom of the will in the light of Jewish teaching
is to be found in Rabbi E. L. Dessler's *'Mikhtabh Me-'Elijahu'*, ed.
L. Carmel and A. Halpern, London, 1955, Part II, pp. 111 f.
and Part III, pp. 278 ff. Dessler calls attention to determinist
philosophers who belie their own theories by demanding praise for
their achievements. Can one praise a machine? (p. 278). Determinists would probably retort with the by now familiar distinction
between self-determinism and mechanical determinism. Dessler
tellingly quotes Bahya, 'Duties of the Heart', V, Chapter 5, that
the 'evil inclination' entices man to believe in determinism in order
to escape the consequences of sin and yet, at the same time, entices
him to believe in free-will when it comes to his business concerns
and the satisfaction of his needs and desires. As we have seen,
Bahya's own view is that with regard to choosing virtue and
rejecting vice man should have the idea of human free-will constantly
in mind, but with regard to other matters He should have complete
faith and trust in God. Among other matters, Dessler develops very
skilfully the idea that each person has his own point or area of
choice.

*   *   *

If we attempt to summarise the results of our survey till
now we find that it yields the following conclusions. No Jewish
teachers reject the tenth and eleventh principles of Maimonides.
They all teach, and in this they follow the Bible and *Talmud*,
that God knows the deeds of men and that He rewards and
punishes. The corollaries to these two propositions are that
God knows *all* the deeds of men, including the deeds they will
do in the future, and that man has free-will. Maimonides states
explicitly in his writings that Judaism teaches that God is
entirely omniscient and that human beings have free-will. But
it is with regard to these two corollaries that the dilemma of

divine foreknowledge versus free-will arises. On this matter there is no complete unanimity among Jewish thinkers. While it may be said that the majority of Jewish teachers accept the views of Rabbi Akiba and Maimonides that both propositions are true, that God is entirely ominiscient *and* man enjoys free-will, there are to be found thinkers who qualify one of these propositions. Thus, as we have seen, Abraham Ibn David (not to be confused with the Abraham Ibn David who offers the above-mentioned stricture to Maimonides) and Gersonides believe that God's omniscience does not extend to the contingent, or, in other words, He is not entirely omniscient. Crescas, on the other hand, believes that the human will is not entirely free. A Jewish follower of a 'limited' Deity, after the manner of E. S. Brightman, could, therefore, claim that he is in the good company of Abraham Ibn David and Gersonides, at least so far as God's lack of knowledge of the contingent is concerned, while a Jewish determinist (not, be it noted, *fatalist*) could claim the company of Crescas. It remains true, nonetheless, that both 'finitism' and determinism are at variance with normative Jewish thinking. In spite of Crescas it is very difficult indeed to see how God can reward or punish creatures whose actions are determined. If predetermination is true then Omar Khayyam is right:

'O Thou, who didst with Pitfall and with Gin
Beset the road I was to wander in,
Thou wilst not with Predestination round
Enmesh me, and impute my Fall to Sin?'

As for 'finitism' there is something more than a little bizarre about a God whose purposes may not be fulfilled. Such a being would not be God. If it be argued that although God does not know the contingent He knows enough to make sure that His purpose for man will not be frustrated by man's deeds, the obvious difficulty then is, how can this be possible? If God really lacks knowledge of the future so far as man's free acts are concerned, how can He be sure that man will not do something to set at nought all of God's purpose? It will not do to reply that man has not been given this power for if that were true then God does know the contingent, since he knows that man cannot in his contingency go beyond a certain point. It similarly

will not do to speak of God's knowledge as being 'general' not
'particular' for if He does not know the 'particular' how can He
be sure of the 'general' which is made up of the particulars?
The most plausible approach to the problem as well as the
most satisfying to the religious mind, is to seize boldly, as
Maimonides does, both horns of the dilemma. If the notion
of eternity be added, as above, a faint glimmer of light is
shed on how the two concepts of divine foreknowledge and
human free-will need not be incompatible.

This is one of those theological questions which have been
so widely discussed from every angle in the Middle Ages, by
Jews, Christians and Muslims, that there is very little which
modern thinkers have been able to add. There have been, of
course, many discussions of the problem. Some logical analysts
have considered this to be a pseudo-problem and have naturally
extended to it their general mistrust of metaphysics. The discussion in modern religious philosophy generally centres
around the three points of logical analysis, determinism versus
indeterminism, and the question of a 'finite' God. It is interesting to find a twentieth century thinker, W. R. Sorley, accepting,
like Maimonides, both horns of the dilemma, and doing so by
postulating, like Moses Almosnino and the other thinkers we
have mentioned, that God's knowledge is not in time but in
eternity. Sorley ('Moral Values and the Idea of God', The
Gifford Lectures, Third. ed., Cambridge University Press,
1924, pp. 465–6) says: 'The event which we perceive is never
strictly instantaneous; it has a certain duration, very short,
indeed, but not infinitesimal. This is our time-span, and in it
we see at a glance what is really a succession. If this time-span
were considerably enlarged, we should have immediate knowledge of a longer series, for example, of a succession of actions
in which a resolution is made and carried out. Within the time-
span differences of past and future do not interfere with immediacy. Why then should not all time be seen as one by an
infinite intelligence? Assuming that God's knowledge is not
limited to a finite span of the time-process, the whole course
of the world's history will be seen by him in a single or immediate intuition. The question how a particular event, such as
the action of a man, comes about – whether by free will or
mechanical necessity – will make no difference to the immediacy

of that intuition. What we call foreknowledge will be just knowledge: past and future, equally with present, lie open to the mind of infinite time-span'. Sorley concludes: 'For this reason it appears to me that freedom is not related to foreknow-ledge in the same way as it is to pre-determination. Universal determination contradicts freedom; universal knowledge does not. And we cannot suppose that God, to whose view all time lies open, would call into existence spirits whose activity would frustrate his purpose in their creation'. Jacob Kohn ('The Moral Life of Man' Philosophical Library, New York, 1956, pp. 77 f.) has similarly pointed out that there is a fallacy in the contention that because God knows all things in all time God's knowledge of today includes His foreknowledge of tomorrow. What we really mean by God's omniscience is, however, that God knows eternally both today and tomorrow but not that His knowledge of today includes that of tomorrow. They remain two items in His eternal wisdom. God's knowledge of all time is due to the fact that all time is in God, not God in time. God knows both today and tomorrow in an eternal knowledge the form of which transcends our own.

*   *   *

EXCURSUS

St. Augustine was one of the first writers to deal at length with the dilemma of divine foreknowledge and free-will, *v.* '*De Libero Arbitrio*', III, 1 ff, given in 'Historical Selections in the Philosophy of Religion', ed. Ninian Smart, SCM Press, London, 1962, pp. 40–49. Augustine's argument is, in the main, the stock argument of those thinkers who believe that the problem is to be solved by pointing out that God's foreknowledge is not determinative. 'Just as you apply no compulsion to past events by having them in your memory, so God by His foreknowledge does not use compulsion in the case of future events'. The *coup de grâce* was given to this argument by Jonathan Edwards (1703–1758). Edwards observes that it is immaterial whether divine foreknowledge *causes* the event or no. 'Whether prescience be the thing that *makes* the event neces-sary or no, it alters not the case. Infallible foreknowledge may *prove* the necessity of the event foreknown, and yet not be the thing which *causes* the necessity. If the foreknowledge be absolute, this *proves* the event known to be necessary, or proves that it is im-possible but that the event should be, by some means or other, either by a decree, or some other way, if there be any other way; because, as was said before, it is absurd to say, that a proposition is known to be certainly and infallibly true, which may yet possibly prove not true'. This is similar to Abraham Ibn David's remarks, mentioned above, in his stricture to Maimonides, that the 'non-determinative' solution is 'not worth anything'. For Edwards *v.* 'Approaches to the Philosophy of Religion', ed. Daniel J. Bronstein and Harold M. Schulweis, Prentice-Hall, New York, 1954, pp. 308 ff. In this work a useful selection of discussions on the whole subject is given in pp. 292–366. Another selection of value is given in 'A Modern Introduction to Philosophy', ed. Paul Edwards and Arthur Pap, George Allen and Unwin, London, 1957, pp. 310–383, with a full bibliography. *Cf.* 'A Modern Introduction to Ethics', ed. Milton K. Munitz, George Allen and Unwin, London, 1958, pp. 252–432; David Elton Trueblood: 'Philosophy of Religion', Rockliff, London, 1957, pp. 275–290; W. K. Wright: 'A Student's Philosophy of Religion', rev. ed., Macmillan, New York, 1950, Part II, Chapter XXI: 'God and Human Freedom', pp. 402–427. On 'finitism' reference has been made in a previous chapter to E. S. Brightman, *v.* his 'A Philosophy of Religion', Skeffington, London, n.d., and 'The Problem of God', Abingdon Press, New York, 1930. For a treatment of the problem from the point of view of linguistic analysis *v.* 'Divine Omnipotence and Human Freedom' by Antony Flew in 'New Essays in Philosophical Theology', ed. Antony Flew and Alasdair Macintyre, SCM Press, London, 1955, pp. 144–169. *Cf.* John Hutchinson: 'Faith Reason and Existence', New York, Oxford University Press, 1956, pp. 69 ff.

*   *   *

Apart from divine foreknowledge, the tenth principle implies God's present and constant concern with the deeds of men. Unlike various ancient philosophies and the Deists, whose views we have previously noted, Judaism teaches that God has not abandoned the world He has created. There is hardly a page of the Bible in which this idea is not expressed. Terms like 'Father' and 'King' used of God serve to emphasise God's regard and love for man, His justice as evidenced in the world and in human history, and His lovingkindness and mercy. Like other concepts, that of Providence is not given a special name in either the Biblical or the Rabbinic literatures but the idea behind the term pervades the whole of those literatures. The mediaeval Jewish thinkers did use a special term for Providence – the term *hashgahah*, meaning 'special care', 'intense concern'. The word is found, in fact, with the same connotation but in verbal form, in Psalm thirty-three:

'The Lord looketh from heaven;
He beholdeth all the sons of men;
From the place of His habitation *He looketh intently* (*hishgiah*)
Upon all the inhabitants of the earth;
He that fashioneth the hearts of them all,
That considereth all their doings'

(Ps. xxxiii. 13–15).

As we have noted, the Bible is so full of the idea of divine Providence that it is almost as futile to quote passages in which this doctrine is mentioned as to quote passages in which God is mentioned. Yet a few references may be made to Biblical passages in which special attention is called to God's providential care and concern. In Psalm one hundred and thirty-nine we read:

'Thou knowest my downsitting and mine uprising,
Thou understandest my thought afar off.
Thou measurest my going about and my lying down,
And art acquainted with all my ways'

(Ps. cxxxix. 2–3).

In Psalm one hundred and four God's care is said to extend to all creatures on earth:

'All of them wait for Thee,
That Thou mayest give them their food in due season.
Thou givest it unto them, they gather it;
Thou openest Thy hand, they are satisfied with good.
Thou hidest Thy face, they vanish;
Thou withdrawest their breath, they perish,
And return to their dust.
Thou sendest forth Thy spirit, they are created;
And Thou renewest the face of the earth'

(Ps. civ. 27–30).

Similarly, in Psalm one hundred and forty-five the same theme is developed:

M

'Thou openest Thy hand,
And satisfiest every living thing with favour.
The Lord is righteous in all His ways,
And gracious in all His works.
The Lord is nigh unto all them that call upon Him,
To all that call upon Him in truth'

(Ps. cxlv. 16–18).

God's answer to Job out of the whirlwind (Job xxxviii) is
a sublime statement of God's constant creative power. In the
book of Jeremiah there is the vivid description of the potter's
wheel with its implication that man in the hands of God is like
clay in the hands of the potter (Jer. xviii). That everything is
in the hands of God is expressed in the book of Isaiah:

'I form the light, and create darkness;
I make peace, and create evil;
I am the Lord, that doeth all these things'

(Is. xlv. 7).

Whatever man plans, the book of Proverbs says, it is God
who directs his steps (Prov. xvi. 9). Man should not glory in
his own power for all power is from God (Deut. viii. 17, *Hag.*
ii. 8).

Psalm twenty-three is the classic illustration of how God's
tender care extends to those who trust in Him so that they
have no excuse to fear for He is their 'Shepherd'. Great movements of history are interpreted as God's work. Assyria is the
'rod' of God's anger (Is. x. 5); God removes kings from their
thrones and sets up others (Dan. ii. 21); He plucks up kingdoms and destroys them but repents of the evil He had thought
to do if they turn from their evil ways (Jer. xviii. 7–8); when
Israel sins he witholds the rain from them (Amos iv. 7); He
leads Israel and cares for them 'as an eagle that stirreth up her
nest' (Deut. xxxii. 11). It is abundantly clear from these and
numerous other passages that the theme of divine Providence,
with all its variations, runs right through the pages of the Bible.

The Rabbis, similarly, have this as a dominant theme in
all their thinking. As in the Bible, there is no attempt in the
Rabbinic literature to fashion a philosophical system, and it
would be practically impossible to deduce from the teachings

we have a Rabbinic 'theology' with particular reference to
Providence, but it remains true that the idea of God's constant
and permanent direction of human affairs is everywhere assumed
in the whole of the Rabbinic literature. It is because of this that
one can freely quote passages in which the theme is discussed,
even though they may be separated from each other by centuries.
The saying of one of the Rabbis that no man injures a finger
down below unless it has been decreed above that he should do
so (*Hull*. 7b) is typical of Rabbinic ideas on this subject. Everything which God does is for a good purpose (*Ber*. 60b) is a
similar typical saying and the Rabbis love to dwell on the way
in which the saints tried to live in the light of this belief.
Everything which God has made has some purpose, even though
this may not be apparent to man. Even flies, fleas and mos-
quitoes are not superfluous (*Eccl. R.* to v. 8). In the old prayer
'*Yotzer 'Or*' God is said to 'renew continually the work of
creation' (Singer's Prayer Book, p. 39). God feeds the whole
world from the horned buffalo to the brood of vermin (*A.Z.* 3b).

The mediaeval Jewish thinkers, influenced by ancient Greek
and contemporary Islamic speculation, discuss the whole
question of divine Providence in great detail, particularly the
question of whether Providence extends only to the general
(*hashgahah kelalith*) or even to the particular and the individual
(*hashgahah peratith*). We have touched on their theories in
connection with the doctrine of divine foreknowledge but here
it is fitting to record Maimonides' analysis of the different
views on Providence ('Guide', III, Chapter 17–19). Maimonides
mentions five different theories which have been held in
connection with the doctrine of Providence. The first of these
is that there is no such thing as Providence. This is the theory
of the Epicureans, according to whom chance rules all. The
second theory, attributed by Maimonides to Aristotle, is
that there is a general Providence and the universe did not come
into being by chance but that the accidents which befall individuals of species are not governed by Providence. For Aristotle
there is no difference between the falling of a leaf or stone and
the loss of a ship at sea. The third theory is that of the Islamic
Ashariyah. This is the extreme view that even the leaf which
falls does so because God has decreed that it should fall. There
is no concept of 'natural law' in this view. The wind blows and

the leaf falls both by the direct decree of God. This is an attitude of complete fatalism. There is no such thing as the *possible*. Everything is either necessary or impossible. When a person is born blind or leprous, the upholders of this theory say it is the will of God. If the justice of God in this matter is questioned the reply they give is that it is proper that God should afflict the innocent and do good to the sinner. On this view all divine commands are really meaningless since all is preordained. The fourth theory is that of the Islamic Muʿ tazila. This theory, like the previous one, holds that God is directly responsible for the falling leaf but that man has some degree of free-will so that divine commands are not meaningless. According to this view it is proper for the mouse to be torn to pieces by the cat for God will reward the mouse for its sufferings in the World to Come. The fifth theory is that of our *Torah*. There is no injustice in any of God's dealings, on this theory. Man has free-will and he is consequently capable of choosing the good and rejecting evil. The slightest pain suffered by man is a punishment for sin, the slightest good a reward for some virtuous act. Maimonides, developing this fifth theory, states that he agrees with Aristotle that there is only general, not special or individual, Providence, so far as all creatures other than man are concerned. But for man there is individual Providence because man has free-will. Thus, it is by chance that a certain spider catches a certain fly, not because God has directly decreed it. But when a ship goes down it is not because of chance, so that if the passengers and crew had stayed at home nothing would have happened to them. No man suffers or obtains pleasure of any kind unless it has been directly decreed by God. Maimonides states that there is no unequivocal statement of this theory in so many words in the earlier Jewish sources but his reading of those sources convinces him that this is the true teaching of the Jewish faith.

Other thinkers discuss the difficulty involved in the idea of man's freedom in a world governed by cause and effect (*v.* Albo *'Iqqarim*, Book IV, Chapters 1 ff.). This problem is particularly acute in the light of modern scientific theory, with its emphasis on cause and effect, and has been a major topic of discussion among modern Theists. We have noted earlier that Bahya Ibn Paqudah ('Duties of the Heart', III. 8) addresses himself to this question, rather than the more conventional one of divine foreknowledge and free-will, and accepts by an act of faith that somehow both determination and freedom are possible. As we have seen, Bahya does not attempt to explain how the two can be reconciled but believes that this is part of the mystery involved in comprehending the divine will and knowledge. If God had wished us to know the solution, or if there were any advantage to us in such knowledge, God would surely have revealed the truth to us. Albo follows Maimonides in adopting a somewhat similar view that God's knowledge is not ours.

The modern believer cannot go very far beyond this point. The emphasis in scientific thinking on such things as 'natural law', 'cause and effect', a 'closed system', does not really affect the basic problem dealt with by the mediaeval thinkers though it certainly serves to highlight the problem. It will not do for the believer to try to escape the problem by speaking, as some believers have done, of 'gaps' in our knowledge, 'gaps' through which God can be seen at work. For a God of the gaps is no God at all. The believer should rather welcome the picture of a universe obeying 'laws', proceeding in an orderly system, itself ordained by God. There is no reason for denying either the possibility of the miraculous or the efficacy of prayer for these are not to be seen as 'breaks' in the order but as part of the order. God is not bound by the laws of His own making. The system, on the Theistic view, is sufficiently flexible to allow for deviations from it. Both the natural order and the deviations all belong to God's purpose, all have their place in it. It is true that human beings cannot see fully how this interaction between the natural and the miraculous is possible but then this has long been recognised as a necessary element in the human condition.

An example may be given from the investigations of a modern historian into the past. If he is loyal to his craft the historian will exercise in his work a rigid addiction to the causes and effects he discovers. He will seek to account for all that has happened in the period under investigation by considering the forces which were operating on the characters whose lives he studies. It will not do for him, as an historian, to attempt to 'solve' difficulties by postulating that no reason can be discovered for this or that event but that God simply willed it so. It is his task as an historian to discover how God's will came into operation through the workings of the human mind and in the human situation. But as a believer he will recognise that the dimension of faith is there above and beyond the historical processes and is indicative of the divine working in and through those processes. Seen in this light the study of science and history is the study of the workings of the divine Mind. This after all was said by Maimonides long ago when he taught that the Rabbinic 'Deeds of Creation' refers to the physical sciences and the 'Deeds of the Heavenly Chariot' to metaphysics and divine Providence (*v. Yad, Hilkhoth Yesode Ha-Torah*, Chapters 1–4).

Although, to my knowledge, the passage is not quoted by any of the great mediaeval authors who deal with the question of Providence, there is a remarkable anticipation of the problem in a Talmudic passage of apparent naivety but of real depth. There (*Ber.* 10a) it is said that King Hezekiah was on his deathbed when the prophet Isaiah came to visit him and to rebuke him. Isaiah told the king that he would die because he had refused to have children. (The story is certainly the more pointed when it is realised that in the Jewish tradition Hezekiah as a scion of the house of David, was the ancestor of the Messiah). Hezekiah replied that he had seen by means of the holy spirit that the children issuing from him would be wicked. Whereupon Isaiah retorted: 'What have you to do with the secrets of the All-Merciful? You should have done what you were commanded to do, and let God do that which pleases Him'. In other words, there is a realisation that the whole scheme of human history has, in a sense, been worked out, as it were, by God right from the beginning, but this should not act as a deterrent to human endeavour. Somehow there is room for human self-determination within God's plan and His purpose for the universe so that when man acts in response to the call of duty he is not frustrating the divine purpose but helping to fulfil it.

The question we are considering has been brilliantly discussed by W. R. Matthews ('The Purpose of God', Nisbet, London, 1935, pp. 131 ff.). Matthews remarks that the Theist cannot accept the view that history has no purpose. Indeed,

such a view would make the writing of history impossible since
all historical writing can only be engaged in by a selection of the
facts in obedience to the author's aim or purpose in writing
the history. Every historian believes that something is 'going
on' in history. At the same time it cannot be argued that the
whole of human history has been pre-ordained as part of a teleological order. For one thing there is the element of chance;
the man of destiny, for example, killed by an accident. No doubt
Maimonides would retort that the 'accident' was a direct
decree of God but even if this be so it is clear that there is a
random element in human history. Matthews concludes that
Providence seems to work in the sphere of history by persuasion
and not by compulsion. What is 'going on' in human history
is the progressive creation of man.

It should be said that this idea of God's purpose finding
fulfilment through men's deeds is basic to the Jewish outlook.
We shall be obliged to consider it in detail in the chapter
on the Messianic idea. But since Judaism teaches that each
individual is precious in the eyes of God it follows that, in
the Jewish view, it would be incorrect to see the progressive
fulfilment in time of God's purpose as the sole aim of human
history. The worth of former generations is not to be seen solely
on the grounds that they prepared the way for us any more
than our worth is to be measured solely in terms of what we
will do to make the world a better place for posterity. Each
generation and each individual has a place in God's purpose.
'One generation shall laud Thy works to another, And shall
declare Thy mighty acts' (Ps. cxlv. 4). As Matthews rightly
says: 'It would be a grave misconception to regard the successive
ages of the human adventure on the earth as having no intrinsic
worth or interest but as deriving their significance solely from
the fact that they are stages in the progress towards some future
"far-off distant event" '.

Implied, indeed, in Maimonides' tenth principle is the idea
that the individual counts in himself, not as a means to an end.
God knows the deeds of *each* man, every individual is significant
in His eyes. The opinion that in the Bible, at least in its earlier
parts, the notion of individual responsibility and significance
is entirely subordinate to that of corporate responsibility,
requires considerable qualification. If the individual counted

for as little as some Bible scholars would have it, it is hard to see how so much importance became attached to the individual characters in the Bible. Every one of the early heroes and heroines, as well as the villains, is a person in his own right with his own characteristics. The following quotations from Rabbinic literature speak for themselves.

When one sees a crowd of six hundred thousand he should recite this benediction, say the Rabbis: 'Blessed is He who discerneth secrets' (*Ber.* 58a). The reason given for the benediction is that just as the face of each is different from that of the other so the mind of each is different from that of the other. Today we know that there are no two men with the same fingerprints. In a well-known passage in the *Mishnah* (*Sanh.* IV. 5) there is a discussion on the procedure to be adopted by the ancient Court of Law in warning the witnesses to a capital charge of the sacredness of human life. A man was on trial for his life and though it was their duty to testify against him, if he were guilty, they must not embark on this without a full realisation of the enormity of destroying an innocent human life. The witnesses were to be referred, says the *Mishnah*, to the Genesis story of Adam and Eve, in which all mankind is descended from one human couple. This is how the *Mishnah* puts it: 'Therefore but a single man was created in the world, to teach that if any man has caused a single soul to perish Scripture imputes it to him as though he had caused a whole world to perish; and if any man saves alive a single soul Scripture imputes it to him as though he had saved alive a whole world. Again (but a single man was created) for the sake of peace among mankind, that none should say to his fellow: "My father was greater than thy father"; also that the heretics should not say: "There are many ruling powers in heaven". Again (but a single man was created) to proclaim the greatness of the Holy One, blessed be He; for man stamps many coins with the one seal and they are all like one another; but the King of kings, the Holy One, blessed is He, has stamped every man with the seal of the first man, yet not one of them is like his fellow. Therefore every one must say, For my sake was the world created'.

No two men are alike, the birth of one man is the birth of a world, therefore every man must say, For my sake was the world created. What clearer evidence is required that while Judaism centres around a *people* it considers the individual to be of supreme importance? In another passage in the *Talmud* (*Pes.* 25b) the story is told of a man who came before Raba (299–352 C.E.) and said to him: 'The governor of my town has ordered me: "Go and kill so-and-so; and if not I will kill you" ' Raba replied: 'Let him kill you rather than that you should commit murder; what reason do you have for thinking that your blood is redder? Perhaps his blood is redder'. The same *motif* appears in the Talmudic anecdote (*Pes.* 50a) concerning the Rabbi who was transported to the next world, where he observed a 'topsy-turvy world', the insignificant on earth of great significance there, and the significant on earth, of no significance there.

*   *   *

EXCURSUS

Among the many works published recently in which there are discussions of the relationship of modern scientific theories and the doctrine of divine Providence, the following should be noted: William Temple: 'Nature, Man and God', Macmillan, London, 1940; C. A. Coulson: 'Science and Christian Belief', Oxford University Press, London, 1955; F. Sherwood Taylor: 'The Attitude of St. Thomas to Natural Science', Blackfriars, Oxford, 1944; F. R. Tennant: 'Philosophical Theology', Cambridge University Press, Vol. I, 1928, Vol. II, 1930; C. E. Raven: 'Natural Science and Christian Theology', Cambridge University Press, 1953; A. F. Smethurst: 'Modern Science and Christian Beliefs', Nisbet, London, 1955; E. L. Mascall: 'Christian Theology and Natural Science', Longmans, Green, London, 1956; Karl Heim: 'The Transformation of the Scientific World View', SCM Press, London, 1953; and: 'The World, Its Creation and Consummation', Oliver and Boyd, Edinburgh and London, 1962; Robert E. D. Clark: 'Christian Belief and Science', English Universities Press, London, 1960; R. T. Miles: 'Religion and the Scientific Outlook', George Allen and Unwin, London, 1959.

[12]

THE ELEVENTH PRINCIPLE
Reward and Punishment

MAIMONIDES' formulation of the eleventh principle reads:
'*The eleventh Principle of Faith.* That He, the exalted
one, rewards him who obeys the commands of the
Torah, and punishes him who transgresses its prohibitions.
That God's greatest reward to man is "the future world", and
that his strongest punishment is *kareth*, "cutting off". We have
already said sufficient upon this theme. The scriptural verses
in which the principle is pointed out are: "Yet now if thou wilt
forgive their sin – ; but if not, blot me out of thy book" (Ex.
xxxii. 32). And God replied to him: "Whosoever hath sinned
against me, him will I blot out of my book" (Ex. xxxii. 33).
This is a proof of what the obedient and the rebellious each
obtain. God rewards the one and punishes the other'.

The eleventh principle in the *Yigdal* formulation reads:
'He bestoweth loving kindness upon a man according to his
work; He giveth to the wicked evil according to his wickedness'.
In the '*Ani Ma'amin* formulation the principle is given as: 'I
believe with perfect faith that the Creator, blessed be His name,
rewards those that keep His commandments, and punishes
those that transgress them'.

Friedländer dealing with this principle observes: 'The
immediate reward and punishment for our conduct we receive
in the pleasure and happiness we experience in doing something
good, and in the belief and remorse we ought to feel on learning
that we have displeased the Almighty by our conduct. As a
rule, every good act leads to further good acts, and every sin
to further sins; and our Sages say therefore: "The reward of a
good act is another good act, and the punishment for a transgression is another transgression". But when we speak of the
principle of Retribution, we generally mean such reward and
punishment as is given in addition to the feeling of happiness

or unhappiness inseparable from our actions . . . The acts of Divine justice recorded in the sacred literature serve as a warning to the evil and an encouragement to the good. They are all of a material character, as only in this shape can they be perceived by man. But by no means do they exhaust all the ways of God. The Divine retribution so frequently referred to in the Law points mostly to the good or evil consequences which the conduct of the Israelites will bring upon the whole community or state, because the whole community is benefited by the virtues and injured by the misconduct of each of the members composing it; it is the duty of the authorities, by watchfulness and well-defined punishments, to prevent the spread of disobedience to the Divine Law. What other rewards or punishments await the individual in this life or after death we do not know. But there are, especially in the Psalms, numerous indications that the pious sufferer was sure that everlasting happiness would more than compensate for the absence of material and transient success in this life'.

Werblowsky formulates the principles as follows: '11. *Reward and Punishment.* The belief in individual reward and punishment is stated without explanatory details. The reference is, however, clearly not to the Biblical idea of material prosperity or misfortune in this life, nor to the belief in a national collective, justice, but to the soul as the immortal part of the individual and to its fate in the hereafter. The traditional doctrine is that most souls are purged of their sins during one year of Purgatory; thereafter they are removed to Paradise. For the Kabbalists heaven and hell were too "static" as means of reward and punishment; they merely settled accounts, as it were, but did not allow for more dynamic change. They therefore accepted the belief in *gilgul* or the transmigration of souls which they regarded as a further manifestation of God's love for his creatures. Even after death God is prepared to give the sinner a fresh start and the possibility not only to expiate and repair his sins but also to acquire merits. According to most Kabbalists three times is the maximum number for *gilgul*. As in most religions, the rather lurid descriptions of hell to be found in mediaeval texts were understood more or less literally according to the degree of sophistication or religious temperament of the believer. Modern, nineteenth-century liberal theologians tried to explain hell and purgatory away but continued, with remarkable inconsistency, to cling to the belief in an eternal blessedness in one form or another. It need hardly be pointed out that this manifestation of modern religiosity merely bespeaks a total loss of understanding of the religious dimensions of sin and guilt. Other attempts at mitigating the "crudity" of the idea of hell include its interpretation in a negative form. Hell or punishment thus means the exclusion from the positive bliss of the blessed vision'.

It is clear from the above that the eleventh principle can only be treated as part of the doctrine of the after-life. We must therefore touch upon the doctrine in our examination of the principle in this chapter. However, a more detailed consideration of the doctrine of the after-life is reserved for the chapter on the resurrection of the dead. In this chapter we shall try to see what the doctrine of reward and punishment has meant in the past and what its significance is for Jewish religion today.

There is hardly a page of the Hebrew Bible in which the doctrine of reward and punishment is not either stated explicitly or implied. It is treated as axiomatic by all the Biblical writers that God rewards those who keep His commandments and punishes those who transgress them. This is not to say that there is no awareness of difficulties inherent in the doctrine, chief among them why the righteous suffer and the wicked prosper. These difficulties are stated in the Psalms, in the books of Job and Ecclesiastes, and in other parts of Scripture, but while this certainly suggests that for the Biblical authors the question was far from simple their basic belief in retribution was not really affected. Since God is the God of justice He must give each man his just deserts. Here we can only note some of the more famous passages in the Bible which call special attention to reward and punishment. From the view of the Bible we have sketched in the earlier chapters of this book it is clear that we cannot speak of one, uniform Biblical viewpoint but rather of many points of view expressed in the collection of books we call the Bible. For all that, and in spite of differences even here, in this matter of reward and punishment there does emerge a kind of common opinion among all the Biblical writers.

Among the rewards promised in the Pentateuch for the

observance of God's laws is length of days. This is stated to
be the reward both for obedience in general (Deut. v. 30; xi. 21)
and specifically for honouring parents (Deut. v. 16) and sending
away the mother bird before taking the young (Deut. xxii. 6–7).
The relevance of this particular reward in the latter two
examples appears to be that one who has reverence for the
parents who gave him life and for all life as evidenced in the
care of the young in the animal kingdom will himself enjoy
the blessing of long life. The Rabbis, however, tend to interpret
the reward in somewhat different fashion. Honouring parents
is an elementary expression of gratitude, sending away the
mother bird involves little loss, and if even for the carrying out of
such obvious and easily performed precepts the *Torah* promises
long life how much more so for the carrying out of more difficult
and demanding precepts? (*v. Jer. Qidd.* I. 7 and *Hull.* 142a).
The fact that good people die young compelled the Rabbis to
interpret the verses as referring to the After-life, 'the world
where life is only good and where life is only long'. Thus R.
Jacob asks, what if a father sent his son to obtain some young
birds and he did so and, in addition, sent away the mother bird,
but fell down to the ground and was killed. Here after fulfilling
two precepts for which long life is promised the lad meets his
death. What becomes then of the *Torah's* promise? To which
he gives the answer that the promise finds its fulfilment in the
After-life (*Qidd.* 39b).

The whole of the book of Deuteronomy speaks of God's
love for Israel and the corollary that He wishes to reward them
for keeping His commandments but that He will not fail to
punish them if they fall short of the standards demanded. In
this book (Deut. xxviii. 15–68), as well as in the book of
Leviticus (Lev. xxvi. 14–45) occurs the *Tokhahah*, the stern
warning of utter devastation and complete downfall which
awaits a faithless Israel. Typical of Deuteronomy is the idea
of the choice before Israel: 'Behold, I set before you this day a
blessing and a curse: the blessing, if ye shall hearken unto the
commandments of the Lord your God, which I command you
this day; and the curse, if ye shall not hearken unto the commandments of the Lord your God, but turn aside out of the
way which I command you this day, to go after other gods,
which ye have not known' (Deut. xi. 26–28). In Deuteronomy,

too, is found the 'Song of Moses' with its teaching that God 'hides His face' when Israel sins (Deut. xxxii. 20), because His 'work is perfect' and 'all His ways are justice' (Deut. xxxii. 4).

From beginning to end the Hebrew Bible dwells on this theme in one form or another. After Adam and Eve had sinned their punishment was announced to them (Gen. iii. 16–19). The first murderer, Cain, is told by God of his punishment for the grievous sin he had committed (Gen. iv. 11–12). When God sees that mankind has become corrupt He resolves to destroy men by bringing a deluge but He saves Noah who is righteous (Gen. vi). And so on right through the books of the Bible the righteous are vindicated by God, the wicked punished by Him. In the first Psalm the reward of the good man is vividly depicted (Ps. i. 3) while the fate of the wicked is similarly foretold (Ps. i. 4–6). All the prophets return again and again to this theme. Amos castigates both his own people and the surrounding nations and warns them of God's stern justice (Amos i f.). In the book of Isaiah it is said that 'there is no peace for the wicked' (is. lvii. 21). Jeremiah speaks of the man who trusts in the Lord and the serene rewards that will be his (Jer. xvii. 7) although in the book of the same prophet (Jer. xii. 1) the problem of why the wicked prosper is agonis-ingly presented. Hereditary responsibility is implied in the Decalogue (Ex. xx. 5) and corporate responsibility in other parts of Scripture (e.g. Josh. vii and II Sam. xxiv) but in the book of the prophet Ezekiel (xviii) there is the famous proclamation that each man is responsible for his own deeds and that none perishes for the sins of others.

It is generally held that the real shift of emphasis from this-worldly to other-worldly sanctions for the good life took place during the Maccabean period when the 'saints' were being slaughtered in the name of their faith. In the face of such direct contradiction to the doctrine of reward and punishment here and now faith could only be maintained by seeking recompense and retribution in the After-life. The book of Daniel speaks of 'Many of them that sleep in the dust of the earth shall awake, some to everlasting life, and some to reproaches and everlasting abhorrence. And they that are wise shall shine as the brightness of the firmament; and they that turn the many to righteousness as the stars for ever and ever' (Dan. xii. 2–3). This other-

worldly sanction is entirely dominant in the whole of the
Rabbinic literature. It should, however, be noted that it is a
severe error to interpret Rabbinic Judaism as a faith which
held out no hope of happiness for the righteous here on earth. It
seems clear from the many Rabbinic statements on the question
that for the Rabbis the aim of the good life, the life of *Torah*,
was not only to equip men to enjoy everlasting bliss in the
Hereafter but to bring blessing and happiness to them here on
earth.

To attempt even to cover the whole range of Rabbinic views
on the subject of reward and punishment is virtually an impossible task. Scholars like Max Kaddushin and I. Heinemann have
in any event noted that Rabbinic thinking is 'organic' rather
than 'systematic' so that one cannot try to construct a system of
Rabbinic thought on this and kindred subjects. But typical
Rabbinic sayings on the question are to be found in the *Mishnah*,
which, because of its universal acceptance, is the best source for
authoritative Rabbinic teaching. Deeds like honouring parents,
practising benevolence, peace-making and the study of the
Torah are said to store up capital for man in the After-life while
enabling him to enjoy the interest on this capital even in this
world (*Pe'ah* I. 1). The rich man who pretends to be poor in
order to receive poor relief will, before he dies, be reduced to
poverty, while the poor man who refuses to accept poor relief
and manages with the little he has will become rich before he
dies (*Pe'ah* VIII. 9). If a man performs but a single commandment it shall be well with him and he shall have length of days
and he shall inherit the Land; but if he neglects a single
commandment it shall be ill with him and he shall not have
length of days and shall not inherit the land (*Qidd.* I. 10).
R. Nehorai said that he would set aside all crafts and teach his
son only the *Torah*, for man enjoys the reward of the *Torah* in
this world while the capital is reserved for him in the Hereafter
(*Qidd.* IV. 14). A criminal about to be executed for his crimes
was urged to confess his sins, for everyone that makes his
confession has a share in the After-life (*Sanh.* VI. 2). If the
Torah promises reward to one who refrains from eating blood
which is abhorrent to man's soul how much more will a reward
be given to one who keeps himself apart from robbery and
sexual immorality. The merit such a one gains is for himself

and for the generations of his generations to the end of all generations (*Makk.* III. 15). Not that the performance of the precepts for the sake of reward is the highest ideal. One of the earliest teachers whose views are recorded in the *Mishnah* taught that men should not serve God like slaves who minister to their master in the hope of receiving a bounty (*'Abhoth* I. 3). Another teacher said that the reward of a good deed is a good deed and the reward of a transgression a transgression (*'Abhoth* IV. 2). R. Tarfon used to say: 'If thou hast studied much in the *Torah* much reward will be given thee, and faithful is thy task-master who shall pay thee the reward of thy labour. And know that the recompense of the reward of the righteous is for the time to come (*'Abhoth* II. 16). Akabya b. Mahalaleel said that if a man wishes to avoid sin he should reflect on the fact that he will be obliged to give account and reckoning for what he does before God (*'Abhoth* III. 1). R. Jonathan said that one who fulfils the *Torah* in poverty shall in the end fulfil it in wealth; while one who neglects the *Torah* in wealth shall in the end neglect it in poverty (*'Abhoth* IV. 9). R. Joshua b. Levi said that in the Hereafter God will reward every righteous man with three hundred and ten worlds (*'Uqtzin* III. 12). One could go on quoting passages of this nature but sufficient material has been noted to provide the clearest possible evidence that the great teachers of the *Mishnah* believed in the doctrine of reward and punishment as applying both to this life and to the Hereafter.

Particular reference should be made to the Rabbinic doctrine of 'measure for measure' – *middah keneged middah* –according to which the Rabbis interpret many Scriptural passages and many of life's situations. God rewards the righteous in the exact manner in which they themselves behave and punishes the wicked in the manner in which they behave. The classical statement of the 'measure for measure' doctrine (C. G. Monte-fiore calls it the 'tit-for-tat' doctrine) is in the *Mishnah* of tractate *Sotah*. Here it is said that with 'what measure a man metes it shall be measured to him again.' A number of illustrations are given from that of the adulterous woman who is laid bare (Num. v. 11–31) because she laid herself bare, to Samson whose eyes were put out because he lusted after his eyes. Similarly because Miriam waited beside the ark of Moses the Israelites waited seven days for her (*Sot.* I. 7–9). Montefiore

finds particularly offensive the detailed application of the principle so that certain kinds of suffering are attributed to certain
kinds of sin. In the *Mishnah* (*Sabb.* II. 6) we read, for instance:
'For three transgressions do women die in childbirth: for
heedlessness of the laws of the menstruant, the Dough-offering,
and the lighting of the Sabbath lamp.' The words of George
Foot Moore ('Judaism', *op. cit.*, Vol. II, pp. 249–250) are wise
in this connection: 'It is unnecessary to expand further on this
topic; most of the opinions recorded are mere *midrash*, which is
not to be taken more seriously than it was meant. So far as they
have any other motive, it is not to serve as an inventory of
crimes and penalties, but to be a warning against transgression
or negligence . . . To whatever uncharitable judgments this led
when it was applied to others, it had its merits when a man was
led by affliction to examine himself, with a view to repentance
and amendment.' There is no doubt that the Rabbis really
believed that God works in this manner and that some suffering
is the direct result of sins and that the payment is in due proportion. But we must not think of this as a systematic proposition which is intended to cover all cases. Rabbinic thinking is
not of the systematic order at all. It is to be understood as a
response to the complex situations of life in the light of Jewish
teaching concerning God's justice. The Rabbis did not attempt
to work out a theodicy. Even when they say that this offence
meets with this punishment and this good deed with this reward
they did not mean to suggest that all this formed part of a
divine plan which man could fathom. They were not really
concerned with understanding God's ways philosophically but
with practical homilies in which the truth concerning God's
justice could be applied to life's situations.

Because of the nature of Rabbinic thinking to which we have
alluded the Rabbinic passages in which much is made of a
weighing of merits and sins are probably best understood as
spontaneous preachment rather than hard and fast rule. Thus
the Rabbis say that a man should always regard himself as
though he were half guilty and half meritorious. If he carries
out one precept he weighs himself down in the scale of merit, if
he commits one transgression he weighs himself down in the
scale of guilt. R. Eleazar b. R. Simeon said that the world as
well as the individual is weighed in the scale of merit. It is

therefore possible that an individual who performs one good
deed may weigh down by virtue of that deed the world in the
scale of merit whereas one bad deed may have the opposite
effect (*Qidd.* 40a–b). However, Maimonides, like many other
mediaeval teachers, takes the whole doctrine quite literally as
an exact description of God's dealings with the world. We must
here state Maimonides' detailed *scheme*, a scheme constructed
on the basis of passages such as the foregoing.

Maimonides begins (*Hil. Teshubhah*, III. 1) by observing
that every human being has both merits and sins. One whose
merits exceed his sins is a righteous man. One whose sins
exceed his merits is wicked. Where the two are equally balanced
he is an average man. The same applies to a country or province.
If its inhabitants possess collectively more merits than sins it is
a righteous country. If their collective sins exceed their merits
it is a wicked country. Where the two are equally balanced it is
an average country. Finally, the test is applied to the world as
a whole. If at a given period there are more virtues than vices
in the world then that age is a righteous age. If the vices exceed
the virtues the age is wicked. Where the two are equally
balanced the age is average. As soon as the sins of an individual
outweigh his merits he dies for his sins. Similarly, as soon as the
sins of a country or province outweigh its virtues it is destroyed.
And when the whole world is wicked in the sense that there are
more sins than merits the world is destroyed, as in the days of
the Deluge. Maimonides is too sharp a thinker to be content
with this simple, mechanical assessment. Obviously, it is not
true to experience that the man with a preponderance of sin
dies immediately. To cope with this difficulty Maimonides
suggests that not all sins and merits are treated in the same
fashion. It is not the quantity of the deeds which matter but
their type and quality. It is possible, for instance, for a good
man to be guilty of a single evil deed which in itself outweighs
all the good he has done, just as it is possible for a wicked man
to have performed a good deed of such high quality that it
outweighs all the evil he has done. All this can only be assessed
by God (*ibid.* III. 2). Following the Talmudic passage in
tractate *Rosh Ha-Shanah* (16b), Maimonides goes on to state
(*ibid.* III. 3) that each New Year is a time when this assessment
is made by God. If as a result of God's assessment a man

emerges as righteous he is 'sealed' in the book of life. If he emerges as wicked it is decreed that he die. If he emerges as an average person time is given to him to repent until the Day of Atonement. If he repents he is 'sealed' in the book of life. If he does not repent death is decreed for him. It is clear that Maimonides takes the Rabbinic sayings in this connection quite literally. As to the question of our experience – good people do die after the New Year and wicked people live on – Maimonides, as we have seen, refers to the quality of the deeds and this can only be known by God. The problem of experience which contradicts the Rabbinic teaching about the New Year assessment was a constant source of embarrassment to those teachers in the Middle Ages who took the Rabbinic sayings literally. Nahmanides ('Sha'ar Ha-Gemul', the last part of his 'Torath Ha-'Adam', Warsaw, 1840, p. 57) attempts to get round the difficulty in a way different from that of Maimonides. According to Nahmanides, following Rabbinic parallels, it is possible that death or suffering is decreed for the good man in order that his sufferings here on earth may atone for the sins he has committed and in this way he can enter Paradise purged of his sins. Conversely, it is possible that a wicked man whose fate it is to be condemned to Hell has, nonetheless, carried out certain good deeds for which he deserves to be rewarded here on earth. Consequently, at the New Year, God assesses whether the individual is to receive death or suffering, perhaps because he is righteous and requires the purge of suffering, or to have success and happiness, perhaps because he is wicked and requires to be rewarded here on earth. It is, of course, also possible that the good man may be rewarded here on earth with prosperity and the wicked punished here on earth. The result of all this is that the terms 'righteous', 'wicked' and 'average' are not used by the Rabbis in an absolute sense but refer to the particular New Year assize. One who, for whatever reason, is to be acquitted on the New Year is called 'righteous', since at this trial he has been acquitted. Similarly, one who, for whatever reason, is to be condemned on the New Year is called 'wicked', since at this trial he has been declared guilty.

On the basis of the foregoing Maimonides (*ibid.* III. 4) gives his famous interpretation of the command to blow the ram's horn on the New Year festival. Although, says Maimonides, it

is a divine decree that the ram's horn is blown on this festival
(and, therefore, one need not look for 'reasons') yet it hints at
the following. The stirring, shrill notes of the *Shophar* call man
to awaken from his sleep to examine his deeds and repent. It is
necessary, concludes Maimonides, to see himself as if his merits
and sins were equally balanced and the sins and merits of the
world equally balanced. One sin will cause both him and the
whole world to be outweighed in the scale of sin while one
good deed will cause both him and the whole world to be outweighed in the scale of merit. It is for this reason, he says, that
it is the custom of Jews everywhere to engage in good deeds
during the period from the New Year festival to the Day of
Atonement to a greater extent than during the rest of the year.
It is their custom, too, to rise at night and frequent the Synagogue where they offer prayer and supplication until the rise of
dawn.

The question of reward and punishment exercised the minds
of all the great mediaeval thinkers. It is hardly necessary to
consider all their views in detail but a useful summary of
these opinions is to be found in Albo's '*Sepher Ha-'Iqqarim*'
(Book IV, Chapters 29 ff., ed. Husik, Philadelphia, 1946, pp.
273 ff.). According to Albo the belief in reward and punishment
is one of the *three* principles of the Jewish faith (the others
being the existence of God and Revelation). The sayings
of the Rabbis, remarks Albo, regarding the idea of virtue
for its own sake must not be taken to mean that there is no
reward or punishment but to emphasise that the man who truly
loves God is indifferent to considerations of rewards beyond
the greatest reward of all, the privilege of serving the Creator.

Surveying the opinions held in this matter, Albo observes
that there are four such opinions. Some thinkers reject the
whole doctrine of reward and punishment. Others believe that
reward and punishment is both corporeal and spiritual, i.e.
there is physical reward and punishment in this world and
spiritual reward and punishment in the next. Others again
believe in corporeal reward and punishment but not in spiritual
reward and punishment. Finally, there are those who believe
in spiritual reward and punishment but not in corporeal
reward and punishment.

The first opinion, says Albo, would treat man as if he were

no different in essence from the animal, so that it is as absurd to reward him or punish him as it is to apportion blame and responsibility to animals. But this opinion is rejected both by the philosophers and by the followers of the *Torah*. Man is a free, responsible being and he can therefore be praised or blamed for what he does.

The second opinion denies any kind of spiritual reward and punishment in the After-life because it denies that the human soul is immortal. According to this view there can be no such thing as a soul without a body. Man is different from the animal and he deserves to be rewarded and punished in this world but nothing of him lives on after the death of his body. This was the opinion of the Sadducees who endeavoured, moreover, to prove their contention from the fact that in the Law of Moses only physical and material rewards are promised and there is no reference to spiritual reward and punishment in a life Hereafter. Albo refutes this view and states that it is at variance with the Jewish faith.

The third opinion thinks of reward and punishment as confined entirely to the Hereafter. This view is held by some of the Rabbis who say that there is no reward for the *mitzwoth* in this world (*Qidd. 39b*). Many Jewish thinkers adopt this view because they conceive of true perfection and happiness only in spiritual terms.

The fourth opinion, which for Albo is the true Jewish doctrine, is that there is reward and punishment both in this world and in the next, that reward and punishment are both corporeal and spiritual. Albo is surely right here in interpreting the opinions of the Rabbis. As we have seen, while the Rabbis certainly believed, without exception, that the final end of man is only realised in the After-life they, nonetheless, believed that the *Torah* gives happiness to man even in this world. It is this fact, as Max Kaddushin has well said, which prevents us from seeing Rabbinic Judaism as a religion of salvation. Albo quotes from the *Siphre* (to Deut. xi. 21): ' "That your days may be multiplied" – in this world; "And the days of your children" – in the times of the Messiah; "As the days of the heavens above the earth" – in the world to come'.

The question of reward and punishment is discussed with reference to the earlier sources in M. H. Luzzatto's *'Mesillath*

Yesharim' (Chapter 4, ed. Kaplan, Philadelphia, 1936, pp. 29 ff.). Luzzatto observes that people of great intelligence need no incentive to live the good life. For them it is sufficient that perfection is the only thing worth striving for and failure to attain it the greatest calamity. Those of more limited intelligence need ambition as an incentive, hence the appeals to ambition, particularly to spiritual ambition, in the Rabbinic literature. These people require the appeal to their ambition as an incentive. 'Would they in this world, which is only transient', asks Luzzatto, 'bear with equanimity the sight of one of their comrades attaining greater honour and rank than they, and acquiring domination over them, especially one of their own servants, or some beggar whom they hold in contempt? Would they not feel chagrin? Would not their very blood boil with indignation? . . . Now, since men find it unbearable to be inferior to others in a world where differences in rank are but illusory and deceiving, where inferiority is only an appearance of things and high rank futility, how can they bear to find themselves in a lower class than those whom they looked upon as their inferiors, and that in a world where differences in rank are real, and glory is eternal?' For the masses, Luzzatto goes on to say, the only incentives are reward and punishment. 'Seeing the far-reaching character of divine judgment, one cannot help being always in fear and trepidation. Who can abide the Judgment Day, and who is righteous in the presence of his Creator, whose gaze scrutinizes all things both great and small, and "who declareth unto man what is his thought?"' Luzzatto quotes a number of Rabbinic passages in which God's severe judgment is spoken of with trepidation. Even the frivolous talk between man and wife is held against him on Judgment Day (*Hag.* 5b). God is exacting with His saints even to the extent of a hair's breadth (*Yeb.* 121b). Even the Patriarchs were punished by God whenever they deviated from the right path. 'In the same manner as the Holy One, blessed be He, allows no good deed, however inconsiderable, to go unrewarded, so He allows no evil deed, however trivial, to pass unjudged and unpunished. This should be a warning to those who delude themselves with the thought that the Lord, blessed be He, does not take into account matters of small importance, and does not include them in His reckoning'. In this connection two Rabbinic passages are quoted. In the one it is said that if the evil inclination tells man to sin and God will pardon him he should not listen (*Hag.* 16a). In the other (*B.Q.* 50a) it is said that if a man argues that God is lax in the execution of judgment such a man's life will be treated loosely, i.e. such a man jeopardizes his very existence. If it be argued, continued Luzzatto, that all this fails to consider that God is merciful, the reply is that God's mercy never has the effect of setting justice aside completely. Mercy provides a respite before punishment is executed. It also has the effect of softening the punishment and it is because of God's mercy that repentance is possible. For all that, divine punishment is a stern reality. 'Though God be long-suffering, He exacts payment' (*Jer, Ta'an.* 12.1).

Thus the picture which emerges from the writings of the mediaeval teachers on reward and punishment is that these operate by inexorable laws, even though their full workings cannot be grasped by humans. God is merciful and loves His creatures but in spite of this love (the mediaeval authors would say rather because of it) He does not fail to chastise those who sin as He does not fail to reward the virtuous. All these teachers know of the higher type of religion in which good is embraced for its own sake and for the love of God, but this is never interpreted as a denial of God's strict justice and His goodness in rewarding His creatures for the good they do.

*　　*　　*

EXCURSUS

On the Rabbinic sources *v.* G. F. Moore: 'Judaism', *op. cit.*, Vol. II, Chapter IV, 'Chastisement', pp. 248–256; Montefiore and Loewe: 'A Rabbinic Anthology', *op. cit.*, Chapter VIII, pp. 202–232; A. Cohen: 'Everyman's Talmud', *op. cit.*, Chapter III, 'Reward and Punishment', VIII, pp. 110–120. On the Rabbinic doctrine of 'measure for measure' *v.* in addition to the sources quoted above, *Mishnah, 'Abhoth,* V. 8–9; *Sabb.* 32b–33a; *Ned.* 20a–b; *'Arak.* 16a. Although many thinkers in the Middle Ages reject the doctrine of the transmigration of souls – *Gilgul* – it was widely adopted by others partly as an explanation of why the innocent suffer, i.e. this was explained as due to their sins in a previous existence, *v.* Alboi *'Iqqarim, op. cit.*, Book IV, Part II, Chapter 29, p. 287 and note of Husik, and JE, Vol. XII, pp. 231–234. Saadiah, ' *'Emunoth We-*

De'oth', V. 1–8, trans. Rosenblatt, Yale University Press, 1948, pp. 205 ff., deals at length with the question of reward and punishment. According to Saadiah, following the Rabbis, the good man is punished here for the few bad deeds he has done in order to be rewarded in the After-life, the converse being true of the wicked. But some of the sufferings of the righteous are not due to sin at all but are a means of increasing their reward in the After-life because of the trials they withstood. A wicked man may be rewarded in this life in order to give him time to repent, or in order to enable him to beget good children, or to use him as tool to punish someone more wicked than he, or for the sake of his righteous relatives. Crescas, ' '*Or 'Adonai*', III, 3, 1–3, ed. Vienna, 1859, pp. 72–75, divides reward and punishment into two kinds, corporeal and spiritual. The purpose of the first kind is to enable man to achieve perfection. Thus the good man enjoys prosperity in order to make it easier for him to acquire perfection while the evil man, who rejects perfection, suffers so that he is moved out of his apathy to attain it. *Cf.* Maimonides, *Yad*, Hil. *Teshubhah*, IX, 1–2. On the views of Crescas and others *cf.* S. B. Urbach: 'The Philosophic Teachings of Rabbi Hasdai Crescas' (Heb.), Her. 1961, pp. 363–371.

*   *   *

The difficulties of moderns with regard to this principle of the faith are partly caused by the fresh interest in penal reform during the past hundred years or so. Punishment as retaliation in a vindictive sense has been largely abandoned. The value of punishment as a deterrent and for the protection of society is widely recognised. But all the stress today is on the reformatory aspects of punishment. Against such a background the whole question of reward and punishment in the theological sphere is approached in a more questioning spirit. It is true that many of the ancients refuse to allow that God is vindictive but it cannot be denied that in some of the literature of Jewish piety the impression is gained that punishment is retaliatory. Insofar as this suggests an inferior conception of the Deity it must be rejected. Furthermore, most thinkers today would be far more reticent than those of the Middle Ages in even attempting to describe the *scheme* by which God allots rewards and punishments. Nor does it seem compatible with God's justice that little children should suffer or die because of the sins of their parents. Because of all these factors the doctrine of reward and punishment is frequently interpreted nowadays in terms of natural progress rather than tit-for-tat. It is pointed out that unless religion is to become a mere sentimental feeling for the divine it must teach that evil is evil and hateful in God's eyes. A God who tolerates a Hitler would be as little deserving of worship and as little capable of being worshipped as a God who wantonly inflicts cruelty on His creatures. Hence the emphasis in present-day religious thought on wickedness as carrying the seeds of its own destruction. We prefer to leave the details to God, who in His wisdom 'searcheth all hearts', but so to conduct ourselves that all the ancient teachings on reward and punishment are still of the utmost relevance to our lives. The eleventh principle of the Jewish faith means for us that in every possible way it is *ultimately* better for us to lead the good life and reject an evil life. When we pursue evil we are at variance with God's purpose and this can never succeed in any ultimate sense. When we pursue the good we are doing God's work and for all the suffering this involves we find complete trust in the knowledge that one who is a co-partner with God is on the 'right side'.

Although the idea of collective guilt and responsibility is difficult to accept, seemingly postulating an inferior notion of the Deity and His justice, (hence the protest of Ezekiel), yet it is not entirely dead. Two aspects of the doctrine have become especially relevant in our day, in ways inconceivable to the ancients. First, the increase of communications has made the world one to an extent beyond the imagination of earlier times. For better or for worse all men today are involved with each other. A minor squabble in some obscure trouble spot can result in global war. The kind of life we choose to lead is not without its repercussions upon men everywhere. It requires neither doctrinal narrowness nor dogma incapable of proof to perceive that the sin of nuclear warfare, or even of the testing of nuclear weapons, is visited upon posterity. Secondly, modern psychological studies and researches have shown beyond doubt that the character of parents or grand-parents is in some measure transmitted to their offspring; that it is more difficult for people with bad hereditary influence and environment to lead decent, useful lives and far easier for the descendants of righteous ancestors to do so. The old Rabbinic doctrine of *zekhuth 'abhoth*, 'the merit of the fathers', is sound psychology. It is not suggested that the Rabbis anticipated twentieth-century psychology, nor is it suggested that the older doctrine was always free from the idea of a semi-magical transmission of guilt and virtue. But moderns who dismiss the whole notion are guided by sentimentality rather than clear insight into the realities of life. It can be asked, of course, why God who is good should have made us part of each other in this way. In reply all we can say is that this belongs to the wider question of why the good God tolerates evil in His creation and that however little we can understand His mysterious ways the facts are that He has made us so that for good or ill our deeds influence others. We can see only a faint glimmer of why the world should so be constituted that my deeds affect others and their deeds me, but is not this very fact a constant reminder that God wants man to belong to his fellows and possess a sense of responsibility to them? All higher religion stresses the supreme value of the individual. This is religion's great protest against totalitarianism. But an unbridled individualism, in which man lives only in and for himself, is morbid, inhuman and self-destructive. The individual who lives in himself alone is not even a true individual. There are sins of society for which the individuals who comprise that society are responsible as there are social virtues for which individuals are responsible. For all that the problem of reconciling any interpretation of corporate responsibility with God's justice is still acute and is expressed in a number of sublime Biblical passages. Two of the most important and best-known of these are Abraham's cry: 'Wilt Thou indeed sweep away the righteous with the wicked?' (Gen. xviii. 23) and Moses' and Aaron's protest: 'O God, the God of the spirits of all flesh, shall one man sin, and wilt Thou be wroth with all the congregation?' (Num. xvi. 22).

*　　　*　　　*

EXCURSUS

On the theological difficulties in the doctrine of reward and punishment *v.* Kaufmann Kohler: 'Jewish Theology', Macmillan, 1918, Chapter XLV, pp. 298–309; Morris Joseph: 'Judaism as Creed and Life', Macmillan, London, 1902, pp. 122 ff.; Solomon Schechter:

'The Doctrine of Divine Retribution in Rabbinic Literature', Studies in Judaism, First Series, Philadelphia, 1911, Meridian Books, New York, 1958, pp. 105–122; Jacob Kohn: 'The Moral Life of Man', Philosophical Library, New York, 1956, Chapter 5, pp. 145–217; Isidore Epstein: 'The Faith of Judaism', London, Soncino Press, 1954, Chapter XIII, pp. 251–313.

[13]

THE TWELFTH PRINCIPLE
The Coming of the Messiah

MAIMONIDES' statement of the twelfth principle is, in Abelson's translation, as follows: '*The twelfth Principle of Faith*. The days of the Messiah. This involves the belief and firm faith in his coming, and that we should not find him slow in coming. "Though he tarry, wait for him" (Hab. ii. 3). No date must be fixed for his appearance, neither may the scriptures be interpreted with the view of deducing the time of his coming. The Sages said (*Sanh.* 97b) "A plague on those who calculate periods" (for Messiah's appearance). We must have faith in him, honouring and loving him, and praying for him according to the degree of importance with which he is spoken of by every prophet, from Moses to Malachi. He that has any doubt about him or holds his authority in light esteem imputes falsehood to the *Torah*, which clearly promises his coming in "the chapter of Balaam" (Num. xxiii–xxiv) and in "Ye stand this day all of you before the Lord your God" (Deut. xxx. 1–10). From the general nature of this principle of faith we gather that there will be no king of Israel but from David and the descendants of Solomon exclusively. Every one who disputes the authority of this family denies God and the words of His prophets.'

In the *Yigdal* formulation the principle reads: 'He will send our anointed (our Messiah) at the end of days, to redeem them that wait for the end – His salvation'. The *'Ani Ma'amin* formulation is: 'I believe with perfect faith in the coming of the Messiah, and, though he tarry, I will wait daily for his coming'.

Friedländer describes the principle in these words: 'A special spot was selected for them (for Israel) where they should, in seclusion from the rest of the world, be trained in the true worship of God and in the practice of virtue. Zion and Jerusalem became in course of time the religious centre from which "instruction came forth and the word of the Lord". The Israelites became negligent in their mission and faithless to their holy charge. Instead of leading other nations to the true worship of God, they allowed themselves to be misled by them to idolatry; instead of living a pure life of justice and righteousness, they yielded to luxury and lust, and committed acts of injustice and oppression. They were punished. Troubles followed troubles; they lost their independence and their religious centre. The men of God, the prophets, from Moses to the last of the prophets, Malachi, foretold the catastrophe, but at the same time added words of comfort and encouragement, pointing to a distant future, when "her appointed time of trouble will be complete and her guilt atoned for"; when Israel will be restored to his land, and under the guidance of the Messiah, "the Anointed of the Lord", he will be filled with the fear of the Lord and an earnest desire to do that which is just and right . . . In the days of the Messiah all people will unite in the proclamation of the Unity of God and in His worship'.

Werblowsky puts the twelfth principle in this way: '12. *The Coming of the Messiah.* The meaning of Messianism is not explained nor is there any indication of what it is from which redemption is desired. In general it can be said that the historical national reference of the Messianic faith has been preserved in most theological writings. Redemption, whatever else it may mean, always also means the actual, physical liberation of Israel from persecution and humiliation, its return to its ancient homeland, the restoration of the Davidic dynasty, the re-building of the Temple in Jerusalem and the recognition by all nations of Israel's election and calling. Whatever the spiritual significances attached to these hopes, they were never allowed to dissolve the concrete historical core into pure spirituality. The reality of Israel's historic consciousness and, we may add, the reality of Anti-Semitism, saw to it that the spiritual or mystical "interiorizations" of Judaism never lost their touch with reality; redemption from evil and sin was always regarded as connected with the conquest of evil in the historical, that is, the political and social spheres. For some thinkers historical Messianism was a major concern; they obviously thought in terms of an historical salvation and the Kingdom of God. For others, including Maimonides, the Messianic kingdom was merely the background for the ideal contemplative life. In Lurianic Kabbalism the Messiah is no Redeemer at all in the normal sense of the word; his appearance merely signifies that Israel has achieved the great work of "restoration" and of repairing the primordial catastrophe or fall. For some of the eighteenth and nineteenth century Hasidim who sought communion with God almost to the point of the "annihilation of all being" and the ecstatic submergence of consciousness in the divine, historical categories were obviously irrelevant. Certain modern trends (democracy, socialism, Zionism) provided secular substitutes for the historical ideals of religious Messianism'.

The Messianic belief was a source of hope and comfort to Jews throughout their history. It arose without parallels in the ancient world as a unique doctrine. With no Golden Age in the past to inspire them the Hebrews dreamed of such an age in the future. Before we can even begin to discuss the relevance of the Messianic doctrine for Jews today it is necessary to examine the history of the idea and the different interpretations successive generations of Jewish thinkers have given to it. Fortunately, we are able to execute this task with a great degree of accuracy because of the many scholarly investigations of the subject, the most noteworthy of which is Joseph Klausner's 'The Messianic Idea in Israel' (translated from the third Hebrew edition by W. F. Stinespring, George Allen and Unwin, London, 1956).

It is more than a little difficult to trace the idea in its historical development since there are considerable differences of opinion among scholars on the dating of some of the sources. Nonetheless, it is possible to see how the idea developed and progressed from its earliest beginnings to its full flowering in the prophets, and then through the apocalyptic and Rabbinic literature down through the Middle Ages to the present. Indeed, there are few great Jewish ideas the study of which demonstrate as effectively as a study of Messianism the evolving character of Jewish beliefs.

The term *Mashiah* ('the anointed one') is first found, in the sense of a redeemer from bondage sent by God to His people, in the apocalyptic literature, but the idea itself is much earlier, receiving emphasis of various kinds in the writings attributed to the great prophets. In the Bible the term '*Mashiah*' refers to persons anointed with sacred oil for the purpose of high office, the king and high priest for example. From this it is but a step to the use of the term for any person for whom God has a special purpose. It is used in Deutero-Isaiah (xlv. 1) for Cyrus of Persia. Since the prophets had spoken of a great leader who would one day guide his people and mankind as a whole to the true worship of God and bring about his people's redemption from servitude and oppression it was natural for the older term to be applied to this leader. The era to be ushered in under God by this leader was one of bliss and perfection. Consequently, the later sources dwell sometimes on the era ('the days of the Messiah') in addition to the person of the Messiah. As we shall see, there has been a considerable degree of tension between the hope for the Messianic age itself and the belief that this must be brought about by a particular person. Much of the theological discussion, which has been carried into the modern period, on this article of faith centres around the question of whether the principle must be interpreted, as Maimonides interprets it, as a demand for belief in a personal Messiah or whether the belief that one day God in His wisdom will allow the Messianic age to be attained suffices for acceptance of this article of faith. Klausner (p. 9) thus describes the difference between the *Messianic expectation* and the more explicit *belief in the Messiah*. His definition of the Messianic expectation is: *The prophetic hope for the end of this age, in which there will be political freedom, moral perfection, and earthly bliss for the people of Israel in its own land, and also for the entire human race.* His definition of the belief in the Messiah is: *The prophetic hope for the end of this age, in which a strong redeemer, by his power and his spirit, will bring complete redemption, political and spiritual, to the people of Israel, and along with this, earthly bliss and moral perfection to the entire human race.*

Klausner's brilliant survey of the Messianic idea in the prophetic period helps us to see how the idea was variously interpreted by different prophets. There is clearly an evolution of the idea but this is not in a straight line from lower to higher. In the first instance the great literary prophets addressed themselves to their own day and saw their vision of the end of days against, and out of, the historical circumstances of their own time, to say nothing of the individual character of each prophetic message. Consequently, there are differing shades of emphasis among the prophets.

The idea common to all the prophets is that sin brings punishment in its wake. National sinfulness is punished on the great 'day of the Lord', the judgment day when God will make the great reckoning. At this time of judgment there will be tremendous catastrophes such as war, exile and destruction. In later literature these were called 'the birth pangs of the Messiah'. The purpose of these dire events is differently interpreted. For some of the prophets it is simply a judgment upon sinners, but for others it is a means to moral improvement. Following upon these events there will be national repentance, the Hebrew nation returning to God as in former times. This, in turn, will be followed by the redemption. According to some of the prophets (Is. xxvii. 13; Zech. ix. 14) the redemption will be heralded by the blowing of a horn, hence the references in the later literature to 'the horn of the Messiah' (*shophar shel Mashiah*). The 'remnant of Israel', the righteous few who remain faithful to the God of Israel, will be the beneficiaries of the redemption and they will comprise the sons of Judah and of Ephraim, the two kingdoms being reunited once again. Furthermore, there will be at that time an ingathering of exiles who will come back to the holy land from the four corners of the earth. While some of the prophets speak of the political power of Israel at that time the majority of the prophets see the aim of redemption as the establishment of conditions of peace and security for all nations. These nations will exalt Israel not because of its superior political power but because they recognise Israel's spiritual superiority and ethical qualities. Some of the prophets dwell on the conditions of material prosperity in the time of the redemption but others either speak little of this or ignore it altogether, dwelling instead on the spiritual nature of that age. Among the material conditions mentioned are: the abolition of war from the face of the earth, peace even in the animal kingdom (the wolf dwelling with the lamb); unusual productivity of the soil and extraordinary increase of human beings; the healing of the sick and the handicapped and the lengthening of human life. The spiritual welfare which will accompany the redemption is found in nearly all the prophets from Isaiah onwards, but it is only hinted at in Hosea and not mentioned at all in Amos.

The nature of this spiritual welfare embraces the knowledge of the Lord for all peoples (according to most of the prophets). It includes also the creation of a new heart and new spirit resulting in the doing of the right and the practice of justice and mercy. The perpetuity of the nation and of the *Torah* are also emphasised.

Ezekiel adds to the above the idea of the war against Gog, king of Magog (in the later literature 'the wars of Gog and Magog'), which will take place after the redemption (in the later literature before the redemption) and in which the Lord will win a great victory. Daniel adds the idea of personal reward and punishment. There will be a general resurrection of the dead, in which the good and pious will wake to everlasting life and the evil and unholy to reproaches and everlasting abhorrence.

On the question of a personal Messiah there are differing views among the prophets. Hosea, Isaiah, Micah, Jeremiah and Zechariah all speak of an ideal human Messiah with lofty spiritual and ethical qualities. He is not, however, a redeemer (as the Messiah became in the later literature). God alone is the redeemer and the Messiah-king is only the leader of the redeemed people who will execute justice and righteousness upon earth. In Nahum, Zephaniah, Habbakuk, Malachi, Joel and Daniel, on the other hand, there is no human Messiah at all but the Lord alone is the redeemer. In other books (Amos Ezekiel, Obadiah) there is only a collective Messiah, the kingdom of the house of David.

* * *

EXCURSUS

For the literature on the very complicated question of Messianism in the prophets *v.* Klausner, *op. cit.* and the references in his notes; JE, Vol. VIII, pp. 505 ff.; UJE, Vol. VII, pp. 499 ff.; Julius H. Greenstone: 'The Messiah Idea in Jewish History', Philadelphia, 1943. The major references in Scripture are: Gen. xii. 2–3; xxvi. 4; xxviii. 14; Ex. xix. 5–6; Num. xxiv. 17–19; Lev. xxvi. 3–45; Deut. xxviii. 1–68; xxx. 3–10; Amos v. 18–20; viii. 11–12; ix. 8–15; Hos. vi. 1–3; iii. 4–5; xiv. 6–8; Is. ix. 5 f.; xi. 1 f.; ii. 12–16;

N

xxx. 26; ii. 2–4; Micah v. 9–13; Zeph. i. 15–16; ii. 3; iii. 9–12; Jer.
iv. 9; iv. 23–27; xvi. 14–15; xxiii. 7–8; xxx. 16; xxxi. 12; xxxiii.
14–16; Ezek. xx. 32–34; xxxvi. 25–33; xxxvii. 1–14; xxxiv. 23–
24; xlvi. 2–13; Obad.; Is. xl–lxvi; Hag.; Zech.; Joel ii. 17; iii.
5; iv. 18; Mal. iii. 17–21; 22–24; Dan. ii.; vi–ix; xii; Ps. lxxxix;
cxxxii. 11–18; cii. 14–17; xii; xlvi; lxvi; lxviii; cxvii.

*   *   *

We must follow Klausner again for an account of the later
developments in the Messianic idea as reflected in the Apocrypha
and the Pseudepigrapha. Here, too, historical events naturally
influenced the developments of the idea and by this period
there existed the many Scriptural passages which formed the
basis for Messianic speculation. The poets and visionaries
whose views are found in this literature developed in particular
three ideas: the birth pangs of the Messiah, the Days of the
Messiah and the New World. Klausner points out that the
imagination of these writers embellished the original ideas
until finally there was forged a complete chain of Messianic
speculation. Although the separate links are not found in all
the books of the Apocrypha and Pseudepigrapha they are
found in the literature in a definite order and recur in this order
in the Rabbinic literature. The links are: the signs of the Messiah,
the birth pangs of the Messiah, the coming of Elijah, the trumpet
of the Messiah, the ingathering of the exiles, the reception of
proselytes, the war with Gog and Magog, the Days of the
Messiah, the renovation of the world, the Day of Judgment,
the resurrection of the dead, the World to come. Klausner
is undoubtedly right in seeing in all these speculations an
outlet for the poetic imagination of a gifted people as well as
their consolation in severe tribulations. From the Dead Sea
Scrolls we see, too, how widespread these speculations were.
Perhaps the later Rabbis frowned on these writings precisely
because of their excessive fantasies which might have unsettled
a people's faith, to say nothing of their influence on early
Christianity. Side by side with the hope of national freedom
and security we find in these works the universalistic hope of
the days when the world will be renewed and everlasting peace
among the nations be established. It is of great importance to
note, as Klausner does, that the personality of the Messiah

is not mentioned in any book of the Apocrypha. The house of David is mentioned but not the son of David. In the apocalyptic literature, on the other hand, the idea of a personal Messiah comes again into prominence.

* * *

EXCURSUS

The relevant passages in the Apocrypha and the Pseudepigrapha are: Eccl. xxxv. 22–26; xxxvi; xlv. 6–7; xlvii. 22; xlviii. 10; I Macc. ii. 27; iv. 46; II Macc. vii. 9; vii. 11; xiv. 46; xxxvi; Judith xvi. 17; Tobit xiii. 9–16; xiv. 5–7; Baruch ii. 24–35; iv. 36–v. 4; v. 5 to end; Wisdom of Solomon iii. 1–4; v. 15–16; The 'Ethiopic' Book of Enoch; Jubilees i. 8–18; xxiii; Testament of the Twelve Patriarchs: Simeon vi; Levi xvii and xxiii; Judah xxiv; Psalms of Solomon xi; xvii; xviii. 3–9; Assumption of Moses x; the Syriac Book of Baruch; IV Ezra; Biblical Antiquities iii. 10; The Sibylline Oracles. For these details, and much else in this section, I am indebted to Klausner's work.

* * *

In view of the immensity of the material, the many different views contained therein, the reaction of the Rabbinic teachers to the historical events of their time, and the general 'loose' and elastic nature of the Rabbinic Aggadah, it is extremely difficult to describe the Rabbinic view of the Messianic belief. In an oft-quoted passage (*Sanh.* 99a) the Amora R. Hillel even denied a personal Messiah: 'There shall be no Messiah for Israel, because they have already enjoyed him in the days of Hezekiah'. Rashi (*ad loc.*) observes that R. Hillel does not deny the Messianic hope as such, only the belief in a human Messiah. But the belief was, nonetheless, so deeply rooted among the Amoraim that R. Joseph, rebuking him, said: 'May God forgive R. Hillel'. Kaufmann Kohler ('Jewish Theology', pp. 384–5) is right in stating: 'At any rate, no complete system of eschatology existed during the Talmudic age, as the views of the various apocalyptic writers were influenced by the changing events of the time and the new environments, with their constant influence upon popular belief. A certain uniformity, indeed, existed in the fundamental ideas. The Messianic hope in its national character includes always the reunion of all Israel under a victorious ruler of the house of

David, who shall destroy all hostile powers and bring an era of supreme prosperity and happiness as well as peace and good-will among men. The Haggadists indulged also in dreams of the marvellous fertility of the soil of Palestine in the Messianic time, and of the resurrection of the dead in the holy land. But in Judaism such views could never become dogmas, as they did in the Church, even though they were common in both the older and younger Haggadah. These national expectations were expressed in the liturgy by the Eighteen Benedictions, composed by the founders of the Synagogue, the so-called Men of the Great Synagogue; here the prayers for "the gathering of the dispersed" and the "destruction of the kingdom of Insolence" precede those for the "rebuilding of Jerusalem and the restoration of the throne of David" '.

Among the more important passages on the Messiah in the Rabbinic literature are these. Rabbi Akiba recognised Bar Kochba as the Messiah even though he was not of the house of David and had performed no miracles (Jer. T. *Ta'an.* 4. 5, 68d, *Lam. R.* to ii. 2). The third century Babylonian teacher, Samuel, said: 'The Messianic Age does not differ from the present at all except for the fact that in that Age Israel will throw off the yoke of the nations and become free again' (*Ber.* 34b). One of the Rabbis cursed those who calculate the date of the advent of the Messiah (*Sanh.* 97b). There is a well-known statement of the conditions obtaining during the 'birth pangs of the Messiah' (*Sot.* IX. 15): 'With the foot-prints of the Messiah, insolence will increase and dearth reach its height; the vine will yield its fruit but the wine will be costly. There will be none to offer reproof, and the whole empire will be converted to heresy . . . The face of this generation is as the face of a dog; and a son does not feel ashamed before his father. On whom, then, can we rely? On our father who is in heaven'. The reference to the empire being converted to heresy probably means that the Rabbis realised that Chris-tianity would become a world religion, the religion of the world empire of Rome. The name of the Messiah was said to be one of the seven things which existed before the world was created (*Pes.* 54b). The prophet Elijah figures prominently as a herald of the Messiah ('*Ed.* VIII. 7 and freq.). Elijah will solve all problems in *Halakhah*, both those due to doubt regarding the proper decision and those where the facts are in doubt (*v. E.T.* Vol. II, pp. 6–8).

All the above ideas were, of course, known to the great scholars of the Middle Ages. But certain forces were at work in the mediaeval period which themselves helped to shape philosophical investigation into belief in the Messiah. Persecution, of which there was no lack in this period, made the Messianic hope more vivid and significant. At the same time, the rise of rationalism and philosophy at this time resulted in various attempts to interpret the whole idea in spiritual rather than material terms. Joseph Sarachek ('The Doctrine of the Messiah in Mediaeval Jewish Literature', Jewish Theological Seminary, New York, 1932) has written a detailed monograph on this theme, on which the following description relies.

First the view of Maimonides needs to be described in detail. We have repeatedly referred in this work to Maimonides' Commentary to the *Mishnah* of the tenth chapter of *Sanhedrin*, where the sage states his principles of the Jewish faith. This statement is preceded by a lengthy essay on the purpose of the good life which deserves to be described in full because of the light it throws on his conception of the Messianic age and the After-life.

There are differing views among thinkers and the ordinary people who follow them, says Maimonides, on the question of the good which man reaps from the performance of the precepts and the punishment which awaits him if he transgresses them. One class of thinkers believes that the reward for the good life consists in the enjoyment of Paradise. There are houses of precious stones, couches of silk, rivers flowing with wine, fine oils and so forth. Punishment is meted out in Hell, which is a place of fire and torture for the sufferings of the wicked. It is not difficult to quote support for this view from the writings of the Talmudic sages if these be taken literally.

Another class of thinkers prefer to dwell on the Days of the Messiah (Maimonides adds here 'may he soon appear!'). When that time comes all men will be as kings and they will inhabit the world for all eternity. Impossible things are believed to happen at that time, the earth bringing forth bread ready-baked and garments ready woven, for instance. The punishment of evil consists in being deprived of participation in these glorious events. These people, too, have no difficulty in quoting Talmudic support for these beliefs, or, at least, for some of them.

The third class prefers to interpret reward and punishment in terms of the resurrection of the dead. After a man has died he will live again to enjoy for ever the company of his family and friends and never die again. The punishment of the wicked is that they will not live again. These, too, can point to ancient teachings which tally with their view if taken literally.

The fourth group prefer to follow literally the Scriptural passages which speak of reward and punishment in terms of this life. The good will be blessed with every kind of material prosperity, fertile lands, great wealth, many children, long life, good health and so forth, while the wicked will be deprived of these.

The fifth group tries to combine all these ideas. Reward, on this view, consists of the enjoyment of the Days of the Messiah, the resurrection of the dead, the entry of the good into Paradise and their living there forever in good health. The members of this group are the largest.

In truth, Maimonides goes on to say, very few people really stop to consider the proper nature of the hoped-for good in the Hereafter, contenting themselves with trivial questions such as whether the dead will rise from their graves naked or with clothes, whether there will be neither rich nor poor in the Messianic age, or whether there will still be the distinctions between the weak and the strong.

Actually, the whole approach of these groups is faulty in the extreme. A child of tender years, brought to his teacher who wishes to teach the *Torah* to him, will require encouragements of various kinds before he becomes old enough and mature enough to appreciate that the study of the *Torah* is a good, indeed the greatest good, in itself. The teacher, at first, is obliged to bribe him with gifts of nuts and sweets to study at all. The study itself, at first, is a weariness of the flesh but the child submits to it in order to be rewarded with the sweet he really desires. As the child grows older sweets no longer tempt him and the teacher must then promise him things more in accordance with his growing mind, new shoes and clothes for example. Later on only monetary gifts will tempt him and he

studies in order to win money prizes the teacher offers him.
At a still later stage only fame will satisfy him and he studies
in order to win renown as a great scholar. But all this is due to
the weakness of man's character. The ideal is the good life for
its own sake. Man should not study the *Torah* for the sake of
some other good but because learning is the greatest good of all
even though, at first, it is no doubt necessary to utilize the
ulterior motive. No motive other than the desire to serve God
is, in truth, adequate from the ideal point of view. The prototype
of the ideal Jew is Abraham who is described as 'a server of
God from motives of pure love'.

However, man's nature being what it is, few can be expected
to rise to the heights of an Abraham. For most people the self-
seeking motive always predominates. Hence the Sages permit
the 'common people' to perform good deeds in expectation
of reward and to refrain from evil deeds through fear of punishment. In this way truth is gradually comprehended and the
higher aim can come into its own.

Having made these preliminary remarks, Maimonides goes
on to discuss the differing attitudes men have towards the
words of the Talmudic sages. There are three classes here.
The first, and the largest, are those who take everything the
Sages say in a quite literal fashion without giving any thought
to the question of interpretation. Since the members of this
group have no science and little knowledge they believe anything is possible and see nothing incongruous in taking literally
the most outrageous statements. These men really deserve
our pity. They imagine that they are honouring the Sages by
thus deferring to everything they say, without realising that by
failing to apply methods of interpretation to the wisdom of the
Sages they are actually reducing the latter to their own low
level of comprehension.

The second group similarly takes the words of the Sages
literally only to scorn them. These men, philosophers and great
sages in their own esteem, do not hesitate to criticise the Talmudic Sages for what in their opinion are ridiculous opinions.
Their failure to appreciate the deep wisdom of the Sages is due
to their lack of training in the appropriate metaphors to be
used in theological discourse, which prevents them from
penetrating to the true meaning of the Talmudic passages.

The third group refuses to take the words of the Sages literally but realises that these words have an inner and outer meaning and that they contain the profoundest ideas. Such ideas are best expressed by means of the parable, just as the wise king, Solomon, whose work is divinely inspired, teaches by means of the parable. The Rabbis themselves interpreted Scriptural passages as parables, the book of Job, for instance. The reader of his work, concludes Maimonides, who belongs to this third class, will not fail to gain insight into the true meaning of those Rabbinic passages which on the surface appear to be contrary to reason.

We are now in a position, the author observes, to delve deeper into the spiritual content behind the materialistic images of the After-life employed by the Rabbis, since these are really profound parables and are not to be taken literally. Just as a blind man is incapable of forming any adequate idea of colours, bodies cannot comprehend the delights of the soul. We live in a material world and the only pleasure we can grasp, except after deep reflection, is material. Angels and similar spiritual beings, on the other hand, can have no conception of material pleasures and their delight is spiritual. When the pious reach, after death, the spiritual state of the angels they will no longer have any desire for material pleasures but will delight forever in spiritual bliss. They will have as little desire to return to a longing for material satisfactions as a king would wish to divest himself of his royal insignia to play childish games. Even in this world many men prefer to give up mere bodily pleasures in favour of those which partake of a more spiritual nature, the acquisition of fame and honour, for instance. The delights of the righteous in Heaven can only be explained to us in the flesh by means of the parable. Thus we find the Sages (*Ber.* 17a) saying: 'In the world to come there will be no eating and no drinking, no washing and no anointing and no marriage; but only the righteous sitting with crowns on their heads enjoying the splendour of the *Shekhinah*'. This signifies that the soul will be preserved in the intellectual sphere to comprehend the Creator, which is the great bliss of the soul. The punishment of evil consists in the soul being 'cut off', namely the soul of the wicked will perish and fail to attain durability. Those souls which reject the truth while in the body are prevented from participation in the spiritual bliss the righteous enjoy.

If this is the true meaning of reward and punishment, that the souls of the righteous enjoy the spiritual bliss of God's presence forever and that the wicked are deprived of it, what is the meaning of the numerous passages in the Scriptures and the works of the Rabbis where apparently different views of the hoped-for good are described? The promises and threats of the Pentateuch have to be understood not as rewards and punishments but as aids and hindrances to the living of the good life. The good man is promised that if he keeps God's laws God will remove bodily sickness and poverty from his life so that he will be better able to serve God. The wicked will be visited with bodily ailments and troubles so that he will not be able to serve God, since this is the way he has chosen for himself. This is what the Rabbis mean when they say ('*Abhoth* IV. 2): 'The recompense of a precept is a precept, and the recompense of a transgression is transgression'.

Consistent with his view that the bliss of the Hereafter is purely spiritual and the punishment deprivation of this bliss, Maimonides goes on to locate the Garden of Eden and Hell as not in the life to come but in this world. The Garden of Eden is a fertile spot *on this earth*, the location of which will one day be disclosed to the righteous. Similarly, Hell is a place on this earth set aside for the physical punishment of the wicked. The Resurrection of the Dead is one of the cardinal doctrines of the Jewish faith. He who does not believe in it has no religion. But it is reserved only for the righteous. Maimonides is more than a little ambiguous here since he does not state how the Resurrection of the Dead differs, if it does differ, from the spiritual bliss in the Hereafter which in his view is the true reward of the righteous. Cryptically enough Maimonides says here: 'And know that man is bound to die and become dissolved into his component parts'. In fact, even in his lifetime, Maimonides was accused of denying a physical resurrection of the dead and equating the doctrine with that of the immortality of the soul.

Maimonides now turns to the doctrine of the Messiah in the light of all he has said before. There will be no difference between the present and the Messianic Age except that in the Days of the Messiah Israel will be free in its own land,

the Holy Land, and no longer subject to the nations. The king
who will reign at that time will be the Messiah, with Zion as
his capital. The fame of this king will be greater than that
of Solomon. God will destroy whoever rises against him.
However, even though conditions will not be very different
from now it will be far easier then for man to earn his living
and he will therefore have much more leisure time for the
pursuit of God. This is how the references in the Rabbinic
literature to ready-cooked bread and so forth being available
in the Messianic Age are to be understood. Wars will cease
and knowledge will increase. 'For the earth shall be full of the
knowledge of God' (Is. xi. 9). Thus whoever is privileged to
live in that age will be aided immeasurably in attaining true
knowledge and perfection which equip man to enjoy the spiritual
bliss of the Heareafter. The Messiah, being mortal, will die and
his descendants will reign in his stead. The kingdom of the
Messiah will endure for a very long time and men will enjoy
a much longer life than they do in the present age since it is
sorrow, toil and trouble which shorten man's days. The Sages
and prophets did not look forward to the Messianic Age in
order to enjoy the good things of this world but only so as to
have the ease and leisure required for complete devotion to
the acquisition of the knowledge of God.

It can be seen from the above that for Maimonides the whole
Messianic idea is to be interpreted in naturalistic rather than
supernaturalistic terms. There will still be death in that age,
all men will not be equal, and man will still be obliged to earn
his livelihood. However, life will be both longer and easier
than it is at present and this will enable men to attain to a far
greater knowledge of God. The aim of life is not the attainment of the Messianic Age but the spiritual bliss of the soul
in the Hereafter. In his great Code, Maimonides repeats
these ideas, referring once again to the naturalistic aspects of
Messianism and our inability to grasp all its details. 'Altogether the sequence in which these things will transpire and
their details are not cardinal articles of the faith, and a person
should not occupy himself with Aggadic matters nor concern
himself with such as these or similar to them' (*Hil. Mel.* XII.
2).

Opinion during the Middle Ages is divided between those

thinkers who prefer to interpret the Messianic hope chiefly in
naturalistic terms, like Maimonides, and those who dwell on
the supernatural events. Saadiah Gaon belongs to the second
group. Nahmanides and, at a later period, Don Isaac Abarbanel,
also dwell at length on the marvels which will take place at
that time. Unlike Maimonides these thinkers felt that it was
possible for man to know in some detail the exact nature of the
Messianic Age, this knowledge being obtained from the
Talmudic and Midrashic passages on the Messiah which they
were prepared to take in a far more literal fashion than Maimonides was prepared to do. Hasdai Crescas and Joseph Albo, on
the other hand, challenged Maimonides' formulation of the
belief in the Messiah as a cardinal doctrine of the Jewish faith.
It was, indeed, for these thinkers, too, an important Jewish
belief but was not to be considered as a fundamental article
of the faith. Despite Talmudic warnings against calculating
the 'end', many of the mediaeval thinkers did try to fathom,
on the basis of Scriptural passages, the date of the advent of the
Messiah. These attempts continued down to the present
although the rise of various false Messiahs and the subsequent
dashing of Jewish Messianic hopes caused Rabbinic authorities
to frown on this kind of speculation. In reaction against the
Christian claim most of the mediaeval thinkers are careful
to point out that the Messiah has no divine powers. He is a
human being, although God may perform miracles on his
behalf and to substantiate his claims.

The Qabbalists have their own version of the Messianic
drama. In Lurianic *Qabbalah* the whole idea is closely bound up
with the doctrine of the divine 'sparks'. Very briefly, the
doctrine holds that at the time of Creation the divine light was
too powerful for finite things to endure in its presence. The
'vessels' or forms which were created to endow finite things
with existence were broken. As a result of this cosmic flaw
there are divine 'sparks' hidden in all things. These have to
be restored to their source before the work of redemption
becomes completed. Redemption thus means a restoration
of pristine harmony in the whole of God's creation. Every
deed of man performed in purity and with devotion to God has
the effect of re-claiming these sparks. Every such deed helps
to bring the Messiah a little nearer. Soon after the Expulsion

from Spain, the Qabbalists engaged in various exercises, chiefly of a severely ascetic nature, with the avowed aim of reclaiming the 'sparks' and bringing the Messiah. On the basis of the Qabbalistic ideas it was said that even in the divine realm there was an imbalance produced by man's sins. It was the task of redemption to restore the divine harmony. The older Rabbinic references to the *Shekhinah*, the Divine Presence, being in exile were interpreted to mean that God Himself was, as it were, in exile and that the true aim of the redemption was to restore the *Shekhinah* to its Source. These ideas, bordering on the dualistic, as we have seen, are obviously dangerous. It is no accident, as Professor Scholem has pointed out, that some of the followers of Shabbethai Zewi, the false Messiah of Smyrna, continued to believe in him even after his apostasy to Islam. For it was but a step from the idea of the divine 'sparks' in neutral things to the idea that these were to be found even in the dark and demonic side of existence, so that the Messiah could descend even into evil in order to reclaim the 'sparks'. Scholem suggests that ideas such as these produced a wave of anti-nomianism in the Jewish world and that it is not too fantastic to see their results in modern times in movements such as Reform Judaism.

*   *   *

EXCURSUS

For the Qabbalistic ideas of Messianism *v.* Scholem's work, currently being issued, on Shabbethai Zewi and his 'Major Trends in Jewish Mysticism', 3rd ed., Thames and Hudson, London, 1955, Index 'Messiah'. The major mediaeval sources, in addition to Maimonides, are: Saadiah: *' 'Emunoth We-De'oth'*, treatise VIII, ed. Rosenblatt, Yale University Press, 1948, pp. 290 ff.; Crescas: *'Or 'Adonai'*, Treatise III, 8, Chapters 1–3, 3ed. Vienna, 1959, pp. 81a–82b; Albo: *'Sepher Ha-'Iqqarim'*, Book I, Chapter 1, ed. Husik, Philadelphia, 1946, pp. 43–48; Abarbanel: *'Mayene Ha-Yeshua' '*, Amsterdam, 1647; *'Mashmia' Yeshua' '*, 1644, *'Yeshu'oth Meshiho'*, ed. Konigsberg, 1860.

*   *   *

In modern times the Messianic doctrine, so deeply rooted in Jewish thought and tradition, has received new interpretations, some of them extremely provocative of dissent and religious strife. This applies in particular to the Reform interpretations of the idea and the Zionist claim. Both of these were felt by their upholders to be legitimate readings of Messianism in the light of present-day conditions and by their opponents to be betrayals of the old Messianic hope. Reform Judaism in the last century tended to interpret the Emancipation of the Jew and new liberalism in the Western world which brought it about, as the first step towards the realisation of the Messianic dream. But if the dream were to be realised, the early Reformers held, it was necessary for Jews to discard the particularistic elements in it. No longer should the Jew yearn for a restoration in Palestine but he should welcome Germany or France or America or England as his Zion and their respective political leaders, who were guided by liberal ideas of freedom for all, as his Messiah. The story of how, in obedience to the new ideas, all references to a physical return to the ancient homeland were removed from the liturgy, is well-known. Zionism, on the other hand, saw the return to Palestine as the Jewish homeland as the legitimate conclusion to be drawn both from the ancient hopes and prayers and the realities of the unnatural life of the Jews in Western lands. Many religious Jews, however, had by this time become too firmly attached to the old idea of a divine intervention in human affairs to accept a modern political movement as a substitute for the Messianic hope or even as the beginning of its realisation. True, there were religious Zionists who saw nothing irreligious in the political activities of Herzl, Nordau and the other Zionist leaders. These men had no great difficulty in pointing to the well-established principle that God helps those who help themselves. As well consider it irreligious, they argued, for man to seek a livelihood for himself. For all that, even with the establishment of the State of Israel, the debate continues. Most Jews today view the emergence of the State of Israel with joy and welcome it as solving the age-old problems of Jewish homelessness. But, at the most, religious Jews are prepared to see in the emergence of the new State the 'beginning of the Redemption' (' *'Ashalta De-Ge'ulah'*), a term used frequently nowadays. Here is the place to consider in somewhat greater detail the attitude of both Reform and Zionism towards the Messianic hope.

At the second Rabbinical Conference of the Reform Rabbis, held at Frankfort in 1845, Einhorn put forward the view, later to be germinal in Reform thinking, that the dispersion among the nations was not to be seen as a punishment for sin but as a golden opportunity for allowing the Jewish ideal to gain adherents among the nations of the world. This was the doctrine of the 'mission of Israel' which saw the Diaspora not as *Galuth*, 'Exile', but as the prerequisite of Messianism. In the United States of America similar views obtained in Reform Judaism. At the Philadelphia Reform Conference in 1869 various principles were adopted and were accepted at the Pittsburgh Conference in 1885. The principles regarding the Messiah in the so-called 'Pittsburgh Platform' read: 'We recognise in the modern era of universal culture of heart and intellect the approaching of the realisation of Israel's great Messianic hope for the establishment of the kingdom of truth, justice and peace among all men. We consider ourselves no longer a nation, but a religious community, and therefore expect neither a return to Palestine, nor a sacrificial worship under the sons of Aaron, nor the restoration of any of the laws concerning the Jewish state'.

In 1937 a declaration entitled 'Guiding Principles of Reform Judaism' was adopted at a Conference of Reform Rabbis in Columbus, Ohio, to replace the 'Pittsburgh Platform'. It is interesting to see a considerable modification of the 'Pittsburgh Platform' in this latter statement on the question of the Messianic hope. Some Reform Rabbis have been among the most prominent workers for the Zionist ideal and the later statement no doubt reflects their influence. The section dealing with the Messianic question reads: 'In all lands where our people live, they assume and seek to share loyally the full duties and responsibilities of citizenship and to create seats of Jewish knowledge and religion. In the rehabilitation of Palestine, the land hallowed by memories and hopes, we behold the promise of renewed life for many of our brethren. We affirm the obligation of all Jewry to aid in its upbuilding as a Jewish homeland by endeavouring to make it not only a haven of refuge for the oppressed but also a center of Jewish culture and spiritual life. Throughout the ages it has been Israel's mission to witness to the Divine in the face of every form of paganism and materialism. We regard it as our historic task to co-operate with all men in the establishment of the kingdom of God, of universal brotherhood, justice, truth and peace on earth. This is our Messianic goal'.

It is clear from the above that while modern Reform does not give up the purely nationalistic aspects of the Messianic hope it does abandon the supernaturalism associated with it as well as the doctrine of a personal Messiah.

With regard to Zionism the position is more complicated. Non-religious Zionists obviously adopted the naturalistic approach even if they chose to interpret the Zionist idea in Messianic terms. On the whole, religious Zionists looked upon the movement as the harbinger of the Messiah and in no sense a substitute for his coming. For these men the older Messianic hope prevailed in all its supernaturalism, including the doctrine of a personal Messiah. The re-settlement of the Jews in their ancient homeland was seen as a necessary preliminary to divine intervention of a direct kind. This is not to say, of course, that religious Zionists failed to see the hand of God in the Zionist revival and, later, in the events which led to the establishment of the State of Israel. It was common, in the early days of the State, for Jews to speak of the *miracles* which God had wrought for His people in causing the new State to come into being. For the late Chief Rabbi of Palestine, Rabbi A. I. Kook, even the non-religious and the anti-religious members of the *kibbutzim* in Palestine were doing God's work without knowing it. His great and tender love for them and his persistent refusal to accept criticism of them has to be understood against the background of his religious philosophy in which they were paving the way for the Messiah. Rabbi Kook's ideas were, in fact, shared by many religious Zionists. In the year 1836

Rabbi Hirsch Kalischer, a pioneer of religious Zionism, wrote, in a letter to Anselm Mayer Rothschild: 'Let no one imagine that the Messiah will appear suddenly, and, amid miracles and wonders, lead the Israelites to their ancient inheritance. The beginning of the redemption will be in a natural way, by the desire of the Jews to settle in Palestine and the willingness of the nations to help them in this work. After many Jews have settled in Palestine, and Jerusalem has been rebuilt, the Temple re-established, and the "sacrifices are for a sweet savour to the Lord", then will God show them all the miracles in accordance with the description given by the prophets and sages. First a man will appear endowed with great natural abilities, who will bring about, in a natural way, the settlement of Palestine by the Jews, then God will send His prophet and His anointed king'.

For Kalischer and the other religious Zionists there was not the slightest denial of the older Messianic hope. These men differed from their religious opponents only in seeing a natural beginning to the work of redemption. But for their opponents, who numbered some of the most distinguished Eastern European Rabbis, even this concession to naturalism was tantamount to heresy. In the literature of the period there are frequent accusations that Zionism is irreligious because it denies the twelfth principle of Maimonides' Creed.

Having sketched the history of the Messianic idea, we now turn to the consideration of its implications for religious Jews today. It would be too much to expect, in view of the divergent opinions in the classical sources on the nature of the Messianic age, for anything like a uniform attitude among religious Jews. There is unanimity among Jews that the Messianic age has not yet dawned. But how is the hoped-for event to be understood? Does it mean a new world order under God? Does it involve the belief in a personal Messiah? Will the Temple be rebuilt and sacrifices offered? Most modern Jews prefer to interpret the Messianic hope in naturalistic terms, abandoning the belief in a personal Messiah, the restoration of the sacrificial system and, to a greater or lesser degree, the idea of direct divine intervention. Traditionalists, on the other hand, still look forward to all of these though, in the nature of the case, the details of how, when and in what way the new age will dawn are left undefined.

It is interesting to consider the views of modern religious thinkers on this question. Morris Joseph ('Judaism as Creed and Life', Chapter X, pp. 150–173) is typical of the 'middle-of-the-road' approach at the beginning of this century. Joseph quotes the '*Alenu*' prayer, recited at every Jewish service, as evidence of what the Messianic hope really means to Jews: 'O speed the day when Thy glory and might shall be manifested, when Thy kingdom shall be firmly established upon earth, when all mankind shall call on Thy name, and every sinner turn to Thee. Then all the inhabitants of the world shall recognise and know that unto Thee every knee must bend, to Thee every tongue sware fealty. Before Thee, O Lord our God, they shall fall prostrate, and to Thy name they shall give glory. They will all take upon themselves the yoke of Thy kingdom, and to all eternity wilt Thou gloriously reign. For so the Law declares "the Lord shall reign for ever and ever" (Ex. xv. 18); and further it is written "the Lord shall be King over all the earth; in that day shall the Lord be One and His name one" (Zech. xiv. 9)'. It follows from this prayer and similar Jewish sources, remarks Joseph, that the limit of the Jew's outlook for the Messianic age is the universal acceptance of 'the beautiful truths about God and duty which the great souls of his race have conceived and cherished'. But the particularistic part of Judaism, the rites and ceremonies, are for the Jews alone and it is even possible that once the world accepts the universalistic aspects of Jewish teaching these will no longer be necessary even for Jews! For Joseph the Messianic age really denotes the acceptance of Theism as a universal religion. 'We look forward to the world's acceptance of our creed, of our Theism, of those great and simple truths about God and goodness which Israel has preserved with unfaltering fidelity through the ages. God, One, a Spirit, the universal Father; man, heavenly in origin, free, responsible, endowed with the power of lifting himself to God in prayer and purity without extraneous aid – these are the essential truths of Judaism viewed on its universalistic side. They are truths as eternal as God Himself. And it is this kernel of our religion to which we refer when we speak of the triumph of Judaism in the coming time'.

It would be difficult to find a statement of what Jewish Messianism means for modern Jews more thoroughly imbued than this with the Victorian idea of progress. Joseph obviously does not believe that the Golden Age to which he looks forward will be brought about by an act or acts of direct divine intervention but by the gradual realisation of the truth through better education and improved social conditions. 'The world', he holds, 'is progressive; mankind is slowly but surely marching on to a happier time of faith and goodness, when men "shall not hurt nor destroy: for the earth shall be full of the knowledge of the Lord, as the waters cover the sea" (Is. xi. 9)'. There is no need to refer to the terrible events of the first half of the twentieth century which have completely shattered such optimism. In an age which has witnessed the suffering our age has, the kind of optimism as to mankind's future evinced by Joseph sounds incredibly hollow. Joseph recognises that there are many Jews who believe in the Messianic hope in its older interpretation. 'If, then, we meet with Jews who believe in the Return, in national revival, in a personal Messiah, let no one venture to say dogmatically that they are wrong'. But he goes on to say that there are many Jews who cannot believe in the Restoration of the Jewish State and they hold that such an event 'would impede rather than promote the fulfilment of the great purpose for which Israel exists'. It would be unfair to belittle Joseph and those who thought like him because of our present knowledge of what has actually transpired. But the State of Israel is a reality and enjoys the good-will of all Jews. This tremendous fact has to be taken into account in any fresh interpretation of Messianism. Joseph does, however, conclude that the whole question of a personal Messiah and of national restoration is an open question on which there can be more than one point of view. It is the Messianic idea that is one of the essentials of the Jewish Creed. 'If

there is no Golden Age in store for the world, which the Jew
is to bring nearer by his belief and his example, if Israel is
never to behold the triumph of the great principles to which
he has borne such pathetic witness, then Judaism is in vain.
To despair of that triumph is to confess that Judaism has no
purpose to fulfil in God's scheme. It is to deny its truth. If
the dogma of the Divine Unity is the foundation of our religion,
the Messianic Idea is its coping-stone'.

A more modern statement of the 'middle-of-the-road'
position on this matter is that of Israel H. Levinthal ('Judaism,
An Analysis and an Interpretation', Funk and Wagnalls, New
York, 1935, Chapters XI and XII, pp. 177–206). Levinthal
believes that the one movement in modern Jewish life which
remains true to the fundamental ideas of the Messianic hope
is Zionism. Much of the success of Zionism in capturing
the hearts and minds of the Jewish masses is due, according
to this author, to the inherent passion for the Messianic ideal.
'Zionism, thus, may be regarded as the modern garb of the old
Messianic hope, which kept the Jew alive throughout the ages
past, giving him today a fresh impetus and a new will to live
for a better day that is certain to come. It, too, has the two-
fold function preached by the Prophets. It aims to restore the
Jew to his national life in his native land, Palestine; it aims,
too, through a regenerated Israel, to help bring about the
regeneration of all mankind'. Levinthal concludes with a
quotation from Hermann Cohen: 'If the Jewish religion had
done nothing more for mankind than proclaim the Messianic
idea of the Old Testament Prophets, it could have claimed to
be the bed-rock of all the world's ethical culture!'.

Thus, for Levinthal, the meaning of the belief in the Messiah
for the modern Jew is a hope compounded of modern Zionism
and the universalistic ideals of the prophets. Through Palestine
as a national home for the Jew the Jewish ideals of the fatherhood
of God and the brotherhood of man will eventually win over all
mankind. But Levinthal, too, does not appear to think of a
direct divine intervention in order to bring about this state
of affairs. If he believes that the signs of the times give evidence
that this will come about in a purely natural way the obvious
reply is that the events of *our* time give us no such assurance.

Among Orthodox thinkers Dr. J. H. Hertz deals with the

question of the Messiah in his Commentary to the Prayer Book
(p. 254). Hertz observes: 'To the overwhelming majority of
the House of Israel in every generation, the Messianic Hope
has meant the belief in the coming of a Messiah (lit. "the
Anointed One") – an exalted Personality, upon whom shall
rest the spirit of the Lord. He will restore the glories of Israel
in Israel's ancient land. In his days, the people will unite in
acknowledging the unity of God, and there will be cessation
of warfare and the spread of freedom and righteousness over all
the earth. In no sense, however, will he have a hand in the
forgiveness of sins. He is but a mortal leader who, through the
restoration of Israel, will usher in the regeneration of mankind'.
But Dr. Hertz does not tell us whether this 'majority' view is
his own. Indeed, in this very comment he goes on to say:
'Some have held that Israel himself is the Messiah, God's
chosen and suffering Servant among the nations. The later
Mystics added that each Israelite was an atom, a spark, of the
Messiah; and that it was the Jew's most sacred duty to save that
spark from extinction, and fan it into a flame of holiness and
righteousness'. Is the significance of this last passage that the
Jew can please himself whether to follow the 'majority' view?
Dr. Hertz does not enlighten us.

Similarly ambiguous is Dr. I. Epstein ('The Faith of Judaism',
Soncino Press, London, 1954, Chapter XV, pp. 314–359).
Epstein remarks: 'The Messianic age will be ushered in by a
descendant of the Davidic Dynasty, whose triumphs in the
work of peace will be on earth, rather than in heaven. But this
personage is not essential to Messianism; nor is he a supernatural
or divine being, having a share in the forgiveness of sin; much
less is he to be confused with God. Indeed, so concerned was
Judaism lest such confusion should arise, that one Talmudic
teacher went so far as to deny the coming of a personal Messiah,
asserting that God Himself would come to redeem His people.
At the highest, the Messiah is but a mortal leader who will
be instrumental in fully rehabilitating Israel in their ancient
homeland and, through a restored Israel, bring about a regeneration of humanity'. Epstein gives as his source Albo's ' 'Iqqarim',
quoted earlier, but it is certain that Albo does not deny that
there is a personal Messiah, only that the belief is not a fundamental principle of Judaism, as Maimonides would have it.

To say that the belief in a personal Messiah is not a *fundamental* principle of Judaism (in Albo's view a fundamental principle is one without which a religion is inconceivable which, as he says, is true of Christian Messianism but not of Jewish) is very different from saying that the belief is not *'essential'*. In any event Dr. Epstein does not tell us about his own conception of the Messianic age, how it will come about and whether the naturalistic or supernaturalistic aspects are to be stressed. There is a quotation from the Babylonian *Talmud* (*Nidd.* 61b) to the effect that there will be no 'precepts' in the future, which Epstein takes to mean that 'the aim of Messianism itself is, in Jewish interpretation, to makes precepts obsolete'. Epstein goes on to quote tellingly from the letters of Rabbi Kook (' *'Iggeroth Rayah'*, Jer. 1943, p. 173) that by no stretch of the imagination can the world today be said to have reached these Messianic heights. 'It is sheer self-deception to imagine that in our times of general disintegration and decay, the world has risen morally to that height that it can dispense with the spiritual aid which the practical observances provide'.

It is refreshing to find a modern religious thinker facing the real challenge of Jewish Messianism for Jews today, refusing to be content with what the doctrine meant in the past but inquiring seriously what it means now. Steven S. Schwarzschild's article 'The Personal Messiah – Towards the Restoration of a Discarded Doctrine' ('Judaism', Vol. V. 1956, pp. 123–135) is an excellent attempt, including a defence of the personal Messiah, at defining the belief in the Messiah as a valid belief for present-day Jews to hold.

Schwarzschild argues that there are three reasons why nineteenth-century Jewish liberalism was moved to transform the doctrine of the personal Messiah into the doctrine of the Messianic age. The first was the marked anti-nationalistic tendency of nineteenth-century Jewish thought. But Schwarzschild argues that this is really a *non sequitur*. Basically the nationalistic aspects of Messianism are not logically connected with the belief in a personal Messiah and there is no reason for discarding the belief even if the Messianic doctrine is interpreted in more universalistic terms. The second reason is the suspicion in nineteenth-century thought of the idea of the miraculous. But if this is the objection it is just as much a miracle for the new age to dawn through the work of many men as through the efforts of one man. (However, the liberal theologians of the nineteenth century would probably have argued that mankind was progressing towards the Golden Age by means of quite natural processes whereas the belief in a personal Messiah sent by God does partake of the miraculous and the supernatural). In any event, thinkers like Maimonides have described the belief in a personal Messiah in non-miraculous terms. (This, too, is not entirely correct as we have seen earlier in our investigation of Maimonides' views). Finally, there was a marked reaction against the Christian doctrine but, argues Schwarzschild, this is only a reason for denying the Messiah any divine powers, not for denying his very existence. The third reason was, as we have noted, the Victorian belief in progress which made the direct intervention of God unnecessary. This optimism is no longer shared by the majority of thinking men. Schwarzschild concludes: 'If, then, we must discard the third main reason which the liberals of the nineteenth century proffered for the abolition of the concept of the personal Messiah, literally not one of their arguments has been found to withstand critical investigation. Their anti-nationalism has been repudiated by Jewish history; their anti-miraculousness has been refuted by the necessities of their own position, not to speak of the views of others; their optimism has been repudiated by general history'. In the absence, therefore, of any sound reason for denying the traditional doctrine it should stand, particularly since we live in an age when the 'de-personalisation' of man is taking place. All the more reason, therefore, for affirming the belief in a *personal* Messiah. Nor does such a belief necessarily lead to an attitude of religious quietism. There is nothing in the traditional Jewish belief which suggests that man has no part to play in the work of redemption, quite the opposite is true.

For all the importance of Schwarzschild's analysis, it is not true to the facts to suggest that the nineteenth-century liberals simply discarded, without precedence, a hitherto universally-held Jewish doctrine. The Messiah idea has a history, as we have noted in these pages. Some of the prophets do not think of a personal Messiah and even those who do chiefly refer to an actual king of the House of David. There is, after all, the statement of Rabbi Hillel which denies a personal Messiah. There is certainly no *a priori* reason why God should not usher in the redemption by means of a person but it is theologically rash to make this an article of the Jewish faith binding upon Jews. It seems to me that such matters can only be left to God in His wisdom. The really important and significant point in Schwarzschild's analysis is that the redemption can only come about by God's direct intervention, in the sense that He will not allow the world He has created to surrender to darkness and destruction. What our age needs is not so much a total rejection of nineteenth-century optimism as a rejection of the belief that man can bring the Golden Age to birth of himself or that he is automatically progressing towards that goal. If God guides the destinies of mankind, as Judaism teaches, it seems overwhelmingly certain that the belief in His final intervention in human affairs *in miraculous fashion* is a perfectly valid belief. The alternative is to suppose that Israel's dream of perfection was an illusion. But this is very different from equating the dream itself with the modern notion of automatic progress. The millennium is not to be understood as a Utopia of the kind envisaged by William Morris or H. G. Wells but a world-shattering *religious* event in which the new world is perfected under the Kingdom of Heaven.

*   *   *

EXCURSUS

For the statements of the 'Pittsburgh Platform' and subsequent modifications of the Reform position *v.* article 'Reform Judaism' in UJE, Vol. VI, pp. 240–241. A modern analysis in the spirit of Reform Judaism is Ignaz Maybaum's very interesting and penetrating book of Sermons: 'The Faith of the Jewish Diaspora', Vision, London, 1962. For a critique of the Reform position *v.* Rabbi Jacob B. Agus: 'Guideposts in Modern Judaism', Bloch, New York, 1954, pp. 62 f. *Cf.* the same work pp. 97 f. for the Conservative view. Agus quotes Mannheimer, a leader of Austrian Conservatism, who said: 'I am one of those who do not rationalize the Messianic belief; I believe in and defend the national interpretation of this dogma and hope for a national restoration.' For the opposition on the part of prominent Russian and Polish Rabbis to Zionism as a betrayal of the Messianic belief *v.* the letters quoted in the English defence of the *Neture Karta* outlook by I. Domb: 'The Transformation',

London, 1957, pp. 179 ff. Thus Rabbi Meir Simhah of Dvinsk
writes: 'They (the Zionists) talk of redeeming us from exile while
we do not desire redemption at the hands of man, seeing that we
know that its end is – Heaven forbid – destruction and vanity, and
all this comes upon them through the desire for greatness and power
that burns and consumes their hearts like fire. Heaven forbid that we
should hasten the hour. Even were the foundation of a kingdom a
basic commandment and even were we to hear a Voice from Heaven
telling us that it is our duty to hearken to Dr. Herzl, then we should
say that no attention is to be paid to a Voice from Heaven because
this Zionist vision is driving – Heaven forbid – Israel to destruction'. Similarly Rabbi Tzadok Ha-Cohen of Lublin writes: 'Do we
not know that the whole purpose of the Redemption is to improve
our ways so that Israel may observe the *Torah* with all the limits
and fences that our teachers ordained. What hope is there for us if
those who blaspheme the *Torah* should – Heaven forbid – be men
of power and influence among us. The prophets foresaw for us that in
the future Redemption we should not need an assembly of camps
and the ranks of war and from this we can see that such a thing is
opposed to the spirit of Judaism and the hope of Redemption'. That
this attitude persists, even now that the State of Israel exists, is
known from the activities of the Sotmarer Rebbe and the *Neture
Karta*. The present Lübavitcher Rebbe in his letter of recom-
mendation of the work '*Simhath 'Olam*' by Rabbi Meyer Blumen-
feld, New York, 1954, takes the author to task (p. 4) for suggesting
that the emergence of the State of Israel is to be interpreted as 'the
beginning of the Redemption'. A more moderate view obtained, of
course, among many Rabbis of the old school, particularly in the
Mizrachi Movement. An interesting example of a Rabbi defending,
in the last century, the right of Jews to work for the re-settlement of
Palestine without this being considered a betrayal of Messianism
is the work by Rabbi Joseph Jaffe: '*Sepher 'Ahabhath Tzion We-
Yerushalayim*', ed. M. Wallenstein, Jer., 1946. Will Herberg:
'Judaism and Modern Man', Meridian Books and Jewish Publication Society, New York, 1959, deals with the question of Messianism for the Jew of today, pp. 227 ff. Herberg points out that the
'liberal' doctrine of automatic progress towards the Messianic Age,
far from being in accordance with the classical Jewish sources, is
actually at variance with them. The doctrine of the 'woes' which
precede the Messianic Age is hardly compatible with the idea of
'the march of progress ever onward and upward'. History, says
Herberg, describing the Rabbinic view, cannot redeem itself. It
proceeds and ends in catastrophe from which it must be redeemed
by God. Says Herberg: 'Isaiah's or Micah's vision of peace is not

something that can be realised by the United Nations. Even the most perfect world state could do no more than *enforce* peace throughout the world, just as the national state does today within its own borders. But the hatreds and conflicts among men would remain, though prevented from breaking out into open violence. The "peace" of the prophets is something very different: it is an inner harmony and love that needs no external sanctions. As such, it transcends the resources of history to achieve, although every achievement of history must be measured in its terms. To ignore this fact and to attempt to reduce the prophetic vision of perfection to the level of perfectionist utopianism is to throw confusion alike into practical politics and the ultimate insights of religion'.

[14]

THE THIRTEENTH PRINCIPLE
The Resurrection of the Dead

MAIMONIDES' statement of the thirteenth principle is brief in the extreme. He simply says: '*The thirteenth Principle of Faith*, We have already explained this'. The reference is to his earlier comments on the resurrection in this very passage, and these, too, are very brief. Abelson (note 5) remarks: 'From the briefness with which Maimonides dismisses this thirteenth article concerning the Resurrection of the Dead, it has been inferred by many that he was really opposed to classing it among the fundamental dogmas of Judaism, and only did so as an unwilling concession to the current orthodox views of his day.' We shall have occasion to examine in detail Maimonides' views on the subject.

The *Yigdal* formulation reads: 'In the abundance of His loving kindness God will quicken the dead. Blessed for evermore be His glorious name'. The '*Ani Ma'amin* formulation reads: 'I believe with perfect faith that there will be a resurrection of the dead at the time when it shall please the Creator, blessed be His name, and exalted be the remembrance of Him for ever and ever'.

Friedländer says: 'As imperfect as is our conception of a creation from nothing, so imperfect is our notion of the resurrection of the dead. We only perceive the dissolution of the body into its elements, which enter into new combinations and form new bodies; and it is almost impossible for us to imagine a reconstruction of the original body out of its own elements. There is no doubt that the Almighty produces fresh life from death – we need only observe the action of Nature in the world around us to convince ourselves that God is "*mehaye ha-methim*", "that He gives life to things dead". But how this will be done in reference to our own selves, whether we shall enjoy the same life, whether our future life will be an improved edition of

398

the present one, whether *all* will be restored to life, or whether
the new life after death will be enjoyed by the soul alone, or by
body and soul jointly: these and similar questions transcend the
bounds of human knowledge. We know nothing but the bare
fact that God can restore to life that which is dead, and that
a resurrection will take place. But all further descriptions of
this event rest on man's imaginative powers . . . According
to Maimonides, the author of the Thirteen Principles, the doctrine of the resurrection of the dead is identical with that of the
immortality of the soul, calling the life of the soul after separation from the body, resurrection . . . because the immortality
of the soul appeared to him more rational and more acceptable
to thinking man. This may be the case, but we, human beings, a
combination of soul and body, are, in reality, as unable to
conceive the separate existence of our soul as we are to comprehend the resurrection of our body. We are taught that there
exists for us a life beyond the present one. But any attempt
to describe that life must be considered merely as an act of
imagination rather than of knowledge'. We shall see presently
that Friedländer's interpretation of Maimonides' views is
contradicted by Maimonides' essay on the resurrection.

Werblowsky's statement is as follows: '13. *The Resurrection
of the Dead.* Since Pharisaic times the resurrection of the body
was official doctrine. Rabbinic literature insists on it as an
essential dogma. Its problematic relation to ideas of immortality
and a hereafter has been discussed earlier. Here it must suffice
to indicate that modernism has found this dogma to be one of the
most unpalatable. Whereas orthodoxy still holds to it, the
Reform Prayerbook has deleted all references to the
resurrection of the body and substituted the apparently less
objectionable and more "refined" expression "life eternal".
Other theologians do not believe it necessary to have any hard-
and-fast ideas on the subject and deem it sufficient to recognise
the symbol as a confession of the value and significance of
the total human personality (body-and-soul) in the divine
scheme'.

We might profitably begin our discussion of the thirteenth
principle with a detailed examination of Maimonides' own
views on the subject. As we have seen he only touches lightly

on the subject in his Commentary to the *Mishnah*. In his 'Guide for the Perplexed' he does not refer to the subject at all. In his 'Code' he devotes a large section to the doctrine of the immortality of the soul, with only a stray reference to the resurrection. His essay on the resurrection is, as we shall see, a defence of his attitude and a reply to the accusation that by virtually ignoring the subject in his works he denies the resurrection or equates it with the immortality of the soul.

In his *Mishnah* Commentary (*Sanh.* X. 1), Maimonides states that the Garden of Eden is a place on the earth's surface which will be disclosed to man one day. But he does not explain when it will be disclosed and how it is connected with the Messianic Age and the Resurrection. Gehinnom is, for Maimonides, 'an expression for the suffering that will befall the wicked'. Speaking of the Resurrection, he says here that it is 'one of the cardinal doctrines of the Law of Moses'. But he argues that this reward is for the righteous only. His conclusion is particularly noteworthy: 'And know that man is bound to die and become dissolved into his component parts'.

In his 'Code' (*Hil. Tesh.* III. 5) Maimonides follows the Rabbinic ruling that all Israel have a share in the world to come and that the pious of the nations have a share in the world to come. He goes on, however, to record that certain severe offenders have no share in the world to come. For all of these he has Talmudic warrant although his interpretation of the types of persons excluded owes much to his own views. Among the persons excluded is one who denies the resurrection of the dead. This is his sole reference to the doctrine in this section of his work, which deals otherwise entirely with the immortality of the soul. In the whole of this section the term 'world to come' is equated with the immortality of the soul.

Developing this theme, Maimonides (*Tesh.* VIII) states that the good stored up for the righteous is the life of the world to come, life in which there is no death, good in which there is no evil. The reward of the righteous is that they will attain to this bliss, the punishment of the wicked is that they will not attain to it but will be cut off to die. Maimonides then quotes the famous saying of Rab (*Ber.* 17a) that in the world to come there is no body and no pleasures of the body but the righteous sit with their crowns on their heads and bask in the radiance of the Divine Presence. 'There is no body or corporeality in the world to come but the disembodied souls of the righteous alone like the ministering angels. Since there are no bodies there is no eating or drinking, nor is there anything of those things the body needs in this world, nor are there any of the events which befall the bodies of men in this world, such as sitting and standing, sleep and death, misery and frivolity, and so forth. Thus did the early Sages say, in the world to come there is no eating or drinking or sexual relations but the righteous sit with their crowns on their heads and bask in the radiance of the *Shekhinah*. From which it is clear that there is no body there, since there is no eating and drinking. The reference to the righteous "sitting" is figurative, that is to say, the righteous exist there without toil or effort. Similarly, the reference to their "crowns on their heads" means that the knowledge by virtue of which they attained to the life of the world to come is with them there and is their crown, as Solomon said: "Even upon the crown wherewith his mother hath crowned him" (Cant. iii. 11). Behold it is said: "And everlasting joy shall be upon their heads" (Is. li. 11) and surely joy is not corporeal that it should be a thing which rests upon the head. In the same way when the Sages speak of a "crown" they refer to knowledge. What do they mean when they speak of "basking in the radiance of the *Shekhinah*?" This means that they know and comprehend of the truth about God in a manner impossible for them while they inhabit the murky and lowly body'.

Raabad (R. Abraham Ibn David, Maimonides' great critic) adds a severe stricture to this latter ruling of Maimonides (*Hil. Tesh.* VIII. 2): 'The words of this man appear to me to be near to the view that the resurrection of the dead is for the soul alone, not for the body'. *Raabad* observes that this is certainly not the Rabbinic view. Thus, the Rabbis say that the righteous will be resurrected wearing their clothes (*Keth.* 111b). They also give instructions before their death on the kind of garments in which they were to be buried for the same reason (*Sabb.* 114a). They also said that the righteous whom God will resurrect will not return to their dust (*Sanh.* 72a) and that if they had blemishes while alive in this world they would be healed of them in the time of resurrection (*Sanh.* 91a). All these sayings prove that the dead will be resurrected in the body. It is possible, concludes *Raabad,* that the Creator will make the bodies of the righteous as firm and as strong as the bodies of the eagles and as Elijah's body. In that case the reference to the 'crowns' the righteous wear is to be taken literally and not figuratively as Maimonides takes it.

Maimonides (*Hil. Tesh.* VIII. 3) then refers to his 'Aristotelian' view that the immortal part of man is the 'acquired intellect' i.e. the development by means of metaphysical speculation of the intellectual capacities of the soul. This becomes attached to the Divine Intelligence, known as the 'Active Intellect' and in this way becomes immortal. This is not the soul which requires the body for its existence but the 'form of the soul' which is defined by Maimonides as 'the knowledge which the soul has acquired of the Creator according to her capacities'. This life in which there is no death, since death belongs to bodily things alone, is called in Scripture 'the bundle of life' (I Sam. xxv. 29). There is no higher reward and no greater good than this and it is for this that the prophets of Israel longed.

This life is called by many names, such as: 'The mount of the Lord' (Ps. xxiv. 3), 'God's holy place' (*ibid.*), 'the way of holiness' (Is. xxxv. 8), 'the courtyards of the Lord' (Ps. xcii. 14), 'the pleasantness of the Lord' (Ps. xxvii. 4), 'the tent of the Lord' (Ps. xv. 1), 'the temple of the Lord' (Ps. v. 8), 'the house of the Lord' (*ibid.*), and 'the gate of the Lord' (Ps. cxviii. 20). The Sages, speaking figuratively, call this goodness prepared for the righteous 'a feast' ('*Abhoth* III. 15). But generally they call it 'the world to come'. Here again *Raabad* (*Hil. Tesh.* VIII. 4) objects: 'If this is what is meant by the "feast" there is no cup of benediction. It would have been better for him to have kept silent'. *Raabad* refers here to the Talmudic passage (*Pes.* 119b) in which it is said that at the feast which God is destined to make for the righteous He will invite David to take the cup of wine for the recitation of Grace. From this it appears that the reference to the 'cup of benediction' is to be taken literally. The righteous will be resurrected in the body and then the great feast will take place. *Raabad* senses that there is a mystery here but, if that is the case, he appears to be saying that Maimonides ought to have kept silent instead of attempting to explain the whole thing away.

Maimonides goes on to say (*Hil. Tesh.* VIII. 5) that there is no greater punishment than to be deprived of this great glory. Hell, on this point of view, appears to be not a direct punishment in the After-life but a deprivation of the eternal bliss that is stored up for the righteous. The wicked soul is destroyed forever. Maimonides' critics were not slow to seize upon this as a denial of Hell-fire.

Maimonides (*Hil. Tesh.* VIII. 6) is aware that his picture of the After-life as a purely spiritual state is not very attractive to many people, who conceive of happiness only in material terms. 'This type of goodness might seem a light matter in your eyes and you may imagine that the only proper reward for keeping God's commands and being perfect in the ways of truth is to eat and drink well, to have intercourse with beautiful forms, to wear choice woven garments of fine linen, to live in marble palaces and to use gold and silver utensils anod s forth, as the foolish, perverted Arabs, immersed in lust, imagine. But the Sages and those gifted with knowledge are aware that all these things are folly and vanity, without any worth. These things are only valuable to us in this world since we have a body and are corporeal and these are bodily wants. The soul desires them only because the body wants them in order to be healthy. But all these have no value when there is no longer a body to enjoy them'. Maimonides states that the bliss of the world to come, since it is of a spiritual nature, cannot be comprehended at all while we are in the body. We can only attempt to describe it figuratively by drawing upon illustrations taken from our life in the body. But, in truth, there is no comparison between bodily pleasures and the ineffable spiritual bliss stored up for the righteous in the Here-after. Hence David says: 'How great is Thy goodness which Thou hast stored up for them that fear Thee.' (Ps. xxxi. 20). The prophets, in fact, never try to describe this bliss out of the fear that they may decrease its value. All they can say about it is that 'no eye has seen it' (Is. lxiv. 3).

Finally (*Hil. Tesh.* VIII. 8), Maimonides makes the very interesting observation that although the Sages call this bliss 'the world *to come*' this should not be taken to mean that the world of eternal bliss is to come *after* this world has been destroyed, that it is a *future* world. Actually, that world is already in existence but man can only inhabit it after the death of his body. It is for this reason that the Sages call it 'the world to come'. Once again *Raabad* objects that the Sages do speak (*Sanh.* 97a) of the destruction of this world and the creation of a new world.

From his virtual silence on the resurrection, from his opposition (implied by his failure to note the points raised by *Raabad*) to physical descriptions of the world to come, it seems as if Maimonides equates the doctrine of the resurrection with that of the immortality of the soul. This was the construction put on Maimonides' words by some of his contemporaries. They felt that Maimonides' picture of the 'world to come' was of a purely spiritual state into which man enters after death. The Messianic Age, it is true, is an era here upon earth but this will not last forever. Men will die, including the Messiah himself, and the only true reward for observing the commands of God will be to enjoy spiritual bliss in the world of the spirit. It cannot be denied that if Maimonides believed in the importance of the physical resurrection he ought to have given it some prominence in his works, instead of passing it over in virtual silence or, at the most, referring to it in a very casual fashion. However, the matter is further complicated by the fact that towards the end of his life Maimonides wrote his essay on the resurrection in which he vehemently denies that he had ever rejected the belief in a physical resurrection. We turn now to consider this important essay.

At the beginning of his essay on the resurrection ('*Ma'amar Tehiath Ha-Methim*', 'Maimonides' Treatise on Resurrection', ed. Joshua Finkel, American Academy for Jewish Research, New York, Vol. IX, 1939) Maimonides relates the events which led to the composition of this remarkable work of defence. He tells us that his 'Code', the '*Mishneh Torah*', containing his views (described above) on the Hereafter, had become known in many lands. Relying on Maimonides' statements in this work a pupil in the Academy of Damascus had declared his unbelief in the resurrection of the body. At first, says Maimonides, he felt that this could safely be ignored as a flagrant misunderstanding but a letter he received in 1189 from Yemen convinced him that some explanatory essay was called for since the writer of the letter informed him that many

Jews in Yemen entertained heretical views through accepting
Maimonides' statements. In reply to the letter from Yemen
Maimonides stated that he believed in the resurrection of
the body as a fact. This would take place after the advent of
the Messiah but the dead who would be revived would not
live forever in the body. The spiritual life of the soul, to which
he refers repeatedly in his other works, comes both immediately
after death and again it supersedes the death of all men after
the period of life on this earth which follows the resurrection.
Maimonides thought that this would suffice, but in the year
1191 he received a letter from Babylonia stating that an
inquirer from Yemen had sought the advice of Samuel ben Ali,
head of the Babylonian Academy, who composed an essay
criticising Maimonides' views. This convinced Maimonides
that the present Treatise was necessary but he argues that it is
in no way a retraction from anything he had previously said
but only an amplification of his opinions as stated in the 'Code'
and the Commentary to the *Mishnah*.

The new idea, which is here stated explicitly for the first
time (though Maimonides claims that this was his intention
all along) is that there will be a physical resurrection but that
the men revived will die again. His statements in the *Mishneh
Torah* refer to the ultimate state, which is the enjoyment of
spiritual bliss forever. This latter is referred to as 'the world
to come', whereas the resurrection will take place on this
earth some time after the advent of the Messiah. 'And so it
appears to me from these verses that the individuals, whose
souls will return to their bodies, will eat, drink, marry and
procreate, and then die after enjoying that very long span of
life characteristic of the Messianic era' (*par.* 23, p. 16). The
Talmudic statement of Rab that in the world to come there is
no eating or drinking clearly implies, according to Maimonides,
that men will not live forever in the body since there will
be no purpose in the bodily organs. It seems impossible, for
Maimonides, that God should create anything without purpose.
It seems offensive to him to suggest that a body will exist
without bodily functions since this is a kind of denial of God's
wisdom. The miracle of resurrection, he says, will, however,
take place. He does not, of course, deny the possibility of
miracles occurring. Only one who follows Aristotle in believing

o

in the eternity of matter denies that God may intervene in a miraculous fashion. His preference for naturalistic interpretations is not due to any *a priori* rejection of the miraculous but to an indiscriminate literal acceptance by the masses of every fairy tale in the classical sources; this he feels must be combated if the Bible is to be preserved as a book providing a rational world outlook instead of a collection of marvels. When he states that the Messiah will not perform miracles he only means that the Messiah himself is not endowed with miraculous powers. But God will perform the tremendous miracle of the resurrection in the Messianic Age. As to the charge that his extreme brevity on the subject in the *Mishneh Torah* and the Commentary to the *Mishnah* suggests that he really wished to deny a physical resurrection, Maimonides replies that brevity is simply a characteristic of his style. Furthermore, it must be realised that there is very little one *can* say on the subject since it is not a matter to be defended by philosophic investigation but a matter of belief and there the matter ends.

Although here and there traces of a similar idea to that of Maimonides are to be found in mediaeval Jewish literature, Maimonides' statement that the resurrected dead will die again and that only the soul is immortal is nowhere else made with the same degree of unambiguity. Finkel notes that Abraham Ibn Ezra says much the same thing in his commentary to Daniel: 'And many of them that sleep in the dust of the earth shall awake, some to everlasting life, and some to reproaches and everlasting abhorrence' (Dan. xii. 2). Ibn Ezra comments: 'It seems to me that the meaning of this verse is that the righteous who died in exile will be resurrected when the redeemer comes. They will then take their delight of the Leviathan, Ziz and Behemoth (fabulous animals and birds) and will die again to live at the resurrection of the dead while in the world to come. There they will neither eat nor drink but bask in the radiance of the *Shekhinah*'. Ibn Ezra speaks of the resurrected dead dying again but he speaks of their subsequent state as the 'resurrection of the dead'. This seems to accord with Maimonides' opinion, but the latter is explicit that the resurrection of the dead is temporal and the world to come, signifying the spiritual state of the soul, is alone everlasting.

Later mediaeval thinkers either content themselves with quoting Maimonides' views without committing themselves or they take refuge in his authority. Thus, so far as we know, Maimonides was the only philosopher in the Middle Ages to commit himself definitely to the view that the future existence is ultimately incorporeal. Finkel has demonstrated that in the year 1189–90 'Abd al-Latif al-Baghdadi, a friend of Saladin, arrived in Cairo and, after examining Maimonides' 'Guide' in a cursory fashion, denounced it as 'a pernicious book that undermines the principles of *all* faiths by the very means with which it appears to buttress them'. If we add to this the fact that Saladin, at a time when Islam was fighting for its life against the Crusaders, was extremely suspicious of the philosophers, whom he tended to suspect of undermining the faith, it is easy to see that Maimonides had to be extremely cautious in expressing unconventional views on such a matter as the resurrection of the dead which looms very large in Islamic theology. This may have caused Maimonides to write the essay on the resurrection and thus restate his view in such a manner as to lessen its vulnerability. But it would be going far beyond the evidence to suggest that Maimonides was writing with his tongue in his cheek. The probable explanation of Maimonides' ambiguity in the matter of the resurrection is that the great thinker was fully prepared to accept the Rabbinic tradition of a physical resurrection but could not bring himself to believe that it was of ultimate significance. Only the spiritual state of the soul could enjoy that significance. If this is correct, the thirteenth principle of his Creed includes *both* the belief in the resurrection and that of the immortality of the soul, with the latter being of ultimate significance. In fact, in the essay on the resurrection Maimonides claims that he does refer to the doctrine of the resurrection in the *Mishneh Torah* since he records that one who denies the resurrection has no share in the world to come (*par.* 8, p. 6).

Maimonides' actual statement of his belief in the physical resurrection (*par.* 21, p. 15) runs: 'I say that the meaning of the resurrection of the dead – a doctrine renowned and accepted among our people and acknowledged by every one of our group and mentioned moreover frequently in the prayers, narratives and supplications which were composed by the prophets and the great Sages and which fill the pages of the *Talmud* and the *Midrash* – is that the soul will return to the body after it has been separated from it. Among our nation there is no difference of opinion on this matter, no dissenting voice. It is not permitted to place any reliance on any member of our religion who believes in the opposite of this'. For all that, Maimonides says that he cannot believe that the ultimate state of man will be this physical existence. He is prepared to take literally the references to the resurrection in the Rabbinic literature, but the true philosopher will not fail to agree with him that the ultimate state of man is spiritual unless we are prepared to be misled by the kind of homily that is suitable for 'women in a house of mourning'. If it be asked (*par.* 52, pp. 36–37) what purpose can this miracle serve (i.e. since the body returns to dust eventually why was it resurrected at all?) we can only reply that we do not know. This belongs to God's wisdom and it is beyond the capacity of the human mind to grasp it.

Among others, Nahmanides ('*Sha'ar Ha-Gemul*', end of the work '*Torath Ha-'Adam*', Warsaw, 1840, pp. 68–69) disagrees with Maimonides' contention that the revived dead will die again. Here Nahmanides first explains Maimonides' view. He says that for Maimonides the Garden of Eden is a spot on the earth's surface which will be revealed to man either during the Messianic Age or at the resurrection (i.e. when there is a body to enjoy the physical delights of the place) but that the revived dead will die again to live a life of purely spiritual bliss forever. Thus, for Maimonides, when the righteous die they attain that state known as 'the world to come' i.e. they exist in a purely spiritual state until the resurrection when the soul returns to the body. But after a long period on earth the body dies again and the soul reverts to its former state and exists in that spiritual state for all eternity. Nahmanides disagrees with Maimonides and holds that once the dead have been revived they will live on in the body for all eternity, but this body will not be the present body but a specially refined body (p. 67). As for the objection of Maimonides that in a world in which there are no bodily functions there can be no purpose in a body, Nahmanides gives two answers. First, he says, since the body is required in this existence it is only right that it should endure in the future life, albeit in a refined form.

Furthermore, the form of the body contains mighty secrets. This latter reference is to the Qabbalistic view that the body of man is the pale reflection upon earth of mighty spiritual mysteries. For the Qabbalists there is a spiritual entity called a 'hand', for example, of which the human hand is but the tangible expression in this world.

Hasdai Crescas is another mediaeval philosopher to treat this subject in detail referring, in his exposition, to the views of both Maimonides and Nahmanides (''Or 'Adonai', Treatise III, 4, Chapters 1–4, ed. Vienna, 1859, pp. 75a-78a. Cf. S. B. Urbach: 'The Philosophical Teachings of Rabbi Hasdai Crescas' [Heb.], Jer. 1961, pp. 371–377). Crescas begins by pointing to contradictions in the Rabbinic sources. Sometimes the Rabbis appear to equate the Resurrection with the Days of the Messiah. In other passages, however, the two are distinct. There may be a real contradiction, he says, and the view of Samuel (Ber. 34b) that the Messianic Age will witness no change in the order of nature is an individual view not accepted by the other Rabbis. On the other hand it is possible that the Resurrection will take place *after* the advent of the Messiah but during the Messianic Age. If this is correct there are four different stages in man's existence: (1) This world, (2) The world of the souls after death, Heaven, (3) The Days of the Messiah, (4) The Resurrection. Crescas sees a reference to these four stages in the well-known Sabbath hymn: 'There is none to be compared unto Thee, O Lord our God, *in this world*, neither is there any beside Thee, O our King. *for the life of the world to come*; there is none but Thee, O our Redeemer, *for the Days of the Messiah*; neither is there any like unto Thee, O our Saviour, *for the resurrection of the dead*' (Singer's Prayer Book, p. 129). Crescas quotes the views of Maimonides and Nahmanides and agrees with the latter.

Crescas (Chapter 2) has some original ideas on the purpose of the resurrection, i.e. what is the purpose of a reunion of body and soul? First, he says, the dead who return to life will tell those who have not died the truth of the spiritual existence they have experienced and the marvel of coming to life again. It was this that the prophet Malachi meant when he spoke of Elijah turning the hearts of the fathers to the children (iii. 24) i.e. the fathers who have died and been revived will tell of the

wonder to their children still alive. Secondly, it accords with
God's justice that body and soul which have acted together
as a unity should be recompensed as a unity. Thirdly, as a
result of the resurrection the whole world will be perfected
and led to God and this is the purpose of the *Torah*. In Chapter
4, Hasdai deals with the question of how the decomposed body
will be reconstituted. It is not necessarily the same body which
will be given to the soul in the resurrection but one which will
serve the same purpose. The identity of the individual will
not be affected by this since even during a man's life in this
world the body suffers change all the time.

Joseph Albo (*'Sepher Ha-'Iqqarim'*, ed. I. Husik, Jewish Pub.
Soc., Philadelphia, 1946, Vol. IV, Chapter 35, pp. 339–356)
continues the discussion. Albo quotes the opinion of Maimonides
that the resurrected dead will die again and the opposite view
of R. Meir ben Todros Ha-Levi Abulafia (1180–1244) and
Nahmanides that they will, at first, live as long as their natural
capacities permit them, and then their bodies will be transmuted
by purification and will become like the body of Elijah and
they will live forever in their refined bodies. All this may seem
strange, says Albo, but it is not impossible. Albo quotes the
reply of R. Joshua b. Hananiah: 'When they come to life again,
we will consult about the matter' (*Nidd.* 70b) i.e. this whole
matter can safely be left to God. There is no need for us to
concern ourselves with it.

It can be seen from our examination of the views of the great
mediaeval thinkers that there is a good deal of ambiguity about
the whole matter of the resurrection of the dead. This is to be
expected since originally it appears certain that the two
doctrines of the immortality of the soul and the resurrection
of the dead were two entirely different doctrines which were
only combined at a later period. Basically, the two ideas are
quite different. The original belief in the resurrection of the dead
was an eschatological hope bound up with the rebirth of the
nation in the Days of the Messiah. The doctrine of the soul's
immortality, on the other hand, owes much to Greek influence
and refers particularly to the fate of the individual soul after
the death of the body. When the two doctrines were combined,
and were accepted by the Pharisees as being true, there was
bound to be a considerable degree of tension between them.

This helps us to understand why the mediaeval thinkers tortured themselves in trying to explain how the two doctrines can both be included in the belief of the Jew. To see more specifically why this is so it is necessary to examine the history of the two ideas.

It is generally assumed that the Hebrew Bible is silent on the whole question of the Hereafter, with the exception of some few references in the later books. However, it is extremely unlikely that there was no belief in some kind of immortality during the earlier period. All ancient peoples shared a belief in a life after death. The Hebrews must have been aware of the beliefs of their neighbours and it is hard to see how they kept themselves from adopting the idea of an existence of some kind even after the death of the body. Unless such beliefs were held in ancient Israel the Biblical prohibitions against consulting the dead (Deut. xviii. 11) and the story of the Witch of Endor (I Sam. xxviii) would have had no meaning. Further evidence of the belief is provided by the frequent references to the dead being 'gathered unto their people' or 'their fathers'. True, the belief is referred to in the most casual fashion, possibly as a protest against undue preoccupation with the cult of the dead on the part of Israel's neighbours, but it is precarious to read too much out of the argument from silence. It is hard to believe that an Isaiah or a Jeremiah, for instance, had no hope of further communion after their death with the God they worshipped in their lifetime. Scholars are generally inclined to the view that a full belief in immortality came into Judaism at the time of the Maccabees when young men were dying in defence of their faith. It was no longer possible at that time to account for human death and suffering solely in terms of divine retribution and reward in this life, and the complete belief in an after-life was felt to be necessary for theodicy. It is highly significant that there is no clear reference to the immortality of the soul in the book of Job, which probes grandly the whole question of human suffering. It is certain that by the time of the Pharisees the belief in the immortality of the soul had become a fundamental Jewish dogma. By this time, of course, the possibility of Greek influence is not to be ruled out.

The earliest definite references to the doctrine of the resurrection of the dead are in the books of Isaiah and Daniel, both generally held to be of later date. It is possible that this doctrine owes something to Persian influence. The passage in the book of Isaiah reads: 'Thy dead shall live, my dead bodies shall arise/Awake and sing, ye that dwell in the dust/For thy dew is as the dew of light, And the earth shall bring to life the shades' (Is. xxvi. 19). The passage in Daniel reads: 'And many of them that sleep in the dust of the earth shall awake, some to everlasting life, and some to reproaches and everlasting abhorrence' (Dan. xii. 2). This belief in the resurrection of the dead obviously belonged, at first, to the eschatological beliefs associated with the Messianic Age. Unlike the doctrine of the immortality of the soul, the belief in the resurrection was nationalistic rather than individualistic. It was the hope of national revival, which embraced the resurrection. After the restoration of the people to its homeland as a result of the advent of the Messiah there would take place the resurrection of the dead. While there is no necessary contradiction between the two beliefs there is some degree of incompatibility between the idea of a great judgment day to take place after the resurrection and the judgment of each individual after his death. When eventually the two beliefs were fused together there was bound to be some confusion on this matter and a large variety of views as to how the two beliefs can both be true. This helps to explain the many details, sometimes of a contradictory nature, concerning God's final judgment in the Rabbinic literature and, as we have seen, the same difficulties persisted in the Middle Ages. The Pharisees held that both doctrines were fundamental to Judaism; the resurrection offered national hope of survival, together with the idea of the Messiah, while the belief in the immortality of the soul appealed to the individual's need to be assured that he survives death. The Sadducees appear to have rejected both beliefs, although some scholars claim that the frequent references to Sadducean denial apply only to the doctrine of the resurrection, not to that of the immortality of the soul.

In the Rabbinic literature generally there are held to be three distinct stages. The first of these is the state of the soul after death in Heaven. The second is the Messianic Age, 'the Days of the Messiah', here on earth 'at the end of days'. The third is the resurrection of the dead which follows the advent of the Messiah. The term 'The World to Come' often means, in the Rabbinic literature, all three stages, but it is generally reserved for the first and the last, i.e. for the state of the soul after the death of the body and for the resurrection. From this brief sketch it will be seen that Maimonides' idea that the resurrection is for a time and that the ultimate state is that of the immortality of the soul in Heaven is the sage's own contribution and has no real support in the Rabbinic sources.

Maimonides, as he himself remarks in the essay on the resurrection, is moved to stress the immortality of the soul as ultimate rather than the resurrection of the body, in the interests of spiritual religion. The masses, he remarks, conceive only of the material as real. It is this which led many to believe that God is corporeal and it is this which leads them to adopt a lukewarm attitude towards the idea that the soul alone is immortal. For them a non-material existence is no existence at all, so that to affirm the immortality of the soul alone, and not the body, is tantamount to denying immortality. But Maimonides refused to be stampeded into adopting a conception that was at variance with his lofty spiritual view of religion.

What is the attitude of modern Jews to this whole question? On the whole Jewish modernists have preferred the doctrine of the immortality of the soul to that of the resurrection of the dead. Accepting the thirteenth principle they have tended to limit it to immortality. There is no doubt that this is a departure from the traditional concept. But it is doubtful, to say the least, whether this warrants the slur that in the interests of a refined gentility it is preferred to give up the full-blooded doctrine of the resurrection in favour of the more 'refined' but less 'Jewish' doctrine of the immortality of the soul. In fact, modernists prefer to stress the latter doctrine for precisely the same motives which led Maimonides to give his special emphasis. No modernist can affirm the impossibility of a physical resurrection. With God all things are possible. But the question of the purpose of the resurrection, with which the mediaeval thinkers grappled, has not been solved in any satisfactory manner. There are serious philosophical objections, too, in the way of acceptance of the doctrine of the resurrection. One of these is the difficulty of accounting for a body in the eternal life. If,

as many thinkers, Jewish and non-Jewish, have said, eternity is
outside time altogether, how can a body (which by definition
must occupy space and time) exist for all eternity? There is a
fundamental difference between the acceptance of the belief
in immortality and that of resurrection. The only reason the
devout Jew can have for accepting the belief in the resurrection
is that tradition demands it. Whereas, as we shall consider
later in detail, the religious mind wishes to accept immortality
and believe in it chiefly because it cannot see God dooming His
creatures who have longed in life for Him to ultimate death.
If God is non-corporeal the highest form of communion with
Him, as Maimonides observed long ago, is in the spirit. The
whole of this work is written from the point of view which is
convinced that reinterpretation of the thirteen principles is both
possible and greatly to be desired for moderns. In this matter
particularly such reinterpretation is called for, especially since
the way has been paved by such giants as Raba and Maimonides.

In the well-known statement of the beliefs of Reform Judaism
known as the 'Pittsburgh Platform' (1885) the passage relevant
to our theme reads: 'We reassert the doctrine of Judaism that
the soul is immortal, grounding this belief on the divine nature
of the human spirit, which forever finds bliss in righteousness
and misery in wickedness. We reject, as ideas not rooted in
Judaism, the beliefs both in bodily resurrection and in Gehinnom
and Eden (Hell and Paradise) as abodes for everlasting punishment and reward'.

But it is not only Reform Judaism which accepts the need
for reinterpretation of the thirteenth principle. In a remarkable
essay the Orthodox thinker, Dr. Joseph Seliger, attacks the
doctrine of the resurrection of the body as unduly materialistic
and vigorously advocates the belief in the immortality of the
soul ('Writings of Rabbi Dr. Joseph Seliger' [Heb.], ed. Leah
Seliger, Jer., 1930, 'Gan 'Eden We-Gehinnom', pp. 71–96). It is
interesting that an approbation to the work by Rabbi A. I. Kook
is printed at the beginning (p. 20) in which Rabbi Kook
refers to this particular essay and observes that after all speculation on these matters we can only rely on Jewish tradition
and we must realise that these matters are really beyond the
human mind to comprehend! Seliger notes that the ancient
peoples tended to depict the After-life in terms of this life.

Whatever values a people considered significant in this life were projected into the Beyond. Seliger quotes, as examples, the Greek, Muslim and Teutonic Heavens. The Egyptians, he says, believed so strongly in the *bodily* aspect of the Hereafter that they mummified the body and built pyramids to protect it. In Israel alone, he claims (with only partial justification, as we have noted above) the belief in the Hereafter was spiritualised. He then quotes the view of Maimonides in *Mishneh Torah* which breathes the air of an elevated spiritual faith. Seliger admits that it is possible for the physical resurrection to take place but he sees the whole conception as a popular folk-belief not really suitable for the philosophic mind to entertain. Basically, he concludes, this belief has far more in common with the ancient Egyptian belief than with the Law of Moses which rules that the corpse defiles. Seliger, in his very bold defence of the view that the 'resurrection of the dead' (i.e. the thirteenth principle of the faith) does not refer to a physical resurrection but to the immortality of the soul, might have added that whereas a religious faith denuded of the belief in the immortality of the soul loses all its spiritual power, a faith without the doctrine of the physical resurrection is not affected at all. Obviously, it matters a great deal to a religious man whether he believes this life is all or whether he believes it is a school in which preparation is made for the enjoyment of God for all eternity. It matters little to a man's religious life whether his body will live forever or will live at all once it has decayed in the grave.

Dr. J. H. Hertz ('Commentary to the Prayer Book', p. 255) is rather more ambiguous but he gives the impression, nonetheless, that the belief in the resurrection of the dead is of secondary importance and that what really matters is the doctrine of the immortality of the soul. Hertz writes: 'Many and various are the folk-beliefs and poetic fancies in the Rabbinical writings concerning Heaven, *Gan Eden*, and Hell, *Gehinnom*. Our most authoritative religious guides, however, proclaim that no eye hath seen, nor can mortal fathom, what awaiteth us in the Hereafter; but that even the tarnished soul will not forever be denied spiritual bliss. Judaism rejects the doctrine of eternal damnation'. It does credit to Dr. Hertz's Jewish heart that this is his conception of Judaism, but in the interests of historical truth it is necessary to mention, as we shall see later, that mediaeval thinkers like Saadiah do believe in eternal torment in Hell and that even Maimonides, who interprets Hell as deprivation of eternal life, affirms that the 'tarnished soul' will be forever denied spiritual bliss. A sound Jewish apologetic, while building on the insights of the great mediaeval thinkers, will not hesitate to depart from the mediaeval conception on matters such as this as Dr Hertz, indeed, does. But there is no reason for failing to recognise that a departure is being made. Dr Hertz continues: 'Since Maccabean times, the pious have ever believed not only in the soul's survival of death and decay, but that, in God's unfathomable wisdom and in His own time, the body will be reunited with the soul. Many people find Resurrection incredible; yet it is not more of a mystery than birth, or the stupendous miracle of the annual resurrection of plant-life after winter . . . Maimonides and Hallevi make the doctrine of *tehiath ha-methim*, lit. "revival of the dead", identical with that of the immortality of the soul, and explain the Talmudic sayings to the contrary as figurative language'. Here again historically it is incorrect to quote Ha-Levi and Maimonides in support of the substitution of the immortality of the soul for the resurrection of the dead. Ha-Levi in his *Kuzari* is very brief in his references to the Hereafter and nowhere states explicitly that he disbelieves in a physical resurrection. As for Maimonides, we have seen that in his essay on the resurrection he affirms emphatically his belief in a physical resurrection, though he believes it will be for a time only and the soul alone is immortal. The proper attitude for a Jewish modernist to take is to recognise that he is going further than any man in the Middle Ages can have been expected to have gone, but that if Maimonides were alive today it is extremely likely that he would have equated the doctrine of '*tehiath ha-methim*' with that of the immortality of the soul. In any event, Dr. Hertz, for all the ambiguity as to his own views on the matter, does quote Maimonides and appears to suggest to his readers that they can remain devout and believing Jews even if they prefer the doctrine of the soul's immortality.

Some modern theologians tend to suggest that there is something invidious in this preference for the immortality of the soul. But they rarely state what it is precisely they would have us substitute for it and they do not appear to mean the doctrine of the resurrection in its traditional form. Will Herberg, for example, calls the doctrine of the resurrection of the dead a 'symbol' ('Judaism and Modern Man', Meridian Books and Jew. Pub. Soc., New York, 1959, p. 229). 'The symbol, "resurrection of the dead", expresses the depth and dimensions of Hebraic religion in relation to the destiny of mankind more adequately perhaps than any other concept. This becomes clear if we contrast it with the essentially Greek belief in the immortality of the soul, with which it is often confused. The teaching of the resurrection affirms, in the first place, that man's ultimate destiny is not something that is his by virtue of his own nature – by his possession of an "immortal" soul, for example – but comes to him solely by the grace and mercy of God, who "wakes him from the dead". It thus emphasises total dependence on God as against metaphysical self-reliance. It affirms, in the second place, that what is destined to fufilment is not a disembodied soul that has sloughed off its body, but the *whole* man – body, soul and spirit – joined in an indissoluble unity. It affirms, in the third place, that the salvation promised of God is not a private, individual affair that each one acquires for himself upon his death, but the salvation of mankind, the corporate redemption of men in the full reality of their historical existence. The whole point of the doctrine of the resurrection is that the life we live now, the life of the body, the life of empirical existence in society, has some measure of permanent worth in the eyes of God and will not vanish in the transmutation of things at the "last day". The fulfilment will be a fulfilment for the *whole* man and for *all* men who have lived through the years and have entered into history and its making. This is the meaning of the doctrine of the resurrection of the dead; it is a doctrine with which we cannot dispense, no matter how impatient we may be with the literalistic pseudo-biological fantasies that have gathered around it through the centuries'. This passage is quoted at length because it is typical of the desire of some moderns to have their cake and eat it. Herberg admits that 'pseudo-biological fantasies' have gathered around the doctrine of the resurrection through the centuries and apparently rejects these. He does not tell us how we can have the doctrine without these fantasies. Once these are subtracted from the doctrine what is left of it and how does what remains differ from the idea of the immortality of the soul? Herberg's three points regarding the *whole* man and *all* men saved by the grace of God are well taken. But to safeguard these we have only to extend the idea of immortality to the whole person (i.e. the continuation of individual consciousness), to *all* men and to see the process as part of God's grace. The first is definitely the opinion of Jewish tradition on the soul's immortality, which is understood always as the continued existence of the individual rather than that the personality is submerged in a world soul. If Herberg is dissatisfied with this and feels that the actual body of man must live for ever, how can this aim be realised without the 'pseudo-biological fantasies' of which he speaks? As for the need to extend immortality to *all* men the Jewish doctrine, as we shall see, is, on the whole, sufficiently wide to embrace at least the righteous of all nations. If, on the other hand, Herberg wishes life in society to continue forever there is again the difficulty of how this can be possible without the 'fantasies' he appears to reject. Finally, with regard to the grace of God, it can safely be said that the Rabbinic view (Maimonides' idea of the 'acquired intellect' may be an exception here) is of the After-life as a 'reward' by God, given to those who keep His commandments, and is in no way an automatic attainment. Herberg seems to be confusing, in any event, the resurrection of the dead with the Messianic Age. In the Messianic Age, as Jewish tradition has developed the idea, there will be the salvation of the *whole* man and *all* men in the form of society we have now under the grace of God. But for the doctrine of the resurrection to have any meaning apart from the Messianic Age (i.e. for it to be extended to those who have died before the advent of the Messiah) and if we are to reject the 'fantasies' it can only be equated with the immortality of the soul. We need not be afraid of every Greek gift. In any event the doctrine has ample support from *Jewish* sources. One suspects that Herberg would agree to all this, and that his chief aim is to safeguard his three points, but no good purpose is served by speaking of the 'symbol' of the resurrection in this connection. The more straightforward attitude for moderns is to admit that the doctrine of the resurrection is not really significant and that what matters is that the soul of the man who had striven during his lifetime to lead the good life is immortal and near to God for all eternity.

Herberg, in fact, follows here Reinhold Niebuhr ('The Nature and Destiny of Man', Nisbet, London, 1943, Vol. II, Chapter X, 3 'The Resurrection', pp. 304–309). Niebuhr similarly speaks of the resurrection of the body as a 'Biblical symbol'. He observes that modern minds find it the greatest offence and, from the Christian point of view, it has been displaced by moderns by the doctrine of the immortality of the soul. Niebuhr makes the same three points as Herberg in favour of the doctrine though in slightly different words and from the Christian standpoint. But a careful reading of Niebuhr shows that he by no means suggests that the physical body must live on for eternity if the particular aims he mentions are to be fulfilled. What is intended in the doctrine of the resurrection of the dead is, for Niebuhr, and we can surely follow him here, that the whole historical, temporal process is fulfilled 'at the end of days'. 'The doctrine of the resurrection of the body implies that eternal significance belongs to the whole unity of an historical realisation insofar as it has brought all particularities into the harmony of the whole. Consummation is thus conceived not as absorption into the divine but as loving fellowship with God. Since such a perfect relation with God is not a human possibility it depends upon the mercy and power of God'. This, says Niebuhr, is a great mystery, part of the tremendous question of how finiteness can be conceived of in eternity. Does not eternal life annul all finiteness? It is the safeguarding of the paradox that in eternal life the finiteness of man is contained and consummated, but not annulled, that is behind the emphasis on the doctrine of the resurrection. Again Niebuhr remarks: 'In the symbol of the resurrection of the body, the "body" is indicative of the contribution which nature makes to human individuality and to all historical realisations'. This exceedingly subtle and important idea is a far cry indeed from the doctrine of the resurrection conceived in terms of an actual physical body existing for all eternity. This Niebuhr explicitly denies. No doubt Herberg makes the same distinction, hence his objection to the 'pseudo-biological fantasies'. In view of all this it is certainly incorrect to quote

Niebuhr, as Dr. I. Epstein does ('The Faith of Judaism',
Soncino Press, Lond., 1954, pp. 323 f.) in support of the belief in
the resurrection of the *physical* body. The truth of the matter is,
as Niebuhr realises, that the doctrine of the resurrection
implies the salvation of the whole man and that this was
conceived of as an actual resurrection of the physical body.
But this led to tension in early Judaism, deriving from the difficulties inherent in the notion of a body inhabiting eternity. We
have seen that these tensions continued in Judaism right through
the Middle Ages. It was considerations of this sort which led
Maimonides to redefine the doctrine of the resurrection and
by the same token moderns are duty bound to redefine it.
Such fresh definition will probably include a rejection of the
idea that the actual physical body will be resurrected from
the dead but that the meaning of 'body' in this context is that
somehow (and no modernist would wish to probe further than
the recognition demanded of a great mystery) all man's finite
strivings will not be annihilated in eternal life but will be
consummated by God in eternity. We can, if we wish, refer
to this as the 'resurrection of the body' but use the term, as
Niebuhr and Herberg do, as a symbol. It seems to the present
writer that the far more effective and less misleading attitude
is to use for this the term 'immortality of the soul' adding to
the idea the points which Niebuhr and Herberg mention. It is
chiefly a matter of nomenclature but it seems preferable to use
the term 'immortality of the soul' and qualify it to include the
other ideas rather than use the term 'resurrection of the body' and
qualify this by rejecting the biological fantasies. The state of a
soul in eternity with its finite character intact and its finite
experiences embraced seems closer to the description of our
immortal state (so far as it can be described at all) than the
state of a body which is not a real body. It is in this spirit that,
for the rest of this chapter, we will use the term 'the immortality
of the soul' to convey our understanding of what the thirteenth
principle means for moderns.

*   *   *

EXCURSUS

On the whole question of the resurrection in its historical development *v.* the article by Kaufmann Kohler in JE, Vol. X, pp. 382–385
and by I. Husik in UJE, Vol. IX, pp. 141–142. An important essay

is 'The Doctrine of the Resurrection of the Dead in Rabbinic
Theology' in 'Studies in Jewish Theology', Marmorstein Memorial
Volume, ed. J. Rabbinowitz and M. S. Lew, Oxford University
Press, 1950, pp. 144 ff. George Foot Moore: 'Judaism', Harvard
University Press, 1958, Vol. II, Part VII, Chapter 1, pp. 287 f. and
Chapter III, pp. 377 f. are very important surveys of the doctrine
of the resurrection of the dead. Further works to be consulted are:
L. Finkelstein: 'The Pharisees', Jewish Publication Soc., Philadel-
phia, 1940, Chapter VIII, pp. 145 ff.; A. Cohen: 'Everyman's
Talmud', Dent, London, 1949, pp. 357 ff.; I. Epstein, op. cit.,
'Additional Note on the Resurrection of the Dead', pp. 383–386;
Montefiore and Loewe, 'A Rabbinic Anthology', op. cit., Chapter
XXXI, pp. 580 f. Among the ideas found in the Rabbinic literature
on the subject are the following. The second of the eighteen
benedictions refers to the resurrection: 'Thou sustaineth the living
with loving kindness, revivest the dead with great mercy, supportest
the falling, healest the sick, loosest the bound, and keepest Thy
faith to them that sleep in the dust. Who is like unto Thee, Lord of
mighty acts, and who resembleth Thee, O king, Who killest and
revivest, and causeth salvation to spring forth? Yea, faithful art
Thou to revive the dead. Blessed art Thou, O Lord, Who revivest
the dead' (Singer's Prayer Book, p. 45). A favourite Rabbinic
argument for the resurrection is that if those who were not in
existence come to life, how much more will they who have lived
come to life again! (*Sanh.* 91a). There are speculations on such
matters as to whether the dead will arise clothed or naked (*Sanh.*
90b) or whether those with physical blemishes in this life will
possess them when they are resurrected (*Eccl. R.* to i. 4). Although
the modern Orthodox objection to cremation of the dead is based
on such reasons as that cremation is an ancient pagan custom, that
burial is a religious duty, and that it is forbidden to burn a human
body, which is sacred, the literature on the subject sometimes
refers to the doctrine of the resurrection as a reason for forbidding
cremation. *V.* J. M. Tuckechinsky: '*Gesher Ha-Hayyim*', 2nd ed.,
Jer. 1960, Chapter 16, par. 9, pp. 155 f., I. J. Yoffey: 'Cremation:
The Jewish Attitude and a Comparison with that of Other Denomi-
nations' in the 'Jewish Chronicle Supplement', Nov. 1932, p. 1 f.
For the mediaeval period *v.* Joseph Sarachek: 'The Doctrine of the
Messiah in Mediaeval Jewish Literature', Jewish Theological
Seminary, New York, 1932. For the statement of the 'Pittsburgh
Platform' *v.* UJE, Vol. VI, p. 241.

*   *   *

The doctrine of Hell, that the wicked are punished for their sins after death, is, of course, known to Judaism. The classical Rabbinic statement on the question reads (*R.H.*17a) : 'Wrongdoers of Israel who sin with their body and wrongdoers of the Gentiles who sin with their body go down to Gehinnom and are punished there for twelve months. After twelve months their body is consumed and their soul is burnt and the wind scatters them under the soles of the feet of the righteous, as it says, "And ye shall tread down the wicked, and they shall be as ashes under the soles of your feet" (Mal. iii. 21). But as for the *minim* and the informers and the *'epiqorsim* and those who reject the *Torah* and deny the resurrection of the dead, and those who abandon the ways of the community, and those who "spread their terror in the land of the living" (Ezek. xxxii. 23), and who sinned and made the masses sin, like Jeroboam the son of Nebat and his fellows – these will go down to Gehinnom and be punished there for all generations, as it says, "And they shall go forth and look upon the carcasses of the men that have rebelled against me" (Is. lxvi. 24). Gehinnom will be consumed but they will not be consumed, as it says, "and their form shall wear away the nether world" (Ps. xlix. 15)'. In this passage, a *Baraitha* not later than the end of the second century C.E., it would seem that not only is there belief in *Gehinnom* for certain sinners, who will suffer torment there, but also a belief in eternal punishment for certain classes of sinners.

Maimonides (*Hil. Tesh.* III. 6, VIII. 1, 5) quotes the above passage, with certain elaborations of his own as to the classification of the offences listed. It is highly significant that apart from this sage's reference to 'judgment' of the offenders (III. 6) he seems to interpret the idea of *Gehinnom* in terms of deprivation rather than of positive punishment. It is true, as we have seen earlier, that in his Commentary to the *Mishnah* (*Sanh.* X. 1) Maimonides speaks of *Gehinnom* as a place of punishment, but his extreme brevity on this subject in his works suggests that he prefers to understand the punishment even of the worst sinners as deprivation of eternal bliss. The penalty of extirpation (*kareth*) mentioned in Scripture (e.g. in Num. xv. 31) means, according to Maimonides, that the soul of the wicked is 'cut off' i.e. is prevented from enjoying the bliss of the world to come.

Maimonides could hardly have been more explicit than in the following passage (*Hil. Tesh.* VIII. 5): 'The vengeance than which there is none worse is for the soul to be cut off so that it does not merit that life (of bliss in the world to come) as it is said: "That soul shall utterly be cut off, her iniquity shall be upon her" (Num. xv. 31). This destruction of the soul is called figuratively by the prophets "the nethermost pit" (Ps. lv. 24), "destruction" (Ps. lxxxviii. 12), "a hearth" (Is. xxx. 33), and "the horseleech" (Prov. xxx. 15). It is called by every name signifying destruction and annihilation since it is a destruction from which there is no rising and is irretrievable loss'. It is not surprising that some of Maimonides' contemporaries concluded from his statements here and his virtual failure to mention punishment in Hell in any of his works that Maimonides interprets Hell solely as deprivation of eternal bliss. The punishment of the sinner is not torment but annihilation. Nahmanides and others try to defend Maimonides by suggesting that in the *Mishneh Torah* he is thinking of the ultimate fate of the soul, but that he does not deny that before its annihilation the soul will suffer in Hell. Be that as it may the emphasis in Maimonides is clear and was no doubt occasioned both by his refusal to believe that God would inflict torture on the soul after death and his general preference for a spiritual interpretation of man's eternal fate.

Saadiah (' *'Emunoth We-De'oth'*, Treatise IX. 7, Rosenblatt, pp. 344–346) discusses the question of reward and punishment after death at length and comes to the conclusion that the punishment of certain classes of the wicked is eternal. His argument is that reward is forever, in order to provide the strongest possible incentive to lead the good life, and by the same token punishment must be eternal in order to provide men with the strongest possible deterrent for keeping from evil. Saadiah is not unaware of the difficulties of this position. He imagines someone arguing: 'I consider such a policy quite proper in the case of the reward of the righteous, since that consists of well-being and bliss and the bestowal of favours. However, when it comes to punishment and condemnation to perpetual hell-fire, I see therein a mercilessness and cruelty which does not tally with God's nature'. For all that, Saadiah does believe in eternal punishment, considering this as

belonging to God's mercy, since it provides men with the
deterrent which leads them to the good life and thus to enjoy
God's mercy. If God is to go back on His threats afterwards
He would be belying His own words. The threat of eternal
punishment, then, is really an act of kindness and although
once the threat had been effective it could be argued that God
can overlook the need to carry it out yet for Him to do this
would be a denial of His own words. This whole method of
reasoning is typical of religious thought in the Middle Ages,
Jewish and non-Jewish. There is probably no area where
modern man differs more from his mediaeval counterpart than
on this doctrine. We cannot believe in an eternal punishment
for even the worst sinner and we cannot bring ourselves to
discover any justifications for the belief.

Saadiah quotes Scripture in support of his contention that
both reward and punishment are everlasting. 'Some to everlasting life, and some to reproaches and everlasting abhorrence'
(Dan. xxi. 2) clearly implies this, as do the verses in the book
of Psalms: 'In Thy right hand is bliss for evermore' (Ps. xvi.
11), 'They shall never see the light' (Ps. xlix. 20). A theological difficulty suggests itself to Saadiah. If God's creatures
live eternally with Him in the future, and this is implied in the
belief in eternal reward and punishment, why could they not
have been in existence with Him in eternity in the past? The
answer he gives is that the author must precede His work, but
once God has brought His creatures into being there is no
reason why they should not exist with Him for all eternity. If
it be objected that this obliterates the distinction between God
and His creatures the answer is that no one can compare a
being of soul and body, dependent on time and place, to One
who is exalted far above all such things. While other mediaeval
thinkers disagree with Saadiah on the question of eternal
punishment there appears to be general agreement that the
reward of the righteous is eternal so that the righteous exist
with God for all eternity. The exception seems to be the author
of the famous 'Adon 'Olam hymn, who sings:

'Lord of the world. He reigned alone
While yet the universe was naught,
When by His will all things were wrought,

Then first His sov'ran name was known.
And when the All shall cease to be,
In dread lone splendour He shall reign,
He was, He is, He shall remain
In glorious eternity'.

As for the question of which classes of the wicked will be doomed
to eternal punishment, Saadiah (Chapter 9, Rosenblatt, pp.
350–352) says that perpetual torment is reserved for the non-
believers and the polytheists and the impenitent perpetrators
of grave sins. The Scriptural authority for the eternal damnation
of the first two classes is: 'And they shall go forth, and look
upon the carcasses of the men that had rebelled against Me;
for their worm shall not die' (Is. lxvi. 24). As for the unrepentant
sinners of grave sins they are referred to in the frequent
Scriptural and Rabbinic references to people deserving the
penalty of extirpation (kareth) and death at the hands of the
court. Reminiscent of the oft-quoted passages in St. Thomas
Aquinas and Tertullian of the righteous rejoicing at the
sufferings of the damned in Hell, because they have been saved,
is the observation of Saadiah that when the righteous regard
the sufferings of the wicked they will say: 'Praised be He who
saved us from this torment!' And they will be glad and rejoice
at their own condition.

Nahmanides ('Sha'ar Ha-Gemul', op. cit., pp. 57a to end)
deals similarly with the question of punishment in Hell.
Basically Nahmanides differs strongly, as we have noticed
earlier, from the view which seems to be that of Maimonides
that there is no actual punishment in Hell only deprivation,
through annihilation, of the enjoyment of the good. He first
admits that the view is not unreasonable in itself (p. 61b).
Punishment after death cannot affect the body, hence it must
be spiritual. But how can a soul inhabit space to be punished
in a Hell which has a definite location and how can a soul
be burned in fire which can have effect only on material things?
But for all the rationality of the view which sees Hell merely
as a negation of the good it is really a viewpoint grafted on to
Judaism from the influence of foreign (i.e. Greek) ways of
thought, and is at variance with the Torah and Rabbinic
teaching. According to the Torah there is, of course, a penalty

known as 'extirpation' (*kareth*) but this is for some sins only.
Are we to conclude that for lesser sins there is no Hell? If so,
it is contrary to Rabbinic teachings. The Rabbis frequently
speak of punishment in Hell for lesser offences than those
for which the *Torah* prescribes extirpation. The Rabbis speak of
Hell as an actual place of fire (*Men.* 89b) and refer to its
measurements (*Ta'an.* 10a) and its portals (*'Erub.* 19a).
Furthermore, there is a legal discussion concerning cooking on
the Sabbath in the hot Springs of Tiberius, in which it is said
that they owe their heat to the fact that they pass the entrance
to *Gehinnom* (*Sabb.* 109a). It is abundantly clear that these
circumstantial details cannot be figurative and that for the
Rabbis Hell is an actual place. Nahmanides' view, therefore, is
that the sinner is actually burned in Hell but with a fire different
from our fire. The distinction, he says, is made in tractate
Pesahim 54a. Hell-fire is an *elemental* fire. Though of the same
nature as our fire it is, as it were, the essence of fire (62b).
Just as our fire has the power of burning the body, that fire has
the power of burning the soul. The Greek and Islamic thinkers
who scorn the very notion of a soul occupying space are wrong.
Just as the soul is made to occupy the body it can be made to
occupy the place of punishment after the death of the body. The
Rabbis, claims Nahmanides, had at least as much a spiritual
conception of the soul as the Greeks, yet they did not hesitate
to teach that the soul is punished by fire in Hell. The less
wicked are punished for a time in Hell and then are either
raised to Heaven or remain forever in a state in which there is
neither suffering nor bliss. But the very wicked are punished
in Hell forever (63a). Apart from her sufferings in Hell the
soul suffers, too, through her longing to return to her Source
(63a). Nahmanides (63b) now turns to Maimonides' views on
Hell as mere deprivation. He agrees that on the surface
Maimonides' ideas are, indeed, very puzzling. However,
Maimonides in the *Mishneh Torah* does refer to some sinners
who are punished and who yet enjoy spiritual bliss in the
Hereafter and this would seem to mean that their punishment is not merely deprivation but actual punishment in
Hell.

To sum up, says Nahmanides (p. 64b), Hell is a place in
which the wicked are punished for their sins, the pain and tor-

ment being of a severity and intensity unimaginable in this life. For suffering in this life is experienced by man's gross body while the sufferings of Hell are endured by the pure, highly sensitive soul. The pain of a needle prick is more acute than that of a blow with a blunt instrument and the more sensitive the person the greater his pain. Nahmanides (64b) quotes the *Midrash* (*Lev. R. 32. 1*) in which it is said that the righteous in *Gan 'Eden* rejoice when they see the wicked suffering in *Gehinnom*.

Hasdai Crescas ('*Or 'Adonai*, Treatise III, 3, Chapter 4, ed. Vienna, 1859, pp. 73b f. and Treatise IV, Exposition 9, p. 90) grapples, too, with the problem of Hell. Crescas asks how the punishment of the soul in the Hereafter can be justified since such punishment, which cannot be known to others and which takes place when a change of life is no longer possible, cannot act as a deterrent. God's punishment cannot be vindictive. Furthermore, how can tradition speak of the punishment of the wicked in Hell lasting twelve months since the soul in the Hereafter is outside Time? Since body and soul are different, to punish the soul for the offences done while in the body is like punishing an angel for the sins of a man, i.e. how can there be a continuing identity after the soul has left the body? Crescas replies as follows. The soul has a capacity both to acquire knowledge and to enjoy the knowledge it has acquired. But the soul which rejected knowledge during its habitation of the body and is thereby prevented from attaining intellectual perfection in the Hereafter is bound to be doomed to a kind of permanent disharmony. It is not impossible for God to decree a temporal punishment (i.e. twelve months) for a soul not entirely deserving of ultimate annihilation. As for the question of identity, the soul after death is not really different from the soul which inhabited the body. During a man's lifetime the soul occupies the body and after death it becomes separated from the body but essentially it is the same soul. Unlike *Gan 'Eden*, *Gehinnom* is not mentioned in Scripture but it is mentioned frequently in the Rabbinic literature, the Rabbis receiving this belief from tradition. Although the soul is of a spiritual nature it can nonetheless be contained in a special place to suffer severe pain. The cause of this pain may be the fact that the soul has become soiled with materialism and is thus connected in some way with the material world. Crescas adds little to the discussion but does not speak of eternal punishment in Hell.

Joseph Albo ('*Iqqarim*, Book IV, Chapter 33, ed. Husik, pp. 331–335) has an elaborate description of the meaning of Hell and Hell-fire. If a person in his lifetime pursued his desires and physical pleasures at the expense of his spiritual needs, his soul becomes habituated to these pleasures and yearns for them. But after death the physical desires are no longer capable of realisation. Furthermore, by virtue of her own nature, the soul yearns for the nearness of God. Thus, the soul of the sinner is pulled in two directions at once. The bodily pleasures to which the soul has become accustomed pull one way, the desire of the soul for her Source pulls the other. 'Accordingly the soul will be drawn in two directions at once, upwards and downwards, the one by reason of her nature, the other by reason of her habit and custom. But she will have no instruments for obtaining the lower desires and no preparation to obtain the higher. This will cause her great pain and suffering, greater than any pain in the world or any kind of fracture – more pain than the burning of fire or cold and terrible frost, more than the wounds of knives and swords or the stings of snakes and scorpions'. This, according to Albo, is the meaning of the Rabbinic saying (*Sabb.* 152b) that two angels at different ends of the world throw the soul one to the other. The meaning is that the soul is pulled in two opposite directions and this is the cause of her torment. The righteous soul, on the other hand, has no downward desire and she finds rest under the Throne of Glory. Albo, too, believes that some sinners are punished eternally (Chapter 34, p. 336).

From the above sketch of the views of the typical mediaeval thinkers it is clear that they build on the Rabbinic tradition, although they feel free to interpret this tradition in the light of their own ideas and time. For all that many of them not only believe in an actual torment for the wicked (with the exception of Maimonides who appears, on the whole, to favour an interpretation of Hell which would equate it with annihilation of the soul rather than positive torment) but also that for certain types of the wicked this torment will last forever. However, there can be observed a marked tendency to spiritualise

the conception, although so far as the moral difficulty is concerned of a good God condemning any of His creatures to
eternal torment, there is not much point in substituting
spiritual for physical torment, particularly since they are at
pains to point out that spiritual torment is far worse and far
more intense than physical torment.

The history of the doctrine of Hell can be more or less
clearly traced. The usual name for it in the Rabbinic literature
is *Gehinnom*, a name derived from the 'valley of the son of
Hinnom', to the south of Jerusalem, where children were
sacrificed to Moloch (Josh. xv. 8; II Kings xxiii. 10; Jer. ii.
23; vii. 31–32; xix. 6, 13–14). There is no reference in the
whole of the Bible to punishment after death in *Gehinnom*
but by the Rabbinic period the belief was accepted and, as
Nahmanides points out, it is generally taken as referring to a
special *place* of torment. Maimonides (Commentary to the
Mishnah, Sanh. X. 1), true to his conception, laconically says:
'*Gehinnom* is an expression for the suffering that will befall
the wicked. The nature of this suffering is not expounded in
the *Talmud*. One authority there states that the sun will draw
near to the wicked and burn them (*A.Z.* 3b, *Ned.* 8b). He proves
this from the verse "For behold the day cometh, burning as
an oven" (Mal. iii. 19). Another asserts that a strange heat
will arise in their bodies, and consume them (*Gen. R.* VI. 6).
He derives proof of this from the phrase "Your breath as
fire shall devour you" (Is. xxxiii. 11)'. Ultimately, as we have
seen, *Gehinnom*, for Maimonides, is strictly limited in its power,
and the final punishment of the wicked is not physical or spiritual
torment but annihilation. But this is a very unconventional
view and hardly describes the commonly held Rabbinic notions.
In the *Mishnah* (*'Eduy.* II. 10) the opinion of Rabbi Akiba is
quoted that the punishment of the wicked in *Gehinnom* is for
twelve months. His contemporary, R. Johanan b. Nuri said,
only as long as from Passover to Pentecost. Following Rabbi
Akiba, it is customary for a son to recite the *Qaddish* prayer
after the death of a parent only for eleven months. The purpose
of the prayer is to assist the departed in the next world and for
the son to recite it for a whole twelve months is to imply that
the parent belongs to the category of the wicked who suffer in
Gehinnom for twelve months (*Shulhan 'Arukh, Yoreh De'ah,*

376 end). We are told that the great teacher, Rabban Johanan
b. Zakkai wept on his deathbed because he was uncertain
whether he would be led into Paradise or into Hell (*Ber.* 28b).
A curious story is told in the *Talmud* (*Hag.* 15b). When *Aher*,
the Rabbi who became an apostate, died it was at first decreed
that he should not be punished in Hell since he studied the
Torah, but that he should not be allowed to enter Paradise
because of his sins. His disciple, R. Meir, observed that it
were better for him to be punished and then to enter Paradise.
R. Meir said that after his death he would see to it that this
would be the judgment of *Aher*, and when R. Meir died smoke
began to rise from *Aher*'s grave. R. Johanan felt that it ought
to be possible to raise *Aher* to Paradise without excessive
punishment in Hell and when R. Johanan died the smoke
ceased from *Aher's* grave.

Among modern Jewish thinkers the tendency is to give up
the whole conception of Hell, certainly as a place or state of
everlasting punishment. But the older conception has not
entirely died out. One of the great teachers of the *Musar*
school, Rabbi E. Dessler (d. 1955) used to devote some of his
ethical talks (*v.* '*Mikhtabh Me-' Elijahu*', Lond., 1955, '*Gehinnom*', pp. 295–303) to the theme. Although Rabbi Dessler
interprets the whole conception in purely spiritual terms
there is not the slightest attempt to mitigate in any way the
severities of the older idea. Dessler observes that the Rabbis
make many different attempts to explain the torments of
Hell because they are trying to convey what cannot really be
conveyed, the nature of a purely spiritual state. The illustration
of fire is frequently used so as to express the idea that the pain
of separation from God in the Hereafter is far greater than the
torment of fire burning the body. There is a Rabbinic saying,
for instance, that the fire of *Gehinnom* is sixty times as hot as our
fire (*Ber.* 57b). Since a purely spiritual punishment cannot be
conceived by us while we are in the body a tangible reminder is
necessary. R. Israel Salanter, the founder of the *Musar* movement and Dessler's great-grandfather, is quoted as saying
that the way to the fear of Heaven is to depict the torments of
Hell in concrete form. If, for instance, the little finger is placed
in a flame for but a second how great is the pain! How much
more if the finger is left there for two seconds, for three . . . for

a whole year! Then double this fire (there are many flames in Hell), then treble it . . . And each moment seems like a year! This reminds us of nothing so much as the terrible sermon preached by Jonathan Edwards, the famous American religious thinker and divine: 'We can conceive but little of the matter; but to help your conception, imagine yourself to be cast into a fiery oven, or a great furnace, where your pain would be as much greater than that occasioned by incidentally touching a coal of fire, as the heat is greater. Imagine also that your body were to lie there for a quarter of an hour, full of fire, and all the while full of quick sense; what horror would you feel at the entrance of such a furnace! and how long would that quarter of an hour seem to you! And after you had endured it for one minute, how overbearing would it be to you to think that you had to endure it the other fourteen! But what must be the effect on your soul, if you knew that you must lie there enduring that torment to the full for twenty-four hours! And how much greater would be the effect, if you knew you must endure it for a whole year . . .' (Quoted by Percy Dreamer: 'The Legend of Hell', Cassell, Lond., 1929, p. 43). I knew Rabbi Dessler personally as a gentle, kindly soul whose whole life was devoted to preaching the virtues of *hesed*, 'lovingkindness', and yet, such is the power of a cruel dogmatism, that he fails to consider the implications of such a doctrine on our conception of God as the loving Father of mankind.

Before considering the views of modern theologians a word or two should be said about the Jewish mystical descriptions of Hell. The *Zohar* (II, 150b) believes in eternal punishment in Hell but limits this to the wicked who never give a thought to repentance during their lifetime on earth. The fire of *Gehinnom* is said to correspond to the hot power of sinfulness in men. It is the heat of sinful passion in mankind which keeps the flames of Hell burning. There are seven habitations in Hell (the seven *medore Gehinnom* are frequently referred to in the mystical literature) each more severe than the other, in which sinners are cast according to the degrees of their wickedness. Sinners in Hell do have a respite, however, on the Sabbath, with the exception of those who profaned the Sabbath while on earth (151a). Myriads of demons under the direction of the archdemon Duma exist in Hell to punish sinners. These

ideas were kept alive in the writings of some of the moralists
and in the preachments of some of the *Maggidim* in Eastern
Europe until the threshold of the modern period. Hayyim
Tchernowitz ('Autobiography', Bitzaron, New York, 1954, pp.
84–5) describes how these ideas concerning Hell affected a
sensitive youth at the end of the last century in Russia. 'I
began to study the works of the moralists, such as *"Reshith
Hokhmah"* and *"Shebhet Musar"*, with all their descriptions
of the seven habitations of Hell which await the wicked and
about which I had heard so much, in addition to the books,
from the vivid pictures of the preachers. But these neither
moved nor frightened me since my reason did not allow me to
believe in the existence of such things. The first question I
asked myself was how they could know what happens in the
seven habitations of Hell. Had they been there to see it for
themselves?'

Even a strictly Orthodox thinker like Dr. Friedländer is
frank enough to admit, without actually saying so, that all
these ideas have had their day and that there is no room for
them in any modern interpretation of Judaism. In 'The Jewish
Religion' (*op. cit.*, pp. 223–4) Friedländer writes: 'The detailed
descriptions of Paradise and Hell as given in books both profane
and religious are nothing but the offering of man's imagination.
The question has been asked, How long shall the punishment of
the wicked last? Will it be eternal? and if so, is it compatible
with God's goodness? This and similar questions do not concern
us in the least. Our task is to do what the Lord has commanded
us to do, and to trust, as regards the future, in Him, who knows
best to combine goodness and justice. We must bear in mind
that "God's thoughts are not ours" '. One would have expected
a less qualified dismissal of the whole notion of eternal punishment but Friedländer does, at least, attribute the descriptions
in the 'holy books' of 'life' in Hell to man's imagination. He is
bold enough to state, too, that such questions as the ones he
mentions do not concern us, even though they were of great
concern, as we have seen, to the Rabbis and the mediaeval
thinkers.

Much more emphatic is Morris Joseph ('Judaism as Creed
and Life', Macmillan, Lond., 1903, pp. 144 f.). 'Nor do we
believe in a hell or in everlasting punishment. The pictures

of penal fires with which some Jewish writers have embellished
their descriptions of a future life are purely imaginary . . . If
suffering there is to be it is terminable. The idea of eternal
punishment is repugnant to the genius of Judaism. Here and
there a Rabbi may be found advocating the notion; but such
teaching does not represent true Jewish doctrine. Nay, it
does not represent the doctrine of any rational religion. God
is supremely just, and He cannot conceivably inflict upon
fallible man, prone to error, beset by fierce temptations, endless
torments for his sins in this life'. We have seen that the doctrine
of Hell, including eternal punishment, was held by more than
'a Rabbi here and there' but Morris Joseph's noble statement,
while not at all representative of Jewish teaching in the past,
certainly expresses the point of view of most Jewish thinkers
in the present.

C. G. Montefiore ('A Rabbinic Anthology', *op. cit.*, Chapter
XXXI, p. 581) argues: The appalling self-delusion which
could glibly talk of a God of love and yet believe in an eternal
hell was, I think, sooner and more prevailingly lost in Judaism
than in Christianity'. This is probably true. There is nothing
in Judaism to correspond with the doctrine of a Saviour to
deliver mankind from the doom of Hell which must have helped
to keep the idea alive in Christianity. It is also worth noting
that for all the instances we have examined of Jewish teachers
who believed in eternal torment in Hell there are hardly any
references to Hell in the Jewish liturgy. *Rahmanuth*, 'compassion', 'pity', is, after all, a prime Jewish virtue, according
to the Rabbis, one of the distinguishing marks of the Jew,
and, whatever a cruel logic may have compelled thinkers to
accept, the Jewish heart refused to allow the notion of eternal
punishment to gain a real foothold in Judaism.

To sum up, Jews cannot afford to be complacent or smug
about superior Jewish teaching on the question of Hell. If
there are horrible descriptions of Hell in Christian sources
these can be capped with equally horrid accounts in Jewish
sources. But present-day Judaism has for all intents and purposes
abandoned the notion of eternal punishment in Hell and has
virtually abandoned the whole concept of Hell as a place of
torture. Whatever truth there may be in the doctrine (it is
sentimentalism which can calmly tolerate a merciful God who

can easily forgive a Hitler, for example) most Jews feel today that the matter must be left to God. It is not for humans to attempt to pierce the veil.

* * *

EXCURSUS

V. Ludwig Blau: 'Gehenna' in JE, Vol. V, pp. 582–4; Mordecai I. Soloff: '*Gehinnom*' in UJE, Vol IV, pp. 520–21; S.D.F. Salmond in Hastings D.B., Vol. II, pp. 343–6. Percy Dreamer's 'The Legend of Hell', Cassell, London, 1929, is an interesting account of a modern Anglican's opposition to the doctrine. On p. 99 Dreamer remarks that because of the realisation of fatherhood, 'the Jews have for long been able to boast that their belief in the Divine Father has freed them from belief in everlasting punishment'. The famous passage from St. Thomas Aquinas on the just beholding the sufferings of the wicked is in *Summa*, Para III, Supplementum, q. 94, art 1 (Dreamer, p. 34–5): 'That the saints may enjoy their beatitude more thoroughly, and give more abundant thanks for it to God, a perfect view of the punishment of the damned is granted to them'. Tertullian's 'spectacle' passage is well-known from Gibbon's description ('Decline and Fall', Vol. II, 15, Dreamer, pp. 33–4): ' "You are fond of spectacles", exclaims the stern Tertullian, "expect the greatest of all spectacles, the last and eternal judgment of the universe. How shall I admire, how laugh, how rejoice, how exult, when I behold so many proud monarchs, and fancied gods, groaning in the lowest abyss of darkness; so many magistrates, who persecuted the name of the Lord, liquifying in fiercer fires than they ever kindled against the Christians; so many sage philosophers blushing in red-hot flames with their deluded scholars; so many celebrated poets trembling before the tribunal, not of Minos, but of Christ; so many tragedians, more tuneful in the expression of their own sufferings; so many dancers" – But the humanity of the reader will permit me to draw a veil over the rest of this infernal description, which the zealous African pursues in a long variety of affected and unfeeling witticisms'. Dreamer (pp. 83 ff.) skilfully conveys the reasons why good men were able to hold on for so long to the doctrine of Hell. These are: the motive of fear, frightening people into goodness; the idea of exclusive salvation; the mendacity which made the theory of Hell as frightening as could be; the misunderstanding of the Bible; ignorance of the nature of Jewish apocalyptic; excessive credulity; the cruelty of the ancient world; the desire for power; the misunderstanding of pain; and distorted ideas about God. There is no doubt that some of these factors

operated among Jews as well. A useful summary of Rabbinic views
on the subject is to be found in A. Cohen's 'Everyman's Talmud',
Dent, London, 1949, Chapter XI, V, pp. 379 f. Among other points
the following are interesting. Although generally speaking
Gehinnom is spoken of as a place beneath the earth (to *go down* to
Hell) some Rabbis speak of it as above the firmament or as lying
beyond the 'mountains of darkness' (*Tam.* 32b). The seven storeys
of Hell are referred to in *Midrash* Psalms to Psalm xi. 7. Hell is
a place of darkness (*Jeb.* 109b, *Gen. R.* XXXIII. 1). The power of
Hell is said to be ineffective so far as students of the *Torah* are
concerned (*Hag.* 27a). Here perhaps more than elsewhere it is
necessary to point out that these and similar sayings belong not so
much to theological doctrine as to preachments of a more or less
popular nature.

*   *   *

From the above observations it will be clear that in any modern
interpretation of Judaism the emphasis will be on the Hereafter
as a state of the soul. With the reservations noted earlier,
that this should be taken to include the survival of the whole
personality of man, the best way of speaking of the ultimate
fate of man is the immortality of the soul. This whole question,
of the most vital significance for a spiritual religious outlook,
must now be considered.

We begin with the history of the idea. This we have sketched
earlier but here is the place to consider the matter in greater
detail. The most striking thing here is the virtual silence on
the whole question in the earlier parts of the Bible. It is hard
to believe that the great prophets, for example, had no hope
of further communion with the God they served, but they are
certainly silent on the whole question in the literary utterances
which we now have. There are frequent references, as we have
noted, to the dead being gathered to their fathers (Gen. xv. 15;
Judg. ii. 10) and to their people (Gen. xlix. 29–33; Num.
xxvii. 13) and this seems to imply a belief that there was some
kind of society of the dead in the Hereafter. A wider term used
in the Bible is *Sheol*, the abode of the dead. Eventually this term
is made to embrace the final abode of all mankind (Gen. xxxvii.
35; xliv. 31 and freq.). This is also called 'the house appointed
for all living' (Job xxx. 23) and man's 'eternal house' (Eccl.
xii. 5). It is admittedly difficult to know exactly what is meant

by this conception but, judging solely by the references to it in
Scripture, Sheol appears to be a place where the dead enjoy
only a shadowy existence, far removed from the idea of the
whole personality of man surviving death, which came into
prominence in later Judaism.

Among ideas in the earlier books of the Bible which served
as a field in which the seed of the doctrine of a future life of the
soul could grow are the following: the creation of man in God's
image (Gen. i. 26, 27); the conception of a 'tree of life' (Gen. ii
and iii); the translation into Heaven of Enoch (Gen. v. 22–24)
and Elijah (II Kings ii. 11); the restoration of the dead to
life through the instrumentality of the prophets (I Kings xvii.
22; II Kings iv. 35, xiii. 21). In the writings of Ezekiel
(particularly, iii. 16–21; xiv. 12–23; xviii; xxx, 1–20) the
note of individual worth and responsibility is struck with great
emphasis. God's regard for the individual and the latter's
responsibility to Him necessarily lead to a belief that death
is not the end for the individual and that he continues to have a
place in the Hereafter in God's care and providence. The great
probings of the book of Job gave further emphasis to the importance of the individual though, with the exception of one
highly debated text (xix. 25–27), there is still no definite
reference to the idea of individual immortality of a more
complete kind than existence in the netherworld of *Sheol*.
In various Psalms (e.g. xlix and lxxiii) belief in personal
immortality for the righteous appears to be implied. As we have
seen earlier eventually the doctrine of the immortality of the
soul became fused with that of the resurrection, but in the centuries immediately preceding the present era both doctrines
came to be held as dogmas of the Jewish faith, at least among
the Pharisees. (The above account draws on the material
assembled in R. H. Charles' famous study: 'A Critical History
of the Doctrine of a Future Life', Adam and Charles Black,
London, 2nd. ed., 1913).

The Sadducees denied the resurrection of the dead and the
immortality of the soul while the Pharisees accepted both beliefs.
The debate between the Sadducees and Pharisees on the subject
of the After-life is referred to by Josephus (*Antiquities*, xviii,
1, 4) and frequently in the Talmudic literature. In the *Mishnah*
(*Ber.* IX. 5) we read: 'At the close of every Benediction in the

Temple they used to say, "For everlasting" ; but after the heretics (in some versions "the Sadducees") had taught corruptly and said that there is but one world, it was ordained that they should say, "From everlasting to everlasting" '. The *Talmud* (*Sanh.* 90b) tells of a debate between Rabban Gamaliel and the Sadducees on this question in which Rabban Gamaliel tried to prove the resurrection of the dead from Scriptural verses which his opponents did not accept. Although these Talmudic sources refer to the resurrection the idea of the immortality of the soul is generally meant as well, unless we accept the contention of David Neumark (which lacks real proof) that the Sadducees only denied the doctrine of the resurrection but believed in the immortality of the soul. The Gospels, too, refer to the controversy between the Sadducees and Pharisees on this question (Mark xii. 18–27; Matt. xxii. 23–33) in which Jesus and the disciples agree with the Pharisees.

The official doctrine of the *Mishnah* (*Sanh.* X. 1) is that all Israelites have a share in the world to come but this is immediately qualified by the statement that certain heretics are excluded from a share in the world to come. In the second century R. Eliezer and R. Joshua debated whether the righteous of the nations (i.e. Gentiles) have a share in the world to come (*Tos. Sanh.* XIII. 2, and *Sanh.* 105a). R. Joshua's view is that the righteous of all nations have a share in the world to come. (It should be noted as stated earlier that the usual expression 'the saints of the nations of the world' – *haside 'umoth ha-'olam* – found in the mediaeval sources is not found in the *Tos.*, *v.* ed. Zuckermandel, Pasewalk, 1881, where the reading is 'the righteous of the nations of the world' – *tzadiqe 'umoth ha-'olam*). R. Joshua's opinion was everywhere adopted by the later Jewish teachers so that it became axiomatic in Judaism that the good men of all nations enjoy immortality. However, the question arises as to what is considered to be a 'good man'. The answer generally given is that goodness in this context is defined as one who observes the 'seven precepts of the sons of Noah', i.e. one who observes the rules of decent conduct said to have been enjoined on the human race before the Sinaitic revelation. The usual classification of these rules is that they embrace: the prohibition of idolatry, adultery, incest, murder, theft, blasphemy, and the eating of a limb torn from a

living animal; and the setting up of proper courts in which
justice can be administered (*v. ET*, Vol. III, pp. 348 ff.).
This is a remarkably liberal view and was widely held right
through the Middle Ages. However, Maimonides is here a
strange exception. According to Maimonides (*Hil. Mel.* VIII.
11) the 'saints of the nations of the world' (by Maimonides'
time the term 'saints' was used) refers only to those Gentiles
who believe that God commanded the seven precepts to Noah
and that He told this to Moses. But the Gentile who carries
out the seven precepts because his intellect tells him that this is
the proper thing to do does not belong in the category of the
'saints of the nations of the world' and has no share in the world
to come. (*V.* J. Katz: 'Exclusiveness and Tolerance', Clarendon
Press, Oxford, 1961, p. 175, note 5, that Maimonides' source is
'*Mishnah Rabbi 'Eliezer*', ed. H. Enelow, New York, 1934,
p. 121). It is safe to say that in practically every modern interpretation of Judaism the wider view, not that of Maimonides,
prevails.

Some of the more typical Rabbinic views on the Hereafter
may now be given, but first it is necessary to repeat G. F.
Moore's warning: 'Any attempt to systematize the Jewish
notions of the hereafter imposes upon them an order and consistency which does not exist in them. As has already been
remarked, their religious significance lies in the definitive
establishment of the doctrine of retribution after death, not
in the variety of ways in which men imagined it' ('Judaism',
op. cit., Vol. II, p. 389). There is the further complication that
the two concepts of the resurrection and the immortality of the
soul are fused and are both referred to by the term 'the world
to come'.

There is to be discerned on the one hand, in the Rabbinic
literature, a certain reticence about life in Heaven. Even the
prophets of Israel did not 'see' the nature of the spiritual
bliss treasured up for the righteous in the world to come (*Ber.*
34b). On the other hand, there are, here and there, attempts
to pierce the veil in some matters at least. Thus, the world
to come is, in one passage, referred to as a 'topsy-turvy' world
because there, those who are here lowly are elevated while those
of great elevation here are frequently found in a lowly position
there (*Pes.* 50a). Reference has already been made to the

saying of Rab (*Ber.* 17a): 'In the world to come there is neither eating nor drinking, nor procreation of children or business transactions; no envy or hatred or rivalry; but the righteous sit enthroned with their crowns on their heads and enjoy the lustre of the *Shekhinah*'. (Professor Samuel Krauss, 'The Jewish Rite of Covering the Head', *HUCA*, Vol. XIX, 1945–6, pp. 121–168, has, incidentally, pointed out that the concept of the crowns on the heads of the righteous in Paradise has its origin in Persian eschatology). The spiritual bliss of the world to come is sometimes compared to the bliss of the Sabbath, the latter being considered as a foretaste of the former (*A.Z.* 3a, *Ber.* 57b). Another favourite expression for the spiritual activity of the world to come is 'the Heavenly Academy' (*B.M.* 86a and freq.) where the dead scholars study the *Torah*. The idea of Heaven as a place of spiritual progress and activity is implied in the saying (*Ber.* 64a) that the students of the *Torah* have rest neither in this world nor in the next. For which the proof-text quoted is: 'They go from strength to strength, every one of them appeareth before God in Zion' (Ps. lxxxiv. 8). Matters of great intellectual difficulty here will be easy to grasp in Heaven (*Pes.* 50a). There are discussions on whether infants have a share in the world to come, some holding that they do have from the time they answer *Amen*, some from the time they can speak, others from the hour of birth and still others hold from the time of conception (*Sanh.* 110b). It can be said that there is nothing in the Rabbinic literature to correspond with the view among some of the Church fathers that unbaptised infants go to Hell. Even the Rabbi who holds that an infant who dies before he has ever answered *Amen* does not go to Heaven is very far from suggesting that he goes to Hell. In the Hereafter (we have noticed above the difference of opinion among the mediaeval thinkers whether this kind of saying refers to the resurrection – it probably does – or to life after death in Heaven), we are told, God will make a great banquet for the righteous from the flesh of the fish monster called Leviathan (*B.B.* 74b). The righteous will drink wine preserved in the grape from the six days of Creation (*Ber.* 34b). The great banquet of the righteous and the wine they will drink are a favourite theme both of later Jewish folklore and of Jewish mysticism. In one Talmudic passage it is said that in *Gan 'Eden*

God will arrange a dance for the righteous. He will sit in their midst and each one will point to Him with his finger and say: 'Lo, this is our God, we have waited for Him and He will save us; this is the Lord, we have waited for Him, we will be glad and rejoice in His salvation' (Is. xxv. 9) (*Ta'an.* 31a). The famous Rabbi Jonathan Eibeschütz (1690–1764) gave this saying, no doubt without historical warrant, the interpretation that the righteous dance in a circle because the circle is finite but unbounded. This signifies that the finite human mind will receive in the Hereafter unbounded revelations of God's truth. These fancies, including the combat of Leviathan and Behemoth, found their way into the famous Pentecost hymn ' '*Aqdamuth Millin*' (trans. Raphael Loewe, 'Service of the Synagogue', 'Pentecost', Routledge, London, 1954, p. 211):

> 'Then shall Leviathan's enthralling sight
> Divert them, with Behemoth's bovine might
> On mountains bred, fast twin'd in mortal fight.
> As Taurus' lofty horn to gore begins,
> See, leaping Draco parries with his fins:
> Till his Creator wields His wondrous sword –
> And so prepares the righteous' festive board.
> Reclin'd round agate, round carbuncles' glow,
> They'll watch while streams of balsam freely flow;
> Quaffing their nectar, copious cups o'erpour'd,
> Vintage matured in vats Creation stor'd'.

There are said to be different stages and compartments in Heaven so that people there will be 'burned' at the sight of their neighbour's glorious canopy (*B.B.* 75a). The compartment of the martyrs is so elevated that none but they can enter there (*Pes.* 50a).

It would be incorrect, however, to imagine that the Rabbis, for all their other-worldliness, denigrated life here on earth or tended to consider it unimportant. Life on earth was, for them, both the opportunity of acquiring immortal life and a good in itself as a means of serving God. Naturally, they held the world to come to be more important than this life but that was because the world to come was everlasting while this world was transient. We do not find, however, in the Rabbinic literature the sharp antithesis between this life and life in the

world to come, with a resulting scorn for material things and
bodily passions, that we find among many of the mediaeval
writers, influenced by Greek ideas of the war between flesh
and spirit. The Rabbinic view is expressed by the frequent
references to this life as 'life of the hour' and the world to
come as 'eternal life' (*Sabb.* 33b). For the performance of
certain precepts a man receives the 'interest' in this world
while the 'capital' is stored up for him in the world to come
(*Pe'ah* I. 1). It is possible for a man to enjoy 'eternal life'
even in this life. This is the meaning of the famous Rabbinic
blessing (*Ber.* 17b): 'May you find your eternity in your life,
and may your future be in the life of the world to come, and
may your hope last from generation to generation'. Perhaps the
most remarkable and most far-reaching of the Rabbinic opinions
on the Hereafter is the famous saying of R. Jacob (*'Abhoth* IV.
17): 'One hour of repentance and good deeds in this world
is more than all the life of the world to come; but an hour of
bliss in the world to come is more than all the life of this world'.
Nowhere in Jewish literature is the peculiar blending of a this-
worldly and other-worldly religion typical of Jewish teaching
more strikingly and more effectively put than this. The life
of this world is a good in itself, quite apart from its value as a
preparation for the After-life. But God rewards His servants
with such bliss in the world to come that its smallest fraction
outweighs all the joys of this life.

Of all the mediaeval thinkers Maimonides, as we have noted
earlier, has the most spiritualised conception of the After-life.
This is due to Maimonides' general preference for the spiritual
in religion and to his particular doctrine of immortality.
According to the Aristotelians, whom Maimonides follows,
it is only that part of man's intellect which he has acquired
through metaphysical speculation (*ha-sekhel ha-niqheh*, 'the
acquired intellect') which is immortal, as we have noted earlier.
This alone, through its contact with the 'Active Intellect'
emanating from God, survives the death of the body ('Guide',
III. 27, 51–52, 54). To be consistent Maimonides should have
limited immortality, like the Aristotelians, to thinkers and
philosophers, but faced with the Jewish teaching that all Israel
are immortal the sage felt obliged to qualify the full rigours of
his position. He is, as we have noted, careful to point out in his

'Code' that the nature of the ultimate fate of man is to enjoy spiritual, not material, bliss and that even after the physical resurrection of the dead men will die again to live on in the world of the spirit. The Rabbinic references to the great 'banquet' prepared for the righteous are accordingly interpreted figuratively (*Hil. Tesh.* VIII. 4).

Crescas ('*Or 'Adonai*, Treatise II, 5, Chapter 5 and 6, Chapter 1, ed. Vienna, 1859, pp. 49a–56b) takes issue with Maimonides and the Aristotelians. It cannot be true that only the acquired intellect is immortal and enjoys eternal bliss since happiness, joy and bliss do not belong to the intellect but to the emotions. For Crescas the soul is a spiritual substance, immortal by nature. After the death of the body the soul retains its individuality to become merged neither with the 'Active Intellect' nor with other souls into one soul. But if the soul is immortal by nature how can Jewish tradition insist that immortality is a reward for living the good life? To this Crescas gives the novel reply that attachment to God during one's lifetime on earth endows the soul with a kind of cohesive strength which assures its individuality after the death of the body. Crescas' view appears to be that for all the soul's natural immortality it requires an adhesive force to keep its parts together. The harmony and permanence of the separate parts, so that they form one whole, are provided by the virtuous life on earth spent in nearness to God, the Source of all unity. Life on earth is seen as so many opportunities for *individual* worship and it is this which enables individuality to persist after death.

Albo ('*Iqqarim*, Book IV, Chapters 32–34, ed. Husik, pp. 317 ff.) adds his own contribution to the problem of immortality. Albo first discusses why it is that all men fear death. No one wants to die. Everyone shares the sentiments of a Heine who sang, even in the direst distress, of the sweetness of life and the bitterness of death. Does not this instinctive fear of death on the part of man suggest that the death of the body is the end of life? If man's soul is really immortal and death but a door which opens on to a fuller life how is it that men are afraid of death? How is it that nature is so false to reality? Albo's solution is that men do not fear death because it is a passing from existence to non-existence but because man's natural inertia makes any change, even a change for the better, painful to him. On this view, fear of death is really fear of change, fear of the unknown, which is not rendered less potent even by the conviction that what awaits man in the unknown is infinitely more pleasant than anything he can have experienced in this life. There are many examples of this, says Albo, in our own experience. The babe cries at birth, the infant weeps when it is weaned, the man long in darkness fears the light. In all these cases the new state is far more pleasant in every way than the old yet fear is present. Even after death, Albo continues, it is, at first, hard for the soul to become accustomed to the change and she goes up and then down again to the place of the body for the first twelve months, as the Rabbis say (*Sabb.* 152b).

But how can the soul exist without the body since in life she is obviously dependent on the body? Albo gives the interesting illustration of the ship which conveys travellers to their destination. While at sea the travellers cannot live apart from the ship, but once the destination has been reached the ship becomes a prison from which those who travelled on it seek to escape at the first opportunity on to dry land where they can wander at will. If it be asked why the great heroes of the past, like Moses, were so reluctant to die, the reason is certainly not because they believed death to be the end. On the contrary, they loved life here on earth so much and were so reluctant to part from it because it is here on earth that man can acquire greater perfection by his actions and thus acquire a greater degree of existence in the Hereafter.

Dealing with the nature of spiritual bliss in the Hereafter, Albo (Chapter 33) uses an illustration from the dream that is realised. The soul while in the body can only hope to have a very faint glimmer of understanding. From this point of view life on earth can be compared to a dream from which the sleeper awakes after death. If the ideas acquired by the soul during her life-span on earth have little or no correspondence with the spiritual realities which are opened up to her after the death of the body, she comes to realise that she has been inhabiting a dream world and is doomed to miss ultimate reality. We have seen that this is Albo's conception of Hell. But if during her life on earth the soul is near to spiritual truth, then

death is a marvellous awakening to the realisation that the
dream was no dream at all, but an approximation to that which
really exists. The soul which pursued, during her life on earth,
God's service, justice, righteousness and loving kindness, will
experience great delight in the world of truth where she will
perceive that her nature is that of the celestial beings whose
delight it is to praise God. Since, however, this delight is
purely spiritual, it cannot be grasped at all by human beings
on earth. Even the prophets had no comprehension of it, contenting themselves with the knowledge that it is a spiritual
pleasure and delight, in the face of which all human pleasures
as we know them pale into insignificance.

A similar suggestion of the incomprehensibility from our
standpoint of the nature of spiritual bliss was given by Rabbi
Judah Löw, known as the *Maharal* of Prague (b.c. 1525–1609)
in his *'Tiphereth Yisrael'* (new ed., Hachinuch, London, 1955,
Chapter 57, pp. 172 f.) *Maharal* observes that there is no
reference to the world to come in the Bible because the prophetic
faculty only operates with relation to the prophet's own
experience and no human being in this life can have any conception of the world to come. The Sages do speak of it, however,
for the human mind, unlike the prophetic faculty, is capable
of reaching out for truth beyond itself. In this respect, says
Maharal, the Sage is greater than the prophet (*v.* B.B. 12a).
This is an extremely interesting view to be entertained by a
sixteenth-century thinker. The truth of the world to come is
not arrived at by revelation but by intellectual speculation,
since revelation always has reference to, and grows out of, man's
situation in *this* life.

In the eighteenth century, a noble expression of the Rabbinic
and mediaeval viewpoint on the Hereafter was given in the
famous devotional classic of Moses Hayyim Luzzatto, *'Mesilath
Yesharim'*, 'The Path of the Upright' (ed. and trans. by Mordecai
Kaplan, Jewish Publication Society, Philadelphia, 1936, Chapter
I: 'Of Man's Duty in the World', pp. 11–19). Luzzatto observes
that it is necessary for 'saintliness and the perfect worship of
God' to be realised in man's life for him to know clearly the
nature of man's duty and the good for which he should strive
all the days of his life. The Rabbis teach in answer to these
questions that man was created only to find delight in the Lord,

and to bask in the radiance of His Presence. The true place of this bliss is the world to come, which has been specially created for this purpose. The present world is a place of preparation for the goal of eternal bliss in the Hereafter. 'This world is like a vestibule before the world to come' ('*Abhoth*, IV. 16). Before one can enter the hall of eternal bliss one must make the necessary preparation in the vestibule. The means of preparation are provided by the precepts of the *Torah*. Here in this life, by obeying God's laws, man learns to commune with Him and acquire perfection so that in the Hereafter he can be worthy of enjoying forever a more perfect communion. God has placed man in a world in which there are many hindrances to the God-centred life. Tempted by both poverty and wealth man is in a sore predicament. But if, as a true man of valour, he keeps himself near to God through the performance of the precepts, he becomes a perfect man with the privilege of communing with his Maker. Such a man will deserve, when he passes from the vestibule of this world, to enjoy the Light of life. All created things become elevated when man uses them in God's service. The man who in this life obeys the precepts not only elevates himself to be worthy of eternal bliss but brings elevation to the whole of God's creation.

To sum up, the purpose for which man was created is not realised in this world but in the world to come, with this world as a 'school', a place of preparation. Hence this world is compared by the Sages to a vestibule. It is also compared to the eve of the Sabbath, the time of preparation for the eternal Sabbath (*A.Z.* 3a) and to the land on which one makes preparations for a sea voyage (*Koh. R.* to i. 15). No reasonable person, Luzzatto argues, can possibly believe that this world is the purpose of man's creation for no one is truly happy here. Man's life span on earth is moreover so short. If this life is the final end of man why did God endow him with such an elevated soul which is ever dissatisfied with material pleasures? The only conclusion to be drawn is that the chief function of man in this world is to keep God's commandments, to worship Him and to withstand trial and temptation. The pleasures of this world should not be looked upon as ends in themselves but only as the means of affording man the contentment and serenity he requires in order to apply himself without distrac-

Q

tion to the true aim of life, the service of the Creator. Since
man came into the world for the sole purpose of achieving
nearness to God, he should prevent his soul from being held
captive by the things which hinder the realisation of that
end.

It would be a mistake to think of Luzzatto as advocating
a fixed and immovable division between life on earth and life
in the world to come. A foretaste of the spiritual bliss of the
world to come is possible for man even in this life. His chapter
on 'Holiness' (Chapter XXVI, pp. 221–228) advises man how
to rise in spiritual stature until he can behold the Presence
of God even in this world. 'See now the difference between
purity and holiness. One who is merely pure regards his bodily
functions as compulsory, and it is with that fact in mind that he
yields to the necessity of performing them. They are thereby
redeemed from the category of evil, which necessarily inheres
in whatever is physical, and are rendered pure. These functions,
nevertheless, do not belong, as far as he is concerned, to the
category of holiness, since he would prefer to dispense with
them altogether, if he could. But the man who is holy,
he who is always in communion with his God, he whose
soul, filled with the love and fear of the Creator, holds
converse with pure ideas, is accounted as though he beheld
the presence of the Lord, notwithstanding that he is still in
this world'.

We have seen that the doctrine of the immortality of the soul
and the other-worldly emphasis was pronounced right through
the Rabbinic and mediaeval periods in Jewish history. With
the Emancipation and the emergence of the Jew from the Ghetto
Jewish intellect began to stretch itself after the long sleep.
Apart from the general decline in belief in an After-life, which
Jews shared with their neighbours, due to the increasingly
this-worldly emphasis in Western civilisation since the Renaissance, the science versus religion controversies, and other
factors, Jews had special reasons for overlooking the claims
of the Hereafter. The desperate struggle to cope with the new
problems regarding how Jews could live as Jews in Western
society, the allure of new cultural patterns and beckoning
ideals, many of them at complete variance with the traditions
of their fathers, all these served to make Jews into a this-

worldly people. With the rise of modern Zionism, the old Biblical idea of a people-centred faith reasserted itself and the fate of the individual in Heaven was allowed to recede into the background. So powerful were these forces that Jews could be found in large numbers who began to question whether belief in immortality was 'Jewish'. The old Sadducean heresy reasserted itself and its power is still not spent. But two devastating world wars, the horrors of the concentration camps, the threat of total annihilation in mid-twentieth century, have had the same effect on Jews as they have had on religious thinking in general. If this life is all, it is hard to see what God is about. Belief in the immortality of the soul is now seen to be essential for a proper religious estimate of man and the only real safeguard against the de-spiritualisation of religion. Even at the very threshold of the emancipation the older ideas, albeit in a new garb, were sufficiently strong, however, to enable Moses Mendelssohn to compose a treatise, after the manner of Plato, on the immortality of the soul. Mendelssohn's 'Phaedon' was first published in the year 1767 and has since been reprinted often. It is one of the classic philosophical works seeking to prove that the soul is truly immortal, in opposition to mechanistic philosophies. There can be little doubt that it was the influence of Mendelssohn's work which enabled Reform Judaism to retain the belief in immortality as essential to Judaism even though Reform did abandon, as we have seen, the doctrine of the resurrection. Indeed, it might be argued convincingly that thanks to Mendelssohn it was the doctrine of the soul's immortality rather than that of bodily resurrection which came to be stressed even in Orthodox Jewish circles.

The wheel has thus swung full circle. From the faint hopes of immortality in the pre-Rabbinic period, the hope grows in the Jewish Apocalyptic and the Talmudic period, in which it comes into full flower. All the great mediaeval thinkers, for all their difference in conception, put the belief in the Afterlife at the centre of their systems. The reaction against other-worldliness in Jewish life and thought is still with us to some extent but there is enough evidence that the tide is turning. A very good case can be made out for the thesis that the comparative silence of the Bible on the wider hope created a tension between this-worldliness and other-worldliness in Judaism. In this can be seen the genius of Judaism which holds out the prospect of man enjoying God's presence for all eternity without sacrificing the legitimate claims of this life. In reply to the question whether Judaism is this- or other-worldly the correct answer is that it is both.

The religious Jew may wish to speculate on why God in His providence allowed the idea of immortality to come to fruition slowly. It is, indeed, puzzling, as the great mediaeval thinkers say, that there are so few references to the belief in the Bible. Many would be prepared to refuse to speculate on such questions. Who are we, they would say, to understand the mysterious way in which God works? For all that, the human mind is insatiable in its desire to see purpose in history, the religious mind to see not only that God works but to try to grasp how He works. No less a thinker than the late Rabbi Kook accepted the comparative silence of the Bible on this matter as a potent reminder that the individual finds his salvation in society and that the new emphasis on the peoplehood of Israel in modern times is a return for good to the Biblical ideal. Other thinkers have not been so easily satisfied. William Temple's interesting suggestion may here be mentioned. Temple ('The Idea of Immortality in Relation to Religion and Ethics' in 'Religious Experience' by William Temple, ed. A. E. Baker, James Clarke, Lond., 1958, pp. 112–123) tries to see a divine purpose in that order of development in which faith in God as One and as Righteous was already firmly established *before* the idea of the Hereafter became clear. Since the aim of all true religion, says Temple, is to transfer the centre of interest from the self to God, it would be dangerous to reach a developed doctrine of immortality until the doctrine of God is definitely established. Otherwise attention would have been called to the self alone. There is nothing religious in the desire for personal survival taken by itself. It is only when belief in immortality is a corollary of belief in the good God who wishes His creatures to share His goodness forever that it assumes its rich religious meaning. Only when the aim of religion as glorifying God has been established can the doctrine of immortality come into its own as God's means of loving man. The true value of immortality as a religious interest lies in its implication of the righteousness and love of God.

The strongest argument for immortality, as well as the most convincing to the religious mind, is that God is good and will not allow His creatures to spend their lives in efforts at attaining goodness and perfection only to be snuffed out like a candle. Men may work at improving the conditions of life here on earth and earn the blessings of their fellows and of posterity but posterity itself will die. The earth itself will one day become inhospitable to life and all man's dreams and achievements will vanish like smoke. Shakespeare's vision of the 'cloud-capped towers' is true. Luzzatto's argument is still valid. Of what use is man's elevated soul if this life is all there is? For all Judaism's teachings on the values of this life can we believe that God who created this wonderful world will allow man to die forever with his spiritual powers at the best only just beginning to develop? And even if one day mankind discovers the secret of longevity and men live for thousands of years what of the noble men and women who died before the secret was discovered? Judaism never tires of assuring us of the justice of God but how can this justice be realised unless all who have striven for the good eventually find it?

'Thou madest man, he knows not why,
He thinks he was not made to die;
And Thou hast made him: Thou art just'.

The strongest objection to the doctrine that the soul is immortal is the difficulty of conceiving how mind can exist without the bodily organs through with it functions. We see that the mind is so dependent on the brain that when the latter is damaged the mind either ceases to function or works very inadequately. How then can a disembodied existence of the soul be possible? This takes us into speculative realms but it should be realised that all the medical evidence we have only tells us that here on earth body and soul, brain and mind, are interdependent. There is nothing in the evidence to contradict the view that in our present life the mind uses the brain as its *instrument*. We have already referred to Albo's analogy of the ship. A more modern illustration can be given from space-travel. If man will be able to travel to the moon in the not too distant future, space suits will be needed for survival there. The space traveller will be completely dependent on his space suit and will be unable to live for one moment without it *on the moon*. But on his return to earth he will be able to discard this artificial aid and will be able to exist without it. On this analogy man only requires the brain as his instrument here on earth, in the world of matter, space and time. In the realm of eternity the soul can function without these aids.

The best thinkers on this whole subject of immortality have preferred to speak of eternal life as something far more embracing than endless duration in time. The idea of eternity as outside time altogether is no doubt unknown in the classical Jewish sources and appears to be an importation from the Greek, but not a few Jewish thinkers (one thinks of the mystics first) have seen eternity as completely outside time. This is admittedly an exceedingly difficult idea to grasp. Dorothy Sayers' illustration of the novel may be found helpful. The characters in a novel obey a time sequence but their adventures are contained within the pages of the book. We ought not to think of the Hereafter as a second instalment of the novel, when the characters will have further adventures of the same kind, but as a removal from the whole realm of the novel into the realm of its Author.

Great Jewish thinkers like Maimonides denied that it is possible for man here on earth to have any conception of what eternal life is like. As little can a blind man hope to appreciate colour, as man in the body to appreciate the nature of pure, spiritual bliss in the world to come (*v.* Maimonides' Comment. to the *Mishnah, Sanh.* X. 1, and *Hil. Tesh.*, VIII). For all that speculations have been rife on the question. Saadiah ('*Emunoth We-De'oth*, Treatise IX, Chapter 10, Rosenblatt, pp. 353–4) defends the view that there is progress in the Hereafter and the obligation of rendering service to God. Saadiah operates here within the categories of the resurrection of the dead rather than of the immortality of the soul. He is thinking of continued existence here on earth so that he includes among the obligations the command to worship God in a special place on earth. The resurrected dead will have no option but to carry out these obligations yet their reward will be that their further happiness will be abundantly increased. On a more mystical and sophisticated level is the notion of ever increasing spiritual comprehension of God by the soul.

The *Zohar* ('*Midrash Ha-Ne'elam*', *Toledoth*, I. 134a–137a) also operates within the categories of the resurrection of the dead but similarly speaks of spiritual progress in the Hereafter. The righteous will attain a fuller comprehension (*hasagah*) of God. They will know Him in their hearts and He will rejoice in them. It is this which is meant by 'seeing God' and basking in the radiance of the *Shekhinah*. The Zoharic picture is not too distant from that of Maimonides' conception of pure spiritual bliss in comprehension, but the *Zohar* is careful to assert the traditional view that the body, too, will partake of that bliss. The *Zohar* here gives a mystical turn to the verse: 'And these are the generations of Isaac, Abraham's son: Abraham begat Isaac' (Gen. xxv. 19). Isaac represents 'laughter' (from *tzahaq*, 'to laugh'), the delight and bliss of the soul, 'the son of Abraham'. It is Abraham who begets Isaac, i.e. the delight in the Hereafter is the fruit of the soul's experience there of God's nearness. In the same passage there is the interesting comment that the nature of the 'feast' which God will prepare for the righteous in the Hereafter can only be ascertained from the ministering angels, but it would seem to be connected with the verse: 'And they beheld God, and did eat and drink' (Ex. xxiv. 11), i.e. the 'feast' consists in a fuller comprehension of the divine. Of some of the righteous it is said that they benefit (*nehenin*) from the radiance of the *Shekhinah*, of others the far stronger term, 'they feed' (*nizonin*) is used. The former, who have less merit, only have an inferior degree of comprehension while the latter have a full and complete comprehension (*hasagah shelemah*). The wine stored in the grape from the six days of creation is said to be the divine secrets which no man has been shown until God will reveal them to the righteous in the world to come. Although the Rabbis promised Israel that they would enjoy that great feast as a reward for their loyalty to God's law in fact the righteous will rejoice in their nearness to God alone. In this connection the verse is quoted: 'We will be glad and rejoice in Thee' (Cant. i. 4) – 'in Thee' and not in the 'feast'.

There the matter may safely be left. The modern religious Jew believes, like his fathers, that God will not condemn His creatures to ultimate annihilation. Somehow, man will attain to ever greater comprehension of the truth after which he strove in this life. The nature of spiritual bliss in the Hereafter is a tremendous mystery, impossible of appreciation here on earth. But faith is strong that eternal life is all around us and that after the death of his body man will behold his Maker.

*   *   *

EXCURSUS

The literature on the subject of immortality is immense. W. R. Alger's 'A Critical History of the Future Life', 4th ed., Widdleton, New York, 1866, contains a very full bibliography of all works on the subject until 1866. This book contains a good deal of information but is very unreliable in its picture of Jewish doctrine. Alger utilises entirely secondary sources for the Rabbinic period, for example. Ulrich Simon's 'Heaven in Christian Tradition', Rockliff, London, 1958, is a very careful study of the Christian attitude in early times (Simon makes the point, p. 198, that it is hard to believe that the great Hebrew prophets did not have any wider hope of communion with God in the Hereafter) but is rather unfair to Judaism. For instance, on page 204 Simon says: 'Some Rabbis, however, excluded the Gentiles from a portion in the World to Come, whereas they claimed that all Israelites will be saved at the end'. In note 1 on the same page Simon adds 'The opposite opinion, however, prevailed'. Why, then, not put *this* opinion in the text and the rejected opinion in the footnote? It is furthermore simply not true that in the Rabbinic view 'all Israelites will be saved at the end'. The very *Mishnah* in which this is stated (*Sanh.* X. 1) goes on to exclude various classes of Israelite sinners and unbelievers. Israel Lipschütz adds, as an appendix to his famous Commentary to the *Mishnah*, a sermon on immortality which he preached in the year 1842 ('*Derush 'Or Ha-Hayyim*' in his '*Tiphereth Yisrael*',Vilna, 1911, *Seder Neziqin*, pp. 548–569). Lipschütz appeals to man's conviction that he will not die forever and to God's justice and mercy as evidence for the soul's immortality. He quotes: 'Yea, though I walk through the valley of the shadow of death, I will fear no evil, *for Thou art with me*' (Ps. xxiii. 4). Lipschütz quotes, as many have done before him, the evidence from nature. After their death in winter the plants and flowers bloom again, *cf. Sanh.* 90b, bottom of page. The argument is, of course, fallacious since the flowers which bloom in the spring are not the flowers which died in winter, *v.* the sermon 'Ten Reasons for Believing in Immortality' by John Haynes Holmes in 'A Modern Introduction to Philosophy' ed. Paul Edwards and Arthur Pap, the Free Press, George Allen and Unwin, London, 1957, pp. 272 ff. On page 307 in this work there is a full, up-to-date bibliography on the subject of immortality. A recent attack on the doctrine of the soul's immortality is Stephen Findlay's 'Immortal Longings', Gollancz, London, 1961. Findlay admits, however, that if one believes in a good God who is concerned with the well-being of His creatures as individuals a belief in immortality will follow. J. M. Tuckechinsky's *'Gesher Ha-Hayyim'*, 2nd ed., Jer. 1960, is a full account of Jewish laws and customs, governing death and burial, by an Israeli Rabbi. Vol. III, pp. 19 ff. contains the author's defence of immortality. An important essay is A. E. Taylor's 'The Christian Hope of Immortality', The Unicorn Press, London, 1938. Taylor, dealing with the alleged evidence for survival from spiritualism or psychical research, says: 'I do not think it too much to say of the most harmless of these "messages from beyond the tomb" that, if they are what they claim to be, we can only hope that the unseen world, like the seen, has its homes for the feeble-minded, and it is with their inmates that our occultists are in communication'. A great book on the subject is John Baillie's 'And the Life Everlasting', Oxford University Press, 1934. Chapter 20 of David Elton Trueblood's 'Philosophy of Religion', Rockliff, London, 1957, pp. 291 ff. is a good modern summary of the belief in immortality. H. E. Fosdick's 'The Assurance of Immortality', SCM Press, London, 1936, is a similarly useful essay. Various national newspapers have printed series of articles on the subject from time to time. In the *Sunday Times*, for instance, such a series, by believers of different faiths and by unbelievers, was published in the issues from Jan. 6th to March 24th, 1957. These articles have now been published in book form under the title 'The Great Mystery of Life Hereafter', Hodder and Stoughton, London, 1957. The opening essay by Dorothy Sayers contains the illustration of the novel quoted in the text. On the whole question of the nature of eternity there is an excellent discussion from the Jewish point of view in Jacob Kohn's 'The Moral Life of Man', Philosophical Library, New York, 1956, Chapter V, 'Retribution and the Faith in Immortality', pp. 145–217. Rabbi E. Dessler's *' Mikhtabh Me-' Elijahu'*, London, 1955, pp. 283 ff. contains many stimulating ideas, among them how progress, which implies a time process, can be possible in eternity! The mystics speak of a special 'garment' with which the soul is clothed in Paradise. This is very refined but acts as a kind of barrier between God and the soul, otherwise the soul would be engulfed in the divine light and would possess no separate identity and therefore no capacity for enjoying God. *V. 'Qunteros Ha-*

Hithpa'aluth' of Rabbi Dobh Baer of Lubavitch, pub. under the title *'Liqqute Bi' urim'*, with a commentary by Hillel of Poritch, Warsaw, 1868, p. 34b. For a summary of some of the views of mediaeval and later Jewish thinkers on the subject of the Hereafter *v. 'Sepher Nishmath Joseph'*, by Rabbi J. Gad, *Jabhneh*, Jer. 1936.

[15]

SUMMARY AND CONCLUSIONS

THE foregoing investigation has shown, it is hoped, that while each one of Maimonides' thirteen principles gives expression to a permanent Jewish idea, a fresh interpretation of some of the principles is required if justice is to be done to the knowledge which has accrued since Maimonides' day. In the previous pages an attempt has been made to delineate the nature of this reinterpretation. We may now proceed to summarise the conclusions, tentative though some of them are, which have been arrived at in our discussion.

The first principle, belief in God, is, of course, the cornerstone of Judaism. The differences between the modern and mediaeval approach lie not in the belief itself but in the reasons for holding it. Since Hume and Kant, less emphasis has been placed on the formal proofs for God's existence and more on the conviction attained through the experiences of the whole man, not his reason alone. But the formal proofs still have potency in helping to produce conviction through powerful pointers to a faith which alone makes sense of human life and endows existence with meaning and purpose.

The second principle, affirming God's unity, is Israel's special contribution to religion. We have seen how successive generations of Jewish thinkers and teachers have enriched the idea of ethical monotheism and continued to uphold the *Shema'* as the great declaration of Israel's faith.

The third principle, the incorporeality of God, had its detractors, but thanks to the efforts of thinkers such as Saadiah and Maimonides the only interpretation capable of enduring in the post-Copernican age wins the adherence of all believing Jews today. We have noted, however, the attempts of various modernists to reinterpret this principle in non-Personal terms and the inadequacies of their position and its failure to satisfy the religious mind.

455

The fourth principle, the eternity of God, is hardly challenged today. A being who is not eternal would not be God. We have, however, examined the notion of a finite God and suggested that it is incompatible with traditional Jewish Theism.

The fifth principle, that God alone is to be worshipped, is still both as demanding upon Jews and as compelling as ever it was. Superstitions of various kinds have not been completely banished from Jewish life but, on the whole, the traditional view prevails in its purity.

These first five principles present no offence at all to the modern mind. On the contrary, the man of faith is able to see the wonders of the Creator in ways undreamed of by his predecessors who lived in a small universe. The dangers of having too small a God were far more real in the Middle Ages than they are in the twentieth century.

The sixth principle, the truth of prophecy, does raise important questions regarding revelation and inspiration. For all the need for rejecting doctrines like that of verbal inspiration, untenable in the light of the knowledge which demonstrates the human element in the Bible, the great Hebrew prophets still stand out as the men who brought God to the world and emphasised, as never before or since in human history, that He is the God of justice, mercy and holiness. Insofar as the meaning of the prophetic message and the nature of prophetic inspiration are matters of investigation by scholarly techniques, we have suggested that the principle of faith cannot be invoked. We have tried to consider what modern scholarship has to say on these questions. The result is that the idea of the prophets as infallible in all they said has to be abandoned, but far from the basic truths of their message being affected, these stand out with far greater clarity.

The seventh principle, the superiority of Moses, is not at variance with the best modern scholarship. We have adopted a mid-way position between the acceptance of the whole Mosaic record as historical fact and the denial of the historicity of Moses. Moses is the great founder of our faith. All its important institutions go back to him, either directly or indirectly. Where moderns do differ from the men of the Middle Ages in this matter is in the significance for faith in this article of belief. If, as seems exceedingly likely and as we have noticed in chapter eight, there is a polemical tendency in this principle of faith, its real value lies in the affirmation behind it that no other religious leader has, under God's guidance, succeeded in bringing to men a religion to supersede Judaism.

Of all the thirteen principles, the eighth, that the *Torah* is divine, demands the most severe readjustment. As we have seen, there is no doubt at all that for two thousand years what is now called the 'fundamentalist' view prevailed, according to which the Pentateuch was written at divine dictation and is infallible in all its parts. It is the very Word of God, this term being interpreted in a strictly literal fashion. This is still the belief of many believing Jews but, as we have seen, unquestioned though such a belief was in Maimonides' day it is not intellectually respectable today and has been abandoned by all who are aware of the facts. We have followed those thinkers who, consequently, reinterpret revelation in terms of a divine-human encounter, for which human beings found words by which it might be expressed. According to this view, the Bible *contains* the Word of God but its own words are human. This applies to the Pentateuch as well as the rest of the Bible, since it is intellectually dishonest to allow scholarship its head but to stop it from having an opinion on the Pentateuch. The problems the new approach raises for Jewish practice have been considered. Our basic contention is that it is not *origins* which matter but what those institutions have come to mean in Jewish life and their capacity to serve as vehicles for the divine. The Pentateuch and the traditional exposition of its laws are still our *Torah*. The *Sepher Torah* is still held aloft with pride as the supreme document of the *Torah* which comes from Heaven, even though the precise nature in which *Torah* and *mitzwoth* have come from Heaven is conceived of differently by us from the way in which the Jews of the Middle Ages conceived of it.

The two attitudes to the Pentateuch held by Jews today can be called the fundamentalist and the modernist, terms taken, of course, from the controversies in the Church on this very question. Using these terms, it must be said that the author's position is modernistic. However, the term 'modernism' nowadays is frequently used to describe the view which holds that the Bible is inspired only in the way in which Shakespeare or Beethoven are inspired. Such a view is certainly not the present author's. The Bible is a unique book in that through it God has revealed Himself to Israel and to the world. Cumbersome though it is, the term 'non-fundamentalist' is, therefore, the better term to express the point of view we have tried to outline.

With regard to the ninth principle, the immutability of the *Torah*, a good deal depends on how this term is understood. No believing Jew will accept the claims of other faiths to have superseded Judaism. The principle also affirms that Judaism is an eternal faith and that its institutions are permanent. But in the light of historical investigations we are now able to see with far greater clarity than was possible in the Middle Ages that Judaism is a dynamic faith and that there have been internal changes brought about by changing conditions. It is here that the practical problem is presented with the great force. What changes are called for today and how are they to be brought about? There are no easy solutions to this kind of question but we have argued that the more Jews share a dynamic conception of the history of the Jewish religion the better capable we shall be of dealing with this important question with the dynamism which has been typical of Judaism in the past and which has helped it to survive to this day.

The tenth principle, that God knows our thoughts, involves difficult ideas regarding God's providence. We have suggested that, like the mediaeval thinkers, for all their attempts at explaining God's providence, we are obliged to practise a proper humility and to acknowledge that here is an area beyond the grasp of the finite human mind. To this we hold fast, as did our ancestors, that we are all in the hands of God and that we are as stewards in the world He has created.

The eleventh principle, that God rewards and punishes, demands, as we have tried to show, an interpretation which does not conceive of God as vindictive. The central thought here is that God loves His creatures and wishes them to be near to Him that they may share in His goodness.

The twelfth principle, belief in the Messiah, emphasises God's miraculous intervention in human affairs. Here more than in any other sphere many moderns have moved away from Victorian notions, preferring to believe in a more direct divine intervention than was implied in the nineteenth-century idea of automatic human progress towards the millennium.

Finally, the thirteenth principle, belief in the resurrection of the dead, is, we have argued, best interpreted today as belief in the immortality of the soul, provided that this is understood to mean that the whole personality of man, his complete individuality, shares in God's eternal goodness.

The picture which emerges from our investigation is of Judaism as an eternal faith, inspiring its adherents to live righteously in God's presence and share in His goodness for eternity. Implied in the picture is the special role of the people of Israel in the fulfilment of God's purpose and the special function of the *Torah* as advancing that purpose. Here we might try to summarise the views expressed above regarding Jewish tradition and its binding force for present-day Jews.

In order for us to possess an effective attitude to Jewish tradition it would appear that a distinction must be made between traditional *beliefs* and traditional *practices*. A further distinction must be made, with regard to traditional *beliefs*, between beliefs which cannot by their nature be contradicted by new knowledge and beliefs which can be so contradicted.

Of traditional beliefs which cannot be contradicted by new knowledge are the basic ones of belief in God, in His goodness and mercy, in His unity and power, that He has revealed Himself to Israel in the *Torah*, that Israel has a special role to play in the fulfilment of God's purpose, that the Messianic age will dawn, that the soul is immortal, that God is to be worshipped, that man is to practise justice and righteousness and to strive to be holy and feel compassion for others. Of traditional beliefs which can be contradicted by new knowledge are: the Mosaic authorship of the Pentateuch, the Isaianic authorship of the second part of the book of Isaiah, the Solomonic authorship of Ecclesiastes, Proverbs and the Song of Songs and the Davidic authorship of the Psalms, that the Rabbis of the Talmud were infallible supermen, that the world is no more than five thousand seven hundred and twenty-three years old, that the earth is flat and in the centre of the universe.

The basic beliefs, which cannot by their nature be contradicted by new knowledge, are known, in part at least, through tradition, but they are accepted by believing Jews not because they are *traditional* but because they are *true*. Their nature is such that new knowledge – which is knowledge based on the discovery of new *facts* – cannot possibly contradict them since they do not purport to supply information about the structure of the material universe but about the meaning of human life. No amount of fresh investigation into the facts can either prove or disprove the existence of God, for example. The man who believes in God does so not because any *particular* facts or set of facts lead to this belief but because it seems to him to be the only possible explanation of the facts *as a whole*.

The beliefs which can be contradicted by new knowledge are based on traditional opinions about the *facts* of the material universe. Obviously, these beliefs must be abandoned if new knowledge of the *facts* demonstrates that tradition is in error.

In the light of the above, if tradition can be mistaken with regard to the second class of beliefs (the *factual* ones), it is fatuous to ask what guarantee we have that it is not mistaken with regard to the first class (the *interpretive* beliefs). Since tradition can be mistaken it is, indeed, never in itself an adequate guide to belief. The Jew who only holds fast to the beliefs in the first class because his tradition tells him to do so is, indeed, in a sorry plight. He is obliged to defend every detail of traditional lore, for the slightest error in any detail of the tradition causes a question mark to be placed against the tradition as a whole. But the thinking Jew accepts the beliefs of the first class as being in the tradition because they are true, and not 'true because they are in the tradition'.

The validity of the above distinction means that the believer will not feel himself to be inhibited by his belief from engaging in any investigation into the *facts* wherever it may lead –whether they be facts about the physical universe, human history, or literary investigation, and even if the new facts discovered contradict traditional beliefs. He need have no fear of betraying his faith since his basic beliefs are not *factual* at all but *interpretive* and are secure from contradiction by the discovery of new facts. Indeed, the basic beliefs *justify* free investigation of the facts since God is the Author of the facts and their investigation involves both an examination of His handiwork and an approximation to His truth.

If tradition can be wrong in theory why should it be followed in practice? With regard to practices based on the fundamental, *interpretive* beliefs there is no problem. Just as the beliefs are of permanent truth and validity so are the practices based on them. Examples of this group of practices are: the practice of justice, the exercise of the compassionate instincts, prayer and the acknowledgment of God as man's Maker, the functions of the Synagogue, the pursuit of peace, truth and righteousness, integrity and honesty in one's business and professional conduct, the fulfilment of one's obligations as husband, wife, parent, or child. But what of those practices based on *factual* beliefs which new knowledge of the facts has rendered untenable or, at least, open to revision? Examples of this group of practices are: the observance of the Sabbath in its traditional form, circumcision, *Tephillin* and *Tzitzith*, the dietary laws, and the observances connected with the Jewish festivals. These traditional practices are based on *factual* beliefs, the belief in the Mosaic authorship of the Pentateuch and the communication by God to Moses of the traditional details of the observances, for instance.

Here a fundamental distinction must be drawn between theory and practice. Theories as to the facts obviously require revision when new facts are discovered which demand a revision of the older theory. Practices, however, even when they are based on theories which are later seen to be unsound, may come to possess a value quite independent of the original theories. It can be shown that even those practices based on *factual* beliefs can and have become (or, at least, many of them have) vehicles for the furtherance of the values expressed in the basic, *interpretive* beliefs. Judaism is an historical religion. The significance of its institutions are due in large measure to the values they have come to express in Jewish life, particularly the religious values through which man is brought nearer to God.

A few examples must be given in order to clarify this matter. Whether the Sabbath had its origin in the Babylonian *shabbatum* as a period of cessation from work, whether the creation really took place in six days so that there was 'rest' on the seventh (i.e. whether the first chapter of Genesis is historically true), whether all the details of Sabbath observance were given at one time or evolved gradually, these are matters for scholarly

investigation. They belong to the domain of the *factual* and
their truth or falsehood can only be decided by reference to
the facts. Faith cannot be invoked in this era. But, whatever
its origins, the traditional Sabbath has come to serve as Israel's
instrument for divine worship, as a weekly attestation to God
as Creator. The Sabbath had assumed this significance at least
as early as the first chapter of Genesis. The origin of circumcision and the history of the patriarchal narratives in Genesis
are similarly matters for scholarly investigation. But whatever
the results of such investigation circumcision has come to
mean for Jews the symbol of the Abrahamic covenant, and
had assumed this meaning at least as early as the relevant
passage in the book of Genesis. It is a 'sacrament', a visible
'sign in the flesh' of the initiation of new-born males into Israel's
dedicatory service of God. The dietary laws are a further
illustration of the distinction between the origin of an institution
and the values it has come to express. The question of the origin
of these laws belongs to scholarship, to empirical investigation.
But the value these laws have come to assume (from at least
as early a date as the book of Deuteronomy) as an expression
of holiness, of the recognition of God even in the indulgence
of the bodily instincts, is quite independent of questions
regarding origins.

It might be objected that the distinction between theories
as to origins, which may be revised, and practices based on
them, which justify themselves independently of the theories,
implies that God allowed believing Jews to hold false theories
as to origins during a major part of Jewish history. It is not
at all difficult to see where the answer lies to this kind of
objection. First, the *interpretive* beliefs, which are those of the
most fundamental significance, have not changed and it is here
that the continuity of Jewish belief is assured. Secondly, to
expect the Jews of old to have had perfectly sound and irrefut-
able beliefs with regard to the *facts* is to ask why God did not
choose to give mankind all the knowledge there is concerning
the universe all at once. Since God can, of course, do this we
can only say that He evidently did not choose to do so. History
shows that in the *factual* areas God preferred to allow men to
discover for themselves, by trial and error over a long period,
knowledge of the physical universe. If all the knowledge which

men have discovered and won for themselves, together with the knowledge they have still to win, had been given in some miraculous fashion to the prophets and sages of Israel, there would have been no need for a Newton, a Boyle, a Laplace and a Darwin, a Wellhausen, a Freud and an Einstein. History informs us that God has room in His world for the great minds who discover truths about its nature by their own efforts. Since this is so it must follow that divine revelation is confined to the *interpretive* beliefs, which are true for all time, and not to the *factual* beliefs which are always open to revision.

Although the distinction between *interpretive* and *factual* beliefs is perfectly sound there are areas where the two overlap and thus lead to a degree of complication which prevents us from resting content with the simple distinction between the two.

The traditional beliefs that the Exodus from Egypt actually happened and that the Decalogue was given by God to Moses both belong in the category of *factual* beliefs. It consequently follows from our distinction between the two classes of belief that these beliefs are open to revision in the light of fresh empirical investigation. If, therefore, it can be demonstrated that the Decalogue (even in its most rudimentary form) is post-Mosaic and that the Exodus never really took place, this demonstration would have no effect on the role of the Decalogue and the demands it makes and the celebration of the Exodus in institutions such as the Passover festival. If it can be proved conclusively that neither event is historical it will be necessary to argue that, whatever their value as history, the Decalogue and Passover serve as instruments for the expression of such *interpretive* beliefs as the Unity of God and His championing of the cause of the oppressed. It cannot be denied, however, that an interpretation of Judaism which treated both the giving of the Decalogue to Moses and the Exodus as unhistorical would deprive Judaism of a good measure of the support it requires if it is to be considered an *historical* religion. But, in point of fact, after empirical investigation has done its work, the evidence of modern scholarship suggests very strongly that the Decalogue is Mosaic and that the Exodus really took place. This is not to say that there were no later additions to the Decalogue or that the Pentateuchal accounts of the Exodus are historically accurate in all their details. Nor does it preclude the view that in the Passover festival we have an ancient Canaanite agricultural feast adopted to serve the ideas associated with the Exodus. It is perfectly reasonable and logical, therefore, for the believing Jew to hold fast to the conviction that, since none of the evidence contradicts the basic historicity of the two events and much of the evidence seems to support it, the Decalogue was given by God to Moses and the Exodus was a real historical event. This means that in certain areas *factual* beliefs share the untentativeness of *interpretive* beliefs.

Conversely, there are *interpretive* beliefs which nonetheless demand to be revised not so much in the light of new knowledge of the facts but in the name of a more advanced moral sense. An example of this is the belief in eternal punishment in Hell. This is a traditional belief (held by the majority of Jewish teachers in the Middle Ages) and it is, moreover, incapable of being contradicted by any kind of investigation into the structure of the physical world. And yet the modern believer will reject it as incompatible with the nature of God as he understands it.

It is possible to put this as follows. *Interpretive* beliefs cannot be contradicted by new knowledge and are to be accepted because they are eternally true. But what of those *interpretive* beliefs which contradict other *interpretive* beliefs? In the face of such contradiction the less significant must yield to the more significant. Now the belief in eternal punishment in Hell is clearly incompatible with the goodness of God. (That the mediaeval thinkers thought otherwise is a cause for surprise and a realisation that in those days there was less awareness of the contradiction involved. That there is a contradiction is as clear to us as anything can be). Consequently, the *interpretive* belief in eternal punishment in Hell must be rejected for the sake of the infinitely more significant *interpretive* belief in the goodness of God.

In reality, in spite of the qualifications we have just noted, the distinction between *interpretive* and *factual* beliefs still obtains. For if none of the traditional beliefs had ever been contradicted by new knowledge they might all have been considered to be divine and then the problems raised by contradictions might have been pushed away into the realm beyond the grasp of the human intellect. As it is the new knowledge provided by empirical investigation demonstrates that some, at least, of the *factual* beliefs are mistaken. From this it follows that tradition is in itself no guide to truth. It follows further that the traditional sources, which contain both *factual* and *interpretive* beliefs, must be seen as human in part, as the product of a series of divine-human encounters. Once *factual* investigation has compelled us to acknowledge the human element in the Bible and in the other classical sources of Judaism the door is open to a rejection of even the *interpretive* beliefs where these are in contradiction to other *interpretive* beliefs of greater significance.

As a result of the above conclusions we are better equipped to deal with the *moral* difficulties in the Biblical record – the command to stone a rebellious son, for instance, or the command to exterminate Canaanite infants. The simple distinction between *factual* and *interpretive* beliefs does not seem to be of much help to us here. Granted that the Bible may be in error with regard to the *facts* of the material universe can it be in error, too, with regard to moral and religious ideas and, if it can, where is its truth to be found? But there, too, once empirical investigation has demonstrated that there are *factual* errors in the Bible it can be clearly seen that there is a human element in the Bible. Consequently, the offence to the moral sense in certain Biblical passages is seen to be due to its human element. Such a recognition does not, however, lead to relativism. The fundamental *interpretive* beliefs are, after all, taught in the Bible and the other classics of Judaism. It is in no sense a question of the unaided human mind arbitrarily picking and choosing the beliefs it is prepared to accept. It is rather a matter of such fundamental beliefs as that of belief in the goodness and mercy of God taught in the *Torah* (= the Bible as interpreted in Jewish tradition) compelling the human mind to reject certain other traditional beliefs which, although *interpretive*, not *factual*, are nonetheless in contradiction with the belief that God is good. Jewish tradition itself makes the distinction by treating belief in God's goodness as an eternal belief, to be accepted by all Jews at all times, while allowing laws such as the stoning of the rebellious son to pass into oblivion.

If the distinction between traditional *theories* and traditional *practices* be granted certain conclusions flow from it. The traditional *Halakhah* rarely allows historical considerations to obtrude on its own categories. The *Halakhah* knows of 'heavy' and 'light' precepts but this kind of distinction is based on traditional *factual* beliefs, e.g., beliefs as to the origin of the precepts. Since, on our account, it is the historical experience of the people of Israel which serves as the source of the authority, under God, for Jewish observance, it follows that a precept of little significance in the *Halakhah* may come to assume much significance through the emphasis it has received in Jewish life and history. Conversely, a precept of great significance in the *Halakhah* may pass into the background as a result of Jewish life and experience. Thus, the Synagogue and its worship are, from the Halakhic point of view, far less important than the duty of living in the *Sukkah* during the festival of Tabernacles. But judged by the experience of the Jewish people and by the capacity of observances to serve the basic Jewish ideas, the former set of observances are far more important than the latter. (This is not, of course, to denigrate the observance of the *Sukkah*, which also serves as the vehicle for the furtherance of certain basic Jewish ideas). Similarly, in the *Halakhah* the Sabbath is more significant than *Yom Kippur* but in Jewish experience both are of the greatest significance, though it is *Yom Kippur* which has come to possess the greater significance as a test of Jewish loyalty. For the *Halakhah* it is a greater offence to eat leaven on Passover than to marry out of the faith but, historically considered, the latter offence is far greater than the former. For the *Halakhah* it is a more severe religious offence to shave with a razor than to eat forbidden food, but the one offence has frequently been overlooked in Jewish life, while the dietary laws are recognised even by many of those who do not keep them as belonging to an essential Jewish expression of the quest for holiness in life and as a powerful means of self-identification with the peoplehood of Israel.

The non-fundamentalist Jew who accepts our argument is as much a man of faith as the fundamentalist. That he has less simple and direct answers to some of the religious problems of Jewish life than the fundamentalist is to be expected. On the non-fundamentalist view faith should have no voice in matters which can be determined by an investigation of the facts. In these areas the non-fundamentalist is inspired to investigate the facts and make the necessary adjustments in the firm belief that it is this which his faith would have him do since the God he worships is the God of truth who abounds in deeds of goodness and truth. With a far greater liberation of his intellect from the fetters of unreason, he can repeat the well-known prayer with the same fervour as his fundamentalist coreligionist: 'I am the servant of the Holy One, blessed be He, before whom and before whose glorious *Torah* I prostrate myself at all times: not in man do I put my trust, nor upon any angel do I rely, but upon the God of heaven, who is the God of truth, and whose *Torah* is truth, and whose prophets are prophets of truth, and who aboundeth in deeds of goodness and truth. In Him I put my trust, and unto His holy and glorious Name I utter praises. May it be Thy will to open my heart unto Thy *Torah*, and to fulfil the wishes of my heart and of the hearts of all Thy people Israel for good, for life, and for peace'.

INDEX OF PHILOSOPHERS AND THINKERS

(*Exc.* = Excursus)

Abahu, Rabbi: anti-Dualism, 86

Abarbanel, Isaac: His 'Pinnacle of Faith', 23–4; on *Torah*, 24–5

Abraham, Rabbi Yom Tobh ben: martyrdom, 25

Abudraham, David ben Joseph: on the *Shema'*, 106–7

Akiba, Rabbi: on fundamental beliefs, 11; God's knowledge and man's free will, 327

Al-Balkhi, Hiwi: on the Bible, 230–1

Albo, Joseph: His 'Book of Principles', 20–3; God's unity, 107; the immutability of the *Torah*, 304–7; God's knowledge, exc., 335–6; reward and punishment, 360-1; on resurrection, 410; the meaning of Hell, 428; immortality, 442–3

Alexander, Samuel: His 'Space, Time and Deity', 141–4

Almosnino, Moses: God's knowledge, 328

Alshech, Moses: on the *Shema'*, 109

Anatoli, Jacob: on prayer, exc., 174

Anselm, Saint: ontological proof of God's existence, 34–5

Arama, Isaac: his three principles, 23; on the *Shema'*, 107–8

Asher, Bahya Ibn: God's unity, 102

Ashkenazi, Zevi: on Deism, 76–8

Astruc, Jean: Bible criticism, 243

Attar, Hayyim ben Moses Ibn: on the *Shema'*, 111

Augustine, Saint, divine foreknowledge, exc., 339

Bentzen, Aage: prophecy, exc., 197; the Pentateuch, exc., 264

Bonfils, Joseph: commentary to Ibn Ezra, 234–7

Brightman, E. S., on a personal God, 131–2; on evil, 144–7

Broad, C. D.: on a personal God, exc., 133–4

Brooke, Rupert: on a personal God, 129–30

Buber, Martin: his existentialism, exc., 31; on Moses, exc., 213–4

Burgon, Dean: his sermon on the Bible, exc., 228

Caspi, Joseph: on God's unity, 106

Carlstadt, A. B.: on the death of Moses, 238

Cassuto, U.: on the Pentateuch, 262

Chajes, Rabbi Zewi Hirsch: on Moses, 313

Comte, August: his 'religion of humanity', 57

Cordovero, Moses: on Qabbalism and atheism, 53

Crescas, Hasdai: critique of Maimonides, 18–9; on the Trinity, 87–8; on prophecy, 188; on the immutability of the *Torah*, 306–7; human free will and God's omniscience, exc., 335; resurrection, 409–10; on punishment, 427–8; immortality of the soul, 442

Darrow, Clarence: his agnosticism, 60–1

Darwin, Charles: natural selection and God's existence, 42

David, Rabbi Abraham Ibn: on God's knowledge of man, 326–7; on free will, exc., 334; on resurrection, 401–2

de Leon, Moses: the *Zohar*, 103

de Modena, Leon: the *Shema'*, 110

Descartes, René: the ontological argument for God's existence, 36

Dessler, Rabbi E. L.: critique of determinism, 336: on Hell, 430

Dreamer, Percy; Anglican attitude to Hell, exc., 434

Driver, S. R.: on the *Shema'*, 96

Duran, Simon ben Zemah: Creed formulation in Judaism, 19–20

Edwards, Jonathan: on divine foreknowledge, exc. 339–40; sermon on hell fire, 431

Edwards, Paul: on atheism, 60–1

Eliezar, Rabbi: on martyrdom, exc., 26

Elimelech of Lizianka: on the *Shema'*, 116

Epicurus: the term *'epiqoros* derived from him, exc., 11–12

Epstein, Dr. I.: on the Pentateuch, exc., 280–1; the Messianic age, 392–3

Ettlinger, Jacob: on the Sabbath, 311

Ezra, Abraham Ibn: God's unity, 100; Bible criticism, 232–8; resurrection, 406

Farrer, Austin: divine and human will, exc., 333

Feuerbach, Ludwig, his atheism, 56–7

Frankel, Zechariah: his view of Judaism, 296–8

Friedländer, M.: his 'The Jewish Religion', exc., 30; God's existence, 33; God's unity, 70–1; the eternal nature of God, 135; the worship of God alone, 149–50; prophecy, 184–5; on Moses, 208–9; the divine nature of the *Torah*, 217–8; the book of Daniel, exc., 228; the immutability of the Law, 302–3; God's omniscience, 320–1; reward and punishment, 350–1; the Messiah, 368–9; resurrection, 398–9; on Hell, 432

Galloway, George: on God and man, exc., 79

Gaunilo (of Marmoutiers): on God's existence, 35–6

Gaon, Saadiah: on Dualism, 83–4; defence of Judaism and monotheism, 98–9; God's knowledge, exc., 333; on punishment, exc., 364; on Hell, 423–5

Gersonides (Levi ben Gershon): theory of creation, exc., 148; God's foreknowledge, exc., 334–5

Ginzberg, Louis: anthropomorphism, exc., 125

Gombiner, Abraham: on fasts, 312–3

Gore, Bishop: on the Hebrew prophets, exc. 50; 203

Graetz, Heinrich: on Judaism, 1–6; on martyrdom, exc., 25

Guttmann, Julius: on Maimonides, 15

Ha-Am, Ahad: on self-sacrifice, exc., 27; on the Pentateuch, 210

Ha-Cohen, Rabbi Tzadok; on the *Torah*, exc., 396

Ha-Levi, Aaron: on the precepts of the *Torah*, 104–6

Ha-Levi, Yehudah: on prophecy, 188

Ha-Sephardi, Joseph ben Eliezer: see Bonfils, Joseph

Herberg, Will: Messianism, exc., 396–7; resurrection, 417–8

Hertz, Chief Rabbi Dr J. H.: Mosaic authorship of Pentateuch, exc., 227–8; his Commentary, exc., 278–80; precepts of *Torah*, 287–8; the Messiah, 391–2; the immortality of the soul, 415–6

Heller, Yom Tobh Lippmann: the *Torah*, exc., 289; the *Halakhah*, 313–4; on free will, 327–8

Heschel, Abraham J.: observance, exc., 171; the prophets, exc., 198

Hirsch, Samson Raphael: on the Pentateuch, exc., 227

Hobbes, Thomas: 'Leviathan', 238

Holbach, Baron Paul: atheism, 57–8

Horowitz, Isaiah: the *Shelah*, 153–4; mystical commentary to 13 principles, exc., 318

Horowitz, Shabbethai: the divine Jewish soul, 109–10

Hume, David: on a personal God, exc., 128–9

Huxley, T. H.: his agnosticism, 62–3

Inge, Dean: mysticism, 5

Isaac of Uceda, Samuel b.: divine foreknowledge, 328

James, William: on saints, 163–4

Jerome, St.: the Vulgate, 257

Johanan, R.: martyrdom, exc. 26; the *Torah*, 221

Joseph, Morris: the Messianic idea, 389–90; on hell, 432–3

Josephus: on the Pentateuch, 223: on Essenes, Sadducees, Pharisees, 330

Joshua, Rabbi: on the world to come, 437

Joyce, G. H.: teleological proof of God's existence, 41

Judah, Rabbi (the Prince): script of the *Torah*, 250–1

Kalischer, Rabbi Hirsch: Messianism, 388

Kant, Emanuel: God's existence, 35; teleological argument, 41; on morality, 46

Kaplan, Mordecai: his views on Judaism, exc., 30., critique of Reform Judaism, 308

Kara, Simeon: *Midrashim*, 98

Karelitz, Rabbi: attitude to *'epiqoros*, 311

Katz, J.: Judaism and Christianity, exc., 318–9

Katzenellenbogen, Ezekiel: on *Torah*, 313

Kaufmann, Yehezkel: idolatry, exc., 181–2; on prophecy, exc., 197–8

Kierkegaard, Sören: religious existentialism, 64–5

Klausner, Joseph: Messianism, 370–1

Kohler, Kaufmann: 'Jewish Theology',

exc., 30; God's unity, 85–6; Messianic idea, 375–6

Kook, Rabbi A. I.: heresy, exc., 13; martyrdom, exc., 27; on divinity, exc., 126; man's self-worship, exc., 182–3; Messianism, 387–8

Laqish, R. Simeon b.: on the *Torah*, 221–2, 225; free will, 330

Levinthal, Israel H.: Messianism and Zionism, 391

Lipschütz, Israel: on Moses, exc., 215; on the immorality of the soul, exe., 452

Lods, Adolphe: prophecy, exc. 204–5

Löw, Rabbi Judah: on the world to come, 444

Luzzatto, Moses Hayyim: on the *Shema'*, 111–2; on prophecy, 188–9; reward and punishment, 362–3; the hereafter, 444

Maggid, The Dubner: on the *Torah*, 305–6

Maimonides, Moses: on the *'epiqoros*, exc. 12; his principles enumerated, 14; on heresy, 15–17; God's existence, 33 ff.; God's unity, 70 ff.; God's incorporeality, 118 ff.; the eternity of God, 135 ff.; God alone to be worshipped, 149 ff.; prophecy, 184 ff.; the superiority of Moses, 206 ff.; the divine nature of the *Torah*, 216 ff.; the *Torah* is unchanging, 302 ff.; God's knowledge of man, 319 ff.; reward and punishment, 350 ff.; the coming of the Messiah, 368 ff.; the resurrection of the dead, 398 ff.

Malbim, M. L.: on the *Shema'*, 116–7

Manoah, Hezekiah ben: on the *Shema'*, 104

Margolis, Max L.: his 'Creed', exc., 32

Marx, Karl: atheism, 56

Masius, A.: on the Pentateuch, 238

Matthews, W. R.: the teleological argument for God's existence, exc., 44; history and providence, 346–7

McTaggart, J. M. E., on evil, 90–1

Meir, Samuel ben: on God's unity, 100

Mendel, Menahem (of Lübavitch): religious proof of God's existence, 47

Mendelssohn, Moses: on Judaism, 4; on dogma, 8; on the *Shema'*, 114

Mill, John Stuart: on a 'finite' God, exc., 147

Montefiore, C. G.: on punishment, 356–7; on Hell, 433

Moore, George Foot: on the *Torah*, exc, 226; on the Sabbath, 295; on punishment, 357; on the hereafter, 438

Moses, Alexander Süsskind ben: *See* Süsskind.

Mowinckel, Sigmund: on the Old Testament, 273–4; on prophecy, 198–9

Muilenburg, Prof. J.: on the prophets, 196

Nahmanides: anti-Trinitarianism, 87; the Pentateuch, 223; suffering, 359; resurrection, 408; punishment, 425–7

Nahman of Bratzlav: God's eternity, 139–40

Nehemiah, Rabbi: on the *Torah*, 220, 222

Neumark, David: on Moses, 212; on resurrection, 437

Niebuhr, Reinhold: on resurrection, 419–20

Nieto, Haham David: on Deism, 73–4, 76–8

Nietzsche, Friedrich: his atheism, 57

Paqudah, Bahya Ibn: creation, 84; 'Duties of the Heart', 99; anthropomorphism, exc., 133; determinism and free will, exc., 336

Parkes, James: on Steinberg, exc., 69

Philo: articles of faith, 8–10; cosmological proof, 39; on Moses, 222–3

Phinehas of Karetz: on the *Shema'*, 114

Plato: as founder of natural theology, 50–1; on creation, 135

Rapoport, S. J.: on the *'epiqoros*, exc., 11–12

Rashdall, Hastings: the idea of a personal God, exc., 134

Rashi: See Yitzhaqi, Solomon

Ribash: See Shesheth, R. Isaac ben.

Robinson, H. Wheeler: on prophecy, exc., 205

Robinson, T. H.: on creation, exc., 140–1

Rosenzweig, Franz: textual criticism, 275

Roth, Prof. Leon: on reason, exc., 32

Rowley, H. H.: on prophecy, exc., 196

Samuel (of Babylon): on civil laws, 284

Schechter, Solomon: on Judaism, 4, 6, 7; on the world to come, 13; on dogma, 21, 28–9; on the Bible, 231–2; Bible criticism, exc., 277–8

Scholem, G.: on the *Zohar*, 103

Schwarzschild, Steven S.: on the Messiah, 393–4

Seliger, Dr. Joseph: the immortality of the soul, 414–5

Sforno, Obadiah ben Jacob: on the unity of God, 108

Sheshest, R. Isaac ben: on the *Sephiroth*, exc., 174

Simhah, Rabbi Meir: Zionism, exc., 396

Simlai, Rabbi: precepts of faith, 10; three names for God, 86–7; precepts given to Moses, 287

Simon, Richard: on the Pentateuch, 238–9

Skinner, James: on prophecy, exc., 204

Sorley, W. R.: God's knowledge, 338–9

Spencer, John: on comparative religion, 239

Spinoza, Benedict; on pantheism, 75–6, 80; the Pentateuch, 238

Süsskind, Alexander: on the *Shema'*, 113; on worship, 155–163

Taku, Moses: anthropomorphism, 121–2

Temple, William: on immortality, 448
Tillich, Paul: God's existence, 65
Trueblood, David Elton: on a 'finite' God, exc., 147–8

Underhill, Evelyn: on worship, 152–3, exc., 166–8
Urbach, S.: on Maimonides, 15

Van Velthuysen, L.: on Spinoza, 75–6

Waterhouse, Eric S.: God's existence, 36
Webb, Clement C. J.: God and personality, 132
Wellhausen, J.: the Pentateuch, 244–6; textual criticism, 260
Werblowsky, R. J. Zwi: God's existence, 33–4; non-mythical character of God, 119; God alone to be worshipped, 150; prophecy, 185, 188; Moses, 209; divine nature of the *Torah*, 218; the immutability of the *Torah*, 303; the omniscience of God, 321; reward and punishment, 351–2; the Messiah, 369–70; the resurrection of the dead, 399

Yehiel, Asher ben: Moses and laws, 283–4
Yitzhaqi, Solomon (*Rashi*): God's unity, 99–100

Zalman, Schneor: attack on Deists, 72–3, 79–80; God's eternity, 140; idolatry, exc., 183
Zalman, Solomon: on the *Shema'*, 115
Zeitlin, Hillel: on evil, exc., 94
Zimra, David ben Solomon Ibn Abi: on the *Torah*, 24–5; on martyrdom, exc., 25
Zweifel, Eliezer: his book *Sanegor*, 309–10.

INDEX OF MAIN BIBLIOGRAPHIES IN EXCURSI

Atheism, 53–4, 58–9
Biblical Criticism, 262–5
Cremation, 421
Deism, 74
Deity, The theories of, 146–8
Divine Providence, Modern Scientific Theories on, 349
Dogma in Judaism, 7–8
Existence of God, Theories on the, 36–8, 42–5, 68
Free Will and Determinism, 332–6, 339–40
Gehinnom: *See* Hell, Doctrine of
Good and Evil, The problem of, 49–50, 94
Hell, The doctrine of, 434–5
Heresy (the *'epiqoros*), 11–13
Idolatry, 181–3
Immortality and the Afterlife, 452–4
Intermediaries in Judaism, 173–6
Judaism (general principles), 30–2
Judaism and Christianity, 318
Logical Positivism, 69

Martyrdom, 25–7
Messianism:
  General, 373
  Scriptural References, 373–4
  Apocalyptic and Pseudepigraphic References, 375
  Qabbalistic Ideas on, 384
'Middle Way', The, 301
Monotheism, The concept of, 82
Moses, 213–5, 240–2
'Myth', Biblical, 275–81
Personalist View of God, Theories on the, 133
Prophecy, 196–8, 203–5
Redemption, 395–6
Resurrection, The doctrine of, 420–1
Reward and Punishment:
  Rabbinic Sources, 363–4
  Theological Difficulties in, 366–7
Torah, The, 226–9
Trinitarianism, Jewish Views on, 89
Worship, Jewish, 166–71